State of the Apes 2015

C000108869

Industrial Agriculture and Ape Conser~

Social and economic systems worldwide are changing rapidly. These changes are accompanied by an increasing global demand for natural resources, including land, water, minerals, energy sources, food and timber. Today's foremost challenge lies in finding the tools not only to address the complexity of these interrelated trends, but also to implement strategies to balance environmental needs with socioeconomic requirements. This volume of *State of the Apes* contributes to this search by presenting original research and analysis, topical case studies and emerging best practice from a range of key stakeholders to examine the interface between ape conservation and industrial agriculture. In assessing the drivers behind agricultural expansion and land investments, it sheds light on governance challenges and legal frameworks that shape land use.

Aimed at policy-makers, industry experts and decision-makers, academics, researchers and NGOs, this volume is designed to inform debate, practice and policy in ways that will help to reconcile the goals of industrial agriculture with those of ape conservation and welfare, and social and economic development.

This title is available as an open access eBook via Cambridge Books Online and at www.stateoftheapes.com.

State of the Apes

Series editors

Helga Rainer   Arcus Foundation

Alison White

Annette Lanjouw   Arcus Foundation

The world's primates are among the most endangered of all tropical species. All great ape species – gorilla, chimpanzee, bonobo and orangutan – are classified as either Endangered or Critically Endangered. Furthermore, nearly all gibbon species are threatened with extinction. Whilst linkages between ape conservation and economic development, ethics and wider environmental processes have been acknowledged, more needs to be done to integrate biodiversity conservation within broader economic, social and environmental communities if those connections are to be fully realized and addressed.

Intended for a broad range of policy-makers, industry experts and decision-makers, academics, researchers, and NGOs, the *State of the Apes* series will look at the threats to these animals and their habitats within the broader context of economic and community development. Each publication presents a different theme, providing an overview of how these factors interrelate and affect the current and future status of apes, with robust statistics, welfare indicators, official and various other reports providing an objective and rigorous analysis of relevant issues.

Other Titles in this Series

Arcus Foundation. 2014. *State of the Apes: Extractive Industries and Ape Conservation.* Cambridge: Cambridge University Press.

Foreign Language Editions

Arcus Foundation. 2014. *La Planète des Grands Singes: Les Industries Extractives et la Conservation des Grands Singes.* Cambridge, UK: Arcus Foundation. Available from: www.stateoftheapes.com

Arcus Foundation. 2014. *Negara Kera: Industri Ekstraktif dan Konservasi Kera.* Cambridge, UK: Arcus Foundation. Available from: www.stateoftheapes.com

State of the Apes 2015
Industrial Agriculture and Ape Conservation

CAMBRIDGE
UNIVERSITY PRESS

University Printing House, Cambridge CB2 8BS, United Kingdom

Cambridge University Press is part of the University of Cambridge.

It furthers the University's mission by disseminating knowledge in the pursuit of education, learning and research at the highest international levels of excellence.

www.cambridge.org

Information on this title: www.cambridge.org/9781107139688

First published 2015

Printed in the United Kingdom by Bell and Bain Ltd

A catalogue record for this publication is available from the British Library

ISBN 978-1-107-13968-8 Hardback
ISBN 978-1-316-50523-6 Paperback

Credits

Editors
Helga Rainer, Alison White and Annette Lanjouw

Production Coordinator
Alison White

Designer
Rick Jones, StudioExile

Cartographer
Jillian Luff, MAP*grafix*

Copy-editor
Tania Inowlocki

Proofreader
Sarah Binns

Indexer
Caroline Jones, Osprey Indexing

Fact-checkers
Rebecca Hibbin and Melanie Hartley

Referencing
Eva Fairnell

Cover Photographs:

Background: © Ardiles Rante/Greenpeace

Bonobo: © Takeshi Furuichi

Gibbon: © IPPL

Gorilla: © Annette Lanjouw

Orangutan: © Jurek Wajdowicz, EWS

Chimpanzee: © Nilanjan Bhattacharya/Dreamstime.com

Foreword

Last year I visited the Indonesian part of Borneo. One of the highlights was a visit to an orangutan shelter on an island covered by rainforest. There I learned that an orangutan builds a new nest every day, using leaves and branches in the trees. These great apes move around from tree to tree and hardly ever come down to the ground. When it rains, they make "umbrellas" from big leaves. Orangutans share more than 96% of their genetic makeup with humans. In fact, the name orangutan means "person of the forest." Many orangutans have lost their habitat because of deforestation. They have become homeless and dependent upon shelters to survive.

It is widely recognized that humans are altering the natural world at an unprecedented rate. Among the greatest challenges facing us today are understanding how human social and economic systems drive these changes and implementing strategies for reconciling economic development with the protection and conservation of the very resources upon which it depends. Future generations will judge us by how we have changed our behavior to ensure that we can live within the limits imposed on us by climate, water and land. They will also evaluate our efforts to ensure social justice and respect for dignity and life, while safeguarding the beauty and diversity of nature.

The *State of the Apes* series aims to identify and raise awareness of potential solutions for the conservation of biodiversity—and the environment more broadly—within the parameters of ongoing economic development. The tropical forests of Asia and Africa are the natural home of great apes and gibbons. By focusing on apes as flagship species for the conservation of these valuable forests, *State of the Apes* seeks to stimulate dialogue and collaboration, while also informing policy and practice.

Given that tropical forest loss is a significant contributor to climate change, the conservation of these resources is critical to protecting not only the great ape and gibbon populations but also the global human population. Even if tree crops replace the natural forest that has been removed, the impact on climate change will not be countered. And the loss of species diversity will be irreversible.

This volume highlights the deleterious effects of industrial-scale agriculture on ape populations as well as other wildlife species, forests and people in South and Southeast Asia to date. It warns that the shift from small-scale agriculture to industrial agriculture in Africa is likely to follow a similar path.

It also presents detailed case studies that show how governments, the private sector, local communities and civil society can work together to reconcile some of the conflicting agendas. In Liberia, for example, a recent agreement with the Government of Norway for results-based development aid holds significant promise for ensuring that decision-making on agricultural expansion takes biodiversity and land use planning into consideration, thereby protecting ape habitats, local communities and wildlife populations. And in Indonesia, major palm oil companies recently committed to establishing deforestation-free value chains.

Our survival depends on finding solutions that will help to preserve biodiversity while simultaneously securing human development and wellbeing. *State of the Apes* demonstrates that the conservation of flagship species—in this case, our closest relatives—can be achieved in conjunction with economic and social development, through integrated planning and sensitive policy and practice.

Tine Sundtoft

Tine Sundtoft
Minister of Climate and Environment,
Norway

Contents

The Arcus Foundation viii

Notes to Readers viii

Acknowledgments ix

Apes Overview x

Introduction 1

Section 1
Industrial Agriculture and Ape Conservation

1. Economic Development and Conservation of Biodiversity: Understanding the Interface of Ape Conservation and Industrial Agriculture 13

Introduction   13
The Role of Palm Oil in Poverty Alleviation and Land Tenure   18
Industrial Agriculture and Climate Change   19
Impact of Industrial Agriculture on Ape Populations   24
Rescue Centers and Problems Faced with Rescued, Translocated and Reintroduced Orangutans   32
Agricultural Industry Engagement in Ape Conservation and Mitigation Strategies   33
The Roles of Producers, Buyers and Consumers   38
Conclusion   39

2. Encroaching on Ape Habitat: Deforestation and Industrial Agriculture in Cameroon, Liberia and on Borneo 41

Introduction   41
Industrial Agricultural Concessions across Ape Ranges   43
Industrial Crops in Ape Ranges   46
Deforestation and Industrial Agriculture: The Cases of Cameroon, Liberia and Borneo   46
Conclusion   67

3. From Habitat to Plantation: Causes of Conversion in sub-Saharan Africa 71

Introduction   71
Expansion of Africa's Agro-Industry   73
Sources of Investment   85
Drivers of Expansion into Africa   87
Industrial Agriculture and Ape Habitat   92
Sustainable Development   96
Conclusion   102

4. Legal Frameworks at the Interface between Industrial Agriculture and Ape Conservation 105

Introduction   105
Findings from the Trend Analysis   109
Conclusion   131

5. From Process to Impact of a Voluntary Standard: The Roundtable on Sustainable Palm Oil 135

Introduction 135
Launching an Institution with a Global Vision: The Creation, Architecture and Operation of the RSPO 137
Case Studies: Industry Applications of RSPO Principles 143
Obstacles to Success: The RSPO's Operational Challenges 152
Reaching Agreements and Controlling Interpretation: Process-related Obstacles 153
The RSPO's Move Toward Enhancing Conservation Impact 157
Conclusion 162

6. Impacts of Industrial Agriculture on Ape Ecology 165

Introduction 165
Different Crop Types: Different Impacts 167
Different Ape Species: Different Impacts 167
The Varying Impacts of Different Phases of Production 172
Remediation 177
Long-term Impacts 179
The Impact of Socioeconomic and Cultural Values on the Forest–Agriculture Interface 183
Human–Ape Interactions 183
Conclusions on the Need to Incorporate the Human Social Dimension in the General Picture 187
Survey Results: Summary of Main Impacts 188
Conclusions 190

Section 2
The Status and Welfare of Great Apes and Gibbons

Introduction 194

7. Ape Populations over Time: Case Studies from Gombe, Mount Halimun Salak, Sabangau and Wamba 197

Introduction 197
Bornean Orangutans in the Sabangau Peat Swamp Forest 200
The Chimpanzees of Gombe 207
The Bonobos of Wamba in the Luo Scientific Reserve, DRC 215
The Silvery Gibbons in Mount Halimun Salak National Park, Java, Indonesia 221
Final Thoughts 226

8. The Status of Captive Apes 229

Introduction 229
Apes in Captivity in Range State Regions 231
Apes in Captivity in Non-range States of the Global North 241
Discussion 256
Conclusion 258

Annexes 260

Acronyms and abbreviations 264

Glossary 268

References 275

Index 323

The Arcus Foundation

The Arcus Foundation is a private grant-making foundation that advances social justice and conservation goals. The Foundation works globally and has offices in New York City, USA and Cambridge, UK. For more information and to connect with Arcus visit:

- arcusfoundation.org.
- twitter.com/ArcusGreatApes; and
- facebook.com/ArcusGreatApes.

Great Apes Program

The long-term survival of humans and the great apes is dependent on how we respect and care for other animals and our shared natural resources. The Arcus Foundation seeks to increase respect for and recognition of the rights and value of the great apes and gibbons, and to strengthen protection from threats to their habitats. The Arcus Great Apes Program supports conservation and policy advocacy efforts that promote the survival of great apes and gibbons in the wild and in sanctuaries that offer high-quality care, safety and freedom from invasive research and exploitation.

Contact details

New York office:

44 West 28th Street, 17th Floor
New York, New York 10001
United States

+1.212.488.3000 / phone
+1.212.488.3010 / fax

**Cambridge office
(Great Apes program):**

Wellington House, East Road
Cambridge CB1 1BH
United Kingdom

+44.1223.451050 / phone
+44.1223.451100 / fax

Notes to Readers

Acronyms and abbreviations

A list of acronyms and abbreviations can be found at the back of the book, starting on page 264.

Annexes

All annexes can be found at the back of the book, starting on page 260, except for the Abundance Annex, which is available from the *State of the Apes* website:

- www.stateoftheapes.com.

Glossary

There is a glossary of scientific terms and key words at the back of the book, starting on page 268.

Chapter cross-referencing

Chapter cross-references appear throughout the book, either as direct references in the body text or in brackets.

Ape Range Maps

The ape range maps throughout this edition show the extent of occurrence (EOO) of each species. An EOO includes all known populations of a species contained within the shortest possible continuous imaginary boundary. It is important to note that some areas within these boundaries are unsuitable and unoccupied.

Photographs

We aim to include photographs that are relevant to each theme and illustrate the content of each chapter. If you have photographs that you are willing to share with the Arcus Foundation, for use in this series, or for multiple purposes, please contact the Production Coordinator (awhite@arcusfoundation.org) or the Cambridge office.

Acknowledgments

The aim of this second volume of *State of the Apes* is to facilitate critical engagement on current conservation, industry and government practice and to expand support for great apes and gibbons. We are grateful to everyone who played a part, from meeting participants, to our authors, contributors and reviewers and those involved in the production and design of the book.

The support of Jon Stryker and the Arcus Foundation Board of Directors is essential to the production of this publication. We thank them for their ongoing support.

A key element outside of the thematic content is the overview of the status of apes, both in situ and in captivity. We extend our thanks to the captive-ape organizations that provided detailed information and to all the great ape and gibbon scientists who contribute their valuable data to build the A.P.E.S. database. Such collaborative efforts are key to effective and efficient conservation action.

Authors, contributors, reviewers and those who provided essential data and support are named at the end of each chapter. We could not have produced this book without them. Most of the photographs included were generously shared by their creators, who are credited alongside each one. We are also grateful to the organizations that allowed us to include extracts from previously published articles, books and reports. Many others contributed by providing introductions, anonymous comments or strategic advice, helping with essential administrative tasks and providing much-appreciated moral support.

Particular thanks go to the following individuals, organizations and agencies: Stichting AAP, Marc Ancrenaz, Elizabeth Bennett, Alexandra Booth, Keith Boyfield, Cambridge University Press, Kim Carlson, Matthew Cassetta, Greer Chapman, Susan Cheyne, Sebastian Clairmonte, Climate Advisers, Lorenzo Cotula, Doug Cress, Bruce Davidson, Debra Durham, Wendy Elliot, Kay Farmer, Fauna & Flora International, Forest Peoples Programme, Takeshi Furuichi, David Gaveau, Global Witness, the Gorilla Rehabilitation and Conservation Education Center, the Great Apes Survival Partnership (GRASP), Greenpeace, Merril Halley, Alexis Hatto, Tatyana Humle, Glen Hurowitz, the International Institute for Environment and Development, the International Primate Protection League, Justin Kenrick, Sam Lawson, Audrey Lee, Patrice Levang, Matthew Linkie, Andrew Marshall, Jessica Martin, the Max Planck Institute for Evolutionary Biology, Linda May, Shirley McGreal, Matthew McLennan, Erik Meijaard, Susanne Morrell, Rob Muggah, Janet Nackoney, Ginny Ng Siew Ling, Greg Norman, the Norwegian Ministry of Climate and Environment, Olam International, Adam Phillipson, Patti Ragan, Ben Rawson, RESOLVE, Cindy Rizzo, Martha Robbins, Dilys Roe, the Roundtable on Sustainable Palm Oil, Sanaga Yong Chimpanzee Rescue Center, Karmele Llano Sánchez, Simon Siburat, Ian Singleton, Rolf Skar, Tenekwetche Sop, Sheri Speede, Marie Stevenson, Christopher Stewart, Sharon Strong, the Sumatran Orangutan Conservation Program, Tine Sundtoft, Cristina Talens, Ravin Trapshah, the United Nations Environment Programme (UNEP) Global Environmental Alert Service, the UNEP World Conservation Monitoring Centre, Graham Usher, Tim van der Zanden, the Wildlife Conservation Society, Elizabeth Williamson, Wilmar International, Vanessa Woods, the World Wildlife Fund and the Zoological Society of London.

Each volume in this series is an extensive undertaking. We are committed to ensuring that these books are available to as many stakeholders as possible, not least by translating them into French, Bahasa Indonesia, and, beginning with this volume, Mandarin. We are delighted that GRASP has partnered with the Arcus Foundation in this endeavor, taking on the translations and the production of the translated editions, and we are thankful for their invaluable support.

Helga Rainer, Alison White and Annette Lanjouw
Editors

Apes Overview

APES INDEX

Bonobo (*Pan paniscus*)

Location and Population

The bonobo is only present in the Democratic Republic of Congo (DRC), bio-geographically separated from chimpanzees and gorillas by the Congo River. The population size is unknown, as only 30% of its historic range has been surveyed; however, estimates place the population somewhere between 29,500 (Myers Thompson, 1997) and 50,000 (Dupain and Van Elsacker, 2001) individuals, with numbers decreasing. The bonobo is included in the Convention on International Trade in Endangered Species of Wild Fauna and Flora (CITES) Appendix I, and is categorized as endangered (EN) on the International Union for Conservation of Nature (IUCN) Red List (Fruth *et al.*, 2008); for more information, see Box 2: IUCN Red List categories and criteria, and CITES Appendices. Activities causing population decline include poaching for the commercial wild meat trade, civil conflict and habitat destruction (Fruth *et al.*, 2008).

Physiology

Male adult bonobos reach a height of 73–83 cm and weigh 37–61 kg, while females are slightly smaller, weighing 27–38 kg. Bonobos are moderately sexually dimorphic and similar in size and appearance to chimpanzees, although with a smaller head and lither appearance.

The bonobo diet is mainly frugivorous (more than 50% fruit), supplemented with leaves, stems, shoots, pith, seeds, bark, flowers, honey and fungi, including truffles. Animal matter—such as insects, small reptiles, birds and medium-sized mammals, including other primates—accounts for 3% of their diet. The maximum life span in the wild is 50 years (Robson and Wood, 2008).

Social Organization

Bonobos live in fission–fusion communities of 10–120 individuals, consisting of multiple males and females. When foraging, they split into smaller mixed-sex subgroups, or parties, averaging 5–23 individuals.

Male bonobos cooperate with and tolerate one another; however, lasting bonds between adult males are rare, in contrast to the bonds between adult females, which are strong and potentially last for years. A distinguishing feature of female bonobos is that they are co-dominant with males and will form alliances against certain males within the community. Among bonobos, the bonds between mother and son are the strongest, prove highly important for the social status of the son and last into adulthood.

Together with chimpanzees, bonobos are the closest living relatives to humans, sharing 98.8% of our DNA (Varki and Altheide, 2005; Smithsonian Institution, n.d.).

Chimpanzee (*Pan troglodytes*)

Location and Population

Chimpanzees are distributed across equatorial Africa, with discontinuous populations from southern Senegal to western Uganda and Tanzania (Oates *et al.*, 2008a).

Chimpanzees are listed in CITES Appendix I, and all four subspecies are categorized as endangered (EN) on the IUCN Red List (Oates *et al.*, 2008a). There are approximately 70,000–116,000 central chimpanzees; 21,300–55,600 western chimpanzees; 200,000–250,000 eastern chimpanzees; and 3,500–9,000 Nigeria–Cameroon chimpanzees. Populations are believed to be declining, but the rate has not yet been quantified.

Decreases in chimpanzee numbers are mainly attributed to increased poaching for the commercial wild meat trade, disease (particularly Ebola) and mechanized logging (which facilitates poaching) (Oates *et al.*, 2008a).

Physiology

Male chimpanzees are 77–96 cm tall and weigh 28–70 kg, while females measure 70–91 cm and weigh 20–50 kg. They share many facial expressions with humans, although forehead musculature is less pronounced and they have more flexible lips. Chimpanzees live for up to 50 years in the wild.

Chimpanzees are mainly frugivorous and opportunistic feeders. Some communities include 200 species of food items in a diet of fruit supplemented by herbaceous vegetation and animal prey, such as ants and termites, but also small mammals, including other primates. Chimpanzees are the most carnivorous of all the apes.

Social Organization

Chimpanzees show fission–fusion, multi-male–multi-female grouping patterns. A large community includes all individuals who regularly associate with one another; such communities comprise an average of 35 individuals, with the largest-known group counting 150, although this size is rare. The community separates into smaller, temporary subgroups, or parties. The parties can be highly fluid, with members moving in and out quickly or a few individuals staying together for a few days before rejoining the community.

Typically, home ranges are defended by highly territorial males, who may attack or even kill neighboring chimpanzees. Male chimpanzees are dominant over female chimpanzees and are generally the more social sex, sharing food and grooming each other more frequently. Males will cooperate to hunt, but the level of cooperation involved in social hunting activities varies between communities. Chimpanzees are noted for their sophisticated forms of cooperation, such as in hunting and territorial defense.

Gorilla (*Gorilla* species (spp.))

Location and Population

The western gorilla (*Gorilla gorilla*) is distributed throughout western equatorial Africa and has two subspecies: *Gorilla gorilla gorilla*, or the western lowland gorilla, and *Gorilla gorilla diehli*, or the Cross River gorilla. The eastern gorilla (*Gorilla beringei*) is found in the DRC and across its border into Uganda and Rwanda. There are two subspecies of the eastern gorilla: *Gorilla beringei beringei*, or the mountain gorilla, and *Gorilla beringei graueri*, or Grauer's gorilla (also referred to as the eastern lowland gorilla).

Population estimates for the western gorilla range between 140,000 and 160,000, while as few as 300 Cross River gorillas remain (Oates *et al.*, 2008a). All gorillas are listed as critically endangered (CR) on the IUCN Red List, except for the endangered (EN) Grauer's gorilla, whose status will be reviewed in 2015. Population estimates for Grauer's gorilla are between 2,000 and 10,000 (Robbins and Williamson, 2008). Estimates for the mountain gorilla are between 780 and 880 individuals (Roy *et al.*, 2014b). The main threats to both species are poaching for the commercial wild meat trade, habitat destruction and disease (the Ebola virus in particular) (Robbins and Williamson, 2008; Walsh *et al.*, 2008).

Physiology

The adult male of the eastern gorilla is slightly larger (159–196 cm, 120–209 kg) than the western gorilla (138–180 cm, 145–191 kg). Both species are highly sexually dimorphic, with females being about half the size of males. Their life span ranges from 30 to 40 years in the wild. Mature males are known as "silverbacks" due to the development of a gray saddle with maturity.

The gorillas' diet is predominantly ripe fruit and terrestrial, herbaceous vegetation. More herbaceous vegetation is ingested while fruit is scarce, in line with seasonality and fruit availability, and protein gain comes from leaves and bark of trees as well as animal supplements in the form of ants and termites; gorillas do not eat meat. Mountain gorillas are largely herbivorous, feeding mainly on leaves, pith, stems, bark and, occasionally, ants.

Social Organization

Western gorillas live in stable groups with multiple females and one adult male (silverback), whereas eastern gorillas are polygynous and can be polygynandrous, with one or more silverbacks, multiple females, their offspring and immature relatives. Eastern gorillas can live in groups of up to 65 individuals, whereas the maximum group size for the western gorilla is 22. Western gorillas are not territorial and home ranges overlap extensively. Chest beats and vocalizations are used when neighboring silverbacks come into contact, but mutual avoidance is normally the adopted strategy. Gorillas have also been known to adopt offspring from other females (orphans usually) and raise them as their own (Smuts *et al.*, 1987).

Orangutan (*Pongo* spp.)

Location and Population

The orangutan range is now limited to the forests of Sumatra and Borneo, but these great apes were once present throughout much of southern Asia (Wich *et al.*, 2008, 2012). Survey data indicate that in 2004 there were approximately 6,500 remaining Sumatran orangutans and at least 54,000 Bornean orangutans (Wich *et al.*, 2008). As a result of continuing habitat loss, the Sumatran orangutan is classified as critically endangered (CR) and the Bornean orangutan as endangered (EN) (Ancrenaz *et al.*, 2008; Singleton, Wich and Griffiths, 2008). Both species are listed in Appendix I of CITES. The main threats to the species are habitat loss, killings due to human–ape conflict, hunting and the international pet trade (Wich *et al.*, 2008; Gaveau *et al.*, 2014).

Physiology

Adult males can reach a height of 94–99 cm and weigh 60–85 kg (flanged) or 30–65 kg (unflanged). Females reach a height of 64–84 cm and weigh 30–45 kg, meaning that orangutans are highly sexually dimorphic. Sumatran orangutans are generally slighter than their Bornean relatives. In the wild, males have a life expectancy of 58 years and females 53 years.

Fully mature males develop a short beard and protruding cheek pads, termed "flanges." Some male orangutans experience "developmental arrest," maintaining a female-like size and appearance for many years past sexual maturity; they are termed "unflanged" males. Orangutans are the only great ape to exhibit bimaturism.

Their diet mainly consists of fruit, but they also eat leaves, shoots, seeds, bark, pith, flowers, eggs, soil and invertebrates (termites and ants). Carnivorous behavior has also been observed, but at a low frequency (preying on species such as slow lorises).

Social Organization

The mother–offspring unit is the only permanent social unit among orangutans, yet social groupings between independent individuals do occur, although their frequency varies across populations (Wich *et al.*, 2009b). While females are usually relatively tolerant of each other, flanged males are intolerant of other flanged and unflanged males (Wich *et al.*, 2009b). Orangutans on Sumatra are generally more social than those on Borneo and live in overlapping home ranges, with flanged males continually emitting "long calls" to alert others to their location (Delgado and van Schaik, 2000; Wich *et al.*, 2009b). Orangutans are characterized by an extremely slow life history, with the longest interbirth interval (6–9 years) of any primate species (Wich *et al.*, 2004, 2009b).

Gibbons (*Hoolock* spp.; *Hylobates* spp.; *Nomascus* spp.; *Symphalangus* spp.)

All four genera of gibbon generally share ecological and behavioral attributes, such as monogamy in small territorial groups; vocalization through elaborate song (including complex duets); frugivory and brachiation (moving through the canopy using only the arms). Due to their dependence on fruit, gibbons rarely have multi-female groups (polygyny) and instead remain in small monogamous groups with few offspring. They are diurnal and sing at sunrise and sunset, with a significant part of their day dedicated to finding fruit trees within their territories.

Hoolock genus

Location and Population

There are two species within the Hoolock genus: the western hoolock (*Hoolock hoolock*) and the eastern hoolock (*Hoolock leuconedys*). A new subspecies of the western hoolock was discovered in 2013: the Mishmi Hills

▶ hoolock (*Hoolock hoolock mishmiensis*) (Choudhury, 2013). The western hoolock's distribution spans Bangladesh, India and Myanmar. The eastern hoolock's distribution is in China, India and Myanmar. With an estimated population of 2,500 individuals, the western hoolock is listed as endangered (EN) on the IUCN Red List. The population of eastern hoolock is much higher at 293,200–370,000, and it is listed as vulnerable (VU) on the IUCN Red List. Both species are listed in CITES Appendix I, with the main threats identified as habitat loss and fragmentation, and hunting for food, pets and for medicinal purposes.

Physiology

The hoolock's head and body length ranges between 45 and 81 cm; they weigh 6–9 kg, with males slightly heavier than females. Like most gibbons, the Hoolock genus is sexually dichromatic, with the pelage (coat) of females and males differing in terms of patterning and color. The eastern hoolock also differs from its western counterpart in its pelage, in particular because they have complete separation between the white brow markings and a white preputial tuft.

The diet of the hoolock is primarily frugivorous, supplemented with vegetative matter such as leaves, shoots, seeds, moss and flowers. While little is known about the diet of the eastern hoolock, it most likely resembles that of the western hoolock.

Social Organization

Hoolocks live in family groups of 2–6 individuals, consisting of a mated adult pair and their offspring. They are presumably territorial, although no specific data exist. Hoolock pairs vocalize a "double solo" rather than the more common "duet" of various gibbons.

Hylobates genus

Location and Population

Nine species are currently included in the *Hylobates* genus, although there is some dispute about whether Müller's gibbon (*Hylobates muelleri*), Abbott's gray gibbon (*Hylobates abbottii*), and the Bornean gray gibbon (*Hylobates funereus*) represent full species. See Table AO1: Great Apes and Gibbons.

This genus of gibbon occurs discontinuously in tropical and subtropical forests from southwestern China, through Indochina, Thailand and the Malay Peninsula to the islands of Sumatra, Borneo and Java (Wilson and Reeder, 2005). The overall estimated minimum population for the *Hylobates* genus is about 360,000, with the least abundant species being the moloch gibbon, and most abundant being, collectively, the 'gray gibbons' (Müller's, Abbott's and Bornean gray gibbons). All species are listed as endangered (EN) on the IUCN Red List and are in CITES Appendix I. A number of hybrids of these species occur naturally and continue to coexist with the unhybridized species in the wild. The main collective threats facing the *Hylobates* genus are deforestation, hunting and the illegal pet trade.

Physiology

Average height across all species is approximately 46 cm for both males and females and their weight ranges between 5 and 7 kg. With the exception of the pileated gibbon, species in the genus are not sexually dichromatic, although the lar gibbon has two color phases, which are not related to sex or age.

Gibbons are mainly frugivorous, with figs being an especially important part of their diet, supplemented by leaves, buds, flowers, shoots, vines and insects, while small animals and bird eggs form the protein input.

Social Organization

Hylobates gibbons are largely monogamous, forming family units of two adults and their offspring; however, polyandrous and polygynous units have been observed, especially in hybrid zones. Territorial disputes are predominantly led by males, who become aggressive toward other males, whereas females tend to lead daily movements and ward off other females.

Nomascus genus

Location and Population

Seven species exist in the *Nomascus* genus. See Table AO1: Great apes and gibbons.

The *Nomascus* genus is somewhat less widely distributed than the *Hylobates* genus, being present in Cambodia, Lao PDR, Vietnam and southern China (including Hainan Island). Population estimates exist for some taxa: there are approximately 1,500 ▶

western black crested gibbons, 130 Cao Vit gibbons and 23 Hainan gibbons. Population estimates for the white-cheeked gibbons are not available except for some sites, yet overall numbers are known to be severely depleted. The yellow-cheeked gibbons have the largest populations among the *Nomascus* gibbons. All species are listed in CITES Appendix I, with four listed as critically endangered (CR) on the IUCN Red List, two as endangered (EN) and one (*Nomascus annamensis*) yet to be assessed (IUCN, 2014b). Major threats to these populations include hunting for food, pets and for medicinal purposes as well as habitat loss and fragmentation.

Physiology

Average head and body length across all species of this genus, for both sexes, is approximately 47 cm; they weigh around 7 kg. All *Nomascus* species have sexually dimorphic pelage, with adult males being predominantly black while females are a buffy yellow. Their diet is much the same as that of the *Hylobates* genus: mainly frugivorous, supplemented with leaves and flowers.

Social Organization

Gibbons of the *Nomascus* genus are mainly socially monogamous; however, most species have also been observed in polyandrous and polygynous groups. More northerly species appear to engage in polygyny to a greater degree than southern taxa. Extra-pair copulations outside monogamous pairs have been recorded, although infrequently.

Symphalangus genus

Location and Population

Siamang (*Symphalangus syndactylus*) are found in several forest blocks across Indonesia, Malaysia and Thailand; the species faces severe threats to its habitat across its range. No accurate estimates exist for the total population size. The species is present in CITES Appendix I and is listed as endangered (EN) on the IUCN Red List.

Physiology

The siamang's head and body length is 75–90 cm, and adult males weigh 10.5–12.7 kg, while adult females weigh 9.1–11.5 kg. The siamang is minimally sexually dimorphic, but the pelage is the same across sexes. The pelage is black, and the species has a large inflatable throat sac.

The siamang's diet relies heavily on figs and somewhat less on leaves, which allows it to be sympatric with *Hylobates* gibbons in some locations, since the latter focus more on fleshy fruits. The siamang diet also includes flowers and insects.

Social Organization

Males and females call territorially, using their large throat sacs, and males will give chase to neighboring males. One group's calls will inhibit other groups nearby, and they will consequently take turns to vocalize. The groups are usually based on monogamous pairings, although polyandrous groups have been observed. Males may also adopt the role of caregiver for infants.

Ape Socioecology

This section presents an overview of the socioecology of the seven species of non-human apes: bonobos, chimpanzees, gibbons (including siamangs), eastern and western gorillas, and Bornean and Sumatran orangutans. For more detailed information, see Wich *et al.* (2009b), Emery Thompson and Wrangham (2013), Reinartz, Ingmanson and Vervaecke (2013), Williamson and Butynski (2013a, 2013b), and Williamson, Maisels and Groves (2013).

Gorillas are the largest living primate species and the most terrestrial of all the apes. Chimpanzees are the most wide-ranging ape species in Africa, occurring across 21 countries (Oates *et al.*, 2008a). Orangutans are found in Asia—in both Indonesia and Malaysia—and are the only ape to have two distinct male types. Gibbons are the most numerous of the apes, with 19 species across Asia and Southeast Asia.

Great Ape Socioecology

Social organization differs considerably across the three great ape genera.

Both chimpanzees and bonobos form dynamic communities, fissioning into smaller parties or coming together (fusioning) according to food availability and the presence of reproductively active females (Wrangham, 1986). Chimpanzee communities average 35 members, with a known maximum of 150 members (Mitani, 2009). Bonobo communities comprise 10–120 individuals.

Gorillas live in family groups. Their large body size and largely vegetation-based diet enable them to cope with fruit shortages and to maintain stable groups. The median group size is ten: one or more adult "silverback" males with several females and their offspring.

Orangutans are semi-solitary and have loosely defined communities. Flanged adult males, characterized by fatty cheek pads and large size, lead a semi-solitary existence

---

BOX AO1

IUCN Red List Categories and Criteria, and CITES Appendices

The IUCN Species Survival Commission has defined various categories for each species and subspecies (IUCN, 2012). The criteria can be applied to any taxonomic unit at or below the species level. In order to be ascribed a specific definition, a taxon must fulfil a number of criteria. As all great apes and gibbons are placed within the categories of vulnerable, endangered or critically endangered, this text box presents details on a selection of the criteria for these three categories. Full details of the IUCN Red List Categories and Criteria (in English, French and Spanish) can be viewed and downloaded at: http://jr.iucnredlist.org/documents/redlist_cats_crit_en.pdf. Detailed guidelines on their use can also be seen at: http://www.iucnredlist.org/documents/RedListGuidelines.pdf.

A **vulnerable** (VU) taxon is considered to be facing a high risk of extinction in the wild. It will number fewer than 10,000 mature individuals and there will be evidence of continuing decline and a significant reduction (upwards of 50%) in the size of the population over the past ten years or three generations.

An **endangered** (EN) taxon is considered to be facing a very high risk of extinction in the wild. It will number fewer than 2,500 mature individuals and there will be evidence of continuing decline as well as a significant reduction (upwards of 50%) in the size of the population over the past ten years or three generations.

A **critically endangered** (CR) taxon is considered to be facing an extremely high risk of extinction in the wild. It will number fewer than 250 mature individuals and there will be evidence of continuing decline and a significant reduction (upwards of 80%) in the size of the population over the past ten years or three generations.

CITES Appendices I, II and III to the Convention are lists of species afforded different levels or types of protection from overexploitation.

All non-human apes are listed in **Appendix I**, which includes species that are the most endangered among CITES-listed animals and plants. They are threatened with extinction and CITES prohibits international trade in specimens of these species except when the purpose of the import is not commercial, for instance for scientific research. In these exceptional cases, trade may take place, provided it is authorized by the granting of both an import permit and an export permit (or re-export certificate). Article VII of the Convention provides for a number of exemptions to this general prohibition. For more information go to: http://www.cites.org/eng/app/.

Table AO1

Great Apes and Gibbons (adapted from Mittermeier *et al.*, 2013)

GREAT APES		
Pan **genus**		
Bonobo	*Pan paniscus*	■ Democratic Republic of Congo (DRC)
Central chimpanzee	*Pan troglodytes troglodytes*	■ Angola ■ Cameroon ■ Central African Republic ■ DRC ■ Equatorial Guinea ■ Gabon ■ Republic of Congo
Eastern chimpanzee	*Pan troglodytes schweinfurthii*	■ Burundi ■ Central African Republic ■ DRC ■ Rwanda ■ Sudan ■ Tanzania ■ Uganda
Nigeria–Cameroon chimpanzee	*Pan troglodytes ellioti*	■ Cameroon ■ Nigeria
Western chimpanzee	*Pan troglodytes verus*	■ Benin ■ Burkina Faso ■ Gambia ■ Ghana ■ Guinea ■ Mali ■ Senegal ■ Sierra Leone ■ Togo
Gorilla **genus**		
Cross River gorilla	*Gorilla gorilla diehli*	■ Cameroon ■ Nigeria
Grauer's gorilla (eastern lowland gorilla)	*Gorilla beringei graueri*	■ DRC
Mountain gorilla	*Gorilla beringei beringei*	■ DRC ■ Rwanda ■ Uganda
Western lowland gorilla	*Gorilla gorilla gorilla*	■ Angola ■ Cameroon ■ Central African Republic ■ Equatorial Guinea ■ Gabon ■ Republic of Congo
Pongo **genus**		
Northeast Bornean orangutan	*Pongo pygmaeus morio*	■ Indonesia ■ Malaysia
Northwest Bornean orangutan	*Pongo pygmaeus pygmaeus*	■ Indonesia ■ Malaysia
Southwest Bornean orangutan	*Pongo pygmaeus wurmbii*	■ Indonesia
Sumatran orangutan	*Pongo abelii*	■ Indonesia

►

Table A01

Continued

GIBBONS (excluding subspecies)		
Hoolock genus		
Eastern hoolock	*Hoolock leuconedys*	■ China ■ Myanmar
Western hoolock	*Hoolock hoolock*	■ Bangladesh ■ India ■ Myanmar
Hylobates genus		
Abbott's gray gibbon	*Hylobates abbotti*	■ Indonesia ■ Malaysia
Agile gibbon	*Hylobates agilis*	■ Indonesia ■ Malaysia
Bornean gray gibbon	*Hylobates funereus*	■ Indonesia ■ Malaysia ■ Brunei Darussalam
Bornean white-bearded gibbon	*Hylobates albibarbis*	■ Indonesia
Kloss's gibbon	*Hylobates klossii*	■ Indonesia
Lar gibbon	*Hylobates lar*	■ China ■ Indonesia ■ Lao People's Democratic Republic ■ Malaysia ■ Myanmar ■ Thailand
Moloch gibbon	*Hylobates moloch*	■ Indonesia
Müller's gibbon	*Hylobates muelleri*	■ Indonesia
Pileated gibbon	*Hylobates pileatus*	■ Cambodia ■ Lao People's Democratic Republic ■ Thailand
Nomascus genus		
Cao Vit gibbon	*Nomascus nasutus*	■ China ■ Viet Nam
Hainan gibbon	*Nomascus hainanus*	■ China (Hainan Island)
Northern white-cheeked crested gibbon	*Nomascus leucogenys*	■ Lao People's Democratic Republic ■ Viet Nam
Northern yellow-cheeked crested gibbon	*Nomascus annamensis*	■ Cambodia ■ Lao People's Democratic Republic ■ Viet Nam
Southern white-cheeked crested gibbon	*Nomascus siki*	■ Lao People's Democratic Republic ■ Viet Nam
Southern yellow-cheeked crested gibbon	*Nomascus gabriellae*	■ Cambodia ■ Lao People's Democratic Republic ■ Viet Nam
Western black-crested gibbon	*Nomascus concolor*	■ China ■ Lao People's Democratic Republic ■ Viet Nam
Symphalangus genus		
Siamang	*Symphalangus syndactylus*	■ Indonesia ■ Malaysia ■ Thailand

Figure AO1

Ape Distribution in Africa

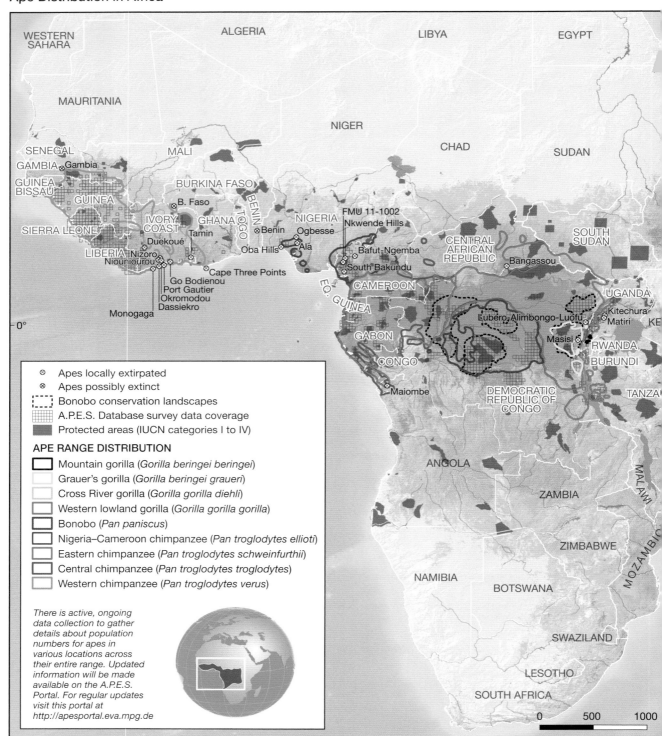

(Emery Thompson, Zhou and Knott, 2012). Smaller, unflanged adult males are comparatively tolerant of other orangutans, and adult females sometimes travel together for a few hours to several days. Sumatran orangutans occasionally congregate when food is abundant (Wich *et al.*, 2006).

Ecology

Most great apes live in closed, moist, mixed tropical forest, occupying a range of forest types, including lowland, swamp, seasonally inundated, gallery, coastal, submontane, montane and secondary regrowth. Eastern and western chimpanzees also live in savannah–mosaic landscapes. The largest populations are found below 500 m elevation, in the vast swamp forests of Asia and Africa (Morrogh-Bernard *et al.*, 2003; Stokes *et al.*, 2010), although eastern chimpanzees and eastern gorillas range above 2,000 m altitude. Most chimpanzees inhabit evergreen forests, but some populations exist in deciduous woodland and drier savannah-dominated habitats interspersed with gallery forest. Although many populations inhabit protected areas, a great number of chimpanzee communities, especially on the western and eastern coasts of Africa, live outside of protected areas, including the majority of individuals in countries such as Guinea, Liberia and Sierra Leone (Kormos *et al.*, 2003; Brncic, Amarasekaran and McKenna, 2010; Tweh *et al.*, 2014).

Great apes are adapted to a plant diet, but all taxa consume insects, and some kill and eat small mammals. Succulent fruits are their main source of nutrition, except at altitudes where few fleshy fruits are available (Watts, 1984). During certain periods, African apes concentrate on terrestrial herbs or woody vegetation, such as bark. Similarly, in Asia, orangutans consume more bark and young leaves when fruits are scarce. Sumatran orangutans are more frugivorous than their Bornean relatives (Russon *et al.*, 2009).

Gorillas inhabit a broad range of habitats across ten African countries. One commonality of gorillas across their range is that they rely more heavily than any other ape species on herbaceous vegetation, such as the leaves, stems and pith of understory vegetation, as well as leaves from shrubs and trees (Ganas *et al.*, 2004; Doran-Sheehy *et al.*, 2009; Masi, Cipolletta and Robbins, 2009; Yamagiwa and Basabose, 2009). Early research suggested that gorillas ate very little fruit, a finding that can be attributed to the fact that initial studies of their dietary patterns were conducted in the Virunga Volcanoes (Watts, 1984), the only habitat in which gorillas eat almost no fruit as it is virtually unavailable; these conclusions were adjusted once detailed studies were conducted on lowland gorillas. While gorillas incorporate a notable amount of fruit into their diets when it is available (Watts, 1984), they are less frugivorous than chimpanzees, preferring vegetative matter even at times of high fruit availability (Morgan and Sanz, 2006; Yamagiwa and Basabose, 2009; Head *et al.*, 2011).

The distance travelled per day by gorillas declines with increasing availability of understory vegetation, varying between approximately 500 m and 3 km per day. As a result of their dietary patterns, they are restricted to moist forest habitats (at altitudes ranging from sea level to more than 3,000 m) and are not found in savannah or gallery forests inhabited by chimpanzees.

Chimpanzees eat mainly fruit, although they present an omnivorous diet, which may include plant pith, bark, flowers, leaves and seeds, as well as fungi, honey, insects and mammal species, depending on the habitat and the community; some groups may consume as many as 200 plant species (Humle, 2011b). Chimpanzees are both terrestrial and arboreal; they live in multi-male–multi-female, fission–fusion communities. A single community will change size by fissioning into smaller parties according to resource

Figure AO2

Ape Distribution in Asia

⊗   Apes locally extirpated

A.P.E.S. Database
survey data coverage

Protected areas
(IUCN categories I to IV)

APE RANGE DISTRIBUTION

Gibbons

Abbott's gray gibbon
(*Hylobates abbotti*)

Agile gibbon (*Hylobates agilis*)

Bornean white-bearded gibbon
(*Hylobates albibarbis*)

Bornean gray gibbon
(*Hylobates funereus*)

Kloss's gibbon (*Hylobates klossii*)

Lar gibbon (*Hylobates lar*)

Moloch gibbon (*Hylobates moloch*)

Müller's gibbon (*Hylobates muelleri*)

Pileated gibbon (*Hylobates pileatus*)

Western hoolock (*Hoolock hoolock*)

Eastern hoolock (*Hoolock leuconedys*)

Northern yellow-cheeked crested
gibbon (*Nomascus annamensis*)

Western black-crested gibbon
(*Nomascus concolor*)

Southern yellow-cheeked crested
gibbon (*Nomascus gabriellae*)

Hainan gibbon
(*Nomascus hainanus*)

Northern white-cheeked crested
gibbon (*Nomascus leucogenys*)

Cao Vit gibbon (*Nomascus nasutus*)

Southern white-cheeked crested
gibbon (*Nomascus siki*)

Siamang (*Symphalangus syndactylus*)

Orangutans

Sumatran orangutan (*Pongo abelii*)

Bornean orangutan (*Pongo pygmaeus*)

Bornean orangutan
subspecies boundaries

*There is active, ongoing data collection to gather
details about population numbers for apes in
various location across their entire range. Updated
information will be made available on the A.P.E.S.
Portal. For regular updates visit this portal at
http://apesportal.eva.mpg.de*

availability and activity (food and access to reproductive females). Parties thus tend to be smaller during periods of fruit scarcity. The most common aggregations are a mixture of males and females with immature offspring. Communities living in forest habitats have annual home ranges of 7–32 km², while in savannah woodland, they range over much wider areas, often exceeding 65 km². Typically, the community's home range is defended by highly territorial males who patrol boundaries and may attack, and even kill, members of neighboring communities. Adult female chimpanzees often spend time alone with their offspring or in a party with other females.

Great apes not only feed, but also rest, socialize and sleep in trees. Being large-brained, highly intelligent mammals, they need long periods of sleep and build nests in which they spend the night. These beds are usually constructed high in trees, 10–30 m above ground (Morgan *et al.*, 2006). African apes are semi-terrestrial and often rest on the ground during the daytime, but orangutans are almost exclusively arboreal. They are not adapted for terrestrial locomotion, although Bornean orangutans also travel on the ground in both primary and degraded habitat (Loken, Spehar and Rayadin, 2013; Ancrenaz *et al.*, 2014b). More or less restricted to the canopy, orangutans do not travel great distances on average. Bornean flanged adult males and adult females move 200 m each day, unflanged adult males usually double that distance. Sumatran orangutans move farther, but still less than 1 km each day (Singleton *et al.*, 2009). The semi-terrestrial African apes range considerably longer distances and the most frugivorous roam several kilometers each day: bonobos and western lowland gorillas average 2 km, but sometimes 5–6 km; chimpanzees travel 2–3 km, with occasional 10 km excursions. Savannah-dwelling chimpanzees generally range farther daily than their forest-dwelling counterparts. See Figure AO3.

Figure AO3

Daily Distances Travelled by Great Apes

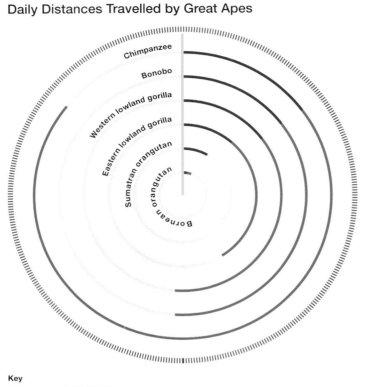

Key

Chimpanzee = 2,000–10,000 m
Bonobo = 2,000–6,000 m
Western lowland gorilla = 2,000–6,000 m
Eastern lowland gorilla = 1,500–5,000 m
Sumatran orangutan = flanged 1,000 m, unflanged unknown
Bornean orangutan = flanged 200 m, unflanged 400 m

Foraging in complex forest environments requires spatial memory and mental mapping. The great apes' daily searches for food are generally restricted to a particular location, an area of forest that an individual or group knows well. Chimpanzees are capable of memorizing the individual locations of thousands of trees over many years (Normand and Boesch, 2009); the other great ape species are likely to possess similar mental capacities. The area used habitually by an individual, group or community of a species is referred to as a home range. The establishment of a home range helps a species to secure access to resources within it (Delgado, 2010).

A male orangutan's range encompasses several (smaller) female ranges; high-status flanged males are able to monopolize both food and females to a degree, and so may temporarily reside in a relatively small area (4–8 km² for Bornean males). Orangutan home-range overlap is usually extensive, but flanged male orangutans establish personal space by emitting long calls (see Figure AO4). As long as distance is maintained, physical conflicts are rare; however, close encounters between adult males trigger aggressive displays that sometimes lead to fights. If an orangutan inflicts serious injury on his opponent, infection of the wounds can result in death (Knott, 1998).

Eastern gorillas range over areas of 6–34 km² (Williamson and Butynski, 2013a), and western gorilla home ranges average 10–20 km²—and potentially up to 50 km² (Head et al., 2013). Gorillas are not territorial and neighboring groups' ranges may overlap (see Figure AO4). Encounters between groups can occur without visual contact; instead, silverback males exchange vocalizations and chestbeats until one or both groups move away. Groups are less vigilant of each other in large swampy clearings where good visibility allows silverbacks to monitor potential competitors from a distance (Parnell, 2002). In contrast, other research finds that mountain gorillas engaged in contact aggression during 17% of studied group encounters (Sicotte, 1993). Physical aggression is rare, but if contests escalate, fighting between silverbacks can be intense. Infections of injuries sustained during intergroup interactions and subsequent deaths have occurred (Williamson, 2014).

Chimpanzees living in forest habitats have home ranges of 7–41 km² (Emery Thompson and Wrangham, 2013), and more than 65 km² in savanna (Pruetz and Bertolani, 2009). Male chimpanzees are highly territorial and patrol the boundaries of their ranges (see Figure AO4). Parties of males may attack members of neighboring communities and some populations are known for their aggression (Williams *et al.*, 2008). Victors benefit by gaining females or increasing the size of their range. Bonobo communities share home ranges of 22–58 km² (Hashimoto *et al.*, 1998). Bonobos exhibit neither territorial defense nor cooperative patrolling; encounters between members of different communities are characterized by excitement rather than conflict (Hohmann *et al.*, 1999).

Wherever gorillas and chimpanzees are sympatric, dietary divisions between the species limit direct competition for food. If the area of available habitat is restricted, such mechanisms for limiting competition will be compromised, but it is thought that both species are more tolerant of each other when they are both attracted to the same highly preferred food source, especially in times of fruit scarcity (Morgan and Sanz, 2006).

Reproduction

Male apes reach sexual maturity between the ages of 8 and 16 years, with chimpanzees attaining adulthood at 8–15 years, bonobos at 10, eastern gorillas around 15 and western gorillas at 18. Orangutan males mature between the ages of 8 and 16 years, but they may not develop flanges for another 20 years (Wich *et al.*, 2004). Female great apes become reproductive between the ages of 6 and 12 years: gorillas at 6–7 years, chimpanzees at 7–8, bonobos at 9–12 and orangutans at 10–11. They tend to give birth to their first offspring between the ages of 8 and 16: gorillas at 10 (with an average range of 8–14 years), chimpanzees at 13.5 years (with a mean of 9.5–15.4 years at different sites), bonobos at 13–15 years and orangutans at 15–16 years.

Pregnancy length in gorillas and orangutans is about the same as for humans; it is slightly shorter in chimpanzees and bonobos, at 7.5–8.0 months. Apes usually give

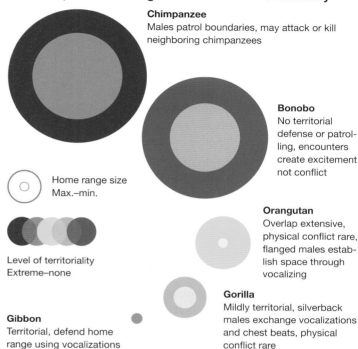

Figure AO4

Size of Ape Home Ranges and Levels of Territoriality

Chimpanzee
Males patrol boundaries, may attack or kill neighboring chimpanzees

Home range size
Max.–min.

Bonobo
No territorial defense or patrolling, encounters create excitement not conflict

Level of territoriality
Extreme–none

Orangutan
Overlap extensive, physical conflict rare, flanged males establish space through vocalizing

Gorilla
Mildly territorial, silverback males exchange vocalizations and chest beats, physical conflict rare

Gibbon
Territorial, defend home range using vocalizations

birth to one infant at a time, although twin births do occur (Goossens *et al.*, 2011). Births are not seasonal; however, conception requires females to be in good health. Chimpanzees and bonobos are more likely to ovulate when fruit is abundant, so in some populations there are seasonal peaks in the number of conceiving females (Anderson, Nordheim and Boesch, 2006), with contingent peaks in birth rate during particular months (Emery Thompson and Wrangham, 2008). Bornean orangutans living in highly seasonal dipterocarp forests are most likely to conceive during mast fruiting events, when fatty seeds are plentiful (Knott, 2005). Sumatran orangutans do not face such severe constraints (Marshall *et al.*, 2009a). Meanwhile, gorillas, who are less dependent on seasonal foods, show no seasonality in their reproduction.

All great apes reproduce slowly, due to the mother's high investment in a single offspring and the infant's slow development and maturation. Infants sleep with their mother until they are weaned (4–5 years in African apes; 5–6 years in Bornean orangutans; 7 years in Sumatran orangutans) or a subsequent sibling is born. Weaning marks the end of infancy for African apes, but orangutan infants remain dependent on their mothers until they reach 7–9 years of age (van Noordwijk *et al.*, 2009). Females cannot become pregnant while an infant is nursing because suckling inhibits the reproductive cycle (Stewart, 1988; van Noordwijk *et al.*, 2013). Consequently, births are widely spaced, occurring on average every 4–7 years in African apes, every 6–8 years in Bornean orangutans and every 9 years in Sumatran orangutans. Interbirth intervals can be shortened by the killing of unweaned offspring by a member of the same species (Harcourt and Greenberg, 2001), typically an unrelated adult male. Infanticide has not been observed in orangutans or bonobos, but if a female gorilla or chimpanzee with an infant switches group, her offspring is likely to be killed by a male in her new group, resulting in early resumption of her reproductive cycle (Watts, 1989).

Long-term research on mountain gorillas and chimpanzees has allowed female lifetime reproductive success to be evaluated. The mean birth rate is 0.2–0.3 births/adult female/year, or one birth per adult female every 3.3–5.0 years. Mountain gorilla females produce an average of 3.6 offspring during their lifetimes (Robbins *et al.*, 2011); similarly, chimpanzees give birth to four offspring, but only 1.5–3.2 survive beyond infancy (Sugiyama and Fujita, 2011).

Key points to be noted are (1) that documenting the biology of long-lived species takes decades of study due to their slow rates of reproduction, and (2) that great ape populations that have fallen off are likely to take several generations to recover (generation time in the great apes is 20–25 years) (IUCN, 2014b). These factors make great apes far more vulnerable than smaller, faster-breeding species. Orangutans have the slowest life history of any mammal, with later age at first reproduction, longer interbirth intervals and longer generation times than African apes (Wich *et al.*, 2009a, 2009b); as a result, they are the most susceptible to loss.

Gibbon Socioecology

Gibbons are the most diverse and widespread group of apes. Currently, 19 species of gibbon in four genera are recognized: 9 *Hylobates* species, 7 *Nomascus* species, 2 *Hoolock* species and the single *Symphalangus* species (IUCN, 2014b). Gibbons inhabit a wide range of habitats, predominantly lowland, submontane and montane broadleaf evergreen and semi-evergreen forests, as well as dipterocarp-dominated and mixed-deciduous (non-evergreen) forests. Some members of the *Nomascus* also occur in limestone karst forests and some populations of *Hylobates* live in swamp forest (Cheyne, 2010). Gibbons occur from sea level up to around 1,500–2,000 m above sea level, although this is taxon and location specific; for example, *Nomascus concolor* has been recorded at up to 2,900 m above sea level in China (Fan Peng-Fei, Jiang Xue-Long and Tian Chang-Cheng, 2009). The *Hylobatidae* are heavily impacted by the extent and quality of forest as they are arboreal (Bartlett, 2007), with the exception of the rarely recorded behavior of moving bipedally and terrestrially across forest gaps or to access isolated fruiting trees in more degraded and fragmented habitats.

Gibbons are reliant on forest ecosystems for food. Gibbon diets are characterized by high levels of fruit intake, dominated by figs and supplemented with young leaves, mature leaves and flowers (Bartlett, 2007; Cheyne, 2008b; Elder, 2009), although siamangs are more folivorous (Palombit, 1997). Reliance on other protein sources, such as insects, birds' eggs and small vertebrates, is likely under-represented in the literature. The composition of the diet changes with the seasons and habitat type, with flowers and young leaves dominating during the dry season in peat-swamp forests and figs dominating in dipterocarp forests (Marshall and Leighton, 2006; Fan Peng-Fei and Jiang Xue-Long, 2008; Lappan, 2009; Cheyne, 2010). Since gibbons are important seed dispersers, their frugivorous nature is significant in maintaining forest diversity (McConkey, 2000, 2005; McConkey and Chivers, 2007).

Each family group maintains a territory that it defends from other groups. Territories average 0.42 km² (Bartlett, 2007), but there is considerable variation and some indication that the more northerly *Nomascus* taxa maintain larger territories, possibly related to lower resource abundance at some times of year in these more seasonal forests. Gibbons have been typified as forming socially monogamous family groups. Other studies, however, have revealed they are not necessarily sexually monogamous (Palombit, 1994). Notable exceptions include extra-pair copulations (mating outside of the pair bond), individuals leaving the home territory to take up residence with neighboring individuals and male care of infants (Palombit, 1994; Reichard, 1995; Lappan, 2008). Research also indicates that the more northerly *N. nasutus*, *N. concolor* and *N. haianus* commonly form polygynous groups with more than one breeding female (Zhou *et al.*, 2008; Fan Peng-Fei and Jiang Xue-Long, 2010; Fan Peng-Fei *et al.*, 2010). There is no conclusive argument regarding these variable social and mating structures; they may be natural or a by-product of small population sizes, compression scenarios or sub-optimal habitats.

Both males and females disperse from their natal groups (Leighton, 1987) and establish their own territories; females have their first offspring at around 9 years of age. Data from captivity suggest that gibbons become sexually mature as early as 5.5 years of age (Geissmann, 1991). Interbirth intervals are in the range of 2–4 years, with 7 months' gestation (Bartlett, 2007). Although captive individuals have lived upwards of 40 years, gibbon longevity in the wild is unknown but thought to be considerably shorter. Due to the gibbons' relatively late age of maturation and long interbirth intervals, reproductive lifetime may be only 10–20 years (Palombit, 1992). Population replacement in gibbons is therefore relatively slow.

Acknowledgments

Principal authors: Annette Lanjouw, Helga Rainer and Alison White

Authors of the socioecology section: Marc Ancrenaz, Susan M. Cheyne, Tatyana Humle, Benjamin M. Rawson, Martha M. Robbins and Elizabeth A. Williamson

Reviewers: Susan Cheyne, Takeshi Furuichi, Benjamin M. Rawson, Melissa E. Thompson, Serge A. Wich and Elizabeth A. Williamson

Biodiversity has essential social, economic, cultural, spiritual and scientific values and its protection is hugely important for human survival. The rapid loss of biodiversity, unprecedented in the last 65 million years, is jeopardising the provision of ecosystem services that underpin human well-being. [. . .] Measures to conserve biodiversity and make a sustainable society possible need to be greatly enhanced and integrated with social, political and economic concerns.

Statement from the Blue Planet Prize Laureates: Gro Harlem Brundtland, Paul Ehrlich, José Goldemberg, James Hansen, Gene Likens, Amory Lovins, Suki Manabe, Bob May, Hal Mooney, Karl-Henrik Robèrt, Emil Salim, Gordon Sato, Susan Solomon, Nicholas Stern, M. S. Swaminathan, Robert Watson, Barefoot College, Conservation International, International Institute for Environment and Development and the International Union for Conservation of Nature. (Brundtland *et al.*, 2012, p. 2)

The one process now going on that will take millions of years to correct is the loss of genetic and species diversity by the destruction of natural habitats. This is the folly our descendants are least likely to forgive us.

E.O. Wilson, *Biophilia* (Wilson, 1984, p. 121)

INTRODUCTION

Section 1: Industrial Agriculture and Ape Conservation

Social and economic systems worldwide are changing rapidly, accompanied by an increasing global demand for natural resources, including land, water, minerals, energy sources, food and timber. In areas where the climate, conflict, human population growth, and human population movements are affecting availability, these changes are tied to a scarcity of natural resources. The impacts of many of these social and economic transformations— many of which are propelled by the forces of globalization—are reflected in changes in the climate; the availability and quantity of water, toxicity and eutrophication of waterways; food scarcity in many areas of the world; a loss of biodiversity; and declining terrestrial and marine ecosystems. Finding the tools to both understand and address the complexity of these interrelated trends, and to implement strategies to balance environmental needs with social and economic requirements, is the foremost challenge facing us today. The *State of the Apes* series is an effort to contribute to this search by providing accurate information on the current situation, identifying viable solutions, and presenting apes as a flagship species that can contribute to the conservation of tropical forest ecosystems worldwide.

Commissioned by the Arcus Foundation and published biennially, *State of the Apes* has a twofold objective: to raise awareness about the status of apes around the world and to present detailed information on the impacts of human activities on apes and ape habitats. Accordingly, the publication comprises two sections. The first of these, the thematic section, focuses on a different key theme in each edition; it presents original research and rigorous analysis of the current situation and highlights selected best practice, with a view to stimulating debate, informing policy and practice, and promoting efforts to integrate economic and social development with conservation of wilderness and wildlife. Section 2 consists of two chapters that consider the status and welfare of apes, in their natural habitat and in captivity. By using apes as an example, the publication also aims to underscore the importance of species conservation.

State of the Apes covers all non-human ape species, namely bonobos, chimpanzees, gibbons, gorillas and orangutans, as well as their habitats. Ape ranges cover countries throughout the tropical belt of Africa and South and Southeast Asia. For details on each ape species, including their ecology and geographic range, see the Apes Overview (page x). Robust statistics on the status and welfare of apes are derived from the A.P.E.S. Portal (Ape Populations, Environments and Surveys) (IUCN SSC, n.d.), with abundance estimates of the different ape taxa presented in the Abundance Annex, available on the *State of the Apes* website at www.stateoftheapes.com.

Apes are vulnerable to many threats posed to their habitats by humans. Many of these threats are linked to the human use of their habitats, as well as more direct interactions, such as hunting and capture.

Since apes are closely related to humans, they are vulnerable to many of the same diseases and stresses. As forests are opened by human encroachment, the proximity between apes and humans is increasing, as is the incidence of direct contact with each other. To promote an understanding of both the impact and extent of these changes with respect to land use, this edition brings together the expertise and experiences of leading scholars and practitioners from various sectors, including civil society, industry and academia, with the ultimate aim of identifying possibilities and potential for avoidance and mitigation of harm.

The first edition of *State of the Apes* presents research, analysis, case studies and

BOX I.1

Industrial Agriculture: Definitions and Usage

State of the Apes defines the term "industrial agriculture" as a method of intensive crop production that is characterized by large monoculture farms and plantations that rely heavily on chemicals, pesticides, herbicides, fertilizers, intensive water use, and large-scale transport, storage and distribution infrastructure. While this edition uses the term "industrial agriculture," it is also referred to as industrial farming, intensive agriculture or farming, plantation agriculture, large-scale agriculture and commercial farming.

Monocultures are a key feature of industrial agriculture; they are part of a strategy to achieve economies of scale and reduce production costs. The term "concession" refers to a relatively large area of land that is allocated to agricultural investors for the industrialized production of crops, generally by a government.

Even though smallholder farmers are known to have significant impacts on tropical forests, including ape habitats (Etiendem *et al.*, 2013), it is beyond the scope of this publication to consider all agricultural sectors. For this reason, this volume only covers smallholder farmers who are part of a system that relies on an industry partner to provide inputs or purchase the commodity, thereby contributing to an expansive monoculture landscape. In these relationships, the farmers are also known as "outgrowers."

On the same basis, this edition considers only the interface of ape conservation and crop production, including agroforestry and tree crops, even though industrial agriculture may also refer to the industrialized production of livestock, poultry and fish. Key commodities such as cocoa, coffee, palm oil, paper and pulp, rubber, sugarcane and tea, produced as a result of large-scale production, are included.

best practice from a range of key stakeholders relating to the interface between ape conservation and the extractive industries. This second edition does the same in relation to the interface between conservation and industrial agriculture (see Box I.1). It examines relevant factors such as the drivers behind agricultural expansion and land investments, governance and the legal framework at this interface, and voluntary standards and certification. By aiming to take an objective approach to the subject matter, this volume is designed to contribute to improvements in current conservation practice and to inform and influence stakeholders, policy and practice in sectors as diverse as commerce (agribusiness, manufacturing and retail), law (legislative protections, industry regulation), civil society and human development—not least by showing how these communities interrelate and affect the status and welfare of apes, and of people. At the policy level, this volume aims to introduce ape conservation into local, national, regional and international policy dialogues; industry policy and practice; and development and economic planning.

This introductory chapter provides a brief overview of the context in which industrial agriculture operates and the broader linkages to ape conservation globally. The specifics of this interaction are more fully explored in the six thematic chapters, which are summarized below.

Industrial Agriculture and Apes

Based on the projected growth of the human population, and anticipated development of global demand for agricultural products, it is estimated that global agricultural production will have to increase by an estimated 60% from 2005 to 2050 to meet the anticipated global demand for agricultural products, such as food and biofuels (Alexandratos and Bruinsma, 2012, p. 7). An estimated additional 700,000 km² (70 million ha) of land will be needed to meet this demand. Since production is expected to decline in developed countries, however, developing countries will be required to make available a projected 1.32 million km² (132 million ha) of land, primarily in sub-Saharan Africa and Latin America (Alexandratos and Bruinsma, 2012, p. 11).

The Institute of Economic Affairs highlights efficient, large-scale industrial agriculture as a solution to these demands (Boyfield, 2013). In stark contrast, the G20 Inter-Agency Working Group on food security points to evidence that large-scale land acquisitions in developing countries to create "megafarms" are the type of investment least likely to generate significant net benefits to host countries and local communities in terms of agricultural development (IAWG, 2011). The Working Group suggests that smallholder farming based on contract farming, outgrower schemes and joint ventures with farmer groups is more conducive to sustainable economic development. The introduction of genetically modified organisms (GMOs) into agricultural production has enormous potential to influence the dynamics of the industry. Although of significant importance in many parts of the world, GMO use remains relatively rare in ape range states across both Africa and Southeast Asia and is therefore not considered in this volume.

The tropical ecosystems in sub-Saharan Africa and Latin America are the primary extensive areas of land left with potential for the development of industrial agriculture (Laurance, Sayer and Cassman, 2014b). The expansion and development of the agricultural estate would not only have obvious implications for forested habitats and wildlife populations, but also significant indirect impacts on humans, not least through the release of greenhouse gases and consequent acceleration of climate change. While Chapter 1 and other sections in this volume touch on the risks and impacts of climate change, this important issue will be addressed in much greater depth in a future edition of *State of the Apes*.

For agriculture to be sustainable and able to meet the demand for food and other commodities, it needs to be considered in the context of a rapidly changing world. It is critical to understand how factors such as urbanization, growing inequalities and divisions between the poor and the wealthy, human migration, climate change, water shortages and floods, environmental degradation, globalization and changing dietary preferences are influencing agricultural production and practice around the world. As this volume demonstrates, industrial agriculture is a major cause of encroachment into tropical forests. Documented effects of forest degradation and clearance on wildlife, including great apes and gibbons, illustrate the impact industrial agriculture can have on biodiversity. The ramifications include local and global food insecurity and pressures on productive capacity as well as entire ecosystems. The complex political, social and economic decision-making that drives the expansion of industrial agriculture needs to consider the environmental factors that underpin the industry, and the diversity of species that is required for ecosystem health. In this context, apes can serve as an indicator species for biodiversity in general.

A significant proportion of tropical forest in South and Southeast Asia has already been converted to serve the needs of large-scale agricultural production systems. In drawing attention to the consequences of this expansion for apes and their habitats, this edition seeks to inform the trajectory of industrial agriculture in Africa, where cultivation rates are relatively low but predicted to increase dramatically in the foreseeable future. Palm oil—used for food, cosmetics, toiletries and biofuels—is the fastest-growing monoculture in the world (Gerber, 2011; FAO, 2014a) and will likely account for a considerable portion of that expansion. Since 42% of Africa's great ape population inhabit areas suitable for oil palm development, and since only a small proportion of that land is protected, the expansion of this crop is certain to have a serious impact on apes (Wich *et al.*, 2014). As reflected in this volume, more research has been carried out on the production of palm oil than on any other commodity. Due to its expansive industrial production, palm oil is the commodity that has had the greatest impact on ape habitats in Asia and that poses the most significant threat to those in Africa. This edition also assesses the impacts of a number of other crops on ape conservation and welfare, including acacia, cacao, rubber, sugarcane and tobacco, thereby speaking to any industrial-scale agricultural production undertaken in ape habitats.

Photo: Palm oil—used for food, cosmetics, toiletries and biofuels—is the fastest-growing monoculture in the world.
© Wilmar International

Chapter Highlights

The first six chapters of this edition of *State of the Apes* focus on the various aspects of

the interface of industrial agriculture and ape conservation. Chapter 1 provides a broad overview of the direct and indirect impacts of industrial agriculture on apes and ape habitat. Chapter 2 discusses the overlap between industrial agriculture and ape conservation and considers contexts within which this interface has developed. Chapter 3 focuses on Africa, the continent whose apes have been least affected by industrial agriculture. Given that this situation is expected to shift significantly in the coming decades, the chapter lays out an in-depth analysis of the context and drivers of agricultural expansion—and of their predicted interaction with apes. Chapter 4 presents an analysis of the legislative frameworks at the interface of industrial agriculture and ape conservation across a number of ape range states and discusses the relevance of engagement with legal instruments to influence the relationship between the two sectors. A discussion of the establishment and evolution of a key voluntary standard, the Roundtable on Sustainable Palm Oil (RSPO), and an assessment of its impact on ape conservation form the basis of Chapter 5. This voluntary standard resonates markedly with ape conservation due to the extensive impact of palm oil production on ape habitats, especially in the Asian context. Chapter 6 puts forward the current understanding of ape ecology in relation to impacts of industrial agriculture. While formal research at this interface remains limited, particularly in relation to African great apes and Asian gibbons, the chapter offers insight based on research in ape socioecology and observations from expert primatologists.

Section 2 is made up of two chapters that focus on broader conservation issues for apes across Africa and Asia (Chapter 7) and for those in captivity (Chapter 8). The chapter highlights are included in the introduction to Section 2 (see page 194).

Section 1: The Interface of Industrial Agriculture and Ape Conservation

Chapter 1: Direct and Indirect Impacts of Industrial Agriculture

As the human population grows and the associated demand for land for cultivation of both food and non-food commodities increases, particularly in the tropics, agriculture will inevitably have an impact on apes and their habitats and affect their chances for survival. The impacts will be felt not only through the clearing of land for large-scale plantations, but also through increasing contact between ape populations that are squeezed into ever-shrinking patches of forest, as well as between apes and humans, as they compete for space

and for food. The mounting frequency of interactions between humans and apes will inevitably lead to the killing and capture of increasing numbers of apes. This chapter explores the direct and indirect impacts of industrial agriculture, evaluating the relevance of industrial agriculture—and palm oil in particular—for poverty reduction and land tenure. It also discusses the interface between industrial agriculture and climate change and—via two case studies, one from Kalimantan, Indonesia, and the other from Bulindi, Uganda—reveals how the development of industrial agriculture affects apes as a result of increased exposure to people and human activity. The final section reviews factors that could motivate the agricultural industry to engage in ape conservation and mitigation strategies—and the means for such engagement.

Chapter 2: Extent of Overlap

This chapter explores the extent to which industrial agriculture overlaps with ape habitats. Through the use of a number of data sets, including the Land Matrix and the Global Forest Watch online platform, several patterns emerge. Comparisons show that in Asia, where a significant amount of land has been allocated to industrial agricultural use, the impact on ape habitats is far greater than in Africa; they also reveal regional differences within Africa, with industrial agriculture concessions seemingly concentrated in West Africa. Other issues, such as agricultural concessions overlapping with protected areas, point to inadequate planning and governance with respect to land use and allocation.

Three case studies—Cameroon, Liberia and on the island of Borneo—explore the evolution of deforestation due to industrial agriculture. A common finding is that industrial agriculture was first established under colonial administrations; yet while significant deforestation linked to industrial agriculture continued across Borneo for decades after the end of colonial rule, this course was not pursued in the other locations, largely due to differing political contexts, including a lengthy civil war in Liberia. In response to a recent resurgence of interest in developing the agricultural sector, however, the allocation of concessions has been on the rise in both Cameroon and Liberia. In Liberia, a recent agreement with Norway for results-based development aid holds some promise for ensuring that decision-making on agricultural expansion takes into consideration areas of significant biodiversity, including ape habitats, and local communities.

Chapter 3: Cause of Conversion—Focus on Africa

The forests of the Congo Basin and West Africa present some of the largest areas suitable for the expansion of industrial agriculture and are also home to important populations of great apes. Agriculture already represents a significant part of sub-Saharan Africa's economy; however, a shift in the composition of this sector—essentially from one dominated by smallholders to one that is increasingly industrial in nature—is likely to have significant implications for the continent's forests and ape habitats. This chapter presents details on the drivers of this shift, including information on the geographic variation and extent of crops that land investments have targeted. Oilseed crops, including oil palm, castor, sesame and sunflower, have attracted the most commercial interest, with oil palm being the second-largest crop in terms of total land area purchased for cultivation. The recent increase in the number of large-scale land acquisitions in Africa has been accompanied by impacts on apes and tropical forest. While the expansion continues to be driven by the increase in the global demand for commodities—as well as by relatively easy access to land and low set-up costs in Africa compared to elsewhere—the development of the industry has been affected by the Ebola outbreak in West Africa and the global decline in palm oil prices. Despite the challenges, investor interest is likely to persist, especially as domestic and regional demand is predicted to increase and current production is not adequately supplying those markets. What remains to be seen is whether African states pursue the Asian model of clear felling large tracts of land to convert to agriculture or look to Brazil for examples of agricultural development that has championed smallholders, an approach that holds greater promise for protecting ape habitats.

Chapter 4: Legal Frameworks

Engaging with legislative frameworks can help to shape how the interface between industrial agriculture and ape conservation is perceived and managed. This chapter focuses on the national legal systems across eight ape range states—Cambodia, Cameroon, the Democratic Republic of Congo, Gabon, Indonesia, Liberia, Malaysia and Myanmar —all of which also have significant agribusinesses. In exploring the extent to which legislation interfaces with ape conservation, it reviews agribusiness tenure arrangements and highlights conflict with conservation, such as requirements that companies make productive use of all land within their concessions despite possible contravention of environmental considerations. The chapter also assesses the process by which agribusiness concessions are allocated, pointing to institutional complexities and power dynamics that influence decisions. It then discusses the role and extent of provisions for environmental protections, such as the Environmental Impact Assessment, and the degree of transparency and monitoring of compliance with legislation on species protection, which is often hindered in the face of competing agribusiness interests. Unsurprisingly, institutional capacity and political economy considerations are at the root of poor environmental protection, a state of affairs that is unlikely to improve in the absence of robust mechanisms to sanction governments. Yet as the chapter's case study demonstrates, legal mechanisms have been used to uphold the enforcement of environmental laws: in Sumatra, such mechanisms proved successful in blocking the attempted encroachment of agribusiness into the Tripa peat swamp forests, which would have resulted in the destruction of ape habitat.

Chapter 5: The RSPO

Voluntary standards and certification have emerged as a dominant avenue for integrating sustainability into commodity production. They have been developed in response to weak or ineffective state regulation and seek to address concerns, primarily driven by consumers, in relation to the social and environmental impacts of commodity production. This chapter assesses a key voluntary standard, the Roundtable on Sustainable Palm Oil, which focuses on promoting the sustainable production of palm oil in the tropics. It presents details on three inter-related issues. First, it considers the RSPO's background and its evolution into a functioning institution that is essentially driven by process, highlighting the tension between the standard's objective to transform the global palm oil market and the resultant need to hold its members accountable. Second, it reviews the challenges facing the RSPO as it aims to ensure adherence to robust environmental and social principles. Specifically, it looks into membership influence on decision-making and the consequences of a lack of scientific clarity on interpretation and on the definition of what exactly should constitute certified sustainably produced palm oil. Third, the chapter analyzes the RSPO's focus on the largest palm oil producers, an approach that presents both an opportunity and a challenge. On the one hand, recent commitments by companies that supply more than 90% of the palm oil industry to "no deforestation, no peatland and no exploitation" policies could significantly enhance the RSPO's impact. On the other hand, poor engagement and inclusion of smallholders and other stakeholders—such as local communities and governments at the regional, national and local levels—may ultimately undermine the recent strides that have been made.

Chapter 6: Ecological Impacts

There are significant gaps in our understanding of the impact of industrial agriculture on ape ecology. To enable a more robust analysis of this issue, this chapter reviews formally published materials and gray literature; it also includes the findings

Photo: Orangutan foraging in an oil palm plantation. © HUTAN - Kinabatangan Orang-utan Conservation Project

from a survey conducted by members of the International Union for Conservation of Nature, the Species Survival Commission, and the Primate Specialist Group's Sections on Great Apes and Small Apes.

Forest clearance and degradation for the development of industrial agriculture have a direct impact on ape populations through habitat destruction and fragmentation, which may lead to stress, increased morbidity and death among apes. By facilitating access to previously remote areas and thereby promoting commercial hunting, including that of apes, industrial agricultural development also has an indirect impact on ape populations. Further, forest clearance can coincide with significant influxes of people into an area, prompting further clearance across the landscape and potentially exposing apes to disease. Of all the apes, gibbons are probably most affected by industrial agriculture, due to their territorial and strictly arboreal nature. While the great apes are likely to fare somewhat better—partly thanks to their ability to enter agro-industrial landscapes to forage, sleep or disperse—they cannot survive in plantations alone and need forest and natural habitat for long-term survival. The ongoing fragmentation of ape populations and the use of ape habitats for industrial agriculture is likely to result in long-term population decline and possible local extinction of species. Changing this course will require specific research on how this industry is affecting apes and their habitats, combined with the implementation of land use planning that incorporates essential ecological functions.

Conclusion

By bringing to the fore the myriad issues associated with both ape conservation and industrial agriculture, this edition of *State of the Apes* takes a first step in identifying perspectives on the interface between large-scale agricultural production systems and biodiversity conservation. A considerable force in economic development, industrial agriculture interfaces with ape conservation in ways that represent a fundamental challenge for natural resource management more broadly.

It is clear that pressure on tropical ecosystems to supply global markets will be enormous. The principal frontiers for the future development of key global agricultural commodities are in Africa and Latin America—which are home to the largest tropical forests that have been identified as "suitable" for agricultural development. In Africa and Southeast Asia, this expansion will have significant impacts on the remaining ape habitats; some ape species risk losing their last remaining pockets of habitat. In presenting an overview of the extent of the impact and interaction between apes and industrial agriculture, this edition provides details on how these interactions are manifested, not only in relation to apes, but also in relation to the development of the industry.

A key finding that resonates throughout this edition is the critical significance of effective land use planning—at the relevant landscape-level scale. By incorporating economic, social and environmental considerations, land use plans can help to ensure equitable and sustainable management of land and resources, in part by identifying key areas to be protected and by securing appropriate corridors to connect forests that are protected and managed in a sustainable manner. Given that land use planning is rarely carried out effectively in any part of the world, the promotion of its application is among the most urgent priorities for the conservation of apes—and of biodiversity in general.

Finally, this edition of *State of the Apes* underscores the lessons learned from the rapid expansion of industrial agriculture in Asia, which, if acknowledged, suggest ways to ensure a more sustainable trajectory of industrial agriculture development in Africa. In this sense, this volume is a timely resource —one that can inform a more responsible approach to future agricultural development and conservation in Africa and influence further agricultural development in Asia. In all affected contexts, better engagement among all stakeholders, including smallholders and local communities, is imperative if shifts in the impacts of industrial agriculture on the natural world are to be achieved.

Acknowledgments

Principal authors: Helga Rainer, Annette Lanjouw and Alison White

CHAPTER 1

Economic Development and Conservation of Biodiversity: Understanding the Interface of Ape Conservation and Industrial Agriculture

Introduction

Tropical ecosystems sustain much of the earth's biodiversity, provide countless natural products and services—both locally and globally—and play critical roles in the regulation of the climate and the carbon and hydrological cycles. The expansion of agriculture into tropical forest ecosystems will therefore have enormous impacts on factors such as human and animal health (Karesh *et al.*, 2012), energy options and prices, biodiversity conservation and infrastructure (see Box 1.1). In addition, this expansion might drive, or be affected by, conflict in areas of resource scarcity. These factors all directly affect human survival and that of countless other species. The rapid expansion of agriculture is the main driver of tropical forest loss (Sodhi *et al.*, 2010). In much of the world, such expansion is led by large-scale, industrial agriculture, although small-scale agriculture also has a significant impact in some countries, particularly those in Africa.

Over the past 50 years, agricultural expansion has primarily been related to the foods and oils that form the basic diet for most of the world's human population: cassava, corn, palm oil, plantain, potato, rice, sorghum, soybean, sugar, sweet potato, wheat and yam. Many other crops, including cacao, coffee, peanuts, rubber, tea and tobacco, as well as various fruit crops, are also grown on industrial plantations. The main vegetable oils produced for global consumption include those made from coconut, cotton, oil palm, peanut, rapeseed, soybean and sunflower (Boyfield, 2013). Only palm oil and coconut oil are exclusively grown in the tropics. Palm oil accounts for 40% of the vegetable oil produced worldwide (Boyfield, 2013; USDA, 2014b).

Tropical forests in Africa and Latin America are the main frontiers for the future development of industrial agricultural plantations, particularly for oil palm. There is agreement within the agricultural development sector that the Amazon and Congo basins hold enormous potential for the creation of large-scale oil palm plantations, with 290,000 km² (29 million ha) of land suitable for oil palm cultivation in the Amazon alone (Corley and Tinker, 2003; Embrapa, 2010, cited in UNEP, 2011). The Institute for Economic Affairs estimates that 2.5–3.0 million km² (250–300 million ha) of land is suitable for food crops in sub-Saharan Africa, where only 1.8 million km² (183 million ha) is currently under cultivation (Boyfield, 2013). As Figure 1.1 shows, all the geographic areas most suitable for new oil palm development are in the tropics (UNEP, 2011). To a large extent, these areas also boast the greatest species diversity and abundance. Yet, due to the relatively high costs of labor and complex social and economic

FIGURE 1.1

Surface Cultivated and Model of Suitability for Oil Palm Plantations

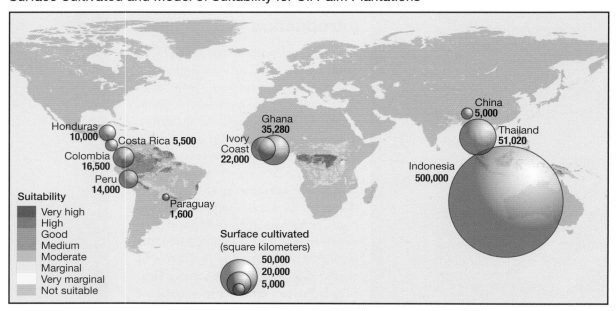

Data sources: Model of suitability for oil palm plantations from IIASA (2002) and FAO (2002). Surface of oil palm cultivated from FAO (2009a)

Source: UNEP (2011)

factors in Brazil and other parts of the neotropics, the palm oil industry is not as likely to see a huge expansion in this region as it is to focus on sub-Saharan Africa.

One means to protect intact tropical moist forests and biodiversity from conversion to agricultural plantations is to cultivate low-carbon-density land (LCDL)—including degraded forests—in both the neotropics and afrotropics. This approach avoids the release of carbon from the conversion of intact tropical forests and protects biodiversity. Sustaining the projected 17–29% increase in the cultivation of the three main commodity crops—oil palm, sugarcane and natural rubber—will require an estimated additional 600,000–660,000 km² (60–66 million ha) of land in the tropical moist forest belt over the next 50 years (Dinerstein *et al.*, 2014).

Much has been studied and written about the history and processes of oil palm development—and about the impacts of the crop on the environment. Far less is known about the impact of other agricultural crops grown at industrial scale. It is clear, however, that industrial cultivation of any commodity that involves the conversion of forest to an agricultural landscape will reduce forest cover and human accessibility to forest resources, including wildlife (see Box 1.2). Given the availability of relevant data and the relatively broad scope of research on oil palm production—as well as the related threats posed to biodiversity—this chapter (and the whole volume) is weighted heavily toward this particular crop and its impacts on tropical moist forests. It also presents findings of research on other industrial agricultural commodities, particularly if these have an impact on ape populations and habitats.

This chapter presents an overview of some of the critical issues at the interface between apes and industrial agriculture. To that end, it is divided into four sections. The initial section assesses the relevance of industrial agriculture—and specifically oil palm and palm oil—to poverty reduction. The second section discusses the impact of industrial agriculture on climate change. The third section, which explores the impact of industrial agriculture on apes, features two case studies that illustrate how the development of industrial agriculture affects apes as a result of increased exposure to people and human activities. The final section addresses the potential motivation for the agricultural industry to engage in ape conservation strategies and to mitigate the loss of ape habitats—and the means to do so.

Key findings of the chapter include the following:

- Oil palm development is not always beneficial to poverty reduction; in fact, it often exacerbates poverty while also degrading the natural resource base on which human livelihoods depend.

- Although the destruction of natural forest to create industrial agricultural plantations involves replacing one vegetation type with another, it does produce net carbon emissions and is contributing to carbon levels in the atmosphere, thereby aggravating climate change.

- The expansion of industrial agriculture into areas inhabited by apes can have multiple repercussions, including the loss of habitat, the killing of apes and an increase in conflict between humans and apes through competition over land and resources.

- While research has identified some management options and practices that agricultural developers can implement to promote the protection of forest habitats and conservation of apes—such as the translocation of resident apes and the maintenance of forest patches and corridors—more studies are required to enhance understanding of the ecological and social impacts of this industry.

BOX 1.1

The Global Roadmap Project

There is a growing need to enhance our general understanding of and our ability to measure and assess the direct and indirect impacts of industrial agriculture on forest ecosystems and ape populations. That is particularly the case with respect to infrastructure development, such as roads (see Figure 1.2). The International Energy Agency anticipates that 25 million km of new roads will be built by 2050—60% more than were built in 2010. Around 90% of these new roads will probably be built in developing countries, largely in tropical forests that sustain exceptional biodiversity and vital ecosystem services (Dulac, 2013). Research shows that roads that penetrate into forests or wilderness often cause significant environmental problems, including habitat loss and fragmentation, overhunting, wildfires and other environmental degradation, often with irreversible impacts on ecosystems and wildlife (Laurance *et al.*, 2001; Blake *et al.*, 2007; Adeney, Christensen and Pimm, 2009; Laurance, Goosem and Laurance, 2009; Laurance *et al.*, 2014a).

In many nations, efforts to plan and zone roads are seriously inadequate (Laporte *et al.*, 2007; Laurance, 2007; Laurance *et al.*, 2014a). Since there is no strategic global system for zoning roads, each road project must be assessed individually, with little information on its broader environmental context (Burgués Arrea *et al.*, 2014; Laurance *et al.*, 2014a).

For these reasons, a group of environmental scientists, geographers, planners and agricultural specialists devised the Global Roadmap Project, a scheme for prioritizing road building around the world (Laurance and Balmford, 2013; Laurance

et al., 2014a; Global Roadmap, n.d.). This large-scale zoning plan seeks to limit the environmental costs of road expansion while maximizing its benefits for human development—especially for increasing agricultural production, an urgent priority given that global demand for agricultural commodities is expected to grow significantly in developing countries over the next few decades (Alexandratos and Bruinsma, 2012).

The Global Roadmap has identified three components—or layers—that are necessary to analyze the design and influence the approval of new roads and road improvements. The first is an environmental-values layer that estimates the natural importance of ecosystems; the second is a road-benefits layer that shows the potential for increased agricultural production, in part via new or improved roads. The third layer shows the distribution of terrestrial protected areas around the world. The Global Roadmap Project argues that protected areas should remain road-free wherever possible to limit the deleterious impacts that such roads often have on natural ecosystems.

Based on the combination of these three components, the Global Roadmap identifies areas of high environmental value, where future road building should be avoided; areas where strategic road improvements could promote agricultural development with relatively modest environmental costs; and "conflict areas," where road building could have sizeable benefits for agriculture but would cause serious environmental damage. The ultimate aim is for the Global Roadmap to be used by governments, stakeholders and environmental groups to help guide road planning. The plan provides a template for the active zoning and prioritizing of roads during the most explosive era of road expansion in human history.

FIGURE 1.2

Global Distribution of Major Roads

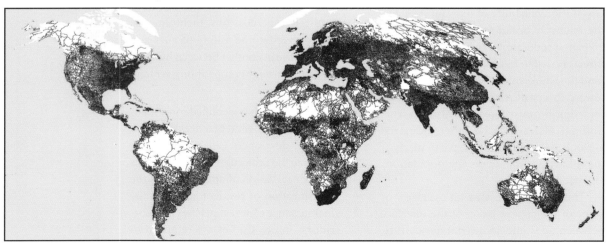

Note: Many illegal or unofficial roads are not mapped; see CIESIN and ITOS (2013).

Source: Laurance *et al.* (2014a, p. 230)

BOX 1.2

Establishing an Industrial Agricultural Estate: Key Phases

The establishment of a plantation project entails three stages of development: initiation, planning and implementation (see Figure 1.3). The phases are generally consistent across a range of crops, despite differing terminology used in the various agricultural sectors (Stewart, 2014). These three phases result in the identification of all potential environmental and social impacts of the project and the development of improved practices and mitigating measures relating to various physiochemical, biological, environmental and social aspects (Corley and Tinker, 2003).

In Malaysia, it is now a legal requirement to carry out formal environmental impact assessments (EIAs) for each new development, in conjunction with the land evaluation process. In general, an EIA sets out baseline data on the geology and soil, water courses and quality, fauna, medical and health services, and other factors. The EIA is followed by an environmental management plan (EMP), which is used as a guide during the development of the agricultural estate, and which sets out the monitoring indicators to determine environmental impacts. This process provides guidelines that highlight the importance of preserving forest fragments and wildlife corridors to maintain biodiversity and wildlife in plantations (Corley and Tinker, 2003). Together with regulations designed to protect the environment and biodiversity in and around plantations, such as maintaining bands of riparian forest along watercourses, these formal requirements could provide an important legal basis for improved sustainability and environmental management. In many countries, however, these guidelines and regulations are frequently ignored, even if they are legal requirements, often due to corruption.

Avoiding and mitigating environmental damage in the early planning stages is far preferable to addressing it later, as it is more difficult and expensive to correct any faults if these are embedded in the plantation layout (Corley and Tinker, 2003). Appropriate actions range from the inclusion of analogous forests with multiple values that can support wildlife, to addressing landscape ecosystems that include plantations as a portion of the broader landscape, together with wildlife habitat, to form a stable system.

FIGURE 1.3

Development Stages of a Plantation Project

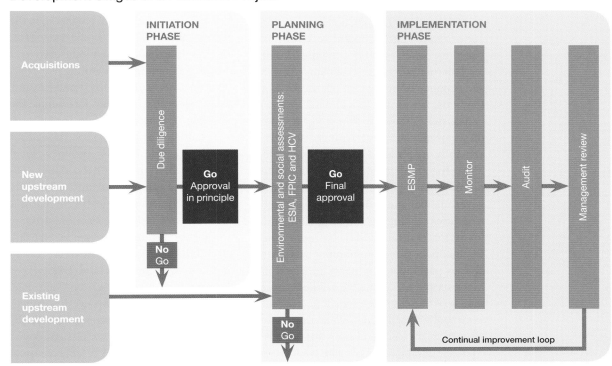

Notes: ESIA: environmental and social impact assessment; ESMP: environmental and social management plan; FPIC: free prior informed consent; HCV: high conservation value.
Source: Stewart (2014)

The Role of Palm Oil in Poverty Alleviation and Land Tenure

Palm oil is the most traded and affordable cooking oil in the world, with a higher yield per hectare than any other major oil crop. It is also used in numerous other products, from foods to biofuel, to toiletries and cosmetics. Oil palm occupies a relatively low percentage (7%) of land cultivated for vegetable oils (Caliman, 2011)—as compared to the much higher proportions of land allotted to soybean (61%), rapeseed (18%) and sunflower (14%); nevertheless, oil palm accounts for 40% of the global production of vegetable oil. Furthermore, its production costs are 20% lower than those of soybean, making it the cheapest of all vegetable oils to produce (Rival and Levang, 2014). As a result, palm oil production is widely thought to contribute to poverty alleviation in the tropics. This claim, however, is controversial (Budidarsono, Rahmanulloh and Sofiyuddin, 2012).

While palm oil production has certainly contributed to government revenue and corporate profit, even boosting the income levels in rural communities in many cases, an audit conducted by the Compliance Advisor Ombudsman for the World Bank in 2009 demonstrates that investment in the palm oil sector may actually have increased poverty in some places (CAO, 2009; Gingold, 2011). The problem does not lie with palm oil production per se, but rather with the governmental and industry processes and structures relating to land acquisition and loans for plantation development, and whether poor rural communities have been able to participate equitably in these. In Malaysia and Indonesia, for example, more than 40% of the surface area of plantations is owned by smallholders. When properly planned, in line with regulations that promote equitable development, oil palm plantations can lead to a decline in rural poverty and improvements in economic development in the regions concerned. Yet given corruption, poor planning or inequitable sharing of benefits, oil palm plantations can have an adverse impact on local populations (Rival and Levang, 2014).

While the World Bank study led to a moratorium on lending to the oil palm sector for two years, the debate over a causal link between the industry and poverty remains unresolved. The labor intensity of oil palm cultivation contributes significantly to employment in many regions, and additional benefits can include higher incomes and access to healthcare and education (Dayang Norwana et al., 2011). A recent assessment of the local impacts of oil palm expansion in Malaysia shows that oil palm smallholders, who have benefited from higher returns than producers of other agricultural products, exhibit the lowest incidence of poverty across all agricultural sub-sectors (Dayang Norwana et al., 2011).

Likewise, a recent assessment of returns to labor showed that oil palm can provide incomes two to seven times higher than the average agricultural wage (Budidarsono et al., 2012), supporting a rural middle class over several generations—something few tropical crops can achieve (Rival and Levang, 2014). In Sumatra, Indonesia, for example, the annual income per hectare over the full cycle of a plantation averages €2,100 (US$2,675) for oil palm, €2,600 (US$3,312) for a clonal rubber plantation and €1,300 (US$1,656) for a rubber agroforest, compared to only €200 (US$255) for a rice field. A comparison of the return on labor is even more striking: €36 (US$46) per day per person for oil palm, €17 (US$22) for clonal rubber and €21 (US$27) for rubber agroforest—vs. €1.70 (US$2.17) per day per person for irrigated rice (Feintrenie, Chong and Levang, 2010, p. 12).[1] It is important to note that these figures refer to smallholders rather than to workers employed by large agribusinesses. A recent economic analysis of palm oil production with respect to per capita income in Indonesia shows that increasing productivity, rather than enlarging the size of plantations, is a more effective means of boosting income and reducing poverty (Nur Rofiq, 2013).

Whether such land conversion always delivers on these claims is highly contested, however, and significant long-term impacts result from trading traditional livelihoods for short-term cash rewards. The ability to adopt oil palm cultivation as a sustainable livelihood strategy depends on the extent of community land loss; such shifts in livelihoods can bring about processes of inclusion and exclusion (Dayang Norwana *et al.*, 2011). Due in part to poor land tenure mapping in Indonesia, conflicts have emerged over both land and tenure. In these contexts, smallholders are often obliged to take out loans to establish plantations; they receive limited technical support and the allocated sites may be suboptimal and distant from the community (Sheil *et al.*, 2009).

It is crucial to recognize that poverty is not simply about having an income below a predefined level; it is about the deprivation of necessities that constitute a minimally acceptable standard of living (Blakely, Hales and Woodward, 2004). The structural causes of poverty are multifaceted, influenced by economic, social and political factors. If country- and project-specific agricultural strategies, including those related to palm oil production, are to contribute to poverty reduction, they must be guided by clear objectives and measured according to their long-term success (CAO, 2009; Gingold, 2011). Until this is done the linkage between industrial agriculture and poverty reduction is by no means guaranteed.

Industrial Agriculture and Climate Change

Industrial agriculture is the second-largest contributor of global greenhouse gas (GHG) emissions, after energy generation, and

before transportation (Stern, 2007); as such, it is an enormously significant factor driving man-made climate change. Perhaps unsurprisingly, this status has led champions of industrial agriculture to present climate-related arguments in favor of its expansion. Based on the fact that all green plants capture carbon in photosynthesis, they frequently—and often erroneously—assert that crops sequester carbon just as natural vegetation does, thus contributing equally to global reductions in GHG emissions and helping to combat climate change. This claim serves as the basis of a commonly argued corollary that is not necessarily accurate either, namely that replacing one type of tree with another has no impact on climate change—that such replacements are carbon-neutral acts. Taking this approach one step further, the Malaysian government successfully lobbied for rubber plantations to be classified as "forest" by the Food and Agriculture Organization (FAO) (Clay, 2004, cited in WWF, n.d.). The inclusion of plantations in a country's "permanent forest estate" can conceal its actual area of natural, biodiverse forest, while allowing lobbyists to promote the plantations that replace them as important carbon sinks.

It should be noted that the claim that plantations absorb carbon from the atmosphere to the same degree as natural forests is erroneous. A plant sequesters carbon while it is standing; accordingly, trees—whether plantation or natural forest species—will sequester carbon longer than annual plants with shorter life spans, such as grasses. In comparison to tropical grassland, tree plantations have the capacity for greater carbon fixation in biomass and soil organic matter as well as a higher rate of absorption of carbon dioxide (CO_2) from the atmosphere; however, these rates are far below those of natural tropical forests on mineral and peat soils (Germer and Sauerborn, 2006).

When oil palm plantations replace grasslands, it is possible that carbon sequestration exceeds carbon loss and that the plantation

thus acts as a net carbon sink (Brinkman, 2009). Yet this ratio depends on the amount of carbon in the soil, as the conversion can release significant amounts of carbon and other GHGs. While forest conversion to create oil palm monocultures causes a net release of about 650 mg of CO_2 equivalents per hectare, the emission from peat forest conversion is even higher, due to the release of CO_2 and nitrous oxide (N_2O) from drained peat (Germer and Sauerborn, 2006). The impact is even greater if the use of fertilizer and emissions from processing are factored in. A new oil palm plantation may grow faster and thus sequester carbon at a higher annual rate than a naturally regenerating forest, but over 20 years the oil palm plantation will store 50–90% less carbon than the original forest cover (Ywih *et al.*, 2009). In addition, plantations are destroyed and

replaced approximately every 30 years, a process that releases significant amounts of GHGs into the atmosphere.

The production of N_2O from the use of nitrogen fertilizers, such as urea, is also among the destructive impacts of industrial agriculture. The global warming potential of N_2O is 300 times greater than that of CO_2 (Stern, 2007). It is estimated that the production and use of nitrogen fertilizer for crops accounts for more than one-third of the GHGs released from agricultural fields (Paustian *et al.*, 2006). In addition, large-scale deforestation, soil erosion and machine-intensive farming methods all contribute to the concentration of carbon and other GHGs in the atmosphere.

It is ironic that palm oil biodiesel, a low-carbon alternative to fossil fuel-based gasoline for vehicles, was once hailed as a solution to climate change. It now represents a small proportion of the uses of palm oil, approximately 74% of which is used for food (USDA, 2010). As stated above, research has revealed that oil palm development, which often involves the clearing of intact forest, can contribute more GHGs to the atmosphere than it helps to avoid. Nevertheless, the sector has been able to exploit ambiguities concerning the type of land converted and the corresponding carbon stocks to make certain claims about emissions.

In practice, however, turning a hectare's worth of palm oil into biodiesel saves only about 6 tons of fossil CO_2 emissions per year, meaning that it would take 80 to 150 years of production to offset the one-off emissions released due to the requisite conversion of forest (Pearce, 2007). If the forest is on peatland—as is the case in parts of Indonesia—the offset requirements are far higher, largely because peatlands are too wet to decompose and thus store vast quantities of carbon. The conversion of a single hectare of Indonesian peatland rainforest releases up to 6,000 tons of CO_2 (Pearce, 2007). The practice of draining and converting these forests is especially damaging for the climate, as these "carbon sinks" store more carbon per unit area than any other ecosystem in the world. Draining peatland also makes it very prone to fires, which release an enormous amount of GHGs into the atmosphere (Trumper *et al.*, 2009).

Some claims and figures regarding emissions will remain disputed, but it is certain that monoculture plantations cannot match the carbon storage properties of natural forests and should not be promoted as though they can. It would be better for plantations to be cultivated on degraded lands, so as to avoid the destruction of natural forests. Some alternative initiatives—such as REDD+ (see Box 1.3)—provide opportunities to derive economic benefit from the sustainable management of natural forest estates, thereby helping to mitigate climate change.

REDD+ as a Tool for Countering Forest Conversion for Agricultural Use

Deforestation and forest degradation account for nearly 20% of global greenhouse gas emissions (UN-REDD, n.d.-b). These are released through agricultural expansion, conversion to pasture, logging, other extraction activities, infrastructure development, fires and other means. At the same time, standing forests provide incalculable ecological benefits to our economies—to the tune of many billions of dollars per year (Krieger, 2001). Nevertheless, the need to provide comparable, tangible financial alternatives to forest conversion has long been a stumbling block for those seeking to conserve biodiversity.

The UN's Reducing Emissions from Deforestation and Forest Degradation (REDD) initiative is an "incentive system" that attempts to calculate a financial value for carbon stored in forests and to motivate developing countries to limit emissions released though the destruction of forested lands. REDD+ goes beyond the single objective of conserving the carbon value in forests by including the goals of biodiversity conservation, sustainable forest management and the enhancement of forest carbon stocks.

Traditional integrated conservation and development projects have aimed to generate income tied to conservation, but the funds leveraged can rarely compete with the economic drivers of deforestation and forest degradation. REDD+ is one of the means proposed to help transform the economy from one that is based on uncontrolled consumption to one that is sustainable (UN-REDD, n.d.-a).

The REDD Programme is the United Nations' collaborative initiative in developing countries, bringing together the Food and Agriculture Organization (FAO), the United Nations Development Programme (UNDP) and the United Nations Environment Programme (UNEP). Other initiatives that engage in REDD+ activities include the World Bank's Forest Carbon Partnership Facility (FCPF), Norway's International Climate and Forest Initiative, the Global Environment Facility, Australia's International Forest Carbon Initiative and the Collaborative Partnership on Forests.

REDD+ projects are under way all over the world, including in ape range states. The government of the Democratic Republic of Congo (DRC), for example, is promoting land use planning and REDD+ as a strategy to reduce deforestation. In addition to joining both the FCPF and the UN-REDD initiative, the government is leading a unique partnership of smallholder cacao farmers, the cocoa producer ESCO, the World Wildlife Fund (WWF) and the Wildlife Conservation Society (WCS) to test market-based alternatives to the conversion of forest into cacao plantations (Makana *et al.*, 2014). The pilot site, Mambasa, is part of the Ituri–Epulu–Aru landscape, an important habitat for chimpanzees.

REDD+ may offer incentive-based models as an alternative to the conversion of forests for industrial agriculture; in practice, however, there are numerous challenges to the success of these initiatives. These include:

- **Market mechanisms:** As there has been no international agreement on REDD, associated project developers can only sell their carbon credits on the voluntary market. If demand is low, an oversupply of credits can result in low carbon prices. At the time of writing, in May 2015, carbon prices stood at US$5 per ton, down from a high of US$17 before the economic downturn of 2008 (World Bank, 2014).

- **Measuring carbon and monitoring compliance:** It is difficult to accurately measure the quantity of carbon stored in a forest—and, consequently, the amount of carbon emissions avoided by preserving that forest. Similarly, it is difficult to assess whether a country is really reducing deforestation. The UNFCCC requires countries to use forest reference emission levels and forest reference levels to assess their performance in implementing REDD+ activities and mitigating climate change.

- **Embezzlement and the equitable sharing of revenues:** Some countries that are rich in natural resources suffer from issues of poor governance, which complicate efforts to ensure that revenue gets to the communities that depend on the forests, rather than, for example, agribusiness companies or local politicians.

Some stakeholders have suggested the creation of advanced market commitments by REDD+ donor countries—by which donors pledge to buy a certain number of carbon credits—and the expansion of existing risk guarantee products to cover market price risk. Other proposals suggest generating investments in certain forest ecosystem benefits that are "bundled" in with carbon, such as water, tourism and non-timber products. This approach would reduce the economic dependence on the sale of carbon credits.

In the absence of a climate change agreement, and with more focus on cutting emissions than on curbing deforestation, many REDD+ projects have been slow to take off. Preliminary analyses indicate that most of these projects are initiated in contexts where sustainable forest management projects were already in place. Yet, while REDD+ is still in its infancy, it has the potential to provide economic alternatives to the business-as-usual scenario of forest conversion into agricultural land. In addition to strengthening existing sustainable forest management projects, REDD+ presents an opportunity for the conservation community to access high political levels within governments, which is not normally possible via more traditional approaches.

A detailed examination of forest ecological services and the initiatives that support them, such as REDD+, is beyond the scope of this edition of *State of the Apes*; a future edition will feature an in-depth analysis of this emerging field.

Conservation Agriculture: A Weapon in the Fight against Forest Destruction

The issue of sustainable productivity has as much to do with crops as with the socioeconomics of the market. The concept of sustainable crop production intensification (SCPI) arises from the pressing need to increase food production to feed growing populations, especially in urban areas. While the Green Revolution, initiated in the 1940s, was able to double grain yields and reduce hunger, malnutrition and poverty, it often did so at the expense of natural ecosystems and the resource base on which sustainability depends (B.G. Sims, personal communication, 2015).

The SCPI paradigm, promoted by FAO, is designed to augment production in a given area of land while simultaneously ensuring the conservation of natural resources, reducing the environmental footprint of agriculture and improving the flow of ecosystem services from the rural sector (FAO, 2011). SCPI endeavors to assist farmers to move from low production on degraded soils to higher, more sustainable production on healthy and improving soils.

Conservation agriculture (CA) forms an integral part of SCPI as it provides the optimum environment for healthy root development in crops, maximizes natural soil fertility and eliminates erosion. It is based on the following three tenets,

which, while being universally applicable, require adaptation to local conditions:

- **Minimum soil disturbance resulting from tillage:** Plowing and cultivation are eliminated.

- **Maintaining organic soil cover:** Soils are kept covered with crop residues and cover crops for as long as possible throughout the year; in this way, they are protected from raindrop energy and insolation.

- **Diversifying species:** Crop, cover crop and associated crop species should be as diverse as possible, so that crop rotations are maintained both for main and cover crops.

Worldwide adoption of CA currently stands at 1.25 million km^2 (125 million ha)—or 9% of arable land—and is increasing by about 70,000 km^2 (7 million ha) per year (Jat, Sahrawat and Kassam, 2013). The main drivers of its adoption are the control of soil and water erosion and drought mitigation, although reducing production costs is particularly attractive to individual farmers and agribusinesses.

In Tanzania and other ape range states, smallholder farmers who cannot afford to invest in costly agricultural machinery are increasingly opting to rent machines as the need arises (Kienzle, Ashburner and Sims, 2013). In Tanzania's Arumeru district, members of a farmer field school are CA practitioners and also offer mechanized CA services to neighboring farmers. CA farmers in nearby Karatu district have brought their land back to its original condition—the state it was in before it was plowed; and since less labor is required for land preparation and weed control, children can now attend school more regularly and women can devote more time to other activities, including vegetable gardening. In addition, the reduced use of herbicides means that net incomes have increased (Sims, 2011, pp. 13–14).

The CA-led improvement of ecosystem services—especially with respect to cleaner water, reduced runoff and sedimentation, and aquifer recharge—has helped to promote the adoption of CA among farmers around the world (FAO, 2011). The rate of take-up remains slow but could be accelerated through sound government policies that support farmers and favor environmentally sensitive crop production. In turn, CA could make a major contribution to the protection of biodiversity and wildlife, including apes and gibbons.

Photo: A member of a farmer field school in Arumeru district, Tanzania, providing contract CA services. © Brian Sims

Impact of Industrial Agriculture on Ape Populations

Industrial agriculture affects ape populations in numerous ways, both directly and indirectly. The destruction of ape habitat for the expansion of the agricultural estate is one of the three principal threats to apes, together with hunting and disease. Indirect impacts result from the construction of roads for the development of agricultural lands and transport of goods, the erosion and contamination of waterways on which apes and other wildlife depend, and the influx of people who hunt and capture apes to supplement their incomes or kill animals who are perceived as threats to safety or to their crops. The frequency of human–wildlife interactions is increasing significantly as people enter more areas that are adjacent to or inside traditional ape territories and plant crops that are either palatable to wildlife or that are destroyed by wildlife as they move through land that is part of their range.

With the expansion of industrial agriculture, natural landscapes are being replaced with large monoculture plantations that are inhospitable to many species and inhibit animals from reaching the remaining patches of natural forest. The result is that wildlife becomes isolated in small fragments of forest, with insufficient food, shelter and access to other individuals to maintain the genetic diversity necessary for survival of the species. For more details on the impact of industrial agriculture on ape ecology, see Chapter 6.

Given that the oil palm is most productive in its first 20 years—with peak yields between 13 and 14 years—plantations are generally rotated (destroyed and replanted) at 25–30-year intervals (UNEP, 2011; Rival and Levang, 2014). The process of planting reduces freshwater and soil quality and, by destroying or degrading natural vegetation, adversely affects local human and wildlife populations that are dependent on natural resources. One of the most damaging effects of oil palm is the drainage of peat swamps for conversion to plantations, which, as indicated above, has significant impacts on GHG emissions. Estimates indicate that between 1990 and 2005, 55–60% of oil palm expansion in Malaysia and Indonesia resulted in the destruction of tropical forests (Koh and Wilcove, 2008a, 2008b; WWF, n.d.).

An area that presents extensive opportunities for development is the intensification of production on currently cultivated land, such as through the implementation of CA practices (see Box 1.4). This approach counteracts the need for continuous conversion of more land for oil palm cultivation. Significant variability exists in the yields of plantations, from 2 to 10 tons of oil per ha (Carrasco *et al.*, 2014). Yield intensification has great potential as it satisfies the goals of both growers and conservationists (Rival and Levang, 2014; B. Dahlen, personal communication, 2015); yet, improved yields may also lead to higher interest in oil palm cultivation and, consequently, an increase in the demand for land.

Case studies 1.1 and 1.2 provide an overview of some of the impacts on apes resulting from the expansion of agriculture and the influx of people into areas that are also used by apes, or that border on ape ranges.

It is clear that industrial expansion of oil palm, even by companies that seek to take a more sustainable approach, has a direct negative impact on orangutan populations in Borneo and Sumatra. By displacing so many wild orangutans, oil palm expansion drives up the number of orangutans in need of rescue and protection in orangutan centers. Since 75% of the known orangutans live outside of protected areas (Meijaard *et al.*, 2010; Wich *et al.*, 2012b), understanding if and how the species could be effectively accommodated in an agro-industrial landscape is crucial to the long-term survival of these apes.

CASE STUDY 1.1

Human–Wildlife Interactions: Orangutan Rescues in Kalimantan, Indonesia

On the island of Borneo, in the Indonesian province of West Kalimantan alone, 326 oil palm concessions occupy 48,000 km² (4.8 million ha) of land—one-third of the total land area of 144,000 km² (14.4 million ha) (Hadinaryanto, 2014). In the southern part of the province, in Ketapang district—home to the Orangutan Rescue and Rehabilitation Centre of the International Animal Rescue (IAR)—there are nearly 100 concessions, all of which have significantly affected the natural forests (Sánchez, 2015; see Figures 1.4 and 1.5).

To address some of the challenges related to the capture of orangutans in plantations, the IAR Indonesia Foundation established the Orangutan Emergency Centre in 2009 and the Rescue and Rehabilitation Centre in 2013, with associated outreach activities. The aim of the foundation is to return captured orangutans to a life in the forest, thereby contributing to the species' survival in the wild. Rehabilitation and reintroduction programs provide a potential, albeit very expensive, solution to the problem of displaced or "refugee" orangutans living in rescue centers. They can also help to increase the

FIGURE 1.4

Map of Concessions in Ketapang District

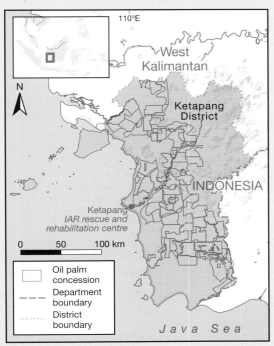

Data sources: WRI (2014c, 2014e)

FIGURE 1.5

Land Cover Sources for Oil Palm Plantation Establishment and Total Planted Oil Palm on Mineral and Peat Soils in Ketapang District, 1994–2011

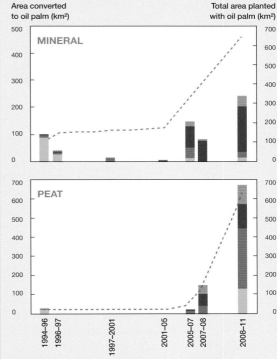

Legend:

▨ Intact forest ▨ Logged forest ▮ Agroforest ▨ Burned/cleared and bare

- - - - - - - Total

Source: Carlson *et al.* (2012, p. 7561)

viability of populations in areas where wild orangutans might be at risk of extinction or inbreeding; in some cases, they can even help to create new populations in areas where orangutans have been extirpated, provided the conditions that led to their extirpation are removed or addressed.

The IAR Indonesia Foundation reports that almost half (43%) of the 120 orangutans rescued between September 2009 and December 2014 came from villages where they were kept illegally by local people; 31% were rescued directly from oil palm plantations; 12% originated from local community agricultural landscapes (including rubber, rambutan, coconut and rice fields), often adjacent to oil palm plantations; 9% were transferred from other facilities; and 1% were recovered from the illegal wildlife trade (see Figure 1.6). Some of the orangutans that were rescued from captivity in villages might have

FIGURE 1.6

The origin of 120 Orangutans Rescued in Ketapang, September 2009–December 2014

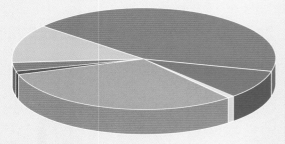

Legend:

■ Local community agricultural landscape (14 = 12%)
■ Mining area/company (4 = 3%)
■ Unknown (1 = 1%)
■ Oil palm plantation (37 = 31%)
■ Illegal wildlife trade (1 = 1%)
■ Transferred from other facility (11 = 9%)
■ Village (52 = 43%)

Courtesy of IAR

been originally captured as a result of conflict between orangutans and people in oil palm landscapes. Figure 1.7 shows the sites of IAR rescues in West Kalimantan and the Borneo Orangutan Survival Foundation (BOSF) rescues in Central Kalimantan, in relation to oil palm and wood fiber concessions.

In Ketapang, 13–25 orangutans have been rescued every year since 2009, with an annual average of 20 for that period. In Central Kalimantan the rescue rates have been higher; BOSF has reported an average of 67—or anywhere between 13 and 240—orangutans per year since 1999 (BOSF, personal communication, 2014). On the Indonesian island of Sumatra, the Sumatran Orangutan Conservation Project (SOCP) has rescued an annual average of 26 orangutans since 2002, recovering 9 to 37 individuals per year (I. Singleton, personal communication, 2014). All these areas have been subject to rapid expansion of industrial agriculture, a likely a factor in the high rates of rescue.

To promote better understanding of the drivers behind human–orangutan interactions, the IAR Indonesia Foundation categorized its findings as follows: the pet trade; conflict between orangutans and local agro-communities; and conflict between orangutans and oil palm plantations.

Pet trade. To capture baby orangutans, people involved in this illegal trade will either seize infants from their mothers or kill the mothers so as to capture the orphan. The captive apes are sold or kept as pets until they die or are handed over to the authorities. The hunting of orangutans for food (Meijaard *et al.*, 2011) may inadvertently be providing infants for the pet

trade; IAR concludes that such captures most likely occur on an opportunistic basis.

Of the former owners or traders of captive orangutans rescued by the IAR Indonesia Foundation, 39% claimed to have "found" the baby or infant orangutan, while 29% admitted to having bought theirs. The remaining 32% of respondents did not wish to answer the question or the information obtained from them was unreliable (Sánchez, 2015).

The fact that none admitted to having killed the orangutan's mother may not adequately represent the extent of human involvement in the injury and death of orangutan mothers. As young orangutans rarely leave their mothers, it is likely that all the mothers were injured or killed before their offspring were taken. Captures may have occurred as a result of conflict, in the context of competition for food, as acquisitions for trade, or for other reasons. Owners who voluntarily handed over their orangutans reported that they had paid anywhere between 500,000 and 1.5 million Indonesian rupiah (US$50–150) for a baby orangutan. The fact that the infants were acquired locally suggests that they originated from a nearby location.

Conflict between orangutans and community agricultural landscapes (local agro-communities). The increased frequency with which people kill orangutans is thought to be a result of the intense deforestation and land clearance for agriculture, as people encroach into previously inaccessible forest and encounter orangutans more often. Furthermore, as the availability of natural foods decreases, orangutans increasingly enter villages, gardens and local plantations to crop raid or "pass through," leading to a higher incidence of conflict with people.

Conflict between humans and orangutans is not only driven by economic factors, but also driven by local perceptions and legends surrounding these animals (Campbell-Smith *et al.*, 2010). Local people are often afraid of orangutans, particularly if they are walking on the ground, which can lead people to harm or kill the apes.

A solid understanding of the perceptions of those who live in and around orangutan habitats, particularly areas where human–ape conflict is common, is key to the development of mitigation techniques that can effectively reduce the conflict and killings, and build trust in and encourage support for wildlife among local populations.

Conflict between orangutans and oil palm plantation owners and workers. The frequency of human–orangutan interactions tends to grow as oil palm plantations move through the successive stages of development. During the first stage of development, degraded forest or agricultural land is utilized, or natural forest is clear-cut or burned. If people encounter orangutans during land clearance, they generally kill the mothers so that their babies can be captured and used as household pets or sold; alternatively, they may kill all the orangutans they come across. During the seedling phase,

FIGURE 1.7

IAR and BOSF Orangutan Rescues in Relation to Agricultural Concessions

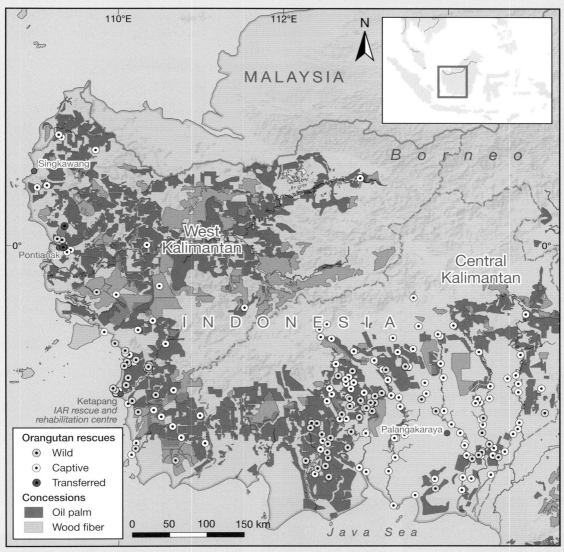

Data sources: rescue data: IAR and BOSF; data for base map: WRI (2014c, 2014e)

conflict occurs when orangutans pull out and eat the palm shoots. Orangutans are then seen as a pest and chased off, injured or killed.

When orangutan habitat is destroyed, the survival rate of female orangutans and their offspring is impacted directly by the reduction in their home range and subsequent starvation. Orangutan males fare marginally better as they are able to migrate to remaining forest areas (van Schaik, 2001; Wich *et al.*, 2012b). However, such migration may result in increased competition among individuals in the new area and overcrowding of habitats, which may exceed their carrying capacity (Wich *et al.*, 2012b); it may also heighten the risk of orangutans entering gardens, villages or other plantations, which can lead to further conflict (Meijaard *et al.*, 2011). For more information on the impacts of industrial agriculture on ape ecology, see Chapter 6.

One mechanism that is used for managing biodiversity risk in extractive industries—and in other development projects—is the mitigation hierarchy (see Box 1.5). This planning tool is designed to help reduce negative impacts on biodiversity from extraction and exploitation of natural resources, and to identify compensation and mitigation measures in the absence of alternatives. However, the applicability of the mitigation hierarchy to industrial agriculture requires further investigation. Unlike the exploitation of mineral, oil and gas deposits, crop production is not tied to specific sites, so avoidance—a key step in the mitigation hierarchy—should be much easier. There is a growing understanding that the application of the mitigation hierarchy should be linked closely to multi-stakeholder, landscape-scale land use planning. That approach is especially important with respect to industrial-scale agriculture, as the siting of new projects may have a much greater negative impact on biodiversity than the establishment and management of a concession once its location has been decided. So while the principle of no net loss (or a net gain) of biodiversity might still be applied, there is a need to develop a new approach that combines the mitigation hierarchy with broad-scale and systematic land use planning (M. Hatchwell, personal communication, 2015).

> **BOX 1.5**
>
> ## The Mitigation Hierarchy
>
> The mitigation hierarchy is a best practice approach to managing biodiversity risk. It advocates applying efforts early in the development process to prevent or avoid adverse impacts to biodiversity wherever possible; then minimizing and reducing impacts that cannot be avoided; and then repairing or restoring impacts that cannot be avoided, minimized or reduced. Only once project developers have taken these initial actions do they respond to any remaining residual effects, preferably by creating a "biodiversity offset". If an offset is not possible, some other form of compensation may be needed (Arcus Foundation, 2014, pp. 144–5; see Figure 1.8).

FIGURE 1.8

The Mitigation Hierarchy and Biodiversity Impact

(developed by WCS for State of the Apes: Extractive Industries and Ape Conservation)

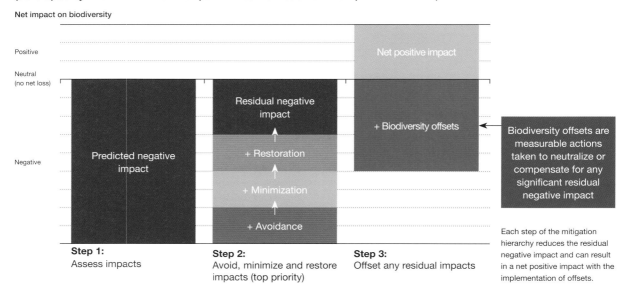

Source: Arcus Foundation (2014, p. 145)

Changing Agricultural Practices and Human–Chimpanzee Interactions: Tobacco and Sugarcane Farming in and around Bulindi, Uganda

The Budongo and Bugoma Forest Reserves of western Uganda (Figure 1.9) support two of Uganda's largest populations of eastern chimpanzees (*Pan troglodytes schweinfurthii*), with more than 500 individuals in each group (Plumptre *et al.*, 2010). The two reserves are separated by 50 km of landscape that is densely populated by people and dominated by agriculture (McLennan, 2008). Nevertheless, the landscape has conservation value as a "corridor" linking chimpanzee and other wildlife populations in Budongo and Bugoma. Its corridor potential rests primarily on the network of small forest fragments that run alongside watercourses throughout the intervening area. These riparian fragments are mostly on local people's land and lack formal protection; they are inhabited by multiple groups—or communities—of wild chimpanzees who live outside the reserves, in close proximity to villages. These "village chimpanzees" may number as many as 260 individuals (McLennan, 2008). Conserving the corridor forests is critical to the survival of these chimpanzees and to maintaining gene flow between chimpanzee populations in the main Budongo and Bugoma forest blocks (McLennan and Plumptre, 2012).

FIGURE 1.9

Budongo and Bugoma Forest Reserves in Western Uganda and Small Riparian "Corridor" Forests in the Intervening Region

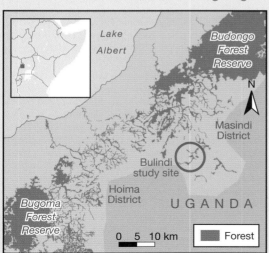

Notes: Most of these small riparian forests are on private land. The Bulindi study site is encircled.

Courtesy of Matthew R. McLennan

The best-known community of "village chimpanzees" is Bulindi's, studied since 2006 (McLennan and Hill, 2010). Bulindi parish, in Hoima district, lies 25 km south of Budongo and 40 km northeast of Bugoma, along the main road between Hoima and Masindi towns. Human population density in Hoima district is high, estimated at 159 persons per km² in 2014.[2] More than 90% of the district's residents live in rural areas and practice a combination of subsistence agriculture with cash cropping (UBOS, 2007). Like other communities in the Budongo–Bugoma corridor, the Bulindi chimpanzees range within a network of unprotected forest fragments on agricultural land. Local households own these small forests according to customary tenure, a common traditional system whereby clans control land and allocate plots to members; thereafter, the land is inherited patrilineally (Place and Otsuka, 2000). Few local households have formally registered land. Most villagers in Bulindi and elsewhere in Hoima district are native Banyoro who traditionally do not eat primates, enabling chimpanzees to persist in dwindling forest amid expanding agricultural systems (McLennan, 2008).

This case study considers how recent agricultural practices in Bulindi and the surrounding region—particularly the shift to commercial tobacco (*Nicotiana tabacum*) and sugarcane (*Saccharum officinarum*) farming—have driven rapid, extensive land use cover changes, meaning the conversion of unprotected forest to agricultural land. The resulting alterations in human–chimpanzee interactions are threatening the survival of the region's chimpanzees.

Recent Causes of Forest Loss

In Uganda, where most forest loss occurs on land that is not managed by the government, the deforestation rate is among the highest in Africa—2.6% in 2000–10, as compared to 1.0% in Cameroon, 0.7% in Liberia and -0.2% in the DRC for same period (MWLE, 2002; McLennan, 2008; FAO, 2011). Widespread clearance and fragmentation of unprotected forest within the Budongo–Bugoma corridor has recent origins, having gained momentum in the 1990s and continued to the present day (Mwavu and Witkowski, 2008; Babweteera *et al.*, 2011). Factors contributing to these land-cover changes are complex and should be viewed in the context of Uganda's Plan for Modernisation of Agriculture, part of the government's Poverty Eradication Action Policy, which focuses on the modernization and transformation of subsistence agriculture into commercial agriculture (MAAIF and MFPED, 2000).

As is well documented in the development literature, when farmers shift farming strategies to increase their income, or to adjust to declining income from existing cash crops, they generally increase the area under crops rather than adopting more intensive farming systems, inevitably putting natural habitat at risk (Bashaasha, Kraybill and Southgate, 2001; Pendleton and Howe, 2002). The rapid conversion of forest to farmland around Budongo and Bugoma has numerous causes, including the promotion of commercial farming alongside rapid human population growth—whether due to natural increase or immigration; a thriving local timber industry; insecure land tenure; inadequate law enforcement; and corruption at various administrative levels (Mwavu and Witkowski, 2008; McLennan and Hill, 2013).

Cash cropping combined with subsistence farming is not a new activity for local farmers. Commercial tobacco production began in Bulindi in 1927, promoted by the colonial administration as a lucrative alternative cash crop to cotton (Doyle, 2006). Back then, farmers cleared grasslands to grow tobacco, whereas now, the only land available to most farmers to clear is forested. In the 1960s, farmers in Bulindi, as elsewhere in Hoima district, planted cacao (*Theobroma cacao*) in riparian forest. Given that cacao grows best under shade, only the understory vegetation was cleared for plantations. The introduction of cacao marks the first reported appearance of conflict with resident chimpanzees, as they quickly learned to exploit the sweet-tasting pods (McLennan and Hill, 2012). Most plantations were abandoned in the 1970s and 1980s, following the breakdown in Uganda's cocoa industry (Kayobyo, Hakiza and Kucel, 2001). Unmaintained, the understory regenerated around the cacao trees, which continued to produce pods. As recently as 2012, cacao was among the main forest foods for chimpanzees in Bulindi (McLennan, 2013). Since then, however, the last of the abandoned cacao was cleared, principally for tobacco and rice (*Oryza* species (sp.)).

Banana (*Musa* sp.) and coffee (*Coffea* sp.) are also cash crops for local farmers, but neither is associated with extensive forest clearance. Dessert bananas and banana beer can be sold at local markets, but in 2000 a new banana wilt disease arrived, destroying plantations (Kalyebara et al., 2007). A new coffee wilt disease arrived at the same time (Rutherford, 2006), destroying smallholder coffee plantations. Farmers were advised to destroy all infected banana and coffee plants and not to replant these same crops on affected land for at least 10–15 years. The combined effect of these new crop diseases has been an important factor in household decisions to clear remaining forest and plant alternatives such as tobacco and rice, both of which were promoted locally by agricultural extension services (Agricultural Extension Office, Hoima district, personal communication, 2007). Moreover, neither tobacco nor rice is susceptible to wilt disease and both produce a crop in the first year, offering quick returns.

Tobacco farming is an aggressive driver of deforestation, requiring large amounts of wood for curing and for the construction of drying barns (Geist, 1999). Local farming traditions maintain that tobacco requires fertile (virgin) soil, such that the only available source for most farmers is forest land. Tobacco seedbeds are established by clearing riverbanks to facilitate access to water. Currently, 76% of Uganda's tobacco is produced by British American Tobacco (BAT) (DD International, 2012), with which most Bulindi tobacco farmers are registered.[3] The growth of tobacco farming in Bulindi and its impact on forests are plain to witness. Seeking to maximize production, growing numbers of farmers clear-cut all but the swampiest parts of forest on their land, exposing riverbanks and wetlands, and selling the timber.

In 2006, five riparian fragments used habitually by the chimpanzees averaged 0.3 km² (30 ha) each. These small forests were already substantially reduced; clearance had been under way since around the year 2000. By 2014 these fragments had been further reduced by an estimated 80% (Lorenti, 2014). Thus, in fewer than 15 years, virtually all the chimpanzees' natural habitat had been converted to farmland. Households that have retained some forest on their land generally have sources of income in addition to farming, or prefer not to cultivate tobacco because of personal principles or because they consider it too labor-intensive.

In neighboring Masindi district, chimpanzee habitat has also disappeared rapidly, although there industrial sugarcane production has had more of an impact. Kinyara Sugar Works Ltd. (KSWL) is Uganda's second-largest manufacturer of sugar, operating over much of the area north of Bulindi up to Budongo. First established in the 1960s, KSWL's factory and plantations were rehabilitated in the mid-1990s and expanded quickly thereafter. The ensuing employment opportunities led to an influx of workers from elsewhere in Uganda (Reynolds, 2005; Zommers, Johnson and Macdonald, 2012). To increase production, KSWL operates an outgrower scheme whereby farmers are contracted to plant their own fields with sugar (Zommers et al., 2012). Between 1988 and 2002 the area under sugarcane increased more than 17-fold: from 6.9 km² to 127 km² (690 ha to 12,729 ha), with a corresponding loss of 47 km² (4,680 ha) of forest (8.2%) (Mwavu and Witkowski, 2008, p. 606).

Impact on Human–Chimpanzee Interactions

The major land cover changes taking place around Budongo and Bugoma Forest Reserves have profoundly altered interactions between villagers and resident chimpanzees, changing the relationship from one of coexistence to one of competition. The loss of riparian forests precipitated a sharp increase in people's interactions with chimpanzees. According to Bulindi residents, chimpanzees previously remained within the forests and were seldom seen; yet, as the forests quickly shrank and fragmented, sightings of apes on agricultural land became commonplace, fuelling the prevalent local belief that the chimpanzee population has increased dramatically (McLennan and Hill, 2012).

The extensive forest clearance inevitably caused a critical reduction in wild food (such as through the removal of large fruit-producing trees). However, chimpanzees have flexible diets and quickly learn to exploit agricultural foods (Hockings and McLennan, 2012; McLennan and Hockings, 2014). Chimpanzees reportedly "raid" crops throughout the Budongo–Bugoma corridor (McLennan, 2008). At Bulindi, cacao, guava (*Psidium guajava*), papaya (*Carica papaya*), mango (*Mangifera indica*) and sugarcane are among the chimpanzees' most important foods (McLennan, 2013). Yet crop damage by chimpanzees is not new. The Bulindi chimpanzees have eaten certain crops for decades, most notably the forest cacao. They also ate bananas and mangoes where these were grown at forest edges, but occasional losses of such fruits were apparently accepted. Residents note that the more persistent incursions into village areas by foraging chimpanzees are a recent development, concomitant with clearance of local forests (McLennan and Hill, 2012).

Farmers in this region are generally tolerant of chimpanzees, perceiving them as less destructive to crops and possessing a "better character" than other wildlife, particularly baboons (*Papio anubis*) (Hill and Webber, 2010; McLennan and Hill, 2012). But as farmers experience improved economic returns from cash cropping sugarcane and tobacco (and increasingly rice), their willingness—or capacity—to tolerate crop losses to chimpanzees and other wildlife declines (Hill and Webber, 2010). Around KSWL this is particularly the case with regard to chimpanzees foraging on sugarcane (Reynolds, Wallis and Kyamanywa, 2003; Webber and Hill, 2014). Outgrower plantations now extend right up to the southern border of Budongo and chimpanzees from the reserve, as well as in the fragments, have been killed for damaging sugarcane (Reynolds, 2005). Chimpanzees do not eat tobacco, but farmers may not wish to tolerate the apes treading on seedlings, in part because the resulting non-consumptive damage to cash crops is viewed in terms of monetary loss. In contrast, previous low-level feeding by apes on domestic fruits, such as mango or guava—traditionally seen as snack food for children—had little impact on household economics (McLennan and Hill, 2012).

The decline in tolerance of chimpanzees is not merely a reflection of changing socioeconomic conditions. Chimpanzees are large-bodied and sometimes threaten or attack people (Hockings and Humle, 2009; McLennan and Hill, 2013). In Bulindi, adult male chimpanzees frequently display aggression on encountering researchers and villagers, for example by "mobbing," charging and pursuing them (McLennan, 2010; McLennan and Hill, 2010). Residents claim that such behavior is recent (McLennan and Hill, 2012). Chimpanzees may direct aggression against humans in response to intensifying disturbance and increasing competitive interactions with people, including over access to crops; moreover, it is not uncommon for people to harass apes in Bulindi, be it by shouting or throwing stones at them, or by chasing them with dogs.

Chimpanzees who range near villages occasionally attack humans physically, particularly children. Five attacks on children have been documented in Bulindi since 2006; while none was fatal, children did sustain serious injuries in three of the cases and required medical treatment at a hospital. Similar chimpanzee attacks—including several fatal ones—have occurred elsewhere within the Budongo–Bugoma corridor (Reynolds *et al.*, 2003; Reynolds, 2005; McLennan, 2008). Although verifying facts can be difficult, in at least some cases chimpanzees seem to have retaliated in response to provocation. Nevertheless, intentional predation on children by chimpanzees has been documented elsewhere in Uganda where forest has been lost to agriculture (Wrangham, 2001). Declining tolerance for chimpanzees therefore has as much to do with fear of physical aggression as crop damage (McLennan and Hill, 2012; Hockings, McLennan and Hill, 2014). Villagers object to the threatening presence of chimpanzees around their homes, even if they do not themselves experience crop losses (McLennan and Hill, 2012).

Changes in chimpanzee behavior are challenging formerly benign attitudes towards them. Even if people do not hunt them for food, as in this part of Uganda, a "conflict threshold" exists beyond which people are unlikely to tolerate living with chimpanzees unless benefits outweigh costs substantially. This threshold is fast looming in Bulindi and elsewhere in the fragments, as reflected in an apparent increase in retaliatory killings and the use of lethal crop protection methods, including large steel "mantraps" (Reynolds, 2005; McLennan *et al.*, 2012). While mantraps are usually intended for other wildlife, some farmers use them to protect cash crops such as sugarcane from chimpanzees—something they apparently would not have done previously (McLennan and Hill, 2012). Snares and traps seem to be taking a toll on the fragmented chimpanzee population; in Bulindi, for example, at least five individuals—or roughly 20% of this small community—were trapped within four years (McLennan *et al.*, 2012).

Unless upward trends in forest clearance and interactions between people and apes are reversed, survival prospects for the "village chimpanzees" are bleak, negating the corridor value of the riparian forests (McLennan and Plumptre, 2012). Any intervention strategy must ensure effective protection of remaining habitat alongside planned and sustained forest restoration to provide an adequate resource base for the existing and future chimpanzee population. Such an approach would require tobacco and sugarcane companies to commission environmental impact assessments, to be conducted by independent, external agencies. In addition, culturally sensitive education programs are needed to encourage human behavior that reduces aggressive interactions with apes (Hockings and Humle, 2009).

Effective crop protection measures are also required to help farmers safeguard their livelihoods. Around Budongo, on-farm trials have tested methods such as barriers, alarms, repellents and systematic guarding (patrolling farm boundaries); guarding was identified as the most effective for reducing crop losses to chimpanzees. Full-time guards were the most valuable, but part-time, randomized guarding schedules were also effective at reducing crop losses to non-human primates (Hill and Wallace, 2012).

Such crop-protection methods are labor-intensive, however, as they require an adult presence on farms for extended periods during daylight hours. Consequently, farmers often combine guarding with other farming tasks; yet, to be effective, guarding should be the main activity of the person tasked with it. In the short term, external financial support to employ full-time guards, deployed at key sites, and operating a randomized guarding schedule, could reduce crop losses and help prevent further escalation of aggressive interactions between people and apes. In the longer term, research is needed to develop alternative, cost-effective crop protection strategies.

Important lessons can be learned from interactions between humans and carnivores, in which people's willingness to tolerate large-bodied predators is often linked to deep-rooted social beliefs rather than perceived or experienced threats (Marchini and Macdonald, 2012). Increasing people's willingness and capacity to tolerate apes requires a combination of awareness raising and financial and social incentives (Treves and Bruskotter, 2014).

Another mechanism is the transloca-tion of wild orangutans, generally from a site where they are considered a problem, to a site where they will not come into conflict with humans; as described below, however, this option is deemed a partial solution (Beck *et al.*, 2007). Indeed, conservation-ists advocate that this option be used only as a last resort, as it carries considerable risk for the animals and people involved. Nevertheless, it is often regarded as the only solution to save the lives of animals threat-ened by deforestation and the rapid develop-ment of industrial oil palm monocultures.

Rescue Centers and Problems Faced with Rescued, Translocated and Reintroduced Orangutans

As described in Case study 1.1 on orangutan rescues in Indonesia, rehabilitation centers in Borneo have rescued an average of 20 orangutans every year since 2009 in West Kalimantan and an average of 67 every year since 1999 in Central Kalimantan; on Sumatra, the average stands at 26 orangu-tans every year since 2002. Given the large number of rescues and the ongoing need to assist orangutans in captivity, rescue and rehabilitation centers across Indonesia are functioning at full capacity. While the cent-ers aim to release orangutans back into the forest, the process is costly and difficult; in some cases, orangutans cannot be released as they have been irreversibly damaged by their experiences and would no longer be able to survive in their native habitats.

Reintroduction sites must meet a num-ber of criteria outlined by the International Union for Conservation of Nature (IUCN) and rescue centers must also abide by Indonesian guidelines before releasing an

orangutan into the wild. One of the most important regulations stipulates:

> Re-introduction should not endanger resi-dent wild ape populations [. . .,] populations of other interacting native taxa, or the eco-logical integrity of the area in which they live (Beck *et al.*, 2007).

If unprecedented deforestation is occur-ring at an alarming rate, however, finding a suitable reintroduction site where no resi-dent wild orangutan population resides is challenging.

In 2009, in an effort to safeguard orangu-tans, the Indonesian government developed and signed the Orangutan Indonesia Con-servation Strategies and Action Plan 2007–2017 (MOF Indonesia, 2009). This action plan pledges to stabilize all remaining wild populations of orangutans by 2017 (Wich *et al.*, 2011, 2012b). One of the goals of this plan was the release of all rescued orangutans into the wild by 2015. While this aim was theoretically feasible at the time of the development of the plan, several practical considerations made the 2015 target unre-alistic. These include the lack of suitable orangutan reintroduction sites; the pres-ence of resident wild orangutans in most of the remaining suitable forests; and the large number of forested areas that are earmarked for conversion, being converted or already converted into oil palm plantations.

One way to facilitate the reintroduction of captive orangutans into the wild is to develop public–private partnerships to secure the use of concessions as release sites. This approach would require each oil palm and timber company to establish not only conservation areas within its concessions, but also human–orangutan conflict rescue units in each subsidiary plantation, to allow for rapid responses to conflict situations. Companies would also be called on to develop strategies for conservation management of orangutan populations at the landscape level; in so doing, they would need to involve different stakeholders, including other companies and concessions. Furthermore, as advocated in the Best Practice Guidelines for the Prevention and Mitigation of Conflict between Humans and Great Apes (Hockings and Humle, 2009), companies should also develop and implement standard operating procedures, not least to foster best practices and procedures for the mitigation of human–orangutan conflict in each concession. These steps would contribute to a more sustainable future for orangutan populations in a landscape of continued agricultural development.

The Roundtable on Sustainable Palm Oil (RSPO) principles and criteria are a good starting point for making oil palm cultivation more compatible with a government's goals of maintaining viable populations of threatened orangutans (Wich *et al.*, 2012b). Following these principles and criteria would also help to reduce the number of orangutans who need to be rescued as a result of oil palm development. However, the implementation of RSPO procedures for sustainability is not yet optimal and has proven a challenge. For an assessment of the RSPO's functions and impact, see Chapter 5.

The killing of orangutans displaced by plantation development or other forms of destructive land use, together with the fragmentation of the remaining intact forest, constitutes a conservation emergency for these great apes (Nellemann *et al.*, 2007), as demonstrated by the rates at which orangutans continue to enter captivity. The situation is further complicated by the complexity of rehabilitation, translocation and reintroduction. A response to this crisis requires commitment from and participation of all stakeholders involved in industrial agriculture, including producers, manufacturers, retailers, investors, consumers, local people, and governments.

Agricultural Industry Engagement in Ape Conservation and Mitigation Strategies

Agricultural Practices and Land Use Management

Understanding the requirements of both displaced and isolated ape populations is essential for effective land use and conservation planning and management (Sha *et al.*, 2009; Hoffman and O'Riain, 2012). Indeed, it is vital to understand where wild apes and other threatened wildlife overlap with protected areas and areas propitious to large-scale development, such as industrial agriculture, so as to be able to inform conservation planning (Wich *et al.*, 2012b). Land use planning can provide the direction needed to coordinate economic development across a region and to regulate the conversion of land and property uses (UNECE, 2008). This includes decisions on balancing social and economic development, enhancing communication networks, accessing information and knowledge by all affected stakeholders, reducing environmental damage and enhancing protection for natural resources, natural heritage and cultural heritage. Comprehensive, landscape-wide planning could enable stakeholders—including governments, industry, civil society, communities and individuals—to assess competing claims for land use in the context of planned changes to habitats.

In many countries, the laws and regulations regarding the protection status of forests are contradictory and unclear (see Chapter 4). In Indonesia, for instance, the laws and regulations regarding the destruction of forest and conversion of peatland need to be harmonized with the legislation that protects orangutans and outlaws killing them. Specifically, the expansion of agricultural activities into legally protected orangutan

> " Land use planning can provide the direction needed to coordinate economic development across a region and to regulate the conversion of land and property uses. "

ranges represents a breach of national laws on species protection. Urgent efforts are needed to focus on improving yields in current plantations and on expanding concessions in already deforested areas (Wich *et al.*, 2012b)—goals achievable through the use of improved varieties of crops and more effective agricultural practices, such as conservation agriculture (see Box 1.4).

In Africa, the challenge is that in some countries with the right conditions for oil palm and other large-scale agricultural development—such as Angola, the DRC, Gabon, Ghana, Ivory Coast, Liberia, the Republic of Congo and Sierra Leone—more than two-thirds of areas suitable for oil palm development outside of protected areas overlap with ape distribution (Wich *et al.*, 2014). Many of these areas, especially across West Africa, already represent degraded landscapes, where chimpanzees have in some cases been surviving for generations, ironically, it seems, thanks to the presence of wild oil palms, which may be a keystone species for some of these communities (Brncic *et al.*, 2010).

Wherever apes can survive and thrive on natural resources available to them and share the landscape with people, agricultural development needs to focus on maintaining natural resources, forest patches and ecosystem services; preserving and promoting connectivity to ensure population viability; and managing negative attitudes toward apes and crop loss (Koh and Wilcove, 2008a; McShea *et al.*, 2009; SWD, 2012; Ancrenaz *et al.*, 2015). Such management strategies and schemes may vary according to the growth stage of the commercial crops. Once oil palms reach maturity in a plantation, for instance, cultivators can remove measures such as trenches and strips of bare land that act to protect oil palm saplings from orangutans; to promote species conservation, these elements can be replaced with bridges to encourage orangutan dispersal, nesting

and low-impact foraging on fruit (Ancrenaz *et al.*, 2015). In fact, the effectiveness of trenches and bare strips of land in protecting plantations from apes and other wildlife remains to be ascertained. Further research is also required to assess the value of implementing other types of buffers around plantations with respect to different ape species, particularly with regard to plant species composition and recommended width.

Another way of preventing crop losses or damage is to switch land use activities or promote low- or potentially low-conflict crops (Hockings and McLennan, 2012). Such strategies may not always result in equal or greater economic benefit to farmers or landowners; however, some crops can help balance both economic and conservation objectives. Research findings demonstrate that cashew nut (*Anacardium occidentalis*) production across a forested agricultural matrix around the Cantanhez National Park in Guinea-Bissau, West Africa, benefited both wild chimpanzees and people, providing an example of co-utilization. While this tree species is of high economic value, it is also nutritionally beneficial to wild chimpanzees. The apes focus on the fleshy part of the fruit, leaving behind the valuable casing for farmers to harvest; the seed—that is, the

cashew nut—is found in the casing (Hockings and Sousa, 2012). Although this crop species appears to meet both livelihood and conservation objectives, it must be noted that unmanaged expansion of cashew plantations or any other low-conflict crop of high market value could result in significant habitat loss for wild chimpanzees and other apes; such expansion can also affect market prices, thus affecting the crop's value to farmers.

Translocation and Other Mitigation Strategies

In areas where orangutans live, wildlife translocations—the "human-mediated movement of living organisms from one area, with release in another" (RSG and ISSG, 2012, p. 1) —have generally been implemented only as a last resort to save individual apes, as noted above (Yuwono *et al.*, 2007).

Translocations often involve individual orangutans in extremely poor physical and psychological condition (Hockings and Humle, 2009). As such individuals often require veterinary support, they tend to be placed in rehabilitation centers, which can facilitate their recovery and potential future release back into the wild. In other cases, orangutans may be rescued after plantation workers or local people signal their presence to local non-governmental organizations or authorities (G. Campbell-Smith and I. Singleton, personal communication, 2014). In some cases, these orangutans are directly translocated elsewhere, without prior assessment as to whether the situation at the site of origin is truly unmanageable— meaning that the negative impacts on apes and people cannot be mitigated or prevented by other means—and without consideration of the full implications of their release at the destination site (S. Wich, personal communication, 2014). By offering quick-fix solutions to problems between people and endangered wildlife, such initiatives

> 66 Releasing individuals into areas that are already populated by conspecifics can lead to intra-specific aggression and disease transmission. 99

can effectively prevent consultation among all stakeholders and expert assessments aimed at understanding, reducing and mitigating the issue.

Unplanned and mismanaged translocations are often carried out without prior assessment of the chances of survival of individuals to be released or the impact of their presence on wild conspecifics and other wildlife at the release site. Releasing individuals into areas that are already populated by conspecifics can lead to mortalities as a result of intra-specific aggression—especially among male chimpanzees (Goossens *et al.*, 2005b; Humle *et al.*, 2011)—or disease transmission, if at-risk individuals are not appropriately quarantined and tested prior to being released (Beck *et al.*, 2007; Kavanagh and Caldecott, 2013). Such translocations can also disseminate "conflict issues" if relocated individuals had habitually foraged on crops or approached human settlements in their area of origin. Such "bad habits" can get passed on to other individuals at the release site and cause problems with the surrounding communities.

Finally, it is clear that any post-release monitoring or pre-release site assessment and translocation initiatives are financially and logistically costly (Hockings and Humle, 2009). It is therefore essential to develop a coherent strategy around ape translocations, not only to ensure sustained funding, but also to integrate expert assessments of suitable release sites that are unlikely to incur future large-scale development and conflict issues with local people, as well as adequate post-release monitoring techniques and methodologies (Colin *et al.*, 2014). Nevertheless, it should be borne in mind that translocations and relocations are rarely useful or feasible options, given that suitable habitats are often scarce and the processes are ethically and logistically complicated, especially for great ape species that live in complex social groupings, such as bonobos, chimpanzees and gorillas (Hockings and Humle, 2009).

Deterrents

To date, very few studies have tested alternative mitigation approaches and deterrent techniques; the ones that have been undertaken focus on small-scale farms, which are more vulnerable to damage than large-scale commercial plantations. Still, their results can serve to inform mitigation approaches applicable to industrial agriculture. As indicated in Case study 1.2, experimentation has identified different locally appropriate techniques aimed at reducing crop damage by primates. While systematic guarding proved the most successful in reducing primate crop damage, other helpful techniques included the use of impenetrable living jatropha hedges, multi-strand barbed wire fences combined with camphor basil (*Ocimum kilimandscharicum*) planted along the bottom of fences and rope fences coated with chili paste. On their own, however, barbed wire fences were not always effective and simple ropes with bells were entirely ineffective. These measures vary in their costs and practical implementation, as a barbed wire fence is expensive and a hedge cannot readily be moved around in a landscape characterized by shifting agriculture, although such an approach could potentially be highly effective in protecting permanent gardens (Hill and Wallace, 2012).

While the large-scale use of hedges and barriers, such as fences, can be effective in terms of reducing crop damage, it can be problematic for wildlife as it can interfere with ranging and dispersal behaviors (Hayward and Kerley, 2009). Therefore, the implementation of such boundaries requires careful analysis and prior understanding of the ecology and local ranging of different wildlife species in the area. Research into effective barriers to protect crops from wildlife has also shown that the implementation of tested measures can lead wildlife to unprotected neighboring farms, displacing the issue and thereby highlighting the importance of implementing mitigation schemes simultaneously across landscapes, including all neighboring farms and agricultural developments. Persistent efforts could eventually lead to a significant decrease in crop damage events, so long as individual apes have adequate natural forage available. Year-round availability of, and access to, natural foods should therefore be assessed in advance, to ensure that preventing access to crops does not nutritionally compromise ape survival (Hill and Wallace, 2012).

In Sumatra, trials have been undertaken to test the effectiveness of noise deterrents and netting of trees to keep orangutans from foraging on fruit orchards in an agro-forestry landscape. The implementation of these measures improved local farmers' attitudes towards orangutans. A comparison of pre-trial and post-trial raiding events revealed that netting of trees, as opposed to noise deterrents, proved highly effective across farms where these approaches were tested; on control farms where no deterrents were employed, there was no difference between pre-trial and post-trial crop damage incidents. Although netting trees proved most effective, as it resulted in a significant increase in crop yield, farmers failed to persist in employing this technique after the trials ended, probably due to the related expense and logistical complexity (Campbell-Smith, Sembiring and Linkie, 2012).

Another way to mitigate instances of aggression is to change people's behavior towards apes (Hockings and Humle, 2009). In some cases, preventing surprise encounters via maintenance of shared paths to increase visibility can act to reduce aggressive incidents (Hockings and Humle, 2009). Educating plantation workers and people in the locality about apes and advising them on how to behave when they see an ape can also minimize the likelihood of aggression and reduce the risk of any escalation during encounters.

The Roles of Producers, Buyers and Consumers

The previous sections place much emphasis on the responsibility of growers and producers of commodities to improve the ability of apes to utilize and move through plantations; however, it is also important to highlight the role of the large-scale buyers and consumers of these commodities in terms of promoting and incentivizing better management practices. Since the current price of RSPO-certified palm oil is not significantly higher than that of non-certified oil, producers do not have much of an incentive to comply with certification requirements, including species-tolerant practices (see Chapter 5). Yet the adoption of such practices could be encouraged through a variety of approaches, including the promotion of no-deforestation and "no-kill" plantation policies, demands from consumer companies and the establishment of effective enforcement and monitoring of adherence to such policies. See Chapter 5 for an analysis of the role and impact of the RSPO in the conservation of apes in an industrial landscape.

Conclusion

Agricultural expansion across ape ranges, especially on an industrial scale, affects apes in two fundamental ways: through the destruction of their habitat (which also provides increased access to previously remote forests) and through increased competition over crops and land, which leads to negative interactions between people and apes. The latter is especially critical for ape species and populations that are likely to utilize cultivated crop species and venture close to human areas in modified landscapes, such as chimpanzees and orangutans.

There is an urgent need for ape range countries to balance industrial agricultural development with the protection of habitat and endangered species. Although it is illegal to kill apes in all the countries in which they are found, agriculture leads to significant population declines, through habitat destruction as well as direct killing. Land use plans do not adequately consider aspects such as conservation value, species diversity or abundance in the identification of areas for agricultural development—even though these factors are critical. Land use management could be improved through the integration of reliable empirical data on ape distribution and occurrence in environmental impact assessments. Including the mitigation hierarchy in decision-making is also critical, as the approach emphasizes the strategies of avoidance, mitigation, restoration and biodiversity offsets.

At the local level, any large-scale industrial agricultural activity should be informed by a solid understanding of how human–wildlife interactions affect people's livelihoods and shape people's perceptions, attitudes and the value they attach to apes. Moreover, effective strategies for preempting human–ape conflict require a firm appreciation of ape ecology and ranging behavior. In this context, it is just as important to ascertain how barriers can effectively mitigate crop damage as it is to recognize that they can also displace problems to areas where mitigation strategies cannot be implemented. Such informed approaches can help to prevent or manage any escalations and retaliatory behaviors resulting from human–ape interactions. In an effort to minimize cumulative impacts and risks to both people and apes, it is useful to adopt a broad perspective—one that will allow for assessment of all the impacts of industrial-scale agricultural developments and related operations. Clearly, such efforts require appropriate interdisciplinary and cross-disciplinary expertise, as well as strong local participation and engagement of all stakeholders.

Acknowledgments

Principal author: Annette Lanjouw

Contributors: Great Apes Survival Partnership (GRASP), Catherine M. Hill, Tatyana Humle, International Animal Rescue (IAR), Bill Laurance, Matthew R. McLennan, Olam International, Adam Phillipson, Johannes Refisch, Karmele Llano Sánchez, Brian Sims and Christopher Stewart

Case Study 1.1 Indonesia: Karmele Llano Sánchez, IAR

Case Study 1.2 Bulindi, Uganda: Matthew R. McLennan and Catherine M. Hill

Reviewers: Bjorn Dahlen, Kimberley J. Hockings, John F. Oates, Alain Rival and Rolf Skarr

Endnotes

1 Conversions were calculated using the yearly average currency exchange rate for 2010: 0.785, as per IRS (n.d.).

2 The figure is calculated by dividing the current population—573,903 (UBOS, 2014, p. 7)—by the total land area; however, there is no consensus on land area of the district. Land area is thus calculated based on the total population and population density as reported in the 2002 census, yielding an area of 3,602 km² (UBOS, 2006, pp. 47, 53).

3 At this writing, British American Tobacco Uganda was reportedly ceding its leaf growing operations to another company (*Sunday Monitor*, 2014).

Photo: Crops found in ape ranges include acacia, cacao, coffee, eucalyptus, maize, oil palm, peanuts, rubber, sugarcane and tea. © Ulet Ifansasti/Greenpeace

Encroaching on Ape Habitat: Deforestation and Industrial Agriculture in Cameroon, Liberia and on Borneo

Introduction

The expansion of industrial agriculture is a primary driver of tropical forest loss (Kartodihardjo and Supriono, 2000; Abdullah and Nakagoshi, 2008; Sodhi *et al.*, 2010). Tropical forests harbor high levels of terrestrial biodiversity and are the principal habitat for apes in Africa and Asia (Junker *et al.*, 2012). Numerous agro-industrial crops are found in ape ranges, including oil palm, peanut, rubber and sugarcane, as well as banana, cacao, coffee, corn, sorghum and tea. This chapter places a particular focus on oil palm cultivation as its impact on tropical forests and various endangered species has been under the loupe far more than that of other crops, particularly in Southeast Asia.

Oil palm (*Elaeis guineensis*) is the most rapidly expanding industrial crop in the world (Miettinen *et al.*, 2012; FAO, 2014a), driven by a growing global market for palm oil for food, cosmetics, fuel and other industrial uses (Nantha and Tisdell, 2009). The global land area of mature oil palm rose from 35,000 km² (3.5 million ha) in 1975 to 131,000 km² (13.1 million ha) in 2005 (Wicke *et al.*, 2011). Although oil palm originated in Africa, it has not been as extensively planted or intensively produced there as it is in Asia; however, a recent increase in investments in Africa suggests that the continent is likely to witness future expansion (Greenpeace International, 2012). Large areas of industrial land purchases for oil palm have recently been negotiated or are under negotiation across Africa (Carrere, 2010; Rainforest Foundation, 2013; see Chapter 3). The Congo Basin and West Africa have been identified as the continent's most suitable areas for oil palm expansion (see Chapter 1). Yet these areas overlap significantly with ape ranges (Wich *et al.*, 2014), raising concerns that their development will lead to biodiversity losses similar to those seen in Southeast Asia.

Indeed, it is highly likely that the future development of industrial agriculture will have a significant deleterious impact on ape habitats globally. Effectively addressing that threat calls for a solid understanding of the context within which industrial agriculture has evolved; to that end, this chapter presents spatially explicit information on the current overlap of ape habitats and industrial agriculture, based on research conducted by the United Nations Environment Programme World Conservation Monitoring Centre (UNEP-WCMC). The WCMC utilizes a number of data sets, including:

- the Land Matrix, a global, independent land monitoring initiative (Land Matrix, n.d.); and

- Global Forest Watch (GFW), whose online platform provides spatial data on land use and agro-industrial concessions. The source data of GFW are based on a combination of government documents, satellite imagery and GPS data.

The bulk of the chapter then focuses on the evolution of deforestation due to industrial agriculture across two countries—Cameroon and Liberia—as well as on the island of Borneo, which is divided among the countries of Brunei, Indonesia and Malaysia.

Key findings from this chapter include:

- Agro-industrial development is a major threat to ape populations across their ranges.

- While the drivers of deforestation are complex, the cause is largely attributable to a combination of poor planning and ineffective governance in relation to land use and tenure.

- Industrial agricultural estates are expected to expand, increasing pressures on ape habitats and existing populations—be it through loss and fragmentation of habitat, increased hunting or intensified conflict between ape and human populations.

- Oil palm and rubber are the crops that have caused the most significant levels of deforestation in Southeast Asia and are leading to the same in Africa.

- Liberia has the highest potential for oil palm expansion in Africa, yet 94.3% of the area suitable for oil palm lies in ape ranges that are unprotected.

- Findings indicate that crops as diverse as rubber, cotton, cacao and sugarcane affect the integrity of ape habitats across their entire range. This diversity implies that efforts to reconcile ape conservation with industrial agricultural development should consider broader responses in addition to addressing specific impacts of individual commodities.

Industrial Agricultural Concessions across Ape Ranges

There is a dearth of data on industrial agriculture—particularly spatially explicit data. The Land Matrix partnership provides data on transnational land deals (see Table 3.1 in Chapter 3, page 75). Precise geospatial information on land deals from the Land Matrix was available for 20 out of 30 countries that have ape ranges within their borders. In an analysis involving all 30 countries, land deals were attributed to the province or state level. Land deals were then classified by size and mapped accordingly. The precise geospatial information that was available for 20 countries was used in a separate, more detailed analysis (see Figures 2.1 and 2.2). However, due to paucity of comprehensive data on land deals, this analysis provides a conservative indication of the overlap between ape habitat and industrial agricultural concessions.

As of August 2014, the Land Matrix Global Observatory had information on approximately 1,800 land deals globally. The Matrix records 877 land deals among the countries that are home to habitat; meanwhile, 352—or 20% of all known land deals—are within or very near ape ranges in Africa and Asia (see Figures 2.1 and 2.2). The contract area of land deals is generally larger in Africa than in Asia; however, the number of deals is larger for some Asian countries, most notably Indonesia, which has 114 recorded deals, and Cambodia, which has 87. Deals in both countries show significant overlap with ape ranges and protected areas that host apes (see Box 2.1). In Africa, most land deals are found in Liberia (17) and Sierra Leone (20).

FIGURE 2.1

Contracted or Intended Land Deals in Ape Ranges in Africa

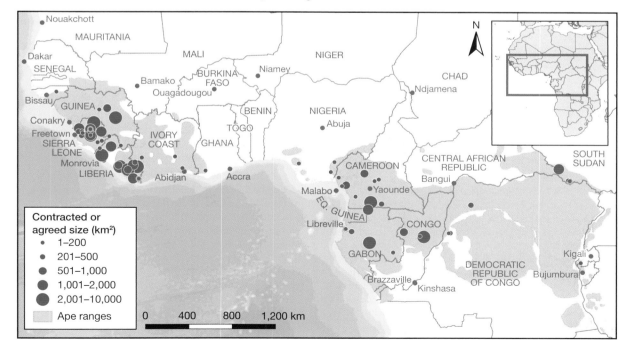

FIGURE 2.2

Contracted or Intended Land Deals in Ape Ranges in Asia

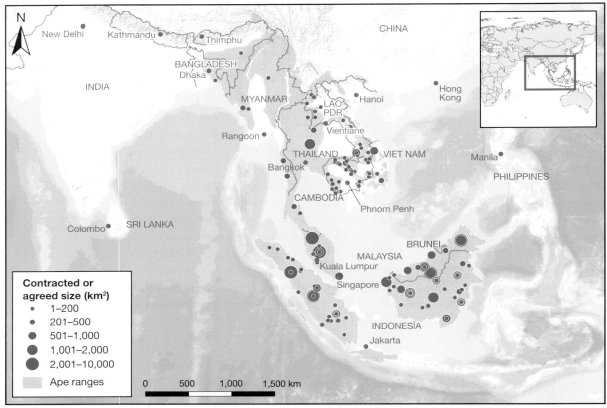

Contracted or agreed size (km²)
- 1–200
- 201–500
- 501–1,000
- 1,001–2,000
- 2,001–10,000
- Ape ranges

0   500   1,000   1,500 km

Notes for Figures 2.1 and 2.2: The size of land deals was defined as the reported contract size or, if this information was not available, the production size. If neither the contract nor the production size was available, the intended contract size was used.

Data sources for Figures 2.1 and 2.2: Land Matrix (n.d.); IUCN (n.d.)

Courtesy of UNEP-WCMC

BOX 2.1

Conflicting Interests in Cambodia: Protected Areas and Land Deals

Even though Cambodia has one of the highest deforestation rates in the world (Hansen *et al.*, 2013)—with total forest cover that shrank from 72% to 48% from 1973 to 2014 (Open Development Cambodia, 2015b)—there is little information on the impacts of agricultural expansion on the country's apes. Cambodia's traditional industrial crop is rubber, which occupied about 2,800 km² (280,000 ha) in 2012; an additional 8,000 km² (800,000 ha) were earmarked for exploitation between 2012 and 2017. The Cambodian government has prioritized the development of economic land concessions, issuing a formal order to a number of government institutions

to strengthen engagement in management systems, land allocation and land use (Cambodia, 2014). Increases in investments in both oil palm and rubber had already been observed before the order was issued (Colchester *et al.*, 2011).

Oil palm plantations have expanded into forested regions through the allocation of economic land concessions on state land to private companies, covering 1,180 km² (118,000 ha) in 2009 (Colchester *et al.*, 2011). When it comes to the current total area of concession land, figures diverge: the Ministry of Agriculture, Forestry and Fisheries indicates that just over 12,000 km² (1.2 million ha) of land had been given out as of June 2012, yet some non-governmental organizations put that figure closer to 20,000 km² (2 million ha) (Open Development Cambodia, 2015a). Growers have planted additional crops, such as corn, soybean, cassava and mung bean (Cambodia, 2014).

FIGURE 2.3

Overlap of Ape Ranges in Cambodia with Protected Areas, Agro-industry and Certified RSPO Sites

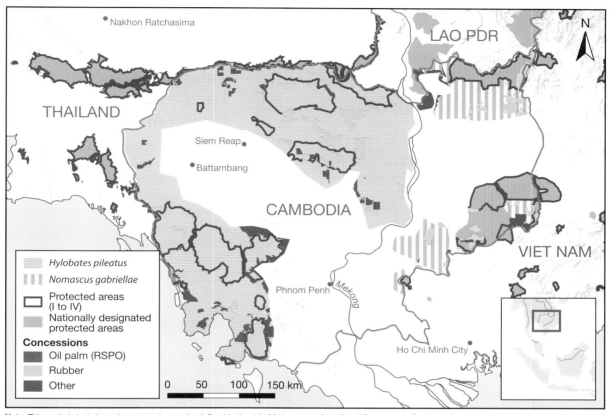

Note: This analysis includes only protected areas (as defined in the July 2014 version of the World Database on Protected Areas) with national protection designation; proposed protected areas are not included.

Data sources: WRI (2013); IUCN (n.d.); IUCN and UNEP (2014); Open Development Cambodia (2014)

Courtesy of UNEP-WCMC

It is estimated that the area of rubber in non-rubber growing areas in Southeast Asian countries, including Cambodia, could quadruple by 2050, replacing mainly evergreen broadleaf forests and vegetation that is currently under shifting cultivation (Fox *et al.*, 2012).

Cambodia has two gibbon species on the Red List of the International Union for Conservation of Nature (IUCN), the pileated gibbon (*Hylobates pileatus*) and the southern yellow-cheeked crested gibbon (*Nomascus gabriellae*). A third species, the northern yellow-cheeked crested gibbon (*Nomascus annamensis*), has been identified but has not yet been assessed by the IUCN. It is found in the northernmost block of the area currently identified as inhabited by the southern yellow-cheeked crested gibbon (B. Rawson, personal communication, 2015).

More than 100 of the 190 spatially explicit concessions for agro-industry in Cambodia are specific concessions for rubber

plantations or mixed concessions of rubber and other crops (mainly acacia and sugarcane, with some oil palm). Rubber plantations occupy a total area of 5,566 km² (556,620 ha), which account for nearly 6% of ape ranges; other plantations take up an additional 4,875 km² (487,550 ha), or 5% of the range, bringing the total area of agro-industrial concessions in ape ranges close to 11%. Of the 239 km² (23,890 ha) dedicated to oil palm concessions in Cambodia, only one was RSPO-certified in 2013 (see Figure 2.3).

Several land deals appear to be located in Category I–IV protected areas and nationally protected areas (see Box 2.2); nearly all of these are rubber plantations. Agricultural concessions are not legally permitted in these categories but are now found in most of Cambodia's protected areas (Cambodia, 2014); as a result, the threat to the habitat they provide for apes and other species is significant.

BOX 2.2

Protected Area Categories

The World Database on Protected Areas—the most comprehensive global spatial database on protected areas—is jointly produced by the IUCN World Commission on Protected Areas and the World Conservation Monitoring Centre of the United Nations Environment Programme (IUCN and UNEP, 2014). The protected areas are classified by IUCN management category, as follows:

- Category Ia: strict nature reserve
- Category Ib: wilderness area
- Category II: national park
- Category III: national monument or feature
- Category IV: habitat or species management area
- Category V: protected landscape
- Category VI: sustainable use of natural resources

These categories are distinguished by differences in the management approaches undertaken within protected areas (Dudley, 2008). Industrial agriculture is restricted in protected areas classified as IUCN Categories I through IV.

Industrial Crops in Ape Ranges

The degree to which agro-industry affects apes depends on the types of crops being cultivated in, and adjacent to, ape ranges. Apes may utilize crops for food, in competition with humans—which may result in human–wildlife conflict; humans may also destroy the forest habitat to make space for cultivation. Crops as diverse as oil palm, coffee, rubber and cotton impact the integrity of ape habitats across their entire range (see Table 2.1). In Uganda, the land used for sugarcane plantations underwent an 18-fold increase between 1988 and 2002, exerting a direct impact on chimpanzee behavior and survival (see Case Study 1.2 in Chapter 1, page 29). In Guinea-Bissau, monoculture cashew nut plantations are highlighted as a threat to the habitats of western chimpanzees (Carvalho, Marques and Vicente, 2013). Given the diversity of crops and their impacts, efforts to reconcile ape conservation with industrial agricultural development need to

consider factors relating to particular crops as well as broader issues that are shaped by commodities in general.

Deforestation and Industrial Agriculture: The Cases of Cameroon, Liberia and Borneo

The context within which industrial agriculture manifests itself in ape range states can provide important insights into drivers that go beyond economic demands. This section presents a detailed analysis of the evolution and current situation of industrial agriculture and its overlap with ape habitats in Cameroon, Liberia and on the island of Borneo.

The countries of Cameroon and Liberia were selected because both are home to important ape ranges on a continent that has been experiencing recent expansion of industrial agriculture and that is likely to witness ensuing impacts on ape habitats and populations. Both these countries are important for apes, and civil society actors have scrutinized their performance and exposed related social and environmental impacts of the ongoing expansion of the palm oil industry. In contrast, Borneo has long experienced rapid and extensive deforestation due to industrial agriculture, which has been a key feature of economic development across the island since colonization. As Borneo is governed by three countries, it offers lessons based on differing trajectories, some of which can serve to inform how the industry might evolve in Africa in the absence of adequate mitigation measures.

Cameroon

Forest and Ape Status

The Republic of Cameroon lies in western Africa's Gulf of Guinea and is bordered by the Central African Republic, Chad, Equatorial

TABLE 2.1

Summary of Impacts of Agribusiness Development on Ape Habitats in Ape Range Countries

Country	Industrial and cash crops*	Developments and coverage details	Impacts	
Africa				
Burundi	Forest plantations for wood	Plantations replaced natural forests	41% of forest cover was lost from 1990 to 2010 (Nduwamungu, 2011)	
Central African Republic	Coffee, cotton, tobacco, tree crops (IMF, 2008; FAO, 2014a)	Industrial crop production decreased in 2001–06 (IMF, 2008)	0.8% of forest cover was lost from 1990 to 2005 (Hansen et al., 2013)	
Democratic Republic of Congo	Cacao, coffee, oil palm, rubber, tea (FAO, 2014a)	Commercial agriculture is limited, but a high demand for oil palm is reportedly causing conversion of forests (Rainforest Foundation, 2013)	Currently the main threat is the hunting of apes for meat, which is exacerbated by habitat fragmentation (Hickey, Carroll and Nibbelink, 2012)	
Gabon	Cacao, coffee, oil palm, rubber, sugarcane (FAO, 2014a)	Large-scale industrial agriculture is under development (Rainforest Foundation, 2013)	No direct impacts on ape populations reported, although they declined by more than half between 1983 and 2000, due to commercial hunting facilitated by logging (Walsh et al., 2003)	
Ghana	Cacao, coffee, oil palm, rubber (FAO, 2014a)	57% of the country is agricultural land (Oppong-anane, 2006)	Impacts of industrial agricultural development on apes not reported	
Guinea	Coffee, fruits, oil palm, peanuts, rice (FAO, 2014a)	Guinea does not have any large oil palm plantations; most production comes from natural oil palm groves (Carrere, 2010)	None reported	
Guinea-Bissau	Cashew nuts (Economy Watch, 2010)	Monoculture cashew nut plantations are possibly increasing (Economy Watch, 2010)	Intensive agriculture and commercial tree plantations have affected habitats suitable for western chimpanzees (Carvalho et al., 2013)	
Ivory Coast	Cacao, coffee, cotton, oil palm, rubber, sugarcane (Aregheore, 2009)	Cultivated land covers 21.8% of the country; the forest area produces the most export crops (Aregheore, 2009)	Severe deforestation in the past due to intensive logging and agriculture expansion (GRID-Arendal, 2005); decline in western chimpanzees due to hunting and habitat loss (Campbell et al., 2008b)	
Nigeria	Cacao, oil palm, rubber (Chapin Metz, 1991)	Oil palm and rubber predominate in the southeast and south-central areas (Chapin Metz, 1991)	Ape ranges are in the same areas as most oil palm and rubber plantations; apes are threatened by logging, hunting and agriculture, including plantations (USAID, 2008)	
Republic of Congo	Cacao, coffee, oil palm, sugarcane, tobacco (FAO, 2014a)	Oil palm is increasing in importance (Carrere, 2010; FAO, 2014a); a single concession of 4,700 km² (470,000 ha) has been granted for oil palm plantations (Rainforest Foundation, 2013)	The area is the habitat of chimpanzees and western gorillas (Rainforest Foundation, 2013), both of which are already affected by disease epidemics and commercial wild meat hunting (Walsh et al., 2003)	
Rwanda	Coffee, tea	Industrial agriculture is limited, except tea and coffee (Rwanda, 2004); 50% increase in tree cover due to plantations developed in 1990–2005 (Butler, 2006; FAO, 2010)	50% of natural forest cover and woodland habitat was lost in 1990–2005 (Butler, 2006)	

Country	Industrial and cash crops*	Developments and coverage details	Impacts
Senegal	Cotton, peanuts	Agriculture is expanding inland	450 km² (45,000 ha) of forest is lost annually (New Agriculturalist, 2008)
Sierra Leone	Cacao, coffee, oil palm (IMF, 2011)	Exports of cacao, coffee and oil palm increased in 2008–12 (IMF, 2011); the number of oil palm concessions is growing (Carrere, 2010)	Much of the original forest cover was probably lost and the deforestation rate remains high (FAO, 2010) and is likely to have impacted ape populations
South Sudan	Peanuts	Large-scale land acquisitions have been made for timber and oil palm plantations (Future Challenges, 2011)	Developments are leading to deforestation (Future Challenges, 2011)
Tanzania	Cashew nuts, coffee, cotton, sisal hemp, tobacco	A government task force was set up in 2006 to promote oil palm production (Carrere, 2010)	Hunting and habitat loss have been the main factors affecting chimpanzee populations in their range in the Ntakata region (Ogawa, Moore and Kamenya, 2006)
Uganda	Coffee, sugarcane	The area of sugarcane plantations adjacent to Budongo Forest Reserve grew more than 18-fold, from 7 km² to 127 km² (690 ha to 12,729 ha) in 1988–2002 (Mwavu and Witkowski, 2008)	Forest loss is due to agricultural expansion (Mwavu and Witkowski, 2008); there are indications that ape populations persist in forest agriculture mosaics (Tweheyo, Lye and Weladji, 2004)
Asia			
Bangladesh	Jute, sugarcane (FAO, 2014a)	Land conversion and illegal logging are the main causes of deforestation (Kibria et al., 2011; Islam and Sato, 2012)	Hoolock gibbon populations are affected by agricultural expansion and declines in natural forest areas (Muzaffar et al., 2011)
China: Hainan province	Betel palm, cacao, cashew nuts, coconut, coffee, lemongrass, oil palm, pepper, rubber, sisal hemp, sugarcane	More than 90% of the land is under cultivation, including rubber plantations (Zhou et al., 2005)	The Hainan gibbon is threatened by forest clearance: 7% of the habitat of the (estimated) remaining 20 individuals of the species was cleared in 1991–2008 (Zhang et al., 2010)
China: southern Yunnan province	Rubber, sugarcane, tea, tobacco	The size of agricultural patches increased in 1965–92; cash crops replaced traditional agriculture (Fox and Vogler, 2005)	Loss of primary forest poses risk to gibbon survival (Fan Peng-Fei et al., 2009)
India: the northeast	Coffee, rubber, tea	Assam state produces 53% of India's tea (Choudhury, 2009)	Agricultural encroachment, extractive industries and timber are the major threats facing the hoolock gibbons' survival (Das et al., 2003; Choudhury, 2009)
Indonesia	Oil palm, rubber, tree plantations	Rubber, oil palm and pulp and paper plantations are primary agricultural crops; small-scale agriculture accounts for a significant proportion of forest loss (see the section on Borneo)	Between 2,383 and 3,882 orangutans have been killed annually; the killings seem more prevalent in areas of deforestation and plantation development (Meijaard et al., 2012)
Lao People's Democratic Republic	Coffee, rubber	The government encourages foreign investment in rubber plantations (Hicks et al., 2009); permanent intensive agriculture is spreading (Thongmanivong and Fujita, 2006)	None reported
Malaysia	Oil palm, rubber	Oil palm and rubber plantations cover around 60% of all agricultural land in Malaysia (Chee and Peng, 2006; Koh et al., 2011)	Development of agricultural crops is a major cause of forest loss (Abdullah and Nakagoshi, 2008); conversion to oil palm threatens the survival of the Borneo orangutan (Nantha and Tisdell, 2009)

Country	Industrial and cash crops*	Developments and coverage details	Impacts
▶ Myanmar	Beans, jatropha, oil palm, pulses, rubber, sugarcane (ADB, 2013; FAO, 2014a)	Concessions for rubber plantations and oil palm are in development stages; more than 7,000 km² (700,000 ha) of concessions for industrial agriculture were granted by 2010—4,050 km² (405,000 ha) of which was for oil palm, including in the Tenasserim Division (Burma Environmental Working Group, 2011), home to the world's last remaining intact lowland dipterocarp rainforests (Geissmann et al., 2013); agricultural concessions are sometimes granted inside protected forests (KDNG, 2010)	Forest conversion and plantation concessions are threatening the Hoolock and white-handed gibbons' habitat and associated biodiversity (Geissmann et al., 2013)
Thailand	Cassava, coconut, corn, oil palm, rubber, sugarcane	Traditional subsistence farming systems are giving way to cash crops (Entwisle et al., 2005)	Crop expansion is leading to forest fragmentation and large-scale deforestation (Entwisle et al., 2005)
Viet Nam	Coffee, cotton, peanuts, rice, rubber, sugarcane, tea	Government aims to boost foreign investment in agriculture (Vietnam Briefing, 2014)	Past large-scale land use change has probably impacted gibbon populations; most, if not all, gibbon populations are highly fragmented and in decline (Rawson et al., 2011)

Notes: * For all crops except palm oil, this table lists single-crop data from FAOSTAT rather than aggregates. Different crop categories can refer to oil palm, including fruit, kernels and "oil crops primary." A review of online country-specific resources was used to determine whether a crop is an industrial or cash crop, although that distinction is not always straightforward.

Guinea, Gabon, Nigeria and the Republic of Congo. It is home to more than 23 million people, with the highest human population densities found in southwestern Cameroon, near the border with Nigeria. The extent of forest cover in Cameroon has steadily declined, from about 243,000 km² (24.3 million ha) in 1990 to just under 200,000 km² (19.9 million ha) in 2010, a loss of roughly 18% with an average annual forest loss of 2,200 km² (220,000 ha) (FAO, 2010). An estimated 1.4% of Cameroon's dense forests—those with more than 50% tree canopy cover—were destroyed between 2000 and 2012; much of this forest loss was concentrated near the coast in southwestern Cameroon (Hansen et al., 2013). For a detailed layout of land allocated to agro-industries in Cameroon, visit the World Resources Institute's Forest Atlas of Cameroon (WRI, n.d.-a).

Cameroon's forests are home to at least four ape subspecies: the Nigeria–Cameroon chimpanzee (*Pan troglodytes ellioti*), the central chimpanzee (*Pan troglodytes troglodytes*), the Cross River gorilla (*Gorilla gorilla diehli*) and the western lowland gorilla (*Gorilla gorilla gorilla*). These populations are distributed throughout the lowland and montane forest zone of southern Cameroon, including the administrative regions of Northwest, Southwest, Littoral, Center, South, and East (see Figure 2.4). Apes have been observed in 47 forest sites across Cameroon, including in 11 national parks, which provide apes with the highest legal protection (Arcus Foundation, 2014). Cameroon is an especially important site for the conservation of Nigeria–Cameroon chimpanzees and Cross River gorillas, as these subspecies are endemic to Nigeria and western Cameroon and are among the most threatened ape taxa.

The Development of Industrial Agriculture in Cameroon

Industrial agriculture has a long history in Cameroon, having been conceived and promoted by its colonial rulers, who developed

an extractive and export economy (Gerber, Veuthey and Martínez-Alier, 2009). Starting as early as 1885 and continuing throughout German rule (1884–1916), German companies were awarded land primarily in today's Southwest region, along Cameroon's coastal area and around the fertile, volcanic soils of Mount Cameroon (Nguiffo and Schwartz, 2012b). Plantations were developed for growing bananas, oil palm, rubber and tea, all of which were primarily destined for the export market. The conversion of large tracts of land for agro-industrial development involved the expulsion and relocation of the indigenous people from the concession areas to "native reserves" (Konings, 1993; Njoh, 2002). People—both indigenous and from afar— were then brought in to serve as laborers in the plantations. Commercial plantation agriculture in coastal areas led to a large influx of migrant workers, who lived in company towns (Njoh, 2002).

Following Germany's defeat in World War I, the League of Nations divided German Kamerun into a British-mandated territory (Northern and Southern Cameroon, along the border with Nigeria, 1918–60) and a larger French-administered territory. Both colonial rulers continued the German tradition of developing large-scale, agro-industrial plantations and continued to enact laws that dispossessed indigenous people of their land by converting it into colonial property and instituting forced labor practices (Njoh and Akiwumi, 2012). Many of the former German plantations in the French territory were purchased by European private companies and later transferred to the agro-industrial company Société Africaine Forestière et Agricole du Cameroun (SAFACAM), established in 1897 as a rubber company and taken over by the Bolloré Group, a French private investment company, in 1997 (Oyono, 2013). The British inherited and retained most of the German plantation lands and, after World War II, they subsumed most of the plantations into a parastatal enterprise called Cameroon Development Corporation.

After independence in 1960, Cameroon invested in state-owned plantations and reaffirmed state control over land and forest (Oyono, 2013). By the 1980s, however, a deep economic crisis led to structural adjustment policies imposed on the Cameroonian government by the World Bank, the International Monetary Fund and bilateral donors that aimed to privatize dozens of state-owned companies, including major agro-industries (World Bank, 1996). The goal of privatization was to increase the efficiency of agro-industrial production, increase domestic production and exports, and attract foreign investors (World Bank, 2004).

Together with these interventions, the development of Cameroon's land tenure and forest policies spurred agro-industrial expansion into the country's forests. Although the government is officially the "trustee" of most lands, the state apparatus acts as owner of all lands and regularly uses eminent domain (compulsory purchase) to displace local communities in order to grant national or private lands to foreign investors. Rural communities in Cameroon's forested zones exercise customary land tenure, but they lack legally recognized land rights on their individual lands and commons (Alden Wily, 2011). This legal framework facilitates state and investor control over forested lands and has laid the foundation for the expansion of agro-industrial development throughout Cameroon's forest zone.

While several government development strategies call for the expansion of large agro-industrial plantations (MINEPAT, 2009; MINADER, 2014), various complex external economic factors and domestic reforms are behind the most recent wave of land acquisition for plantation development in the country. Among these are:

- changing land use policies in Indonesia and Malaysia, which have led companies to diversify into Africa (Feintrenie, 2013);
- growing demand for biofuels (Danielsen, Beukema and Burgess, 2009);

- China's strategic partnership with the Government of Cameroon (Khan and Baye, 2008; Jansson, 2009);
- the perception that there is political stability in Cameroon (Feintrenie, 2014); and
- new foreign direct investment incentives and protections (MINEPAT, 2009; Hawkins and Chen, 2011).

All of these factors have contributed to the high demand from agro-industries for Cameroonian land.

As a result, Cameroon has witnessed a substantial increase in the scale of industrial agriculture in the 1990s and even more so in the following decade. Numerous agro-industries now operate throughout Cameroon's forest zone, primarily producing palm oil and rubber and, to a lesser extent, tea, rice, bananas and sugar, which, together, cover more than 3,000 km² (300,000 ha) of land (Feintrenie, 2014).

Agro-industry Development by Commodity

This section details the rise and expansion of Cameroonian agro-industries by commodity, with a particular focus on palm oil, rubber and sugar. It also considers how agro-industrial growth is likely to impact ape populations.

Palm oil

Cameroon has made agro-industrial oil palm development an economic priority. The government aims to increase palm oil production to 300,000 metric tons in 2015 and 450,000 metric tons by 2020 (Hoyle and Levang, 2012). Although artisanal processing will account for some of this increased production, the government is focused on expanding the total area under industrial oil palm development. It aims to accomplish this goal, in part, by leasing large tracts of fertile land to foreign agro-industrial investors. Cameroon has thus positioned itself at the heart of a "new wave" of large-scale, industrial oil palm development in the African forest zone (Linder, 2013). This situation is especially unfavorable for ape conservation, as most agro-industries tend to clear primary and secondary forest for the development of oil palm plantations (Richards, 2013; Nkongho, Feintrenie and Levang, 2014).

Cameroon hosts three privately held agro-industrial oil palm producers—Société Camerounaise de Palmeraies (Socapalm), SAFACAM, and Société des Palmeraies de la Ferme Suisse—and two publicly owned ones—Cameroon Development Corporation and Pamol. In addition, at least eight other foreign agro-industries either currently lease or are attempting to acquire land for oil palm development in the country (Greenpeace International, 2012; Hoyle and Levang, 2012). These companies are targeting the same "fertile crescent" lands that colonial-era companies coveted, not only because of the rich soil, but also in view of the proximity to major urban and industrial centers as well as the Atlantic coast for export.

Sithe Global Sustainable Oils Cameroon (SGSOC), owned by the US agribusiness Herakles Farms, was the first of these agro-industries to be awarded a contract. This land acquisition, originally for 731 km² (73,086 ha) but finally reduced to 200 km² (20,000 ha), has proved to be the most controversial oil palm development in the recent resurgence of industrially produced palm oil in Africa. Cameroonian and international non-governmental organizations declared the deal a "land grab" based on details that came to light on the history of the SGSOC development (Linder, 2013). Of particular importance to this case study is the plantation's location in high-conservation-value forest. The SGSOC plantation is in the Southwest region, close to a Pamol oil palm plantation; it is flanked by four protected areas known to harbor key populations of the endangered Nigeria–Cameroon chimpanzee (Morgan *et al.*, 2011).

Sugar

Cameroon's sugar industry is controlled by the Société d'Organisation de Management et de Développement des Industries Alimentaires et Agricoles (SOMDIAA), a French conglomerate, via two affiliates: Société Sucrière du Cameroun (SOSUCAM) and the Cameroon Sugar Company (CAMSUCO), which operate in the Center region, approximately 100 km north of the capital, Yaoundé. Founded in 1965, SOSUCAM possesses a land lease for 101 km² (10,085 ha) in the Mbandjock area (Nguiffo and Schwartz, 2012b). CAMSUCO was launched in 1977 as a state-owned company in Nkoteng. It was acquired by SOMDIAA in 1998, following production stoppage and financial difficulties (Tchawa, 2012).

SOMDIAA currently exploits 187 km² (18,700 ha) of sugar plantations and has announced its intention to add another 70 km² (7,000 ha) by 2017 (SOMDIAA, n.d.). The forested zones of Mbandjock and Nkoteng have largely been converted to agricultural land for sugar production; the remaining forested zones are likely to be purchased by Chinese and Korean companies that are already developing about 100 km² (10,000 ha) of new rice plantations in the area (Nguiffo and Schwartz, 2012b). The Indo-British-Cameroonian consortium, Justin Sugar Mills SA, has also announced plans to develop a sugar plantation near Batouri, in Cameroon's forested East region. The project's future is in doubt, however, as it has yet to receive all necessary permits and lacks capital (Mbodiam, 2014).

Rubber

New investment in the rubber sector presents a major threat to the forested areas of

Cameroon's South region. The Chinese company Sinochem controls two major rubber companies, HEVECAM and Sud Cameroun Hevea. HEVECAM already cultivates 180 km² (18,000 ha) adjacent to Campo Ma'an National Park and has announced plans to augment the production area by 200 km²

(20,000 ha) (Gerber, 2008; Biy, 2013). In 2010, Sud Cameroun Hevea obtained a land concession of more than 410 km² (41,000 ha) adjacent to the UNESCO World Heritage site Dja Faunal Reserve (Bela, 2014); the company has already cleared 30 km² (3,000 ha) of forest to establish rubber nurseries

FIGURE 2.4

Overlap of Agricultural, Oil Palm and Logging Concessions with Protected Areas and Chimpanzee and Gorilla Ranges in Cameroon

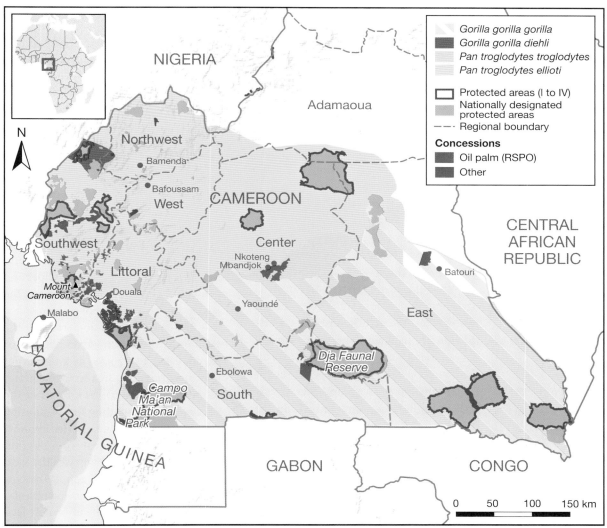

Notes: The range area for chimpanzees overlaps with the gorilla range. The size of land deals was defined as the reported contract size or, if this information was not available, the production size. If neither the contract nor the production size was available, the intended contract size was used.

Data sources: IUCN and UNEP (2014); WRI (2014a, 2014b); IUCN (n.d.)

Courtesy of UNEP-WCMC

and related infrastructure. Both Campo Ma'an National Park and the Dja Faunal Reserve are home to considerable populations of chimpanzee and gorilla and have been designated as high priority areas for their conservation (Tutin *et al.*, 2005).

The Current Situation

In Cameroon, agricultural plantations are allocated by the Ministry of Economy, Planning and Regional Development to private entities under long-term, renewable contracts that are then monitored by the Ministry of Agriculture and Rural Development.

All agricultural concessions in the country lie within ape ranges. Fourteen oil palm concessions fall within gorilla ranges, totaling 1,697 km² (169,740 ha), which is 1.0% of the total gorilla range in Cameroon. Another 65 oil palm concessions are found within chimpanzee ranges, totaling 3,928 km² (392,770 ha), or 1.4% of the total range. Logging concessions are also all located in gorilla and chimpanzee ranges, accounting for a total area of 98,612 km² (9.9 million ha) (see Figure 2.4).

While the current extent of industrial agriculture concessions within ape ranges is relatively low, the apportionment of concessions in ape habitats contravenes national environmental legislation that provides for the protection of endangered species such as Cameroon's great apes. Moreover, industrial agriculture is prohibited within the national forest estate (CED and RELUFA, 2013; WRI, 2014a).

In the light of past transgressions, it is unclear whether future allocations of agricultural concessions will comply with environmental legislation. Of particular concern are areas that are suitable for oil palm plantations that lie within Cameroon's ape ranges, as 48% of that land is outside protected areas (Wich *et al.*, 2014).

> " The proximity of agro-industrial plantations to protected areas is of particular concern as these parks and reserves serve as strongholds for apes and other endangered wildlife populations. "

Conclusion for Cameroon

Agro-industrial expansion is developing into a significant driver of deforestation in areas of chimpanzee and gorilla habitats. In particular, agro-industrial companies continue to target forested lands in Cameroon's "fertile crescent"—from the Southwest region through the Littoral and Center regions and into the South region, as well as the lands farther from the Atlantic coast that are near large urban centers and new transport infrastructure. This region contains some of the largest populations of the Nigeria–Cameroon chimpanzee, the most endangered chimpanzee subspecies, distributed across several protected areas that have been designated exceptional priority sites for the conservation of this taxon (Morgan *et al.*, 2011). This analysis indicates that the expansion of oil palm and rubber plantations will be the primary cause of agro-industrial deforestation in Cameroon, given that these industries require vast areas of forested land to be economically viable.

The proximity of large-scale, agro-industrial plantations to protected areas is of particular concern as these parks and reserves serve as strongholds for apes and other endangered wildlife populations. The creation and maintenance of such protected areas is a core conservation strategy. The extent of deforestation surrounding protected areas is recognized as a significant predictor of protected area ecological health (Laurance *et al.*, 2012). As a result of the clearance of surrounding forest, hunting intensifies in protected areas, fueled by growing demand for wild meat from migrant workers and an increasingly wealthy local population (Poulsen *et al.*, 2009). The synergistic effects of habitat fragmentation and intense hunting of wildlife ultimately lead to the depletion of large-bodied mammals in protected areas (Brashares, Arcese and Sam, 2001; Gonedelé Bi *et al.*, 2012; Benchimol and Peres, 2013).

Cameroon's government seems willing both to allow agribusinesses to circumvent national laws and to convert high conservation value forest into monoculture plantations (Nguiffo and Schwartz, 2012a; Linder, 2013). This conduct reflects a neopatrimonial approach to the governance of natural resources, whereby legal, technical and environmental factors such as environmental and social impact assessments are given little or no consideration in the decision-making process (Médard, 1977; Nguiffo, 2001). This situation is compounded by a lack of recognition of community land and forest rights, which enables the state to continue to use expropriation to accelerate deforestation and forest degradation for agro-industrial and related infrastructure developments (Stevens et al., 2014).

Liberia

The Republic of Liberia is a West African country bordered by Guinea to the north, Ivory Coast to the east and Sierra Leone to the west. It is home to 4 million people and emerged in 2003 from two civil wars that destroyed its economy. In 2014–15, the Ebola crisis stretched its public services to the breaking point. Liberia currently harbors around 42% of the remaining Upper Guinea Forest, in two large forest blocks that consist of evergreen lowland forests in the southeast and semi-deciduous mountain forests in the northwest (Christie et al., 2007). The tropical forests of the Guinea region are among the world's priority conservation areas and are believed to incorporate several major Pleistocene refugia. Boasting extraordinary levels of biodiversity, including the highest diversity of mammals in the world, the Upper Guinea Forest is host to high numbers of endangered and endemic species. The forest extent for the countries within the Upper Guinean Forest system

has declined to just 15% of its original area (CEPF, 2000).

Evidence suggests that agricultural expansion has been the primary cause of long-term forest loss and degradation in West Africa, and a significant proportion of formerly forested land (80%) is now an agriculture–forest mosaic (Norris et al., 2010). In addition to commercial and subsistence agriculture (including tree crop plantations), the significant drivers of deforestation and forest degradation are timber extraction, mining (commercial, artisanal and small-scale) and post-conflict population migrations (CEPF, 2000).

Great Apes in Liberia

The western chimpanzee (*Pan troglodytes*) is one of the most threatened subspecies of chimpanzee and is the only great ape present in Liberia. A recent nationwide survey estimates that Liberia, with its relatively large and un-fragmented forest cover, hosts more than 7,000 chimpanzees, making it home to the second-highest number of chimpanzees in West Africa (Tweh et al., 2014). Liberia's National Forestry Reform Law (2006) commits the country to setting aside at least 30% of its forests (about 15,000 km² or 1.5 million ha) as a network of protected areas. Yet, to date, the government has officially declared only 3,000 km² (300,000 ha) protected land; it has been divided into three areas, each of which has very limited management activities taking place on the ground. Complicating matters, an estimated 70% of Liberian chimpanzees live outside protected areas (Tweh et al., 2014).

Significant and growing threats to the chimpanzees include habitat loss through deforestation, wild meat hunting and the pet trade (Anstey, 1991a, 1991b; Greengrass, 2011; Bene et al., 2013). Illegal hunting, whose rates are closely correlated with those

> Evidence suggests that agricultural expansion has been the primary cause of long-term forest loss and degradation in West Africa.

of deforestation, represents the most significant threat to chimpanzee populations in Liberia (Christie *et al.*, 2007; Greengrass, 2011; Tweh *et al.*, 2014). Although taboos surround the consumption of chimpanzee meat in some regions of Liberia (Anstey, 1991a, 1991b; Greengrass, 2011), reports suggest alarmingly intense chimpanzee hunting practices. One study finds that in just one month, hunters at a camp adjacent to Sapo National Park killed 75 chimpanzees and captured seven live infants (Greengrass, 2011).

Industrial Agriculture in Liberia

Given Liberia's favorable soils and climate, the agriculture sector has long been central to the country's economy, with arable land accounting for 28.1% of the total area (World Bank, 2015b). Contributing 10% of the gross domestic product (GDP) in the late 1970s, agriculture (including fisheries) became a mainstay of the economy during the civil wars and currently contributes more than one-quarter of Liberia's GDP (IMF, 2014). The agriculture sector is also a dominant contributor to export trade and earnings as well as a major source of employment, with nearly 70% of the economically active population engaged in the sector (MOA Liberia, 2008).

Liberia's agriculture sector is dominated by traditional subsistence farming systems that are characterized by labor intensity, shifting cultivation, and low-level technologies and productivity (MOA Liberia, 2008). Cassava is the most widely grown subsistence crop in Liberia, with approximately 500,000 tons grown in 2012, followed by paddy rice and sugarcane, both of which yield about half the yearly production of cassava (FAO, 2014b). Agricultural activities in Liberia—whether commercial or concession-based—have been almost exclusively plantation estates of rubber, coffee, cacao and oil palm. Rubber was a chief

export in 2013, delivering 22.0% of total export earnings. Cocoa beans and coffee made up 9.9% and 0.1%, respectively. Since the majority of active oil palm plantations are five years old or younger, significant export of palm oil has yet to commence (CBL, 2014).

Rubber

The first rubber concession agreement in Liberia was held by a British firm in 1890 for the extraction of latex from wild rubber

trees. It was followed in 1910 by an agreement with another British-owned company, the Liberia Rubber Corporation, for commercial cultivation of rubber at Mount Barclay. In 1926, these were dwarfed by the Firestone concession agreements, which allowed Firestone to cultivate a 4,050 km² (405,000 ha) concession for a 99-year period (Chalk, 1967). Covering 4% of Liberia's land mass and 10% of its arable land, this vast concession became the world's largest industrial rubber plantation and left the country's economy highly dependent on one crop. In April 2005, the company's lease was extended until 2041 to secure the opportunity to harvest rubber from newly planted trees (SAMFU, 2008). Today, Firestone has 8 million rubber trees planted on 520 km² (52,000 ha) of its total concession (FNRC, 2014).

Foreign investors, including Firestone, own and operate four large rubber plantations totaling 1,080 km² (108,000 ha) under production (LISGIS, 2004). In addition, several smallholder-owned medium and small

Photo: Rubber remains Liberia's largest agricultural export. Source: USAID on www.public-domain-image. com. Title: liberia-aerial-view-of-rubber-plantation-45463

private farms (<0.4 km²/40 ha) account for an estimated 2,000 km² (200,000 ha) currently under rubber production, the majority as monoculture (International Development Association, 2012). In general, however, the sector has seen a reduction in production and rubber factories are operating below capacity (The Inquirer Newspaper, 2012). The majority of the rubber trees currently under cultivation are between 30 and 60 years old and coming to the end of their productive life, so that large-scale replanting is needed to make the plantations economically viable in the future (MOA Liberia, 2008). This aging is reflected by the national decrease in rubber production, which fell from 63,074 to 55,020 tons between 2012 and 2013; the drop is also attributed to an ongoing decline in international natural rubber prices (CBL, 2014).

Nevertheless, rubber remains Liberia's largest agricultural export, delivering about US$120 million of export earnings in 2013 (CBL, 2014). It continues to be a major source of formal employment, with approximately 18,500 workers employed on commercial rubber farms (MOA Liberia, 2007).

Cocoa and coffee

Together with sugarcane, coffee was the first export-oriented crop introduced in Liberia, in the mid-19th century (IITA, 2008). However, since the 1980s, international prices have discouraged farmers from planting new coffee tree stocks, such that coffee makes up only 0.09% of Liberia's foreign export earnings. An estimated 202 tons was produced in 2013 (CBL, 2014); the more profitable rubber and cacao trees reportedly drew resources away from the rehabilitation of coffee farms.

An estimated 40,000 households grow cacao in Liberia (MOA Liberia, 2007), with 8,337 metric tons produced in 2013 (FAO, 2015). While other tree crops (especially rubber) are mostly planted in pure stands, cacao is planted along with secondary food crops, allowing for diversification of enter-

prise (MOA Liberia, 2008). The vast majority of cacao trees in Liberia are more than 20 years old, an age after which economic productivity decreases.

Between 1989 and 2005, the value of the Liberian coffee and cocoa sectors fell by 90.8% and 79.5%, respectively (IFAD, 2011). The major constraints for cocoa and coffee production lie in the maturity of the trees, limited availability of new plant stock, infrastructural restrictions and lack of capital (English, 2008). Since 25 years of war came to a close, little replanting has taken place and plantations have largely degenerated into secondary forest; there is yet to be any significant increase in any export commodity (FAO, 2015).

The Liberian government, in its efforts to address food insecurity, recently secured a US$24.9 million loan from the International Fund for Agricultural Development to revitalize 150 km² (15,000 ha) of existing cacao and coffee plantations in Lofa county, targeting smallholders with farms of less than 0.02 km² (2 ha). Given the low cost of rehabilitating plantations, as opposed to generating new sites, the focus is on increasing yields and the quality of existing plantations rather than clearing forest for new planting (IFAD, 2011).

Oil palm

Oil palm is native to West Africa. Its production has traditionally been managed as part of a mixed farming practice throughout West and Central Africa. Following the British abolition of the slave trade in 1807, palm oil became the most exported commodity from West Africa to the United Kingdom, feeding the industrial revolution prior to the wide uptake of mineral oils. Imports grew from 114 tons per year at the start of the 19th century to a peak of 64,159 tons in 1895 (Lynn, 1997).[1]

In the 1970s, the government of Liberia embarked on a major oil palm development program by establishing several state-owned industrial plantations and a number of small- and medium-scale private farmer plantations. An estimated 270 km² (27,000 ha) were planted, although up to 600 km² (60,000 ha) were reportedly allocated to various additional operators (IFC, 2008). The full extent of this proposed development was never realized, however, due to the onset of civil war in the late 1980s. During the height of the conflict era, many industrial post-harvest facilities suffered significant damage or destruction; on the whole, the civil unrest left oil palm plantations in a state of deterioration. Liberia has since moved from being a crude palm oil exporter to a net importer (Winrock International, 2010).

Today, most production in Liberia is expanding by way of industrial-scale monoculture. Between 2008 and 2010 the government signed concession agreements that potentially span an area of 6,200 km² (620,000 ha)—6.3% of Liberia's land area and more than twice the area that is currently protected (Liberia, 2008, 2009b, 2010a, 2011). Modern oil palm cultivation is generally characterized by large monocultures of uniform age structure, low canopy, sparse undergrowth, a low-stability microclimate and intensive use of fertilizers and pesticides (Fitzherbert *et al.*, 2008).

The operators of the three largest concessions—Equatorial Palm Oil, Golden Veroleum and Sime Darby—are all members of the Round Table on Sustainable Palm Oil (RSPO), a global, multi-stakeholder initiative that aims to promote the growth and use of sustainable palm oil through cooperation within the supply chain. Problems have arisen with respect to the interpretation of criteria for high conservation value and the credibility of certification assessments of the RSPO (see Chapter 5). Furthermore, the management responsibilities for high conservation value within gross concession areas are currently unclear between the state, concessionaires and local communities

(R. Brett, personal communication, April 2015). Yet, the conditions outlined in a recent Norway–Liberia deal move beyond RSPO standards (see Box 2.3); the agreement stipulates that decisions regarding land clearance are to be assessed along with criteria established under the high-carbon stock approach.

RSPO members are obliged to acquire adequate free, prior and informed consent (FPIC) from the communities in which they intend to operate. Stakeholders have filed complaints with the RSPO against Equatorial Palm Oil, Golden Veroleum and Sime Darby concerning inadequate implementation of the FPIC procedure (SDI, 2010, 2012a, 2012b; FFI and Forest Trends, 2012; FPP, 2012b; Green Advocates and FPP, 2012; Rights and Resources Initiative, 2012). They exposed the lack of an integrated development strategy, little to no land use planning, inadequate participation and representation of communities and civil society, poor transparency, weak monitoring and enforcement and a lack of clarity of land tenure and local user rights (Green Advocates and FPP, 2012).

The abovementioned Norway–Liberia deal also considers the social impacts of industrial agricultural development, with the Liberian government committed to upholding adequate safeguards for communities that risk being affected by industrial development (see Box 2.3).

Implications for Liberia's Chimpanzees

Liberia has the highest potential for oil palm expansion in Africa and 94.3% of the area suitable for oil palm within ape ranges is not protected (Wich *et al.*, 2014).

The chimpanzee range covers a large part of the country (80%). Within that range, 17 oil palm plantations occupy a total area of 5,129 km² (512,940 ha), or 7% of the range

> Liberia has the highest potential for oil palm expansion in Africa and 94.3% of the area suitable for oil palm within ape ranges is not protected.

and four rubber plantations have a combined area of 144 km² (14,420 ha), including two rubber plantations that do not overlap with oil palm plantations. The agro-forestry dataset registers another three plantations that have a combined total area of 85 km² (8,530 ha) (see Figure 2.5).

It should be noted that chimpanzees inhabiting forested areas in close proximity to palm oil plantations are at exceptionally high risk of extirpation (Linder, 2013). The elevated risk is due to increased chimpanzee vulnerability to hunting while nesting in and feeding on oil palms that become contiguous with forest edges (see Chapter 6).

Conclusion for Liberia

In focusing on natural resource extraction as the linchpin of economic recovery and poverty reduction, Liberia relies on rapid infrastructure development (Liberia, 2010c). The enormous potential for growth and job creation in the country's agro-based industries has long been recognized, with ambitious policies in land intensification and the development of related agro-industries currently being implemented to drive further economic growth. The most recent International Monetary Fund country report on Liberia outlines a number of policy approaches aimed

FIGURE 2.5

Overlap of Agro-industry and Protected Areas with Ape Ranges in Liberia

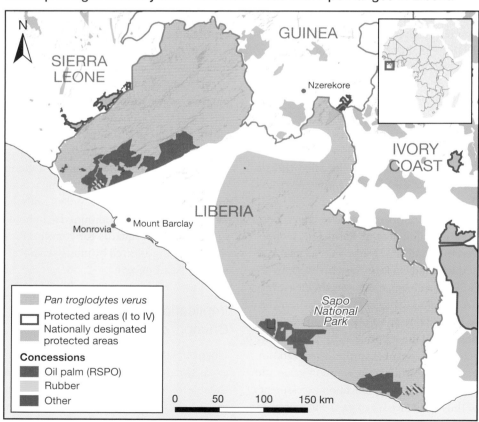

Notes: The size of land deals was defined as the reported contract size or, if this information was not available, the production size. If neither the contract nor the production size was available, the intended contract size was used.

Data sources: IUCN and UNEP (2014); WRI (2014c); IUCN (n.d.)

Courtesy of UNEP-WCMC

at boosting agricultural productivity to support inclusive economic growth in the country (IMF, 2014). While rubber, cocoa and coffee remain important export products, the current investment focus for these crops is on the rehabilitation of aging plantations located on brownfields.

Meanwhile, the aggressive and rapid expansion of oil palm concessions is of considerable concern. As a result of a "new wave" of large-scale industrial oil palm plantations, developed through land-lease or multinational agribusiness concession agreements, Liberia now faces a shift in deforestation drivers. This is expected to significantly impact Liberia's apes, the majority of whom are outside of protected areas. Industrial agriculture constitutes a major threat to their survival, through the direct loss of habitat as well as increased hunting as a result of fragmentation and the influx of migrant workers.

The recent Norway–Liberia deal holds some promise in terms of ensuring that decision-makers consider areas of significant biodiversity, including ape habitats, and secure appropriate consent from and inclusion of human communities in the process of expanding industrial agricultural activity (see Box 2.3). This approach could also be applied to guide industrial expansion in other African states, but it is too soon to tell how effective it will be at fostering well-considered development in Liberia.

The Island of Borneo

The island of Borneo is divided among three countries: Brunei and Malaysia in the north and west, and Indonesia to the south and east. It is the third-largest island in the world, located in the center of Island Southeast Asia. It is at the heart of Southeast Asian biodiversity, with the majority of species and evolutionary lineages from the broader region originating on Borneo (de Bruyn *et al.*, 2014).

BOX 2.3

The Norway–Liberia Deal

Liberia is home to much of West Africa's remaining rainforest and some of the last viable populations of western chimpanzee. In the wake of Liberia's civil war and in the midst of significant governance challenges, large international palm oil, rubber and timber companies obtained thousands of square kilometers (hundreds of thousands of hectares) of concessions throughout the country. Many of these concessions overlap with chimpanzee habitat and other forest, raising concerns that this latter-day wave of commodity expansion could threaten Liberia's forests and communities. More recently, the Ebola epidemic introduced a new set of challenges for Liberia.

Despite government constraints, the country may be poised to lead the way in Africa in dramatically reducing deforestation with the help of results-based development aid. In September 2014, Norway and Liberia announced a landmark agreement to improve forest governance and reduce emissions from deforestation and forest degradation in the West African country. The deal, which will run through 2020, commits Norway to paying Liberia up to US$150 million to preserve its forests. Of this amount, US$70 million will be disbursed in the initial years of the commitment period to assist Liberia in developing the necessary policy measures and institutional capacity to govern its forests. The remaining US$80 million will be paid upon independent verification of reduced emissions from deforestation (Norway, 2014).

Although there is flexibility in the specific actions Liberia can take to eliminate the destruction of its forests, the Norway deal commits the country to several specific actions. These include:

■ declaring a moratorium on all new logging contracts until an independent body reviews existing concessions to ensure their legality;

■ placing at least 30% of Liberia's forests under protected status, as stipulated in Liberia's National Forestry Reform Law of 2006;

■ piloting a project of direct payments to communities that sustainably manage their forests;

■ developing a reporting system for carbon emissions from forests; and

■ identifying measures to address all key drivers of deforestation in the country.

Importantly, the agreement also provides safeguards for the respect of land rights, including customary rights, and adherence to the principles of FPIC (Norway and Liberia, 2014).

The development of a deforestation-free agricultural sector forms a key pillar of the agreement. In an example of how private sector policy can contribute to government reform, multinational companies that aim to do business in Liberia will be required to issue ambitious zero-deforestation policies—as defined by a letter of intent that is at least as strong as palm oil trader Wilmar's "no deforestation, no peat, no exploitation" policy. Meanwhile, a newly commissioned study is exploring alternative models of agricultural investment, including small- and medium-scale enterprises, and an overarching strategy to be developed by Liberia's government will guide the allocation of land for agricultural use.

While the signing of the agreement is a major step forward for a country long plagued by legal and illegal forest destruction, the results—in terms of forests left standing and climate-changing carbon emissions avoided—will be the true measure of success in the years to come.

Some of the Bornean plant lineages can be dated back as far as 130 million years, to a time well before the last dinosaurs became extinct.

Borneo is estimated to have lost more than 30% of its forest between 1973 and 2010. Fire and conversion to plantations—mainly oil palm (*Elaeis guineensis*) but also other tree crops (such as *Acacia* species (spp). and rubber)—were the greatest drivers of forest loss. In 2010, the island accommodated nearly 65,000 km² (6.5 million ha) of oil palm plantations and 10,537 km² (1.1 million ha) of other tree plantations, which together occupied 10% of its total land area (Gaveau *et al.*, 2014; see Figures 2.6 and 2.7).

A History of Deforestation

Borneo has been occupied by humans for at least 40,000 years (Brothwell, 1960) and deforestation of the island's forests started during the early iron age. The impact of these activities remained relatively small until the 17th century, when deforestation, primarily for timber extraction, gained in both intensity and spread, with log and processed timber exports departing from most Bornean ports (Knapen, 2001). What limited the impact of such harvest on forest stands was a shortage of the labor required to transport and process the trees (Knapen, 2001).

More and more, however, timber extraction and the opening up of land for agriculture started to push back the forest boundary. Valuable species such as ramin (*Gonostylus bancanus*), ironwood (*Eusideroxylon zwageri*) and sandalwood (*Santalum album*) had disappeared from large parts of south-east Borneo by the mid-19th century. Similarly, in west Borneo, along the Kapuas River, large areas had been cleared by the 19th century through unsustainable land clearing practices, the use of fire and artisanal mining (Teysmann, 1875; Gerlach, 1881; Enthoven, 1903). By the middle of the 19th century, an estimated 5% of Borneo had been deforested, mostly along the major rivers and wetlands (Brookfield, Potter and Byron, 1995).

By the early 20th century, the major economic interests of the colonial powers—Great Britain and the Netherlands—in north Borneo shifted away from spices and other primary products, to tin and rubber as the two major commercial commodities to be traded with the British Empire, Europe and the United States (Pryer, 1883). In 1910, the Dunlop Research Station was established in Malaysia, and the British rulers encouraged private companies to develop vast tracts of land to produce rubber. Easily accessible forests close to the coast and major rivers were preferentially converted to rubber plantations. To bring rubber and other agricultural products to the market, developers built extensive roads and railways in Sabah and Sarawak, thus facilitating access to the forests in the interior of the island.

Industrialization and the invention of the one-man chainsaw, the outboard motor and more powerful vehicles designed following the end of World War II led to a rapid increase in timber exploitation and deforestation (Brookfield et al., 1995). After forests are depleted of their high-value timber resources, they are often converted to agricultural land (Gibbs et al., 2010). For orangutans, such crops are of very limited utility (Meijaard et al., 2010; Ancrenaz et al., 2015); for fully arboreal gibbons, they are of no use.

Land conversion processes started in Malaysian Borneo and subsequently began on the Indonesian side of the island. After independence in 1957, Malaysia established the Federal Land Development Authority (FELDA) scheme to settle poor, rural smallholders into newly developed areas to grow cash crops. In 1966, the Federal Land Rehabilitation and Consolidation Authority (FELCRA) was created to boost agricultural production in the country by allocating and developing land, especially idle land and degraded forests, for agricultural purposes. At this time, smallholders were also encouraged to switch from subsistence crops to cash crops, such as rubber and oil palm. In early 1970, there were 1,230 km² (123,000 ha) of oil palm compared to 13,150 km² (1.3 million ha) of rubber in Malaysia. Most of these plantations replaced natural forests.

In the 1970s, FELDA and FELCRA intensified and expanded their programs with an emphasis on oil palm expansion to eradicate poverty (Parid et al., 2013). Agricultural development was concomitant with timber extraction and forest conversion. In the eastern states of Malaysian Borneo, it focused primarily on lowland forest areas; during the period from 1970 to 2010, deforestation rates reached 39.5% in Sabah and 23.1% in Sarawak (Gaveau et al., 2014). Most of these forests were replaced with oil palm plantations and other crops. From 1990 to 2010, more than half of all oil palm development throughout all of Malaysia replaced forests through direct deforestation (Koh and Wilcove, 2008a).

Quantified Forest Loss and the Role of Agro-industry

A recent analysis mapped forest extent and deforestation for the period 1973–2010 for the whole island of Borneo at medium spatial resolution (Gaveau et al., 2014). In 1973, about 76% of Borneo was still under natural forest cover (558,060 km²/55.8 million ha); only 53% was still forested in 2010 (389,567 km²/39.0 million ha), mostly in the mountainous center of the island (see Figure 2.6). Intact forests represent only 54% (209,649 km²/21.0 million ha) of the total remaining forest area—or 28% of the whole of Borneo. Among the different geopolitical units on the island, Brunei has the highest proportion of intact forest area (57%), in stark contrast to the significantly lower rates in Kalimantan (33%), Sabah (19%) and Sarawak (15%). Over the past 40 years, Borneo has witnessed a loss of tropical forests amounting to 168,493 km² (16.8 million ha)—an area about four times the size of Switzerland.

FIGURE 2.6

Borneo's Forest in 1973 and Forest Loss between 1973 and 2010

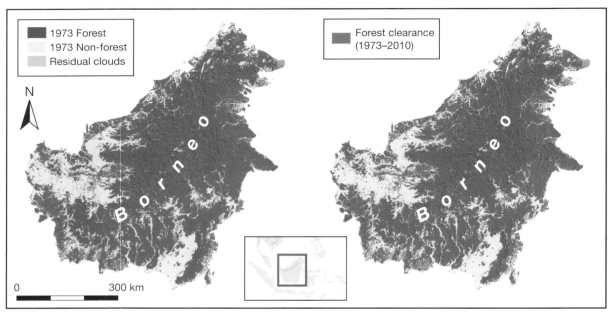

Reproduced from PLoS One (Gaveau *et al.*, 2014, p. 6).

Although timber harvest levels are currently dropping, the expansion of logging has not stopped. Especially in Sarawak, the development of logging roads in interior highlands indicates a further shift of the logging boundary (Gaveau *et al.*, 2014). In all regions of Borneo, conversion to industrial and small-scale agriculture—rather than timber exploitation—currently drives deforestation (Miettinen, Shi and Liew, 2011; Abood *et al.*, 2015). The expansion of the oil palm sector has drawn considerable atten-

tion from environmentalists and human rights activists for its major social and environmental impacts, especially in lowland areas. Even so, roughly one-third of Sabah's workforce (up to 376,000 people) is involved in agriculture—mostly in oil palm, which is the second-largest employer in the Malaysian state, after services (ETP, 2010).

By 2010, about 65,000 km² (6.5 million ha)—or about twice the size of Belgium—was planted with oil palm throughout Borneo, and an additional 10,537 km² (1.1 million ha)

TABLE 2.2

Target Proportions of Land Earmarked for Oil Palm, Industrial Tree Plantations and Forest Cover in Borneo, by Political Division

Divisions		Target oil palm	Target ITP	Target forest cover
Brunei		0%	0%	75%
Indonesia	Kalimantan	15%	4%	45%
Malaysia	Sabah	29%	5%	50%
	Sarawak	16%	2%	50%

Data source: Runting *et al.* (2015)

was converted to industrial tree plantations (ITPs) (Gaveau *et al.*, 2014). Although approximately 10% of Borneo is currently planted with oil palm or ITP (such as acacia, eucalyptus and rubber), the drive for further expansion of industrial agriculture is strong. Sabah has 14,000 km² (1.4 million ha)—or 20% of its land area—planted with oil palm and plans to increase the proportion to 29% (about 20,000 km²/2 million ha), with ITP taking up 5%; that expansion would leave a forest cover comprising intact and selectively logged forest of just over 50% of the state (Runting *et al.*, 2015). Table 2.2 shows targets for Sabah and the other political divisions of Borneo.

Most of the forests that have been converted for agricultural purposes used to serve as prime habitat for Borneo's apes, mainly in the coastal lowland areas (see Figure 2.7).

An unpublished study on oil palm development in different parts of Borneo indicates that the two Malaysian states have a more deliberate approach to deforestation, especially with regard to developing oil palm.[2] Between 1973 and 2010, 56% to 81% of Sabah and Sarawak's oil palm was primarily established in areas of logged and intact forest. In contrast, the rate in Kalimantan varied between 27% and 45%, with the majority of oil palm established in non-forest areas before 1973 or areas destroyed by wildfires in 1982–83 and 1997–98. These data suggest that, unlike Malaysia, Indonesia largely restricted oil palm development in Borneo to land that was already degraded or that became available after fire removed standing forests.

Nevertheless, from 2000 to 2010, ITPs, logging from natural forest, oil palm and mining—in that order—accounted for 45% (66,000 km²/6.6 million ha) of forest loss in the Indonesian states of Kalimantan, the Moluccas, Papua, Sulawesi and Sumatra. This finding indicates that most of the deforestation in these states—the remaining 55%—cannot be directly attributed to the activities of the four main industries (Gaveau *et al.*,

FIGURE 2.7

Borneo's Remaining Forest in 2010 (Intact and Selectively Logged) and Areas of Industrial Plantations

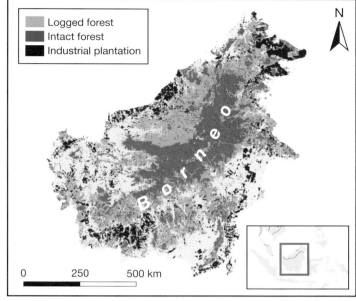

Reproduced from PLoS One (Gaveau *et al.*, 2014, p. 6).

2013, 2014). Additional factors, such as illegal logging outside concessions, fire and small-scale agriculture also play a large role in deforestation. The major industries, and especially those associated with large-scale land conversion—such as the pulp and paper business and oil palm cultivation—may be the most visible components of deforestation, yet they are not necessarily its main drivers in Indonesian Borneo (Kalimantan).

Drivers of Ape Decline: Forest Loss and Hunting

The population of Mueller's gray gibbon (*Hylobates muelleri*) has been conservatively estimated at 250,000–375,000 individuals,[3] but no total population estimates exist for the island's other species, the Bornean white-bearded gibbon (*Hylobates albibarbis*). Gibbons are deeply affected by forest degradation, loss and hunting, although actual impacts on population trends are poorly understood (see Chapter 6).

The Bornean orangutan (*Pongo pygmaeus* spp.) is found mainly in West and Central Kalimantan and the Malaysian state of Sabah. The most recent orangutan population estimates date back to 2008 and put the total population at more than 54,000 individuals, with a total distributional range of 155,000 km² (15.5 million ha) (Wich *et al.*, 2008, 2012b). As a result of recent technological advances, such as satellite imagery and statistical programs, future population estimates for Bornean orangutans may be revised upwards. Regardless, it is undeniable that Bornean orangutan populations are in rapid decline. The annual loss of orangutan habitat in Borneo between 1990 and 2005 was around 3,000 km² (300,000 ha) (Meijaard and Wich, 2007); based on estimates that these forests were occupied by orangutans at average densities before conversion, that decline in habitat corresponds to an average annual loss of 2,000 to 4,850 individuals (Meijaard

FIGURE 2.8

Overlap of Current and Planned Agro-industry, Certified RSPO Sites and *Pongo pygmaeus* in Indonesian Borneo

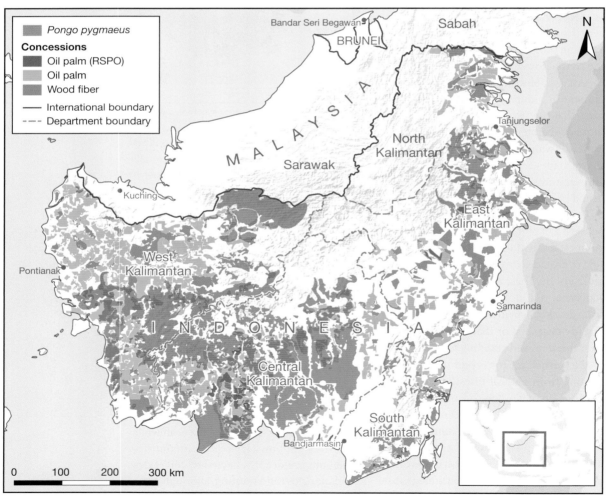

Data sources: WRI (2013, 2014c, 2014e); IUCN (n.d.)
Courtesy of UNEP-WCMC

et al., 2012). While an estimated 750–1,800 orangutans were directly killed in Kalimantan alone in 2007 (Meijaard *et al.*, 2011), many of these deaths are associated with deforestation and agricultural development. If people see orangutans destroying young palms, for instance, they may perceive them as a threat to agricultural production and kill them (see Chapter 1). In some cases, oil palm companies have paid a bounty for orangutans to be killed (Kusuma, 2011).

A recent study shows that 19% of the modeled potential Bornean orangutan distribution range in West Kalimantan lies in undeveloped oil palm concessions and 6% in undeveloped tree plantation concessions. Moreover, 24% of the Bornean orangutan distribution occurs outside of protected areas and concessions. If all agricultural concessions—oil palm and tree plantations—were to be fully developed, an estimated 49% of the remaining orangutan range would be lost (Wich *et al.*, 2012b). These estimates are based on modeled species ranges, which may explain why this study finds a greater overlap than does the analysis using IUCN taxa range maps in Figure 2.8.

Despite the rapid losses of Bornean apes, there is hope for their survival. Orangutans have shown remarkable ecological resilience and can survive, at least over short time frames, in degraded areas (Ancrenaz *et al.*, 2010; Meijaard *et al.*, 2010; Campbell-Smith *et al.*, 2011b). Gibbons are ecologically more vulnerable, but they do survive in degraded forests if hunting can be controlled. If a minimum area of forest were retained and if reduced-impact logging techniques were applied, both gibbons and orangutans could survive. Connectivity between these populations is vital for facilitating gene flow (Goossens *et al.*, 2005a); it also allows apes to adapt to altering ecological conditions brought about by regional and global climate change (Gregory *et al.*, 2014; Wich *et al.*, 2014; see Chapter 6).

Conclusion for Borneo

The differences in the rates of deforestation across the three states that occupy the island of Borneo reflect varying governance contexts. Malaysia's policies emphasize agricultural development and facilitate deforestation for that purpose, whereas Indonesia has been promoting the use of degraded lands, such as areas that have been burned or logged, for agricultural activities. Further analysis of Borneo's different governance structures and policies could provide additional insight into the impact of government policy on rates of deforestation in valuable ape habitats.

Given the fact that industrial agriculture is among the causes of forest loss across Borneo, engaging with industry on agricultural development is one way of helping to curb deforestation. Oil palm plantations alone occupied 10% of the entire island in 2010 and were encroaching on important ape habitats. Findings in relation to ape ecology point to the value of retaining ecological connectivity, underscoring the importance of adequate land use planning. This type of planning calls for strong collaboration at the international level—at a minimum, among the three countries that govern the island—if the ecological function across the island is to be conserved. Ultimately, the correlation between the rate and extent of forest loss and the decline of ape populations on the island of Borneo since 1975 is a stark example of a fundamental connection between economic development and ape conservation.

Conclusion

The increased demand for commodities to supply growing global human populations requires intensified and expanded agricultural practices, which are generally accompanied by a plethora of detrimental impacts on terrestrial biodiversity and wider socio-ecological and environmental systems.

Given the scale of agricultural expansion in Liberia, projected changes will have dramatic impacts on the diversity, composition and functioning of the remaining natural ecosystems—unless mitigation strategies are put in place at the beginning of operational planning. Otherwise, these changes will pose insurmountable challenges in biodiversity conservation and result in the extirpation of Liberia's vulnerable, forest-dependent large mammal species, such as the elephant and chimpanzee. As part of its recent agreement with Norway, Liberia has

committed to taking specific actions that surpass even the RSPO's Principles and Criteria. While it is too early to assess the impact of this model, its potential success may have implications for Cameroon and other African countries that are also pursuing agricultural development.

The case of the Herakles plantation in Cameroon has demonstrated that apes and their habitats are being impacted by the recent wave of industrial agricultural development in Africa. In this context, the allocation of concessions in proximity to protected areas is of particular concern. Unless the Cameroonian state incorporates adequate

land use planning and establishes robust regulations to ensure that future allocations take significant sites of biodiversity into consideration, unchecked deforestation will likely become the norm.

In contrast, Borneo has already suffered rapid and extensive forest loss and degradation as a result of industrial agriculture. In Malaysian Borneo, policies that prioritized agricultural development resulted in the highest rate of forest loss across the island, highlighting the influence of aggressive government policies that do not adequately consider the environmental and social implications of such action.

In Borneo and elsewhere, two strategies could be adopted to ensure adequate protections for the environment and the local populations it serves:

- First, land use planning should be used to establish sufficient buffer zones between agro-industrial sites and protected areas so as to maintain the integrity of ape habitats (Laurance *et al.*, 2012).

- Second, governments should implement moratoria on the granting of new agro-industrial concessions until they have instituted or reformed land use planning processes to be transparent and to entail strict criteria for allocation (Hoyle and Levang, 2012; Nguiffo and Schwartz, 2012a).

Adequate land use planning is at the core of mitigating the negative impacts of industrial activities in environmentally critical landscapes. The case of Cambodia is instructive with respect to problems that can arise due to conflicting land use designations and the disregard for the value of conservation in relation to economic development.

Future research could usefully analyze the consequences of industrial agricultural expansion in terms of the social, economic and environmental costs and benefits of different land use options.

Acknowledgments

Principal authors: Helga Rainer and Annette Lanjouw

Contributors: Marc Ancrenaz, Katherine Despot Belmonte, Max Fancourt, Fauna and Flora International, Chloe Hodgkinson, Joshua M. Linder, Erik Meijaard, Rebecca Newham, Marieke Sassen, Brendan Schwartz, Kathryn Shutt, Arnout van Soesbergen, and the United Nations Environment Programme World Conservation Monitoring Centre

Figures 2.1–2.5 and 2.8: UNEP-WCMC—Marieke Sassen and Arnout van Soesbergen—with assistance from Max Fancourt, Rebecca Newham and Katherine Despot Belmonte

Reviewers: John F. Oates, Charles Palmer and Nancy Lee Peluso

Endnotes

1 In the 19th century, the Windward Coast that runs from Freetown to Monrovia was an important site for the production of hard palm oil, which was used for industrial purposes (Lynn, 1997). It is not possible to convert export tonnage of those days into modern equivalents.

2 Based on unpublished data by D. Gaveau, seen by the authors.

3 Based on unpublished data compiled by the contributor and V. Nijman.

CHAPTER 3

From Habitat to Plantation: Causes of Conversion in sub-Saharan Africa

Introduction

Agriculture is a major part of sub-Saharan Africa's economy, but its expansion poses significant threats to great ape habitats and forests. The sector accounts for nearly one-quarter of the continent's gross domestic product (GDP) and, in one way or another, it employs nearly two-thirds of its labor force (UNECA, 2013, 2014).[1] The production of agricultural commodities—for both sub-sistence and export—has been an important contributor to economic growth over the past several decades and will likely continue to be a key driver of future development, as indicated by nascent shifts in the composition of agricultural activity on the continent.

Historically, sub-Saharan Africa's agri-cultural sector has been fragmented and dominated by smallholder farms. While the definition of a "smallholder farm" varies regionally, it typically refers to small-scale plots—often less than 0.01 km² (1 ha) but sometimes up to 0.1 km² (10 ha)—cultivated both for subsistence purposes as well as to grow a limited number of cash crops (Dixon, Tanyeri-Abur and Wattenbach, 2004). While large-scale, foreign-owned plantations persisted throughout the colonial period, their prevalence declined during the second half of the 20th century, in part because of the increased risks due to instability and regulatory ambiguity that arose in the post-colonial period (Smalley, 2013). Some plantations were taken over by governments while others were abandoned.

In addition to the decline of large-scale plantations, frequent civil unrest, remoteness, poor infrastructure and other destabilizing factors have reduced efforts to conserve the continent's forest resources and ape habitat to a level of "passive protection" (Megevand, 2013). At particular risk are the dense tropical forests of the Congo Basin, which are among the last largely intact forest areas in the world. They represent nearly three-quarters of Africa's forest cover and a large portion of its biodiversity (Hourticq and Megevand, 2013). Central and West Africa are also home to four of the world's six great ape species. Detailed information on the species and ranges of African apes is provided in the Apes Overview in this edition of *State of the Apes*.

African apes already face numerous pressures, including the impact of extractive industries, the expansion of smallholder farming and the illegal hunting of wild meat (Arcus Foundation, 2014). These and other factors have contributed to the shrinking of ape habitat and have led to substantial declines in ape populations over the past several decades (Junker *et al.*, 2012). Although large-scale commercial agriculture—the subject of this edition—has not yet been a leading driver of the decline of African ape species,

important shifts in the composition of sub-Saharan Africa's agricultural sector are likely to have significant implications for the continent's forests and ape habitat.

Since the turn of the 21st century, sub-Saharan Africa has seen a new wave of agro-industrial land investment. Foreign companies, for a long time reluctant to invest in large-scale operations on the continent, have shown increasing interest in acquiring African land for the production of food, biofuels and animal feed. Over the past 15 years, hundreds of land deals—involving both foreign and domestic investors, as well as partnerships between foreign companies and African governments—have resulted in the allocation of thousands of square kilometers (millions of hectares) of land for industrial-scale agricultural cultivation. While these projects—many of which have not yet started operation—have the potential to provide substantial economic opportunities to some of the poorest regions of the world, they could also have significant negative consequences for sub-Saharan Africa's forest resources and local communities, unless they are managed appropriately.

This chapter presents an in-depth look at the recent expansion of industrial agriculture in ape range states and the extent to which it may affect sub-Saharan Africa's forest resources and ape habitats. The first section provides an overview of the expansion of the continent's agro-industry, including a description of recent trends in large-scale land acquisitions and an in-depth look into the development and market for specific commodities, particularly palm oil. The following section explores the sources of agricultural land investment in the region, including the geographic distribution of investor companies, as well as their sources of funding. The third section discusses the drivers of the recent trend in land acquisitions, while the fourth dives deeper into the current and potential effects of large-scale agricultural development on ape habitat.

> "Since the turn of the 21st century, sub-Saharan Africa has seen a new wave of agro-industrial land investment."

The final section considers the expansion of industrial agriculture from the perspective of sustainable development and identifies key factors that can encourage ecologically sustainable and equitable economic growth. Key findings include:

- The cultivation of oil palm has been one of the most widespread and most visible objectives of land investments in sub-Saharan Africa during the most recent wave of land acquisitions (from 2000 onward). The crop accounts for the largest portion of active investments, both in terms of project quantity and land area acquired.

- Unlike in Southeast Asia, the primary markets for commodities derived from oil palm are domestic, reflecting increasing demand for vegetable oil in sub-Saharan Africa. Palm oil exports are relatively small and most often destined to regional trading partners.

- The drivers of the expansion of industrial agriculture include an increase in demand for agricultural commodities, both domestic and international, relatively easy access to land on the African continent and lower set-up costs, thanks to government incentives intended to attract foreign investment. Increases in land prices and the perception of declining land availability in Southeast Asia have also driven agricultural investment toward Africa.

- To date, industrial agriculture has not been a leading driver of deforestation in sub-Saharan Africa, although planned investments, if fully developed, could substantially threaten the continent's forests, including ape habitats.

- There is a pressing need to assess current and planned industrial agriculture projects to determine the specific impacts on ape populations and habitat in sub-Saharan Africa.

Expansion of Africa's Agro-Industry

Overview of Broad Trends

Agriculture is the largest driver of economic activity in sub-Saharan Africa. The sector —including subsistence and smallholder farms as well as large estates—accounts for approximately 25% of the continent's GDP and nearly two-thirds of its employment (UNECA, 2013, 2014). Sub-Saharan African countries are major producers of cash crops such as cocoa, coffee, tobacco, sugar and cotton. Agricultural production and its contribution to the region's economy has expanded steadily over the last few decades: the annual rate of growth of agricultural GDP rose from 2.16% in the 1980s, to 2.95% in the 1990s and 3.44% during the first decade of the 21st century (Fuglie and Rada, 2013). This growth in output has been paralleled by a rise in employment. According to the Food and Agriculture Organization (FAO), approximately half of the increase in employment in sub-Saharan Africa between 1999 and 2009 can be attributed to the expansion of the agricultural sector (FAO, 2012b).

The growth in agricultural production has had significant land use implications. Since per-hectare yields and technological inputs have undergone little change (FAO, 2009b), the majority of the region's output increase has been driven by greater use of natural resources, namely, an expansion of the total land area under cultivation. FAO data show that the area under temporary and permanent crops in sub-Saharan Africa increased by 36% between 1990 and 2012. The rise has been particularly pronounced in Mali (230%), Sierra Leone (206%), Benin (83%), Ghana (76%) and Burkina Faso (70%) (FAOSTAT, n.d.). The vast majority of this expansion can be attributed to the proliferation of smallholder farms rather than industrial-scale operations, and small-

> **"** FAO data show that the area under temporary and permanent crops in sub-Saharan Africa increased by 36% between 1990 and 2012. **"**

scale plots continue to dominate agricultural activity. In fact, 85% of Africa's farms occupy less than 0.02 km² (2 ha) (Jayaram, Riese and Sanghvi, 2010).

While smallholders remain the principal drivers of agricultural production on the continent, agribusiness has shown increasing interest in acquiring African land since the turn of the century. According to the Land Matrix, an independent repository of global land deals, the pace of acquisition[2] in Africa was relatively slow until about 2005, at which point it accelerated substantially, peaking in 2009 (Land Matrix, n.d.; see Box 3.1). The number of signed contracts appears to have dropped off since then, although this decline may be as much a reflection of companies' reluctance to publicize deals under negotiation as a real hesitation to undertake large land acquisitions on the continent (Anseeuw *et al.*, 2012b).

Accurate figures for the total land area acquired for large-scale agriculture across sub-Saharan Africa are difficult to obtain, largely because details on concluded land deals are not publicly available. According to the Land Matrix database,[3] some 114,000 km² (11.4 million ha) have come under agro-industrial contract since 2000. This figure is most likely an underestimate as the database includes only deals that have been made public. The figure also excludes plantation-style timber and pulpwood contracts (Land Matrix, n.d.).

A separate, recent analysis found that up to 227,000 km² (22.7 million ha), an area nearly the size of Ghana, has been acquired across sub-Saharan Africa since 2005.[4] Large-scale agricultural projects comprise approximately 85% of this land area, while plantation forestry accounts for the remainder. The mean contract size is approximately 404 km² (40,368 ha), although this figure is skewed upward by several large acquisitions—half of all land deals are smaller than 123 km² (12,300 ha) (Schoneveld, 2014a). A smaller-scale study of land allocated to large-scale plantations in Central Africa found that more than 15,000 km² (1.5 million ha) were under agro-industrial concession in Cameroon, the Democratic Republic of Congo (DRC), Gabon and the Republic of Congo (hereafter Congo) as of the end of 2013 (Feintrenie, 2014). Although this figure includes several plantations that were in operation before the recent wave of land investments, the majority of projects either obtained a new owner or were wholly initiated after 2000.

A good deal of agricultural land investment has been directed toward ape range states[5]—Central and West Africa account for approximately 9% and 30% of the total land area acquired, respectively (Land Matrix, n.d.). Table 3.1 provides several estimates of these acquisitions by country. Within Central Africa, Congo has received the most investment interest in terms of land area, with as much as 9,000 km² (900,000 ha) under commercial contract. In West Africa, Ghana, Liberia and Sierra Leone have been the largest recipients of new land investment, collectively accounting for up to 45,000 km² (4.5 million ha) under contract.

In addition to geographic variation, agricultural investments have also targeted

BOX 3.1

The Land Matrix

The Land Matrix is an independent initiative that monitors and catalogs land deals around the world. Coordinated by the International Land Coalition, the Land Matrix's Global Observatory aggregates information on intended, concluded and failed attempts to acquire land through concession, lease and purchase. The database covers deals greater than 2 km² (200 ha) that were initiated after 2000 and entail plans to convert forests, smallholder farms and other land types to commercial production. For maps showing land deals in some ape range states, see Chapter 2.

Information on land deals is drawn from a variety of sources, including research publications, media reports, government records and company materials. Although attempts are made to ensure accuracy, some of the information may be unreliable or incomplete. Land deals often lack transparency since many completed deals are not publicly reported, and the scope and size of actual projects may differ from that reported in the database.

TABLE 3.1

Land Acquired in Selected Ape Range States

Country	Land Matrix (n.d.)		Feintrenie (2014)		Schoneveld (2014a)	
	No. of projects	Contract area (km²)	No. of projects	Contract area (km²)	No. of projects	Contract area (km²)
Central Africa						
Cameroon	6	1,281	3	3,045	14	3,715
Central African Republic	2	140	–	–	2	138
Congo	4	6,140	5	7,422	8	8,939
DRC	7	2,075	2	2,833	11	3,560
Gabon	3	732	4	2,194	5	3,998
West Africa						
Ghana	27	7,511	–	–	45	20,662
Guinea	5	1,090	–	–	5	12,495
Ivory Coast	6	681	–	–	5	1,132
Liberia	8	6,157	–	–	11	10,759
Nigeria	27	2,471	–	–	42	7,838
Senegal	16	2,592	–	–	24	6,174
Sierra Leone	16	10,423	–	–	19	12,948

Notes: Columns are not fully comparable, as Land Matrix (n.d.) and Feintrenie (2014) data include agro-industrial contracts signed since 2000 and exclude plantation forestry contracts, while Schoneveld (2014a) includes both agro-industrial and plantation forestry contracts concluded since 2005. Moreover, the Land Matrix reports publicly available data while the two other sources include primary and confidentially obtained information.

multiple crops. Oilseed crops, including castor, oil palm, sesame and sunflower, have piqued the most commercial interest, accounting for more than 60% of all land area acquired on the African continent since 2005. Oil palm alone represents approximately 22% and is the second-largest crop after jatropha in terms of total land area purchased for cultivation. After oilseed crops, sugarcane has attracted the most commercial investment, accounting for approximately 13% of the total land area purchased; cereals represent another 6% (Schoneveld, 2014a).

Agribusiness investment in traditional African cash crops such as cocoa, coffee, tea, tobacco and cotton has been relatively low (Schoneveld, 2014a). This is the result of a mix of factors, including their history as largely smallholder-grown commodities—whose cultivation continues to be strictly governed by contract arrangements between small-scale producers and commodity buyers—the relative maturity of the markets for these crops, and a general preference for fungible investments such as oilseed crops and sugarcane, as a hedge against price volatility.

Land continues to be attractive across sub-Saharan Africa and, despite the marked decrease in the number of land acquisitions since 2009, several large-scale leases remain in negotiations (Land Matrix, n.d.). Information on the scope of these projects is often sparse and unreliable, however. Even when negotiations are concluded successfully, the land area eventually contracted is

The Rise and Fall of Jatropha

Jatropha, a perennial tree whose seeds can be crushed to produce oil, has led commercial land investment over the past decade. Drought-resistant and able to grow in poor-quality soil, jatropha saw significant commercial interest for a few years starting around 2004, as mandatory biofuel blend requirements came into effect in European and other developed nations (von Maltitz and Stafford, 2011). At its peak, nearly 100 projects and more than 30% of the total land area acquired on the continent was set aside for jatropha cultivation (Schoneveld, 2014a).

The jatropha bubble burst in 2009, when the global financial crisis restricted credit availability and dampened the demand for biofuels. Many jatropha projects were shelved; those that entered production experienced disappointing yields and were either abandoned or sold (von Maltitz and Stafford, 2011). Today, international interest in jatropha cultivation is limited and very few projects remain active in sub-Saharan Africa.

often far smaller than originally planned by the investor or reported in the media. It is thus difficult to predict with any certainty how much land is in the pipeline for commercial agricultural development in the coming years.

Oil Palm

Plantation Area

Investment in oil palm in sub-Saharan Africa has garnered significant international media attention due to both the quantity and size of reported land deals. The crop has been the second-biggest target of foreign agricultural land investment over the past decade and, since the decline of jatropha (see Box 3.2), it has risen to dominate commercial agricultural interest.

Varying estimates exist for the extent of commercial oil palm leases in the region, as it is not always easy to isolate palm oil from the broader set of land acquisitions. According to the Land Matrix, contracts that list oil palm as an intended crop encompass 27,000 km² (2.7 million ha) across sub-Saharan Africa. However, this figure may overestimate the total land area leased for oil palm cultivation because it includes large multi-crop plantations that do not provide a crop-specific breakdown of their concessions. Among monocrop projects, oil palm land deals comprise about 14,000 km² (1.4 million ha) (Land Matrix, n.d.). Either or both of these figures may also underestimate the true land area allocated to industrial-scale oil palm cultivation, as some land deals may not be included in the Land Matrix database.

Other estimates have also been put forth. Schoneveld (2014a) concludes that land transfer agreements for oil palm finalized since 2005 comprise at least 36,000 km² (3.6 million ha) across sub-Saharan Africa, while another study finds that 18,000 km² (1.8 million ha) of land have been leased for the crop's cultivation in West and Central Africa alone (Economist, 2014). Based on these estimates, it is clear that leases for oil palm account for at least 14,000 km² (1.4 million ha), that another 10,000 km² (1 million ha) or more have been leased for multi-crop plantations that include oil palm and that both of these estimates could be low.

The vast majority of the continent's oil palm concessions lie in West Africa and the Congo Basin. In terms of land area, investment has been concentrated in Congo, Liberia and Sierra Leone. The Congo total is dominated by one single land deal—the 4,700 km² (470,000 ha) Atama plantation, located in the Cuvette and Sangha provinces. Cameroon has also attracted a substantial amount of investor interest, as indicated by the size of announced oil palm plantation projects, but the area leased to date remains relatively small (Land Matrix, n.d.). For more information on the historical development of industrial agriculture in Cameroon, see Chapter 2, page 46.

Production

Sub-Saharan Africa has been a palm oil producer for decades—in fact, the crop traces its origin to West Africa—but its output has been a tiny fraction of the global total and has been dominated by smallholder farms. Even today, as much as 80% of the land area planted with oil palm is occupied by plots ranging from 0.02 km² to 1 km² (2–100 ha) (Wich *et al.*, 2014). To a lesser degree, large estates have also been involved in oil palm cultivation in countries such as Cameroon, DRC, Ghana and Ivory Coast (Kim *et al.*, 2013; Ecobank, 2014; Feintrenie, 2014).

Of the new wave of large-scale land investments, a relatively small fraction of the total contracted land has been planted and an even smaller portion has seen the start of production. Land Matrix data show that of the 27,000 km² (2.7 million ha) that

have come under contract since 2000, a large portion has not yet been planted and fewer than 2,000 km² (200,000 ha) are currently in production. Although this figure may underestimate the true total due to incomplete information and missing data, evidence suggests that the majority of recent projects have either not broken ground or are at very early stages of development (Land Matrix, n.d.).

Due to the limited output from newly established estates, sub-Saharan Africa remains a marginal player in the global palm oil market. Although the continent's overall production—both on large-scale plantations and smallholder farms—has increased steadily over the past decade, from 1.7 million tonnes in 1992 to 2.4 million tonnes in 2013, this accounted for just 4.4% of the global market (FAOSTAT, n.d.; see Figure 3.1).

The region's palm oil production is dominated by Nigeria, which has been responsible for approximately half of the continent's total output for much of the past two decades (FAOSTAT, n.d.). The vast majority (more than 90%) of this oil comes from wild oil palm groves cultivated by local farmers; planted estates—whether small, medium or large—represent a very small share of total production (Gourichon, 2013).

Beyond Nigeria, a handful of other countries have also contributed to African palm oil's modest growth in recent years. With total output of 415,000 and 225,000 tonnes, respectively, Ivory Coast and Cameroon were the continent's second- and third-largest producers in 2013 (FAOSTAT, n.d.). Ivory Coast's rise as a palm oil producer can be attributed, at least in part, to the PALMCI group, the country's largest commercial oil palm grower. The company, which is majority-owned by locally based Société Immobilière et Financière de la Côte Africaine (SIFCA) (52.5%) and the Wilmar–Olam joint venture Nauvu (25.5%), controls close to 400 km² (40,000 ha) of

Photo: Drought-resistant and able to grow in poor-quality soil, jatropha saw significant commercial interest for biofuel from 2004 to 2009. © Angkawijaya92 | Dreamstime.com - Jatropha Curcas Fruit Photo

FIGURE 3.1

Palm Oil Production in Sub-Saharan Africa, 1992–2013

Key: ■ Nigeria ■ Ivory Coast ■ Cameroon ■ DRC ■ Ghana ■ All other states

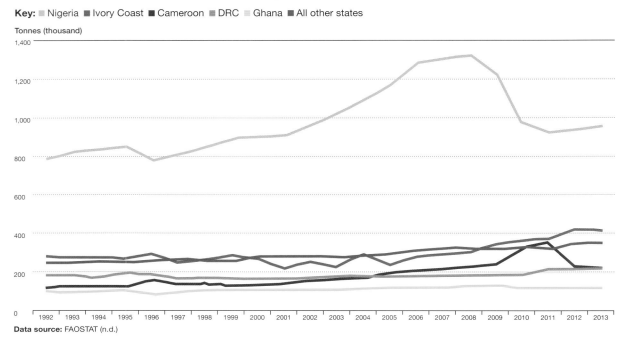

Tonnes (thousand)

Data source: FAOSTAT (n.d.)

industrial estates and 1,330 km² (133,000 ha) of outgrower plots. PALMCI's annual output of roughly 300,000 tonnes of crude palm oil represents nearly 80% of the Ivory Coast's total production (PALMCI, 2012).

Agro-industry is somewhat less dominant in Cameroon, where approximately half of the total palm oil output is produced on agro-industrial estates and one-third on independent smallholder plots; the rest comes from supervised smallholder plantations (Hoyle and Levang, 2012). Four commercial ventures currently lead the country's agro-industrial production: Luxembourg-based Société Financière des Caoutchoucs (SOCFIN) partially owns two local companies, Société Camerounaise de Palmeraies (SOCAPALM) and Société Africaine Forestière et Agricole du Cameroun (SAFACAM), while the government of Cameroon wholly owns another two estates, Cameroon Development Corporation and Pamol. Although the country has attracted significant com-

mercial oil palm interest in recent years, virtually all of its current agro-industrial production comes from these older estates.

Ghana and the DRC are the only other African producers with annual outputs greater than 100,000 tonnes; all other nations collectively produce just under 350,000 tonnes of palm oil—a nominal quantity compared to giants such as Indonesia which, in 2013, supplied 26 million tonnes of the commodity (Rusmana and Listiyorini, 2014; FAOSTAT, n.d.).

Trade

In contrast to sub-Saharan Africa's relatively steady production, demand for palm oil on the continent has expanded rapidly over the last decade (FAO, 2013). This has led to a surge of imports, largely from global producers such as Indonesia and Malaysia, yet also from regional suppliers. Between 2000 and 2011 sub-Saharan Africa's imports of crude

FIGURE 3.2

Sub-Saharan Africa's Palm Oil Trade, 1992–2011

Key: ■ Export ■ Import ■ Production ■ Consumption

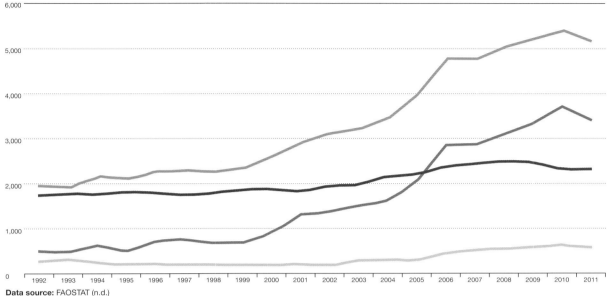

Tonnes (thousand)

Data source: FAOSTAT (n.d.)

palm oil increased nearly threefold, while production rose by a little more than one-quarter (FAOSTAT, n.d.). Today, sub-Saharan Africa remains a large net importer of palm oil, with domestic demand far outstripping supply (ZSL, n.d.-a; see Figure 3.2).

Exports of palm oil are still very limited. Although several producer countries send some quantity of the commodity abroad, trade is typically confined to regional partners. For example, exports of palm oil from West Africa—primarily from Ivory Coast—are mostly destined for neighboring Burkina Faso, Ghana, Mali, Nigeria, Senegal and Togo. In Central Africa, Cameroon, the region's largest producer, exports palm oil to Gabon and the Central African Republic (CAR), among a few others (USDA FAS, n.d.).

With growing production and relatively small domestic demand, Ivory Coast is sub-Saharan Africa's only net-exporter of palm oil (see Figure 3.3). The country's primary export market is regional as well, although

it also sells a small quantity of palm oil to Europe and the United States. Germany is by far Ivory Coast's largest non-regional client, purchasing 12% of the country's total exports in 2011 (USDA FAS, n.d.).

Future Expansion

Large-scale land acquisition for oil palm development in sub-Saharan Africa has proceeded rapidly over the past decade. Yet despite the myriad agreements and flurry of media reports, the land area currently under agro-industrial oil palm cultivation remains small in comparison to that suggested by announcements of land deals. Once contracts are concluded, the process to identify suitable land, complete environmental impact assessments and secure the necessary materials and workforce is lengthy (RFUK, 2013). The future of oil palm development on the continent is therefore uncertain, with the continued attractiveness of abundant land

FIGURE 3.3

Geographic Distribution of Ivory Coast's Palm Oil Exports, 2011

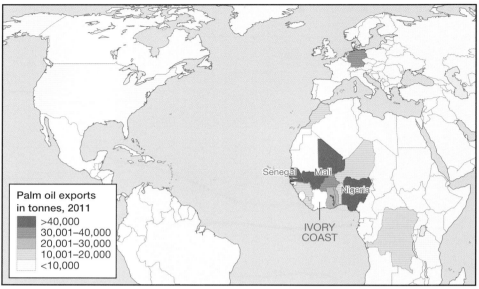

Palm oil exports
in tonnes, 2011
>40,000
30,001–40,000
20,001–30,000
10,001–20,000
<10,000

Data source: USDA FAS (n.d.)

complicated by difficult operating conditions and a host of other challenges.

Several recent developments, in particular, have reduced interest in oil palm cultivation on the continent. The 2014 Ebola outbreak slowed economic activity and investment—including in the palm oil sector—throughout West Africa, particularly in the most heavily affected countries (World Bank, 2015a). Executives of palm oil companies active in the region have even noted that the Ebola crisis led to a *de facto* moratorium on new deforestation in affected areas.[6] Although the outbreak is now contained, fears may continue to repress interest from international investors for some time.

Another factor that has inhibited oil palm investment on the continent is the global decline in the price of crude palm oil. Despite sharp dips in late 2008 and early 2009 as a result of the global economic recession, the price of crude palm oil remained at a historic high through the end of the decade, reaching an average monthly peak of US$1,292 per tonne[7] in February 2011 (Mongabay, n.d.).

Since 2011, however, prices have declined sharply, fluctuating between US$800 and US$900 per tonne during most of 2013 and dipping below US$800 per tonne in August 2014 for the first time in five years; at this writing, the price per tonne stood at well below US$700 (Agrofin, n.d.).

Industry experts predict continued price declines due to abundant global supplies of edible oils (Pakiam, 2014). For example, there are large soybean crops in the United States and there has been a massive expansion in the planted area in Southeast Asia over the past few years. Many plantations have reached maturity at the same time, flooding the global market with edible oils. Although the majority of palm oil produced in sub-Saharan Africa is sold locally, and local palm oil prices are typically higher than those a producer is able to obtain on the international market, as discussed below, the persistence of low international prices may reduce the appetite of commodity companies to make relatively high-risk investments in Africa.

While challenges abound, some investor interest in large-scale oil palm cultivation is likely to persist, due to both growing domestic demand for the commodity as well as government-led campaigns to attract greater foreign direct investment. In fact, governments across the region are actively promoting commercial agricultural investment, especially in oil palm, due to its potential to promote economic growth, local employment and poverty alleviation (see Chapter 1). Cameroon's Rural Sector Development Plan, for example, aims to increase production to 450,000 tonnes by 2020 through both industrial and smallholder operations (Hoyle and Levang, 2012), double the amount that it produced in 2012 (FAOSTAT, n.d.). The Congolese government, meanwhile, has said that it plans to develop plantations covering 10,000 km² (1 million ha) by the early 2020s (Tsoumou, 2011). Finally, in Gabon, the government's Strategic Plan for an Emerging Gabon calls for the conversion of the country into Africa's largest producer of palm oil, most of which is to be facilitated by Olam's plan to plant 1,300 km² (130,000 ha)[8] of oil palm by 2018–19 (Fern, 2013). For more information on Olam's activities in Gabon, see Chapter 5.

Overall, intended deals in sub-Saharan Africa cover 8,500 km² (850,000 ha), with the majority located in Cameroon (Land Matrix, n.d.). Yet, as noted in Box 3.1, reliable information on specific deals under negotiation is difficult to obtain. Media reports can be inaccurate and companies may keep plans from becoming public, especially before an agreement is reached, due to the recent wave of negative publicity around "land grabs" on the continent (see Chapter 4). Many of the projects known to be under negotiation have not progressed and may not materialize, while other, unpublicized deals may be proceeding behind closed doors.

Africa's choice

The African model of agriculture—characterized by the predominance of smallholder farms using low-quality stock and achieving lower yields—has many advantages, particularly for smallholder farmers and their communities. It provides broadly distributed benefits and allows farmers more flexibility in managing agriculture to meet their needs and those of their communities. Since the African model is not conducive to large concentrations of capital, it may even keep the expansion of agriculture into forests in check. Despite these benefits, pressure from international agribusiness and state actors to develop a larger commercial plantation sector is likely to continue at some level for the foreseeable future. If these plans actually pass from the project negotiation phase to large-scale development, African countries and communities will face a choice about which model of large-scale tropical agriculture they want to adopt: the Asian or the Brazilian model.

In the Asian model, rapid development would be accompanied by massive forest clearance and significant associated impacts on great apes, as well as on local communities.

Although oil palm is native to West Africa, its home base remains undisputedly Southeast Asia. Indonesia and Malaysia have tripled their production over the past 15 years and currently account for about 85% of the global total (FAOSTAT, n.d.). The rapid expansion in the crop's cultivation has had a devastating impact on Southeast Asia's environment and communities. Palm oil producers have cleared several hundred thousand square kilometers of native forests to expand plantations, contributing to significant increases in carbon dioxide emissions and putting immense pressure on local populations of orangutans, gibbons, Sumatran tigers and other species (Sheil *et al.*, 2009). In Indonesia, fires set annually to help clear forests and peatlands—largely to make way for oil palm plantations—have created dangerous haze that routinely spreads to neighboring Malaysia and Singapore (Varkkey, 2013). Moreover, lax law enforcement and unclear land ownership have led to social conflicts. In 2012, for instance, 59% of Indonesia's 1,000 palm oil companies were found to be connected to land conflicts with local communities (Hadinaryanto, 2014). Without stronger regulations, large intact forests across the Congo Basin could experience the same fate as the "paradise forests" of Borneo, Sumatra, Sulawesi, peninsular Malaysia and even parts of New Guinea.

The other option is the Brazilian model, which can serve to promote the protection of forests and the growth of agriculture. While the model was imperfectly applied in the beginning, the Brazilian government subsequently joined with key agriculture companies and civil society to implement strong forest protections that have reduced the rate of deforestation by more than 70% since 2004 (INPE, 2013). This success can be attributed to factors such as the soy industry's voluntary moratorium on new deforestation (following campaigns by non-governmental organizations (NGOs)), similar commitments in the cattle sector, improved law enforcement, recognition of indigenous land rights and the creation of new protected areas (CLUA, 2014). These steps have not inhibited agricultural development; in fact, they may even have made it more efficient and profitable. By concentrating development on large areas of degraded land and improving yields, Brazil has managed to achieve steady increases in the production of soy, cattle and other commodities even as it has made great strides in protecting forests (Strassburg *et al.*, 2012).

Whether Africa follows the Asian or Brazilian model for commodity agriculture will be determined by many forces, including whether governments show the political will to protect forests and communities, whether international corporate agriculture players adopt and implement strong forest conservation policies, and the extent to which African civil society can join with international NGOs to scrutinize commodity expansion efforts in Africa.

Other Agricultural Commodities

The recent wave of investment in oil palm plantations has been one of the largest and most visible components of active land acquisitions in sub-Saharan Africa. Yet foreign direct investment in crops is by no means limited to oil palm. Sugarcane, rubber and cereals (especially rice) have also piqued investor interest, as discussed below.

Sugarcane

Although sugarcane is grown across the continent, traditional areas of large-scale cultivation are located in East and Southern Africa. In sub-Saharan Africa, South Africa is by far the largest producer, accounting for about one-quarter of total output;[9] Kenya, Mauritius, Swaziland and Zimbabwe are also significant producers (FAOSTAT, n.d.). Although these regions contain far less ape habitat, some human–wildlife conflict has been reported around sugarcane plantations in Uganda (see Case Study 1.2 in Chapter 1). The land area under sugarcane cultivation has increased markedly over the past two decades, from 9,310 km² (931,000 ha) in 1992 to 13,000 km² (1.3 million ha) in 2013. Madagascar and Nigeria were responsible for a large portion of the increase, although traditional growers, including Kenya, Mozambique, South Africa and Zimbabwe, also saw significant expansions in land area harvested (FAOSTAT, n.d.).

Over the past decade, investor interest in sugarcane has been in part driven by the projected growth in demand for biofuels; the vast majority of projects concluded since 2000 aimed to produce for both the food and biofuel markets (Land Matrix, n.d.). Investment in the crop represents approximately 13% of the total land area acquired over the past decade (Schoneveld, 2014a). The most popular destinations of recent international land investments have been Ethiopia, Mozambique and Tanzania, in terms of both the number of projects as well as the total land area acquired. Areas where the crop has not traditionally been cultivated have also seen some sugarcane investments, including approximately 450 km² (45,000 ha) in Sierra Leone, 200 km² (20,000 ha) in Cameroon and 150 km² (15,000 ha) in Ivory Coast. South African companies such as Illovo Sugar[10] and Crookes Brothers have sought land outside of the country, investing in plantations in Congo, Mali, Mozambique, Swaziland and Zambia. As with oil palm, however, only a small portion of the total area acquired has actually been cultivated (Land Matrix, n.d.).

Large-scale investment in sugarcane plantations appears to have dropped off over the last couple of years—the majority of deals recorded in the Land Matrix were concluded prior to 2011. Little information exists on new projects under negotiation; this suggests slowing investor interest but can also be a reflection of a more limited willingness to publicize incomplete contracts.

Rubber

In sub-Saharan Africa, the principal producers of natural rubber are located in West and Central Africa, the largest of which are Cameroon, Ivory Coast, Liberia and Nigeria (FAOSTAT, n.d.). Between 2000 and 2012, the total area harvested for rubber cultivation increased by approximately 1,150 km² (115,000 ha), with the majority of that increase coming from Cameroon, DRC and Ivory Coast. The crop is produced both by smallholder farms as well as large plantations, the latter principally located in Cameroon, DRC and Gabon (Hourticq and Megevand, 2013). Trade in rubber is still relatively limited—only Cameroon, Ivory Coast and Nigeria export any significant quantity of the commodity, while imports are nominal across the region (FAOSTAT, n.d.).

Rubber producers, however, have been turning increased attention to West Africa, which has a climate suitable for rubber cultivation as well as a significant pool of agricultural workers (Hawkins, 2012). A number of land deals concluded over the past decade have targeted rubber production, amounting to a contracted land area of about 7,700 km² (770,000 ha) (Land Matrix, n.d.). The majority of these have set aside land for the cultivation of rubber and one other commodity, most often oil palm because the site requirements for the two crops are similar (FAO, 2001). It is unclear how much of the land area will be dedicated to rubber production specifically.

Liberia has the greatest number of concluded deals, with approximately 3,000 km² (300,000 ha) under contract. The Sime Darby rubber and oil palm plantation covers nearly two-thirds of that total. The development of these areas, however, may be significantly impacted by the newly concluded Norway–Liberia agreement on reducing emissions from deforestation and degradation, as discussed below (see Box 2.3 in Chapter 2). Other companies are reportedly seeking land in Cameroon, the DRC and Gabon (Land Matrix, n.d.).

Cereals

Cereal crops are harvested across sub-Saharan Africa, largely by smallholders for domestic

consumption. In terms of production volume, the most common crops are corn, rice, wheat and sorghum. Corn is grown in some quantity in virtually all sub-Saharan African countries, although Ethiopia, Kenya, Malawi, Nigeria, South Africa, Tanzania and Zambia are the largest producers. The crop has been the fastest-growing cereal in terms of total area under cultivation, increasing by approximately 70,000 km² (7 million ha) from 2003 to 2013. This has resulted in a substantial rise in output, from 45 to nearly 71 million tonnes during the same time period. Producer countries export limited quantities of corn; in 2011, approximately 5% of total production was exported (FAOSTAT, n.d.).

Investors have shown some interest, albeit limited, in commercial corn cultivation in sub-Saharan Africa. This is evidenced by the conclusion of several dozen land deals since 2000; the majority of which cover relatively small land areas—with a mean of 130 km² (13,000 ha)—and target multiple commodities, with corn as one of four or more planted crops. The most popular destinations for investment—Ethiopia, Mozambique, Tanzania and Zambia— have limited or no ape habitats, although several land deals have also been concluded in ape range states, such as the DRC, Ghana, Nigeria and Senegal (Land Matrix, n.d.).

The second most widely cultivated cereal, rice, is largely grown in West Africa, Tanzania and Madagascar, although smaller quantities are produced across the continent. Production increased rapidly during the past decade, from just under 19 million tonnes in 2003 to 29 million in 2013 and the total land area under cultivation expanded by approximately 30,000 km² (3 million ha). As with corn, sub-Saharan Africa exports a limited quantity of rice—approximately 1% in 2011; the vast majority is consumed within the region (FAOSTAT, n.d.).

The scale of investor interest in rice cultivation has been commensurate with that of corn in terms of the number of land deals concluded, although rice is much more likely to be the sole crop planted. The average project size is also relatively small, at approximately 180 km² (18,000 ha). The largest number of land deals involving rice have been concluded in East and West Africa, particularly in Ethiopia, Ghana, Mozambique, Nigeria, Sierra Leone and Tanzania (Land Matrix, n.d.).

Wheat and sorghum, the two other cereals that are widely grown in sub-Saharan Africa, are almost entirely produced for local consumption and have received very little investor interest (FAOSTAT, n.d.; Land Matrix, n.d.).

Sources of Investment

Broad Trends

The wave of recent land acquisitions has substantially increased foreign direct investment in sub-Saharan Africa's agriculture. Although capital comes from a variety of entities, including private companies, governments, international financial institutions and sovereign wealth funds, foreign companies dominate land-based investments (Farole and Winkler, 2014). An analysis of 520 projects across all agricultural commodities found that 86% of primary investors—actors directly involved in land acquisition and project implementation— were of foreign origin; ranked in terms of land area acquired. In regional terms, European investors account for roughly 40% of the total land under contract, while Asian and North American actors represent 19% and 15%, respectively (Schoneveld, 2014a).

There are, however, important differences in the purpose of investment across country of origin. Acquisition of land for biofuel production[11] is particularly common among European and North American investors; nearly 60% of land purchases for biofuels have been made by firms of European origin. Jatropha investments, in particular, were dominated by European and US actors, often small new ventures funded by venture capital, private equity funds or alternative stock exchanges (Schoneveld, 2014a). Thriving before the financial crisis of 2008-9, these small and often poorly capitalized firms were the hardest hit by the global economic downturn and accompanying credit restrictions. Lacking adequate financial backing —and seeing poor yields—many have since withdrawn from the continent (von Maltitz and Stafford, 2011).

Agricultural investment in food crops, such as cereals, roots and tubers, and vegetables—which comprise only a small fraction of the total land area acquired over the past decade—has come from a much more diverse range of sources, including the Middle East, North Africa, China, India and, often, Africa itself. Sub-Saharan companies have also been an important source of investment in land for food production. In fact, nearly 40% of land deals entered into since 2000 have involved a regional actor, either as the sole investor or in partnership with a foreign entity (Land Matrix, n.d.).

Oil Palm

Sources of outside capital for specific projects are difficult to determine, reflecting not only the complicated ownership structure of many commodity growers and traders, but also the fact that a substantial number of companies that are privately held and do not make their transaction details public. Moreover, funding flows may vary based on the type of company seeking to fund operations. Broadly, oil palm investors can be categorized into three groups:

Photo: Across sub-Saharan Africa, cereal crops are largely grown by smallholders for domestic consumption. The most common crops are corn, rice, wheat and sorghum. © Jabruson, 2015. All Rights Reserved. www.jabruson.photoshelter.com

1. **Plantation owners who wish to grow their operations:** These include state-owned enterprises (such as the Cameroon Development Corporation) and regional palm oil companies (such as Ivory Coast-based SIFCA), as well as primarily foreign entities with a long-standing presence on the continent (such as the Belgium-based Siat Group).

2. **Large Asian agribusinesses that aim to expand into Africa:** Often cited in media reports on land acquisitions in Africa, this group includes companies that already own oil palm estates in Southeast Asia —such as Golden Agri-Resources (GAR), Sime Darby and Wilmar—as well as traders seeking to enter upstream production (such as Olam International). Large European and US companies, including Bunge, Cargill and Unilever, have thus far not expanded production in Africa, as far as public data show (Land Matrix, n.d.).

3. **New ventures with plans to grow oil palm for the first time:** Mostly foreign-owned, these are relatively small and unknown enterprises aiming to enter the palm oil marketplace, both for food and biofuel production, for the first time; they include Atama, Biopalm Energy, FRI-EL Green Power and Herakles Farms.

Well-capitalized and profitable from large-scale operations in Indonesia and Malaysia, many Asian agribusinesses have used revenue to fund expansion into sub-Saharan Africa rather than relying on specific project finance. There are exceptions. Golden Agri-Resources, for example, received a US$500 million loan from the China Development Bank Corporation to finance its plantation in Liberia (Bank Track, n.d.). Olam International, meanwhile, received a US$228 million loan from the Development Bank of Central African States and several other lenders—including BGFI Bank of Gabon, the African Export–Import Bank, and Africa's leading banking group, Ecobank—to develop an oil palm and rubber plantation in Gabon (Agence France-Presse, 2012). For more information on Olam's activities in Gabon, see Chapter 5.

Companies already operating on the continent have also received some funding from African financial institutions to extend their operations. In 2007, the African Development Bank provided a €10 million (US$13 million) loan to Siat to expand its oil palm and rubber estates in Gabon (AFDB, 2008). Meanwhile, the private equity fund African Agriculture Fund—capitalized by European and African development finance institutions—has made equity investments worth US$19.5 million in Feronia's oil palm estate in the DRC (Phatisa, n.d.). Through its subsidiary Golden Oil Holdings, the equity fund now owns a 32.5% share in Feronia (Bloomberg, n.d.).

The role of international development banks in oil palm development in sub-Saharan Africa has been the subject of some debate. Although media reports attribute several large-scale deals to these institutions—including the ones described above—others have found that only a small fraction of all concluded agreements have received international development bank financing (Schoneveld, 2014a). The World Bank, which has funded some palm oil projects in West Africa though its private-sector lending arm, the International Finance Corporation, issued a revised palm oil lending policy in 2011 following an 18-month suspension on new lending to the sector (World Bank, 2011). Although the policy does not wholly preclude the financing of palm oil, it refocuses lending to smallholder projects and activities that increase land productivity. In general, the perception that international development bank involvement has been significant may simply reflect the fact that information on these transactions is much more readily available than it is on those involving private financial institutions.

Financial Institutions and Sustainable Lending

In general, private financial institutions appear to be aware of deforestation as a serious concern in oil palm development (Hays and Hurowitz, 2013). Although other social and environmental issues overshadowed palm oil as top priority in the past, the commodity has since become the most visible sustainability topic. A number of industry players, including BNP Paribas, Citi, Credit Suisse, ING, Rabobank and Standard Chartered have already adopted specific policies for palm oil or broader agribusiness lending (CLUA, 2014), yet the extent to which these policies are applied remains both unclear and difficult to study due to the absence or weakness of disclosure practices. Other banks continue to operate without or with weak policies on palm oil or other agricultural commodities.

To help make more responsible investments, private financial institutions claim to need better data on corporate performance and adherence to established sustainability standards. The most commonly used indicator, membership in a body such as the Roundtable on Sustainable Palm Oil (RSPO), has not been sufficient to prove adherence, because verifying on-the-ground compliance of RSPO-certified companies remains difficult (see Chapter 5). Moreover, in cases where certain criteria were not initially met, obtaining real-time information on progress—changes in corporate operations that may make them more or less likely to qualify for funding under certain sustainability requirements—is challenging (Hays and Hurowitz, 2013).

It is important to note, however, that some observers question the presence of an "information gap" in the financial industry in view of the immense number of resources that institutions have available for data collection and due diligence.

Wherever gaps do exist, the NGO community can play an important role in the provision of timely data on corporate performance to the financial sector. Although such work is already under way, financial institutions cite the lack of a common language as a persistent barrier to stronger partnerships. Specifically, financiers note that information regarding corporate environmental practices must be less rhetorical, more detached and more analytical if it is to be valuable as input into financial decisions—in contrast to the style often used by the NGO community to sensitize the public to a particular topic. By adopting terminology and language that is more familiar to the financial industry, NGOs may be able to increase their ability to inform funding decisions (Hays and Hurowitz, 2013).

> " By adopting terminology and language that is more familiar to the financial industry, NGOs may be able to increase their ability to inform funding decisions. "

Drivers of Expansion into Africa

The drivers of increased agricultural land investment in sub-Saharan Africa can be generally grouped into three categories:

1. an increase in global demand for agricultural commodities;
2. easier access to land on the African continent; and
3. lower set-up costs.

These are further described below.

Increased Demand for Agricultural Commodities

The Shift from Fuel to Food

Demand as a driver of large-scale land acquisition in sub-Saharan Africa has experienced a marked shift between the initial years of the boom—from about 2005 to 2010—and the post-financial crisis period. While the earlier period was characterized by a rise in land acquisition for the cultivation of biofuel feedstock, the post-crisis years saw a decline in biofuels development in favor of food production.

Influenced by a decline in easily recoverable oil reserves and national pushes to diversify supplies of vehicle fuels, the global demand for biofuels has risen considerably since 2000 (Hourticq and Megevand, 2013). Aiding this growth has been an increase in demand for transport fuel from emerging markets such as China and India, as well as the implementation of national policies around the world to promote the development of renewable energy (Cotula, 2013).

European nations, in particular, have driven the biofuel-based land purchases since the adoption of the 2003 Biofuels Directive. The directive, which required that 5.75% of all transport fuels used in the European Union (EU) come from renewable sources by 2010 (EU, 2003), had important implications for Europe's biofuel industry. As imports supplied roughly 40% of Europe's domestic consumption (Gerasimchuk, 2013), European companies began looking outward to secure new sources of raw materials to meet future growth in demand. This trend is reflected in the composition of the concluded land deals in sub-Saharan Africa, more than half of which represent investments that involve Europe-based companies and either partially or fully target the biofuel market (Land Matrix, n.d.). Europe, however, has not been the only source of growing demand for biofuels—several dozen countries around the world have also adopted biofuel targets or mandates over the past decade (CFS, 2013).

Although demand for biofuels continues to grow globally (Schroeder, 2014), the rush for African land to cultivate biofuel feedstock has waned since 2009. First, the 2007–08 food crisis highlighted the attractiveness of investment in food crops as a way of ensuring global food security and shone

a harsh spotlight on the use of food crops as a biofuel feedstock (ActionAid, 2012). Second, the global financial crisis has significantly depressed demand and credit availability for biofuel projects (IEA, 2009). This is particularly true of jatropha cultivation, which, as described above, drove large-scale land acquisitions in Africa until the bubble burst in 2009 (see Box 3.2). Lacking

experienced staff and poorly capitalized, many projects have been postponed or abandoned entirely. Investors in oil palm plantations largely survived the financial downturn—although their numbers have also declined—but due to limits on entering the biofuel market, as described below, as well as the growing demand for cooking oil on the continent, these have since turned their attention towards cultivating oil palm for food.

Finally, more recent European policy changes have dampened the attractiveness of obtaining land for biofuel production. In 2009, the 2003 Biofuels Directive was repealed and replaced by the Renewable Energy Directive, which set a minimum 10% target for renewable transport fuels by 2020

(EU, 2009). Importantly, the law also put in place a sustainable biofuels requirement that the feedstock generate a net reduction in greenhouse gas emissions without negatively impacting biodiversity or land use. In October 2012, the European Commission went even further, publishing a proposal to limit food crop contribution to no more than half of the 10%. After nearly two years of deliberations, the EU's Council of Energy Ministers agreed to a 7% cap on food-based biofuels (ICCT, 2014).

Domestic versus International Demand

The final destination of food crops produced on African agro-industrial estates varies by crop. Cereals, roots and tubers, and vegetables are grown for both domestic consumption and export. Companies from the Middle East and North Africa, for example, have sought to acquire land to supplement domestic food production, while others have looked for new market opportunities. Some Chinese and Indian companies, for instance, see agricultural expansion into Africa as an opportunity to establish a foothold for product sales on the continent (Schoneveld, 2014a).

Palm oil, however, has been primarily cultivated to supply domestic or immediate regional demand. Consumption of palm oil, which is largely used directly as cooking oil, has risen rapidly across sub-Saharan Africa (see Figure 3.2), a trend that is expected to continue well into the next decade (Ofon, 2014). Even with increased production, local supplies have not been sufficient to meet the growing demand. In West Africa alone, the excess demand for palm oil grew from 250,000 tonnes in 2002 to 1.2 million tonnes in 2012 (FAOSTAT, n.d.). The figure is projected to rise further—to 1.5 million tonnes by 2020, according to one estimate (ITC, 2012), although this may be an underestimate given the current growth rates. Across the continent,

palm oil consumption is expected to grow by 60% between 2014 and 2030 (Ofon, 2014).

This rate of growth in demand is difficult to match with domestic production. Given the current levels of palm oil consumption in sub-Saharan Africa—approximately 5.2 million tonnes in 2011—a 60% increase would necessitate more than a threefold increase in production by 2030 to meet the domestic demand with local supplies.[12] While this is not entirely impossible, achieving such rapid growth will be exceedingly difficult given that production over the last decade increased by only 16% (FAOSTAT, n.d.). Therefore, in the short term, almost all expansion in regional production is likely to be absorbed by countries in sub-Saharan Africa, with the remaining gaps satisfied by imports (ITC, 2012).

Beyond the ready local market, companies that produce palm oil in the region are further incentivized to sell the commodity to domestic consumers because they are likely to obtain a higher price within sub-Saharan Africa than on the international market. The difference between world and West African palm oil prices, for example, has widened over the past two decades, from a differential of approximately 3.3% in 1993 to nearly 55% in 2011 (Dublin-Green, 2013). This is a reflection of the region's significant excess demand—propped up by relatively low yields and increasing preferences for palm oil for cooking compared to other vegetable oils—high cost of transport and the prevalence of import tariffs (ITC, 2012).

Easier Access to Land

The focus on sub-Saharan Africa as a destination of large-scale agricultural land investment is primarily a reflection of substantial land access, in terms of both perceived availability and the relative ease of acquisition. The continent has the greatest availability of non-cultivated arable land in the world, accounting for approximately half of the world total (Jayne *et al.*, 2014). The Congo Basin countries alone represent roughly 40% of the total uncultivated, unprotected and sparsely populated land suitable for agriculture in sub-Saharan Africa—and 12% of such land globally (Hourticq and Megevand, 2013). When it comes to solely non-forested land, the Congo Basin accounts for one-fifth of all suitable agricultural land area in sub-Saharan Africa and 9% of such land worldwide.

It is important to note, however, that some of the land cited as "available" is subject to competing claims. In particular, portions of it may already be in use by local communities, but complex and confusing land tenure laws allow governments to cede tracts to agribusiness; the ramifications can include tensions between governments, business and civil society, the loss of land and livelihoods, and direct conflict (Cotula *et al.*, 2009). For more information on land tenure and relevant legal frameworks, see Chapter 4.

Despite these challenges, foreign companies continue to turn to the continent to bypass the real and perceived constraints on expansion at home. These include increasing protection of the rights of local and indigenous peoples, and awareness of the environmental impacts of forest conversion, such as climate emissions and threats to biodiversity. Moreover, even when degraded land is available, the investment necessary to cultivate it—engaging in long and costly administrative or legal proceedings and carrying out consultations with local communities—is greater than that required in sub-Saharan Africa, where regulation is poor and local community rights are even weaker than those in Southeast Asia.

Lower Set-up Costs

Although it may be as or more expensive to operate in sub-Saharan Africa than in Southeast Asia or other parts of the world, myriad incentives designed to attract companies have substantially lowered the cost of establishing agro-industrial projects on the African continent. The main incentive is the remarkably low price of land. Annual lease rates rarely surpass US$5 per hectare (Schoneveld, 2011), in comparison to about US$150 to US$300 in Latin America and US$250 to US$500 in Indonesia (Manciana, Trucco and Pineiro, 2009; Olam, 2010). In contrast, a hectare of land in the United States can cost more than US$1,600 (USDA, 2014a). In some cases, developers are not asked to pay annual rental fees; rather, the economic development and regional job creation is taken as payment for the land (Cotula, 2011).

Total acquisition costs, including other acquisition expenditures such as negotiation, land surveying, legal and corporate expenses as well as any compensation for local communities, have been estimated at US$825 per hectare in sub-Saharan Africa, compared to US$1,000 in Indonesia (Ofon, 2014). Although the overall cost of plantation management is similar to that encountered in Southeast Asia, and profits are typically smaller due to lower yields, African labor is often cheaper and the corporate taxes levied on profits from producing plantations are either low or entirely negligible (ITC, 2012). Therefore, overall returns to investment are often comparable.

Governments in sub-Saharan Africa have also enacted numerous incentives aimed at attracting foreign agricultural investors and facilitating the ease of doing business. Beyond low land-lease fees, incentives include low taxation rates and tax holidays, flexible labor regulation and rights to water, minerals and timber in the concession area (Linder, 2013). International trade policies have also extended privileges to African producers. Under the EU's Everything-but-Arms arrangement and the Africa Growth and Opportunities Act in the United States, products derived from sugar and palm oil are exempt from tariffs and quotas when

> It is important to note that some of the land cited as "available" may be subject to competing claims.

they originate in African least developed countries (European Commission, 2014; USITC, 2015).

Despite ample demand and financial incentives, the cost of operating in sub-Saharan Africa can still be prohibitively high. While unskilled labor is abundant, skilled local personnel can be scarce and expensive. Risks to operations frequently include corruption, unstable institutions, inadequate transport infrastructure and poor communication networks, as well as violence and general political instability (von Maltitz and Stafford, 2011). All of these factors can raise costs, increase risk and discourage large-scale investment.

Industrial Agriculture and Ape Habitat

Unlike in the tropical zones of Latin America and Southeast Asia, deforestation in sub-Saharan Africa is still principally caused by expansions in smallholder farming (Rudel, 2013). This is particularly evident around the peripheries of urban centers in densely populated areas (Hourticq and Megevand, 2013). In general, the most forested regions of Africa—such as the Congo Basin, which represents 70% of the continent's forest cover—have not yet experienced the scale of industrial agricultural expansion[13] and associated deforestation that has been observed in other tropical areas around the world (Rudel, 2013). It is important to note that although large-scale agriculture has thus far not had widespread effects on forests in the Congo Basin, the effects of industrial and artisanal timber harvesting have been significant. For more information, see *State of the Apes: Extractive Industries and Ape Conservation* (Arcus Foundation, 2014).

Given the recent rise in large-scale land acquisition, greater attention is being placed on the potential impacts of industrial agricultural expansion on forest degradation and loss. For example, one recent study suggests that fully developing one of the large oil palm plantations that have already broken ground in three countries—Herakles in Cameroon, Olam in Gabon and Atama in Congo—would increase the annual deforestation rate by 12%, 140% and 50%, respectively (Lawson, 2014).

Of equal concern is the international "leakage" of deforestation, as financial incentives and policy directives aimed at reducing deforestation are increasingly preventing companies from clearing forests in their traditional regions of operation and thus encouraging them to move into sub-Saharan Africa, where arable land is abundant and regulations are relatively weak (Wich *et al.*, 2014). This threat is particularly salient for palm oil investments as large oil palm corporations are more likely to convert remote native forests than revive old estates or operate on degraded land (Koh and Ghazoul, 2010).

Additionally, to speed up the land acquisition process and minimize the possibility of land use conflicts wherever land tenure systems are ambiguous, investors may decide to operate in areas that were not previously owned by other entities. Evidence also shows that some investors specifically target densely forested areas to recover some of the initial investment costs by harvesting timber within the concession (RFUK, 2013).

The extent to which agricultural expansion threatens forests varies across regions. Although some overlap between suitable arable land and forest areas is evident in West Africa, especially in Guinea, Ivory Coast and Liberia, the majority of intact forest landscapes—unbroken expanses of natural ecosystems of at least 500 km^2 (50,000 ha) that are minimally influenced by human economic activity—lie in the Congo Basin, namely in Cameroon, Congo, the DRC and Gabon (Mackey *et al.*, 2015). In Gabon and Congo, approximately 93% and 85% of suitable arable land, respectively, lies under forest cover (Schoneveld, 2014a).

The pressures on ape species also vary across regions. In West Africa, chimpanzees have already suffered significant population losses due to forest clearance and hunting. In Central Africa, where large tracts of native forest remain intact, apes have been threatened by the international trade in wild meat, which is often linked to commercial logging operations that facilitate access to their habitat. Cross River gorillas, a subspecies of western gorilla, have seen approximately 60% of their habitat disappear in the last two decades; meanwhile, eastern gorillas have lost half of their traditional range since the early 1990s. Bonobos, who live only in the DRC, have seen nearly 30% of their habitat destroyed (Junker *et al.*, 2012). All species of African apes are threatened: the western gorilla (both subspecies) and the mountain gorilla are critically endangered, while Grauer's gorilla and all species of the chimpanzee are endangered (IUCN, 2014a).

Oil palm plantations are most likely to have an impact on ape habitats, not only because concessions to cultivate the crop account for the largest portion of acquired land area, but also because they often lie in densely forested areas. According to a recent analysis, approximately 60% of the land currently allocated to oil palm concessions overlaps with great ape habitat. The principal areas of intersection appear in Cameroon, Gabon and Liberia (Wich *et al.*, 2014).[14] Yet, since spatial data for oil palm concessions are rarely available and development to date has been sluggish, it may be more instructive to look at the proportion of great ape habitat that is suitable for oil palm cultivation. According to the same analysis, the average overlap between the great ape range and land suitable for oil palm is 40%, excluding areas under official protection. Regional variations abound. In countries with significant ape habitat—more than 50,000 km² (5 million ha)—the overlap ranges from 20% in CAR, to nearly 75% in the DRC and Congo, to 94% in Liberia (Wich *et al.*, 2014; see Figure 3.4).

The extent to which different great ape species are threatened by oil palm development also varies. Eastern gorillas (including lowland and mountain gorillas) are least threatened, as the overlap between their ranges and unprotected oil palm-suitable land amounts to less than 10%. Chimpanzee habitat exhibits the second-smallest amount of overlap, averaging around 39%. A much

FIGURE 3.4

Proportion of Great Ape Habitat Suitable for Oil Palm

Key: ■ OP suitable (not protected) ■ OP suitable (protected) ■ Not OP suitable

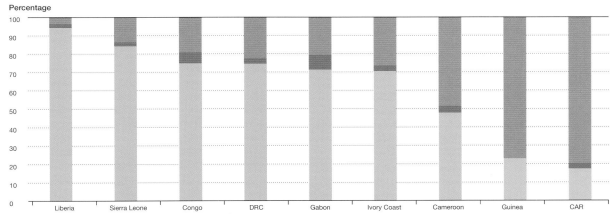

Note: The figure includes countries with more than 50,000 km² (5 million ha) of ape habitat.

Data source: Wich *et al.* (2014)

BOX 3.3

Documented Impacts from Large-scale Palm Oil Expansion in Africa

Industrial agriculture regularly has a negative impact on natural forests, great apes and other wildlife populations and local communities in Africa. Industrial logging remains the largest driver of forest degradation and poses an enormous threat to great apes due to habitat destruction as well as poaching and its related wild meat trade.

Evidence shows that the consequences of recent industrial agricultural development projects can be harmful in multiple ways. A number of projects have attracted the attention of local and international NGOs, the media and other stakeholders because of their destructive impact on environmentally significant locations and local communities as well as their apparent immunity from prosecution and disregard for best practices.

Table 3.2 outlines nine agricultural expansion projects in six different West and Central African countries and indicates what is known about associated forest clearance and impacts. Almost all of these projects are in early stages of development, during which the clearance of natural forest begins. They vary in size, with some plantations as large as 3,000 km² (300,000 ha). Six of the projects have already been documented as having a negative impact on great ape habitat. This includes direct habitat destruction—coupled with the indirect effects caused by the influx of workers and families into these once densely forested areas—which could endanger the very survival of great apes in Africa.

The Atama palm oil project in Congo is to cover an area encompassing large tracts of primary and swamp forest (RFUK, 2013). According to a recent mission report, Atama has been selectively logging in a forested area of approximately 50 km² (5,000 ha) and had fully cleared and planted 5 km² (500 ha) by the end of 2013 (Wah Seong, 2013; WWF-CIRAD, 2014). The Atama project's development is threatening forests which have been found to be habitat for record densities of western lowland gorillas (WCS, 2014). The plantation could also produce severe indirect impacts on the surrounding forests.

Government inspectors and the officially mandated independent monitor—the Independent Monitoring of Forest Law Enforcement and Governance (IM-FLEG)—have repeatedly found Atama's operations to be in violation of a range of laws, for example because they failed to have the legally required environmental impact assessment, cleared forest many kilometers outside the area licensed for clearance, laundered illegal timber, subcontracted illegally and failed to pay due taxes. IM-FLEG has repeatedly recommended that the company's operation be suspended (IM-FLEG, 2013, 2014).

In Cameroon, two plantations operated by Herakles Farms and Sud-Cameroun Hevea are poised to replace a total of 650 km² (65,000 ha) of the Congo Basin rainforest with oil palm and rubber. While a total of less than 45 km² (4,500 ha) has been cleared to date, the Herakles Farms plantation alone is set to destroy the habitat of 23 different mammals, including a rare subspecies of the chimpanzee (Waltert, 2013; Kupsch et al., 2014). Both projects have also been beset by conflict with local communities: there is evidence that Herakles Farms violated procedures of free, prior and informed consent (FPIC) (Oakland Institute, 2012); operated illegally, including by cutting timber illegally (Greenpeace USA, 2013; Greenpeace International, 2014b); assaulted and harassed an opponent of the project (FPP, 2014a; Jacquemart, 2014); and drew accusations of corruption (Greenpeace and Oakland Institute, 2013). Meanwhile, Sud-Cameroun Hevea is accused of operating illegally by clearing rainforests in the periphery of the Dja Faunal Reserve on permanent forest estate in south Cameroon (CIFOR, 2015; UNESCO, n.d.).

The Olam project in Gabon may be one of the largest industrial agriculture plantations in the region. To date, about 200 km² (20,000 ha) have reportedly been developed. Although Olam returned a portion of the land it originally acquired to the government of Gabon to protect high conservation value (HCV) habitats, further research will be required to assess potential indirect impacts on great ape habitats, such as through the influx of workers and wild meat hunting (Olam, n.d.). Social conflict, including corruption and harassment of civil society groups, has also been reported (Publish What You Pay, 2013). For more information on Olam's activities in Gabon, see their case study in Chapter 5, page 147.

Liberia has allocated vast amounts of land to industrial agriculture plantations in recent years. Three palm oil plantations—Liberia Palm Developments (LPD) (also known as Equatorial Palm Oil), Sime Darby and Golden Veroleum Liberia (GVL)—could together cover more than 6,000 km² (600,000 ha). Forest clearance and plantation development for any of these three is likely to impact great ape populations.

Liberia Palm Developments, which potentially overlaps with a protected area, is threatening the last littoral forest in West Africa (Small, 2013; BirdLife International, n.d.). Sime Darby's concession is close to or borders on five protected areas, thereby increasing the likelihood of direct and indirect impacts on endangered wildlife in the Upper Guinean Forest ecosystem, including great apes (Bene et al., 2013; Evans and Griffiths, 2013). Golden Veroleum Liberia borders the Taï-Sapo-Cestos biodiversity hotspot and is near Sapo National Park, which has the largest remaining forest block in West Africa and is home to an important population of the endangered western chimpanzee. Destruction of chimpanzee habitat has been documented and additional direct and indirect impacts are likely (Dowd et al., 2014); on a more positive note, GVL has agreed to halt all development of chimpanzee habitat, which covers approximately half of the proposed development area.

All three plantations have elicited complaints from local communities. Specifically, all three have violated FPIC procedures (FOE Europe, 2013; FPP, 2014b, 2015); both LPD and GVL

TABLE 3.2

Selected Projects' Impacts on Forests and Ape Habitat as of November 2014

Project	Location	Plantation size (km²)	Commodity	Forest clearance so far	Impacts on great apes?
Atama	Congo	1,800 (180,000 ha) (Lawson, 2014)	Palm oil	At least 5 km² (500 ha) and selective logging of tens of km² (WWF-CIRAD, 2014)	Yes (WWF-CIRAD, 2014)
Golden Veroleum Liberia	Liberia	2,200 (220,000 ha) (Kenrick and Lomax, 2013)	Palm oil	At least 30 km² (3,000 ha) (FPP, 2015), including at least 0.5 km² (50 ha) of high conservation value chimpanzee habitat (Dowd et al., 2014)	Yes (Dowd et al., 2014); further monitoring needed
Herakles Farms	Cameroon	200 (20,000 ha) (Mongabay, 2013)	Palm oil	Roughly 10 km² (1,000 ha)*	Yes (Waltert, 2013; Kupsch, Serge and Waltert, 2014)
Liberian Palm Developments (plantation also known as Equatorial Palm Oil)	Liberia	1,690 (169,000 ha) (Equatorial Palm Oil PLC, 2010; KLK, 2015)	Palm oil	Unknown; 1,470 km² (147,000 ha) expansion under way (Equatorial Palm Oil PLC, 2010)	Further research needed; indirect impacts likely
Olam	Gabon	3,000 (300,000 ha) (RFUK, 2013)	Palm oil and rubber	208 km² (20,808 ha) has been developed, of which 188 km² (18,793 ha) has been planted (Olam, 2014)	Yes (RFUK, 2013)
Sime Darby	Liberia	2,200 (220,000 ha) (Sime Darby, 2013)	Palm oil and rubber	Unknown; plantation size exceeds 100 km² (10,000 ha) (Sime Darby, 2013)	Yes (Bene et al., 2013)
Sud-Cameroun Hevea	Cameroon	450 (45,000 ha) (GMG, n.d.)	Palm oil and rubber	33 km² (3,274 ha) cleared as of November 2014*	Yes (UNESCO, n.d.)
Wilmar	Nigeria	270 (27,000 ha) (Wilmar, 2013b)	Palm oil	Unknown; at least "several thousand hectares" (several dozen km²) of natural forest lost (FOE Europe, 2014)	Further research needed; indirect impacts likely
Wilmar	Uganda	400 (40,000 ha) (FOE Europe, 2014)	Palm oil	Unknown; approximately 36 km² (3,600 ha) of natural forest cleared to date in highly biodiverse areas (FOE International, 2013)	Further research needed

Note: * Clearance information is drawn from unpublished sources, including maps, that were reviewed by the authors.

have played a role in assaulting and harassing opponents (All Africa, 2014; FPP, 2014b); and reports indicate that GVL has further jeopardized local food security (Forest Trust, 2013).

Wilmar has plantations in Nigeria and Uganda that could cover up to 670 km² (67,000 ha). Although more research is needed on the impact of these operations, assessments show that a significant area (several thousand hectares) of natural forest in regions of high biodiversity has already been lost to these plantations in each country (FOE International, 2013; FOE Europe, 2014). The company's plantation in Nigeria potentially overlaps with a forest reserve and the Cross River National Park (ProtectedPlanet, n.d.-a, n.d.-b); moreover, it is likely to have direct and indirect impacts on associated wildlife (FOE Europe, 2014). Wilmar is facing social conflict, including renewed concerns over the failure to observe FPIC processes in both locations (FOE International, 2013; FOE Europe, 2014).

The environmental and social problems caused by these nine plantations are not unique. They point to the potential consequences of industrial agriculture throughout the African continent if corporate best practices are not implemented and if legal and governance reforms, including adequate land use planning, are not passed and enforced by national governments.

greater degree of overlap is observed for the western gorilla in Cameroon, Gabon and Congo (65% in all three countries), and the bonobo in the DRC (91%) (Wich *et al.*, 2014). The extent to which ape habitats are threatened by specific projects is discussed above in Box 3.3.

Beyond demonstrating the significant amount of overlap between ape habitats and areas suitable for oil palm cultivation, this analysis illustrates that only a small fraction of vulnerable habitat is currently under protection across sub-Saharan Africa. Even when official protections are in place, the development of adjacent areas still poses an indirect threat due to increases in the local population and a subsequent rise in the number of incursions into protected forest, illegal logging and hunting of wild meat (Linder, 2013).

Sustainable Development

Powerful forces are driving commodity expansion to Africa. Agriculture is a key driver of economic activity in sub-Saharan Africa and will likely continue to play an important role in the economy. Although smallholders have thus far dominated agricultural production, large-scale plantations could also have a role to play in future development, especially as a source of new financial capital, skills, technologies and—if planned responsibly—local and regional employment. If agriculture is to play a positive role in Africa's development, strong company and government policies will be needed to avoid deforestation and promote greater respect for the rights and livelihoods of local residents.

Thus far, forests in a number of countries have enjoyed "passive protection" due to their remoteness, poor infrastructure and history of political instability (Hourticq and Megevand, 2013). This situation may change rapidly, however, as governments, companies

and populations make inroads into previously inaccessible territories. The Congo Basin, which contains the largest remaining stretch of relatively untouched forest, is already experiencing substantial development as its vast land area and investor-friendly governments facilitate large-scale agricultural land acquisitions across multiple crop categories. Given the recent interest in land in the region, as well as its abundant agricultural potential, there is a distinct need to ensure that development projects are undertaken responsibly, such that environmental and social costs are kept to a minimum while substantial benefits accrue to the local communities. The following three approaches are among the ways to increase economic activity while minimizing social impacts:

- **Cultivate non-forested or degraded lands:** There is substantial potential to expand agricultural activity in sub-Saharan Africa without threatening vulnerable habitats. In the Congo Basin alone, cultivated land area can nearly double without the conversion of forests (Hourticq and Megevand, 2013), although deeper analysis is required to determine how much land is truly free of conflicting claims. Potentially available land includes old plantations and other formerly cultivated areas that have long been abandoned. Developing oil palm projects on non-forested or degraded lands can produce economic benefits without threatening great apes or other regional biodiversity (Wich *et al.*, 2014). To encourage investment, governments can tie some established financial incentives to the cultivation of less vulnerable land.

- **Engage smallholder farms:** Small-scale oil palm cultivation is already common across sub-Saharan Africa and many older estates source a portion of their fresh fruit bunches from associated smallholder farms. The crop's cultivation is particularly attractive to small-scale growers due to its low susceptibility to pests and diseases, relatively small input requirements, and the need for a large workforce (Hoyle and Levang, 2012). A number of new concessionaires have also discussed developing operations according to the nucleus estate–outgrower model in order to involve local communities and leverage existing human resources (TechnoServe, 2011). Despite its promise, the practice remains largely in the conceptual phase and few (if any) new plantations have significant smallholder components. If properly implemented, however, greater smallholder involvement can be a practical way to prevent the myriad negative social impacts that often accompany large-scale oil palm cultivation and help ensure that the benefits of "development" are truly felt at the local level.

- **Increase yields from existing plantations:** Annual yields of oil palm fresh fruit bunches average 7.8 tonnes per hectare across sub-Saharan Africa—less than half of the average annual yield from oil palms planted across Southeast Asia (Wich *et al.*, 2014). While low yields have traditionally plagued smallholder farms with limited access to inputs and technology, agro-industrial plantations across the continent are also facing similar challenges. In Cameroon, for example, smallholder farms produce an average of 0.8 tonnes of crude palm oil per hectare while agro-industry yields approximately 2.3 tonnes per hectare. In contrast, the global industrial average is 4.0 tonnes per hectare (Hoyle and Levang, 2012). The low yields result from a number of factors, including less consistent rainfall than in Southeast Asia, a lack of proper inputs such as fertilizer—a common constraint among smallholder farms—as well as the prevalence of low-yield-variety oil palm (ACET, 2013). Raising yields could help encourage economic growth and meet domestic demand without requiring significant additional land cultivation—but this is far from assured. By contributing to profits, greater yields could also further incentivize agricultural expansion and deforestation in the region (Gutiérrez-Vélez *et al.*, 2011). In the absence of strong forest conservation measures and improved governance, a pure yield improvement program runs the significant risk of driving unsustainable expansion of agriculture with a variety of negative impacts. Yet this risk can be mitigated, for example if financial support to increase yields is tied to agreements that farmers will refrain from clearing forest for the expansion of crops.

A number of corporate and political forces can enable the development of responsible agro-industry. In particular, large agricultural growers, traders and consumer companies can undertake voluntary commitments to eliminate deforestation and other abuses from their supply chains. This is already happening on a significant scale, particularly within the palm oil industry. After facing harsh criticism of its operations in Indonesia, Wilmar, the largest trader of palm oil globally, released its "no deforestation, no peat, no exploitation" policy in early December 2013 (Wilmar, 2013a). While a handful of such commitments had been announced in preceding years—Nestlé, for example, made the first zero-deforestation commitment in 2011—Wilmar has gone further. In addition to applying the policy on its own plantations, the company has extended it to all of its third-party suppliers. Moreover, rather than focusing solely on palm oil, the commitment covers all commodities Wilmar produces and trades around the world. For information on Wilmar's growing commitment to sustainability, see their case study in Chapter 5, page 144.

Wilmar's announcement was succeeded by a host of similar corporate commitments. In February 2014, Golden Agri-Resources, which had already adopted a no-deforestation policy for its own plantations, expanded it to third-party suppliers (Butler, 2014). By mid-2014, US-based company Cargill had announced a similar commitment for palm oil, and Bunge followed suit in October (Bunge, 2014; Cargill, 2014). A number of consumer companies have also adopted similar policies for their suppliers (CLUA, 2014).

Despite the recent proliferation of important zero-deforestation commitments, much of the industrial agricultural development in Africa remains to be covered by the new policies. With respect to oil palm development, the majority of ongoing and planned projects that are likely to impact great ape territory are not yet bound by zero-deforestation commitments, largely because a substantial proportion of African production is consumed on the continent and does not flow through large international traders and procurers. One exception is Wilmar, which is among the few traders that also own plantations in Africa. It is possible that zero-deforestation approaches could spread to smaller producers and regional traders that want access to global markets; alternatively, large global players that have made such commitments may convince governments to enforce policies more broadly, or extend their reach by purchasing small players. Even without such global trade pressure, the region's large palm oil producers can do much more to ensure that their operations do not negatively impact sensitive forest areas.

Corporate commitments are an important first step in ensuring responsible and sustainable agricultural practices. On-the-ground practices, however, must adhere to written policy. Environmental groups have continued to draw attention to ongoing violations on large plantations and in supply chains in Africa and elsewhere, demonstrating the difficulty of changing entrenched agricultural practices (see Box 3.4).

" Corporate commitments are an important first step in ensuring responsible and sustainable agricultural practices. On-the-ground practices, however, must adhere to written policy. "

BOX 3.4

Toward More Responsible Practices in Industrial Agriculture in Africa

The expansion of industrial agriculture is very difficult to reconcile with wildlife conservation. Establishing plantations always involves the large-scale removal of existing vegetation, which often entails the loss of dense natural forests that serve as the habitat of great apes and other wildlife. In addition, such development tends to be accompanied by a massive influx of workers and their families to these once remote forested areas, increasing the demand for wild meat and related hunting and poaching; these factors have an indirect, yet severe, impact on the surrounding forest even if it remains standing (Linder, 2013).

Industrial agriculture is also increasingly provoking conflict over land and human rights abuses, as a rise in land acquisition threatens local communities' livelihoods and access to land. If new agricultural development is not managed properly, the destruction that large-scale palm oil has caused in Southeast Asia over the past years is set to be replicated on the "new frontier" for industrial agricultural production: Africa (Greenpeace International, 2012; RFUK, 2013).

It is therefore crucial that those involved in industrial agriculture adopt and implement strong policies to avoid deforestation and respect the rights and livelihood of local residents. First and foremost, it is the role of governments to engage in proper land use planning and establish strong environmental and social safeguards before industrial plantation concessions are allocated. Where governance is weak and law has not achieved these safeguards in practice, corporations must be especially careful to adhere to external standards and be fully transparent and responsible, especially toward local communities (Global Witness, 2012).

In Africa, corporations and governments have been slow to recognize the need for and to ensure the implementation of best practices in industrial agriculture. However, a few global producers and traders are taking initial steps toward limiting the negative environmental and social impacts of industrial agriculture in Africa.

Both Wilmar and Golden Veroleum Liberia, the latter through major shareholder Golden Agri-Resources, have made global commitments to follow no-deforestation policies that include respecting the rights of local communities (Golden Agri-Resources, 2011; Wilmar, 2013a). In both cases, however, implementation has been slow at best, which has meant ongoing adverse environmental and social effects (Greenpeace International, 2014a; FPP, 2015; Greenomics Indonesia, 2015).

In February 2011, GAR announced a forest conservation policy, which committed the company's global operations to protect forests, peatlands and the right of local communities to give free, prior and informed consent (Golden Agri-Resources, 2011). GVL has taken steps to set aside HCV forests and protect wildlife (Wright and Tumbey, 2012). Assessments to identify high carbon stock (HCS) forests are also under way; in fact, GVL has pioneered the HCS methodology in Africa as a tool for the identification and protection of forests (Greenpeace International, 2013). However, GVL's implementation has faltered at times. Specifically, the company destroyed some HCV chimpanzee habitat, although it put a halt to clearance in that area in January 2013. In addition, GVL provoked several incidents of severe social conflict (Dowd et al., 2014); it has also continued to violate communities' rights to FPIC procedures (FPP, 2015).

Established in December 2013, Wilmar's "no deforestation, no peat, no exploitation" policy includes forest and social protections similar to GAR's (Wilmar, 2013a). In the first year of implementation, Wilmar reported on efforts in the company's plantations in Nigeria and Uganda (Wilmar, 2013b); however, international and local NGOs have accused the company of continuing to clear forests—including in globally recognized key conservation areas—and of perpetuating social conflict in both countries (FOE Europe, 2014). Although Wilmar has "reaffirm[ed] its commitment to open, transparent and considerate practices" (Wilmar, 2013b), the company still needs to respond to accusations and dramatically improve the transparency of its implementation process.

A third global company, Olam, has taken some noteworthy steps toward responsible practices in its plantation in Gabon. The Gabonese government offered Olam areas of primary forest inside intact forest landscapes, as well as areas recognized as Ramsar wetlands for conversion. It was thanks to Olam's voluntary policies—not Gabonese government policy—that parts of the concession area that were ecologically most important were not converted and instead returned to the government (Olam, n.d.; C. Stewart, personal communication, 2014).

Olam conducted HCV assessments, which revealed that only a fraction of the total land bank was appropriate for palm oil development (Proforest, 2014). To date, Olam has followed the recommendations based on these assessments and protected the identified HCV areas (RFUK, 2013); however, the company does not recognize, nor protect, HCS forests, which include areas adjacent to narrowly defined HCV land that would provide important buffers from poaching and habitat fragmentation. Olam's plantation is thus still likely to impact great apes and other large mammals; it will also continue to have indirect impacts—including through increased poaching—on endangered species in and around its land bank (RFUK, 2013).

While the policy commitments that GVL and Wilmar have made are steps in the right direction, they are both struggling with on-the-ground implementation. Many stakeholders are currently hailing the Palm Oil Innovations Group (POIG) as the most groundbreaking and comprehensive model for best practice in the palm oil sector. Its criteria, which should be easily applicable to other industrial agriculture, go beyond the requirements of the RSPO and cover plantation creation and operation with considerations for environmental responsibility, partnerships with communities, and corporate and product integrity (POIG, 2013).

At the national level, some steps are being taken toward providing needed reforms. In Cameroon, for instance, the government is preparing a national palm oil strategy, which could—provided adequate safeguards are incorporated—serve as a foundation for limiting the harmful impact of palm oil development on forests and local communities. In the same vein, the Cameroonian government is reviewing land use planning processes (Gwinner, 2013). A solid national palm oil strategy should be based on strong land use planning laws; in parallel, participatory and transparent processes with local communities are needed to prevent conflicts over environmental and social issues.

Cameroon is also revising several sectoral regulations, including the Forest Code and Mining Code (FPP, 2012a). In view of the fact that land concession decisions and requirements for industrial agriculture companies are dictated by several ministries without inter-agency consultation, efforts need to be made to establish clear environmental safeguards and cross-sectoral integrated policies, as these will be critical for the long-term health of the country's forests and great ape populations.

Ultimately, Congo Basin countries need to develop palm oil national strategies that not only lay out strict social and environmental safeguards, but also require full transparency in land acquisition processes. These strategies need to be based on proper participatory land use planning processes that are developed with all stakeholders and that promote full civil society engagement.

In Liberia, another model of legislative and governance reforms appears to be under way. In September 2014, the governments of Liberia and Norway signed an agreement to cooperate on reducing emissions from deforestation and degradation. The agreement stipulates that corporations will be allowed to do business in the Liberia only if they implement commitments that are at least as strong as Wilmar's policy to protect forests and respect local communities. It also provides a road map for the recognition of customary land use rights and the inclusion of strong environmental and social safeguards, including no-deforestation standards, into the national legal framework (Norway and Liberia, 2014). Liberia has in past years allocated vast land areas to large-scale agricultural concessions that have led to deforestation and numerous conflicts; if implemented, this agreement could integrate much-needed safeguards into national law. For more information on the Norway–Liberia deal, see Box 2.3 in Chapter 2.

No one political prescription is a cure-all for every country. These examples, however, can provide a basis for understanding how legislative and regulatory reforms can fundamentally change where and how industrial agriculture operates in African countries. As stressed above, establishing country-specific legal and regulatory reforms is not enough; they must be accompanied by proper enforcement. Governance reforms aimed at eradicating corruption and ensuring transparent legal enforcement are critical. As long as corruption and the lack of transparency remain dominant features of forest governance in African countries, it is unlikely that any voluntary commitment will have the desired effect of limiting the negative impact on the forests, wildlife and people.

Moreover, corporate action alone is not enough. Governments must create an enabling environment for sustainable development, not least by enacting clear and strong legal structures around forest governance and stamping out corruption. Among nations' top priorities must be creating and enforcing fair and transparent processes for the granting of concessions and the resolution of competing claims to land. This includes recognizing the land rights of local communities and indigenous groups, as well as consistently requiring project developers to obtain free, prior and informed consent from affected populations.

To prevent illegal deforestation and hunting of wild meat, governments must create a solid legal framework that eliminates impunity for those who illegally obtain and trade timber and wildlife. Although several such laws exist across the continent, enforcement is often poor due to inadequate resources and expertise, as well as a tendency to accord a low priority to environmental crimes (Lindsey *et al.*, 2012). Legislation must be backed by a legal system that has the capacity to police and prosecute perpetrators.

As noted above, local and national-level authorities must construct a level playing field for agribusiness by rooting out corruption. When one company or set of actors is able to benefit from bypassing regulations or paying bribes, it becomes difficult for its peers to remain economically competitive without engaging in similar activities. Despite corporate players' best intentions, the prevalence of corruption perpetuates a race to the bottom in terms of environmental and social standards. By disincentivizing irresponsible operations, governments can create a business environment that rewards sustainable practices and ensures that competition engenders greater protections for communities and ecosystems.

Conclusion

Sub-Saharan Africa has experienced a substantial increase in agricultural land investment over the past decade. Looking to take advantage of easier access to land, lower set-up costs and a growing demand for key agricultural commodities, foreign companies—both alone as well as in partnership with domestic governments—have received access to thousands of square kilometers (millions of hectares) of land for the cultivation of crops such as oil palm and other oilseeds, sugarcane, cereals and a variety of fruits and vegetables. During the first decade of the 21st century, the anticipated growth in global demand for biofuels drove scores of companies, large and small, to invest in a then little-tested but seemingly promising crop called jatropha and encouraged others to cultivate more traditional biofuel feedstocks such as oil palm and sugar. By 2010, the jatropha bubble had burst and concerns about land use and food security impacts linked to traditional biofuels have since pushed many of the original oil palm and sugar investors to turn their attention to food-oriented markets. Still, interest in African land has remained intact, although companies have increasingly chosen not to publicize deals concluded or under negotiation in an effort to escape the negative media attention that followed earlier investors.

Development of acquired land has proceeded slowly, curtailed by confusing land tenure regimes, insufficient infrastructure,

regional unrest and, in some instances, opposition from local communities. While these factors have slowed the land use and ecosystems impacts of the new wave of agricultural investment, they have not eliminated them completely. Several environmental costs are already becoming apparent. Moreover, the costs associated with future land development are potentially significant, as a few large-scale projects are threatening ape habitat. Since large portions of land suitable for oil palm cultivation overlap with forest areas, the rapid and unchecked spread of agricultural estates could result in widespread deforestation and loss of habitat for vulnerable ape species on the scale seen in parts of Southeast Asia. Meanwhile, the local population growth that often accompanies the development of a new industry can exacerbate already common threats, such as the illegal hunting of wild meat.

Agriculture is a key driver of economic activity in sub-Saharan Africa. A significant portion of the new agro-industrial production, especially that of palm oil, is and will likely continue to be used to satisfy the growing demand for food and fuel on the continent. The need to promote responsible development is thus pressing. As this chapter describes, efforts must be made to ensure that agribusinesses commit to avoid razing HCV and HCS forests, governments incentivize the regeneration of abandoned plantations and the inclusion of smallholder farms, and communities become empowered to demand change when their livelihoods are threatened by poorly planned large-scale land development. While some progress is already being made, a great deal more will have to be done. With the new wave of large-scale agricultural expansion still in its early stages, a variety of economic and political factors have aligned to make the current moment one filled with opportunity to ensure this expansion is achieved without inflicting irreversible damage on Africa's forests, wildlife and people.

> " With the new wave of agricultural expansion still in its early stages, a variety of factors have aligned to make the current moment one filled with opportunity to ensure this is achieved without inflicting irreversible damage on Africa's forests, wildlife and people. "

Acknowledgments

Principal authors: Maria Belenky and Michael Wolosin with Climate Advisers, and Glenn Hurowitz, formerly with Climate Advisers

Boxes 3.3 and 3.4: Amy Moas and Rolf Skar, both with Greenpeace US

Reviewers: Sam Lawson, Ivo Mulder and Michal Zrust

Endnotes

1   This chapter uses the term "continent" to refer to sub-Saharan Africa. Unless specifically mentioned, North Africa is outside the scope of this analysis.

2   Throughout this report, "land acquisition" or "land contracted" implies the concession, lease or purchase of land from a government or government entity to a third party, either public or private, for commercial use.

3   All Land Matrix figures cited in this chapter are current as of November 2014.

4   This figure is based on the sum of what the analysis terms "category 1" (more accurate) and "category 2" (less accurate) data. The category 1-only total is about 179,240 km² (17.9 million ha).

5   Ape range states include Angola, Burundi, Cameroon, Central African Republic, Congo, Ivory Coast, DRC, Equatorial Guinea, Gabon, Ghana, Guinea, Guinea-Bissau, Liberia, Mali, Nigeria, Rwanda, Senegal, Sierra Leone, South Sudan, Tanzania and Uganda (GRASP, n.d.).

6   Author communication with palm oil executives at the Liberia Roundtable on Forest-Friendly Palm Oil, Cocoa, and Paper & Pulp Development, 2014.

7   The figure includes the cost of purchase, insurance and freight to Rotterdam.

8   Of the total 1,300 km² (130,000 ha), 300 km² (30,000 ha) are to be allocated to smallholders.

9   If North Africa were also taken into account, Egypt would be Africa's largest producer of sugarcane.

10 Illovo ended its engagement in Mali in May 2012 due to incomplete funding and security concerns.

11 A number of crops, particularly oil palm and sugarcane, but also corn, sorghum, soybeans and others, are fungible and can be channeled to food- and non-food-related industries. Producers can and often do allow market conditions to determine the end use, shifting between food and biofuels according to demand.

12 The estimate of current consumption was derived by adding sub-Saharan Africa's net imports in 2011 (the last year for which data are available) to its 2011 level of production, assuming stable standing stock. The source of both figures is FAOSTAT (n.d.). The calculation is as follows: With a 60% increase in consumption, sub-Saharan Africa's 2030 demand will be approximately 8.2 million tonnes. As current production is about 2.3 million tonnes, production will have to grow more than threefold to meet domestic demand in 2030.

13 For the purposes of this chapter, "industrial agriculture" excludes logging and forestry operations.

14 These areas only include concessions for which spatial data was available (ten units across five countries). Because of gaps in coverage, the true overlap may be significantly different.

CHAPTER 4

Legal Frameworks at the Interface
between Industrial Agriculture and
Ape Conservation

Introduction

This chapter discusses the legal frameworks
relating to the interface between agribusiness investment and ape conservation. It
assesses how applicable rules, and the institutions that implement them, address this
interface in a range of countries that host
important ape populations.

If policy is often the primary driver of
change, laws constitute the framework via
which government policies are implemented
and relevant stakeholders can lawfully operate. Analyzing such legal frameworks can
provide a useful understanding of formal
policy goals, as well as of existing pressure
points and leveraging tools that can help to
drive change from within the system. It also
serves to identify both inconsistencies and

bottlenecks in a country's laws, affording an opportunity for reform. Yet since laws and regulations are only one aspect of policy frameworks, it is also crucial to develop an overall view of existing policies to thoroughly understand a specific context.

The interface between agribusiness investment and ape conservation has become the object of animated policy debates. These debates raise issues relating to options for reconciling the objectives of conservation and economic development, the rights and role of local communities in habitat conservation and productive activities, the most appropriate levels of decision-making authority, and the different models of land tenure and conservation schemes.

In a sense, law is crystalized policy, and many of the issues discussed in policy debates are regulated, in one way or another, in legislation that frames property rights, decision-making, environmental safeguards and compliance procedures, among other mechanisms. At the same time, a legal analysis is inevitably a snapshot of the normative arrangements adopted by a given society at a given point in time. It takes prevailing policy choices largely as a given and does not preclude the possibility of change in future policy preferences. In fact, some of the countries reviewed in this chapter are currently considering legislative reforms in relevant policy areas.[1]

Similarly, while a discussion of legal trends reveals much about the formal policy goals that a society has set for itself, it says little about the extent to which legal arrangements are actually implemented on the ground, how compliance is monitored and how the failure to comply is sanctioned. While the gap between the statute books and the realities on the ground represents a notorious challenge, a discussion of legal frameworks can be pivotal to addressing critical shortcomings. As this chapter demonstrates, the individual features of

legal frameworks can fundamentally shape interactions between industrial agriculture and ape conservation.

Recent developments in international environmental law have strengthened conservation efforts significantly and enhanced their coordination across borders. Indeed, several multilateral treaties set out obligations that are directly relevant to ape conservation, at both the global and the regional level (see Table 4.1). Yet, none of these international measures will be effective unless individual states ratify them and establish the institutional systems required for their implementation.

The conservation of apes and their habitats—a matter of global concern—is thus largely dependent on national measures and their governing legal frameworks. Consequently, it is important to assess the preparedness of national legal systems and institutions to assist in mitigating the pressures that agribusiness investments place on apes and ape habitats. In that vein, this chapter explores national laws that establish and govern environmental protection measures. It identifies important gaps between national law and practice, as well as factors that lead states to allow the conversion of ape habitats into industrial plantations. To explore these issues, the chapter presents a trend analysis and a case study.

The trend analysis focuses on legislative frameworks in eight key ape range states: four in Southeast Asia—Cambodia, Indonesia, Malaysia and Myanmar—and four in West and Central Africa—Cameroon, the Democratic Republic of Congo (DRC), Gabon and Liberia. These countries were selected due to the density of their ape populations and the presence of significant agribusiness developments. For each of the countries under review, the section presents findings from the authors' systematic review of national legislation on the management of land, forests and other natural resources, investment

TABLE 4.1

State Ratification of Multilateral Treaties Relevant to Ape Conservation, as of May 2015*

Instrument	Area of cooperation	No. of parties	Cambodia	Cameroon	DRC	Gabon	Indonesia	Liberia	Malaysia	Myanmar
Global										
Convention on Biological Diversity (UN, 1992)	Establishment of general principles of conservation at the global level	195	Yes	Yes	Yes	Yes	Yes	Yes	Yes	Yes
Convention on International Trade in Endangered Species of Wild Fauna and Flora (CITES, 1973)	Regulation of the import and export of endangered species	180	Yes	Yes	Yes	Yes	Yes	Yes	Yes	Yes
Convention on Conservation of Migratory Species of Wild Animals (CMS, 1979)	Establishment of standards of conservation with a focus on individual species	120	No	Yes	Yes	Yes	No	Yes	No	No
International Tropical Timber Agreement (UN, 2006)	Promotion of international trade of timber and sustainable management of timber-producing forests	69	Yes	Yes	Yes	Yes	Yes	Yes	Yes	Yes
Regional										
African Convention on the Conservation of Nature and Natural Resources (African Union, 2003)	Coordination of conservation measures and establishment of types of protected areas	59	n/a	Yes	Yes	Yes	n/a	Yes	n/a	n/a
Treaty on the Conservation and Sustainable Management of Forest Ecosystems in Central Africa and to Establish the Central African Forest Commission (COMIFAC, 2005)	Harmonizing national sustainable forestry policies, instruments and certification systems	10	n/a	Yes	Yes	Yes	n/a	n/a	n/a	n/a
Agreement on the Conservation of Nature and Natural Resources (ASEAN, 1985)	Coordination of development planning and conservation of species and ecosystems	6	Yes	n/a	n/a	n/a	Yes	n/a	No	Yes

Notes: * Yes = the state has signed and ratified the convention; No = the state is not party to the convention; n/a = the regional convention is not applicable to the state.

governance, environmental protection and redress mechanisms. The analysis relies on a review of primary legal documents and available secondary literature, including gray literature, both for commentary on features of national legal frameworks and for insights into the relationship between law and practice.

The case study considers how the multiple elements of legislation studied in the trend analysis interact in practice. In particular, it examines the experience of instigating judicial proceedings against agribusiness companies in Aceh province, Indonesia. The case study offers guidance on how best to bridge the gap between law and practice and suggests ways in which conservation groups can use legal arrangements to protect apes and ape habitats.

The conclusion of the chapter distils key insight from the analysis and develops recommendations for moving forward.

Findings from the Trend Analysis

Land and Resource Tenure and the Agribusiness–Conservation Interface

Forests—the primary ape habitats—are the resources that are most directly at stake in transactions promoting industrial agriculture. To operate lawfully, a company that establishes an agro-industrial plantation typically needs legal authorizations to use the land and clear the forest.

The legal frameworks governing tenure of land and forests determine who owns or controls these resources, who has the legal authority to allocate resources to agribusiness investments, and how. Tenure regimes also govern the nature and extent of the rights of individuals and groups that use

land and natural resources, such as small-scale farmers and forest communities. While national legal frameworks vary considerably across countries, the trend analysis shows that three specific factors—widespread ownership or control by central government agencies, weak local rights, and inadequate mechanisms for transparency and accountability—facilitate large-scale land acquisitions for industrial agriculture and enable deals that flout social and environmental concerns, thereby potentially threatening apes and ape habitats.

In most of the countries under review, a constitutional provision sets key principles concerning the status of land and natural resources (see Table 4.2). The core principle in a majority of the constitutions examined is that the state owns or otherwise controls these resources, while public institutions are tasked with enacting implementation laws.[2] Some of the newer constitutions go further and explicitly affirm the right of government authorities to allocate land and resources through concessions, in particular in order to ensure the productive use of these resources.[3] Comparable regimes of centralized state ownership and control are also present in countries whose constitutions are silent on the matter of allocating concessions.[4] Relevant laws on land and forestry tend to echo this principle and set the framework for more detailed provisions on implementation.

This is not to say that private land ownership is prohibited. On the contrary, with very few exceptions,[5] most of the laws reviewed enable private property ownership as well as the conversion of permanent use of land into officially recognized title, as a way of establishing private ownership rights[6] (see Table 4.2). However, the registration procedures required for this conversion are often costly and cumbersome, or otherwise inadequately adjusted to rural contexts. As a result, only relatively small shares of the national territory are privately owned in most of the countries reviewed, and the state ends up controlling most of the land, even if the statute books allow private land ownership (Rights and Resources Initiative, 2014).

In most ape range states under review, communities hold rights to the land owned by the state. In fact, the majority of them have legal arrangements that allow for the recognition of traditional communal rights—which could potentially play a positive role in the conservation process (Stevens *et al.*, 2014)—and that limit the allocation of land to industrial agriculture. However, the extent of this legal recognition varies significantly from country to country, as does the effectiveness of the associated legal protection. In most cases, the legal recognition of community land rights does not provide strong safeguards against government decisions to allocate lands to agribusiness investments (see Table 4.2).

A brief discussion of a few specific issues illustrates these limitations. First, legal protection may be subject to formalization requirements, although these vary across countries. In some states, such as Cameroon and the DRC,[7] customary occupancy is protected and no collective action is required for a community to enjoy formal protection. However, such recognition does not typically entail a high level of protection of community rights (van Kempen and Mayifuila, 2013). Moreover, most countries provide for higher formalization requirements, including registration-type procedures that create communal title to land.[8] Some observers find that these solutions provide greater land tenure security for the community, but that they also create significant procedural hurdles, many of which are too difficult for rural residents to overcome. Multiple approaches may coexist in the same jurisdiction; for example, mere occupancy may be nominally protected while registration procedures are available

to convert customary rights into full-fledged land ownership.[9]

Second, in most countries under review, communities are able to secure their land tenure in the face of industrial agriculture only if they can show they are engaged in the productive use of the land themselves (see Table 4.2).[10] In Cameroon, for example, land legislation explicitly conditions legal protection to proof of evident productive use. Land that is claimed by local communities that use it for grazing, hunting and gathering, or hosting sacred sites can potentially be allocated to agribusiness operators, as can land that has been set aside for future generations. While it is difficult to come by reliable estimates, areas that are used by communities for non-productive purposes are thought to account for a substantial share of communal lands. As the protection of local land rights is often tied to productive use requirements, ape habitats—which are typically among the least cultivated areas—are particularly at risk of being allocated to agribusiness investments. Such requirements might also create perverse incentives for communities to clear land, although there is as yet little empirical evidence of the extent to which these incentives are affecting ape conservation in practice.

Furthermore, most of the countries reviewed have enacted far-reaching laws on expropriation, which often date back to the early post-colonial era. Such laws allow governments to acquire land on the basis of vague concepts—such as "public purpose" in Gabon or "national interest" in Indonesia—which tend to receive the widest interpretation from implementing administrations (Alden Wily, 2012).[11] As a result, public authorities can—and often do—compulsorily invalidate local tenure rights to pave the way for agribusiness investments.

Another important variable in the tenure structure relates to the types of rights over land and resources that agribusiness operators themselves can acquire, and to the mechanisms established to enable businesses to access those rights. Virtually all countries under review have taken steps to facilitate access to land for agribusiness operators, often through long-term land leases or concessions and joint venture agreements on state-owned land. However, important differences in relevant regulatory frameworks exist, particularly between the countries that are old hands at hosting agribusiness estates, such as "traditional" palm oil or rubber exporters, and the newcomers,

TABLE 4.2

Land and Resource Tenure

Instrument		Cambodia	Cameroon	DRC	Gabon	Indonesia	Liberia	Malaysia*	Myanmar**
Global									
Does the national constitution set out the principles of ownership over land and natural resources?		Yes	No	Yes	No	Yes	Yes	Yes	Yes
Is the state designated as the principal owner of all natural resources?		Yes	Yes	Yes	Yes	Yes	Yes	Yes	Yes
Is private ownership of land permitted by law?		Yes	Yes	No	Yes	Yes	Yes	Yes	No
Is private ownership of forest permitted by law?		Yes	Yes	No	No	Yes	Yes	No	No
Are customary rights to land recognized by the constitution?		No	No	Yes	No	No	No	Yes	No
Are customary rights to land recognized by primary legislation?		Yes	Yes	Yes	Yes	Yes	Yes	Yes	No
Are customary land rights legally protected if they are not formally registered?		Yes	No	Yes	No	No	No	No	n/a
Are communal forest rights legally protected if they are not formally registered?		Yes	No	Yes	No	No	No	No	n/a
Is the protection of communal land rights conditioned on productive use?		No	Yes	No	No	No	No	Yes	n/a
Are there legal arrangements that facilitate the transfer and use of land for commercial agriculture (joint venture agreements, financing institutions, etc.)?		Yes	No	No	Yes	No	Yes	Yes	Yes
Is there a legal requirement for the productive use of land by the concessionaire of the land?		Yes	No	Yes	Yes	Yes	Yes	Yes	Yes

Notes: * The information on Malaysia reflects a focus on the Sabah region, one of the two autonomous regions that has full competency to make decisions concerning land and natural resource management (and therefore functions under a distinct set of state regulations), and that also hosts the most extensive ape population in the country. ** n/a = not applicable. Since the law does not recognize communal or customary rights in Myanmar, these issues remain unregulated.

Sources: Alden Wily (2007, 2012): Cambodia (1993a, 2001, 2002, 2003); Cameroon (1974, 1992, 1994, 1995b); DRC (2002, 2006c, 2008a, 2008b, 2011a, 2011c); Gabon (1961, 1967, 1987a, 1991, 2001, 2004, 2007, 2008); Indonesia (1945, 1960, 1999, 2006a, 2010); Kennedy (2011); Liberia (1904, 1956, 1984, 2000, 2006, 2009c, 2010b); Majid Cooke (2006); Malaysia (1930, 1957, 1965a, 1968a, 1968b); Myanmar (1894, 1992, 2008, 2011, 2012c); Nguiffo, Schwartz and Hoyle (2012); Oberndorf (2006, 2012); USAID (2010a, 2010b, 2011); van Kempen and Mayifuila (2013)

meaning countries whose engagement with agricultural investors has occurred relatively recently.

Malaysia is an example of an old hand. The country has implemented several generations of elaborate schemes to promote agribusiness operations (Majid Cooke, Toh and Vaz, 2012). The consequence of this complex legal set-up is the rapid conversion of undeveloped areas into plantations across Malaysia. At the same time, these well-established instruments also seem to provide a more defined space for regulation, while creating at least some legal safeguards for local farmers.

At the other end of the spectrum, the relative newcomers to large-scale industrial agriculture include countries such as Gabon and Myanmar, as well as Cameroon and DRC, with the exception of some major concessions that date back to the colonial era. These countries have vast forest resources available for industrial logging, as examined in the first edition of *State of the Apes* (Arcus Foundation, 2014). Yet, although they are increasingly turning to the agricultural sector as another viable source of income and economic development, their legal frameworks continue to reflect the needs and concerns of industrial logging, rather than those of commercial agriculture. As effective institutional arrangements to manage forest conversion processes are often lacking, agribusiness developments are taking place in an uncontrolled and largely unplanned manner, which in itself can threaten apes and ape habitats.

An additional area of concern relating to tenure arrangements for agribusiness companies relates to productive use requirements. A number of countries have adopted legislation or negotiated concession contracts that require companies to make productive use of the land leased (see Table 4.2). Non-compliance with this commitment would entitle government authorities to impose sanctions, including the termination of the concession agreement.[12] These requirements have a clear rationale in terms of discouraging speculative land acquisitions and ensuring that leased land is used productively. However, the requirements can create perverse incentives, as they might make it more difficult for companies to set aside conservation areas even if they are willing to do so. In Indonesia, for example, some palm oil companies that are committed to "zero deforestation" have claimed they have had issues trying to set aside areas of high conservation value and high carbon stock forest due to productive use requirements. Yet, such claims should be treated with some caution, not least because if environmental impact assessment legislation is properly implemented, conditions attached to environmental permits may enable, and in fact require, conservation in specified concession areas.

To sum up, notwithstanding the great diversity of contexts and applicable rules, certain recurring features of national legal frameworks tend to facilitate large-scale land acquisitions for agribusiness investments, both in the countries reviewed and beyond (Alden Wily, 2012; Anseeuw *et al.*, 2012a). Centralized government control, coupled with weak local land rights, means that governmental authorities have extensive discretion in decisions on conversion of forests to industrial agricultural purposes—which can be problematic if decision-making on forest conversions and on the allocation of agribusiness concessions lacks transparency and accountability. Other aspects of tenure arrangements also raise direct concerns about ape conservation, including in relation to the perverse incentives that may be associated with poorly conceived productive use requirements and the overall level of preparedness of tenure arrangements to deal with the issues raised by rapid agribusiness developments in sensitive habitats.

Decision-making on Allocation of Agribusiness Concessions

The aforementioned finding that governments play a central role in land allocations raises a number of important issues about the mechanics of decision-making regarding agribusiness concessions, including the distribution of decision-making authority among different government bodies, and opportunities for public scrutiny and accountability. Indeed, the ways in which decision-making authority is distributed among government agencies, and between different levels of government—local to national—can have important implications for the overall coherence, coordination and effectiveness of government action in addressing the interface between agribusiness investment and ape conservation. By reducing the scope for rent-seeking behavior, transparency and downward accountability can also have important reverberations for the effectiveness of conservation efforts.

All of the national legal frameworks reviewed in this chapter include different sets of laws that potentially play a role in regulating, to different degrees, decision-making on agribusiness concessions in forest areas, with varying degrees of coherence and coordination. The main set of laws is the one that regulates allocation of rights to land (land laws). When the land is forested, laws governing the regime for forest protection, exploitation and conversion (forestry laws) and laws on wildlife protection also play a role. In most countries, land allocation for agribusiness investments appears to be taking place at the intersection of all of these regulations, each of which has a distinct rationale, principles and instruments of implementation, and, in most instances, a dedicated administrative institution.

The interplay between the different sets of legislation—particularly those on land and forestry—is generally a contested matter that has created much confusion in the practice of issuing agricultural concessions, with important repercussions for the interface between agribusiness and ape conservation. One example relates to the national authority responsible for making decisions on land allocations for agribusiness concessions, particularly where forestlands are at stake. Some companies have reportedly used multiple institutional routes to obtain concessions, whereby several institutional authorities in the same countries have signed different contracts. In Cameroon, for example, three different ministries are in charge

of issuing relevant concessions (Nguiffo *et al.*, 2012).

The balance of negotiating power among different ministries is another important issue. The balance tends to vary considerably across countries, in accordance with the national context, political will, contracting processes and other aspects. Broadly speaking, however, ministries and agencies charged with agribusiness development tend to be particularly powerful, especially in comparison to bodies that are charged with environmental protection. The latter, judging from their competencies under national law, tend to be marginalized in decision-making processes; they cannot fulfill their mandate as effectively because they intervene relatively late in the process, their economic resources are more limited and they cannot rely on relevant backing from the highest level of government (Oberndorf, 2006; Alden Wily, 2007). Owing to the dynamic nature and high economic stakes in the agribusiness sector, decision-making generally emphasizes the prerogatives of the executive; even in Liberia, where recent agribusiness concessions have been approved by the parliament,[13] contract negotiations, terms and monitoring have all been driven by the executive.

Indonesia is characterized by a vertical distribution of power through which its regions enjoy autonomous decision-making powers. As the case study below illustrates, this power structure raises a distinct set of issues; in particular, regional governments are incentivized to exploit natural resources for the purpose of fostering economic development, which then might—and, in the case of Indonesia, did—result in fast-paced commercialization of forested areas. All in all, the trend analysis illustrates that in the context of decentralization there is no "golden rule" of vertical power distribution within the state that would foster the responsible use of natural resources and ensure adequate conservation efforts. Instead,

Photo: Malaysia has implemented generations of schemes to promote agribusiness operations, resulting in the spread of plantations across the country. © HUTAN - Kinabatangan Orang-utan Conservation Project

natural resources are clearly highly vulnerable to any changes of power distribution within the state—which is why every internal governance reform has an equal chance of creating positive results or accelerating the pace of habitat conversion.

Finally, another important issue concerning the allocation of agribusiness concessions relates to mechanisms to ensure transparency and accountability in decision-making processes. Transparency can provide an important safeguard against arbitrary or illegal decision-making, as it facilitates public scrutiny and challenges to government action. There have been some important legislative advances in transparency requirements concerning environmental impact assessments (EIAs, as discussed below) and in transparency requirements concerning public revenues, particularly in a number of laws regulating investments in the extractive industries (Arcus Foundation, 2014).

Nevertheless, transparency requirements affecting broader decision-making on agribusiness investments remain limited in most of the countries reviewed. The Liberia Extractive Industries Transparency Initiative Act of 2009, which covers agribusiness and forestry, as well as extractive industries, is one of the few examples of legislation that mandates the disclosure of agribusiness concession agreements.[14] The DRC also provides for some limited transparency through a 2011 decree that requires the publication of forestry contracts (in addition to mining and oil contracts), although it is not clear whether this covers the agribusiness sector and whether contracts are indeed being systematically published (DRC, 2011a). Yet, even if contract disclosure is required, it occurs after key decisions have already been made; moreover, in contexts characterized by high illiteracy rates and significant capacity challenges, disclosure alone is unlikely to make a significant difference

unless it is accompanied by complementary support for civil action.

Overall, patterns in decision-making authority vary considerably across the countries examined, including with respect to the extent of decentralization; transparency and public participation requirements; and the nature of relationships between different agencies of central and local government. Beyond this diversity, however, prevailing legal and institutional contexts point to significant challenges affecting the interface between agribusiness and ape conservation. In particular, there seems to be a general lack of clarity about roles, powers and procedures in allocating agricultural concessions; imbalances of power between government agencies with different mandates; and inadequate arrangements to ensure transparency and public accountability. This situation tends to undermine the coherence, coordination and the effectiveness of government action to pursue ape conservation in the face of agribusiness expansion.

General Provisions on Environmental Protection

The previous sections discuss key trends in ownership, control and decision-making regarding resources that have a direct bearing on facilitating, or regulating, the interface between industrial agriculture and ape conservation. This section considers the nature and effectiveness of mechanisms designed to protect the environment, focusing on generally applicable legislation, and specifically on the obligations with which agribusiness projects need to comply. This section is followed by an exploration of conservation measures put in place to protect ape species and habitats.

All of the countries under review in this study have stand-alone laws that deal exclusively with issues of environmental protection, which, by their very nature, should contribute to the protection of apes and ape habitats.[15] In broad terms, the content of these provisions has become more elaborate and comprehensive over time, and more recent environmental laws tend to include global best practice in their regulatory approach.[16] However, this trend still depends largely on the political environment that prevails in each state; Myanmar, for one, has drawn repeated criticism for adopting a "weak model" of environmental protection in its relatively recent national environmental law (Burma Environmental Working Group, 2011).

The analysis of prevailing trends shows that good environmental laws are usually in place, and that they mandate government authorities to protect the environment, require EIAs for major development projects and include sanction and monitoring mechanisms. Nevertheless, these laws do not necessarily result in more stringent environmental protection on the ground, largely because of significant problems in implementation and enforcement, yet also due to some legal design issues.

One problem that is especially apparent in post-conflict settings, such as the DRC, is the design of environmental provisions that do not match a country's institutional capacity to implement them and thus prove unrealistic (Bwiza, 2013). This is not to say that a "weak model" of environmental protection is preferable; yet, if lawmaking does not fully factor in institutional capacity to enforce legislation on the ground, challenges in implementation and enforcement may prove insurmountable, and legislation will be unlikely to make any difference at the local level. In this respect, environmental regulation runs a serious risk of regulatory failure.

Moreover, some of the most comprehensive laws, with highly ambitious and elaborate environmental goals, only serve as a framework for further action, rather than as an effective institutional apparatus through which sound environmental policies can be readily implemented; such laws are rarely implemented further through secondary legislation. An example of this problem is Cameroon's 1996 Law on Environmental Management, which, as comprehensive as it is, also contains a whole array of provisions that require the government to enact further implementing decrees and regulations—some of which have not yet been adopted, nearly 20 years after the adoption of the primary text (Cameroon, 1996; Fuo and Semie, 2011). Similar regulatory gaps exist in Cambodia and the DRC (De Lopez, 2002; Moutondo, 2008).

Environmental impact assessments—which are probably the most important procedural safeguards—have become a standard tool of environmental protection that potentially promotes ape conservation. Depending on the degree of protection they establish, EIAs might also include a social impact assessment (SIA) and result in an environmental management plan (EMP). The EMP normally identifies measures necessary to protect the environment and comply with applicable legislation.

An EIA is usually required before a governmental authority can issue a license or permission, or grant a contract for certain types of development projects, including significant agribusiness developments. All countries reviewed require some procedure of this sort, with the exception of Myanmar (see Table 4.3). While Myanmar has now established the competency for its Ministry of Environment to regulate these matters and has adopted draft rules concerning EIAs, these rules have not yet been adopted by the ministry and are therefore not yet in force.

There is significant variation among countries with respect to the kind of impact assessment required, including in relation to whether local consultation, public hearings or a full-fledged SIA are mandated; the types of legal instrument that ensure mitigation

> Good environmental laws do not necessarily result in more stringent environmental protection on the ground, largely because of significant problems in implementation and enforcement.

of risks (an area in which EMPs are particularly important); and the range of projects for which this procedure is mandatory (see Table 4.3). Within this diversity, the more stringent procedures do not necessarily result in more effective protection in practice. Instead, mandatory requirements for "heavy" EIAs are often merely disregarded by public officials, and consequently fail to be effective—as has been documented in Cameroon (Fuo and Semie, 2011).

In almost all of the countries reviewed, national legislation requires a degree of transparency in EIA procedures (see Table 4.3). Transparency clauses vary significantly, however. In some countries, the government must simply publish EIA reports that have already been accepted; elsewhere, the government is required to disclose draft reports before approving the EIA, a process that is more likely to allow stakeholders to provide input and influence decision-making. Some countries also require companies to engage in public participation while preparing an EIA, which potentially allows affected people to voice their concerns. By its very nature, transparency regulation is a process of opening up decision-making to external scrutiny and allowing civil society to monitor developments—a precondition for advances in any area. Yet much remains to be done to translate these openings into real change.

The value of the law rests primarily in its practical application. This study thus examines to what extent countries under review have established legal mechanisms to promote proper implementation, including through the allocation of responsibilities and the stipulation of procedures for monitoring compliance with environmental standards—and for dealing with non-compliance.

All of the countries considered in this study have established some process for monitoring compliance with environmental standards. In addition, national environmental laws tend to designate an institution—or

several of them, in the case of decentralized decision-making[17]—that is responsible for this process (see Table 4.3). In practice, monitoring compliance requires significant resources and strong institutional capacities, particularly if agribusiness concessions cover very large areas in remote parts of the country. Many observers have noted the lack of human, financial and technical resources in forest administrations—in particular in ape range states in West and Central Africa (Nguiffo et al., 2012). This lack is known to affect crucial matters such as the demarcation of boundaries between protected and convertible forest areas, and institutional capacity to gather evidence of environmental non-compliance (Oates et al., 2007).

By and large, environmental legislation in the eight ape range states under review tends to satisfy the requirements of good environmental regulations. With respect to EIAs, the laws seem to reflect a general trend toward more transparency and public participation, as evidenced to varying degrees across the countries. Tighter transparency requirements do not mean that decisions are necessarily made transparently in practice; however, they do provide benchmarks on how companies and officials should behave. As noted above, it is important to recognize that more stringent laws are not always more effective in practice. In the worst cases, stringent laws can create an impression of environmental commitment, despite the absence of the institutional apparatus necessary to back it up.

Protected Areas and Species

All countries under review have adopted legislation that allows for the creation of protected areas (Morgera, 2010); Table 4.4 reveals the percentage of protected areas in national territory (land) in all eight states. This legislation is primarily embodied in laws relating to environmental protection,

> " The value of the law rests primarily in its practical application. "

TABLE 4.3

Legal Aspects of Environmental Impact Assessments

Instrument		Cambodia*	Cameroon	DRC	Gabon	Indonesia	Liberia	Malaysia***	Myanmar****
Types of rules that govern EIAs									
Is the EIA procedure required by primary legislation (enacted by the highest authority within the state)?		Yes	Yes	Yes	Yes	Yes	Yes	Yes	No
Is the size and type of project that must undergo EIA procedures set out in primary legislation?		No	No	Yes	Yes	Yes	No	Yes	No
Are there official guidelines for implementing primary legislation that governs EIAs?		Yes	Yes	No**	No	Yes	No	Yes	No
Scope of obligation									
Is an SIA a mandatory part of the EIA?		Yes	Yes	Yes	No	No	Yes	No	n/a
Is an EMP a mandatory part of the EIA?		Yes	Yes	Yes	No	Yes	Yes	Yes	n/a
Are there explicit requirements with regard to the specific content of the EIA?		Yes	Yes	No	No	Yes	Yes	Yes	n/a
Is an authoritative institution charged with assessing the quality and content of the EIA before it is accepted?		Yes	Yes	No	No	Yes	Yes	Yes	n/a
Is there a requirement for a competent authority to consent to the measures set out in the EIA before the project can be implemented?		Yes	Yes	No	Yes	Yes	Yes	Yes	n/a
Transparency									
Is there a requirement to inform the public about the intention to initiate the EIA?		No	No	Yes	No	Yes	Yes	No	n/a
Is there a requirement to hold public consultations during the preparation of the EIA?		No	Yes	No	No	Yes	Yes	No	n/a

although laws dealing specifically with protected areas do exist. Other legislation may also be relevant, particularly forest laws, which may include provisions that deal with the zoning of forest resources for both productive and conservation purposes. Despite the close interrelationship between forest codes and laws regulating protected areas, explicit cross-referencing between them is frequently missing,[18] which generally makes it difficult to assess whether or not they overlap, and if so, to what extent (Oberndorf, 2006).

The most important practical implication of such overlap between environmental and forest legislation may be that various institutions implement these laws, which means that it might not be entirely clear which agency is ultimately responsible for effective results on the ground. Moreover, it has been noted with regard to several national frameworks that the agencies charged with conservation efforts tend to be relatively weak in terms of their institutional capacity—and hence not able to enforce stringent protection regimes over

TABLE 4.3

Continued

Instrument	Cambodia*	Cameroon	DRC	Gabon	Indonesia	Liberia	Malaysia***	Myanmar****
Is there a requirement to hold consultations with affected communities during the preparation of the EIA?	No	Yes	Yes	No	Yes	Yes	Yes	n/a
Is there a requirement to publish the EIA and EMP?	No	No	No	No	Yes	Yes	Yes	n/a
Implementation and enforcement								
Is there an explicit requirement for the authorities to monitor the implementation of the EIA?	Yes	Yes	No	Yes	Yes	Yes	Yes	n/a
Does the law explicitly state that failure to implement the EMP (or other operational parts of the EIA) should result in termination of the concession?	No	No	No	No	Yes	No	No	n/a
Are there specific sanctions for state officials who fail to implement requirements relating to the EIA?	Yes	No	No	No	Yes	No	No	n/a
Are there specific sanctions for companies that fail to implement requirements relating to the EIA?	Yes	Yes	No	No	Yes	Yes	Yes	n/a

Notes: * The assessment is based on the Law on Environmental Protection and Natural Resource Management, its implementing sub-decree on the EIA process and Prakas on General Guidelines for Initial and Final Environmental Impact Assessment Reports (Cambodia, 1996, 1999, 2009). At the time of writing, the new draft law on EIAs was in the process of being adopted.

** No general guidelines are applicable to all sectors (including agriculture); however, there are some sector-related guidelines, such as those that are applicable to mining projects in the DRC.

*** The information on Malaysia reflects a focus on the Sabah region, one of the two autonomous regions that has full competency to make decisions concerning land and natural resource management (and therefore functions under a distinct set of state regulations), and that also hosts the most extensive ape population in the country.

**** n/a = not applicable. Since EIA procedure is not regulated in Myanmar, questions regarding the relevant scope, transparency, implementation and enforcement cannot be answered.

Sources: Cambodia (1996, 1999, 2002, 2009); Cameroon (1996, 2005, 2011, 2013); DRC (2002, 2006b, 2011b, 2011c, 2011d); Fuo and Semie (2011); Gabon (1993, 2001, 2005, 2007); Indonesia (1999, 2007, 2009, 2010); Kennedy (2011); Liberia (2000, 2002a, 2006, 2009a, 2009c, 2010b); Malaysia (1968b, 1974, 1987, 2000, 2002, 2010); Myanmar (1994, 2012a, 2012b); Syarif (2010); Tieguhong and Betti (2008)

the vast protected areas that they may be overseeing (ICEM, 2003).

National laws on protected areas vary considerably, both within and across countries, including in the degree of protection that is accorded to flora and fauna, and in the conditions under which the status of protected areas can be revoked or changed. This study shows that, generally speaking, national parks are not only subject to the most stringent conservation regimes, but are also designated by the highest authorities of the state.[19] This means that national

parks cannot easily be converted back into production areas—a finding that underscores the need to prevent external interventions in such territories to ensure the protection of wildlife and its habitat.

That said, national parks do not necessarily provide the most effective and sustainable ways of protecting endangered species in the long term. There are long-standing debates about the restrictions on communities that live in national parks or use resources located within park boundaries (Alden Wily, 2012). It is often difficult for state officials to enforce such strict regulations; only one country among those under review—Gabon—has set up the kind of institutional infrastructure through which effective administration of extensive national park territories is feasible (ITTO, 2011).

In many contexts, the density of the population is such that forbidding all forms of human activity in protected areas cannot be sustained in the long run. Most countries have enabled the creation of other types of protected areas, in which some agricultural, hunting and even logging activities are allowed (Morgera and Cirelli, 2009; Morgera, 2010; Morgera and Tsioumani, 2010). Less stringent regulations apply to such areas, whose protected status is generally easier to change, partly depending on the state of the forest. If, for instance, a forest has been overexploited and its conservation value has dropped, it could be "reclassified" as a production area instead.[20] Evidence shows that community forestry can be more effective than conventional protected areas in protecting forests.[21]

Many studies note that protected areas often do not cover the full range of forests where primates live, such that many primates actually live outside these formally protected territories (Arcus Foundation, 2014; Dunn *et al.*, 2014). It therefore becomes important to consider to what extent the individual animals and their species enjoy direct protection under the law—and what kind of protection this entails.

Most of the countries reviewed have passed legislation, often in connection with ratification of the Convention on International Trade in Endangered Species of Wild Fauna and Flora (CITES), placing apes under the highest level of protection accorded to endangered species. While CITES only regulates international trade, and trade in apes is a relatively minor driver of their loss, ratification of CITES can indirectly lead countries to take legislative action at the national level. Indeed, legislation to protect

apes typically prohibits hunting and killing apes, keeping them in captivity, and engaging in any related trading activities (Morgera and Cirelli, 2009; Morgera and Tsioumani, 2010). However, the enforcement of these provisions is often undermined by a number of factors, including corruption, vested interests, inadequate resources and capacities, and the absence of powerful pressure groups, which could otherwise create political incentives for government agencies to enforce applicable norms.

Moreover, national legislation on protected areas and species faces real challenges in tackling the interface between agribusiness investments and ape conservation, as norms that prohibit the killing of apes are of relatively little effectiveness in contexts where the principal threat is in the form of habitat conversion for agribusiness developments. In most of the countries reviewed, there is no explicit prohibition against the clearing of forests outside protected areas (see Table 4.4). In other words, while the killing of individual apes is strictly forbidden,[22] a severe intervention that destroys the habitat on which the survival of apes depends could be entirely legal—as

TABLE 4.4

Protected Areas and Recognition of Apes as Protected Species

	Forests as % of national territory (land)*	Protected areas as % of national territory (land)*	Agricultural land as % of national territory (land)*	Can communal forests be established in protected areas?	Do apes fall under the most stringent protection regime applied to individual species?
Cambodia	55.7	26.2	32.6	Yes	Yes, via adherence to CITES classification
Cameroon	41.2	11.0	20.6	No	Yes, as "Class A" under national law
DRC	67.7	12.0	11.5	Yes	Yes, as "wholly protected game" under secondary legislation
Gabon	85.4	19.9	20.0	No	Yes, as "strictly protected" under secondary legislation
Indonesia	51.4	14.7	31.2	Yes	Yes, as "endangered protected species" under secondary legislation
Liberia	44.3	2.5	28.1	No	Yes, as "protected" under secondary legislation and via adherence to CITES classification
Malaysia	61.7	18.4	23.6	No	Yes, as "totally protected" under provincial law
Myanmar	47.7	7.3	19.3	No**	Yes, as "completely protected" under secondary legislation

long as activities take place outside protected areas and on the basis of prescribed procedures.

An exception to this approach appears in Indonesian legislation, which regulates the protection of endangered species in terms of individual animals as well as their habitat (Indonesia, 1990, art. 6). Unfortunately, these provisions have not yet been fully implemented through subsequent regulations, and therefore their effectiveness in practice cannot be tested.

Most of the countries under review have adopted legislation that creates protected areas and provides direct protection of ape species. However, the implementation and enforcement of such norms are often undermined by a lack of institutional capacities, ambiguities concerning institutional responsibilities, and limited human, financial and technical resources. Moreover, legislation that protects species is poorly suited to deal with the interface between industrial agriculture and ape conservation since the main threat to ape conservation in an agribusiness context stems from ape habitat destruction rather than the killing of individual animals.

TABLE 4.4

Continued

What protection is granted to apes (beyond prohibition of illegal trade and export as stipulated in CITES)?	Are there protection mechanisms beyond the focus on individual animals and outside protected areas?
Prohibition of hunting	No
Prohibition of hunting	No
Prohibition of hunting; it is justifiable to kill an animal only if it threatens a person's life or property	No
Prohibition of hunting and keeping in captivity; it is justifiable to kill an animal only in defense of human life, livestock or crops	No
Prohibition of catching, injuring, killing, keeping in captivity, possessing and transporting animals in live and dead condition; it is justifiable to kill or injure an animal only if it endangers human life	Yes, the conservation of endangered species is also regulated "ex situ," and the law requires protection of "life support systems" by both holders of land rights and institutions administering the land
Prohibition of hunting and keeping in captivity; it is justifiable to kill an animal in the process of taking "reasonable measures" to protect human life, livestock or crops	No, although the law requires constant monitoring of endangered species
Possession only with authorization; it is justifiable to kill an animal in the process of taking "reasonable steps" to protect human life, livestock or crops	No
Capture and possession only with authorization; prohibition of hunting	No

Notes:

* The figures reflect 2012 World Bank development indicators based on the following definitions:

Forest area: "land under natural or planted stands of trees of at least 5 meters in situ, whether productive or not, and excludes tree stands in agricultural production systems (for example, in fruit plantations and agroforestry systems) and trees in urban parks and gardens."

Protected areas: "totally or partially protected areas of at least 10 km^2 (1,000 ha) that are designated by national authorities as scientific reserves with limited public access, national parks, natural monuments, nature reserves or wildlife sanctuaries, protected landscapes and areas managed mainly for sustainable use."

Agricultural land: "the share of land area that is arable, under permanent crops, and under permanent pastures. [. . .] Permanent pasture is land used for five or more years for forage, including natural and cultivated crops."

** There is no legal mechanism that recognizes or enables communal forests in Myanmar.

Sources:

indicators: World Bank (n.d.-b);

definitions: World Bank (n.d.-a, n.d.-c, n.d.-e);

legislation: Alden Wily (2007, 2012); Cambodia (1993b, 1994, 1996, 2002, 2003); Cameroon (1978, 1994, 1995a, 1995b, 1996); CITES (1973); Cotula and Mayers (2009); DRC (1969, 1975, 1982, 2000, 2002, 2006a, 2011d); Dunn *et al.* (2014); Gabon (1987b, 1993, 1994a, 1994b, 2001, 2004, 2007); ICEM (2003); Indonesia (1990, 1999, 2006a, 2009); Liberia (1988, 2002b, 2003, 2006, 2009c); Majid Cooke (2006); Malaysia (1963, 1965b, 1968a, 1968b, 1973, 1980, 1984, 2002, 2008, 2010); Morgera (2010); Morgera and Cirelli (2009); Morgera and Tsioumani (2010); Myanmar (1992, 2012b); Nguiffo and Talla (2010)

Issues of Enforcement and Legal Opportunities to Challenge Decision-making

The issue of implementation and enforcement is a fundamental concern in all areas of environmental protection, including ape conservation. As emphasized in the previous sections, it is not enough to have good laws—they must also be put into practice. Sound environmental practice requires an ongoing effort not only on behalf of the entire state administration, but also on behalf of other stakeholders engaged in conservation and accountability.

In the ape range countries reviewed, legislation typically tackles several enforcement-related issues:

(a) sanctions for environmental damage caused in violation of environmental legislation;

(b) institutional responsibilities to monitor and ensure compliance and to impose the applicable sanctions;

(c) rules that regulate the exercise of public authority in these matters; and

(d) norms empowering citizens and stakeholders to challenge decision-making.

Rules that establish sanctions and enforcement mechanisms can be a part of the general regime of criminal and administrative responsibility and civil liability, that is, a regime set in the constitution or in civil or administrative codes; alternatively, they can be tailored regimes based on legislation that creates specific sanctions for wrongdoing in environmental matters. While general state institutions—such as the police or prosecution services—tend to enforce common rules of responsibility and liability, specialized institutions[23] are often established to monitor compliance and to investigate breaches of environmental law.

With regard to environmental sanctions, there is a noticeable trend in environmental laws to criminalize specific types of environmental damage. Most countries reviewed have introduced criminal provisions that prescribe penalties for illegal forest use or unlicensed exploitation of land. However, only a few countries have explicitly criminalized the failure to comply with some of the key requirements of environmental procedural safeguards; in the DRC, for example, it is illegal to provide misleading information in the preparation of an EIA (DRC, 2011d, arts 72–73).

Another important issue concerning industrial agriculture is the extent to which environmental violations can justify the termination of the agribusiness concession. In most of the countries reviewed, national law does not unequivocally empower the government to terminate a concession if environmental obligations are not complied with. There are exceptions—such as provisions in Cambodia's Law on Forestry that allow the government to terminate logging contracts for environmental violations (Cambodia, 2002, arts 17, 88)—but they do not seem to apply to agribusiness. A lack of explicit provisions effectively deprives administrative agencies committed to conservation of important legal backing. Moreover, investors are less likely to challenge government action to revoke permits or terminate contracts if sanction clauses are integrated in legislation. Yet, even if countries have adopted provisions allowing termination, they do not necessarily apply them.

The discussion in the previous sections highlights that many problems are rooted not in the formulation of laws, but in institutional capacity challenges or political economy considerations that affect the political and administrative will to apply the law. An important enforcement issue thus concerns the extent to which legislation establishes mechanisms to review and sanction the exercise of government powers in relation to compliance with procedural requirements or the outcome of decision-making processes. In this regard, the trend analysis reveals gaps in accountability and sanction mechanisms. While enforcement norms often establish administrative and criminal sanctions for malpractice by low-level officials, they seldom address abuse of authority by high-level decision-makers. There are important exceptions; for example, the Forestry Code of the DRC explicitly limits the discretionary powers of the minister to issue harvesting concessions—although the application of this provision has never been tested in practice (DRC, 2002, art. 5; Lawson, 2014). Indeed, it is very difficult to hold high-level officials to account, for both legal and political reasons.

A final point that needs to be considered in this review of national frameworks is the availability and nature of legal mechanisms that rights holders can use to foster compliance with legal requirements. In several countries, forestry laws and environmental legislation allow public interest litigation or legal "action on behalf of the community," thereby establishing an opportunity for actors to challenge government action without having to prove they have been directly affected by the decision in question.[24] In Cameroon, where no such explicit clause exists in the relevant laws, a similar outcome has been reached by a court decision, which concluded in 2009 that a local non-governmental organization (NGO) had the right to question the legality of an investment project that did not undergo the necessary EIA procedure (Fuo and Semie, 2011).[25]

In contrast to this positive trend, certain legal arrangements limit access to justice, including in relation to land matters. In Malaysia, for example, farmers who participate in joint venture agreements with agribusiness are required to waive their right of access to courts in relation to the agribusiness venture (Majid Cooke *et al.*, 2012). Similarly, Myanmar's Farmland Law

Protecting Orangutan Habitats on Sumatra, Indonesia, Using Legal Action

This case study focuses on "law in action"—that is, practical experiences that highlight the opportunities and challenges of using legal mechanisms for ape conservation purposes. Based on the experience of taking legal action to protect orangutans on Sumatra, Indonesia, it highlights the advantages and limitations inherent in the use of judicial proceedings.

Indonesia ranks 107 out of 174 countries in the 2014 Corruption Perceptions Index[26] and is well known for the lack of law enforcement within the forestry and plantation sectors. Yet, as this case study shows, enabling conditions have led to partial enforcement of some of Indonesia's environmental laws in the Tripa peat swamp forests of the Leuser Ecosystem in Sumatra's Aceh province (see Figure 4.1).

To date, Indonesia has sanctioned one oil palm company by revoking its plantation permit, sentencing its owner and manager to jail terms, and imposing a multi-million dollar fine. Meanwhile, seven civil and criminal cases are ongoing or in preparation against four other palm oil companies operating in Tripa's peat swamps. These cases are rare examples of how—despite the odds—the law can be used effectively to challenge, and potentially halt or even reverse, decisions leading to the destruction of ape habitat in Indonesia. Understanding these early successes and the conditions that enabled them is fundamental to any efforts at replication elsewhere.

FIGURE 4.1

The Tripa Peat Swamp Forests, within the Leuser Ecosystem in Aceh Province, Sumatra, Indonesia

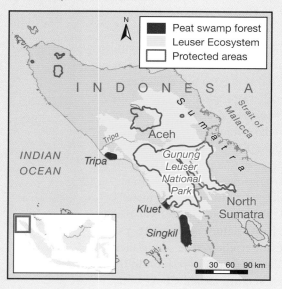

The enabling conditions for these cases of law enforcement fall into three main categories:

- accurate documentation of illegal activities;
- a public campaign that demands action from the government; and
- government agencies that are willing to act in response to the documentation of illegal activities.

Background

Along with the two other remaining peat swamp forests in Aceh, namely the Kluet and Singkil swamps, Tripa harbors the highest densities of orangutans recorded anywhere in the world. In the late 1980s Tripa was covered by around 600 km² (60,000 ha) of primary peat swamp forest and was home to at least 3,000 orangutans. At that time, however, it was removed from Indonesia's national forest estate and reclassified as "land for other uses"—commonly known by its Indonesian acronym, APL, which stands for areal penggunaan lain. Beginning in 1990, several major oil palm concessions were progressively awarded, and the companies proceeded to clear forests, drain the peat and plant oil palms. By 1999, about half of the peat swamp forest had been cleared and large tracts of the cleared areas were already planted. Yet then a dramatic increase in hostilities between Aceh's separatist rebels and Indonesia's central government led to a cessation of activities in all of the concessions. During the ensuing few years, the plantations were effectively abandoned and vegetation began recovering naturally until peace was finally restored in 2005, in the aftermath of the December 2004 tsunami.

Plantation activities gradually began to resume in the years following the 2005 Helsinki peace accord between the warring factions and a return to near normalcy in Aceh province. Between mid-2007 and the end of 2009, almost 80 km² (8,000 ha)—or 28% of the remaining forests—were lost, mostly to the concessions of just three companies. Despite considerable lobbying by local communities and environmental groups, no action was taken to stop the burning or land clearing.

By this time, a number of other developments relevant to Tripa's land status had also occurred. Even though it was no longer part of the national forest estate, in 1998, Tripa was included in the newly established Leuser Ecosystem, an area that covers more than 26,000 km² (2.6 million ha) of mostly upland primary forests and that also contains the last remaining lowland forest habitats of any significance in Aceh and North Sumatra. The Leuser Ecosystem is one of the richest expanses of tropical rainforest in Southeast Asia and the only place on earth where the Sumatran elephant, Sumatran rhinoceros, Sumatran tiger and Sumatran orangutan live side by side.

The importance of protecting the Leuser Ecosystem was emphasized in National Law No. 11/2006 on Aceh Governance (Indonesia, 2006b).[27] In Article 150 of this law, the Aceh government was specifically obligated to protect the 80% of the ecosystem that lies within Aceh. The protected status of the Leuser Ecosystem was further strengthened when it was designated a national strategic area (NSA) based on its environmental functions in Government Regulation 26/2008 on the National Spatial Plan, a derivative of National Law No. 26/2007 on Spatial Planning (Indonesia, 2007, 2008).[28]

In May 2011, as a direct result of a US$1 billion pledge by the government of Norway to help Indonesia reduce its carbon emissions from deforestation and degradation, then president Susilo Bambang Yudhoyono signed a moratorium preventing new concessions from being granted in primary forests and peatlands. The moratorium included a map, which the Ministry of Forestry was to revise every six months, the PIPIB or Peta Indikatif Penundaan Izin Baru (map indicating areas for which no new concession permits may be granted for the duration of the moratorium). The first editions of this map included significant tracts of Tripa that had not already been allocated for concessions.

In August 2011, the then governor of Aceh issued a new plantation concession permit for 16 km² (1,600 ha) of previously unallocated peat swamps to a palm oil company. This same area was clearly identified on the PIPIB as "protected peatland." It was also inside the Leuser Ecosystem, which by then was an NSA for environmental functions, within which concessions that damage environmental functions are prohibited.

The Resistance Begins

On these grounds, a group of NGOs spearheaded by Walhi Aceh (an affiliate of Friends of the Earth) filed a legal challenge to the new permit in Aceh's administrative court in November 2011. In April 2012, the court dismissed the challenge, but Walhi Aceh instantly appealed the decision to the high court in Medan, North Sumatra.

Around the same time, a group of local community representatives also filed a complaint against the same permit with Indonesia's National Police in Jakarta, alleging that the new concession was a criminal breach of National Spatial Planning Laws and Aceh's own Governance Law, all of which prevent new concessions from being granted inside the Leuser Ecosystem. This complaint was passed on to the Aceh police force and was taken no further.

While the case was still at the administrative court in Banda Aceh, the palm oil company at the heart of the case continued to clear land, as did four other companies with major oil palm concessions in Tripa. In response, concerned NGOs organized a press conference and prepared a press release that featured dramatic footage of the clearing fires; the issue soon made headlines in the national and international media. During the rest of 2012 and much of 2013, Tripa was in the national news almost daily and international news items were an almost weekly occurrence. Petitions launched by the environmental groups became news items in themselves, as local and national government figures and agencies received numerous demands for intervention. The degree of news coverage helped considerably in focusing public attention on the legal cases and significantly reduced the potential for corruption to interfere in the legal process.

On 30 August 2012, the High Court in Medan ruled in favor of Walhi Aceh and instructed Aceh's new (and current) governor to cancel the permit, which he did on 27 September 2012. The company appealed the decision, taking the case to the Supreme Court in Jakarta on 6 November 2012. Their appeal was rejected on 25 April 2013, the Medan High Court decision was upheld and the concession permit remains cancelled.

Due largely to these privately initiated legal actions and the massive national and international attention focused on the cases via mass and social media, Indonesia's national government began to take notice. In particular, the president's Sustainable Development Unit, known locally as UKP4, set up under the pledge agreement with Norway, dispatched fact-finding investigative teams to the field on several occasions, starting in early 2012. UKP4 lawyers also met with the Aceh provincial government's dedicated Leuser Ecosystem Management Authority and with local NGOs, which provided several years' worth of temporal and spatial information on land clearing and burning activities in Tripa. Teams from UKP4 and Indonesia's Ministry of the Environment then investigated the legality of all the oil palm concession permits in Tripa and cross-checked the NGO reports on illegal activities within each concession, finding them both accurate and verifiable. The teams paid special attention to the large-scale, highly publicized fires raging on most of the concessions at the time and found them in contravention of National Law 32/2009 on the Protection and Management of the Environment, which specifically prohibits the use of fire to clear land and the clearance of peat more than 3 m deep.

These investigations led public authorities to file additional legal cases against all of the major palm oil companies operating in Tripa. They included several civil cases filed by the Ministry of Environment against two of the companies and criminal cases brought by the state against these and two (and eventually three) other companies and some of their key personnel, mostly based on the illegal use of fire to clear land.

Lessons Learned

There are two ways to look at the Tripa case study. The conservation perspective places weight on the fact that Indonesia continues to experience forest clearance and loss of biodiversity. Many observers argue that the Tripa peat swamp forest and its orangutan population were already a lost cause when the area was taken out of the national forest estate in the late 1980s, and certainly by the time large-scale oil palm concessions were being issued in the 1990s. Indeed, there is a widespread perception in Indonesia that large companies and powerful individuals essentially have a free hand to do whatever they want on APL lands, and that it is better to focus conservation efforts on areas with more obvious legal control or protection, such as within the national forest estate and in formal protected areas. By extension, however, this mindset writes off all but the broadest brushstrokes of

spatial planning and environmental management. Laws and regulations that forbid the burning of land, require the maintenance of riparian zones and other environmentally sensitive areas, and protect endangered species should be enforced wherever they are applicable, be it within the forest estate or on APL lands.

The other way to look at the Tripa case is to recognize the capacity to create conditions under which at least some of the abovementioned laws can be enforced. An illegal oil palm concession has been successfully cancelled, a plantation owner and manager have been sentenced to prison terms, their plantation has been handed a multi-million dollar fine and further legal cases are ongoing or in the pipeline. In January 2014, following intense local lobbying, the provincial government began to block the drainage canals created by the company in the cancelled concession area; plans are also in place for a large-scale swamp forest restoration program. While the rehabilitation of a large, significant area of the Tripa peat swamp forests will take many years, legal precedents have been set and some first successes have been achieved.

As noted earlier, three main factors have contributed to these successes. The first is precise, accurate and verifiable data collection and reporting on variables such as peat depth, hotspots (fires), deforestation and environmental infractions. This documentation has allowed for the development of strong, clear legal cases against the companies based on largely indisputable evidence.

The second key enabling factor has been the successful use of this information by a consortium of many actors, including environmental, social and human rights NGOs and local community members, to publicize the issues. This joint effort eventually developed into a major national and international campaign that gained and maintained global public interest, putting significant political pressure on key government actors to pursue legal action and helping to minimize opportunities for interference in the legal process.

The third main enabling factor is the presence of a government agency (or agencies) with the political will to take action. In this case, the now defunct UKP4, the Ministry of Environment and the Public Prosecution Service took the wealth of evidence and data on environmental wrongdoing and—under public scrutiny and pressure—used it to prepare and prosecute cases.

Arguably, this third factor—namely the presence of government agencies that are willing to enforce environmental laws—is the most crucial. While communities and NGOs can file class action suits and administrative cases, only the Public Prosecution Service can argue criminal cases in Indonesian court. Donors interested in promoting better environmental law enforcement in Indonesia would do well to direct results-based support toward the legal arm of the Ministry of the Environment and Forestry and the Public Prosecution Service.

While current environmental legislation in Indonesia is not perfect, it does provide an adequate foundation for improving environmental management in the country. This will not happen overnight, but if further efforts are made to establish legal precedents, jail and fine senior offenders and sanction concessionaires, it should be possible to turn the tide.

effectively blocks access to courts by those who wish to challenge decisions made under that law (Oberndorf, 2012).

Commentators have argued that the general process of judicial review would normally allow for legal challenges to environmentally unsound acts, even if specialized laws are silent about this possibility (Oberndorf, 2006, 2012). Nevertheless, few court cases have involved challenges to government decisions that potentially harm the environment. Multiple factors may help to explain this situation, including the fact that local communities are not normally recognized as legal persons; costly and inaccessible procedures; inadequate institutional capacity in government and civil society; and the limited independence and impartiality of the judiciary—as well as the resulting lack of faith in the court system. As described in Case Study 4.1, however, environmental litigation is not unheard of, at least in some of the covered countries, and one important task is to assess the effectiveness of legal action and understand the conditions that make it possible.

Conclusion

This chapter has explored the legal frameworks that regulate the interface between industrial agriculture and ape conservation. It has drawn on an analysis of trends in eight ape range states—including four in Central and West Africa, and four in Southeast Asia. It has also presented a case study that illustrates both the challenges affecting those legal frameworks in practice, and the opportunities that are being pursued to harness the law for ape conservation.

Overall, the analysis reveals multiple issues in the design of applicable laws and their operation in practice. There is an inherent tension between industrial agriculture and ape conservation, as goals and beneficiaries differ significantly. Legal rules, and

the institutions mandated to apply them, provide a basis for managing this tension. The approaches pursued in different countries vary depending on the institutional structures of the states, the laws that govern them and the division of competencies in decision-making. In most cases, such approaches have led to unsatisfactory solutions that not only fail to resolve existing tensions, but also result in the significant loss of apes and ape habitat.

A common characteristic across the countries under review is the concentration of power in state institutions. This aspect is primarily due to the fact that land and forest ownership in most of these countries is predominantly public, while collective land and resource rights based on customary laws are not sufficiently strong to protect communities. Concentration of power is also linked to the extensive prerogatives of the executive, and the limited opportunities for democratic scrutiny through parliament, public participation and other deliberative and accountability mechanisms. This legal context facilitates very large land deals that fly in the face of social and environmental concerns.

Similarly, shortcomings in the articulation between land and forest legislation and decision-making create spaces for abuse by governments and companies, while productive use requirements can create perverse incentives and unintended consequences for ape conservation. World-class environmental legislation may be designed in ways that are difficult to implement, particularly in resource-constrained countries. And legislation aimed at protecting individual species provides few, if any, remedies to address the destruction of ape habitats, which industrial agriculture has exacerbated. In other words, the design of legal frameworks, not just their implementation, matters a great deal in tackling the interface between industrial agriculture and ape conservation.

At the same time, the agribusiness–conservation interface is also affected by gaps

Photo: Public authorities filed legal cases against the major palm oil companies operating in Tripa, mostly based on the illegal use of fire to clear land.
© Ian Singleton, SOCP

in the capacity of government institutions to implement and enforce legislation, by political economy considerations affecting incentives for government agencies to apply and enforce legislation, and by uncoordinated government or legislative action that creates legal uncertainty capable of undermining conservation efforts. In these contexts, mechanisms to ensure transparency, public scrutiny and accountability become crucial in advancing ape conservation.

Overall, there is an urgent need to strengthen both procedural and substantive safeguards—in terms of their design and their implementation—to ensure that ape conservation considerations are properly factored into decision-making about development pathways, including in relation to industrial agriculture. Procedural safeguards include not only impact assessment studies, such as project-specific EIAs and SIAs, but also strategic environmental assessments for macro planning decisions, and mechanisms to translate findings of these impact assessments into operational risk-mitigation tools. Substantive safeguards are designed to strengthen local rights to land and resources, which would make it more difficult for governments to allocate very large areas of land; they also involve the rethinking of approaches for the protection of apes in contexts where the main threat is not to individual apes as a protected species, but to their habitat. The case study from Aceh, Indonesia, highlights that some of the more promising enforcement mechanisms may come not from legislation that specifically protects apes from killing or hunting, but from forest fire regulations or public moratoria that indirectly protect ape habitats.

The case study also suggests that three specific factors can help to promote better law enforcement, namely accurate documentation of illegal activities; public campaigns that call on action from the government; and government agencies that are willing to

act on the documentation of illegal activities. The case study shows that in contexts of limited enforcement and widespread impunity, effective action for ape conservation is possible and can deliver some tangible results.

Ultimately, the country reviews highlight the pressing need to develop regulatory and enforcement strategies that can stem a tide underpinned by strong economic interests. This task requires not only imaginative solutions, but also political action and alliances among multiple stakeholders to give real leverage to legal arrangements.

> " Ultimately, the country reviews highlight the pressing need to develop regulatory and enforcement strategies that can stem a tide underpinned by strong economic interests. "

Acknowledgments

Principal authors: Lorenzo Cotula, Giedre Jokubauskaite and Philippine Sutz, all with the International Institute for Environment and Development (IIED), and Ian Singleton, with the Sumatran Orangutan Conservation Programme (SOCP)

Case study 4.1: Ian Singleton, with SOCP

Reviewers: Sam Lawson, Elisa Morgera, Nancy Lee Peluso and Denis Ruysschaert

Endnotes

1   For example, Myanmar is debating a new National Land Use Policy, which, if adopted, would lead to reform of land legislation; see Myanmar (2014).

2   See Cambodia (1993a, art. 58); DRC (2006c, art. 9); Indonesia (1945, art. 33); Liberia (1984, art. 7); Malaysia (1957, art. 76; pt. IV, ch. 4); and Myanmar (2008, art. 37).

3   See DRC (2006c, art. 9) and Myanmar (2008, art. 37).

4   For relevant regulatory instruments, see Cameroon (1974, 1994); see also Cotula and Mayers (2009). In Gabon, the land tenure regime is set out in a range of decrees, while Gabon (2001) regulates forestry; see also Alden Wily (2012).

5   The countries that do not allow private land ownership are Myanmar (Oberndorf, 2012) and the DRC (USAID, 2010a).

6   This observation applies to the ownership of land; private ownership of forests is explicitly allowed only in Cambodia (Oberndorf, 2006), Cameroon (USAID, 2011) and Liberia (USAID, 2010b).

7   The relevant laws are Cameroon (1974, art. 16) and DRC (2011c, arts 16–25).

8   For relevant regulations, see Gabon (1967, 1987a); Indonesia (1999, arts 5, 67); Liberia (1904, 1956); Malaysia (1930, 1965a); and Sarawak (1958).

9   Cameroon (1974) is one example.

10   For instance, it has been noted that communities in Myanmar are required to harvest certain valuable plant species in the forest. While this approach makes the forests better suited for commercial purposes in the long run, such "productive use" is of little benefit to the community, which perceives it as a "price" for securing their land tenure (Burma Environmental Working Group, 2011). Similar productive use requirements feature in relevant legislation in Cambodia, the DRC and Indonesia (Indonesia, 1960; Cambodia, 2002; DRC, 2011c).

11   The examples refer to Gabon (1961, art. 1) and Indonesia (1999, art. 4).

12   Concession contracts from Liberia and Cameroon, reviewed by the authors.

13   See Liberia Extractive Industries Transparency Initiative (LEITI n.d.).

14   See, in particular, Liberia (2009a, art. 5.4).

15   The two most recently adopted stand-alone general laws on environmental protection are the DRC's Law on Basic Principles of Environmental Protection of 2011 and Myanmar's Environmental Conservation Law of 2012 (DRC, 2011d; Myanmar, 2012b).

16   Indonesia (2009) is an example of the inclusion of "best practice." For a thorough overview, see Syarif (2010).

17   Malaysia, which is a federal state, has transferred much of the competency on these matters to its autonomous states; in contrast, Indonesia has drawn up separate EIA processes for each of its autonomous regions. See Indonesia (1945, 1960, 1999, 2009); Malaysia (1930, 1957, 1965a, 1968a, 1968b, 1980, 1984, 2002); and Syarif (2010).

18   For instance, the DRC's Law on Basic Principles of Environmental Protection of 2011 makes no reference to the areas set out in the Forest Code of 2002, nor does it explicitly state how areas designated under the Protected Areas Decree of 2008 link back to the protected forest zones regulated under the forest legislation (DRC, 2002, 2008b, 2011d).

19   The following countries clearly single out national parks as separate areas that require the highest level of conservation, and therefore particular procedures for their designation: Cameroon, where parks are established by a decree of the prime minister (Tieguhong and Betti, 2008); Gabon, where all national parks are designated or changed by law based on the National Parks Law (Gabon, 2007, art. 4); Indonesia, where changes of "significant impact, scope and strategic value" can be made by the House of Representatives based on the National Law on Forestry (Indonesia, 1999, art. 19); and Liberia, where they are established by recommendation of the Forest Development Authority,

through the declaration of the president, and adopted by the legislature, based on the National Forestry Reform Law (Liberia, 2006, ss. 9.2–9.5).

20   Examples of this sort of decision-making procedure are the rules on forest zoning set out in Cambodia's Law on Forestry of 2002, which specifies that the physical condition of a forest is the sole factor that determines to which zone— production or conservation—the area belongs (Cambodia, 2002, art. 12), and Indonesia, where the decision is based on the outcome of "integrated research," as stipulated in the Regulation on Procedure for Changing Function of the Forest Zone (Indonesia, 2010).

21   See Stevens *et al.* (2014).

22   Exceptions apply in rare circumstances, when apes are perceived to threaten human life or property; see Table 4.4.

23   There are some exceptions; in Indonesia, for example, the EMA clearly mandates general institutions to monitor environmental compliance (Indonesia, 2009).

24   See, for example, DRC (2002, art. 134); Gabon (2007, art. 72); Indonesia (2009, arts 91–93); and Liberia (2006, s. 20.10).

25   The case was *Foundation for Environment v. China Road and Bridge Corporation*; for an extensive analysis, see Fuo and Semie (2011).

26   See Transparency International (2014).

27   National Law No. 11 was essentially the Aceh Special Autonomy Law required in the 2005 Helsinki peace agreement.

28   The National Law No. 26/2007 on Spatial Planning is part of the ongoing reversal of the decentralization trend that occurred in the years following the fall of President Soeharto (apparently his preferred spelling, "Suharto" is more commonly used in the international English-language media) in 1998, under which wide powers to allocate and grant permits to use land were devolved to the provincial and especially to the district level. Recent legislation, such as the abovementioned Law No. 26, has increasingly required local governments to conform to national guidelines on land use allocation and permits, even in areas with special autonomy, such as Aceh. National legislation such as the ban on the use of fire for land clearing, the ban on the conversion of deep peat, the requirement to maintain riparian buffers in plantations and other concessions, the criteria for determining areas requiring environmental protection (including national strategic areas for this purpose) and national conservation legislation protecting species and habitats should now be universally followed. While some confusion and apparent contradictions remain in the legislation and regulation of different sectors, there is no doubt that today's wealth of legislation can be employed to enforce better environmental practice in Indonesia.

Photo: Two countries alone account for 85% of the global palm oil production: Indonesia (54%) and Malaysia (31%). Riau, Indonesia. © Kemal Jufri/Greenpeace

CHAPTER 5

From Process to Impact of a Voluntary Standard: The Round-table on Sustainable Palm Oil

Introduction

Industrial agricultural production in the tropics is known to have adverse social and environmental impacts (CBD, 2010). Firms —especially the ones exposed to consumer preference, such as retailers, processors and consumer goods manufacturers—are increasingly responding to these concerns. Nations in the tropics have established comprehensive political, legal and institutional frameworks to conserve biodiversity, including additional protections for great apes and gibbons; however, they continue to face challenges with respect to fulfilling their obligations under international environmental treaties such as the Convention on International Trade in Endangered Species (CITES), the Convention on the Conservation of Migratory Species, the Convention on Biological Diversity, the Convention on Wetlands of International Importance (Ramsar Convention) and the World Heritage Convention (Adams, 2004; Ruysschaert, 2013). Furthermore, as a majority of agricultural development occurs on remote forest frontiers, the enforcement of compliance tends to be poor.

Over the past ten years, firms and nongovernmental organizations (NGOs) have responded by pushing for global sustainable standards for a range of agricultural commodities—with the aim of transforming global markets towards sustainability. One result has been the establishment of a number of roundtables that include private stakeholders of a supply chain, such as the Roundtable on Sustainable Palm Oil (RSPO), the Roundtable on Responsible Soy, the Better Sugar Cane Initiative, the Better Cotton Initiative, the Roundtable on Sustainable Biomaterials (for agro-fuels) and the Sustainable Natural Rubber Initiative. The global standards promoted by these roundtables are complemented by the work of various organizations with specific social or environmental focuses. One of them, the Rainforest Alliance—which was established in 1987 and today counts 35,000 members—works with growers of commodities such as cocoa, coffee, palm oil and tea to conserve natural resources and ensure the long-term economic health of communities.

The most important voluntary standard in relation to great apes and gibbons, and perhaps for tropical biodiversity generally, is currently the palm oil standard governed by the RSPO. Palm oil accounts for about 40% of the global supply of vegetable oil (approximately 70 billion tons per year)— 36% from the fruit of the palm and 4% from the palm kernel, the seed. Oil palm is grown in 27 tropical rainforest countries, but two alone account for 85% of the global palm oil production: Indonesia (54%) and Malaysia (31%). Palm oil demand continues to rise at rates of more than 6% per year (USDA, 2015).

> In Asian contexts, great ape habitats are considered a part of agricultural landscapes, as opposed to landscapes that are being negatively affected by agriculture.

Oil palm grows mainly in lowland humid areas (up to 1,000 m), which also serve as the natural habitats of most great apes and gibbons in Asia and Africa (Wich et al., 2011, 2014). In Southeast Asia, there is direct competition between land use allocation for agricultural expansion and forest conservation, which also covers orangutans and gibbons (Fitzherbert et al., 2008). Widespread oil palm expansion is considered the most significant threat to apes, especially the Sumatran orangutan, far outweighing other dangers such as hunting, live animal trade and diseases (Wich et al., 2011).

This chapter explores in detail how the RSPO approaches the daunting task of effectively protecting biodiversity, especially apes and gibbons, considering the huge demand for agricultural expansion for oil palm cultivation.

The key findings include:

- In Asian contexts, great ape habitats are considered a part of agricultural landscapes, as opposed to landscapes that are being negatively affected by agriculture. A similar trend is being observed in Africa, raising questions about long-term ecological viability, especially in view of the absence of effective land use planning at the national level.

- Certified sustainable palm oil (CSPO) represents a mere 20% of global palm oil production; only half of it is sold with the CSPO label, which commands premium pricing. The remainder is sold as conventional oil without any premium, reportedly due to insufficient demand for sustainable oil, largely because only Western countries purchase CSPO and there is a lack of confidence in the certification process.

- The RSPO process involves a wide range of private stakeholders along the supply chain and follows key democratic principles, including participation, inclusivity and consensus. As a consequence, the process of reaching agreements that strengthen social and environmental indicators tends to be slow.

■ Despite the implementation of the RSPO guidance document—the Principles and Criteria for Sustainable Palm Oil Production—efforts to protect biodiversity are not necessarily effective, due to a number of factors. In particular, only a small number of growers are members of the RSPO and undertake certification; the guidance leaves room for interpretation, which allows growers to reduce conservation areas; provisions do not apply to non-members, meaning that they are free to clear-cut forests that the RSPO has earmarked for conservation; not all local actors, smallholders or small-scale producers are included in the RSPO; and, in certain contexts, state regulations negate RSPO agreements.

■ After ten years of existence, the RSPO has acknowledged internal structural weaknesses that have kept it from preventing habitat destruction and securing ecologically viable conservation areas; accordingly, it has shifted its focus to raise global demand for CSPO and to enhance the credibility of the CSPO certification process, primarily by improving traceability and transparency across the entire supply chain, as well as by promoting RSPO+, which provides additional social and environmental safeguards.

■ The RSPO continues to face major challenges in identifying effective ways to factor local, socioecological contexts into its approach.

The chapter is split into three main sections. The first describes the RSPO: its history, architecture and operation as a democratic institution with a global vision. The second presents details on the challenges the RSPO faces in its efforts to achieve impact. The final section discusses the RSPO's decision to shift its emphasis toward transparency and traceability across the entire supply chain in order to achieve the desired impacts on the ground. This chapter also features two case studies on how two leading agribusinesses—Wilmar and Olam—interpret and implement RSPO principles and criteria.

Launching an Institution with a Global Vision: The Creation, Architecture and Operation of the RSPO

Palm oil is currently the most widely used vegetable oil and demand is expected to continue to rise due to growth in global human populations and improved standards of living. Demand is likely to increase for food and non-food uses, including biofuel (Vis *et al.*, 2012). Oil palm is the most efficient crop with which to produce vegetable oil (USDA, 2015). It thrives in tropical climates, which is also where some of the most biologically diverse ecosystems on earth are found (Fitzherbert *et al.*, 2008).

Traditionally, oil palm cultivation took place in palm groves and as part of mixed farms in Africa; it originated in the humid tropical forests along the Gulf of Guinea in West and Central Africa. It was brought to Asia in 1848, and the first large plantations were planted in Sumatra in 1911 (Corley and Tinker, 2003). The industry developed in Indonesia and Malaysia, where significant improvements were made in plant material and management practices, enabling crop production at significant economies of scale. Although African-grown palm oil still supplies much of the domestic and regional demand in some areas (see Chapter 3), most countries are now importing the oil from Asia, with Malaysia and Indonesia dominating the world supply (USDA, 2015).

> " Widespread oil palm expansion is considered the most significant threat to apes, especially the Sumatran orangutan. "

The RSPO was initiated in 2001 by Migros, the largest consumer goods manufacturer and retailer in Switzerland, and facilitated by the World Wildlife Fund (WWF). It was created after a group of European retailers, processors and consumer goods manufacturers became increasingly worried about their public image in connection with news about deforestation in Southeast Asia; beginning in 1997, the international media had begun to report on large-scale forest fires that were producing extensive smoke and haze (Ruysschaert, 2013). The Swiss public was particularly concerned as Bruno Manser, a national activist who had led an international campaign highlighting rainforest destruction in Malaysia, disappeared in those forests in 2000 (BMF, n.d.). In addition, a number of downstream firms are based in the Netherlands, Switzerland and the United Kingdom, which also host the headquarters of some of the most powerful conservation NGOs, such as Friends of the Earth, Greenpeace and WWF. Firms therefore sought both to protect their reputation and to secure their long-term supply by seeking partnerships with the environmental sector (de Man, 2002).

The European firms secured the participation of some of the world's biggest palm oil producers and traders, especially in Malaysia, as well as the Malaysian Palm Oil Association and the Indonesian Palm Oil Association. These stakeholders and some key NGOs, such as WWF and Oxfam Novib, then established the RSPO as a yearly roundtable in 2003, and as an association with about 50 members the following year (RSPO, 2004a). RSPO membership has steadily grown, reaching approximately 1,100 ordinary members as of February 2015 (RSPO, n.d.-d). The members are divided into seven categories: oil palm growers; palm oil processors; consumer goods manufacturers; environmental NGOs; social NGOs; banks and investors; and retailers.

RSPO Principles and Criteria

In 2011, the RSPO adopted a global vision to "transform markets to make sustainable palm oil the norm"; however, its basic objective is more humble, namely promoting the growth and use of sustainable palm oil (RSPO, 2004b, n.d.-e). While there is no agreed definition of sustainability, the results are assumed from the application of the following eight principles:

1. commitment to transparency;

2. compliance with applicable laws and regulations;

3. commitment to long-term economic and financial viability;

4. use of appropriate best practices by growers and millers;

5. environmental responsibility and conservation of both natural resources and biodiversity;

6. responsible consideration of employees and of individuals and communities affected by growers and mills;

7. responsible development of new plantings; and

8. commitment to continuous improvement in key areas of activity (RSPO, 2013b).

These principles, with their associated criteria and indicators, constitute a detailed guidance document—the Principles and

Criteria for the Production of Sustainable Palm Oil, which is also known as the P&C, the RSPO standard or the RSPO agreements. The document was approved at the RSPO General Assembly (GA) of 2007, after a two-year trial period. Further refinement during a round of negotiations in 2012–3 strengthened its environmental criteria and indicators. The next round of negotiations is expected to review this document after another five years (RSPO, 2013b). In this context, sustainability can be understood as a working concept to be improved over time, as each stakeholder category defends its own interests while all strive to advance together.

Following the RSPO GA approval of the guidance document in 2007, the RSPO introduced CSPO to the market in 2008. Certification enables downstream firms to label the final branded product with a distinctive CSPO trademark. Certification involves a two-step process in which the oil palm plantations and the mills—both of which are generally operated by large-scale producers—must be RSPO-certified. Growers are certified once an RSPO assessor has checked that they successfully implemented the principles and criteria of the guidance document in establishing and then managing their plantations.

The implementation of the detailed criteria and indicators associated with Principles 5 and 7 in particular ensures that RSPO certification contributes to the conservation of biodiversity. Principle 5 deals explicitly with biodiversity conservation, requiring the grower to conserve species and habitats and to control hunting. Individual ape species are not mentioned, but they are included in the more general wording, which stipulates that "rare, threatened or endangered species [. . .] shall be identified and [. . .] maintained and/or enhanced" (RSPO, 2013b, p. 25).

Principle 7 deals with new plantings—the stage at which there is a potential impact on ape habitats. It specifies that, as of November 2005, new plantings cannot replace primary forest or high conservation value (HCV) areas, which are particularly important to apes (RSPO, 2013b). For new plantation developments, planters must also comply with the RSPO New Planting Procedure, which requires independent environmental and social impact assessments (ESIAs) and HCV assessments. The latter have to be conducted by assessors who are approved by the HCV Resource Network, a group of organizations and certification bodies (HCV Resource Network, n.d.). These assessments must consider the presence and status of primary forests, HCV areas, peatlands and land owned by local people; they must also be posted alongside relevant management plans on the RSPO website for a 30-day public consultation period. The RSPO considers comments within this period and any serious or sustained objections must be resolved before field operations commence (RSPO, n.d.-c).

RSPO Architecture

Over time, the RSPO developed into an institution composed of three main bodies:

- the GA;
- the Board of Governors; and
- the Secretariat.

The RSPO GA is the main body and meets each November. Every ordinary member may present resolutions to advance its agenda and may cast one vote; GA endorsement requires a simple majority. In practice, three broad groups can be distinguished in the area of conservation: environmental NGOs, which present draft resolutions with a view to enhancing implementation of the guidance document to realize conservation gains, especially for ape habitat conservation, as discussed below; growers, who are often opposed to such resolutions due to the direct economic cost of implementing them; and downstream firms, which demand CSPO, are indifferent to production requirements and do not bear the direct costs associated with implementing the resolutions (Ruysschaert and Salles, 2014).

In practice, the environmental NGOs get support from most of the downstream firms that form the bulk (close to 80%) of RSPO members and therefore control the GA. As a result, their resolutions usually pass despite the growers' opposition and the underrepresentation of environmental NGOs, which account for less than 3% of the RSPO members (RSPO, n.d.-d).

Two of these resolutions have contributed to ape conservation by according enhanced protected status to two specific ape habitats, thereby preventing RSPO members from converting those forests into plantations. The first of these, presented by the PanEco Foundation at the GA in 2008, concerned "the primary rainforests of Tripa"—600 km² (60,000 ha) of peat swamp forest on the coast of Aceh, Sumatra. Tripa is an integral part of the world-famous Leuser Ecosystem, which is known for harboring the highest densities of orangutans globally. The second resolution, introduced by the Sumatran Orangutan Society at the GA in 2009, related to the "Bukit Tigapuluh Ecosystem," an orangutan reintroduction area on Sumatra.

Other regulations have affected ape conservation indirectly. The New Planting Procedure, which was proposed by WWF at the 2008 GA, requires growers to conduct a transparent public consultation for new permits on forestland before the land may be converted into oil palm plantations. This process allows stakeholders—especially NGOs and affected communities—to raise concerns before it is too late, for example if a planned conversion were to entail the destruction of ape habitat. At the 2009 GA, Wetlands International proposed the "establishment of a working group to provide recommendations on how to deal with existing plantations

TABLE 5.1

RSPO Board of Governors, February 2015

Category of members	Number of members	Names of members
Palm oil growers: one each from Malaysia, Indonesia, small-scale producers and other parts of the world	4	United Plantations Bhd PT Agro Harapan Lestari FELDA Agropalma
Palm oil processors	2	AarhusKarlshamn (AAK) IOI Loders Croklaa
Consumer goods manufacturers	2	Unilever Mondelēz International
Retailers	2	Retailers' Palm Oil Group Marks & Spencer
Banks and investors	2	Rabobank HSBC
Environmental NGOs	2	WWF International Conservation International
Social NGOs	2	Oxfam Novib Both ENDS
Total members	**16**	

Data source: RSPO (n.d.-a)

on peatlands," largely to minimize oil palm expansion into peatlands, but also to prevent expansion into HCV forest. As a consequence, the guidance document was reworded to require efforts to minimize greenhouse gas emissions. This regulation supports apes as they live on high-carbon peatlands and in high carbon stock (HCS) forests, such as primary forests (Wich *et al.*, 2011).

Between GAs, a 16-member Board of Governors[1] provides the strategic direction of the RSPO, negotiating the implementation of GA decisions, giving instructions to the Secretariat to implement decisions and representing the organization. During the GA, members from each category are elected to serve on the board for a two-year period (see Table 5.1).

The Secretariat manages the RSPO, organizing the yearly roundtable associated with the GA, promoting the RSPO worldwide and implementing the Board's decisions. It manages the RSPO's operational structure, which consists of four permanent Standing Committees (SCs) made up of RSPO members. These are the SC on Standards & Certification, Trade & Traceability, Communications & Claims, and Finance (see Figure 5.1). Working groups set up to deal with long-term issues support the committees, while

FIGURE 5.1

RSPO Structure Highlighting Bodies that Focus on Biodiversity

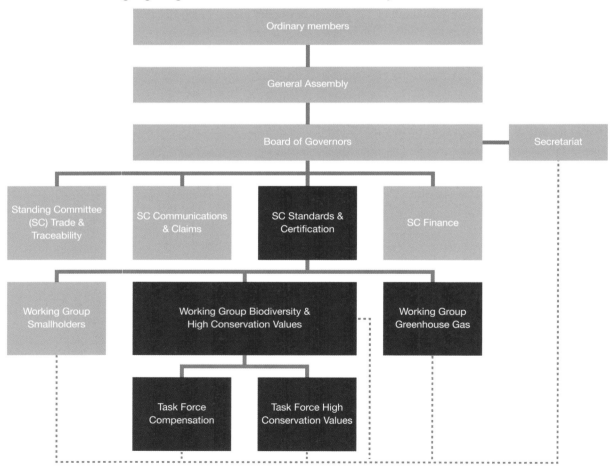

Source: Ruysschaert (2013)

short-term task forces are established to deal with specific issues. The Permanent Committee on Standards and Certification—through its Working Group on Biodiversity and High Conservation Values, Working Group on Greenhouse Gas and the Task Force on Compensation and Task Force on High Conservation Values—contributes directly to issues related to ape conservation (see the bodies marked in red in Figure 5.1).

The Quest for Legitimacy

As with other voluntary schemes with a global vision to transform a market, the RSPO is confronted with a dual challenge: to establish itself as a legitimate global standard while also holding its members accountable for their commitments (Ruysschaert and Salles, 2014). To meet that challenge, all the working groups and task forces function based on three principles:

- inclusive participation in each member category;
- consensus-building in reaching agreements; and
- transparency during the negotiation process and with respect to decisions made.

The implementation of these principles is intended to ensure the legitimacy of the agreements and to make members accountable for their actions in the implementation process, since they are the ones that negotiate and endorse the agreements.

To achieve environmental effectiveness and thus encourage growers to be accountable, the RSPO has made special efforts to ensure transparency, which is reflected in RSPO Principle 1. It has established a user-friendly system based on a database of member profiles, a public consultation procedure for new plantings and a complaints procedure (which is used to apply sanction mechanisms). In addition, members are

required to provide an "annual communication of progress" (ACOP); this information is accessible on the RSPO website and is used in RSPO reports that benchmark the members (RSPO, 2014a).

In addition to adhering to operational principles, debates among stakeholders consider issues such as:

- accountability;
- additionality;
- feasibility;
- flexibility;
- inclusiveness;
- pragmatism;
- rationality; and
- scientific robustness.

The management structure seeks to depoliticize the debate among the members (Boltanski and Chiapello, 2011; Cheyns, 2012). This approach facilitates communication among the stakeholders, as the terminology used in debates is compatible with the working styles of companies as well as NGOs (Persey *et al.*, 2011; Ruysschaert and Salles, 2014).

Case Studies: Industry Applications of RSPO Principles

The case studies presented in this section focus on two main industrial agricultural companies whose operations have had a direct impact on deforestation and forest degradation. Case Study 5.1 considers Wilmar International's management of oil palm plantations in areas of significant biodiversity, while Case Study 5.2 examines the process by which Olam International selects new sites for development and CSPO production according to the RSPO standard.

Conservation in an Agricultural Landscape: Wilmar International

Wilmar International was founded in 1991. It has since risen to be Asia's leading agribusiness group with business activities encompassing the entire value chain of agricultural commodity processing, from the field to branding, marketing and distribution of a wide range of agricultural products. Wilmar and its joint venture plantations have a total of 2,860 km² (286,000 ha) of planted area in Indonesia, Malaysia and Africa. In addition, Wilmar also manages approximately 410 km² (41,000 ha) of schemed smallholders in Indonesia, under the Indonesia Plasma Scheme, and 1,370 km² (137,000 ha) of smallholders and outgrowers under a joint venture arrangement in Ivory Coast and Uganda. In the oil palm sector, Wilmar is not only one of the largest palm oil producers, it is also the main palm oil trader, holding 40% of the international market.

In 2005, soon after the RSPO was established, Wilmar International became an RSPO member. It actively participates in the RSPO's various working groups, including the ones that address conservation issues. While learning to become sustainable on the ground and implementing the RSPO's principles and criteria, Wilmar has been the target of a number of environmental NGO campaigns. Some NGOs filed complaints directly with the RSPO complaints panel, for example regarding Wilmar's operations in Nigeria in 2012, while others have made findings public, such as Greenpeace, which issued a press release in 2013 to point the finger at the company for clearing forests and endangering wildlife in Indonesia (Greenpeace, 2013; RSPO, 2013a).

Wilmar's sustainability commitments have been strengthened over time, largely in response to those campaigns. Wilmar not only assesses and manages HCV areas as required by the RSPO (see Box 5.1), but also announced a corporate policy of "no deforestation, no peat, no exploitation" in 2013. The policy is aimed at protecting forests, peatlands and human and community rights. The implementation of the policy requires assessments to be conducted for HCV forest areas, as well as for HCS areas, prior to the clearing of any land. Wilmar's assessment process—which includes stakeholder consultations—is designed to help the company minimize the impact of its operations on local communities and biodiversity. In 2015, Wilmar became the first agricultural commodities firm to disclose the names and locations of all of its suppliers in its Indonesian and Malaysian supply chain, in an effort to raise transparency and address deforestation (TFT, 2015).

Wilmar engages in the management of HCV areas in a number of ways, such as by participating in a state-run conservation program, in which Wilmar staff members are appointed as honorary wardens and rangers (see HCV Initiative 1); by partnering with conservation NGOs to implement conservation activities, monitoring and evaluation of the HCV areas (see HCV Initiatives 2 and 4); and by providing managed sites for the reintroduction of captive apes (see HCV Initiative 3).

HCV Initiative 1:
Honorary Wildlife Rangers in Sabahmas Plantations

In East Malaysia, which is also known as Sabah, Wilmar has an enforcement unit whose members have been appointed as honorary game wardens or honorary wildlife rangers. As such, they have the authority to prevent any illegal wildlife hunting and transportation in Wilmar's plantations and in the adjacent areas.

Wilmar gives high priority to the honorary wildlife rangers initiative in its Sabahmas Plantations, as the western border of the plantation is adjacent to the Tabin Wildlife Reserve, a 1,200-km² (120,000-ha) Class 1 (totally protected) area. It is home to the critically endangered Sumatran rhinoceros (*Dicerhorinus sumatrensis*) and other endangered species, such as the Bornean orangutan (*Pongo pygmaeus morio*), Bornean pygmy elephant (*Elephas maximus borneensis*), banteng (*Bos javanicus*), Malayan sun bear (*Helarctos malayanus*) and the Bornean clouded leopard (*Neofelis diardi borneensis*).[2]

Photo: In Sabah, Wilmar has an enforcement unit whose members have been appointed as honorary game wardens. They have the authority to prevent any illegal wildlife hunting and transportation in Wilmar's plantations and adjacent areas. © Wilmar International

In 2001, Sabahmas Plantations established its own conservation area of 5.27 km² (527 ha) consisting of a contiguous secondary forest ridge and adjacent flat areas that extend into the Tabin Wildlife Reserve. The conservation area was subsequently named the Sabahmas Conservation Area (SCA). Planting of oil palm was deferred because several herbivorous species—such as the banteng, sambar deer (*Rusa unicolor*) and Bornean bearded pig (*Sus barbatus*)—were observed grazing in the area. While the SCA provides a safe haven for wildlife, the challenge is to ensure the continued security of this area. The discovery of a Sumatran rhinoceros carcass by the side of a highway in 2006 highlighted the need for stronger enforcement around the SCA and Tabin Wildlife Reserve and gave rise to the collaboration between Wilmar International and Sabah's Wildlife Department.

In September 2008, a unit of 16 honorary wildlife rangers was established for the SCA. The unit conducts daily patrols on the road and waterways that lead into and out of the Tabin Wildlife Reserve. In addition, the unit sets up roadblocks on the access roads in an effort to reduce the removal of prohibited forest products, particularly poached wildlife. Within the first four months of operation, about 20 arrests were made; the integrity of the unit was further established by their involvement in special sting operations conducted by the Sabah Wildlife Department. Since then, there has been a reduction in the number of arrests, possibly linked to a reduction in poaching incidents; between 2012 and 2014, no arrests were made.

BOX 5.1

HCV Areas

The Forest Stewardship Council introduced the concept and definition of HCV as a means to identify and manage environmental and social values in forest production landscapes. It has since been used as a tool in other production landscapes (Brown *et al.*, 2013). As Figure 5.2 illustrates, there are six defined HCVs.

FIGURE 5.2

The Six High Conservation Values

Photos: © Alison White

HCV 1 Species diversity
Concentrations of biological diversity, including endemic species and rare, threatened or endangered species, that are significant at the global, regional or national level.

HCV 2 Landscape-level ecosystems and mosaics
Large landscape-level ecosystems and ecosystem mosaics that are significant at the global, regional or national level, and that contain viable populations of the great majority of the naturally occurring species in natural patterns of distribution and abundance.

HCV 3 Ecosystems and habitats
Rare, threatened or endangered ecosystems, habitats or refugia.

HCV 4 Ecosystem services
Basic ecosystem services in critical situations, including protection of water catchments and control of erosion of vulnerable soils and slopes.

HCV 5 Community needs
Sites and resources fundamental for satisfying the basic necessities of local communities or indigenous peoples (such as livelihoods, health, nutrition and water), identified through engagement with these communities or indigenous peoples.

HCV 6 Cultural values
Sites, resources, habitats and landscapes of global or national cultural, archaeological or historical significance, and/or of critical cultural, ecological, economic or religious/sacred importance for the traditional cultures of local communities or indigenous peoples, identified through engagement with these local communities or indigenous peoples.

Source: HCV Resource Network (2013, p. 3)

HCV Initiative 2:
SMART for HCV

One of the core activities related to management of HCV areas is the regular monitoring and patrolling of HCV areas by specially designated teams. Since a large amount of data is collected during each monitoring session, Wilmar has had to introduce a system to analyze and manage this information. To do so, the company partnered with the Zoological Society of London in 2013 to develop and field test the use of the Spatial Monitoring and Reporting Tool (SMART) in Central Kalimantan on the island of Borneo. SMART is designed to measure, evaluate and improve the effectiveness of wildlife enforcement patrols and site-based conservation activities. Wilmar has pioneered the use of SMART in a production landscape; to enable the teams to analyze and determine potential vulnerabilities within their HCV sites, the data are displayed in a spatial format. SMART is being piloted at a number of sites and there are plans to review its effectiveness and potential for replication in other plantations with HCV areas. Wilmar has also partnered with a number of academic institutions to study the effect of HCV areas on biodiversity in a production landscape.

HCV Initiative 3:
Gibbon Conservation in Sumatra

In 2008, Kalaweit, a gibbon conservation project in Indonesia, approached PT Kencana Sawit Indonesia, a subsidiary of Wilmar, with a request to reintroduce gibbons into the company's HCV areas. Subsequently, in April 2014, Kalaweit and the subsidiary signed a partnership agreement to reintroduce a population of siamangs (*Symphalangus syndactylus*) into an HCV management area. The selected area is located at Bukit Tengah Pulau, in West Sumatra, and covers roughly 3.6 km² (360 ha). This HCV area was selected based on two criteria: the forest provides a suitable habitat for the siamangs and there is no existing siamang population in the area, hence no possibility of conflict with other gibbons. In addition, Kalaweit is confident that the HCV areas within Wilmar's plantations provide adequate protection from illegal activities due to the company's established monitoring and patrolling programs. At the time of writing this report, the siamangs were in pre-release cages on site, as part of the acclimatization phase prior to release.

Photo: Wilmar engages in the management of HCV areas in a number of ways, such as providing managed sites for the reintroduction of captive apes. 'No hunting' signs written in both Bahasa Malaysia and Iban.
© Wilmar International

HCV Initiative 4:
Tripartite Collaboration on Best Management Practices for Orangutan Conservation in Central Kalimantan

Wilmar's Central Kalimantan Project is a contiguous plantation area on Borneo that is separated into seven land holding companies. Three of the seven plantations have populations of orangutans and cover approximately 107 km² (10,700 ha).

In 2011, as part of managing these orangutan populations, Wilmar collaborated with the Central Kalimantan Provincial Government and the Borneo Orangutan Survival Foundation to develop best management practices (BMPs) for orangutans in oil palm plantation landscapes (see Box 5.2). The BMP initiative had two key objectives:

- to obtain agreement with local communities on HCV management; and
- to obtain legal status of the HCV area as an orangutan habitat.

One of the plantations with orangutan populations was selected as a pilot project and four activities were conducted to reach the objectives:

- information awareness sessions for the local communities, to increase their knowledge and understanding of HCVs and orangutans;
- development of partnerships with local communities for HCV area management;
- development and distribution of publications on HCVs and orangutan conservation; and
- program monitoring and evaluation.

In addition to the BMPs, biodiversity surveys and nest censuses are being conducted to obtain baseline information for monitoring changes in habitat quality. The Central Kalimantan Project uses standard operating procedures for the management of orangutan areas and actions to be taken when orangutans are spotted. The results have included the demarcation of a 25-meter HCV buffer zone, orangutan habitat enrichment planting, and education and social awareness activities for the workers and local communities.

The most common threats are land clearance, logging and mining, all of which are prohibited in the plantation areas. In 2012, there were more than 50 recorded incidents of each of

BOX 5.2

Best Practice Guidelines for Orangutan Conservation on Plantations

In 2010, the Orangutan Conservation Services Program, with the support of the US Agency for International Development (USAID), issued *Best Management Practices for Orangutan Conservation*, a guide that details how orangutan conservation can be secured within oil palm concessions (Pedler, 2010). Aimed at companies that have orangutans on their concessions, it advises general and environmental managers on how to provide the necessary conditions for orangutan survival. It is also intended to inform local and international financial institutions, local communities and government agencies about environmental and social risks, as well as actions that can help to conserve orangutans in concessions.

The guide highlights that land use planning must be informed by an adequate understanding of the ecological and behavioral requirements of orangutans. It recommends that companies take four key steps to effect and demonstrate sustainable oil palm development and management practices, namely that they:

■ articulate a corporate commitment to protect orangutans;

■ comply with laws and regulations;

■ develop an orangutan-sensitive conservation management plan, which is implemented and monitored; and

■ collaborate with government, communities and other private-sector land managers to conserve orangutans both inside and outside concessions.

Image: © USAID. http://pdf.usaid.gov/pdf_docs/Pnady485.pdf

---

these activities. By 2013, the number of logging and land clearance incidents had dropped by about 50% and 30%, respectively, while mining incidents had fallen by more than 25%, from 69 to 51 cases (see Figure 5.3).

While large intact forest areas are required for biodiversity conservation, some studies have shown that retaining and maintaining forest fragments within oil palm landscapes can provide ecological benefits to the plantations, such as biological control and pollination (Foster *et al.*, 2011). In addition, such fragments contribute to the survival of wildlife by better enabling them to roam and migrate, thereby helping to maintain genetic diversity in isolated populations (Struebig *et al.*, 2011). For more information, see Chapter 6.

FIGURE 5.3

Trends in Number of Reported Incidents of Conflict in HCV Areas*

Key: ■ Land clearance ■ Mining ■ Logging

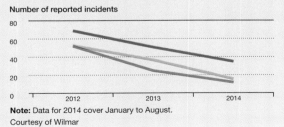

Note: Data for 2014 cover January to August.
Courtesy of Wilmar

CASE STUDY 5.2

Industrial Agriculture and Apes: Olam International in Gabon

Site selection is by far the most important decision in the development of a plantation, as it determines the plantation's overall future environmental and social impact—factors that should be primary drivers for rational site selection. It is also a determining factor in the economic viability of a plantation; however, modern techniques have enabled oil palm plantations to be profitable in areas that would previously have been considered marginal or undesirable.

Such techniques tend to have harmful consequences for the environment, as has been documented in Southeast Asia, where competition for land has led agricultural companies to develop plantations on difficult terrain. In peat swamp forests, including very deep peat on Sumatra and Borneo, these companies have carried out extensive drainage; on steep slopes (>20°), they have developed large-scale terracing; and wherever soils are extremely nutrient-poor, such as in the white-sand areas in South and Central Kalimantan, they have engaged in heavy fertilization using imported organic matter. In contrast, landscapes with broad climatic suitability for oil palm agriculture allow many technical or economic constraints on oil palm production to be alleviated or overcome.

Gabon in Context

Gabon is a highly forested nation, with 88% forest cover and one of the lowest deforestation and forest degradation rates in Africa, averaging 0.12% and 0.09% per year, respectively (Blaser *et al.*, 2011). The population of Gabon is highly urbanized (ca. 87%) and very small relative to land area—there are about 1.67 million people to 257,670 km² (25.8 million ha) (World Bank, n.d.-d). Rural populations are extremely sparse (0.86 people/km²) and mainly concentrated along road axes, such that Gabon still has extensive remote areas where human pressures are extremely low, as compared to neighboring countries.

In November 2010, the government signed a joint venture with Olam International to develop up to 1,000 km² (100,000 ha) of industrial oil palm plantations, 300 km² (30,000 ha) of smallholder oil palm and 500 km² (50,000 ha) of rubber plantations, in two phases. Olam, a Singapore-listed company, is a global leader in food ingredients and agricultural supply chain management; it has 25 years of experience working closely with small-scale farmers in Africa. Olam's national joint venture subsidiaries Olam Palm Gabon and Olam Rubber Gabon are responsible for the day-to-day management of the businesses, bringing in plantation expertise from Asia and elsewhere in the region.

Olam has committed to 100% compliance with the international standard set by the RSPO, which covers all aspects of plantation development; it includes requirements to complete a comprehensive and independent ESIA, to subject any proposed new plantings to stakeholder consultation, to obtain the free, prior and informed consent (FPIC) of local communities, and to avoid primary or HCV forests (see Figure 5.4). In addition, Olam's Palm Policy supplements the RSPO requirements, most notably with a commitment to invest in local communities, to minimize the carbon footprint of its oil palm operations by avoiding HCS forests and peatlands, and to support national land use planning processes.

Significantly for Olam, and for any plan to expand agriculture in order to meet national development needs, most of the land suitable for oil palm expansion in Gabon is forested. Some areas of savannah and gallery forest are in the south of the country, but only a small proportion of these receive sufficient rainfall for sustained economic yields. Therefore, Olam has been working with the government and national conservation organizations to identify suitable alternatives, such as areas of secondary vegetation, significantly degraded and over-hunted forest, and agriculturally suitable savannah. In this context, the objectives of site selection are to maximize the economic and social benefits of plantation developments, minimize impacts on biodiversity and vulnerable communities (through a landscape approach, which considers a range of land uses over an appropriate unit, and HCV assessments), and limit carbon emissions from land conversion (through HCS assessments).

In November 2010, the government of Gabon allocated an initial 519 km² (51,920 ha) of land for palm development in Estuaire province, in three separate concessions. It was soon apparent, however, that a large majority of the land bank did not meet RSPO requirements because of the presence of swathes of primary forest, large-scale seasonal flooding and overlapping designations, including a Ramsar site. Once independent national and international teams had carried out regulatory ESIAs, HCV assessments and stakeholder consultations, Olam returned two concessions to the government.

The company retained a single concession of 200 km² (20,030 ha) of partially logged-over, degraded forest known as the Awala plantation or Lot 8, of which 71 km² (7,134 ha) were initially considered suitable for development following the RSPO New Planting Procedure. FPIC negotiations were then conducted with local villagers to obtain local consent to use land to which they had traditional access and use rights. Planting in the Awala plantation was completed in 2014: 65 km² (6,502 ha) were planted and the remaining area was set aside for the conservation of HCV forests, steep areas and riparian buffer zones (Proforest, 2014). The plantation covers less than 13% of the land originally allocated. This experience highlights the need for improved agricultural land use planning, which has gradually been implemented for successive projects.

By September 2014, Olam in Gabon had completed three ESIA, HCV and FPIC processes for its palm plantations, totalling 870 km² (87,000 ha). A further suitable 238 km² (23,780 ha) have been identified and are in the second stage of land development, as discussed below. Olam expects to develop 510 km² (51,000 ha) or 45% of this total land area by 2018–19, having already planted 157 km² (15,700 ha) of palm between 2011 and 2014. Most of the HCV areas comprise large, contiguous forest blocks. Olam has followed a similar process for the 290 km² (29,000 ha) rubber plantations in the north of the country.

Apes, Wildlife Management and Oil Palm in Gabon

In addition to being a global conservation priority, great apes—particularly the central chimpanzee and western lowland gorilla—are flagship species in Gabon and more widely in Central Africa. Ape species can be found in low to medium densities in most suitable habitats across Gabon, and scattered individuals or small groups even live close to major cities, such as in the Mondah Forest, a few km from Libreville (L.J.T. White, personal communication, 2014).

Excluding all potential ape habitat from development would effectively preclude any kind of agricultural expansion, which is not compatible with the goals of the government's "Gabon Emergent" strategic plan; classifying habitat as HCV on the sole basis of the presence of any number of apes—rather than significant populations or concentrations—would have a comparable effect, precluding any responsible company from investing in Gabon and perhaps opening the door to less scrupulous developers. For Olam, the challenges inherent in conducting agricultural operations in Gabon include avoiding major ape concentrations altogether; safeguarding or improving the status of viable ape populations wherever they are found, through suitable habitat conservation and management measures; and developing land in ways that avoid doing harm to individual apes, either directly or indirectly. Such factors should also be considered in Gabon's forthcoming national land use plan.

FIGURE 5.4

Spatial Zoning of Olam's Mouila Lot 1 Palm Plantation

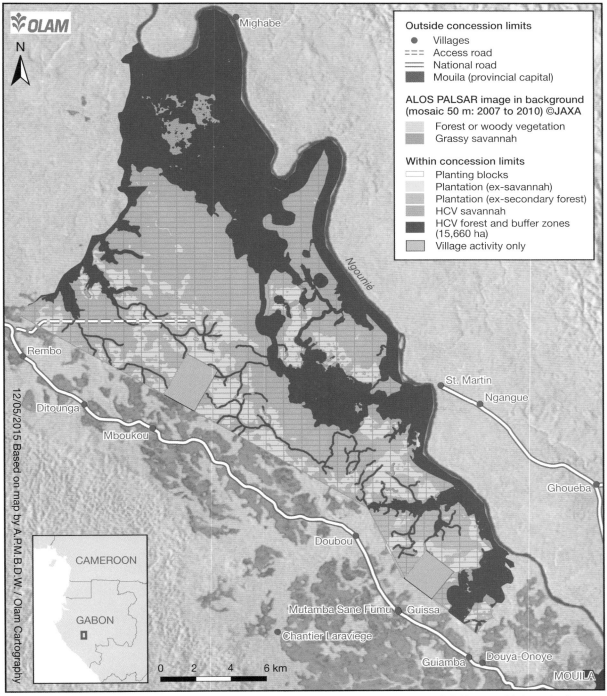

Note: The map shows the extensive and contiguous network of protected HCV blocks, corridors and riparian buffers that provide habitat connectivity for species of conservation concern in Gabon. The large habitat block to the northwest is connected to contiguous forest cover extending into the interior forests of Gabon.

Courtesy of Olam International

Olam has included great ape surveys in the ESIAs for all of its sites, none of which is within the current great ape priority landscapes that have been identified in the Regional Action Plan for the Conservation of Western Lowland Gorillas and Central Chimpanzees 2015–2025 (IUCN, 2014c). In the concession known as Mouila Lot 1, HCV assessors found that faunal transects and anecdotal evidence indicated that both ape species were sparsely present across the concession as a whole, with more ape signs far from the main road and in less accessible, swampy areas (see Figure 5.4). They also came across direct evidence of great apes being hunted and eaten by local villagers. Encounter rates were much too low in this survey to attempt a population estimate, but based on the sparse data, habitat evidence, home range requirements and expert views, the assessors concluded that resident ape populations had probably been severely reduced by hunting and that they were significantly smaller than their habitat's carrying capacity.

Based on the analyses, the assessors recommended that Olam set aside and rigorously protect an initial 139 km² (13,868 ha) of suitable habitat in the first instance, in two major HCV forest blocks connected by a network of riparian buffer zones (of variable widths) and broad conservation corridors (with a minimum width of 300 m). The largest HCV block to the north of the concession is contiguous with an unbroken forested landscape, allowing free movement of animals into and out of the concession. The assessors suggested a tentative estimate of 20 to 40 individuals of each species, in one to two groups, as a potential target for fully protected populations in these HCV areas. The conservation organizations consulted during the New Planting Procedure required Olam to conduct further faunal surveys and to develop an ape management plan prior to entering potentially sensitive areas.

Preliminary results of the additional faunal surveys found ape signs in a previously under-sampled area. On the advice of the zoologist in charge of the surveys, Olam set aside a further 10 km² (1,000 ha) of suitable ape habitat in a third forest block, which is connected to the first two by a 1 km-wide riverine forest corridor. The

company subsequently completed surveys across the entire concession, which, together with photographic analysis, confirmed that the gorilla presence was limited to a very small number of individuals and that it was unclear whether there was a reproducing family unit within the concession. The surveys also confirmed that habitat occupancy by chimpanzees was somewhat higher than expected, and camera analysis suggested the presence of two potentially distinct chimpanzee groups with home ranges overlapping with the main HCV blocks (almost all of the signs were either inside HCV areas or within 1.25 km of the set-asides). The two groups may also be fissioned subgroups of a larger family clan; further monitoring may be able to provide answers.

As advised, Olam developed an ape management plan, which is being implemented to ensure further protection of ape populations as economically viable operations continue. The implementation of the plan formalizes the development process and identifies actions that are still needed to safeguard great ape individuals and groups at risk from oil palm development. The ape management plan comprises six pillars that consider how best to:

- allocate areas of intact habitat (HCV areas) for preservation;
- ensure robust baseline and ongoing monitoring protocols;
- require scheduling of land preparation to enable wildlife to move into HCV areas;
- implement protocols that mitigate the potential for disease transmission between humans and apes;
- impose hunting controls and raise awareness among local communities; and
- support the development of subsistence programs to promote alternatives to hunting.

Photo: The western lowland gorilla is a flagship species in Gabon. Excluding all potential ape habitat from development would effectively preclude any kind of agricultural expansion, which is not compatible with the goals of the government's "Gabon Emergent" strategic plan.
© Martha M. Robbins/MPI-EVAN

Obstacles to Success: The RSPO's Operational Challenges

This section provides details on three broad types of operational challenge the RSPO faces in its efforts to achieve its goals:

- There is no economic incentive for growers to become RSPO members or to produce CSPO, as the price premium paid by downstream firms is too low. As a result, certification is limited to a handful of the biggest palm oil growers that target Western markets and widespread CSPO production remains a challenge.

- The RSPO guidance document leaves certified growers too much scope for interpretation, largely because the RSPO's modus operandi—specifically, procedures aimed at consensus building and inclusiveness—stands in the way of reaching agreement on tougher environmental standards.

- The RSPO is not set up to hold non-RSPO growers or even its members to account for non-compliance with the RSPO standard.

All of these challenges are linked to the voluntary nature of the RSPO and its operational structure. Moreover, all of them dramatically reduce the impact of the RSPO in terms of ensuring effective ape habitat conservation (Ruysschaert and Salles, 2014).

Barriers to Widespread CSPO Production

On the surface, the RSPO scheme appears to have the makings of a "bargaining model" (Coase, 1988). Ideally, the growers participate voluntarily because they receive financial compensation or a premium that is higher than the additional costs they have to bear to conserve HCV areas and to certify their palm oil. In theory, the three main transaction costs are low enough to make the RSPO model attractive. First, certification information is provided by the RSPO Secretariat for only €2,000 (just over US$2,000) per member per year. Second, negotiation costs are kept to a minimum, as online discussions are promoted and physical meetings only take place twice per year (RSPO, 2004b). Finally, NGOs undertake external supervision at no cost to growers or downstream firms (Ruysschaert and Salles, 2014).

In reality, however, downstream firms pay large-scale oil palm producers very low premiums in comparison to the costs these growers have to bear. As a result, producers have no interest in joining the RSPO or certifying their palm oil. Indeed, downstream firms pay only about US$2 per ton when they adopt the "Book & Claim" traceability system; this approach appears to be the method they prefer, as more than 50% of CSPO was sold in this way in 2014 (RSPO, 2015a).

The Book & Claim method is based on a trading program that was developed by the palm oil processor AarhusKarlshamn. With its palm oil certified as CSPO, the grower receives GreenPalm certificates that can be sold on a dedicated certificates market. The downstream company buys these certificates to combine with its purchase of uncertified palm oil on the open market. In this context, the conventional supply chain is used and CSPO is mixed with non-certified oils. The final product can be branded "sustainable" with a CSPO label although it often consists of insignificant amounts of CSPO, as CSPO only makes up a small part of the global palm oil market.

For downstream firms, it does not make economic sense to separate CSPO from other palm oil since the former is produced in small amounts and sourced from numerous locations that would have to be delinked from the usual downstream supply chain. By maintaining separation throughout the supply chain, they would incur additional logistical costs, reducing potential for efficiency and cost reduction through economies of scale. Downstream firms thus tend to favor GreenPalm over other, costlier certification categories, which can reach US$30–50 per ton for full traceability (see Box 5.3). It seems that downstream firms only adopt a full traceability policy when pressured by NGOs. A case in point is Ferrero, which adopted full physical separation after a Greenpeace-led campaign against its Nutella brand (Ferrero, 2014).

For growers, certification that requires ape habitat to be conserved is extremely costly. It costs more than US$10 per ton of CSPO to conserve an orangutan in a 100-km² (10,000-ha) oil palm concession, and much more for a smaller concession as the proportion under conservation is much higher. The grower must accept the economic opportunity cost—that is, the loss of potential economic gain associated with converting ape habitat into oil palm plantation, which depends directly on the size of the conservation area. For species such as the orangutan, whose population densities are as low as one individual per km² (100 ha), the costs are particularly high. Individual females are territorial within a home range of 1 km² (100 ha) and males are semi-nomadic, with a territory that can reach more than 100 km² (10,000 ha) (Singleton *et al.*, 2009; Wich *et al.*, 2011). In addition to this direct economic loss, growers must cover the annual certification costs: US$2–9 per ton of CSPO for the initial year, and US$1–3 per ton thereafter (Levin *et al.*, 2012).

As a result of the lack of economic incentives and the costs of getting certified, the only palm oil producers that pursue certification are the ones that are seeking access to the Western palm oil market, which represents only 13% of the global market (USDA, 2015). These are primarily large-scale producers that hold close to 40,000 km² (4 million ha) on lease; among them are 20 of the 25 biggest oil palm pro-

---

BOX 5.3

Categories of RSPO Certification

From lax to strict, the four RSPO certification categories are:

- **GreenPalm:** allows CSPO and conventional oil to be mixed, without separation or traceability;
- **mass balance:** allows the mixing of CSPO with non-certified palm oil, but requires traceability of the CSPO tons along the supply chain;
- **segregated:** allows the mixing of CSPO from different origins, but requires traceability from these plantations to the final product; and
- **density preserved:** requires separation and traceability of CSPO from each specific plantation to the final product.

---

ducers in the world, which could potentially supply more than 25% of the world market (WWF, 2013b; ZSL, n.d.-b). Yet, in Indonesia, certified RSPO growers represent less than 3% of the oil palm estates that exceed 0.5 km² (50 ha) and do not include the small-scale producers, which account for 40% of the country's production (BPS, 2012).

Reaching Agreements and Controlling Interpretation: Process-related Obstacles

The RSPO's efforts to strengthen the guidance in relation to biodiversity conservation are complicated by the very nature of its multi-stakeholder negotiations, as these are designed to reach compromises. Additional factors, including the scientific community's lack of consensus on certain biodiversity issues, preclude agreement on matters such as how to identify areas to be protected (Borges, 2003; Struebig *et al.*, 2011). The difficulty in reaching agreement was highlighted during the European RSPO meeting in London in June 2014, when the chair of the Biodiversity and HCV Working Group noted that a seemingly obvious and fundamental term such as "deforestation" remains entangled in internal debate.

The indicator that is most directly linked to the conservation of ape habitats has been the prohibition of clearance of primary and HCV forests as of November 2005. In practice, this prohibition is difficult to implement, as current RSPO members seem to justify actions that appear to contravene the prohibition, for example by arguing that they cleared primary forest before joining the RSPO or before 2007, when the prohibition was formally adopted as a rule.

Meanwhile, the temporary bodies set up to deal with biodiversity issues have essentially given rise to semi-permanent bodies: the Biodiversity and HCV Working Group (which grew out of the Biodiversity Technical Committee established in 2006), the Greenhouse Gas Working Group that was formed in 2009 and the Compensation Task Force that was established in 2010. Each of these bodies seems to achieve only minimal results without reaching a conclusion, as each step forward uncovers a new issue for extensive debate (McCarthy, 2012).

The complex HCV concept, which is at the core of biodiversity conservation in the guidance document, remains a somewhat qualitative tool that is subject to case-by-case interpretation. Moreover, the RSPO guidance document does not explicitly rule out deforestation. It prohibits the conversion of primary and HCV forests but protection of other types of great ape habitat—such as secondary or degraded forest—is much more problematic, even though the RSPO recognizes that they can be HCV forests, which require protection (RSPO, 2010b). Despite the revision that was introduced in 2013, the guidance document is still not sufficiently restrictive with respect to biodiversity and forest conservation (RSPO, 2013b). It limits planting on peat, a major issue in Southeast Asia, due to peat swamp forest carbon emissions; it also requires planters to avoid "land areas with high carbon stocks and/or sequestration options" and asks producers to "plan to minimize greenhouse

gas (GHG) emissions" (RSPO, 2013b, p. 54). Yet, as there are no measurable objectives or deadlines, these plans can be postponed or scaled down for reasons of technical feasibility or economic viability.

This lack of clarity in the guidance document regarding biodiversity gives growers the opportunity to interpret the criteria to their advantage, especially if the technical assessment and consultative processes are weak. For example, a grower can subjectively reclassify primary forest as secondary forest, which is suitable for development, as there is no agreed definition. Growers have also been known to conceal the existence of apes on their concessions, especially if the relevant species have very low population densities. Such was the case with the RSPO member PT Sisirau, which converted orangutan habitat on the edge of Sumatra's Gunung Leuser National Park—part of the Leuser Ecosystem—into an oil palm plantation on the grounds that it was a secondary forest without biodiversity value (RSPO, 2010a; Mongabay, 2012). Having been identified as "transmigrants," the resident orangutans were moved to the Gunung Leuser National Park with logistical support from RSPO member NGOs. Although this translocation was presented as an achievement, it ushered in the destruction of the orangutans' natural habitat and could compromise the socioecology of existing orangutan populations in the national park (Rijksen and Meijaard, 1999).

Furthermore, even when the guidance document is implemented in a manner that would be considered favorable for conservation, it does not fully account for the ecological needs of apes. The RSPO certification process creates conservation areas within intensive oil palm agribusiness plantations and cannot compensate for a lack of large-scale zoning for conservation. Such plantation areas are ecological barriers to biodiversity in general and apes in particular (Fitzherbert *et al.*, 2008; see Chapter 6). Whereas research indicates that maintaining forest patches

within plantations can contribute to conservation, the long-term effectiveness of these areas in industrial agricultural landscapes remains in doubt; more research is needed to bridge this knowledge gap (SEnSOR, 2012).

To tackle these issues, the RSPO has established a task force to define a compensation mechanism. The task force has confronted a number of contentious issues, such as a lack of scientific information, diverging views regarding the methods used to decide which areas should be used for planting oil palm and ambiguity surrounding the responsibility of the grower. While the compensation mechanism is a work in progress that has elicited tense internal debate, its latest version includes financial compensation for clearing HCV forests, which in practice means ratifying historic deforestation (RSPO, 2014c).

This option has been preferred to expelling members or applying heavy fines, which would have been at odds with the inclusive, consensus-building spirit of the RSPO.

Limitations of Membership of the RSPO

Membership and certification are the means by which the RSPO aims to protect biodiversity from the adverse effects of the oil palm industry. In practice, three main challenges undermine this approach. First, certain RSPO rules conflict with some state regulations. Second, since the RSPO standard applies only to members, the growers that have not become members cannot be enjoined to pursue sustainable practices.

Third, uncertified RSPO members benefit from the "sustainable" label by association, without acquiring certification. Examples of each of these limitations follow.

Conflicting regulations

One country where RSPO rules have been in conflict with national regulations is Indonesia, where entire concessions—including areas that should be conserved according to RSPO rules—are earmarked for development as "land for other uses" (more commonly known by its Indonesian acronym, APL, which stands for *areal penggunaan lain*; see Chapter 4). If the land is not developed, local or central government actors—who may seek economic development or income from taxes —can reallocate it to other growers in Indonesia, the majority of whom are not RSPO members, or to local community members. Yet even if an RSPO grower has earmarked an HCV area within a concession, that area can potentially be reallocated to a non-RSPO grower, especially if the government supports this reallocation. As a consequence, RSPO growers tend to focus on areas that have minimal conservation management requirements; at the same time, non-RSPO growers —such as local communities, smallholders or large-scale estates—may simply convert forest that would have been protected under RSPO rules (Colchester *et al.*, 2009).

Recognizing the need to find a solution, the RSPO established an Indonesian task force on HCV, of which Wilmar is a member. The task force had two objectives. The first was to explore the means to secure HCV areas in oil palm development concessions in Indonesia, in line with the RSPO P&C. This goal pertained especially to HCV areas identified in location permits during HCV assessments. The second objective was to explore options to reform local and national laws and procedures to secure HCV areas and abide by the RSPO P&C (RSPO, 2012). The task force identified potential synergies

and gaps between the RSPO P&C and Indonesian policies, laws and regulations. While the task force has since been disbanded, its report was submitted to the RSPO for further lobbying action, which will most likely affect only RSPO members.

Inadequate coverage of stakeholders

The case of the Tripa peat swamp forests in the Indonesian province of Aceh demonstrates that partial coverage of stakeholders limits the impact of the RSPO, as evidenced by the fact that non-RSPO members are still able to establish oil plantations on biologically significant areas. Since the 2004 peace agreement, Aceh has seen rapid economic development. In the Tripa peat swamp forests of the Leuser Ecosystem, oil palm producers—none of which were RSPO members— converted habitat of Sumatran orangutans into five large-scale oil palm plantations (Wich *et al.*, 2011; Tata *et al.*, 2014). Although a 2008 RSPO GA resolution recognized Tripa as an HCV area and thus should have prevented this development, the resolution only applied to RSPO members; non-RSPO producers thus continued to expand into Tripa (Ruysschaert and Salles, 2014).

Freeloading and non-compliance

Nearly half of the RSPO growers do not actively engage in the certification process. Indeed, only 57 of 119 of registered growers have certified mills (Mongabay, 2015); nevertheless, they remain RSPO members to benefit from "sustainable" branding. Moreover, uncertified growers are particularly unlikely to submit compulsory ACOPs; when they do, they often provide very limited information.

In March 2015, the RSPO responded to such freeloading and non-compliance by expelling all RSPO members that had not provided ACOPs for the previous three years and suspending those that had failed to submit them for the previous two years (RSPO, n.d.-f). The RSPO had long been reluctant to implement this decision, as it runs counter to its vision of transforming the global market.[3]

In the absence of an established external policing institution, social and environmental NGOs have taken on monitoring roles. Due to financial and technical limitations, however, these NGOs are only able to focus on selected cases in which RSPO rules have been violated. Complicating matters is the power of growers, who often dismiss the value of securing the necessary long-term community support and who can successfully conceal non-compliance. Consequently, many cases are not reported to the RSPO or remain unnoticed (Ruysschaert and Salles, 2014). The cases that do come to light can take a number of years to resolve. One example involves a complaint filed by the Sumatran Orangutan Society against PT Sisirau, which was initiated in October 2012 but remained unresolved in July 2015 (RSPO, n.d.-b).

The RSPO's Move Toward Enhancing Conservation Impact

The RSPO is at a crossroads. CSPO, all of which is produced by RSPO growers and producers, accounts for only 20% of global palm oil (RSPO, 2015a); CSPO producers trade palm oil at a net economic loss owing to inadequate financial compensation, in contrast to non-RSPO growers and RSPO downstream firms (Ruysschaert and Salles, 2014). At the same time, firms are reluctant to buy CSPO due to the lack of credibility of the standard, as it still has not put a halt to deforestation. Only 50% of available CSPO was bought in 2014, most of it through GreenPalm certification, which provides only a small premium for the grower (RSPO,

2015a). Some environmental NGOs, such as Greenpeace, still question the ability of RSPO certification to preserve rainforests (Greenpeace, 2014).

The RSPO has acknowledged that its focus on an inclusive, consensus-building process among all members has only been able to yield compromises, thus restricting its potential conservation impact. In 2014, after a decade of work and under great pressure from NGOs to demonstrate its conservation impact, the RSPO adopted a new, two-pronged approach: it shifted its emphasis toward the worldwide promotion of CSPO as well as traceability and transparency through the whole supply chain. This dual effort is reinforced though other initiatives that focus directly on enhancing the RSPO's conservation impact.

Increasing Global Demand for CSPO

In order to raise global demand for CSPO, the RSPO is initially focusing on the European palm oil market—with the intention of capturing 100% of the market for CSPO. To achieve this goal, the RSPO established a European office in Brussels, began to hold yearly European conferences in 2013 and started facilitating a palm oil debate on the *Guardian* newspaper homepage. Given that European legislation mandates distinct labeling for palm oil vs. other vegetable oil on packaging as of 2015, educating Europe's 500 million consumers about CSPO is of critical importance. To prevent the European consumer from boycotting CSPO, an effective campaign is needed to combat the poor perception associated with palm oil production.

The RSPO's efforts are supported by the European Commission policy that grants CSPO (all but GreenPalm certification) access to the European biofuel market (European Commission, 2012).

> The RSPO has acknowledged that its focus on an inclusive, consensus-building process has only been able to yield compromises, thus restricting its potential conservation impact.

In some countries, such as the Netherlands, buyers have joined forces and agreed to buy only CSPO from 2015 (Halliday, 2010). Individual downstream European and US companies have also committed to trading exclusively in CSPO. More than two-thirds (36 out of 52) of the European retailers have made commitments to use only CSPO by 2015 (WWF, 2013a, p. 24). A number of key retailers are already at 100% CSPO, including IKEA, Marks & Spencer, Migros, Sainsbury's and Tesco, whereas others, including Johnson & Johnson, Lindt & Sprüngli, Premier Foods and Unilever, are committed to achieving 100%. The RSPO has also partnered with the United Nations Environment Programme to raise global awareness about sustainable palm oil and to generate market demand (UNEP, 2014). In parallel, the RSPO is reaching out to other large markets, such as India and China, which together consume more than one-third (or 15 billion tons per year) of all the internationally traded palm oil (USDA, 2015).

> Full traceability and transparency means that all stakeholders in the supply chain—not only the palm oil producers—are accountable for the commitments they made.

Toward Full Traceability and Transparency

In addition to creating sufficient demand for CSPO, the RSPO is placing emphasis on full traceability and transparency of physical palm oil throughout the whole supply chain. Besides boosting the credibility of the RSPO standard, this move could lead to an increase in the global production of CSPO. Indeed, more growers would be likely to certify their palm oil plantations, as the premium for fully traceable CSPO is considerable and exceeds the cost of certification.

In practice, full traceability and transparency means that all stakeholders in the supply chain—and not only the palm oil producers—are accountable for the commitments they made; in turn, these commitments are expected to result in the desired conservation impact on the ground. In this vein, the RSPO GA endorsed a Unilever resolution entitled "Declaration of Mills" in 2014; by requiring full transparency throughout the supply chain, the resolution is forcing the GreenPalm certificate platform to disclose information about the origin of traded certificates, at least at the mill level (RSPO, 2014b).

The full traceability and transparency approach has the support of a number of environmental NGOs in the RSPO. The World Resources Institute (WRI), co-chair of the Biodiversity and High Conservation Values Working Group, has established the Global Forest Watch platform, which will initially focus on palm oil-related concerns in Indonesia (WRI, n.d.-b). The platform aims to monitor forest trends—such as deforestation rates and fire hotspots—through remote sensing, by gathering all the available data from a wide range of partners and by making it easily accessible. WRI also partnered with Unilever to increase transparency of the latter's key commodity supply chains in an effort to stop the company and its suppliers from engaging in deforestation (WRI, 2014d).

The Zoological Society of London (ZSL), another prominent environmental NGO in the RSPO, launched the Sustainable Palm Oil Transparency Toolkit (SPOTT) at the RSPO annual meeting in November 2014. The tool may be seen as a complement to the Global Forest Watch platform, as it allows investors, manufacturers and other stakeholders to assess oil palm growers based on the information that they make publicly available about the sustainability of their operations. SPOTT combines satellite-mapping technology with environmental performance assessments for the 25 largest publicly listed companies that have oil palm plantations, including 21 RSPO members (ZSL, n.d.-b).

Complementary Initiatives: "No Deforestation" and RSPO+

Frustrated by the RSPO's apparent inability to prevent continued deforestation, a number of prominent environmental NGOs, including Greenpeace and WWF, have partnered with large growers that have historically been targeted by Greenpeace campaigns —including Asia Pulp and Paper, Golden Agri-Resources and Wilmar International —to break the link between oil palm expansion and deforestation. The firms have committed to "no deforestation" and have, with their NGO partners, established the Palm Oil Innovations Group (POIG), whose aim is to put a complete halt to deforestation and to ensure respect for human rights (POIG, 2013). In developing a process by which to achieve their objective, they introduced the HCS concept and made commitments to preserve carbon-rich areas. Firms that are POIG members are thus barred from clearing peatlands and forests above a certain carbon stock threshold (TFT, 2014).

To address the complexity of local social and ecological contexts in relation to HCS, POIG members joined a broader group to form the High Carbon Stock Approach Steering Group. In May 2015, the group launched a toolkit that is designed to "enable the widespread adoption of the HCS Approach" (Greenpeace, 2015).

Meanwhile, a group of prominent Malaysian and Indonesian growers and traders, which considered POIG and its Steering Group too NGO-led, signed the "Sustainable Palm Oil Manifesto" in 2014; this alternative initiative also focuses on halting deforestation, protecting peat and ensuring the equitable distribution of benefits to local communities (SPOM, n.d.). While POIG members are actively adopting the HCS approach, however, the manifesto signatories are still undertaking a study to define what actually constitutes HCS (HCSS, n.d.).

These NGO- and business-led HCS initiatives complement the RSPO in two ways. First, they reduce the amount of subjectivity in the interpretation of the HCV concept. In contrast to the RSPO's approach to HCV, which is open to different interpretations among stakeholders, the HCS approach focuses on clear quantitative indicators within the HCV concept, thus reducing the room for negotiation and facilitating cost-effective monitoring using tools such as remote sensing. In addition, the HCS strategy should be able to preserve significantly more areas of ape habitat and biodiversity, as it aims to conserve most forests and all peatland.

Second, the "no deforestation" commitment emphasizes traceability and transparency along the supply chain. Through traceability, the product path can be traced back along the suppliers to the plantation and sustainability can be introduced as a quality control element on the supply chain. Theoretically, the "no deforestation" commitment should be able to support supply chain hubs—such as refineries and ports— and should cover all relevant social actors and ecological factors. In its implementation, however, the HCS approach may face the same limitations as the RSPO, particularly regarding its ability to appreciate and respond to social and ecological needs, such as those of the great apes and gibbons of Africa and Asia.

The "no deforestation" commitment has already attracted leading consumer brands, such as Ferrero, Mars, Nestlé and L'Oréal. Some of the largest producers—such as Golden Agri-Resources and Wilmar—and most of the trading companies—such as Cargill and Olam—have committed to "no deforestation" policies as a result of campaigning by prominent civil society actors, such as Greenpeace (Greenpeace, 2014). These companies account for more than 96% of the palm oil that is traded internationally (Finkelstein, 2014). In May 2015, in response to growing interest in the HCS approach, the RSPO launched RSPO+, a voluntary addendum to the RSPO standard that will "strengthen the standard on peat, deforestation and social requirements." The final addendum is currently under development (RSPO, 2015b).

> " The HCS approach focuses on clear quantitative indicators within the HCV concept, thus reducing the room for negotiation and facilitating cost-effective monitoring. "

BOX 5.4

Smallholders or Industrial Agriculture: Which Is the Better Development Model?

Oil palm cultivation can generate a high and stable source of income and support a rural middle class over several generations, accomplishments few tropical crops can achieve today (see Chapter 1, p. 18).

In terms of fruit and oil yield, industrial agriculture tends to be more efficient than family farming. Transaction costs are lower and state involvement may be limited to the granting of easy terms to investors. In addition, it is easier to deal with a small number of big enterprises than thousands of unorganized or poorly organized smallholders, especially with respect to duties and taxation or the monitoring of compliance with environmental rules (such as RSPO certification or pollution control) and social standards (such as workers' rights).

Nevertheless, family farming can potentially sustain more biodiversity than agribusiness cultivation. Indeed, while large-scale producers segregate protected lands from oil palm plantations on their concessions, smallholders tend to integrate biodiversity into their palm oil cultivation plans, such that one does not exclude the other.

In addition, family farming has proved more effective in the promotion of social justice, job creation and the reduction of poverty. While permanent employees of industrial agricultural plantations usually enjoy good working conditions — with regular salaries, housing, and health and education benefits — labor-intensive operations are generally competitively outsourced to contractors that typically exploit their workers by paying low wages, offering piecework and failing to offer benefits. These workers tend to be packed into low-cost housing and have no choice but to buy all their food at the company store. In stark contrast, family farms provide labor opportunities to the whole family, cash income is redistributed to all members — albeit seldom equitably or according to the labor provided — and most of the consumed food is produced on the farm. Work discipline is less tight, and the farmer remains his or her own boss (Barral, 2012; P. Levang, personal communication, 2014).

In Cameroon, where small- and medium-scale farmers manage approximately 1,000 km^2 (100,000 ha) of oil palm plantations, average annual yields are very low (0.8 ton of crude palm oil/ha) because of difficult access to improved seedlings, the steep price of fertilizer and poor management techniques (Nkongho et al., 2014). Considering that Indonesian and Malaysian smallholders can reach annual yields of 4 tons of CPO/ha, there is huge scope for progress. By increasing the average yields to just 2 tons/ha, Cameroon, which currently imports 50,000–100,000 tons every year, would regain self-sufficiency in palm oil and even become a net exporter.

Increasing smallholder yields is feasible, but it has a cost and requires political will. Rather than providing credit and subsidies for inputs such as improved seedlings or adequate extension services to improve management techniques, many governments prefer to offer attractive conditions to international investors (Nguiffo and Schwartz, 2012a).

Photo: In terms of fruit and oil yield, industrial agriculture tends to be more efficient than family farming. Nevertheless, family farming can potentially sustain more biodiversity than agribusiness cultivation and has proved more effective in the promotion of social justice, job creation and the reduction of poverty. Oil palm trucks near forest fires in Sumatra.
© Ulet Ifansasti/Greenpeace

Conclusion

In its early years, the Roundtable on Sustainable Palm Oil relied on its operational approach—which emphasized inclusiveness, transparency and broad stakeholder participation along the supply chain—to gain legitimacy as a global standard. As its membership grew, the RSPO established an ambitious global vision of transforming the market to make sustainability the norm. Its inability to achieve this central goal can be attributed to interlinked factors, all of which stem from the way the RSPO was initially set up. Three main challenges can be identified.

First, the global production of CSPO remains insufficient. To date, certification has been pursued only by leading oil palm producers whose sights were set on selling CSPO to Western markets. For all other growers, the economic incentives of certification—the premium accorded to CSPO—is far too low compared to the costs of certification; as a result, many do not become RSPO members and those that do have no interest in seeking certification.

Second, questions persist with respect to the actual sustainability of CSPO, as the guidance document is ambiguous in this regard. In particular, the guidance can be interpreted to allow deforestation and plantation on peatland, which can be of vital importance to the conservation of biodiversity, including of apes.

Finally, the RSPO standard fails to provide effective guidance on how to factor local contexts into oil palm production plans. At the ecological level, this means that even if growers implement the guidance document with the genuine intention of conserving apes and biodiversity more generally, they will find that the HCV concept has not been effectively tailored to address relevant environmental needs. At the social level, the growers are not systematically encouraged to engage with key country-level actors, such as smallholders, communities and ministries.

> If conservation goals are to be met, the oil palm sector could encourage producers to develop already degraded land that presents real agricultural potential.

Given the absence of effective engagement with local stakeholders, it is not surprising that HCV areas continue to be allocated or reallocated for development purposes, be it for political, legal or economic reasons.

By 2014, the RSPO had recognized the need to boost global demand for CSPO, raise the credibility of the standard and better address the local context to propel the market towards sustainability. To address these challenges and, more generally, to enhance its conservation impact while maintaining an inclusive process, the RSPO began to pursue three complementary approaches. First, to raise global demand for CSPO, it began to implement an outreach strategy to win markets, beginning with the European market. Second, to raise the credibility of the CSPO standard, it started to promote the RSPO+ concept—as a means of better integrating the consideration of social and environmental factors into the standard. Third, to raise global demand for CSPO as well as credibility of the standard, the RSPO is fostering traceability and transparency along the whole supply chain. This last step is likely to persuade more growers to certify their production, as CSPO producers with full traceability should be able to attain a significant premium, which would easily cover certification costs.

If conservation goals are to be met, however, the RSPO—along with the rest of the oil palm sector—will need to shift into a higher gear at the local level. To do so, these actors could take four relatively workable steps that would go a long way in promoting sustainability. In particular, they could:

- Encourage producers to develop already degraded land that presents real agricultural potential; in Indonesia, for instance, such land accounts for more than 73,000 km² (7.3 million ha) (JPNN, 2010; Ruysschaert *et al.*, 2011).

- Assist smallholders by providing support in the form of seedlings, technology and market access. Smallholders currently produce half the yields (about 2 tons/ha) of agribusiness firms (Jacquemard *et al.*, 2010; Jacquemard, 2011; see Box 5.4).

■ Become familiar with the factors that inform local decision-making, including land tenure, palm oil prices, biofuel subsidies, support to smallholders for better yields and market access.

■ Redouble their efforts to engage with local communities, not only to bolster urgently needed poverty eradication programs, but also to promote the conservation of biodiversity. For it is the exclusion of communities from their own land that drives them to destroy remaining forests in pursuit of economic survival.

The RSPO has made promising advances to boost global demand and raise credibility of the standard. However, some stakeholders concede that, as a global private standard, it may not be equipped to respond effectively to differing socioecological contexts and, as a result, it may not have the reach to transform the market and tackle deforestation "at the scale needed to have a big enough positive impact on the planet" (TFT, 2014, p. 11). At present, the RSPO's chief impact involves bringing the biggest palm oil producers into the Western agrofuel, cleansing agent and agri-food industries; in the process, the RSPO is forcing these companies to adopt much more stringent environmental and social safeguards to ensure compatibility with the values and objectives of fundamental Western standards, as set out, for example, by the European Union (EU, 2000).

It remains to be seen whether the proposed approaches will effectively drive the entire palm oil market towards sustainability. For apes, such a transformation would translate into secure habitats in large territories and adequate interconnectivity. For communities and smallholders, it would

mean benefiting from the value chain thanks to structural reforms. Achieving these goals requires sustained progress in the three complementary areas mentioned above: boosting consumer demand for CSPO, promoting the production and supply of CSPO as a way of factoring in social and environmental costs along the supply chain, and advocating the use of effective socioecological land use planning at the local and national levels. The alternative to taking these steps would be business as usual.

Acknowledgments

Principal authors: Denis Ruysschaert and Helga Rainer

Contributors: Patrice Levang, Ginny Ng Siew Ling, Olam International, Simon Siburat, Christopher Stewart, Wilmar International

Case Study 5.1: Wilmar International – Ginny Ng Siew Ling, Syarial Anhar Harahap, Surya Purnama, Simon Geh, Marcie Elene Marcus Jopony, John Alit and Simon Siburat

Case Study 5.2: Olam International – Christopher Stewart

Reviewers: Hilde de Beule, Elizabeth Clarke, Michelle Desilets and Carl Traeholt

Endnotes

1   The Executive Board was renamed Board of Governors to show that the Secretariat was taking over management responsibilities.

2   The classifications are derived from the Red List of the International Union for Conservation of Nature (IUCN, n.d.).

3   Based on comments made by the RSPO Secretary General at the 12th annual RSPO meeting, Kuala Lumpur, 19 November 2014.

CHAPTER 6

Impacts of Industrial Agriculture on Ape Ecology

Introduction

Agro-industrial landscapes represent a significant and increasing part of the ranges occupied by apes in Africa and Asia. The changes caused by the transformation of the natural habitat of apes have profound impacts on food availability, activity patterns, natural dispersal and ranging patterns, social systems, exposure to new pathogens and risks linked to close proximity with people and infrastructure development (specifically roads). Suitable habitat for gorillas across central Africa has declined by approximately 30%–50% over the past two decades (Junker *et al.*, 2012); this trend is likely to continue as various types of development expand in Africa. Indeed, approximately 43% of the area where African apes currently occur is suitable for oil palm production and much of that is outside of protected areas, which translates into a real likelihood that current ape habitat will be converted to agriculture (Wich *et al.*, 2014). Industrial-scale oil palm plantations have had well-documented, devastating effects on orangutan populations in Southeast Asia and could soon have a serious impact on African apes (Meijaard *et al.*, 2011; Wich *et al.*, 2012b).

Overall, forest clearance and degradation have a direct impact on all ape populations through habitat destruction and fragmentation. Logging and large-scale agricultural development also have indirect effects on these populations, specifically by facilitating access to previously remote areas, which can promote commercial wild meat hunting, including that of apes (Poulsen *et al.*, 2009). Forest clearance tends to be accompanied by significant influxes of people into an area, which can expose apes to disease (Laurance *et al.*, 2006; Leendertz *et al.*, 2006b; Köndgen *et al.*, 2008). Moreover, it can lead to further forest clearance across the landscape to sustain the newly established human populations (Cuaron, 2000; van Vliet *et al.*, 2012).

All available evidence—especially what is known about the plight of apes in Southeast Asia—shows that agro-industrial plantations cannot sustain viable ape populations in the long term, even though there is increasing evidence that apes may be making use of agro-industrial plantations as supplemental food sources, sleeping sites or corridors in the short term (Ancrenaz *et al.*, 2015). Apes use agricultural habitats primarily in the absence of an alternative, as their natural forest is cleared for agricultural and other uses.

To identify whether and how apes are using these different landscapes, and to assess whether that behavior can serve to promote ape conservation, it is essential to better understand how these newly created artificial landscapes impact apes and how they affect the interaction between people and apes. This information can then be used

to formulate appropriate recommendations for regulating and overseeing bodies—such as governments, the Roundtable on Sustainable Palm Oil and industry—and to better engage agribusinesses, plantation owners and grower communities in managing these areas for more positive ape conservation outcomes.

There remains a dearth of information, knowledge and understanding of the real impact of agriculture-induced landscape transformations on ape ecology, adaptation and long-term survival. Much more is known about the impact on apes in Asia than in Africa, largely due to the greater intensity of industrial agriculture in Asia compared to Africa over the past few decades. Doubtless, the situation will change quickly in Africa, especially as large-scale oil palm production is expanding rapidly (RFUK, 2013; Wich *et al.*, 2014). In Asia, more information is available for orangutans than for gibbons.

This chapter aims to provide an overall picture of the impact of industrial agriculture on ape ecology by summarizing formally published reports and gray literature; information gathered from experts, through discussion; and presenting the results of a 28-question online survey that was completed by the International Union for Conservation of Nature, the Species Survival Commission, and the Primate Specialist Group's Sections on Great Apes and on Small Apes.

Key findings:

- Habitat conversion for agricultural purposes can result in the local extinction of ape populations either directly, through the destruction of ape habitat, or indirectly, by facilitating the killing, capture or starvation of apes.

- Habitat conversion to other types of land use, including industrial agriculture, has resulted in the decline of the range of orangutans and gibbons in Southeast Asia and is today a major driver of the decline of all ape populations. The conversion of

> 66 All available evidence shows that agro-industrial plantations cannot sustain viable ape populations in the long term. 99

ape habitat is expected to accelerate in Africa, due in part to the expansion of industrial agriculture.

- Although great apes are able to enter agro-industrial landscapes to forage or disperse, they cannot survive in plantations alone and they need forest and natural habitat for their long-term survival.

- The survival of all apes is under serious threat unless 1) key habitats are taken into consideration in land use planning, 2) industry players and other stakeholders implement best management practices and 3) human communities that share the same habitat with apes tolerate this cohabitation. If we fail with any of these approaches, the future of all apes is seriously threatened.

Different Crop Types: Different Impacts

A variety of crops are grown in ape habitats. Cultivated fields range from small-scale cash crops to medium-sized mosaics of agroforest plantations—which produce crops such as banana, cashew, cloves, cocoa, coconut, coffee, corn, passion fruit, pepper, rice, sugarcane, sweet potato and tea—to commercial harvesting of agarwood (*Aquillaria* spp.) or pine trees, to extensive agro-industrial monocultures that cover tens or hundreds of thousands of hectares, for crops such as oil palm (*Elaeis guineensis*), sugarcane and tea, to industrial tree plantations.[1]

In comparison to natural forests, agricultural landscapes have a simplified structure and composition: tree density and diversity are impoverished, the number of tree canopy layers is reduced (they lack the multi-dimensional characteristics of tropical forests that occur within 28 degrees north or south of the equator), and they present a uniform tree age structure with sparse undergrowth. In case of annual crops

(crops harvested on a yearly basis, such as corn or rice), all canopy layers are completely absent. Depending on the type of crops cultivated, agricultural landscapes provide either a source of food for animals (mostly non-tree crops), or opportunities for shelter (non-edible tree crops) or both. Topsoil is leached or stripped by erosion or damaged by compaction, and microclimate conditions become drier and hotter (van Vliet *et al.*, 2012). Impoverished ecosystems found in agro-industrial monocultures possess a far lower floral and faunal diversity than natural forest ecosystems. Plantation assemblages are typically dominated by a few abundant generalist species and invasive species that replace endemic and forest-specialist taxa (Fitzherbert *et al.*, 2008).

Agricultural land is managed for the production of crops for humans and not for the maintenance of a diverse, natural ecosystem. Regeneration of these areas following the cessation of human exploitation requires intense management due to colonization by generalist and invasive species, with a very low likelihood for rapid and natural regeneration to the original forest composition. However, some ape species can temporarily use these altered landscapes as a food source, for nesting purposes or for travelling (whether for dispersing or ranging) between isolated patches of natural habitats.

Different Ape Species: Different Impacts

The current understanding of great ape ecology and behavior in agricultural and industrial landscapes is still very limited; much of the information comes from gray literature or anecdotal reports, although there is somewhat more research on orangutans (Meijaard *et al.*, 2010; Campbell-Smith *et al.*, 2011a, 2011b; Ancrenaz *et al.*, 2015). Research on the impacts of agro-industrial

> " The current understanding of ape ecology and behavior in agricultural landscapes is still very limited. "

practices on gibbons and African great apes is urgently needed. Numerous variables interact to determine how well apes are able to survive in agricultural landscapes. These include the intensity and extent of agricultural operations; whether the plantation is a monoculture; the resident population's former reliance on the converted area for keystone species or fallback foods; the degree of competition with sympatric taxa; and the severity of any additional anthropogenic impacts such as hunting, road access, human influx and associated agricultural expansion. It is therefore not surprising that clear themes on the impacts of large-scale agriculture on apes are difficult to isolate, especially given the large geographic range over which the different taxa occur.

In the long term, agro-industrial landscapes alone cannot sustain ape populations that are not connected to a larger metapopulation found in a more natural environment. It is important to remember that short-term survival of individual great apes cannot be equated with long-term success of a population. Indeed, research is needed to determine whether apes use landscapes that have been modified by human activity as part of their regular home range (by occasionally entering plantation areas), whether they are only transients in search of new forest habitat or whether they are taking part in a re-colonization process from nearby forests.

Orangutans

For a long time, scientists assumed that orangutans were very sensitive to forest disturbance (Rijksen and Meijaard, 1999; Delgado and van Schaik, 2000). However, recent studies have shown that orangutans are able to survive in exploited forests in Borneo and in a mosaic agroforest landscape in Sumatra (Ancrenaz et al., 2010; Campbell-Smith et al., 2011a, 2011b; Arcus Foundation, 2014). Recent surveys also show that orangutans have been found in large industrial acacia

and oil palm plantations in Borneo (Meijaard et al., 2010; Ancrenaz et al., 2015). Given the drastically simplified structure of these agricultural landscapes, it is not surprising that the behavior and ecology of orangutans in these altered landscapes differ markedly from those in natural forests.

In the mosaic landscape of northern Sumatra, orangutans spend more time resting and less time feeding, as well as less time eating fruits and more time consuming bark; they also have a smaller home range than conspecifics in the forest (Campbell-Smith et al., 2011a, 2011b). This strategy, called "sit and wait", is usually characteristic of periods of fruit scarcity, when orangutans rely heavily on substitute plant species to survive (Morrogh-Bernard et al., 2009). However, during a two-year study, natural fruits still contributed about 80% of their diet, suggesting that continued access to natural forest food sources is a strong determinant of the future of this population. In Kinabatangan, north Borneo, orangutans who are living in natural forests are regularly seen entering plantations and feeding on ripe fruits produced by mature palm trees and on young palm leaves (Ancrenaz et al., 2015).

In acacia and eucalyptus plantations, orangutans reportedly have longer daily travel distances than their wild counterparts.[2] The duration of the daily period during which orangutans are active—the time between leaving a night nest in the morning and building a new one in the evening—has also been noted to have changed for those living in and around plantations; they remain active later into the night to exploit plantation crops after humans have left (Campbell-Smith et al., 2011b; Ancrenaz et al., 2015). These patterns are similar to those of other crop-raiding non-human primate species in Africa and Asia (Krief et al., 2014). Orangutan nests can also be found in acacia and eucalyptus trees and in mature oil palms when no other trees are available for nesting (Meijaard et al., 2010; Ancrenaz et al., 2015).

Gibbons

Although gibbons do occur in forest patches within agricultural matrices, the consensus among questionnaire respondents is that gibbons do not generally use industrial landscapes as sleeping sites or as main sources of food; in particular, unlike the other apes, gibbons do not consume pith. Nor are gibbons normally targeted directly by humans in human–wildlife conflict over crop raiding, as perceptions of gibbons are generally positive; however, they do fall victim to hunting and the pet trade, as discussed below.

The impacts of agriculture on gibbons are somewhat difficult to assess as there are very few studies focusing on gibbons in an agricultural landscape. Due to their territorial and strictly arboreal nature, gibbons may be more affected by the immediate impacts of agricultural regimes than many other wildlife species (Asquith, 1995; Kakati, 2004). Specifically, the expansion of industrial agriculture affects gibbons by fragmenting their habitat and, in some cases, by clearing all the trees from a plantation (Vasudev and Fletcher, 2015). A lack of connectivity in the forest limits accessibility for immigration and emigration into an area, which affects dispersal from birth groups; it can also restrict ranges, reduce access to food, heighten territorial competition, increase isolation and restrict the gene pool.

Gorillas

Western and eastern gorillas—also known as lowland gorillas—are typically found at higher densities in secondary forests than in primary forest (Bermejo, 1999; Rogers *et al.*, 2004; Head *et al.*, 2012), which is likely linked to their reliance on understory vegetation. Gorillas have been observed in abandoned plantations, probably also because of the greater abundance of herbaceous vegetation in these forest clearings (Tutin, 1996). The two locations where mountain gorillas

live, Bwindi Impenetrable National Park, Uganda and the Virunga Massif of Rwanda, Uganda, and the Democratic Republic of Congo (DRC), are currently protected by national park status, which presumably buffers their habitat against industrial agriculture, but these areas are small and the gorillas do exit the national parks to crop raid. While little is known about Grauer's (eastern) gorillas, it is clear that they inhabit large areas of unprotected forest interspersed with human settlements, so they are likely impacted by agriculture. Both western and eastern gorillas, including mountain gorillas, are hesitant to cross roads, but they may venture more than half a kilometer outside of forests when areas of their former range have been removed.

Little is currently known about how gorillas respond to habitat changes brought on by agricultural landscapes. This knowledge gap mainly reflects the fact that there are relatively few industrial agricultural landscapes in areas occupied by gorillas, but the need for research is great as agricultural expansion in Africa is expected to increase dramatically in the foreseeable future (Wich et al., 2014). Few systematic studies have been done; among them are investigations of crop raiding on small-scale subsistence farms by mountain and western lowland gorillas. This research reveals that gorillas consume many crops, but primarily banana plants (the pith, but not the fruit), eucalyptus bark, pine tree bark and, occasionally, coffee, corn, passion fruit and sweet potatoes (Kalpers et al., 2010; Fairet, 2012; Seiler and Robbins, 2015).

Chimpanzees and Bonobos

In general, there is limited understanding as to how chimpanzees and bonobos manage in degraded or mono-dominant landscapes and what factors may compromise their survival and their ability to adapt to rapidly changing landscapes, such as those typi-cally imposed by industrialized agriculture. Nevertheless, it is evident that such landscapes may raise the frequency of encounters between apes and people; threaten ape survival and habitat; and challenge coexistence between people and apes locally. The risks vary across species, however. While the bonobo range across Africa is mainly restricted to the south of the Congo River in the DRC, in areas dominated by forest (IUCN and ICCN, 2012), chimpanzees inhabit a wider array of habitat types that range from primary forests to savannah, woodland and fallow, to agriculture-dominated landscapes across areas of West, Central and East Africa (Oates et al., 2008b).

Chimpanzees are indeed highly flexible in their behavior and can readily adapt to mixed agroforest landscapes with small-scale farming by foraging on crops, travelling along human paths and crossing roads to access different areas of their range (Hockings, Anderson and Matsuzawa, 2006; Hockings, 2007; Hockings and Humle, 2009). However, more research is required to determine whether and how such landscapes are able to sustain chimpanzees in the long term. Crop foraging potentially favors chimpanzee survival in such landscapes, as it provides the apes with dense clusters of highly nutritious foods. Wild chimpanzees have been reported to consume as many as 51 different parts from 36 different species of cultivars across their range (Hockings and McLennan, 2012). However, some crops with commercial value, such as banana, cacao, corn, mango, oil palm, papaya, pineapple and sugarcane, have been identified as "high-conflict" crops—that is, people are less tolerant of apes when they eat or damage these high-value crop types. Another study finds that chimpanzee communities that faced high levels of disturbance to their home ranges also experienced greater levels of harassment from people (Wilson et al., 2014b). Such situations run the risk of exacerbating retaliatory killings or the capture of apes (Brncic *et al.*, 2010). For an example of this, see Case Study 1.2 in Chapter 1 (page 29).

Although some bonobo populations are known to forage in secondary vegetation alongside agricultural fields (J. Thompson, personal communication, 2014), these apes tend to avoid areas of high human activity and fragmented forest, and the presence of humans significantly reduces effective bonobo habitat (Hickey *et al.*, 2013). Bonobos may also consume banana, palm pith, pineapple and sugarcane, but their crop consumption remains less studied than that of chimpanzees (Hockings and Humle, 2009; Furuichi *et al.*, 2012; Georgiev *et al.*, 2013); research may be limited simply because many bonobo populations occur in more remote areas dominated by primary forest, with relatively low human densities and levels of activity (IUCN and ICCN, 2012). As seen with chimpanzees, bonobo reliance on commercial (and subsistence) crops for food and nesting is likely to increase with the expansion of primary forests loss, land conversion and habitat fragmentation (Dupain and Van Elsacker, 2001; Myers Thompson, 2001); however, the extent of these changes will depend primarily on the type of crops grown locally.

The impact of industrial agriculture is of growing concern with respect to the status of both chimpanzees and bonobos across their ranges—be it linked to new developments or to the reclamation or reactivation of historical plantations of crops such as oil palm, rubber or sugar (see Box 6.1). In African countries whose conditions are propitious to oil palm and other large-scale agricultural development—such as Angola, the DRC, Gabon, Ghana, Ivory Coast, Liberia, the Republic of Congo and Sierra Leone—more than two-thirds of the land suitable for oil palm development is located outside protected areas and overlaps with great ape habitat (Wich *et al.*, 2014). Many of these areas, especially across West Africa, already represent degraded landscapes, where chimpanzees, in particular, have been thriving for generations, ironically, it seems, thanks to human tolerance and the presence of wild oil palms, which may be a key species for some chimpanzee communities, as they serve both nutritional and nesting purposes (Humle and Matsuzawa, 2004; Leciak, Hladik and Hladik, 2005; Brncic *et al.*, 2010; Sousa *et al.*, 2011).

In areas where wild oil palms persist, it remains unclear whether chimpanzees or bonobos would significantly target commercially grown palms, even if they knew the oil

BOX 6.1

Reclamation of Abandoned Plantations: Impact on Bonobos and Chimpanzees

In the DRC, many commercial plantations—whose crops include banana, cassava (also known as manioc and tapioca), coffee, oil palm, quinine, root crops, rubber, sugarcane, tea and tobacco—date back to the early 20th century and colonial times. Although most are located outside the bonobo range and have remained dormant as a result of decades of military and political insecurity, international companies, such as Feronia Inc., are now increasingly reclaiming abandoned oil palm, rubber and sugarcane plantations and reviving the commercial industry (J. Thompson, personal communication, 2014). Some of the areas they have targeted are within the bonobo range, such as those in Equateur province and along the Congo River. Although the large distances and the lack of overland infrastructure have greatly limited and concentrated plantation locations in specific areas, the probability of a rejuvenated industry looms on the horizon (FAO, 2012a); the risk of expansion into more pristine forest areas is thus high.

A similar pattern is apparent in Nigeria, especially in Cross River state, a key area for the Nigeria–Cameroon chimpanzee. Rural transformation in Cross River state is driven by the privatization of defunct plantations and the crowding out of smallholder production systems by agricultural investors (Schoneveld, 2014b).

Across three of Feronia's reclaimed oil palm concession areas in the DRC, road infrastructure increased by 34% in less than three years between 2011 and 2013 (Feronia, 2014). A rubber plantation has recently been reactivated in the DRC's Luo Scientific Reserve, which is part of the bonobos' current natural range (T. Furuichi, personal communication, 2014). However, there is no evidence to date to suggest that the Wamba bonobos use rubber trees for food or nesting, nor do they seem to use coffee or oil palm, which also occur in the area; what is known is that bonobos forage locally on subsistence and cash crops (Furuichi *et al.*, 2012).

The main concern for the apes in these landscapes is habitat loss and degradation, as well as increased hunting as plantations are reactivated and road infrastructure is expanded.

palm as a resource (Humle and Matsuzawa, 2004; Hockings and Humle, 2009); if they did, the risk of "conflict" with plantation owners would certainly be heightened. Their behavior may ultimately depend on what other natural resources are available to them across the seasons, as crop consumption, at least for chimpanzees, is often inversely correlated with the availability of natural foods in their habitat (Hockings, Anderson and Matsuzawa, 2009). Nesting patterns are also likely to depend on what other suitable species are available.

Although oil palm development is not as much of a concern in East Africa, other developments, such as sugarcane plantations, pose a potential threat to chimpanzee habitat and their coexistence with people in the region (T. Furuichi, personal communication, 2014).

The Varying Impacts of Different Phases of Production

Infrastructure Development

The development of agro-industrial plantations has resulted in increased remodeling and fragmentation of the natural habitat and ape populations. Examples include the removal of trees that border small tributaries and the digging out of drains and trenches, both of which create new barriers that are impassable to apes as none of the ape species can swim. This process of fragmentation will further threaten ape survival unless natural or artificial connection bridges are constructed (Ancrenaz, Dabek and O'Neil, 2007; Das *et al.*, 2009). Other infrastructure development, including roads, train tracks, electricity cables, human settlements and fences, also make the landscape less navigable for wildlife.

Where forest is fragmented, apes may be forced to travel on the ground to cross to different fragments due to the loss of canopy continuity, or because of isolation, such as if families or individuals are stranded in a small number of trees. Increased time on the ground makes the apes, and particularly gibbons, vulnerable to predation. Fragmentation can also lead to malnutrition and increased parasite loads in the medium term, and population decline in the long term (Das *et al.*, 2009).

In Central Africa and in Indonesia, the decline in ape densities has been linked to the growing number of roads and human settlements (Kuehl *et al.*, 2009; Marshall *et al.*, 2009b). This correlation largely reflects an increase in hunting for wild meat and the pet trade, as areas become more accessible to subsistence and commercial hunters, and transportation from remote areas to major cities becomes easier (Wilkie and Carpenter, 1999; Wilkie *et al.*, 2000; Poulsen *et al.*, 2009).

Wild apes, including those habituated to human presence, are likely to behave cautiously when close to human landscape features such as crop fields or roads. The effects of road infrastructure on forest composition and structure depend on road network density, width, spatial layout and traffic intensity (Malcolm and Ray, 2000; Wilkie *et al.*, 2000; Blake, 2002). Although secondary roads may be smaller and less frequented than primary transport roads, the former may occur at higher densities within the landscape and thus represent an impediment to natural patterns of habitat utilization in apes.

Chimpanzees are known to be more nervous and are more vigilant when entering crop fields to forage than when they are in the forest; they also stay closer together when crossing roads, especially wider ones (Hockings, Anderson and Matsuzawa, 2006, 2012). Recent observations in the Kinabatangan, on the island of Borneo, showed that wild habituated orangutans who were followed both inside and outside the forest were more wary of the presence of observers and more difficult to follow in oil palm landscapes (F. Oram, personal communication, 2014).

In the long term, the fragmentation and isolation of ape communities, groups and populations that result from significant landscape changes made for infrastructure development are likely to cause genetic inbreeding, which would significantly impact population viability. The heightened presence and activities of humans may also act as deterrents to dispersal and further erode the genetic health of the local population. Among chimpanzees, young adolescent females resident in less disturbed areas may be dissuaded from immigrating into semi-isolated communities if these exhibit high rates of encounters between humans and apes, thus further impacting the long-term survival of such communities (Matsuzawa, Humle and Sugiyama, 2011).

Habitat Destruction and Clearance

In most cases, the development of industrial crops involves the removal and conversion of natural forest, whether primary or already disturbed (Wilcove and Koh, 2010; Gaveau *et al.*, 2014). Overall, the impact of forest conversion on ape populations is dramatic for all species, and it should be stressed that populations that survive the initial forest conversion stage continue to decline after the establishment of the plantations (Bruford *et al.*, 2010). Nevertheless, some differences across taxa are expected when the natural habitat of apes is converted to industrial crops.

Orangutans: Forest clearance has the worst impact on the long-term survival of orangutan populations. Genetic studies in Kinabatangan, on the island of Borneo, show that 95% of the original orangutan population was lost over the past 200 years; that decline can be attributed to human activities, mostly hunting and forest clearance

for oil palm development and other crops (Goossens *et al.*, 2006). Forest conversion results in the death of nearly all resident and territorial orangutans—namely adult females and flanged males—either through direct killing and open-burning practices, or as a result of starvation (Rijksen and Meijaard, 1999). However, non-territorial, unflanged adult male orangutans can move away from disturbed areas and take refuge in undisturbed areas (MacKinnon, 1972; Ancrenaz *et al.*, 2010); the result is a transitional "excess" of males in remaining forest patches (Bruford *et al.*, 2010).

Gibbons: Undisturbed gibbon groups change and expand their territories as part of their natural behavior, suggesting that they may be able to move to avoid human disturbance such as forest clearance (O'Brien *et al.*, 2003; Cheyne, 2008a, 2010; Fan Peng-Fei and Jiang Xue-Long, 2008; Savini, Boesch and Reichard, 2008; Kim, Lappan and Choe, 2010). However, there are limits to the distance a group can move and to available forest for establishing new territories, depending on the level of disturbance and the number of groups affected; that is, a small number of groups may be able to move, yet the carrying capacity of the destination forest area may soon be reached (Akers, Islam and Nijman, 2013). If a group cannot establish a new territory, the most likely outcome is a breakup of the group or the death of an adult. The surviving adults and offspring may be unable to defend the territory, leading to group breakdown, reduced reproductive opportunities and possibly the associated deaths of the remaining group members (Choudhury, 1991; Kakati, 2004; Savini *et al.*, 2008; Cheyne, 2010; Cheyne, Thompson and Chivers, 2013).

Gorillas: The loss of nearly all naturally occurring vegetation renders habitat unsuitable for gorillas. To date, no studies have been conducted on the impact of large-scale clearing on gorillas, but in all likelihood it

Photo: In most cases, the development of industrial crops involves the removal and conversion of natural forest. Stranded orangutan being rescued by IAR in Indonesia.
© Alejo Sabugo, IAR Indonesia

would result in the death by starvation of the majority of the individuals if there are no remaining forest fragments or nearby areas of intact forest in which the apes can seek refuge. Small-scale subsistence farming can involve the clearance of the majority of native plant species, but some trees and under-story plants may remain. If such plants are present and the area borders on intact forest, gorillas are likely to continue to attempt to forage in this area if it previously constituted a part of their home range, particularly if they are habituated for tourism or research purposes (Kalpers *et al.*, 2010).

Chimpanzees and bonobos: Extensive clearing can cause a decline in chimpan-zee density and shifts in their home range, as evidenced by large-scale clearance con-ducted as part of commercial logging activi-ties (Johns and Skorupa, 1987; Chapman

and Lambert, 2000; Chapman *et al.*, 2000; Morgan and Sanz, 2007). The ramifications can include severe social disruption, as a result of increased competition, conflict and stress, with potential long-term consequences for the reproductive and general health of the population (White and Tutin, 2001; Emery Thompson *et al.*, 2007a; Kahlenberg *et al.*, 2008). Similar patterns are expected among the bonobos, although related data are more limited.

Young Plantations

In a mosaic landscape or close to the border between natural habitat and agro-industrial crops, animals who live in nearby forests or remaining forest patches are prone to using newly established plantations, especially

during periods of fruit scarcity in the forests. The likelihood of foraging on young plantations increases with the crops' proximity to the apes and depends on the type of crop.

In mosaic habitats, small forest patches, isolated trees or edge areas may still attract apes into plantations for feeding, even if they do not make regular use of these plantations. When forest patches are not producing food, some individuals tend to enter plantations to feed on resources that are available to them to survive. Orangutans typically feed on fruits cultivated by smallholders and cambium of acacias and other trees (Salafsky, 1993; Yuwono *et al.*, 2007); gibbons eat young leaves of acacia or the petiole (growing tip) of agarwood trees (S. Spehar, personal communication, 2014; U. H. Reichard, personal communication, 2014); chimpanzees and bonobos are known to pull out young fronds of wild oil palms for consumption of the petiole, making it likely that knowledgeable individuals might perform a similar foraging behavior if exposed to young saplings of commercially selected and grown oil palms or other plant species (Humle and Matsuzawa, 2004; Hockings and Humle, 2009).

The impact of young plantations on gorillas is unknown. Their response would likely depend on whether the understory or the ground vegetation is kept clear or if plants eaten by the gorillas are able to regrow. For example, herbaceous vegetation consumed by gorillas can grow in both young tea plantations and stands of eucalyptus trees (Kalpers *et al.*, 2010; Seiler and Robbins, 2015). As gorillas are unlikely to feed on the seedlings of eucalyptus or tea, this should not directly impact these crops.

Animals can cause significant economic losses on newly established plantations (Ancrenaz *et al.*, 2007; Campbell-Smith *et al.*, 2011b). Many of them are either killed or captured and translocated to other places (Hockings and Humle, 2009).

Mature Plantations

As with recently cleared areas and young plantations, the impact of mature plantations on apes depends on the planted crops, the management of the plantations and the presence of nearby forest patches.

Orangutans: Over time, orangutans who live in forests that are close to industrial plantations start to use mature plantations for dispersal, as a supplementary source of food or for nesting. As orangutans are mostly arboreal, it is no surprise that all age and sex classes have been recorded roaming and dispersing in acacia, eucalyptus and other tree species plantations (Chung *et al.*, 2007; Meijaard *et al.*, 2010). However, recent studies in Kinabatangan show that orangutans are also found in mature oil palm landscapes (Ancrenaz *et al.*, 2015). The animals bend and break large fronds to build their nests in the central part of the plant (Ancrenaz *et al.*, 2015). Orangutans who venture into oil palm plantations feed on young shoots and ripe fruit of mature oil palm plants, which they pick from bunches on the ground or take directly off the palm.

Recent fieldwork and surveys in the Kinabatangan floodplain reveal that these activities had no negative impact on the fruit productivity of the mature palms (Ancrenaz *et al.*, 2015). As a result, orangutans are not considered a major pest for mature oil palms (those that are at least five years old), although they can inflict significant damage when the plants are younger, as discussed above. In Kinabatangan, the vast majority of orangutan signs were found within 50 m of forest patches, suggesting that they are reluctant to disperse in oil palm plantations,

as has already been documented on Sumatra (Campbell-Smith *et al.*, 2011a). In this landscape, orangutans often walk on the ground to travel faster and to avoid detection (Ancrenaz *et al.*, 2014, 2015).

In industrial tree plantations, orangutans eat tree bark of acacias (Chung *et al.*, 2007; Meijaard *et al.*, 2010). In eastern Kalimantan, acacia plantations established close to Kutai National Park suffered a tree mortality rate of 5%–10% because of bark stripping by orangutans (Meijaard *et al.*, 2010).

Gibbons: Much of the focus of gibbon studies has been on tree plantations and little is known about the impact of low-level plantations, such as cocoa, rice and sugarcane. Gibbons are predominantly arboreal, much more so than the larger apes. While gibbons can walk bipedally for short distances, they are not likely to cross areas that are devoid of trees or covered by mature palms. Consequently, gibbons are not seen in areas of low-level crops, where there are no trees. Such plantations likely act as barriers to gibbon movement. Gibbons have not been shown to inhabit oil palm plantations, although they are sometimes present in isolated patches of forest left within a plantation. They do not consume the oil palm fruit or the pith of the young leaves. Gibbons may, however, enter acacia plantations and consume leaves (S. Spehar, personal communication, 2014). It is possible that mature plantations, even ones with trees, act as a barrier to dispersal; there is a need for more studies on the presence of gibbons, as no information is currently available on their long-term persistence in plantations, nor on their impact on mature plantations of any type.

Gorillas: Plantation management—which involves either the clearing of herbaceous understory vegetation that is consumed by gorillas, or tolerance of its growth among the crops—and the presence of nearby intact forest determine how mature plantations affect gorillas. Certain crops—such as banana and eucalyptus trees, which are highly sought after by gorillas—may in fact attract the apes as they reach more advanced stages of maturity (Seiler and Robbins, 2015).

Chimpanzees and bonobos: To date, there is no evidence that either chimpanzees or bonobos can thrive in mature plantations. While more research and reporting is urgently required, it may be assumed that their survival depends on the availability of other vegetation types and forested habitats within the landscape, human attitudes, pressures and density; another factor is the extent to which apes can use crops as a resource, such as mango, oil palm, oranges, pineapple and sugarcane. If chimpanzees have knowledge of the oil palm as a resource, the crop could potentially help them meet most of their nutritional needs. In some areas, chimpanzees are known to consume the rich oily fruit and the kernel of the nut throughout their range, using natural stone or wooden objects to crack open the hard-shelled nut. They also eat the tip end of young fronds, the pith of mature fronds, and potentially the oil palm heart[3] and beetle larvae contained in the dead trunk of the palm (Humle and Matsuzawa, 2004). The oil palm can also act as a highly preferred nesting species for chimpanzees in areas where oil palms are relatively abundant in the landscape, as in Guinea and Guinea-Bissau (Humle, 2003; Sousa et al., 2011). In Guinea, for example, Bossou chimpanzees spent nearly one-quarter of their feeding time consuming wild or feral oil palm parts; they also preferentially nest in wild or feral oil palms, especially at night (Humle, 2003; Soumah, Humle and Matsuzawa, 2014).

As yet, there is no indication that chimpanzee nesting or foraging on wild or feral oil palms has any significant impact on oil palm survival or fruit productivity (Humle and Matsuzawa, 2004; Soumah et al., 2014). However, this may depend on which part is preferentially consumed; consumption of oil palm flowers could, for instance, severely impact oil palm production and the frequency of use could affect palm survival over time (Soumah et al., 2014). However, when chimpanzees consume oil palm fruit, they often ingest the seed, which is then evacuated whole in the feces, a favorable environment for sapling growth (Lambert, 1998; Humle and Matsuzawa, 2004). Chimpanzees can also disperse the seeds of other crop species such as cacao, mandarins and oranges, thus promoting the growth and the distribution of these high-value species (Lambert, 1998; Hockings and Matsuzawa, 2014).

Conclusions on the Impacts of Different Phases of Production

As discussed, the different phases of agricultural development and production have variable impacts on ape populations. Forest conversion has the most negative impact on the short-term survival of the animals—through habitat loss, destruction of natural food sources and an increased rate of killing. By using newly established plantations, apes who survive forest conversion can cause significant economic losses and conflicts with people, which can lead to retaliatory killings, as discussed below. As crops mature, the extent of conflict may decrease significantly, partly due to the reduced ape population density in the area. At some stage, these plantations may simply act as "corridor" areas between fragmented forest patches, as long as the apes' ability to travel in these planted landscapes is not impeded and is tolerated by workers and plantation owners.

Remediation

Set-aside versus Total Clearance

As discussed, current information suggests that agro-industrial plantations cannot sustain viable orangutan populations in the long term (Meijaard et al., 2010; Ancrenaz et al.,

> **❝** By using newly established plantations, apes who survive forest conversion can cause significant economic losses and conflicts with people, which can lead to retaliatory killings. **❞**

2014); this conclusion is likely the case for all ape species. However, these landscapes could at least provide essential connectivity between populations in areas of natural forest (Wich *et al.*, 2012b); they could also maintain some basic ecosystem functionality (Wilson *et al.*, 2007a; Koh and Wilcove, 2008a; McShea *et al.*, 2009; Meijaard *et al.*, 2010; Ancrenaz *et al.*, 2015; Mendenhall *et al.*, 2014).

A conservation paradigm for apes in an agro-industrial landscape must include the preservation or restoration of small patches of forest—a system known as "set-aside"—as opposed to the total clearance of forest. Used as corridors or stepping stones, these forest patches—even if degraded—play an important role in sustaining ape populations by providing dispersal, nesting or food resources. All remaining forests and forest patches located within an industrial landscape should be identified as high conservation value forests (HCVF) and should be maintained as natural forests. Indeed, retaining forests within an agro-industrial landscape is the key to maintaining ecosystem functionality, because it ensures the viability of meta-populations of many wildlife species by facilitating dispersal and survival (Maddox *et al.*, 2007; McShea *et al.*, 2009).

Challenges to Rehabilitating Agricultural Lands

Deforested areas are very challenging environments for the natural growth of seeds and seedlings. The underlying soil or peat has been damaged and eroded: its nutrients have been depleted; the soil and water tables and waterways have often been polluted with artificial chemicals; the ground layer is open, compacted and exposed to a high amount of sunlight; much of the area is exposed or flooded during the wet season; forest soil seed stocks have been destroyed; and seed dispersal into the area is low. These problems

are particularly severe in peatlands, which suffer from additional impacts of disruption to natural hydrology and subsequent increased fire risk when converted (Page *et al.*, 2009).

Natural regeneration in these areas is often very slow, with much of the land colonized by sedges, rushes and low-growing shrubs, which are generalist or invasive species that can provide a barrier to subsequent secondary succession. The overall focus needs to be on assisted regeneration, including identifying species that would be suitable for large-scale reforestation projects. These species should be able to grow quickly to form a closed canopy, thus creating shade to make the habitat more hospitable to other tree species, and attracting seed-dispersing fauna to the area. This helps to speed up the rate of natural (unassisted) regeneration and, in the long term, to re-establish a forest that resembles its original state. Young secondary forest habitats resulting from a regeneration process can provide important fallback foods for bonobos (Hashimoto *et al.*, 1998; Terada *et al.*, 2015); they can also act as an essential source of food and nesting species for chimpanzees in modified landscapes (Humle and Matsuzawa, 2004; N. Bryson-Morrison and T. Matsuzawa, personal communication, 2015).

In the past, many reforestation projects have concentrated on commercial tree species or have adopted methods that are expensive—such as the use of fertilizer—or labor-intensive. Resources for most conservation projects are generally quite restricted, and therefore high costs are likely to reduce the scope and scale of planting. High-intervention projects are also less transferable to other sites, so any lessons learned are of less value to the conservation community. Therefore, a clear focus should be placed on identifying species that are naturally suited to growing in these conditions, and that require as little human intervention as possible (Matsuzawa *et al.*, 2011; OuTrop, 2013). As these reforestation activities usually

occur decades after a plantation begins operation, a clear long-term plan and commitment
is needed from agro-industrial companies.

It is important to stress that reforestation
is a very lengthy and expensive exercise. In
every case, it is always more economical to
avoid cutting down the forest than to initiate
a reforestation program after damage caused
as a consequence of poor land use planning.

Long-term Impacts

Ongoing population fragmentation, especially outside of protected areas, is a major
issue for most ape populations in Asia and
in Africa. Habitat fragmentation following
agricultural development leads the original
meta-population to be split into a number
of smaller subpopulations, as has been the
case among Cross River gorillas (Bergl *et al.*,
2008). These small populations become more
vulnerable to genetic drift and inbreeding,
and unpredictable events triggered by climate changes or anthropogenic pressures
(Shimada *et al.*, 2004; Bergl *et al.*, 2008; Xue
et al., 2015).

When forests are transformed into non-
forest landscapes without adequate large-
scale land use planning, which would include
provisions for the survival and population
connectivity of apes and other wildlife, the
impact on the original biodiversity in general and resident ape populations in particular is devastating. Many designated high
conservation value areas are too small or
too isolated from other forests to be viable
long-term habitats for apes. When forests are
replaced with crops, most animals disappear, as described above. The compression
effect—meaning the compaction of the habitat available to wildlife, which is sometimes
referred to as the "crowding effect"—occurs
when animals are exposed to disturbance in
part of their range and thus start to use their
home range differently; that is, they increase
the use of parts that have not been affected.

Photo: When forests are transformed into non-forest landscapes without adequate large-scale land use planning, which would include provisions for the survival and population connectivity of apes and other wildlife, the impact on the original biodiversity in general and resident ape populations in particular is devastating. © Greenpeace/Oka Budhi

Habitat loss is therefore expected to result in the compression of groups into undisturbed areas or "refuges" (Shimada *et al.*, 2004; Bergl *et al.*, 2008).

Most ape species present some degree of range overlap: male and female orangutans; family groups of gibbons, with estimates ranging from 11% to 64%; gorilla groups; and chimpanzee or bonobo communities (Idani, 1990; Reichard and Sommer, 1997; Singleton and van Schaik, 2001; Wrangham *et al.*, 2007; Bartlett, 2008; Cheyne, 2010; Robbins, 2010; Furuichi, 2011; Nakamura *et al.*, 2013). After the cessation of logging activities and other disturbances, individuals may return to their former range if some forest or other suitable habitat still remains (MacKinnon, 1971; Johns and Skorupa, 1987); however, there is great variation across the species and among individuals.

If crowding occurs for a short period of time or during periods of high seasonal fruit abundance, many animals may survive agricultural development in the short term. For chimpanzees, however, the situation is risky as they face a high risk of aggressive encounters with members of neighboring communities (Wrangham *et al.*, 2007); within a community, such compression could also result in heightened levels of competition and aggression among females (Miller *et al.*, 2014). In comparison, bonobos are more tolerant of neighboring groups (Furuichi, 2011).

If the crowding is long term and the compressed population exceeds the carrying capacity of the habitat, members of the resident population, as well as the displaced apes, run the risk of starvation, as has been observed among orangutans (Rijksen and Meijaard, 1999). The longer a population remains compressed, the more marked this effect will be. Many populations in forests and fragments today are likely undergoing a compression effect, as many wildlife species, including apes, are being pushed into small forest patches or fragments between burned or otherwise cleared areas. As a consequence,

> If crowding exceeds the carrying capacity of the habitat, members of the resident population, as well as the displaced apes, run the risk of starvation.

population densities increase beyond the carrying capacity of habitats and are unsustainable in the long term, due to a lack of space and food and, in some species, heightened levels of aggression, stress and susceptibility to disease. The likely long-term result is population decline, possibly followed by the local extinction of the species.

The following summaries provide the little information that is currently available about the long-term impacts of agricultural development on the various ape taxa.

Orangutans

In Kinabatangan forest, on Borneo, conversion resulted in a temporary influx of adult unflanged males into nearby patches of forests and therefore in a temporary male excess. These excess males dispersed into nearby agricultural landscapes after a few years, in search of new territories (Bruford *et al.*, 2010). There is, however, a risk of animals entering newly established plantations when there are not enough fruits in the natural forest patches. This results in conflicts and exacerbates retaliatory killings of orangutans because the apes destroy people's crops or because people are afraid of the orangutans (Abram *et al.*, 2015). The long-term consequences of a diet that is altered to include fruits and other parts of cultivated plants need to be investigated.

Gibbons

There is insufficient information about dispersal distances for subadult gibbons to determine maximum distances over which gibbons would disperse, perhaps with the assistance of canopy bridges to cross barriers such as roads, power cables or large forest gaps (Das *et al.*, 2009). The wide dispersal of groups that occurs at low densities could lead to a lag in new group formation due to an imbalance in available dispersing offspring, such as through the stochastic impacts of a male bias in any given dispersing generation. This situation would result in more males than available females, an imbalance that prevents many males from forming a new group with a female. Limited information is available about genetic relatedness among wild gibbon populations, but the available data suggest that the level of relatedness is naturally high (Liu *et al.*, 1989; Reichard and Barelli, 2008; Zhou *et al.*, 2008; Reichard, 2009; Kenyon *et al.*, 2011). The impacts of forest loss, population compression and reduction into fragments can thus be expected to have a long-term influence on the genetic viability of an affected population.

Gorillas

In case of compaction, gorilla groups that arrive in an area that is already occupied by another group or groups will face serious social and ecological challenges. Males compete intensely for females, both by retaining female group members and by attempting to get more females to join their group. Loss of habitat, which leads to greater crowding of individuals in a particular area, would likely result in higher rates of intergroup interactions and increased aggression among adult males. In turn, this could cause an increase in adult male mortality. The death of the dominant male of a one-male group of gorillas can also result in infanticide of unweaned infants, who are still dependent on milk, by other adult males, meaning that increased mortality among adult males has far-reaching consequences for other age and sex classes and group stability (Robbins and Robbins, 2004; Robbins *et al.*, 2013).

The ability of gorillas to move through a matrix of subsistence farming or industrial agriculture, which has implications for their ability to disperse as well as for genetic diversity, depends largely on the distance between suitable forest patches. However, the ability to retain connectivity between

patches, as well as the level of genetic diversity within and between patches, depends on more than absolute distance, as dispersal patterns differ for males and females. Female gorillas always disperse directly between social units and do not travel on their own, but males disperse alone and travel greater distances (Yamagiwa, Kahekwa and Basabose, 2003; Harcourt and Stewart, 2007; Guschanski *et al.*, 2009; Arandjelovic *et al.*, 2014; Roy *et al.*, 2014a). As a result, males may have more of an impact on gene flow within populations and among isolated subpopulations (Bergl *et al.*, 2008; Guschanski *et al.*, 2009; Roy *et al.*, 2014a). Human disturbance is believed to have resulted in an abrupt reduction not only in population size, but also in genetic diversity in Cross River gorillas, emphasizing that the impacts of altered landscapes are far more complex than only having fewer apes (Bergl and Vigilant, 2007; Bergl *et al.*, 2008).

Chimpanzees and Bonobos

As a result of habitat compression and increased home range overlap between neighboring communities, chimpanzees are likely to commit intercommunity lethal attacks on both adults and infants (Watts *et al.*, 2006; Williams *et al.*, 2008; Wilson *et al.*, 2014b); however, such events are unlikely to arise among bonobos, among whom records of conspecific killings remain extremely rare (Wilson *et al.*, 2014b). If forced into areas dominated by agricultural crops, chimpanzees may have to forage on crops to meet their nutritional needs (Hockings *et al.*, 2009). They may also become more visible—though not necessarily more habituated—to local people, thereby potentially exacerbating people's fear of chimpanzees and heightening the risk of retaliation from farmers or plantation workers (Hockings and Humle, 2009). All these factors necessarily imply increased competition and stress,

BOX 6.2

The Road to Extinction: The Bossou Chimpanzees in Guinea, West Africa

The Bossou chimpanzee community in southeast Guinea, West Africa, lives about 6 km from the Nimba Mountains, which are home to several chimpanzee communities. This group inhabits an agroforest matrix and is semi-isolated from its neighbors. Research shows that the community is likely to become extinct. The threats to their survival include the following:

- a lack of immigrant females;
- the disappearance of natal females (that is, over the years, as expected, some of the younger females may have emigrated from the community, possibly to join neighboring communities in Nimba, although this assumption remains unconfirmed);
- the aging of its members (some are over 50, and older females no longer reproduce) (Sugiyama and Fujita, 2011); and
- sporadic mortality events associated with outbreaks of respiratory infection predominantly affecting infants and older individuals (Humle, 2011a).

It may be too risky for females from other communities in the Nimba Mountains to travel through an open savannah or agricultural forest matrix from their more contiguous and pristine natal primary forest. These Nimba females are much more likely to disperse to known neighboring communities along the massif than to immigrate into a community exposed to high levels of human presence and disturbance, whose existence is potentially unknown to them, such as Bossou.

It is ironic that—in spite of the evident risk of extinction of this community, as associated with longer-term cumulative genetic erosion, reproductive senescence and respiratory epidemics—until recently, Bossou chimpanzees showed significantly shorter interbirth intervals and higher infant survival rates than conspecifics more dependent on wild foods for their survival (Sugiyama and Fujita, 2011); this pattern was attributed to their significant reliance on highly nutritious crops available to them in their habitat. However, the chimpanzees at Bossou also have an extremely diverse diet comprising more than 200 plant species, which represent 30% of all available plant species in their heterogeneous environment (Humle, 2011b). While rapid habitat conversion, especially on a large scale, can have significant negative effects on the reproductive success and survival of individual apes and populations, feeding on crops may, in some cases, actually benefit the reproductive success of particular populations in the short term, provided there is no retaliation from people and the landscape is a mixed agricultural forest mosaic that enables dietary diversity, rather than one dominated by monocultures.

This example highlights the heightened vulnerability to epidemic outbreaks of small gregarious groups of apes and the importance of ensuring gene flow between groups or subpopulations and maintaining a landscape propitious to dispersal.

which impact ape health and reproduction (Pusey, Williams and Goodall, 1997; Emery Thompson *et al.*, 2007b). Such patterns are also expected among bonobos.

Should bonobo and chimpanzee ranging and dispersal be constrained by landscape features and habitat quality—as determined by food abundance and distribution, not only year-round but also seasonally—then it is likely that lactating females and especially their offspring could suffer from nutritional stress (Markham *et al.*, 2014); moreover, the population's reproductive and genetic viability would be impacted significantly. If they are unable to expand or shift their range during times of food scarcity, chimpanzees are forced to rest more and travel less (Takemoto, 2002, 2011); alternatively, they may have to compete more aggressively for food (Miller *et al.*, 2014). In addition, in areas where chimpanzees are at risk of being hunted or killed, they vocalize less and drum less on trees than they do in undisturbed areas (Hicks, Roessingh and Menken, 2013). Such a reduction in communication patterns could have a significant impact on dispersal success and on sociality; that is, it may compel the community to be more gregarious, thus heightening competition for food among community members, which potentially forces increased reliance on highly nutritious and highly abundant crop species or shifts in activity patterns, such as nighttime crop raiding (Krief *et al.*, 2014). Increased densities of apes and other wildlife could also imply increased risk of parasitic infection and ill health, thus exposing the community or population to added risk (Gillespie and Chapman, 2006).

Conclusions on Long-term Impacts

In all likelihood, the transformation of natural forest to non-forest landscapes results in increased physiological and ecological stressors that impact the short- and long-term survival of ape populations. The decline of food resources has a negative impact on breeding success—such as ovarian function and overall reproductive success and survival rates (Knott, 1999; Knott, Emery Thompson and Wich, 2009). It increases inter- and intra group competition for resource access and, in some cases, inter group or inter-individual aggression. Stress also affects the immune system and general health of the animals (Muehlenbein and Bribiescas, 2005). In addition, habitat fragmentation and any associated barriers to natural dispersal are likely to hinder gene flow and contribute to the reproductive senescence of these populations (see Box 6.2). Combined, these factors can lead to a negative growth rate, to a decline in overall population size and, ultimately, to local extinction.

The Impact of Socio-economic and Cultural Values on the Forest–Agriculture Interface

Human presence is greater in agricultural lands than in natural forests; a hectare (0.01 km²) of industrial oil palm plantation sees human presence 56 days per year, on average (Ginoga et al., 2002). This presence introduces new risks and challenges for surviving wildlife, such as emerging diseases, more frequent encounters and conflicts with domestic animals and people, and, consequently, more frequent killings of apes and other wildlife. The survival of viable populations of apes and other wildlife in heavily transformed landscapes ultimately depends on the general perception of human communities that share the same environment.

The public perception and acceptance of wildlife reflect a complex combination of factors. These are frequently related to economy: is wildlife perceived as a source of loss because of conflicts or a source of gain through ecotourism and other services? Or are wild animals valued for other reasons, such as an individual appreciation of an animal's proximity for recreation, the place of animals in traditional culture and folklore, and awareness of their role in maintaining health of the ecosystem (Meijaard et al., 2013)?

The presence of wildlife in newly created human-made (anthropogenic) landscapes, such as agricultural lands, often results in crop-raiding activities and an increase in conflicts. These conflicts lead to emotional distress and occasionally to significant economic losses (Nepal and Weber, 1995; Ancrenaz et al., 2007; Chung et al., 2007; Campbell-Smith et al., 2011b, 2012). Worse, the occurrence of conflicts creates a negative perception of wildlife and becomes a major impediment to building local support for conservation (Webber, Hill and Reynolds, 2007; Marchal and Hill, 2009; Aharikundira and Tweheyo, 2011; Campbell-Smith et al., 2012; Gore and Kahler, 2012).

Successfully addressing conflicts between wildlife and humans requires the design and implementation of technical solutions that decrease or suppress the damage (Hockings and Humle, 2009). For a strategy to yield long-term success, however, it also needs to integrate the underlying social and stakeholder dimensions of the problem (Ancrenaz et al., 2007; Dickman, 2010, 2012).

Human–Ape Interactions

Agriculture Development and Crop-raiding Activities

Apes who are living within or close to plantations can cause substantial damage to people's crops, as discussed above. Orangutans, for example, kill acacia trees by stripping bark and cambium (Meijaard et al., 2010); they also pull out stems and destroy young palms to feed on the heart of the plant (Yuwono *et al.*, 2007). In addition, they can consume entire fruit crops in orchards that belong to local villagers (Campbell-Smith *et al.*, 2011b); in this case, orangutan crop-raiding activities are better explained by the presence of ripe cultivated fruits than the scarcity of wild fruit. Most of the raiding activities take place less than 500 m from forest edges (Ancrenaz *et al.*, 2015). Gibbons have not been identified as a major crop-raiding species and are generally not subjected to retribution killings. Studies have reported the presence of subsistence foods and crops, such as cloves, coconut, rattan, sago, sweet potato and taro, around gibbon habitat, but the local gibbons did not use any of them (PHPA, 1995; Quinten *et al.*, 2014; gibbon experts, personal communication, 2014).

In Africa, studies in Bwindi, Uganda indicate that crop raiding by gorillas appears to be primarily influenced by the presence of palatable crops or native species growing in the understory of eucalyptus, pine and tea plantations—and not by food availability within the park (Seiler and Robbins, 2015). In Kibale National Park, which is also in Uganda, forest-dwelling wildlife, including chimpanzees, are more likely to forage on crops in fields located within 500 m of the forest edge than further afield (Naughton-Treves, 1997, 1998). Chimpanzees, in particular, can be responsible for significant damage (Hockings and McLennan, 2013).

Disease Risk

Diseases can play a significant role in the decline and extinction of apes and other wildlife (Leendertz *et al.*, 2006a). The occurrence of emerging infectious diseases is also a major threat to global public health, with high economic impacts. These diseases result from complex demographic and anthropogenic environmental changes, including global climate change, urbanization, increased

> " The increased risk of disease transmission between humans and apes who live in human-modified landscapes originates from physical proximity and elevated levels of stress. "

presence and incursions of people in natural ecosystems, international travel and trade, land use change and agricultural intensification, poaching for wild meat and the live animal trade, and the breakdown of public health (Daszak *et al.*, 2013). The increased risk of disease transmission between humans and apes who live in human-modified landscapes originates from physical proximity between humans and apes and associated elevated levels of stress that could impede an individual's immune system from combating disease and infection (Muehlenbein and Bribiescas, 2005).

In the case of Asian apes (orangutans and gibbons), increased terrestrial locomotion in a human-made matrix increases the susceptibility to contamination with pathogens of human origin (H.B. Hilser, personal communication, 2011; Ancrenaz *et al.*, 2014). In general, the current state of knowledge on pathogens and diseases of wild orangutans and gibbons is limited, except for some studies on intestinal parasites (Mul *et al.*, 2007; Labes *et al.*, 2010). Therefore, the epidemiology and dynamics of emerging diseases that could potentially affect these species in human-made landscapes need to be investigated (Gillespie and Chapman, 2006; Travis *et al.*, 2008; Muehlenbein and Ancrenaz, 2009).

Disease transmission is a major threat to gorilla and chimpanzee populations across sub-Saharan Africa (Köndgen *et al.*, 2008). Less is known about bonobos, but their susceptibility to diseases is expected to be similar to that of chimpanzees.

Chimpanzees and gorillas are prone to a variety of diseases, including Ebola and a range of typically human-borne diseases ranging from pneumonia to polio (Formenty *et al.*, 2003). All African apes are particularly vulnerable to respiratory disease outbreaks, especially where regular and close proximity to humans is prevalent (Sakamaki, Mulavwa and Furuichi, 2009; Humle, 2011a; Palacios *et al.*, 2011).

There is also strong evidence that chimpanzees and gorillas harbor greater parasite loads and share several types of intestinal parasites with humans in areas occupied and disturbed by people (Rwego *et al.*, 2008; McLennan and Huffman, 2012). One study suggests that increased ecological overlap may promote microbial exchange between chimpanzees and humans (Goldberg *et al.*, 2007); since some bacteria are pathogenic—meaning that they can induce illness—and infections can sometimes be fatal (such as *Escherichia coli*), this study stresses the value of strategies aimed at limiting inter-mixing of gastro-intestinal bacteria in order to benefit both human health and ape conservation.

Intense exploitation and heavy human presence in agricultural landscapes that are used by apes definitely increases the risk of disease transmission between taxa. It is vital, therefore, to promote good sanitary and health standards of people living near ape populations, and to implement a thorough health monitoring program of the wild populations that are in close contact with humans. Failure to do so can have catastrophic consequences (Köndgen *et al.*, 2008; Humle, 2011a; Reed *et al.*, 2014).

Retribution Killings

In most places where apes cause damage, people are resentful and can be very upset by crop-raiding animals foraging in their fields. In some areas of Borneo, subsistence farmers consider orangutans the most damaging crop-raiders (Hockings and Humle, 2009); in many human-modified landscapes, killing the "pest" animals is often seen as the ultimate solution to conflicts with orangutans (Davis *et al.*, 2013; Abram *et al.*, 2015). The effects of industrial agriculture on African great apes are still mostly unknown, but the likely impacts can be estimated based on those of small-scale subsistence farming. In places where raiding is not tolerated or

people fear great apes, they are chased off, injured by snares and other devices, or killed in retribution (Brncic *et al.*, 2010; Kalpers *et al.*, 2010; Fairet, 2012).

Foraging in planted fields, plantations or orchards is potentially high-risk behavior for all species of apes (Hockings *et al.*, 2009). Consequently, animals may shift their active period and enter the crops in the early morning or late afternoon, when people are not around (Ancrenaz *et al.*, 2015; Krief *et al.*, 2014). In most of the chimpanzee range in Africa, adult males tend to be the ones who forage on crops, since they are more likely to exhibit risk-taking behavior than are adult females or subadults (Hockings, 2007; Wilson, Hauser and Wrangham, 2007b).

It should be noted that retaliatory killings are not the only way that apes who live close to plantations are killed. Indeed, recent interview surveys conducted in Kalimantan, the Indonesian part of Borneo, reveal that animals were also killed for a number of other reasons, including the illegal trade in meat, pets and traditional medicine, as well as due to fear and ignorance. Research has identified a complex interplay of variables that predict the risk of orangutans being killed at the local level; among these, religion is the prime indicator and Christian people are the most likely to kill orangutans (Davis *et al.*, 2013; Abram *et al.*, 2015). These surveys also concluded that between 2,000 and 3,000 orangutans have been killed every year over the past three to four decades in Kalimantan (Meijaard *et al.*, 2011); the rate is well above what the species can sustain (Marshall, 2009). These findings indicate that many orangutan populations will go extinct within a human lifetime (60 years) if killing continues at the current rate (Meijaard *et al.*, 2012). In some regions of Africa, wild meat hunting represents a major threat to ape populations and also fuels the pet trade, since infants are also often captured as a by-product of such activities (Tutin *et al.*, 2001; Poulsen *et al.*, 2009; Ghobrial *et al.*, 2010).

> **"** In places where raiding is not tolerated or people fear great apes, they are chased off, injured by snares and other devices, or killed in retribution. **"**

The Need for Better Land Use Planning

The best way to limit the negative impacts of agricultural and industrial development on wild ape populations is to prevent any large-scale development where major ape populations occur. When all or part of the range of an ape population is designated for land conversion, it is crucial to undertake a sound and precise land use planning program that considers the needs of apes (and other wildlife) before any new development takes place. HCVF and other important unprotected forest patches, as well as corridors, have to be identified, marked and set aside at the earliest stages of land use planning (Ancrenaz *et al.*, 2015). It is also essential to evaluate the entire landscape structure and to incorporate other types of land use in proximity to plantations to minimize fragmentation and the potential exacerbation of conflict with ape species that are likely to forage on commercially grown or subsistence crops. In addition, management plans that try to use connectivity between forest fragments as a strategy need to consider not only the distance between forest patches (structural connectivity), but also the quality of the area between the patches and the level of human activity within connecting areas (functional connectivity) (Kindlmann and Burel, 2008).

In addition, a zero-tolerance policy on the killing of apes and other harmful acts needs to be enforced at all management levels in agro-industrial plantations. The opening of ape habitat for oil palm and other plantations increases conflicts between humans and apes across their range, and allows increased access to poach apes for the pet trade and for wild meat. The killing of apes —either as a retaliatory means to protect people's crops or for meat—has a knock-on effect on reproductive success and significantly affects the long-term survival of

ape populations. Indeed, studies have shown that orangutan populations cannot withstand annual killing rates of more than 1% of reproductive adults without going extinct (Marshall *et al.*, 2009b). This is linked to the fact that apes exhibit a slow reproductive rate, as a result of long interbirth intervals and slow maturation of youngsters to adulthood (Williamson *et al.*, 2013).

Conclusions on the Need to Incorporate the Human Social Dimension in the General Picture

More information is urgently required on the drivers and patterns of crop foraging in apes, the impact of humans on their social, foraging and ranging behavior, and the drivers and extent of killings for all species, whether retributive or for meat, in anthropogenic landscapes.

Human–ape conflict leads to emotional distress in apes and occasionally to significant economic losses for humans (Nepal and Weber, 1995; Chung *et al.*, 2007; Campbell-Smith *et al.*, 2012). The occurrence of conflict creates a negative perception toward wildlife and becomes a major impediment to building local support for conservation (Webber *et al.*, 2007; Marchal and Hill, 2009; Campbell-Smith *et al.*, 2012; Gore and Kahler, 2012). The successful mitigation of conflict between apes and humans requires the design and implementation of technical solutions that decrease or suppress the damage done to both sides (Hockings and Humle, 2009). But for a strategy to yield long-term results, it also needs to integrate the underlying social and stakeholder dimensions to the problem (Dickman, 2010). There is thus an urgent need to disentangle the real from the perceived cost of ape foraging on crops, and to assess the socioeconomic and political dimensions of conflict among local stakeholders that could have an impact on ape survival.

As the needs and aspirations of local communities are the ultimate drivers of conservation successes or failures outside protected forests, it is clear that they should be encouraged and assisted in order to become engaged actors in—and not only beneficiaries of—conservation efforts (Steinmetz, Chutipong and Seuaturien, 2006; Meijaard *et al.*, 2012).

Survey Results: Summary of Main Impacts

Following the International Primatological Society meeting in Vietnam in August 2014, the authors of this chapter developed a questionnaire using the online survey tool SurveyMonkey. The main purpose was to

TABLE 6.1

Impact of Industrial Agriculture on Apes and Ape Use of Crops Based on Questionnaire Responses and Expert Opinions

Ape species		Bonobos	Chimpanzees	Gibbons	Gorillas	Orangutans
Number of respondents		2	9	17	2	8
Countries represented		DRC	Guinea-Bissau, Republic of Congo, Tanzania, Uganda	Bangladesh, China, India, Indonesia, Malaysia, Thailand	Republic of Congo	Indonesia, Malaysia
Apes are known to forage on commercial crops		Yes	Yes	No	Yes	Yes
Apes are known to nest in some plantation tree species or oil palm		Unknown	Yes	Not available	No	Yes
Ape habitat loss reported as a result of agro-industry – in the last 10 years		Yes	Yes	Yes	Yes	Yes
Increased habitat fragmentation occurring – in the last 10 years		No	Yes	Yes	No	Yes
Plantations result in a decrease in the apes' natural foods – in the last 10 years		Yes	Yes	Yes	Yes	Yes
Shift in ape range and ranging patterns – in the last 10 years		Yes	Yes	Yes	No	Yes
Increased ape–human interaction – in the last 10 years		No	Yes	Yes	No	Yes
Increased number of ape rescue interventions – in the last 10 years		No	Yes	Yes	No	Yes

canvass ape researchers, conservationists, and rehabilitation and reintroduction practitioners with respect to the key ways in which agro-industry threatens and affects apes.

Table 6.1 summarizes the predominant impacts of agro-industry on apes based on 30 responses to the questionnaire and other expert opinions, following in-person discussions of the questionnaire with researchers and primatologists. As only a few respondents provided information about gorillas and bonobos, the "no" responses for those apes should be interpreted as site-specific, not as representative of the species' full ranges. It should also be noted that the answers to these questions would probably change according to the intensity of agricultural development in ape ranges, such as if the oil palm industry expands in sub-Saharan Africa.

The respondents to the questionnaire identified key threats and important questions for the conservation of apes in these landscapes, which are summarized below. This list is not exhaustive; site-specific responses are available in Annex I.

Economic impacts

- Apes destroy subsistence or staple crops by foraging, thus affecting people's access to food and income.
- Opportunity costs are incurred if people miss work or fail to engage in other economic activities because they need to protect their crops from apes.

Genetic diversity and health

- Agro-industry expansion could lead to the degradation of genetic diversity.
- What are the causes and the potential means of preventing disease transmission between people and apes?

Ape behavioral ecology

- In zones where ape habitat and plantations overlap, what food resources are the apes consuming?

- How flexible is ape ecology and life history? What can be learned from comparing ape populations in intact versus disturbed areas? How much of their diet comes from plantation crops, and how much from wild foods found in secondary forest patches?
- Have apes drastically changed their energy budgets to accommodate the change in environment? If so, are the adapted budgets sustainable in the long term?
- Is the use of landscapes gendered? Are females using small areas, or are they moving between secondary forest patches? Do males have different patterns?
- What is preventing apes from surviving long term in fragments?
- Is normal dispersal taking place in any fragmented habitats?

Ape population and home range sizes

- What are the population sizes of apes in modified landscapes?
- What are the minimum requirements of species-specific home ranges, including tree and feeding tree densities? To what extent do home ranges fluctuate over time?
- How can ape populations be maintained, helped to recover or reintroduced in protected areas in mosaic agricultural landscapes?
- What are the carrying capacities of plantations?
- Endocrinological studies would allow for analysis of ape energy budgets and stress levels, and how these factors affect reproductive capacity.
- What is the effect of habitat compression in the remaining forest on the natural socioecology of apes?
- The collection of demographic information could inform population viability analyses and other modeling.

Photo: A significant part of the current range occupied by apes will be profoundly transformed by agriculture within the next decades, as range countries intensify their commercial agricultural activities to bolster their economies and to address the needs and demands of the growing human population. Stockpiles of plantation timber at a pulp and paper plant on Sumatra.
© Daniel Beltrá/Greenpeace

Mitigation of negative human–wildlife interactions

- What is the frequency of interactions, conflict and killings between apes and people?

Land use planning

- How can land use planning be improved?
- How can habitat be secured and corridors established?

Conclusions

A significant part of the current range occupied by apes will be profoundly transformed by agriculture within the next decades, as range countries intensify their commercial agricultural activities to bolster their economies and to address the needs and demands of the growing human population.

Scientists alone will not change how the world evolves or how human development progresses. There is, however, an urgent need for the results of research to reach stakeholders beyond academic circles—to ensure that all social groups are informed: politicians, local communities, private industry, the media, civil society and others. To reach a wider audience, multi-disciplinary engagement is required (Johns, 2005; Meijaard *et al.*, 2012).

The future of apes—and of many other species—very much depends on the long-term security of strictly protected forests and already established agroforest matrices where illegal logging, natural resource extraction and poaching are efficiently controlled and where ape populations are large enough to cope with potential catastrophic events, such as fires and disease (Meijaard *et al.*, 2011). These forests must have the ecological gradients that contain key resources to ensure that apes are able to adapt to climate change (Gregory *et al.*, 2012). Across wider

landscapes, scientifically based, regional land use planning is needed to delineate the zones of interaction around protected forests or important forest patches for apes and their surroundings, which also provide irreplaceable hydrological, ecological and socioeconomic services to people (DeFries *et al.*, 2010).

Ideally, these core forest areas should remain connected with other forests, which could potentially be used for commercial timber extraction. Indeed, well-managed timber concessions result in significantly lower levels of forest conversion than those associated with industrialized agricultural activities (Gaveau *et al.*, 2012, 2013); this finding highlights the possible value of the timber industry in maintaining ape populations in the long term (Arcus Foundation, 2014). Some agricultural companies already have certain attributes that are useful for biodiversity conservation: well-trained staff, significant financial resources, and clear and strong operation protocols for managing their activities. Therefore, it is urgent to engage with these stakeholders to improve their practices.

Natural forest areas could also be buffered by low-intensity plantations such as acacia, pulp and paper, and other mosaic industrial tree plantations (McShea *et al.*, 2009). These landscapes could then be connected to high-intensity use areas, such as other agro-industrial schemes and areas where infrastructures, roads and small-scale agriculture dominate alongside human settlements (Wich *et al.*, 2012b).

The design of such dynamic landscapes must be approached across the whole landscape rather than at the site or species level (Morrison *et al.*, 2009; Sayer *et al.*, 2013). The focus needs to be shifted from conserving specific sites and species to respecting landscapes and processes; that shift involves envisioning a larger-scale landscape approach. The resulting ecological benefits extend far beyond just apes. Conserving ecosystem functions and services can only happen if environmental concerns are considered at the beginning of the planning process. The best chance of achieving this goal requires full engagement from and collaboration among scientists, NGOs, government agencies and the private sector (Doak *et al.*, 2014).

Regardless, it is inevitable that agro-industrial landscapes will have a predominantly negative impact on apes. In newly created agro-industrial landscapes, the long-term impact of human disturbance on biodiversity is strongly influenced by the general configuration of the landscape after habitat loss and alteration (Fischer and Lindenmayer, 2006; Forman, 2006; Hilty *et al.*, 2006). While apes may be able to modify their behavioral ecology by incorporating plantation crops into their diet, little is known about their long-term adaptability to human-created landscapes, the long-term impacts of industrial agriculture and the loss of biodiversity and ecosystems. What remains abundantly clear is that apes depend on natural vegetation, which is normally incompatible with large-scale plantations. More research is needed to understand the most effective strategies for conserving apes in a human-modified landscape. It is therefore imperative to investigate whether and how industrial-scale agricultural landscapes can serve the conservation of apes and biodiversity. At the same time, it is important to ensure that agricultural landscapes retain some functional ecological role to guarantee a minimum level of ecosystem services (Foster *et al.*, 2011).

> "What remains abundantly clear is that apes depend on natural vegetation, which is normally incompatible with large-scale plantations."

Acknowledgments

Principal authors: Marc Ancrenaz, Susan M. Cheyne, Tatyana Humle and Martha M. Robbins

Reviewers: Takeshi Furuichi, Mark E. Harrison, Andrew J. Marshall and Melissa Emery Thompson

Endnotes

1 Industrial tree plantations grow timber species such as *Acacia* spp., *Eucalyptus* spp., *Albizia* spp. (silk tree), *Hevea braziliensis* (rubber tree) and *Neolamarckia cadamba* (known as Kadam or Laran).

2 S. Spehar, unpublished data, reviewed by the authors.

3 To get to the oil palm heart, chimpanzees reportedly use a modified frond as a pestle; this behavior is known as "pestle pounding" and has been recorded in Bossou, southeast Guinea, and less frequently elsewhere (Ohashi, 2015).

INTRODUCTION

Section 2: The Status and Welfare of Great Apes and Gibbons

Thus section of *State of the Apes* provides details on the status and welfare of all great apes and gibbons, both in situ and in captivity, as well as on broader issues that affect each of these groups. Abundance estimates of the different ape taxa in situ are presented online, in the Abundance Annex, which is available on the *State of the Apes* website: www.stateoftheapes.com. Updated information on the number of apes in captivity is provided in Chapter 8. The regular provision of data and findings in this section is intended to allow for the identification of population trends and patterns over time.

The section is comprised of two chapters; the first focuses on apes in situ and the second on apes in captivity. In this edition, the in situ chapter explores the relevance and findings of long-term monitoring of wild populations of apes. It also considers, through four case studies, what has been learned about key threats and opportunities for influencing ape conservation and welfare. The chapter on captive apes looks at the legal context, status and conditions of apes housed in facilities across the world, the pressures that led to their captivity and the role played by people's perceptions, not only with respect to captive apes, but also in terms of people's support for ape conservation.

Chapter Highlights

Chapter 7: Long-term Trends

This chapter presents long-term case studies on four species of apes in different locations:

- Bornean orangutans in Sabangau Forest, Indonesia;
- chimpanzees in Gombe Stream National Park, Tanzania;
- bonobos in Wamba, in the Democratic Republic of Congo (DRC); and
- silvery gibbons in Mount Halimun Salak National Park, Indonesia.

In exploring long-term datasets across different taxa and contexts, this chapter describes some of the threats to ape populations and the challenges inherent in their conservation. Three of the case studies illustrate the value of long-term engagement on a broad geographic scale, as well as the utility of understanding political and economic contexts in critical ape habitats. The fourth case study highlights the ambiguity and the gaps in our knowledge of many ape species and populations. It also demonstrates the importance of research, consistent survey methods, and the sharing of data in a way that facilitates comparison and the detection of trends, so that the information can then be used to inform and develop appropriate conservation strategies.

While the case studies expose the impacts of logging, armed conflict, habitat loss and agricultural development on the viability of ape populations, they also showcase positive trends among ape populations, particularly those that have resulted from effective protection and the application of natural resource management principles. This research underscores that long interbirth intervals make apes particularly vulnerable to even small declines in their populations; it also reveals that habitat loss, hunting and disease are

the key threats to ape survival. These threats are driven by economic development and are often compounded by political and social dynamics. All of these factors influence the capacity and drive of relevant authorities and organizations to achieve conservation outcomes. Perhaps unsurprisingly, the chapter confirms that finding a balance between economic development and wildlife conservation is an urgent and persistent challenge.

Chapter 8: Apes in Captivity

Apes are found in captivity as a result of a number of factors that range from active breeding and capture, to habitat loss and hunting. Captive apes are housed in facilities that include private residences, research centers, zoos, circuses and sanctuaries. In addition to presenting details on what is known about the number of apes in captivity in range states and adjacent regions, the chapter analyzes some of the factors that contribute to the ongoing demand for captive care. It also provides information on apes in captivity in the consumer countries of the global North, as well as some of the issues that affect their welfare.

The chapter sheds light on the disparities between policies and social attitudes in and outside of range states and considers what these might mean for the future of apes, both in captivity and in their natural habitats. It highlights how differing legislative frameworks that provide varying levels of protection affect the capture and holding of apes in captivity. It also examines how perceptions of apes change in response to how they are portrayed in the media and kept in zoos or other sites of captivity, and how these perceptions influence the extent to which people support conservation in situ. If people feel that apes are not threatened with extinction, or thrive in captivity, they are less likely to engage or push for conservation action. The provision of accurate and appropriate information on the plight of apes could reduce the demand for apes as pets and people's desire to see apes utilized in the entertainment industry. Resulting shifts in public opinion would likely strengthen support for ape conservation.

Photo: Confiscated chimpanzee in the arms of a national park guard, Virunga National Park, DRC.
© Jabruson, 2015. All Rights Reserved. www.jabruson.photoshelter.com

Photo: The overriding threat to the survival of apes is habitat loss. Forest destruction on Sumatra, Indonesia. © Ulet Ifansasti/Greenpeace

CHAPTER 7

Introduction

Our understanding of how changes in ape habitats affect the status of apes is dependent on robust monitoring of population density and distribution as well as ape socioecology. This chapter presents four long-term case studies, selected to be representative of distinct taxa as well as very different contexts. The case studies examine specific sites more closely, to highlight the status of their resident ape communities and evaluate the threats they face as well as the conservation efforts to protect them:

- Bornean orangutans in the Sabangau Forest, Central Kalimantan, Indonesia;

- chimpanzees in Gombe Stream National Park, Tanzania;

- bonobos of Wamba, in the Luo Scientific Reserve, Democratic Republic of Congo (DRC); and

- silvery gibbons in Mount Halimun Salak National Park, Java, Indonesia.

The overriding threat to the survival of apes is habitat loss due to logging, extractive operations and agricultural expansion—especially for palm oil cultivation—followed by hunting and disease. As extensive tracts of forest across Africa and Southeast Asia are lost, the forest ecosystems are degraded or destroyed. Water tables fall, soil fertility decreases as runoff increases, and the canopy that provides shade for other plants as well as food and homes for forest animals is drastically diminished.

The four case studies that follow describe some of the threats to particular ape populations and the challenges facing their conservation, as well as some of the approaches that have been used to prevent habitat loss and degradation, and to protect the apes. The examined threats range from industrial agriculture and logging to civil unrest and poaching. Rather than covering the whole range of issues and responses to those issues, the case studies provide illustrative examples of some of the threats that affect apes and their habitats. They also highlight the value of long-term engagement that considers a broad geographic scale in different political and economic contexts. The Max Planck Institute is currently conducting a temporal analysis of the global trends in demographics of ape populations utilizing data provided in the IUCN SSC APES Database (International Union for Conservation of Nature; Species Survival Commission; Ape Populations, Environments and Surveys Database) (IUCN SSC, n.d.).

In the first case study, Husson *et al.* assess the impact of logging and industrial agriculture on a peat swamp forest in Central Kalimantan, Indonesia. The Bornean orangutans were forced out of part of their historic range when logging commenced in one section of the forest and clearing for agriculture put pressure on another area. Together, logging and agriculture destroyed and fragmented much of the forest habitat. The orangutans retreated from the noise, human disturbance and hunting pressure, which led to crowding in poorer-quality forest that was not able to provide enough food for the increased numbers of animals. These refugee populations came into conflict with resident orangutan populations, in part through competition over limited food resources. Hitherto, little was known about this "compression effect" on orangutan populations; this case study concludes that it was probably the primary cause of a 40% drop in orangutan numbers in the Sabangau area in 2000–1.

There is, however, some encouraging news about the adaptability and resilience of orangutans. In Sabangau, their numbers are on the rise again: orangutans are moving back to forests that are naturally regenerating, and preliminary evidence indicates that orangutan populations can recover over time, as long as they have not been impacted too severely and are left undisturbed. The study strongly supports the idea that, under certain conditions, previously logged forest can support viable orangutan populations; such areas should not simply be dismissed as degraded, as that designation can lead them to be selected for alternative land uses.

In the second case study, Pintea *et al.* look at population trends among the chimpanzees of Tanzania's Gombe Stream National Park. Data going back to the 1960s show that both the chimpanzees' range and numbers have changed significantly in the past five decades, depending on their proximity to or location in the park. Groups whose range is within the park's borders have suffered less decline than those who range in habitats that straddle the park boundary. This demonstrates not only that protected areas can offer conservation benefits, but also that there are limits to what such areas can do to ward off threats to forest habitats and, specifically, to apes. When conservation measures are not in place in the landscape surrounding the protected area, the pressures on natural resources —land, forest products and wildlife—build and potentially cause significant declines in ape numbers. While the park has afforded some protection, the surrounding areas have witnessed rapid changes in land use as people increasingly convert forest to cash-crop agriculture, extract firewood and charcoal, and expand settlements and infrastructure.

The third case study examines the conservation of bonobos in the DRC's Luo Scientific Reserve. The bonobos of Wamba are the focus of Furuichi's study, which uses data going back 40 years. Local people in the Luo area have long sustained a taboo against the hunting and eating of bonobos, but the wars and political and economic upheavals that have plagued the DRC over the past two decades have led to in-migration and associated pressures that have altered local practices. Specifically, changes such as the presence of military and weaponry, as well as the settlement of populations for whom no such taboo exists, have resulted in an increase in hunting. Although bonobos are not deliberately hunted, they can fall victim to illegal snares set for other wildlife, which can result in injury or death. This case study —which is based on a research program that involves long-term community support —highlights the challenges of balancing conservation and the needs of people.

Finally, in the fourth case study, Nijman's review of research on silvery gibbons in Java's Mount Halimun Salak National Park highlights the gaps in our knowledge of many ape species and populations, and particularly gibbons. This study demonstrates the importance of research and the use of consistent survey methods, as well as the sharing of data in a way that makes comparison and the detection of trends possible. Although a number of silvery gibbon population surveys have been undertaken in the park

over the past 30 years, a lack of comparability across the studies—due largely to the use of different survey methodologies as well as varying temporal and geographic focuses—has precluded accurate estimates of population size, density and changes over time. What is certain, however, is that the extent of forest habitat in Halimun Salak decreased by about 2% per year—or by a total of around 200 km² (20,000 ha)— between 1989 and 2004. Growing human populations, competition for resources in a region of high economic growth and corruption in key ministries, including those that oversee forestry and conservation, translate into an urgent need for improved and sustained research and intervention.

The four case studies support broader conclusions from ape conservation efforts across Africa and Southeast Asia, such as the following:

■ Habitat loss, hunting and disease remain the main threats to ape survival in both Africa and Southeast Asia. The pressures vary, but underlying them in all landscapes is the push for development. In much of Africa, the threats are primarily driven by forest clearance for industrial and subsistence agriculture, as well as to accommodate the expanding human population. In other areas, they are linked to extractive industries, energy production, infrastructure and other impacts of economic and social development.

■ Additional drivers of threats in many contexts come from political and state forces. Among them are politicians who advocate land development in advance of elections and armed forces that boost demand for meat from the hunting and trafficking of wildlife.

■ Long interbirth intervals mean that ape populations are slow to recover, making them particularly vulnerable to even small drops in population size. Evidence indicates that certain species are able to

> Long inter-birth intervals mean that ape populations are slow to recover, making them particularly vulnerable to even small drops in population size.

adapt to some extent to disruption and loss of habitat, as long as the forest is left to regenerate at the end of the planned economic activity. While research shows that some orangutans have adapted in such cases, this finding does not necessarily apply to other ape taxa with different social and ranging habits.

■ Long-term research is invaluable to the monitoring of change in ape habitat and populations, and to the design of appropriate conservation interventions. In the case studies where researchers are able to analyze data dating back several decades, it is possible to develop evidence-based recommendations to scale. Wherever monitoring is patchy, inconsistent or interrupted for long periods—such as with respect to the silvery gibbons discussed in the final case study—the knowledge base is correspondingly inadequate, which seriously complicates efforts to design effective interventions.

■ Variations in survey methods make it difficult to compare findings, extrapolate results and make predictions. If the scope of studies varies significantly in terms of the temporal and geographic focus, or if potentially important habitats have been ignored, it is difficult to draw accurate conclusions concerning ape numbers, densities and population trends.

■ High-intensity logging can result in crowding of apes in small forest refuges. Crowding has been a greater driver of declines in their numbers than simply the reduction in food availability or the increase in hunting pressure.

■ Well-managed, low-intensity logging has far less of an impact on apes than uncontrolled, high-intensity logging. The speed and intensity of tree removal affect their survival more than the volume of trees removed.

■ Previously logged forests can support healthy ape populations, depending on the species. They should not be dismissed as degraded and thereby designated for alternative land uses.

■ The permanent or regular presence of people working in a forest for conservation purposes—including scientific researchers, forest monitoring patrols and local communities that manage the forest sustainably—contributes significantly to its protection.

Bornean Orangutans in the Sabangau Peat Swamp Forest

Context and Background

Widespread forest clearance for industrial plantations, cultivation for food, mining, infrastructure and rural development, combined with illegal logging, fire and hunting, has dramatically reduced numbers of the endangered Bornean orangutan, *Pongo pygmaeus* (Rijksen and Meijaard, 1999; Singleton *et al.*, 2004; Wich *et al.*, 2008; Husson *et al.*, 2009). The most recent population estimate, from 2004, counts at least 54,000 Bornean orangutans (Singleton *et al.*, 2004); that number is likely to have declined significantly in the past decade, owing to ongoing forest loss on Borneo, where the forest extent is shrinking by an estimated 10% every five years (Wich *et al.*, 2008). The best habitat is found in sites with a mosaic of habitat types, for example the alluvial–peatland–dryland forest mosaic of Mount Palung National Park, in West Kalimantan, where the highest Bornean orangutan densities have been recorded (Johnson *et al.*, 2005; Husson *et al.*, 2009). These ideal conditions are rare, however, following decades of conversion of the most fertile habitats in Borneo. Over time, peat swamp forests have assumed the role of the most important habitat for conservation in the 21st century, despite

their relatively low productivity and moderate orangutan densities (Cannon *et al.*, 2007; Husson *et al.*, 2009).

Five of the eight largest orangutan populations are found in peat swamp (Singleton *et al.*, 2004). Ongoing agricultural development places these populations at risk; by 2006, 45% of Southeast Asia's peat swamp forests had been deforested, primarily for oil palm plantations (Hooijer *et al.*, 2006). Today, a strong international focus and financial commitment to protect carbon-rich peat soils provide hope for the protection of Indonesia's peatlands (Murray, Lubowski and Sohngen, 2009; Solheim and Natalegawa, 2010).

The Sabangau Forest, which supports the biggest population of the Bornean orangutan, is the largest remaining peat swamp forest on Borneo (Morrogh-Bernard *et al.*, 2003; Wich *et al.*, 2008). The Sabangau catchment covered a total of 9,200 km² (920,000 ha) between the Kahayan and Katingan rivers

in Central Kalimantan prior to 1995 (see Figure 7.1). The largely forested area was designated for logging under the Indonesian concession system, whereby only permit-holding companies could remove timber of a specified size and species for a limited period of time.

The situation began to change in 1996, when the eastern catchment was designated for conversion as part of the disastrous 10,000 km² (1 million-ha) agricultural scheme known as the Mega Rice Project (Notohadiprawiro, 1998). By 2007, widespread drainage and fires had destroyed all but 670 km² of the original 2,300 km² (67,000 of 230,000 ha) of forest (Cattau, Husson and Cheyne, 2014). In the western catchment, the logging concessions began to expire in 1997, but although the law mandated a set-aside period, a massive wave of organized, indiscriminate illegal logging started (Currey *et al.*, 2001). Uncontrolled deforestation continued until

FIGURE 7.1

The Sabangau Catchment between the Kahayan and Katingan Rivers, Central Kalimantan, Indonesia

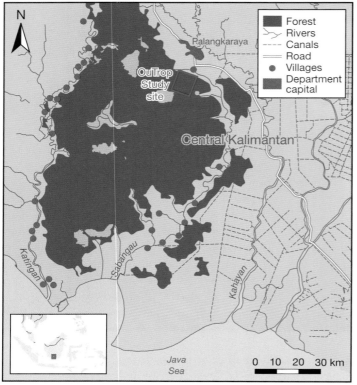

Note: Forest cover is from 2007.

Courtesy of OuTrop

compared to unlogged forests (Rao and van Schaik, 1997; Hardus *et al.*, 2012; Morrogh-Bernard *et al.*, 2014); all of these behavioral changes have a negative impact on an orangutan's energy balance. Research has shown that orangutans move away from sites that are being actively logged and crowd into unlogged areas (MacKinnon, 1974; Rijksen and Meijaard, 1999; Morrogh-Bernard *et al.*, 2003); to date, the long-term consequences of such overcrowding are not well understood.

This case study uses the results of the first 15 years of ongoing research on orangutan densities to assess the impacts of illegal logging on resident orangutans. In particular, it examines why the population declined by focusing on the impact of a prolonged period of logging-induced refugee crowding—also known as the compression effect—and it describes what has happened in the ten years since logging stopped.

Methodology and Results

The research for this case study was carried out as part of a multi-disciplinary research project that is jointly run by the Orangutan Tropical Peatland Project (OuTrop) and the Centre for International Cooperation in Sustainable Management of Tropical Peatlands (CIMTROP) in the Natural Laboratory for the Study of Peat Swamp Forest—an area covering roughly 500 km² (50,000 ha) in the western Sabangau River catchment, in Central Kalimantan. Since 1998, the University of Palangkaraya has managed this integral part of the larger Sabangau Forest for research purposes.

The entire study area is tropical rainforest standing atop a dome of peat whose depth ranges from 0.8 m to 13 m and whose radius is about 15 km. This forest is classified into three major habitat sub-types based on tree species composition and forest structure (Shepherd, Rieley and Page, 1997; Page *et al.*, 1999). Each sub-type occupies a distinct zone along a gradient of peat depth and

2004–5, when the government—supported by non-governmental organizations (NGOs) with a conservation focus—implemented direct action to halt it, following the designation of 5,780 km² (578,000 ha) as the Sabangau National Park (Cattau *et al.*, 2014).

Little is known about the impact of logging on orangutans, other than that densities are predictably lower in logged compared to unlogged forests (Davies, 1986; Felton *et al.*, 2003; Husson *et al.*, 2009). If persistent hunting occurs at the same time as logging, however, the effects of hunting can outweigh those of logging (Marshall *et al.*, 2006). While only a handful of studies have assessed post-logging orangutan behavior, they do provide evidence that orangutans rest less, travel more and feed on lower-quality foods in logged

increasing distance from the river (see Figure 7.2A), as follows:

- **Mixed peat swamp forest (MSF):** This diverse sub-type, characterized by a large quantity of commercial timber trees, is found on the shallowest peat in the region, from the limits of river flooding to 5.5 km inland from the forest edge. The study divides mixed peat swamp forest into two regions: the perimeter (0–2.5 km from the forest edge) and the interior (2.5–5.5 km from the forest edge) because of markedly different logging patterns between these two regions.

- **Low pole forest (LPF):** Relatively stunted and depauperate, these areas are found 5.5–10 km from the forest edge on peat that is 6–10 m deep; they have few trees of commercial timber size.

- **Tall interior forest (TIF):** Productive and diverse, these areas crown the top of the dome on peat that is 10–13 m thick; they have many commercial timber trees.

Orangutan densities have been estimated for each habitat type on an annual basis since 1999, based on local surveys of their sleeping platforms, or "nests," along permanent straight-line transects using standard survey methods and nest parameters (van Schaik, Azwar and Priatna, 1995; Husson *et al.*, 2009). Obtaining accurate orangutan densities from nest surveys is not straightforward (Husson *et al.*, 2009; Marshall and Meijaard, 2009; Wich and Boyko, 2011); nevertheless, nest counts are favored when time or resources are limited and are especially useful for identifying population trends over time.

To identify annual changes and trends in population size, these density estimates were extrapolated across a sample area of 10 km × 13 km centered on the survey locations (see Figure 7.2A). Extrapolating across the entire Sabangau Forest is less reliable because of the very large size of the forest and difficulties in determining the extent of each habitat sub-

FIGURE 7.2

Shifts in Orangutan Distribution in Sabangau Forest, 1997–2004

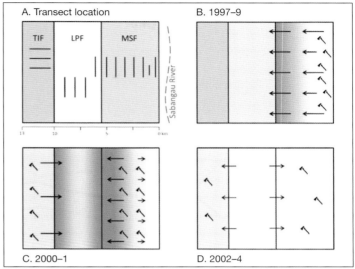

Notes: LPF = low pole forest (stunted and depauperate); MSF = mixed peat swamp forest; TIF = tall interior forest (productive and diverse). Darker shading indicates higher orangutan density. Box A marks the location of each habitat sub-type and survey transects. Boxes B–D show areas of high-intensity logging (axe symbols) and the resulting movement of orangutans (arrows) during three time periods. In B (1997–9), illegal logging had started and was intense near the river, prompting orangutans to move inland, away from the disturbance. In C (2000–1), illegal logging had spread throughout the mixed peat swamp forest and reached the tall interior forest, causing orangutans to crowd into the low pole forest and transition zones. By D (2002–4), the orangutan population had crashed. Logging slowed down during this period and the surviving orangutans moved back to their preferred habitats.

Courtesy of OuTrop

type. Figures 7.2B–D show the changing locations of intensive logging and the subsequent movement of orangutans. Figure 7.3 charts annual orangutan densities for each habitat sub-type and the estimated annual population in the sample area; it includes data from 1996 that pre-date the illegal logging (Morrogh-Bernard *et al.*, 2003).

Discussion

The Orangutan Population of Sabangau and the Impact of Logging Disturbance

Early research identified Sabangau as home to the largest extant population of Bornean orangutans (Morrogh-Bernard *et al.*, 2003).

FIGURE 7.3

Orangutan Density in Each of the Three Habitat Sub-types and Population Size in the Sabangau Forest Sample Area, 1996–2013

Legend: ■ Population size ■ TIF ■ MSF perimeter ■ MSF interior ■ LPF

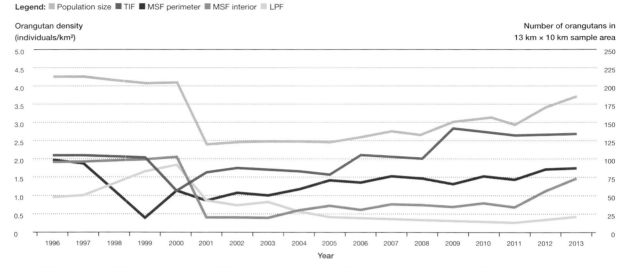

Orangutan density (individuals/km²)

Number of orangutans in 13 km × 10 km sample area

Notes: LPF = low pole forest (stunted and depauperate); MSF = mixed peat swamp forest; TIF = tall interior forest (productive and diverse).

Courtesy of OuTrop

They were concentrated in two of the three main habitat sub-types: the expansive mixed peat swamp forest and the small area of tall interior forest, where they were found at moderate densities of about 2 individuals/km². The low-canopy, nutrient-poor low pole forest, which makes up about one-third of the total area of Sabangau, can support only very low orangutan densities (<1 individual/km²) and is clearly a sub-optimal habitat. Adult males use the low pole forests as a corridor between preferred habitats, and non-dominant or maturing individuals also use it during seasonal periods of higher than normal fruit production (Husson *et al.*, 2009).

No surveys were conducted prior to the start of commercial logging, so it is likely that the first density surveys underestimated the true potential of Sabangau in its pristine state. Nevertheless, the commercial logging of 1993–7 was of low intensity and carried out by a relatively small number of people who were only active in a small part of the forest at any one time, and who targeted a restricted number of tree species. The illegal logging epidemic that started in 1997, by contrast, involved large numbers of people who targeted all species of value, worked in independent groups, used environmentally damaging techniques and left very few refuge areas for orangutans. The tall interior forest in the study area was not reached until 2000, and the low pole forest has not been significantly affected. By 2003, most logging activity was deep inside the forest and was decreasing markedly, due to CIMTROP's anti-logging patrols and the significantly reduced volume of high-value timber left standing. In 2004, the cutting down of large timber was stopped completely in the study area and, by the following year, it had also been brought to a halt throughout most of the western Sabangau catchment.

An orangutan's initial response to logging is to move away from human presence and the noise of chainsaws and falling trees (MacKinnon, 1974). Such movement is easier for the wide-ranging adult males, whereas adult females have stable home ranges, which they appear incredibly reluctant to leave (Husson *et al.*, 2009; Singleton *et al.*, 2009). Female orangutan ranges can exceed 2.5 km² (250 ha) (Singleton *et al.*, 2009); this may allow the apes to escape logging by making biased use of their range. The mass movement of male and female orangutans into unlogged areas results in refugee crowding, particularly if other orangutans are already resident in these areas (Rijksen and Meijaard, 1999). The dramatic drop in densities in the mixed peat swamp forest perimeter between 1996 and 1999, and the corresponding rise in the unlogged low pole forest—while overall population numbers remained stable—is clear evidence of this dynamic.

A behavioral study that was carried out in Sabangau immediately after logging ended shows that orangutans made selective use of their habitat by seeking out areas where tall trees were still standing and by avoiding the most damaged areas (Morrogh-Bernard *et al.*, 2014). The more logged an area was, the less frugivorous was their diet and the more time they spent traveling. This negative impact on their energy balance is presumably the reason for lower population densities in logged forest (Davies, 1986; Rao and van Schaik, 1997; Felton *et al.*, 2003; Husson *et al.*, 2009; Hardus *et al.*, 2012; Morrogh-Bernard *et al.*, 2014). Orangutans demonstrate a high degree of dietary flexibility and can maintain their pre-logging densities in lightly logged or well-managed concessions (Meijaard *et al.*, 2005; Ancrenaz *et al.*, 2010). In Sabangau, however, a highly intense period of logging led to a sudden and dramatic population crash.

Timeline of a Population Crash

The population crash between 2000 and 2001 was preceded by massive shifts in orangutan distribution, as shown in Figures 7.2 and 7.3. Illegal logging started in the mixed peat swamp forest perimeter in 1997–8 and led orangutans to move deeper into the forest, away from the disturbance. By 1999 orangutan density here had declined to one-fifth of its 1996 level, which led to knock-on effects throughout the mixed peat swamp forest; a large number of orangutans were displaced into the sub-optimal low pole forest habitat as competition for resources in the mixed peat swamp forest interior increased. In late 1999, loggers reached the tall interior forest, displacing more orangutans into the low pole forest. Orangutan density in the tall interior forest was halved from 1999 to 2000 and their density in the low pole forest during that time was the greatest ever recorded.

Despite these massive shifts in distribution, orangutan numbers remained constant during this period. Many were now concentrated in the low pole forest and the mixed peat swamp–low pole forest transition zone, which, by late 2000, was the only part of the forest that remained unaffected by illegal logging. This area was acting as a refuge for displaced orangutans, and the crowded population was inevitably overshooting the carrying capacity of this habitat. In 2001, densities in both low pole forest and the mixed peat swamp forest interior declined sharply; the researchers estimated that approximately 40% of the orangutan population died during this short period. They concluded that refugee crowding in this zone had led to starvation for many members of the resident population, as well as for the displaced apes. Refugee crowding caused by high-intensity logging appears to have superseded the direct effects of reduced food availability in logged forest—as well as secondary effects such as hunting—as the main reason for orangutan population decline in Sabangau.

This finding has important implications for forestry management. It is apparent that well-managed, low intensity logging has far less impact on orangutans than uncontrolled, high-intensity logging (Husson *et al.*, 2009; Ancrenaz *et al.*, 2010); in fact, orangutan densities in unlogged areas do not differ significantly from those in sustainably logged areas in Sabah (Ancrenaz *et al.*, 2005). By providing clear evidence that refugee crowding caused a population crash, the study demonstrates that in determining the impact of logging on orangutans, what matters is not necessarily the volume of timber removed within certain limits, but rather the speed and manner with which it is removed.

Population Recovery after Logging

Only after the cessation of illegal logging in 2004 did orangutan densities return to their original rank order by habitat type: primarily tall interior forest, followed by mixed peat swamp forest and then low pole forest. At this stage, the surviving orangutan population was probably living at densities below the carrying capacity of the logged habitat, which, together with natural forest regeneration, made population growth possible. Rapid growth is not expected, as orangutans have a very slow life history, with first reproduction at 15 years of age and a 6–9-year interbirth interval (Wich *et al.*, 2009a); see the Socioecology section, page xv). A slow but steady increase in orangutan density and population size has been recorded during the ten years since the logging stopped. The researchers conclude that this is primarily the result of reproduction but also partly due to net immigration of mature males as a result of continued forest shrinkage at the landscape level. Densities have increased at a faster rate in the best habitat sub-types, and there has been no evident increase in the low pole forest.

Based on nest density surveys conducted in this small sample area, the overall population declined from 212 in 1996 to 119 at its nadir, in 2001, before recovering to 185 in 2013. The ongoing population growth indicates that orangutan densities can return to pre-logging levels if left alone to recover. This finding supports the conclusion of an earlier survey, which found that orangutan densities in a forest that had been logged 22

> Fire remains the greatest threat to the forest in Sabangau, as it is a quick, albeit illegal, way to clear land for agriculture.

years prior to the study were not significantly lower than those in an unlogged forest nearby (Knop, Ward and Wich, 2004). This research underscores the abovementioned point, namely that previously logged forests can support healthy orangutan populations and should not be dismissed as degraded or designated for alternative land uses (Meijaard *et al.*, 2005).

Sabangau at the Landscape Level

If the pattern of refugee crowding and the resultant die-off described above actually occurred throughout the Sabangau Forest —and illegal logging was indeed present throughout—then, based on a crude analysis of the area of each habitat sub-type, it may be assumed that the population was roughly halved, from about 8,700 orangutans before the crash to around 4,800 thereafter.

Of course this only tells one part of the story. Although orangutan populations have been recovering since the logging ended, the area of remaining habitat continues to shrink at the landscape level. The national park's boundary is neither clearly defined nor well known locally, and it is often willfully ignored or rejected. Almost 1,000 km² (100,000 ha) of forest has been lost in fires since 1997, and forest continues to be lost at the margins. Forest loss is driven by human population growth—primarily by the development of settlements and agricultural smallholdings—as well as by the expansion of transport networks and local demand for products such as scaffolding timber and granite rocks. Fire remains the greatest threat to the forest in this area, however, as it is a quick, albeit illegal, way to clear land for agriculture.

This destruction is cyclical and progressive. As areas of heavily burned forest on the margins of settlements are no longer a priority for protection, they are soon claimed by people and developed. Regrowing shrubs are burned off and fire thus spreads deeper into the original forest. Newly acquired fields still flood in the wet season, so more drainage channels are cut, lowering dry-season water tables. Meanwhile, fire prevention and fire-fighting actions are woefully inadequate and underresourced, and law enforcement is virtually absent.

Analysis of Landsat images reveals that the total area of forest in the western catchment declined from 6,700 km² (670,000 ha) in 1991, to 5,500 km² (550,000 ha) in 2000, to 4,950 km² (495,000 ha) in 2007. The rate of loss has slowed since Sabangau was accorded formal protection in 2004, but it has not ceased. Researchers estimate that roughly 6,500 orangutans currently live in the western Sabangau catchment, based on 2013 density surveys and 2007 forest cover estimates. If the period 2007–13 had witnessed forest loss at the previously recorded rate, however, this number could have been as low as 5,800, which would have represented a decline of 15% since the last published estimate of 6,900 individuals in 2008 (Wich *et al.*, 2008).

It thus follows that if Sabangau and its orangutan population are to be protected effectively, encroachment, fires and logging must be halted. Even if these steps are taken, however, conservation efforts are complicated by the fragility and interconnectedness of the tropical peat swamp forest ecosystem. Tropical peatlands form under precise hydrologic and climatic conditions; they are very sensitive to changes at the interface between peat soils and the overlying forest, particularly with respect to hydrologic integrity and nutrient availability (Page *et al.*, 1999). Illegal logging has changed that balance, not least because the hundreds of timber-extraction channels are draining the peatland of its water. Draining one part of a peatland impacts the entire ecosystem, resulting in peat degradation and subsidence throughout, which in turn undermines mature trees and increases fire risk. Climate change is predicted to increase rainfall seasonality and cause drier dry seasons, further exacerbating the problem (Johnson, 2012).

Protecting Sabangau is thus a daunting task, but the forest's global importance as a carbon store and for biodiversity conservation makes this task essential. Effective conservation will require significant and costly peatland rehabilitation and restoration work in order to slow, halt and eventually reverse the effects of drainage and peat degradation, together with improved protected-area management to prevent further encroachment and forest destruction. Many laudable efforts are under way, spearheaded by NGOs and community groups, but there is a need for much greater international attention and conservation action, at a much larger scale.

> " Draining one part of a peatland impacts the entire ecosystem, resulting in peat degradation and subsidence throughout. "

The Chimpanzees of Gombe

Context and Background

Gombe Stream National Park is on the eastern shore of Lake Tanganyika in the Kigoma region of western Tanzania (see Figure 7.4). Established in 1968 and covering a land area of 36 km² (3,569 ha), it was recently extended into the lake to cover an additional 20 km² (2,072 ha) of water. Although small, Gombe is rich in biodiversity, with a mosaic of evergreen and semi-deciduous forests, dense woodlands, open woodlands including Zambesian miombo, grasslands with scattered trees, and upper ridge grasslands with rocks along the crest of the rift escarpment (Goodall, 1986; Collins and McGrew, 1988).

Gombe is the longest continuously running great ape research site in the world. Jane Goodall's studies of wild chimpanzees (*Pan troglodytes schweinfurthii*) began in 1960, focusing on the central Kasekela community. The park also contains two other chimpanzee communities, Mitumba in the north and Kalande in the south. Between

FIGURE 7.4

Gombe Stream National Park and Village Land Use Plans in the Greater Gombe Ecosystem

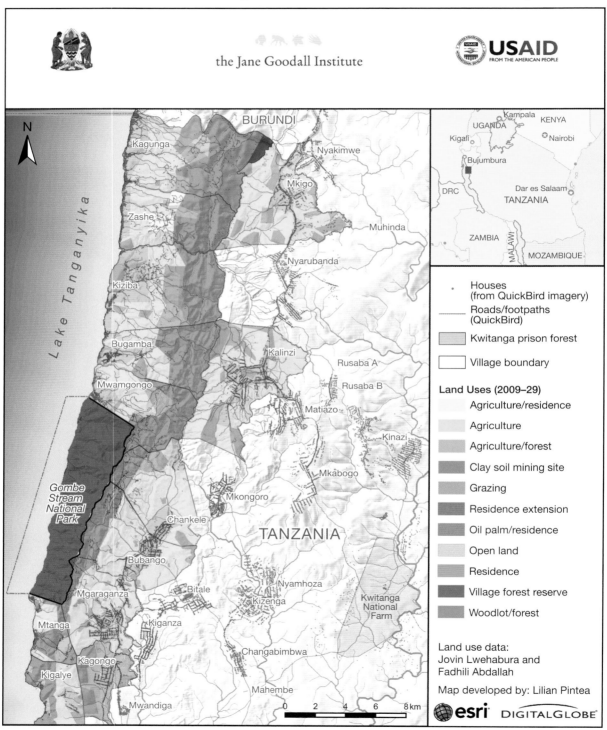

Courtesy of JGI

1972 and 1978, the park was home to the Kahama community, which had split from the Kasekela community in the early 1970s. The park also had a Rift community in the 1960s. Figure 7.5 shows current and historic chimpanzee communities' home ranges and habitat change between 1972 and 2012.

Habituation of the chimpanzees in the Mitumba community did not start until 1985 because of concerns that it would put them at risk of poaching when they ranged outside the park. Full habituation to human observers was achieved in 1994. The Kalande community has been monitored since 1999, but it remains unhabituated to close observation.

Methodology

Population estimates for habituated Kahama, Kasekela and Mitumba chimpanzee communities are based on direct observations. Mitumba community population estimates for the years after 1994 are more reliable, as the apes were fully habituated to human observers by then. Kalande community numbers since 2002 are based on occasional sightings of individuals, genetic monitoring of fecal samples with microsatellites, and extrapolation from the immigrants to Kasekela and the number of bodies found dead from disease, intergroup aggression and poaching (Pusey *et al.*, 2007; Rudicell *et al.*, 2010).

Territorial ranges of habituated Kasekela and Mitumba chimpanzees have been estimated by using geographic information systems (GIS) and by drawing a polygon enclosing 99% of 1973–2004 and 2012–13 location points (Williams *et al.*, 2002). The 1973 Kalande and Mitumba community ranges are estimates based on incidental observations of chimpanzees inside and outside the park. The existence and location of the Rift community is based on a small number of reported sightings that indicated there was a community east of the Rift in the 1960s

(Pusey *et al.*, 2007; J. Goodall, personal communication, 2014; see Figure 7.5). The 2004 and 2013 Kalande community ranges were estimated based on incidental sightings.

Chimpanzee habitat monitoring includes analyses of remote sensing data from as early as 1947, using a combination of historical aerial photos and medium- and high-resolution

FIGURE 7.5

Historic and Current Chimpanzee Home Ranges and Habitat Change

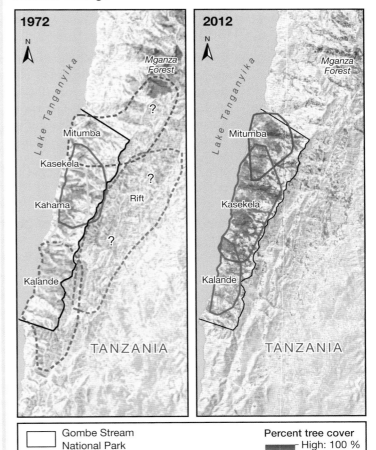

Notes: The tree canopy cover is estimated using Landsat Multispectral Scanner imagery for 1972 (Pintea, 2007) and Landsat Thematic Mapper and Enhanced Thematic Mapper Plus imagery for 2012 (Hansen *et al.*, 2013). Historic chimpanzee community home ranges are from 1973 (Pusey *et al.*, 2007). Current ranges for Kasekela and Mitumba cover 2012–13. The current Kalande range is from 2007, as estimated in Rudicell *et al.* (2010).

Courtesy of JGI

imagery acquired by Landsat, SPOT and other satellite programs (Pintea *et al.*, 2002). Since 2001, vegetation, human infrastructure and land use inside and outside of Gombe have been regularly monitored with very high-resolution satellite imagery (less than one meter) acquired from QuickBird, WorldView and Ikonos satellites (Pintea *et al.*, 2011).

Causes of Change in Population Size and Ranging Patterns

Chimpanzee numbers in Gombe have fallen from a peak of 120–125 at the end of the 1960s to approximately 90 in 2014 (Pusey *et al.*, 2007). In the early 1970s the Kasekela community split to form the offshoot Kahama community, which Kasekela community chimpanzees wiped out by 1978. In 1994, Gombe chimpanzee numbers stabilized at

around 100 individuals, but by 2014 they had declined to 90 individuals. Recently, the Kasekela community experienced a drop, but with five births in 2014, some of this loss has been replaced. Numbers in the Mitumba community have remained relatively stable while the Kalande community has lost most of its members (see Figure 7.6).

Chimpanzee ranging patterns have also changed dramatically since 1960. For the past five decades, the Kasekela home range has been inside the park, but it has fluctuated and increased by 287%—from 5.4 km² (539 ha) in 1973 to 15.5 km² (1,549 ha) in 2004, and to 16 km² (1,600 ha) in 2013 (Pusey *et al.*, 2007; Pintea *et al.*, 2011). In contrast, Mitumba and Kalande community ranges, which covered habitats inside and outside the park, both suffered drastic decreases outside the protected area (see Figure 7.5). The Kalande range has also declined inside the park as a result of the expansion of the Kasekela range.

FIGURE 7.6

Community and Total Population Size (Full Counts) of Gombe Chimpanzees, 1966–2014

Legend: ■ Kasekela ■ Kahama ■ Mitumba ■ Kalande (max.) ■ Sum (min.) ■ Sum (max.)

Number of chimpanzees

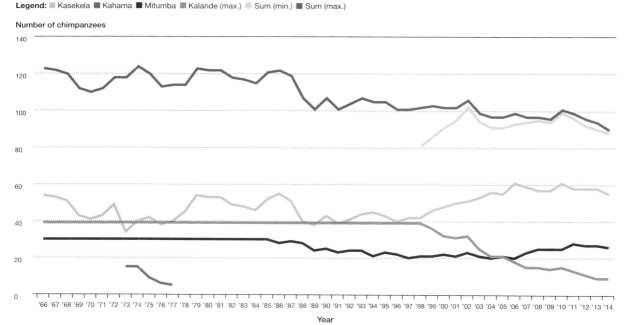

Year

Courtesy of JGI

Causes of Population Changes

Habitat Change and Loss

Rising human populations are the main cause of deforestation in the Gombe region. In Kigoma region, human population density grew from an estimated 12.4 people/km² in 1967 to 17.1 in 1978, to 22.6 in 1988, 44 in 2002 and 57 in 2012 (Pintea *et al.*, 2011; L. Pintea, personal communication, 2015). Habitat within the park has remained relatively well protected, but the loss of forest and woodlands outside the park between 1972 and 1999—driven by rapid population growth and the influx of refugees who fled civil wars in Burundi and the DRC—has had a devastating effect on the park's chimpanzees (Pintea *et al.*, 2002, 2011; Pusey *et al.*, 2007).

There are three main causes of habitat change and loss:

- conversion of habitat to cash crops, such as oil palm, or food crops, such as beans, cassava and corn;

- extraction of firewood and charcoal production; and

- expansion of settlements and infrastructure development (JGI, 2009).

The Kasekela chimpanzees, located in the center of the park, have been the least affected by deforestation, however the Mitumba and Kalande communities have lost key food resources outside the park to agricultural conversion and settlements (see Figure 7.5).

Habitat changes inside the park have also affected chimpanzee communities unequally. Since 1972, because of fire control and protection in the Kasekela and Mitumba community ranges in the northern part of the park, tree canopy density and evergreen vines that contain important chimpanzee foods have increased in the forests and open woodlands on lower slopes (Pintea *et al.*, 2011). That growth is reflected in significant changes in the chimpanzees' diets. Adult Kasekela males dramatically increased their feeding time on forest species in 1997–2001 as compared to 1974–6, consuming the fruits of two vines, *Dictyophleba lucida* and *Saba comorensis* var. *florida*; meanwhile, they substantially reduced their feeding time on open woodland species, such as *Diplorhynchus condylocarpon* (Pintea *et al.*, 2011).

The vegetation in the southern Kalande range inside the park, which has changed the least, is dominated by deciduous miombo woodlands that are still frequently burned. Chimpanzees can live in a variety of vegetation types, from dry savannah woodlands and woodland–forest mosaics to humid-canopy rain forests (Teleki, 1989); in drier habitats, where food tends to be more scattered and fruiting occurs at different times, chimpanzees need larger home ranges (Kano, 1972; Baldwin, McGrew and Tutin, 1982; Moore, 1996; Pruetz *et al.*, 2002). The Kalande community probably suffered the most from habitat changes inside and especially outside the park because of the decrease in both their range size and habitat quality (Pintea *et al.*, 2011).

Disease

Disease is a leading cause of chimpanzee deaths in the Gombe Stream National Park (Goodall, 1986; Lonsdorf *et al.*, 2006; Pusey *et al.*, 2007; Rudicell *et al.*, 2010). Of 130 deaths among Kasekela chimpanzees between 1960 and 2006, 58% were due to illness (Williams *et al.*, 2008). Since researchers are not always able to find chimpanzee remains, they cannot systematically confirm causes of death and must often speculate as to the source of disease. One possible source of disease transmission to chimpanzees is human–chimpanzee interaction, which has been increasing both inside and outside the park (Leendertz *et al.*, 2006b). Moreover, Simian immunodeficiency viruses (SIVcpz) are present in Gombe; the discovery that they are pathogenic in chimpanzees suggests that disease may have had, and may continue to have, more devastating effects than previously expected (Keele *et al.*, 2009; Rudicell *et al.*, 2010).

Deliberate Killing by Humans

During more than five decades of study at Gombe, at least ten chimpanzees are known or suspected to have been killed by poachers (Pusey *et al.*, 2007). The Greater Gombe Ecosystem Conservation Action Plan (GGE–CAP) states that chimpanzees may be killed for a variety of reasons, including:

- to protect crops from crop raiding;
- to protect women and children from real or perceived threats, such as when they spend time in agricultural buffer zones or enter chimpanzee habitat to collect firewood and other natural resources;
- to retaliate when a chimpanzee shows signs of aggression toward a human, or to preempt such aggression;
- for fear that chimpanzees may transmit diseases to humans; and
- to prevent chimpanzee habitat from being co-opted as an extension of Gombe Stream National Park—a common fear that has its roots in the evictions that occurred when Gombe Stream Game Reserve was officially established in 1943.

Poaching for food or body parts has not been considered a major threat, although that could change with an influx of refugees from countries with other cultural traditions. Similarly, the killing of adult chimpanzees to obtain infants for sale is not a threat, but it may become one due to the increasing proximity between humans and habituated chimpanzees on land that is not protected or patrolled by Tanzania National Parks (TANAPA).

Intraspecific Aggression

Chimpanzees cooperate to attack and sometimes kill individuals in neighboring communities (Wrangham, 1999; Wilson *et al.*, 2014b). Intraspecific aggression accounted for 24% of male and 15% of female known deaths in the Kasekela community between 1960 and 2006 (Williams *et al.*, 2008). The Mitumba and Kalande communities, whose ranges previously extended beyond the edge of the park (see Figure 7.5), are especially vulnerable, at risk of being caught in a slowly closing trap of habitat loss, disease and poaching on one side, and increasing pressure from the more powerful Kasekela community on the other (Pusey *et al.*, 2007).

Reducing Threats

In 1994, the Jane Goodall Institute (JGI) began working with local communities outside Gombe Stream National Park through the Lake Tanganyika Catchment Reforestation and Education project, which aims to stop the rapid degradation of the area's natural resources. To promote community engagement in the conservation of the area —which is essential for the success of the conservation and development programs —agriculture, health, social infrastructure, community development and clean water provision were integrated into the project. These interventions initially focused on areas close to village centers, but remote sensing and spatial analysis using GIS from 1972, 1999 and 2003 showed that most habitat loss took place farther away from villages (Pintea *et al.*, 2002). Since 2005, conservation efforts have focused on forest patches that provide the most benefits to people and chimpanzees.

In 2006 JGI and its partners started a conservation action planning process for the Greater Gombe Ecosystem (JGI, 2009). As part of the process, stakeholders agreed on conservation objectives, prioritized strategies to abate the most important human threats and spatially delineated a core conservation area for protection and restoration. The core area was defined by mapping human structures, roads and footpaths from 60-cm QuickBird satellite images and by overlaying chimpanzee sightings outside the park, historical habitat distribution and steep slopes that are important to maintain watersheds and ecosystem services. JGI then facilitated village-by-village land use plans with communities that voluntarily set up village forest reserves in places that had been prioritized by the GGE–CAP. Six years later, in March 2015, key experts and stakeholders convened to undertake a systematic review of the GGE–CAP and its implementation, along with other plans in western Tanzania, using Open Standards for the practice of conservation (CMP, 2013). The participants reviewed information on changes in chimpanzee status and threats, identified future conservation needs and coordinated strategies to meet these needs.

Habitat Loss

The first iteration of the GGE–CAP identified village-level participatory land use planning as one of the most promising and cost-effective conservation strategies for addressing habitat loss and degradation and supporting natural vegetation regeneration outside the park (JGI, 2009). Between 2005

FIGURE 7.7

Natural Regeneration of Miombo Woodland in the Kigalye Village Forest Reserve, as Detected by 2005 and 2014 Satellite Imagery

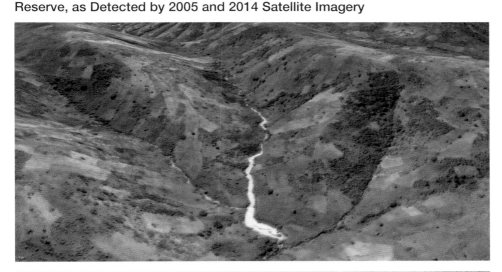

Map data: Google, DigitalGlobe

and 2009, 13 local communities voluntarily assigned 97 km² (9,690 ha) as village forest reserves connected to Gombe (see Figure 7.4). JGI and its partners are now facilitating the establishment of community-based organizations (CBOs), developing by-laws and building local capacity to implement village land use plans to restore and manage village forest reserves. In 2006, initiatives to build village governments' capacity to patrol their own forests were put in place. Since 2005, village forest monitors have been patrolling these reserves using Android smartphones and tablets that are enabled with a Global Positioning System (GPS), as well as Open Data Kit software to facilitate mobile data collection.

Natural regeneration of miombo woodlands can be seen in some village forest reserves using 2005 and 2014 DigitalGlobe satellite imagery on Google Earth (see Figure 7.7). Forest monitors have also recorded evidence that chimpanzees at least occasionally use forests outside the park; the largest number of nest sightings was recorded in 2014 in the village forest reserves close to the border with Burundi. This finding confirms that a northern community still exists outside Gombe and might be using habitats across Tanzania and Burundi's borders. Discussions are now taking place to examine the possibility of extending community forest management, land use planning, and forest restoration and monitoring approaches into Burundi to protect and restore habitats and connectivity across the national borders.

Disease

Conservation efforts have focused on tackling disease and combating transmission among Gombe's chimpanzees; they have also introduced measures to reduce the risk of disease transmission from humans to chimpanzees, including by:

- imposing a minimum observation distance for tourists and researchers;

> **Deliberate killing remains a serious threat to the Gombe chimpanzees.**

- instituting a one-hour observation time for tourists;
- establishing a one-week quarantine for researchers;
- introducing a shift system to reduce the number of people in the park; and
- requiring a routine health check for researchers whenever they return from travels abroad.

A health-monitoring program asks researchers to record signs of chimpanzee illness on daily health sheets and to collect fecal samples for virology and parasitological studies from observation targets. By improving health infrastructure, hiring new staff to keep track of sick individuals, and carrying out more frequent health check-ups and training for JGI and TANAPA staff, disease management will be steadily improved.

Poaching

Deliberate killing remains a serious threat to the Gombe chimpanzees. The fact that the Kalande community—which has not been habituated to human observers—was more severely affected by poaching than the Mitumba and Kasekela communities suggests that the presence of researchers and rangers in the forest plays an important role in protecting chimpanzees; the continuation of the long-term study of Gombe's chimpanzees could therefore be seen as a potential strategy for safeguarding their survival. Participation of local people, such as forest monitors, is also critical to protecting Gombe's chimpanzees and conserving their habitat.

Specific Recommendations

Regular updating and reviews of conservation action plans and management plans enable the assessment of lessons learned by various stakeholders and representatives of different interest groups and highlight the impact of interventions to date. These steps allow for different stakeholders in the landscape to guide the strategic restoration and maintenance of the larger Greater Gombe Ecosystem for the benefit of biodiversity, natural resources and sustainable human livelihoods (JGI, 2009); they are also designed to help to improve strategies and actions for the next five years.

Further research is needed to assess and manage the risks associated with an increase in the rates of human–chimpanzee interactions. This will support the emphasis on law enforcement—raising awareness about the illegality of killing chimpanzees—and foster a stronger understanding of human–chimpanzee coexistence and effective methods of managing conflict.

It is critical to increase the ability of local communities and CBOs to implement village land use plans and to enhance the management of forest reserves. Empowering communities and decision-makers with respect to forest monitoring, through the use of appropriate technologies for remote environments, has been shown to be extremely effective. Numerous mobile, cloud and web-based mapping technologies are adaptable to low bandwidth environments.

The presence of researchers and rangers in the forest contributes to the protection of chimpanzees. Long-term research can thus be considered a tool in a more comprehensive conservation strategy. It is essential, however, that such studies also include and engage local forest monitors and communities.

The Bonobos of Wamba in the Luo Scientific Reserve, DRC

Context, Challenges and Background

In 1973, primatologist Takayoshi Kano travelled by bicycle through a vast area of the Congo Basin—then in a country known as Zaïre, but since 1997 as the DRC—looking for a suitable site to start ecological and behavioral studies of bonobos. It was a difficult mission, as bonobos had already disappeared from some areas. Eventually, he settled in Wamba village, where people welcomed him.

The people of Wamba traditionally believed that in the distant past, the youngest brother in a bonobo family that lived in the forest got tired of eating raw food. He roamed the forest alone, crying, and when god saw him, he helped him by giving him fire with which to cook food. He started eating cooked food and built a village. Wamba tradition holds that he was the ancestor of today's villagers; as a result, they respected bonobos as their brothers and never hunted or ate them. Bonobos thus had little fear of people, which proved to be a significant enabling factor in the development of Kano's research project.

Kano decided to send a student to the site to start a long-term research project, which has now continued for more than 40 years (Kano, 1992; Kano *et al.*, 1996; Furuichi *et al.*, 2012). For the first ten years, the taboo against eating bonobos was well observed; there was no suspected poaching until 1984, when a hunter from outside of Wamba killed a young adult male bonobo. In 1987, soldiers were sent to capture two or three baby bonobos, reportedly as a gift for a visiting dignitary. Spurred by these incidents, the research project, by then known as the Wamba Committee for Bonobo Research (WCBR), submitted a proposal to the Congolese Center for Research in Ecology and Forestry (CREF), and through cooperative efforts, the area was officially established as the Luo Scientific Reserve in 1992. The reserve covers 481 km² (48,100 ha) on both sides of the Luo (Maringa) River (see Figure 7.8).

Since the villagers' traditional respect for bonobos had helped the apes to survive, five human settlements were allowed to remain in the northern section of the Luo

> **Empowering communities and decision-makers with respect to forest monitoring has been shown to be extremely effective.**

Scientific Reserve. Traditional subsistence activities, such as hunting using traditional arrows or snares and rotational slash-and-burn cultivation for cassava and other crops, were also permitted to continue. The idea was to conserve and study bonobos by supporting the traditional coexistence between people and the bonobos.

While the project was initially successful, reconciling the conservation of animals and their forest environment with the wellbeing of local people subsequently proved very difficult, particularly when adverse political and economic factors affected local conditions.

Methodology: Changes in the Number of Bonobos in the Reserve

Since the habituation of a group of bonobos known as the E1 group (then a subgroup of E group) in 1976, researchers have continuously observed their daily ranging from sleeping site to sleeping site. The E1 group ranges in the northern section of the reserve, which also includes human settlements. The number of bonobos in the group has been dramatically affected by changes in political and economic conditions (see Figure 7.9).

FIGURE 7.8

Primary Forest Loss in the Luo Scientific Reserve and Iyondji Community Bonobo Reserve, 1990–2010

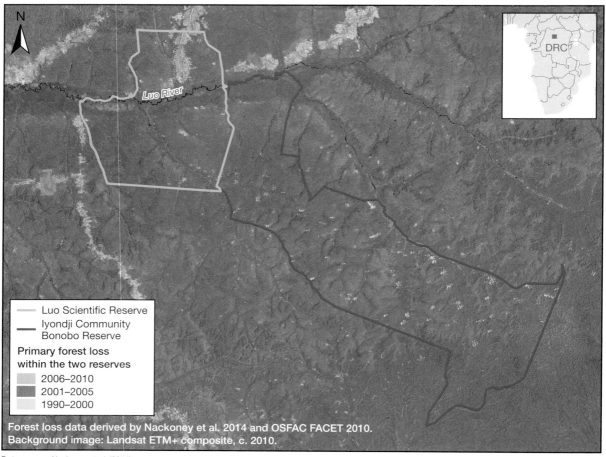

Luo Scientific Reserve

Iyondji Community Bonobo Reserve

Primary forest loss within the two reserves
- 2006–2010
- 2001–2005
- 1990–2000

Forest loss data derived by Nackoney et al. 2014 and OSFAC FACET 2010.
Background image: Landsat ETM+ composite, c. 2010.

Data source: Nackoney et al. (2014)

Courtesy of Janet Nackoney

FIGURE 7.9

Changes in the Number of Bonobos in the E1 Group (Full Counts), 1976–2014

Legend: ■ Adult males ■ Adult females ■ Adolescent males ■ Adolescent females ■ Infantile and juvenile males ■ Infantile and juvenile females

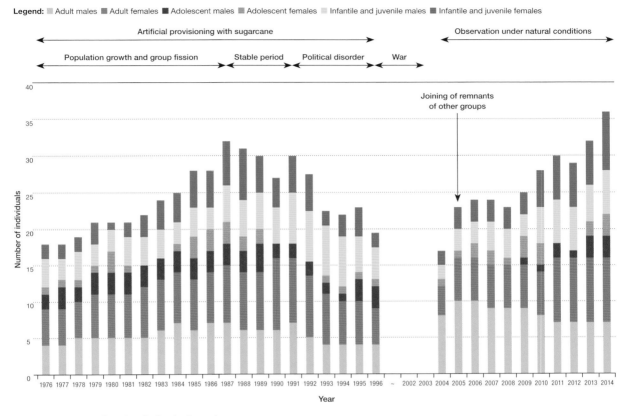

Courtesy of the Wamba Committee for Bonobo Research

Over the course of the first ten years of the project, when poaching pressure was low to non-existent, E1's population increased steadily. Between 1982 and 1983, the E group split into two independent subgroups, E1 and E2. Both groups expanded their ranging area and E1's population continued to increase until 1987. In 1991, however, E1's population began to decrease rapidly. Deteriorating political and economic conditions led to riots in the capital city, Kinshasa, and the Wamba researchers were forced to leave the country. While there is no confirmed information on exactly what happened in Wamba during this period, some people reportedly began to hunt and eat bonobos. They may have abandoned their taboo against killing bonobos due to severe economic conditions,

or, if they had returned to Wamba from the capital to escape the unrest, they may have forgotten or dismissed the taboo. The researchers returned in 1994, but the number of bonobos continued to decrease until 1996, when civil war broke out in the DRC.

During the two periods of war in the DRC—1996–8 and 1998–2003—researchers could do no more than to provide assistance to the bonobo sanctuary in Kinshasa, which founder Claudine André-Minesi had named Lola ya Bonobo. Fearing that logging companies would resume their activities as soon as the war was over, which could have resulted in the extermination of bonobos in many areas, researchers visited Wamba with the support of National Geographic in 2002, when the war appeared to be ending, and resumed their studies immediately following the cease-fire in 2003.

While relieved to find that E1 group numbers had not decreased significantly during the war, the research team eventually discovered that three of the six bonobo groups that had been in the northern section of the Luo Scientific Reserve before the war had disappeared. The total number of bonobos in the northern section had decreased from approximately 250 in 1986 to approximately 100 in 2004. The research team set out to find out what had caused this decrease in the number of groups—and in the total number of bonobos—without seriously affecting the numbers of the main study group.

Perforated Forest: A Stealthy Influence of War

The Wamba researchers assumed that the main cause of the loss of bonobos during the war had been hunting, especially by, or on the orders of, soldiers. Many of the soldiers deployed in the Luo Scientific Reserve were from other areas of the country and did not share the taboo against killing and eating bonobos. In fact, one of the study team's original research assistants was repeatedly ordered by soldiers to guide them to the E1 group's sleeping sites. Although he intentionally guided them to the wrong sites several times, he was finally forced to guide them to a sleeping site after they threatened to kill him.

Local people may also have hunted bonobos, to eat or to sell the meat, as a means of surviving the war. When researchers first visited Wamba after the war, government soldiers were still deployed there, using the research camp as headquarters. Although there was no actual fighting in the Wamba area, the people said that they sometimes fled deep into the forest for fear of the nearby fighting and harassment by government soldiers. Some people had small

houses and cassava fields in the forest, but were forced to return to the village if found by soldiers. Hunting bonobos is not only prohibited by the traditional taboo, but also by law, although control and enforcement was minimal during the war. The research team therefore concluded that the bonobo population had suffered a decline as a result of the movement and hunting activities of people in formerly remote areas.

An analysis of changes in vegetation cover that occurred during the war helped determine the causes of deforestation and increased hunting pressure. On the basis of Landsat Thematic Mapper and Enhanced Thematic Mapper Plus satellite imagery, primary forest loss and degradation rates were compared across two decades, 1990–2010 (Nackoney *et al.*, 2014; see Figure 7.8). The analysis covered both the Luo Scientific Reserve and the Iyondji Community Bonobo Reserve, which had been created in 2012 (Sakamaki *et al.*, 2012; Dupain *et al.*, 2013). The annual rates of primary forest loss between 1990 and 2000—the decade of political disorder and warfare—were more than double the annual rates of the largely post-war decade 2000–10. Satellite images and analysis showed an increased prevalence of small, scattered clearings in the forest during the war. Between 2000 and 2010, however, the number of new forest clearings decreased; instead, clearings around the agricultural areas surrounding settlements expanded. These findings confirm that people who had been forced into the forest by war generally returned to the villages afterwards.

Researchers who surveyed the southern part of the Iyondji Reserve, where a greater number of small clearings appeared during the war, reported that the density of bonobos in that area was very low, compared with the northern part of the Iyondji Reserve and the Luo Scientific Reserve. Although the forest in that area is still intact, small, scattered settlements appear to have a much larger influence on fauna than expected. The Lomako Forest, another long-term study site for bonobos, showed a 75% decline in the bonobo population in just four years during the civil war, demonstrating the now well-documented empty forest syndrome (Redford, 1992). The mechanism by which biodiverse and species-rich forests become empty during war could be explained by an increase of small-scale, scattered forest clearance.

The decrease in the number of bonobo groups in the northern section of the Luo Scientific Reserve has been linked to the increase in hunting deep in the forest, by and on the order of soldiers, and for subsistence by local people. It may also explain why some groups of bonobos ranging farther from human settlements disappeared, while the main study group ranging in the forest around the village did not decrease. Although those bonobos sometimes became targets of hunting by soldiers, they were probably not the primary target for local people. Another possible explanation of the presence of bonobos around the village is the difficulty of hunting illegally without being seen by other people. Furthermore, as illustrated in the case of the research assistant being unwilling to help the soldiers, some people of Wamba were dedicated to conserving the bonobos of the main study group.

Survivorship of Bonobos

The number of bonobos in the main study group, E1, is steadily increasing, and the population is larger now than it was at its former peak in 1987, when the apes were being provisioned artificially during parts of the year. The study team, which has habituated three groups of bonobos in the Luo Scientific Reserve and two groups in the Iyondji Reserve, follows two groups continuously from sleeping site to sleeping site.

Since the ceasefire in 2003, there has been no reported incident of specific hunting of bonobos. Illegal hunting using shotguns (primarily for hunting monkeys) does occur in the reserve, however, and bonobos are often captured in snares set for bush pigs and large antelopes (Tokuyama *et al.*, 2012). In July 2014, while following the E1 group in the forest, the study team observed a newly immigrated young female who was caught in a snare. Although the team helped her to escape from the snare by cutting the stick (the bonobos usually achieve this even without help), the wire was still bound tightly around her fingers. The following morning, one elder female was seen trying to remove the wire while other females looked on (see the photo on page 219). They failed and the study team anticipated that either her fingers or the wire would drop off sometime in the near future. This event illustrates typical female bonobo behavior: they associate and help each other (Furuichi, 2011).

Research activities contribute to the local economy through employment and much of the income goes directly to the local community; however, only a limited number of people directly benefit from employment provided by the research station. Some villagers still engage in poaching, not only for their subsistence but also as a form of protest against the research activities. The frequency of gunshots fluctuates greatly from year to year; the incidence of such illegal activities can serve as an indicator of the extent to which conservation efforts succeed in maintaining the balance between the welfare of local people and the protection of bonobos.

Recommendations

A large proportion of great apes live in isolated patches of forest surrounded by human habitation. Successful conservation requires the protection of such vulnerable and isolated populations. In all forest habitats, even in strictly protected areas in which no humans reside, it is difficult to eliminate illegal and destructive activities. The WCBR encourages involvement of local people from the inception of all conservation activities and the development of programs that directly benefit them, such as tourism, research and support for education, medical services and road maintenance.

Improved and effective communication, trust and understanding between local communities, the CREF, the Ministry of Scientific Research and bonobo researchers would facilitate efforts towards both conservation and development. The strict prohibition of all human activities in protected areas can be counter-productive; through dialogue among all stakeholders, strategies designed to combat illegal hunting and other destructive activities can readily emerge.

It is inevitable, however, that during times of conflict or instability, and in the absence of the rule of law, people will engage in activities that put their short-term needs above those of the longer term and sustainable development. During these periods, the presence of the WCBR and the engagement with the local communities can protect the forest and the wildlife in the reserve.

Building relationships between all stakeholders in the area, including local and national authorities, is essential. Their influence, especially during electoral campaigns —when they speak directly with local people and build alliances with particular groups —has the potential to strengthen or to substantially weaken conservation efforts. It is important that all groups understand the benefits of protecting nature and the possible negative impacts that result from the disappearance of wildlife. Engagement with traditional structures via individuals such as village elders can further strengthen enforcement around illegal activities and build support for conservation. These actions could be complemented by a strengthening of support for the CREF, especially with respect to enhancing law enforcement, such as through patrolling and monitoring of illegal activities in the forest.

The Silvery Gibbons in Mount Halimun Salak National Park, Java, Indonesia

Context and Background

The island of Java—Indonesia's political, economic and industrial center—is one of the most densely populated areas in the world. The silvery gibbon (*Hylobates moloch*) is restricted to the provinces of Banten, Central Java and West Java, excluding the capital, Jakarta. That area, hereafter western Java, is home to some 86 million people who live at an average population density of 1,150 people/km² ; by 2020, the population is expected to increase to 98 million, and the density to 1,300 people/km² (BPS, n.d.). Java is largely deforested and most of the remaining forest fragments cover parts of the volcanoes and mountains on the island. The remainder of the island is a mosaic of rice fields, agricultural land, cities and villages (Nijman, 2013).

Over the past five years, Indonesia's economy has grown at a rate of 6.0%–6.5%; western Java contributes about one-quarter of the country's total growth (BPS, n.d.). Levels of corruption are high: Indonesia ranks 107 out of 175 on the Corruption Perceptions Index (Transparency International, 2014). The Ministry of Forestry is considered to be Indonesia's most corrupt ministry, according to the country's Corruption Eradication Commission (Amianti, 2014).

Photo: Mount Halimun Salak National Park harbors between 25% and 50% of the global silvery gibbon population. © Jaima Smith

Silvery Gibbons in Western Java

Since 1925, all species of gibbon have been protected under Indonesian law (Noerjito and Maryanti, 2001). The hunting of gibbons is not as prevalent in Java as elsewhere in Indonesia, since primate flesh is considered unfit for consumption under Islamic tenets and more than 95% of people in western Java are Muslim (BPS, n.d.). Moreover, the people of Java rely more on agriculture than their neighbors on the islands of Sumatra and Borneo, and few people are directly dependent on forest products for subsistence. Nevertheless, silvery gibbons are traded as pets on Java (Nijman, 2005).

The silvery gibbon is confined to lowland and lower montane rainforest, mostly below 1,600 m, but occasionally up to 2,000–2,400 m (Kappeler, 1984; Nijman, 2004). Most populations can be found in the provinces of Banten and West Java, however a few remain in Central Java (Kappeler, 1984); farther east the dry season is too long to

support the evergreen tropical rainforest on which the species is dependent (Nijman, 1995, 2004).

Mount Halimun Salak National Park harbors between 25% and 50% of the global silvery gibbon population (Kappeler, 1984; Supriatna et al., 1994; Djanubudiman et al., 2004; Nijman, 2004). Situated about 100 km southwest of Jakarta, the park encompasses an area of 1,134 km² (113,400 ha) of forest from lowland to montane; Mount Halimun (1,929 m) and Mount Salak (2,211 m) dominate the area in the west and east, respectively (see Figure 7.10). The link between Halimun and Salak is formed by an 11-km, largely forested area known as "the corridor." There are several large enclaves, such as plantations and villages, inside the park, including in the center the site of the Nirmala tea estate, which covers roughly 10 km² (1,000 ha) and has sharp boundaries with the adjacent forest. Agricultural land and villages border the park on all sides, and gibbon territories abut the agricultural fields.

FIGURE 7.10

Map of Mount Halimun Salak National Park, Java, Indonesia

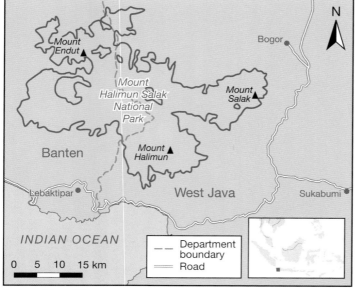

Courtesy of Vincent Nijman

Population Surveys and Monitoring of Silvery Gibbons in Halimun Salak

Population estimates for this species vary greatly, ranging from a few hundred in the late 1970s and again in the mid-1990s, to 2,000–5,000 gibbons at various times in the 1980s, 1990s and into the following decade. The IUCN Red List currently lists the silvery gibbon as endangered, having ranked it as critically endangered in 1996 and 2000, due to the small size of the remaining population fragments (Andayani et al., 2008).

Over the past 30 years, Halimun Salak has seen at least ten attempts to estimate the number of silvery gibbons in the park, each with a distinct approach. The diverse findings are summarized in Figure 7.11; the differences in methodology, among other factors, preclude comparisons of these estimates over time, rendering analysis of the data difficult.

Estimates of group density in Halimun Salak show some variation, but between the elevations of 800 and 1,200 m, the range is 2–4 groups/km²; at higher elevations, up to 1,600 m, the density falls below 1 group/km² (Kool, 1992; Sugarjito and Sinaga, 1999; Sutomo, 2006; Iskandar, 2007). Average group sizes in Halimun Salak range from 2.1 to 4.0, without any apparent temporal or altitudinal pattern (Kool, 1992; Supriatna *et al.*, 1994; Sugarjito and Sinaga, 1999; Iskandar, 2007; Yumarni *et al.*, 2011). Much like the population size estimates, the density and group size estimates reflect different research teams' methodologies and assumptions.

Temporal Changes in Population and Habitat Estimates

As with the population figures, estimates of the amount of habitat available to silvery gibbons in the Halimun Salak area have varied over the years, partly due to changes in the amount of forest that remains, but also as a result of changes in methods used to estimate the proportion of the remaining forest that is actually used by silvery gibbons (see Table 7.1).

Using satellite imagery that covers 95% of the park, researchers established that in 2004 some 625 km² (62,500 ha) of the park's total (1,134 km² or 113,400 ha) was covered in natural forest (Prasetyo, Setiawan and Miuru, 2005). Estimates of forest available to silvery gibbons vary considerably—from about 280 km² to 470 km² (28,000–47,000 ha)—depending on factors such as whether areas >1,500 m above sea level or the first kilometer of the forest's periphery were included (Kappeler, 1984; Supriatna *et al.*, 1994; Campbell *et al.*, 2008a). Most of these estimates were derived from land use (forest) maps.

More recently, two studies combined field observations with GIS and habitat suitability analysis to estimate how much suit-

FIGURE 7.11

Population Estimates of Silvery Gibbons in Mount Halimun Salak National Park

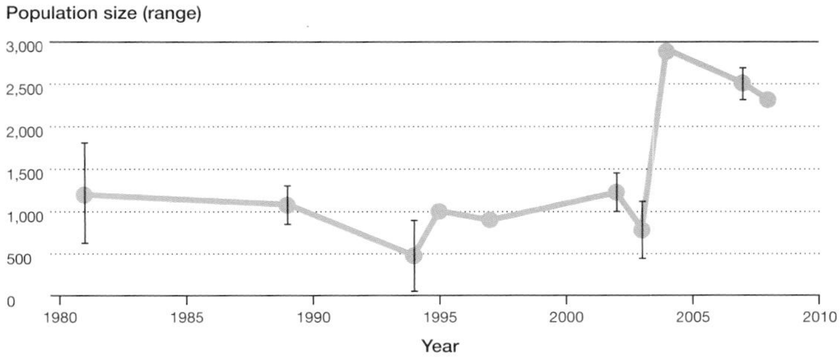

Notes: Error bars give minimum and maximum estimates. Estimates prior to 1992 do not include the Mount Salak part of the park as it was believed at the time that no gibbons were present there.

Data sources: Kappeler (1984); Kool (1992); Supriatna *et al.* (1994); Asquith, Martarinza and Sinaga (1995); Sugarjito and Sinaga (1999); Rinaldi (2003); Djanubudiman *et al.* (2004); Nijman (2004); Iskandar (2007); Campbell *et al.* (2008a)

able habitat is available to silvery gibbons in Halimun Salak. One of them covered the park using satellite imagery from 2001 and field data from 2003; it finds that some 246 km² (24,600 ha) of forest was highly to moderately suitable for silvery gibbons and that an additional 123 km² (12,300 ha) of forest was deemed suitable (Dewi, Prasetyo and Rinaldi, 2007). The other study, covering just Salak, used satellite imagery from 2003 and field data from 2006; it concludes that 78 km² (7,800 ha) was highly to moderately suitable and 33 km² (3,300 ha) was suitable (Ikbal, Prasetyo and Idung, 2006).

The main difficulty in comparing estimates of available habitat is that some researchers only considered forest inside the reserve—be it Halimun or Halimun Salak —as available to silvery gibbons, whereas others included continuous forest outside the reserve as well. Various studies set the altitudinal limit at 1,400 m, 1,500 m and 1,900 m (Kappeler, 1984; Kool, 1992; Sugarjito and Sinaga, 1999); meanwhile, one study excluded some of the best lowland forest as the researchers mistakenly assumed that silvery gibbons did not inhabit the forest periphery (Supriatna *et al.*, 1994).

TABLE 7.1

Estimates of the Forest and Available Habitat for Silvery Gibbons in Mount Halimun Salak National Park

Year	Forest area (km²)	Area available to gibbons (km²)			Method	Source
		H	S	HS		
1981	400 (H)	380	0	380	Satellite imagery	Kappeler (1984)
1994	470 (HS)	235–96	50–70	305–46	Not specified	Supriatna et al. (1994)
1999	360 (H)	240–300	–	–	Land use maps	Sugarjito and Sinaga (1999)
2002	–	270	70	340	Land use maps	Nijman (2004)
2003	379 (HS)	–	–	369	GIS modeling	Dewi, Prasetyo and Rinaldi (2007)
2004	625 (HS)	–	–	–	Satellite imagery	Prasetyo, Setiawan and Miuru (2005)
2006	135 (S)	–	111	–	GIS modeling	Ikbal, Prasetyo and Idung (2006)
2008	–	–	–	283	Not specified	Campbell et al. (2008a)

Notes: HS = entire area; H = only Halimun; S = only Salak; — = not assessed or not found. Varying research methods were applied.

Some data are available on deforestation rates in Halimun Salak; not all of the monitored areas were inhabited by gibbons, however. One study used Landsat data to estimate deforestation rates for an initial forest area of 841 km² (84,100 ha) over the period 1989 to 2004; the results show an average rate of around 1.9% per year. The study observed significantly higher levels of deforestation during the height of the Asian economic crisis in 1998 (3.3%) and in 2001–3 (3.4%), just before the transfer of State Forestry production forest into Mount Halimun Salak National Park. Overall, the park lost some 200 km² (20,000 ha) of forest over the 15 years covered by the study (Prasetyo et al., 2005). While that research clearly demonstrates land use changes within the boundaries of what is now Halimun Salak, including the loss of natural forest, it is not possible to extrapolate the findings directly to the loss of silvery gibbon.

Challenges Associated with Long-term Monitoring

As is clear from the data presented above, no long-term, consistent monitoring of the silvery gibbons has taken place in Halimun Salak. Many of the studies that have been undertaken were of short duration or covered only a section of the reserve, or both (Kool, 1992; Indrawan et al., 1996; Geissmann and Nijman, 2006; Kim et al., 2011, 2012; Yumarni et al., 2011). At best, the different population estimates can be compared with one another, but given that they differ in vital aspects—such as methodology, survey sites, area included and duration—no firm conclusions can be drawn.

While Jakarta's Biological Science Club has maintained a research station in the eastern part of Halimun Salak since the 1980s, and the Cikaniki field station in the center of the park has been operational since the early 1990s, there is no comprehensive trail system in place that allows for monitoring of the park as a whole. The steep terrain is difficult to work in and the amount of rainfall during the rainy season hampers fieldwork, which may explain, at least in part, the absence of permanent research teams.

One of the challenges facing silvery gibbon conservation in Halimun Salak is that no single organization or park has "adopted" the ape as its responsibility or project; rather, many organizations have been making small contributions once in a while. These include the Japanese International Cooperation Agency, which began to work in Halimun in the 1990s, but much of its work focused on the area around the Cikaniki field station. Cikaniki was also the site of a one-year ecological study on three habituated groups (Kim *et al.*, 2011, 2012). One organization, the Silvery Gibbon Project, based out of Perth Zoo, works with the Javan Gibbon Rescue and Rehabilitation Center to support the Javan Gibbon Center at the Bodogol Resort in Mount Gede Pangrango National Park. The project is focused on rescue and rehabilitation, and has little direct effect on the conservation of silvery gibbons in Halimun Salak.

Recommendations and Opportunities

The potential for proper long-term monitoring of the silvery gibbons in Halimun Salak is high: major universities, the Indonesian Institute of Sciences and the Ministry of Forestry, and several major conservation NGOs are situated in the nearby cities of Bandung, Bogor and Jakarta. It is important for monitoring programs to emphasize the use of consistent methods and to share findings, including raw survey data, if possible.

The various studies over the past three decades have shown that the population of silvery gibbons in Halimun Salak is indeed the largest remaining in Java; the amount of

gibbon habitat included in the protected area network has increased substantially over this period, as has our understanding of the distribution of gibbons in the area. Increased protection and effective monitoring and management of this population are critical. Such conservation efforts could eventually be expanded to include populations in more remote locations, such as Ujung Kulon National Park and Mts Dieng.

Final Thoughts

Although the case studies presented in this chapter cover distinct species in different locations, they illustrate at least five cross-cutting themes that are key to conservation work across the board.

First, they underscore the urgent need for sustainable ways to meet the often-incompatible requirements of a growing human population on the one hand, and of the world's wildlife and its habitat on the other. Striking that balance means securing improvements in human health, education and communication to promote social and economic development—a complex process that relies on creative and effective partnerships between government agencies, NGOs and local communities. At the same time, it calls for the engagement of local actors in conservation strategies, transparent and equitable approaches to the sharing of benefits with local communities, and effective enforcement of forest and wildlife protection legislation.

The second point relates to the growing use of technological tools—from satellites and drones to shareware and handheld devices —to record geo-referenced data, monitor forests and wildlife, produce real-time reports and compare environmental conditions over time. Today's low-cost, user-friendly technology can serve as a valuable addition to more sophisticated and expensive satellite technology in the monitoring of forest areas.

> The need for effective land use planning cannot be overstated. At the local, national and regional levels, such planning can benefit biodiversity, natural resources and human livelihoods.

The third theme concerns the value of long-term research. Only when data are gathered using a consistent approach and method, with set survey sites and fixed geographical areas, can researchers hope to identify trends such as population decline, the shrinking of habitats and patterns of deforestation over long periods of time. In conjunction with a solid understanding of the local history and context, analyzing trends can also help to reveal what external factors—such as war or disease—might be at play in the environment under review. Moreover, such quantifiable evidence can inform effective policies to counter adverse effects on biodiversity and human development alike.

A fourth theme revolves around the effective management of protected areas. As the case studies stress, the engagement of governments, communities and other stakeholders is vital to the success of long-term conservation projects. Such engagement can promote the enforcement of laws and the prosecution of illegal activities; similarly, it can encourage local communities to take ownership of conservation goals. During times of political instability or conflict, it is particularly important for local communities to be able to protect the resources and land on which they depend.

Finally, the need for effective land use planning cannot be overstated. At the local, national and regional levels, such planning can benefit biodiversity, natural resources and human livelihoods—while allowing stakeholders to avoid repeating the errors of the past. In this context, partnerships based on shared goals, cooperation and understanding are also central.

Acknowledgments

Principal author: Annette Lanjouw

The Orangutans of Sabangau: Simon J. Husson and Helen Morrogh-Bernard, both with the Wildlife Research

Group at the University of Cambridge; Santiano, Ari Purwanto and Franciscus Harsanto, all with CIMTROP; Claire McLardy, with the UNEP World Conservation Monitoring Centre; and Laura J. D'Arcy, with the Indonesia Program of the Zoological Society of London; all authors are also affiliated with OuTrop

Author acknowledgments: This study was carried out with financial support from the U.S. Fish and Wildlife Service Great Ape Conservation Fund, the Orangutan Project, the Royal Geographical Society, Rufford Small Grants for Nature, Primate Conservation Inc., Peoples Trust for Endangered Species, the Percy Sladen Trust and the International Fund for Animal Welfare. The authors extend thanks to CIMTROP, the University of Palangkaraya, LIPI and RISTEK for granting permission to work in Central Kalimantan, and particularly to Suwido Limin, Jack Rieley and Susan Page for facilitating the research. Many people contributed to data collection, including Mark Harrison, Susan Cheyne, Karen Jeffers, Sahara Alim, Adi, Nico, Kitso Kusin, Agus Israwadi, Sampang Gaman, Agung Daudi, Ella, Twentinolosa Firtsman, Thomas, Zeri, Yudhi Kuswanto, Adul, Abdul Azis, Iwan, Salahuddin, Hendri, Grace Blackham, Rosalie Dench, Ben Buckley, Nick Marchant, Pau Brugues Sintes and Bernat Ripoll Capilla, and Megan Cattau, who provided land-cover figures.

The Chimpanzees of Gombe: Lilian Pintea, Deus Mjungu and D. Anthony Collins, all with the Jane Goodall Institute

Author acknowledgments: The authors thank TANAPA, the Tanzania Wildlife Research Institute and the Commission on Science and Technology for permission to conduct research at Gombe. They acknowledge the support of the US Agency for International Development, Duke University, the University of Minnesota, Esri, DigitalGlobe, Google Earth Outreach, the National Institutes of Health and the National Science Foundation for long-term support.

The Bonobos of Wamba: Takeshi Furuichi, with the Wamba Committee for Bonobo Research

Author acknowledgments: The author is grateful to the Ministry of Scientific Research and the Center for Research on Ecology and Forestry, which provided permission and support for the research and conservation activities at Wamba. Thanks also go to members of the Wamba Committee for Bonobo Research for their dedicated work, as well as the Japan Society for the Promotion of Science, Japan Ministry of the Environment, National Geographic Committee for Research and Exploration and the Toyota Foundation for their financial support.

The Silvery Gibbons in Mount Halimun Salak National Park: Vincent Nijman

Author acknowledgments: The author is grateful to the Indonesian Institute of Sciences and the Directorate General of Forest and Nature Conservation for permission to conduct surveys on Java. Funding over the years has been received from the Zoological Museum Amsterdam, the Society for the Advancement of Research in the Tropics and the Netherlands Foundation for International Nature Protection.

Reviewers: Fiona G. Maisels, Andrew J. Marshall and Elizabeth A. Williamson

Photo: The illicit trade in live apes is driven in part by consumer demand to keep and use apes in captivity. © Greenpeace/Ardiles Rante

CHAPTER 8

The Status of Captive Apes

Introduction

Achieving meaningful protection for apes depends on ethical and legal frameworks that acknowledge the intrinsic value of apes; if the laws were to extend protection to all apes, then rationalizations for their exploitation would be weakened and risks to their protection minimized. Similarly, the policies governing apes in captivity have implications for apes in their natural habitats because the illicit trade in live apes is driven in part by consumer demand to keep and use apes in captivity (Stiles *et al.*, 2013). Evidence suggests that what people believe about apes in captivity can affect their attitudes and actions regarding apes in their natural habitats. For example, what people see at zoos or in pictures can affect what they think about ape conservation (Ross *et al.*, 2008; Schroepfer *et al.*, 2011).

The decisions that people make about anything from agriculture to zoos have the potential to affect apes. Scientists recognize that both risks and protective factors that affect apes vary geographically (Funwi-Gabga *et al.*, 2014, p. 263, fig. 9.7). For example, a review of the entire primate order found that human density was a strong predictor of extinction risk (Harcourt and Parks, 2003). A number of studies have shown that apes living outside of protected areas or near concessions often face different risks than those with a home range deep within protected areas (Chapman and Lambert, 2000; McLennan *et al.*, 2012; Arcus Foundation, 2014).

Where apes are held in captivity also influences the risks that individuals face and many of the factors that impact their welfare. Importantly, the laws governing captivity can vary across and within countries, just as they can differ from the international to the local level. These regulations can address the contexts or conditions in which apes may be held in captivity, factors that strongly influence welfare. Apes used in circuses or other performances or held as private pets face a number of distinct welfare risks, such as isolation or punishment during training; these are absent in professionally run sanctuaries and rescue centers (Durham and Phillipson, 2014, p. 283, table 10.1). Geography and context can also determine other factors associated with welfare, such as the provision of veterinary medical care, food and other resources.

The first edition of *State of the Apes* reviews various forms of ape captivity as well as some of the laws that regulate them (Durham and Phillipson, 2014). Two key observations are that 1) what is allowed or forbidden varies globally, and 2) current standards do not always meet the needs of apes or promote their wellbeing. These findings remain relevant. In some places, laws

> The range of current laws—and lack thereof—can influence not only the number of apes in captivity, but also their quality of life.

do not afford protection to all apes in captivity. In others, municipal regulations, national laws and international conventions form a patchwork of protection. The resulting legal framework can offer strong protection for apes, serve some apes some of the time or, in the absence of enforcement mechanisms, amount to little more than words on paper. The range of current laws—and the lack thereof—can influence not only the number of individuals in captivity, but also their quality of life.

The protection afforded to individual apes is also partly determined by their provenance and the time of their capture. The wildlife laws of range states may apply to all apes, affording protection whether individuals are in their natural habitat or in captivity, or they may apply only to apes in their natural habitat. A wild-born ape might thus have a different status under the law than an ape born in captivity. Similar legal and enforcement disparities may exist with respect to the welfare of apes in captivity. In Indonesia, for example, orangutans are protected by law, but their welfare in zoos has been characterized as poor (Susanto, 2014). Fewer than half of Indonesia's zoos have gone through accreditation and a recent government audit found that only four of the country's 58 registered zoos were deemed "decent and appropriate," with the remainder classified as "less than decent" or "bad" (Saudale, 2015).

Numerous apes are found in captivity in countries adjacent to or otherwise in close proximity to ape range states, as evidenced by the 200 chimpanzees who live in sanctuaries in Kenya, South Africa and Zambia (Durham and Phillipson, 2014). Bilateral, regional or multilateral agreements might serve as the legal framework for protections in such circumstances. In other cases, apes who are in captivity in states outside of their range may not enjoy the same legal protection as native ape species. In Thailand, which is a range state for some gibbons, the law may not afford the same protections to all species under all circumstances (Nijman and Shepherd, 2011). In the absence of strong, comprehensive laws that restrict private and commercial use of all apes in Thailand, animal charities struggle to effect rescue for cases such as orangutans used in performances or a chimpanzee kept as a private pet (Kaminski, 2010; Haynes, 2012; WFFT, 2015).

In addition to location, the form of captivity, qualities of any given site, and interactions with people and other animals have potential implications for apes' welfare. For example, in common, everyday usage the term "zoo" is used to describe a range of facilities from accredited sites with full-time veterinary services and formal welfare programs to roadside attractions without permits or qualified staff. In the United States, businesses may use words such as *preserve*, *sanctuary* or *conservation center* in their name even though they do not technically engage in those activities and revenues come from exhibition or breeding. It is particularly difficult to control the illegal trade and exploitation that occur online because of the global nature of the Internet and related challenges with enforcement and jurisdiction, although this issue has been gaining attention with the World Trade Organization's Doha Declaration and among a number of UN directorates, government agencies and NGOs in many countries (Obama, 2013; Clark, 2014; Environment DG, n.d.).

Beyond any legal requirements, the standards set by professional associations can also impact apes in captivity, often for the better. Both zoos and sanctuaries have professional associations with membership requirements that address captive care and welfare. Membership in a professional organization does not itself guarantee good welfare, but oversight by a third party creates additional opportunities for maintaining and improving performance and keeping practices up to date. Formal and informal standards of practice can play a role in ape

welfare, not only as foundations of regulations and standards, but also with respect to what apes actually experience on a day-to-day basis and how that influences their quality of life.

To expand the discussion regarding the interdependence of the law, captivity and the wellbeing of apes, this chapter explores two general themes. First, it presents recent data on apes in captivity in range states and adjacent regions in the context of some of the factors that contribute to the ongoing demand for captive care. Second, as a comparison, it reports on what is known about apes in captivity and some of the factors that affect their welfare in non-range states in the consumer countries of the global North. The chapter discusses information about apes in captivity within and outside of range states in light of disparities between policies and social attitudes, highlighting what these might mean for the future of apes both in captivity and in their natural habitats.

> " In the United States, businesses may use *preserve*, *sanctuary* or *conservation center* in their name even though they do not technically engage in those activities. "

Apes in Captivity in Range State Regions

Wild ape populations in Africa and Asia have declined sharply in recent years due to factors including habitat loss, hunting and the illicit wildlife trade. Simultaneously, the number of ape residents at rescue centers and sanctuaries has burgeoned (see Box 8.1). Estimates reported in the first edition of *State of the Apes* indicate that nearly 1,000 chimpanzees were living in sanctuaries across Africa in 2011, along with 55 bonobos and more than 75 gorillas (Durham and Phillipson, 2014, p. 296, table 10.7). Of the chimpanzees, approximately 200 were outside of ape range states, namely in Kenya, South Africa and Zambia. An estimated 1,300–1,600 orangutans live in sanctuaries and rescue centers, alongside approximately 500 gibbons (Stiles *et al.*, 2013; Durham and Phillipson, 2014, pp. 296–7, tables 10.7, 10.8).

BOX 8.1

Sanctuaries and Rescue and Rehabilitation Centers

Organizations that provide care for rescued apes are variously called rescue centers, rehabilitation centers and sanctuaries. Although their missions can vary, all of these facilities provide shelter and care for apes. Rescue and rehabilitation centers often specialize in short- and intermediate-term care with the goal of releasing apes back into their natural habitat. By contrast, many sanctuaries focus on long-term or even lifetime care. In practice, these programs often cover a spectrum of care scenarios. A rescue center might be able to translocate a healthy ape within a matter of days, while providing lifelong care for a seriously injured ape. Likewise, a given sanctuary might have several residents fit for release but keep them in residence in the absence of release sites. Yet another sanctuary might provide lifetime care for all residents because the facility is not in a habitat country. In summary, important functions are provided by the full range of facilities that house and care for apes in captivity.

Sanctuary arrival rates vary both over time and from place to place. Retrospective analyses of data from chimpanzee sanctuaries suggest that patterns of arrival reflect a number of factors (Farmer, 2002; Faust *et al.*, 2011; Durham and Phillipson, 2014). In the first half of 2014, the Great Apes Survival Partnership (GRASP) reported that 38 great ape rescues had taken place, a rate almost double that of the prior year (GRASP, 2014a; Platt, 2014). Examples of recent arrivals at ape sanctuaries and rescue centers include the following:

- Two young chimpanzees who had been kept captive at a supermarket in Kinshasa, in the Democratic Republic of Congo, for approximately one year were airlifted to the Lwiro sanctuary after they were confiscated by authorities (GRASP, 2014b).

- In Gabon, three gorillas were transferred to the Fernan-Vas Gorilla Project after spending decades at a research center. As infants, they had been victims of the illicit wildlife trade; subsequently, authorities had placed them at the research facility, where they remained for many years. Now adult (18–33 years old), the gorillas will be able to live out their lives

at the sanctuary. The research center stated that the transfer was part of their efforts to satisfy new US rules regarding the use of apes in biomedical testing (CIRMF, 2014).

- International Animal Rescue (IAR) accepted a scarred and malnourished female orangutan who had been surrendered to local authorities. She had been kept captive as a pet for approximately two years, tethered by a rope around her neck (Francis, 2014).

- The Borneo Orangutan Survival Foundation rehabilitation center in Nyaru Menteng rescued a young male orangutan trapped in a forest fragment adjacent to a farm. Although he was just three and thus too young to be weaned, he was found alone (BOS Foundation, 2014).

Ape Rescues: The Challenges

As the examples above illustrate, the reasons for rescue and experiences in captivity prior to rescue can vary considerably. The differences between local pet keeping and illegal trafficking to consumer countries versus other forms of human–wildlife interactions have implications for sanctuaries. The types of interaction that increase risk for apes are also factors that influence arrival rates and other important rescue outcomes, such as health and rehabilitation success. Thus, it is important to ascertain the origins of rescued apes.

Data collected by the IAR Indonesia Foundation in Ketapang, West Kalimantan, revealed that rescued orangutans come from a variety of backgrounds. The greatest proportion (43%) came from villages where local people kept them illegally; 31% were rescued directly from oil palm plantations; and 12% were caught in local community agricultural landscapes (including coconut, rambutan, rice and rubber fields), very often adjacent to oil palm plantations. Only 1% of orangutans were rescued from the illegal wildlife trade. The remainder (13%) were transferred from other facilities (Sánchez, 2015).

Demands for sanctuary space and services are influenced to some extent by past experiences of ape residents. For example, individuals who were kept as pets can be familiar with or even drawn to people and desensitized to certain risks, while exhibiting specific pathologies as a result of a history of abuse or neglect (Ferdowsian *et al.*, 2011; Freeman and Ross, 2014; see Case Studies 8.1 and 8.3). Importantly, these same factors are also relevant for welfare and sanctuary outcomes. Facilities that deal with residents of disparate backgrounds and experiences face specific demands on their capacity that go beyond the number of apes present; residents arrive with distinct needs for care and rehabilitation that place a wide range of demands on the facility, its programs and staff. Care and rehabilitation activities can be better tailored to residents if their origins and backgrounds are known.

Photo: The reasons for rescue and experiences in captivity prior to rescue can vary considerably. The types of interaction that increase risk for apes are also factors that influence arrival rates and other important rescue outcomes, such as health and rehabilitation success. IAR rescue a mother orangutan and her infant in Peniraman, West Kalimantan. © Feri Latief, IAR Indonesia

Knowledge of resident background may vary more for facilities that serve chimpanzees than those that house orangutans. Not only is the geographic range of orangutans generally smaller, but trade and captivity are also more localized, a pattern explored in more detail below and in Case Study 1.1 in Chapter 1. By the same token, risks are also concentrated, such that the number of orangutans arriving at and passing through rescue centers has been greater than that of chimpanzees (Farmer, 2002; Durham and Phillipson, 2014). Since 75% of known orangutan distribution is found outside of protected areas, understanding whether and how the species could be accommodated in an agro-industrial landscapes is crucial for the long-term survival of these apes (Meijaard *et al.*, 2012). In view of the abovementioned surge in rescues, current patterns could certainly change. In any case, reversing the trend remains vital for both species.

Any estimates for the number of apes in captivity or the arrival rates in habitat countries belie a much larger and more devastating flow of apes from their natural habitats into captivity around the world. The apes who arrive at sanctuaries and rescue centers represent only a fraction of trafficking cases because arrival figures do not account for individuals who reach the intended, albeit illegal, destination, nor for those killed during capture attempts or trafficking. The adult mortality rates associated with the capture of young apes must be added to the infant deaths to estimate the wider number of trafficking deaths; for every captive infant, 1–2 adults die among orangutans and gorillas, while 5–10 adults are killed among chimpanzees and bonobos (Stiles *et al.*, 2013, p. 36). Given that gibbons tend to live in pairs, it would be reasonable to estimate 1–2 deaths for each captured infant.

There is reason to believe the traffickers who get arrested might not be among the most prolific. As GRASP Programme Coordinator Doug Cress recently noted, "We're just catching the losers right now, the guys who aren't good enough to really pull this off" (Platt, 2014). An evaluation of ape trafficking suggests a much larger scale for criminal networks and illicit trade (Stiles *et al.*, 2013). Indeed, as wildlife law enforcement expert Ofir Drori reports, a number of individual traffickers have sold "hundreds of apes" each (Stiles *et al.*, 2013, p. 7). The source and origin of apes held captive in consumer countries may not be systematically recorded or reported. Except where media attention or confiscations in consumer countries bring these cases to light, there may be insufficient evidence to tie countries of origin or traffickers to the illicit trade; similarly, as discussed below, there may not be enough information to link trafficked apes back to their original habitats. Implementing programs to determine the provenance of confiscated apes and return them to their countries of origin is an important goal for future tracking and enforcement (Stiles *et al.*, 2013).

Factors that put ape populations at risk and that ultimately influence the continued demand for sanctuary space and services in habitat countries—such as habitat conversion, the illicit trade and the transmission of disease—are complex and difficult to disentangle (Arcus Foundation, 2014; Carne *et al.*, 2014; Di Marco *et al.*, 2014; Tranquilli *et al.*, 2014; Wilson *et al.*, 2014a). Among these drivers, all of which are anthropogenic, ongoing habitat conversion remains the key cause behind the flow of apes from their natural habitats to captivity.

Case Studies 8.1 and 8.2 illustrate the types of challenges that affect ape sanctuaries as well as the residents in their care; 8.1 focuses on a rescue center in Cameroon, while 8.2 considers gibbon rescues in Indonesia. The next section compares and contrasts the two case studies to highlight potential opportunities and solutions.

CASE STUDY 8.1

Great Ape Rescue in Cameroon: The Sanaga-Yong Rescue Center

Unless otherwise cited, the information for this case study is drawn from author interviews with the Center's founder, Sheri Speede, in September 2014.

General Information

Sanaga-Yong Rescue Center (SYRC), a project of In Defense of Animals–Africa, was founded in 1999 to provide sanctuary for orphaned chimpanzees in their natural habitat. The Center is located northeast of the capital, Yaoundé, in the Mbargue Forest, which still has small populations of chimpanzees and gorillas. Over the past 15 years, the organization has added a range of programs to promote the protection of wild apes and their habitats. Sanaga-Yong has worked with law enforcement authorities across Cameroon to seize chimpanzees who are held captive or traded illegally. The organization has about 25 staff members in Cameroon as well as a small team that works through a US charity affiliate, In Defense of Animals–Africa.

Direct Care for Chimpanzees and Other Programs at SYRC

SYRC has approximately 0.91 km² (91 ha) of forest with facilities that include a veterinary clinic and a camp with staff quarters. The main complex includes six large, fenced enclosures of natural forest where sanctuary residents live. One enclosure is more open and equipped with custom climbing structures and other features for chimpanzees who require specialized care. As of September 2014, 70 chimpanzees were resident at SYRC.

The organization has a number of community and conservation programs. SYRC developed media campaigns focused on decreasing consumer demand for ape meat and recently published a children's book called *Je Protège les Chimpanzés* (I Protect Chimpanzees), which is being used in schools as part of their conservation outreach. For many years, SYRC has had programs to support schools and medical care in communities around the rescue center. Conservation field research recently conducted by SYRC found that apes in the Mbargue Forest are at high risk due to small population sizes, continued habitat loss and degradation, as well as hunting pressure. Social surveys in nearby villages indicated that many communities support the idea of chimpanzee protection and the organization's work.

The very first residents at SYRC were three chimpanzees who had been illegally exhibited at a resort. Once the facility officially opened its doors, the number of residents grew rapidly as the authorities seized more and more chimpanzees. SYRC worked closely with law enforcement on many such cases to rescue chimpanzees, including older individuals who had been captive for decades, and infants who had been for sale in markets or by illegal traders. In recent years, sanctuary staff members have noticed that people are no longer openly displaying apes in public places and fewer orphaned chimpanzees are arriving at the Center. It is not clear whether or not these changes represent decreases in the number of orphaned chimpanzees or in the volume of illegal trade. Nor is it known whether illegal trafficking has simply been driven further underground. The changes could also indicate that a drop in the wild population has slowed the rate of illegal trade or captivity. It is hard to say for certain, since it is difficult to document the illegal activities and a number of complex spatial and temporal factors can affect the demand for sanctuary space and services (Stiles *et al.*, 2013; Arcus Foundation, 2014).

Logging, Agriculture and Human Settlements

For SYRC, commercial logging in the Mbargue Forest has an ongoing impact. Beyond the harvesting of trees by commercial loggers and the illegal logging that followed, the construction of roads by logging companies brought new people to the forest, and some of them settled there. Forest is cleared using the slash-and-burn method to make way for homesteads and fields for subsistence crops, as well as cash crops such as coffee.

Local agriculture is important to the sanctuary for a number of reasons, some of which are positive. For example, SYRC buys most fruit and vegetables for the chimpanzees from farms in nearby villages. Such arrangements are mutually beneficial; farmers have a predictable market for their produce and a reliable source of income, while the sanctuary has a convenient source of food for its residents. These shared interests help the organization foster goodwill and sustain relationships with local communities.

This is not to say that all impacts are positive or that there are no challenges associated with the human settlements and farms in the Mbargue Forest. The large, natural forest enclosures at SYRC provide an excellent setting for rehabilitation and re-release preparation, but no reintroductions have been attempted due to a lack of suitable release sites. The habitat near SYRC, for instance, is close to human settlements and farms and the apes would thus be at risk of experiencing habitat pressures from agriculture and related human–wildlife conflict. The presence of subsistence and smallholder farms in the Mbargue Forest drives habitat loss, fragmentation and degradation, which the wild apes living around the Center are facing as well. Although reintroduced chimpanzees and wild chimpanzee communities in Mbargue Forest could face different risks, it is safe to say that—due to a number of factors, such as sensitivity to human presence and familiarity with the surrounding habitat—ongoing agricultural pressures increase risks for both groups. More

▶

farms, larger plots and less forest increase the chances of encounters, which can be risky for both people and apes.

As discussed in Chapter 1, crop raiding is a significant source of conflict between people and primates, including apes (Campbell-Smith *et al.*, 2010; Strum, 2010; McLennan *et al.*, 2012). Earlier this year, SYRC experienced the devastating consequences of direct conflict, when a male chimpanzee who had escaped from a sanctuary enclosure was later killed at a pineapple farm several kilometers away. In cooperation with Sanaga-Yong and a wildlife law enforcement team from LAGA, the Last Great Ape organization, local authorities executed search warrants, identified the alleged perpetrator and issued a warrant for his arrest. On November 30, 2014, three months after the warrant had been issued, authorities located the suspect in Belabo East, where they successfully arrested him and took him into custody (LAGA, 2014).

While this case was tragic for SYRC, it serves as a compelling example. The sanctuary took the position that a chimpanzee from the sanctuary deserved protection and justice, as do apes in their natural habitat and those who are sold by poachers. In so doing, both the sanctuary and law enforcement authorities demonstrated their commitment to the law and to the intrinsic value of chimpanzees. More broadly, SYRC illustrates how the reach and impact of a sanctuary can extend beyond its walls and fences to bridge gaps in protection, enforcement and social change in ways that can benefit apes in captivity and in their natural habitat.

Photo: The large, natural forest enclosures at SYRC provide an excellent setting for rehabilitation and re-release preparation, but no reintroductions have been attempted due to a lack of suitable release sites.
© Jacques Gillon and Sanaga-Yong Chimpanzee Rescue Center

CASE STUDY 8.2

Gibbon Rescue in Indonesia: Kalaweit

Unless otherwise cited, the information for this case study was drawn from author interviews with A. "Chanee" Brulé of Kalaweit in September 2014.

General Information

Kalaweit is a conservation organization based in Indonesia that rescues gibbons for rehabilitation and reintroduction and provides permanent sanctuary. In addition, Kalaweit has a number of other programs on Borneo and Sumatra. As part of its efforts to protect gibbons and their natural habitats, the organization cooperatively manages two nature reserves through agreements with the Indonesian government. In addition to the founder, Kalaweit employs about 50 people in Indonesia and has one staff member in France.

Programs and Direct Care for Gibbons

Kalaweit was initiated in 1997 and began running activities about two years later, once essential agreements with government authorities were in place. The first rescue residents— 17 gibbons—had arrived at the facility by December 2000. Agreements with and responsibilities to the Indonesian government expanded through 2004, by which time the number of gibbons taken in at Kalaweit had increased to 240 individuals, reflecting a growth of more than 1,400%. Although arrival rates have slowed over time and some individuals have been released back into the wild, the number of individuals in residence is still increasing, as discussed below.

The organization operates facilities to care for gibbons in captivity on both Borneo and Sumatra. Both the Care Center, where the apes receive initial care and housing after rescue, and the Pawarawen Gibbon Conservation Center are located in Central Kalimantan. Kalaweit also operates outreach and radio programs from Borneo. In 2011, the Supayang Gibbon Conservation Center was established in Western Sumatra. The Center is adjacent to the Supayang Reserve, where gibbons occur naturally. Approximately 30 wild gibbons live in the reserve, a site co-managed with the Indonesian government. In addition, six siamangs live in large, pre-release forest enclosures as part of the earliest stage of their reintroduction process. Efforts are currently under way to expand the size of the reserve.

Demand for Sanctuary Space and Services at Kalaweit

The number of gibbons now kept illegally as pets and for entertainment in Java, Kalimantan and Sumatra, the nation's most populous provinces, is estimated at around 6,000. Deforestation, driven by oil palm development and the extractive industries, is a primary facilitator of the illegal regional pet trade in gibbons. Activities associated with industrial agriculture and extractive industries, such as road construction, commercial transportation and the movement of people, can make apes more accessible to traffickers and generally more vulnerable. Farms represent a further risk, as apes captured in the wild are sometimes kept illegally as pets or mascots at company sites. Indeed, three gibbons recently rescued by Kalaweit were confiscated from a palm oil company.

The Supayang facility is one of the few in the world where Kloss's gibbon (*Hylobates klossii*) exists in captivity. If an ambitious government plan to rescue all other Kloss's gibbons kept as illegal pets is successful, Kalaweit will lead efforts to rehabilitate healthy individuals for reintroduction and provide long-term care for those in need.

The organization currently cares for 254 individuals from five endangered gibbon species at rescue facilities in West Sumatra and Central Kalimantan (see Table 8.1). About 25% of the gibbons at Kalaweit are not candidates for release. A particular concern is past exposure to infectious diseases carried by people or other animals. Kalaweit's permanent residents also include gibbons who have disabilities that stem from illness or injury, and those who lack the social and behavioral skills to survive independently. With the exception of these special cases, the majority of gibbons at the centers are candidates for reintroduction, and some are ready to begin the process. Since the number of release sites is extremely limited, however, most of the apes at Kalaweit are expected to remain there for the long term, perhaps even permanently.

Much of the forest where gibbons ranged historically has been cleared to make way for oil palm plantations or extractive industries (Arcus Foundation, 2014). Land cleared and degraded by industrial agriculture and extractive industries has drastically reduced the number and size of potential release sites. Currently, the forests available to Kalaweit have very few or no gibbons but do not meet size, quality or other requirements. In areas where the habitat is suitable, the population density of gibbons is too high to accommodate more apes. The lack of release sites is the greatest challenge confronting the organization. Thus, acquiring forest to protect gibbons in their natural habitat and to provide release sites for residents from the rescue centers is one of Kalaweit's top priorities.

TABLE 8.1

Gibbons in Kalaweit Facilities in West Sumatra and Central Kalimantan, September 2013–September 2014

Taxon	Number of arrivals, September 2013–September 2014	Total number of gibbons, September 2014	% increase from 2013 to 2014
Agile gibbon	2	33	6%
Bornean white-bearded gibbon	6	79	8%
Kloss's gibbon	1	7	14%
Müller's gibbon	2	74	3%
Siamang	5	61	8%
Total	**16**	**254**	**6%**

Data source: A. Brulé, personal communication, 2014

Drivers and Impacts of Ape Sanctuaries

The case studies reveal some of the challenges associated with land conversion. In the Cameroon case study, villagers cleared land for small farms within the forest, causing fragmentation, degradation and the expansion of the human–wildlife frontier —that is, edges where human-dominated landscapes encroach on the sanctuary and surrounding habitat. In Indonesia, Kalaweit has seen extractive industries and industrial agriculture destroy natural forest wholesale. Habitat loss is an immediate issue because apes are stranded on plantations, from where they must be rescued if they are to survive. Factors such as the global markets, trade negotiations and consumer trends are likely to influence industrial farming practice (see Chapter 3); in contrast, smallholder farms are more reactive to population size, human settlement patterns and food security. However, that distinction becomes blurred if smallholder farms are contracted suppliers to agribusinesses.

In both of the sanctuary case studies, habitat destruction and degradation from agriculture and other development activities are reducing the availability of release sites. There is less and less forest area to consider, and what remains does not meet the sanctuaries' needs. With few or no individuals able to leave the sanctuaries through release, arrivals drive the total number of residents up toward the facilities' limits—and beyond.

In addition to these ecological impacts, agriculture, extractive industries and other development activities can affect sanctuary operations, programs and ape health and wellbeing in other ways. As illustrated by the case studies, these activities can have both direct and indirect effects on the demand for sanctuary space and services. Decreasing habitat and expanding human–wildlife frontiers can result in more frequent and riskier interactions, which can lead to conflict. People can cross paths with apes while walking to their fields or to the market, increasing the risk of disease transmission or conflict-related injury.

The sharing of time and space with people heightens the risk that apes may be injured or exposed to illnesses, which, in turn, increases the likelihood that they may need sanctuary care and rehabilitation, further affecting post-rescue outcomes. The following examples shed light on a variety of such threats:

- The use of chemical pesticides, traps and other defenses that farmers use to protect their crops or livestock increases the risk of illness or injury for apes, and thereby augments the likelihood that they could require human care or spend time in captivity. Apes trapped in snares or injured in human–wildlife conflict may be unable to escape human captors and consequently require human intervention to ensure their survival. In either case, such individuals might subsequently require captive rehabilitation or sanctuary care.

- When habitat conversion is accompanied by the introduction or expansion of animal agriculture and increased livestock density, disease-related risks can increase. Direct and complex transmission scenarios warrant concern. Domestic animals such as livestock can contract diseases in one place and subsequently spread them to humans and other animals, including apes, in another place. A recent study reports instances of tuberculosis among wild chimpanzees (Wolf *et al.*, 2014). Cryptosporidiosis and other parasitic infections are also prevalent in some wild chimpanzee populations that live in close proximity to settlements and farms (Ghai *et al.*, 2014; Parsons *et al.*, 2015). Apes who have been exposed to disease and end up in sanctuary care may have specialized needs, such as veterinary medical requirements. Disease status could also exclude apes as candidates for re-release.

- Human–wildlife conflict associated with agriculture is tied to pet keeping and the local pet trade in apes. Apes who are kept as pets locally account for most sanctuary cases involving trade and trafficking. In contrast to the demand-driven illicit international trade in apes, which is discussed below and in Case Study 8.3, the local pet trade seems to be more opportunistic. Survey research at the IAR rescue center in Ketapang indicates that pet keeping is typically a secondary result of conflict. When asked about the origins of pet orangutans surrendered to the rescue center, 39% of the previous owners claimed that they had "found" the orangutans, while 29% admitted to buying them. Those who admitted paying for a baby or infant orangutan reported paying an amount between 500,000 and 1.5 million Indonesian rupiah (US$50–$150) (Sánchez, 2015). Normally the trade is local and the orangutans originate from a nearby location. In some cases, young orangutans are taken as pets after their mothers are killed for food (Meijaard *et al.*, 2011). Although a small number of respondents in the IAR survey admitted to knowing about such circumstances, many did not want to reveal the origins of a pet orangutan at all; 32% of respondents did not wish to answer the question or the information obtained from them was considered unreliable (Sánchez, 2015).

Apes with histories of other forms of human–wildlife conflict and captivity might have unique needs due to injury, illness or psychological status. For example, apes kept captive as pets are more likely to develop behavioral pathologies and less likely to be socially competent than apes raised by their mothers (Freeman and Ross, 2014). Research has also shown that some orphaned chimpanzees exhibit signs of psychological conditions, such as depression or post-traumatic stress disorder (Ferdowsian *et al.*, 2011, 2012). Such individuals may require specialized housing, veterinary care or other sanctuary services. If basic social integration proves difficult, for instance, apes may require special enclosures and added social support from staff.

Apes in Captivity in Non-range States of the Global North

To examine the state of apes in different forms of captivity in non-range states of the global North, this section considers information from Europe and the United States. It relies on official government data, information collected directly from facilities, NGO reports and other published sources. The data reflect gaps in coverage and variations in terms of the level of detail and reliability. While these factors limited the scope and depth of the review for the chapter, they also underscore the importance of maintaining systematic, detailed records and of ensuring transparency in the monitoring of the welfare of apes in captivity.

The data show that most captive apes are living in zoos and sanctuaries. Some of the information reported here is limited to licensed or accredited facilities, which are those that are operated under government authority or have been granted membership in a professional organization. Professional organizations and accrediting bodies include the European Association of Zoos and Aquaria (EAZA) and the European Alliance of Rescue centres and Sanctuaries at the regional level, and the Global Federation of Animal Sanctuaries and the World Association of Zoos and Aquariums at the global level. In this chapter, information that is cited as coming from accredited or member facilities has been sourced from such professional organizations. In addition to establishing their own standards for members, membership organizations can also coordinate practices and the sharing of information across institutions, such as by reporting on the number of individuals or births for a given species. Although such information is primarily for internal use, it is sometimes published or shared externally at the discretion of an organization, as is the case with some of the data in this chapter.

Apes in Captivity in Europe

Some EU member states, such as Austria and Sweden, have adopted strict rules at the national level that forbid testing on apes (Knight, 2008). More broadly, EU law severely restricts testing on apes, with the

only possible consideration limited to a safeguard clause for critical emergencies [2010/63/EC Article 55(2)]. Thus, laboratories in the EU hold a limited number of apes, and captive apes are thus found predominantly in zoos and sanctuaries. A small and declining number of apes are kept legally and illegally as pets or performers. The following sections present information about apes who are kept in zoos, circuses and other entertainment settings, and sanctuaries in the EU.

Zoos

The EU does not engage in the systematic compilation of statistics regarding the number of apes in zoos. Implementation and enforcement of the Zoos Directive 1999/22/EC and related regulations are handled by individual member states, which may also devolve authority to the regional or municipal level (EU, 1999). As noted in the first edition of *State of the Apes*, zoo standards, compliance and reporting vary widely across EU member states (Durham and Phillipson, 2014, pp. 288–9). In Germany, for example, federal authorities do not maintain centralized records that would identify the number of zoos in the country—which is estimated at anywhere between 350 and 850—raising concerns about whether the zoos are licensed (Animal Public eV, Born Free Foundation and Bund gegen Missbrauch der Tiere eV, 2012).

There are more apes in zoos than in any other captive setting in Europe. Thus, knowing how many zoos exist and where they are located is essential to oversight and protection efforts. A full accounting of apes in zoos is key to a better understanding of the scale and nature of the welfare challenges that apes may face. Further, in the EU, individual member states, competent authorities and zoo administrators require such basic information to develop effective ways to address the needs of apes.

In the absence of official EU figures on apes in captivity, the author has compiled information from other sources, including published and unpublished figures and personal communication, which were obtained using methods described in detail elsewhere (Durham and Phillipson, 2014). In particular, the author requested species-holding reports through the online portal of the International Species Information System (ISIS), a voluntary membership organization that represents "more than 800 member zoos, aquariums and related organizations in 84 countries" (ISIS, n.d.). In response to the request, ISIS provided aggregate data indicating the number of apes by taxon from its member facilities in Europe in 2014, though some of the reported figures may represent totals from earlier periods due to varying reporting protocols and technical issues. The data include some facilities in European countries that are not members of the EU, as well as some non-EAZA institutions. Since ISIS membership is voluntary, the provided zoo figures are not necessarily representative of zoo holdings in general, and thus should be considered only a starting point for estimating the number of apes now captive in zoos across Europe.

In total, the figures accounted for 2,284 apes in 204 member institutions, with holdings ranging from 1 to 68 apes per site. The 40 sites with the greatest number of apes accounted for roughly half of the total, while the 40 sites with the smallest number of apes held fewer than 100 apes collectively. The six smallest facilities reported only one individual. Gibbons were the most common taxon in this sample, followed by chimpanzees, gorillas, orangutans and bonobos. Numbers and the proportion of apes in each group are shown in Figure 8.1. The number of solitary apes in the sample was small—29 apes, or 1% of the total. Since apes who lack conspecific companions are a particular welfare concern, even this small number warrants special attention.

FIGURE 8.1

Number and Percentage of Apes in Select European Zoos, by Taxonomic group

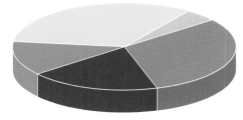

Legend:

- Bonobo (108 = 5%)
- Chimpanzee (698 = 31%)
- Gorilla (424 = 19%)
- Orangutan (300 = 13%)
- Gibbon (754 = 33%)

Notes: Percentages do not add up to 100% due to rounding. Gibbon category also includes siamangs.

Data source: Aggregate data from species-holding reports from select ISIS members, submitted to the author by ISIS in 2014, though some of the reported figures may represent earlier reporting periods.

Circuses and Entertainment

A small number of apes are kept as performers in the EU. EU regulation 1739/2005/EC specifies that circus operators must register with authorities to move animal performers between countries, but it does not address the welfare of animals in circuses or traveling animal shows (EU, 2005). As with the keeping of apes as pets, the use and welfare of apes in circuses and other live performances is governed at the national level; conditions vary across countries, ranging from the absence of a comprehensive law to outright bans on all animals in circuses (Durham and Phillipson, 2014, pp. 282–3, box 10.1). In Greece, for example, the use of all animals in circuses is banned nationwide; in contrast, approximately 140 communities have enacted local circus regulations in Spain, where laws are adopted at the municipal level (Born Free Foundation, 2013; ENDCAP, n.d.). Estonia and Poland ban the use of "wild-caught" animals, while Austria and

Croatia ban "wild" animals, including "non-domestic species" (Eurogroup for Animals, 2010; ENDCAP, n.d.).

While apes are not among the most common species in circuses and live performances, some continue to be exploited in this manner, and evidence suggests their treatment and welfare is poor. The German amusement park Schwaben Park, which features live animal performances and has been investigated on three separate occasions, allegedly maintains chimpanzees in poor welfare and dangerous conditions (Animal Public eV *et al.*, 2012; Nakott, 2012; Animal Equality, 2013). According to these investigations, the facility has approximately 44 chimpanzees, more than are kept by many accredited zoos and ape sanctuaries. A small number of the chimpanzees perform in daily shows promoted on the park's website and social media channels, which at times have featured videos and photos of chimpanzees wearing clothes and doing tricks (Schwaben Park, 2011, n.d.).

In the case of circuses and other live entertainment that features apes, the damage is two-fold. First, the individual apes are at risk of poor welfare and chronic suffering, as demonstrated by a recent study of long-term suffering and negative psychosocial effects (Freeman and Ross, 2014). Second, as a growing body of evidence indicates, exposure to apes in unnatural settings and circumstances—such as posing with people and wearing clothing—often leads people to conclude that apes are not endangered, and not in need of conservation or stewardship (Ross and Lukas, 2006; Ross *et al.*, 2008).

Although circus operators and trainers sometimes sell apes that they cannot or do not want to use in live performances any longer, rescue can be an option. Indeed, sanctuaries have recently rescued some apes from within Europe and nearby areas (AAP, 2011; Monkey World, 2012). Apes who were previously used as performers may

have chronic injuries, behavioral pathologies and other health issues that require specialized care, although this is not always the case. Case Study 8.3 details the rescue of Linda, a chimpanzee who was kept as a pet and performer.

Photo: Mowgli (16) and Kodua (13) were Hollywood performers as babies. They arrived at the Center for Great Apes ten years ago when their owner/trainer agreed to stop working great apes in the entertainment business. © Patti Ragan, Center for Great Apes

Sanctuaries

According to the Global Federation of Animal Sanctuaries, the primary purpose of professionally run sanctuaries is to provide lifetime care for the health and welfare of abused, injured or abandoned animals or for those otherwise in need (GFAS, 2013). The number of apes in sanctuaries is a small but important fraction of the total number of apes in captivity, in part because arrivals of new residents represent decreases in the number of vulnerable apes in high-risk settings (see Table 8.2). The author collected relevant

TABLE 8.2

Number of Apes in EU Sanctuaries in 2014, by Country and Taxon

Sanctuary name	Country	Taxon	Number of apes
AAP Rescue Center for Exotic Animals	Netherlands	Chimpanzees	37
Gut Aiderbichl*	Austria	Chimpanzees	37
Mona Foundation	Spain	Chimpanzees	14
Monkey World	UK	Chimpanzees	59
		Orangutans	16
		Gibbons	23
Monte Adone	Italy	Chimpanzees	13
Primadomus	Spain	Chimpanzees	9
Rainfer	Spain	Chimpanzees	16
		Orangutans	1
		Gibbons	1
Wales Ape and Monkey Sanctuary	UK	Chimpanzees	7
		Gibbons	3

Note: * Estimated figure

Sources: Gut Aiderbichl (2014); Centro de Rescate de Primates Rainfer (n.d.); Monte Adone (n.d.); Wales Ape and Monkey Sanctuary (n.d.-a, n.d.-b); A. Cronin, personal communication, 2014; D. Eastham, personal communication, 2014

CASE STUDY 8.3

EU Case Study: The Rescue of a Chimpanzee Named Linda

Unless otherwise cited, the information for this case study was drawn from author interviews with David van Gennep of AAP in September 2014.

Linda is a female chimpanzee who was probably born around 1978. She was previously kept for use as both a tourist attraction and pet by a private owner in Lanzarote, one of the Canary Islands. Following a complicated rescue, she was flown to a sanctuary in the Netherlands, where she will receive care for the remainder of her life. Details about Linda and what she has experienced epitomize the plight of chimpanzees kept as pets and performers and the challenges that sanctuaries face in their efforts to rescue them.

Linda was purchased as an infant for approximately US$2,240; her owners used her as a tourist attraction by letting people pose for photographs with her for a fee. At the time, Spanish law permitted this type of exhibition, which was so popular that the purchase price of "exotic" animals could be recovered within a matter of days.

Linda was already in captivity when Spain implemented the Convention on International Trade in Endangered Species (CITES) in 1986. Spain has laws pertaining to animals, including Ley 50/1999 regarding the possession of potentially dangerous wild animals and regulations regarding the operation of zoos, all of which address certain aspects relating to the welfare of apes in captivity (Á. Guede Fernández, personal communication, 2014). Spanish support for the protection of apes seems strong; a parliamentary committee passed a resolution in 2008 that recognizes certain rights for great apes (Glendinning, 2008).

Nevertheless, the law was of little help to Linda. Spain has several autonomous communities that operate under self-governance, including the Canary Islands. As a result, the legal framework is partially decentralized; Spanish laws are implemented at the regional level and autonomous regions may adopt their own laws. Two such laws enacted in the Canary Islands during the 1990s were relevant to Linda's welfare. In 1991, Ley 8/1991 (BOE-A-1991-16425) was adopted to protect domestic animals—a term broadly interpreted to mean any animals kept in a home and dependent on people for survival. A second law, enacted in 1994 (BOE-A-1994-12127), increased legal restrictions regarding hawkers and peddlers, including the people who sold photo opportunities, such as the ones who exploited Linda (Á. Guede Fernández, personal communication, 2014).

While these types of regulations might be expected to protect animals such as Linda, they failed to do so in her case. Linda fell into a legal loophole. The new laws meant that her owners could no longer use her as a tourist attraction, but what did they mean for Linda? She was not handed over to a sanctuary or sold by her owners, nor was she seized by the authorities; instead, she was locked away, out of view.

Linda's owners kept her alone in a room for decades before a family member reportedly saw a documentary and contacted the MONA Foundation, a sanctuary near Barcelona. The sanctuary worked for nearly three years to secure her release, a process hampered by limited cooperation from the authorities in the Canary Islands (MONA Foundation, 2013). When the terms were finally agreed, a veterinary examination revealed that Linda was a carrier of the hepatitis B virus (MONA UK, 2014). The rules, requirements and costs associated with her specialized health care needs meant that it was not possible to find a sanctuary placement for Linda in Spain.

As these developments put Linda's rescue in jeopardy, a suitable location was needed urgently. Fortunately, following the Dutch government's ban on biomedical testing on chimpanzees, a sanctuary called AAP had taken in and provided care for the laboratory chimpanzees that had been exposed to human diseases such as hepatitis. AAP was able to offer its considerable expertise and specialized facilities for Linda's care, but the transfer was dependent on a government permit to import her into the Netherlands. After nearly eight months of concerted efforts by AAP, the authorities finally granted permission for Linda's transfer in August 2014. Shortly thereafter, she arrived from Lanzarote to begin the next stage of her life and rehabilitation (AAP, 2014).

At the time of writing, Linda had completed her mandatory quarantine period and integration with a new social group was under way. Despite her prolonged isolation, Linda responded positively to social cues, embracing, holding hands and playing with male chimpanzees named Julio and Jim (AAP, 2015).

The sanctuary plans to estimate Linda's age more precisely with dental and anatomical markers and to identify her geographic origin using DNA once she is thoroughly integrated and has adjusted to the sanctuary. Even given her early progress, the sanctuary expects that Linda may need psychological care as a result of the emotional toll of loneliness, one of the most difficult issues the residents at the sanctuary face during rehabilitation (D. van Gennep, personal communication, 2014). Scientists who work with the sanctuary have found that many residents benefit from treatment, including training, environmental modifications or even psychiatric medication (Kranendonk et al., 2012; Ghosh, 2013).

Linda's case highlights some key issues concerning the welfare and rescue of apes in captivity, especially those used as pets and performers:

■ Purchased as babies, chimpanzees are typically used as performers or kept as pets until they are about five years old, when they begin to act of their own volition (D. van Gennep, personal communication 2014). Due to their physical strength, people can no longer control or handle the apes safely; some even resort to drugging apes or

removing their teeth. The value of keeping and using apes as performers thus changes for the people involved: the costs of housing, managing and handling apes increase, while the benefits—revenue from performance or companionship from holding and playing with them—are in decline or disappear altogether. As a result, some apes are sold or surrendered, while others may be killed. Still others might be transferred to a permanent exhibit, where they are put on display. Some, such as Linda, are hidden away, alone and out of sight, which makes them very vulnerable to abuse, neglect and other welfare risks.

■ The legal mechanisms that many people assume provide different forms of protection for apes in captivity— such as CITES, laws on animal welfare, public safety, wildlife conservation and animal cruelty—can prove insufficient in practice. As noted above, they did little for Linda. Despite her status as a member of an endangered species, she was exploited and remained in harm's way for many years. The law did not provide a mechanism for ensuring her health, protecting her welfare or preventing her pain and suffering.

■ The restriction of business activities was important in Linda's case. Legislation to restrict private ownership and the use of apes in entertainment is essential to stem the illicit trade in apes and the flow of apes from range states to captivity in consumer countries. The very presence of sustained illegal trade demonstrates that the economic incentives are powerful, such that market solutions alone will not be able to reduce consumer demand.

■ Linda was microchipped shortly before her rescue, but prior to that she lacked any permanent identification. Linda's identification raises an important concern regarding age-in-place solutions and other scenarios where private ownership is grandfathered into new regulations: the risk of identity theft. The authorities issued a permit for a female chimpanzee, but it would be extremely difficult to prove that the chimpanzee listed on that permit was the same individual brought to Lanzarote decades earlier, or the chimpanzee now living at AAP. Unique identification is important not only for monitoring the health and welfare of individuals over time, but it is also key to discouraging ongoing trade. Without clear and permanent individual identification, unscrupulous parties could buy apes and then pass them off as individuals named in granted permits.

Photos: Linda – one year on from being rescued, her first time outside, and before she was rescued. © AAP/Rob Schreuder, AAP/Petra Sonius and AAP/Roland J Reinders, respectively

data by collating published and electronic sources, as well as by requesting information directly from sanctuaries. The data show that 235 apes currently live in European sanctuaries, reflecting a small increase (3%) since 2013, when the figure stood at 211 (Durham and Phillipson, 2014, p. 288); the revised figure takes account of apes at two sites that were not included in the previous survey, Monte Adone in Italy and Rainfer in Spain.

Unless large numbers of individuals are transferred from one institution to another, arrival rates at sanctuaries are typically low, as they reflect rescues of individuals or small groups. Sanctuaries can experience temporary increases in arrival rates if, for example, private owners relinquish animals in anticipation of a new law, or in response to enforcement efforts once it is in place. By anticipating increased demand for sanctuary space and services, sanctuaries can prepare in ways that help to minimize barriers to enforcement. For example, in 2014 the Netherlands adopted a positive list—or "white list"—of the only wild animals that may be kept as pets, and apes are not among them (AAP, 2013). Knowing that this rule would come into force in 2015, AAP was able to prepare for the potential arrival of new residents through voluntary surrender and coordination with law enforcement (D. van Gennep, personal communication, 2014).

Apes in Captivity in the United States

In the United States, federal, state and municipal laws have implications for the welfare of apes in captivity. Various federal regulations direct the protection, importation, interstate trade and transport, and minimum welfare requirements for endangered species. These laws explicitly address apes or primates, in addition to other animal species. The frame-

work of federal regulations governing apes in captivity has evolved on a number of fronts in recent years. For example, following a review ordered by the House of Representatives, the federal government adopted a number of new practices regarding experiments on chimpanzees, including improvements to housing and welfare programs (Altevogt et al., 2011).

The same review also dramatically reduced the number of federally owned chimpanzees who were used in experiments—down to 50, through the retirement of more than 300 chimpanzees (NIH, 2013). A number of other ongoing federal policy reviews and proposed laws could have dramatic effects for apes in captivity in the United States. Key examples follow.

Proposed Legislation: S. 1463/H.R. 2856 Captive Primate Safety Act

On August 1, 2013, the Captive Primate Safety Act was introduced into the Senate, one day after being introduced to the House of Representatives (Boxer, 2013; Fitzpatrick, 2013). The proposed legislation aimed to amend an existing law known as the Lacey Act (18 USC 42-43. 16 USC 3371-3378), which limits trade in wildlife, as well as other activities, by further prohibiting interstate commerce in apes and other primates for the exotic pet trade. Although some state laws regulate possession within state borders, they do not restrict out-of-state dealers, nor do they necessarily apply to commercial activities, such as certain auctions or Internet sales (Paquette, 2014). As a result, interstate enforcement remains a challenge. The bill, S. 1463, was referred to the Committee on Environment and Public Works on the day it was introduced. A review by the Congressional Budget Office found that the changes were relatively minor and would have no significant effect on the federal budget.

On July 30, 2014, the Committee on Environment and Public Works reported favorably and on December 11, 2014, it was placed on the Senate Legislative Calendar. The House of Representatives has not taken further action on H.R. 2856 since referring it to the Subcommittee on Fisheries, Wildlife, Oceans, and Insular Affairs on August 6, 2013. No further action was taken during the 113th Congress, which ended on January 3, 2015.

It is noteworthy that some sanctuaries and animal welfare organizations have opposed adoption of the bill on the grounds that the proposed language would allow the use of small New World monkeys as service animals for people with disabilities (Friends of Animals, 2014). While this exemption would not directly affect apes, it could weaken the law intended to protect them by undermining enforcement. The proposed exemption would give legal recognition to a new category of use under the Lacey Act as no corresponding class of registration exists under another important law, the Animal Welfare Act.

The contradiction inherent in simultaneously restricting trade and codifying a new commercial use that could set a precedent for other species and lead to complex interagency enforcement mandates is something that legislators and authorities need to weigh carefully in the context of public health and safety incentives that could be achieved through S. 1463 / H.R. 2856. As written, the proposed legislation would provide additional protections for apes and almost all other species of nonhuman primates nationally, overriding disparate state and local laws (US Senate Committee on Environment and Public Works, 2014). Proponents maintain that achieving increased federal protections for apes and the vast majority of other primates, as well as for public health and safety, while there is a favorable legislative climate outweighs agreeing to concessions in the amendment (Born Free USA, 2013).

Proposed Legislation: H.R. 3556 Humane Care for Primates Act

On November 20, 2013, the Humane Care for Primates Act was introduced to the House of Representatives (Elmers, 2013). The bill addresses the importation of apes and other primates into the United States for the purposes of sanctuary care. While current laws allow importation for zoo exhibition and other commercial activities, there is no provision for humane sheltering. As a result, under current regulations, a sanctuary would have to register with the United States Department of Agriculture (USDA) as an exhibitor in order to receive apes or other primates from abroad. Indeed, a similar issue regarding international transfer was relevant in the case of the chimpanzee named Linda, as discussed in Case Study 8.3. The proposed legislation would obviate the need for this registration by recognizing that sanctuaries are not, in fact, in the business of exhibition at all. The new rule would distinguish sanctuaries from other forms of captivity, such as roadside zoos or attractions, so that they could rescue primates rather than registering as exhibitors. The bill was referred to the House Subcommittee on Health, and no further action was taken during the 113th Congress.

Proposed Rule: Split-listing of the Chimpanzee

While the aforementioned National Institutes of Health (NIH) policy changes regarding experimentation on chimpanzees did not affect individuals who were privately owned, the United States Fish and Wildlife Service (USFWS) recently proposed a rule that could further limit experiments and other commercial uses of privately owned chimpanzees (USFWS, 2013).

Beginning in 1990, the USFWS listed chimpanzees under the Endangered Species

Act; wild chimpanzees were designated as *endangered*, while chimpanzees in captivity were accorded the lower status of *threatened*. As a result of this distinction, commonly referred to as *split-listing*, it was legal to use captive chimpanzees in the United States for various trade and commercial purposes, such as circuses and movie performances, and to engage in interstate commerce of chimpanzees and their parts (USFWS, 2013).

In March 2010, stakeholders petitioned the agency to amend the rule. Following a 90-day review, the USFWS announced its finding in 2011 with a public comment period (USFWS, 2013). After an extended review period, on June 12, 2013 the USFWS published its 12-month petition findings and opened another public comment period on the proposed language for new rules regarding the status of chimpanzees (USFWS, 2013). Two years later, on June 12, 2015, the USFWS announced that it would finalize the proposed rule to classify all chimpanzees, both in the wild and in captivity, as endangered (USFWS, 2015a). The government noted that the vast majority of comments received during the public comment period were in favor of the listing, and that most of the comments opposing the rule had been submitted by parties affiliated with the biomedical industry (USDOI, 2015, p. 34515).

The most significant effect of the new listing is that it makes it illegal for a "person subject to the jurisdiction of the United States" to "take" any listed species, meaning that it is forbidden to "harass, harm, pursue, hunt, shoot, wound, kill, trap, capture, collect" a chimpanzee, or to attempt to do so (USDOI, 2015, p. 34515). The rule also restricts import, export and interstate trade of chimpanzees (USFWS, 2015a).

The US government has emphasized that the new rule does not prohibit ongoing private ownership, normal husbandry or care of legally acquired chimpanzees (USFWS, 2015b). The endangered listing status for chimpanzees will not further restrict exhibitions that are "designed to educate the public about the ecological role and conservation needs of the affected species," so long as such exhibition is not found to harm populations in the wild or in captivity (USDOI, 2015, p. 34518). The agency will continue to consider applications for the "take" of endangered species, including chimpanzees, subject to criteria of the Endangered Species Act. Permits for "take" associated with research, for example, could be permitted under specific circumstances relating to the conservation of endangered species (USFWS, 2015b).

The new rule came into effect on September 14, 2015, 90 days after official publication by the US government (USDOI, 2015).

Petition to the USDA: Rulemaking to Prohibit Public Contact with Big Cats, Bears and Nonhuman Primates

On January 7, 2013, a coalition of stakeholders filed a joint petition with the USDA that would affect apes in captivity (USDA APHIS, 2013). Specifically, it addresses private owners, exhibitors and other entertainment businesses that allow the public to handle or otherwise interact with animals such as apes.

The petition cites a number of reasons why the rules are needed, including factors that directly impact the health and welfare of apes: premature mother–infant separation, excessive handling of young animals, abusive training, and zoonotic disease transfer to and from exhibited animals. There is considerable evidence that these factors have long-lasting, detrimental effects on the health and welfare of apes in captivity.

The period for public comment on the changes came to a close on November 18, 2013. According to the USDA website, 15,335 public comments were submitted. If the changes are adopted, they would have the greatest impact on apes who are kept as pets and performers as well as those who are kept by dealers who trade in apes for these purposes. The USDA has not yet announced the findings of the public review or its response to the petition.

Sub-national legislation

In addition to laws and regulations at the federal level, state and local laws also impact apes in captivity and influence their welfare. Such laws govern a range of activities, from business operations to criminal animal cruelty. For example, state anti-cruelty laws could potentially be invoked if an ape in captivity has been abused or neglected. The captivity of apes could also be restricted or banned under public safety laws that address dangerous wild animals or under public health regulations that pertain to zoonotic disease. State laws are typically enforced by state agencies, but enforcement can also be devolved to counties or cities, which may enact their own rules.

Variations in state and local laws can impede the coordination of federal, state and local enforcement. Indeed, this issue was one of the justifications listed for the abovementioned Captive Primate Safety Act and the petition for rulemaking on public contact with primates and other animals. On the one hand, disparate state laws can produce a geographic concentration of privately owned apes and certain risks for health and welfare in jurisdictions where regulations are weak or non-existent. On the other hand, state-level authority means that incremental legislative efforts to protect the welfare of apes in captivity can be pursued through state laws without having to build national consensus.

Among the most important state laws that deal explicitly with apes—or primates as a whole—are those that regulate the private ownership of apes as performers and pets. Local coverage varies widely—from the absence of any relevant laws to outright bans. Wherever laws do exist, they may not cover all pet keeping or afford the same protections for all apes (see Figure 8.2). For example, Texas has a list of 19 banned species that includes great apes but not gibbons (Texas Statutes, 2001). A number of state laws that restrict apes as pets also include an exemption for parties with lawful federal permits (Paquette, 2014). Thus, some people who keep apes as pets can obtain licenses

---

BOX 8.2

Factors that Support Compliance and Enforcement of New Laws

Delaying adoption of laws that prohibit private ownership or other exploitation of apes without any abatement ultimately increases the number of animals and the cost of implementation and enforcement. That said, sanctuaries and related organizations are aware that rules enacted in haste and without preparation can also lead to problems. When new laws are adopted and implemented, a number of factors that support compliance and enforcement deserve consideration:

■ Public awareness campaigns before, during and after implementation can reduce resistance among stakeholders and allow for transitions in responsibility by the authorities and sanctuaries. When laws that ban exhibition and ownership are implemented hastily, they can drive the people and businesses involved underground, making enforcement more difficult.

■ It is essential to anticipate the capacity needed to re-home animals who are voluntarily surrendered before and after a new law goes into effect. Restrictions that are phased in or activities that are phased out should be matched closely with rescue and sanctuary capacities to remove barriers to effective enforcement and encourage compliance.

■ Training on how to ensure animal safety and care during seizure and the welfare of animals under control of law enforcement plays a role in rescue outcomes, especially when animals cannot immediately be placed in the care of qualified rescue workers.

■ Periods of clemency, during which owners and other people can surrender animals without civil or criminal penalty, may help to minimize the number of animals killed or hidden.

■ When a new law allows owners to keep animals who are already in their possession for a fixed time period or for the rest of their natural lives—through what is known as a grandfather clause—the permits must be for individually identified animals who have a microchip or are otherwise uniquely identified. Any generic permit, such as for "two gibbons," would allow an owner to replace one animal for another of the same species—perhaps repeatedly.

Sources: personal communication with D. van Gennep, the European Alliance of Rescue centres and Sanctuaries, North American Primate Sanctuary Alliance and individual sanctuaries

from the USDA and sidestep restrictions in their state.

State laws can also address the issue of disparity in county or city regulations or limitations in jurisdictions where municipalities do not have the authority to regulate certain activities. Kentucky has one of the strongest laws to prevent the keeping of apes as pets through a focus on trade and importation of wild animals, including apes (301 KY. Admin. Regs. 2:082 - Transportation and holding of exotic wildlife; see Figure 8.2). Before Kentucky enacted this state law, regulation was left to its 121 counties (Truitt, 2014). When the state law was enacted, one section addressed a small number of people who received exemptions to keep apes already in their possession, provided they registered each individual, and subject to strict prohibition on breeding, exchange and replacement (Truitt, 2014). Box 8.2 highlights some challenges and opportunities that are relevant to the adoption of new regulations that impact apes and ape sanctuaries.

State laws on primates as pets can serve as an indicator of major social shifts that have taken place over the past 15 years. Table 8.3 shows the number of states that banned, had some restrictions or lacked laws regarding the keeping of apes and other primates as pets in 2000 and 2014.

The overall trend is positive. During the period under review, the number of states with the strongest laws—that is, bans—nearly doubled, while the number of states without

TABLE 8.3

Number of US States that Banned, Restricted or Lacked Laws Regarding the Keeping of Apes and Other Primates as Pets, 2000 and 2014

Year	States with bans	States with some restrictions	States without laws
2000	14	8	28
2014	26	11	13

Data source: Paquette (2014)

laws dropped by more than half. Another promising pattern is that states that increased protections largely opted for outright bans over more lenient rules. Figure 8.2 depicts US states according to whether state laws prohibited, allowed or did not regulate the keeping of primates (including apes) as pets in 2014.

The Number of Apes in Captivity in the United States

Chimpanzees are by far the most common ape in captivity in the United States, followed by gibbons, gorillas and orangutans. The high ranking of gibbons is due to the fact that all genera and species were aggregated into a single group, *gibbons*. Figure 8.3 shows the percentage of apes in captivity by taxonomic group.

As noted above, some facilities belong to private organizations with distinct standards of care that provide external review and oversight of their members. In the United States, one example is the North American Primate Sanctuary Alliance (NAPSA), which, in addition to its own membership conditions, requires membership and accreditation through the Global Federation of Animal Sanctuaries (NAPSA, n.d.). It is important to note that not all facilities that claim to be sanctuaries seek accreditation or operate to equivalent standards. Given that chimpanzees account for 62% of apes in the United States, it is critical to appreciate how many are captive outside of accredited institutions, where health and welfare risks are often higher.

Relatively few chimpanzees (14%) are kept in accredited zoos. Perhaps more importantly, slightly more chimpanzees (15%) are kept in high-risk settings with limited third-party oversight, under the categories of exhibition, dealer/pet and entertainment. Although biomedical laboratories do have third-party oversight, their missions require them to

FIGURE 8.2

US States that Ban, Allow or Do Not Regulate the Keeping of Primates as Pets, 2014

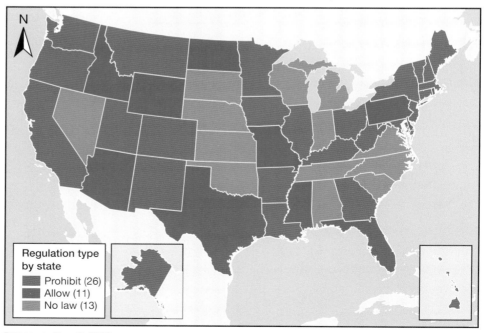

Regulation type by state
- Prohibit (26)
- Allow (11)
- No law (13)

Data source: Paquette (2014)

FIGURE 8.3

Apes in Captivity, by Taxon, 2012

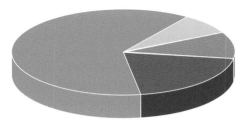

Legend:

▪ Orangutan (246 = 8%)
▪ Gorilla (310 = 10%)
▪ Gibbon* (624 = 20%)
▪ Chimpanzee (1,926 = 62%)

Notes: * Includes all gibbons and siamangs.

Data source: Durham and Phillipson (2014, p. 292, table 10.6)

TABLE 8.4

Reported Number of Chimpanzees in Different Forms of Captivity in the United States, as of September 2014

Captivity type	Number of chimpanzees	Percentage of total
Biomedical labs	794	43%
NAPSA sanctuaries	525	28%
Zoos accredited by the Association of Zoos and Aquariums	258	14%
Exhibition*	196	11%
Dealer or pet	52	3%
Entertainment	18	1%
Total	**1,843**	**100%**

Notes: * Includes individuals who are in sanctuaries that are not NAPSA members.

Data source: ChimpCARE (n.d.)

carry out biomedical experiments that, in spite of being legally authorized, inevitably inflict pain and suffering. The welfare of the 50 chimpanzees the government plans to keep, as well as of the privately owned chimpanzees who are in laboratories, remains a cause for concern. Table 8.4 lists the number of chimpanzees in different forms of captivity.

As of September 2014, more than 600 chimpanzees were in sanctuaries in the United States (see Table 8.5). In contrast to the EU figures presented above, a larger proportion of chimpanzees are in sanctuaries in the United States. The number of chimpanzees in sanctuaries has grown since the publication of the first edition of *State of the Apes*, although this increase did not result from the abovementioned NIH policy regarding experiments on chimpanzees. Indeed, a recent news report indicates that fewer than 2% of 310 eligible chimpanzees have been released from research facilities to sanctuaries, even though "dozens" have reportedly died in the 18 months since the policy was announced (Bonifield and Cohen, 2015). To date, federal authorities have not declared a timetable for releasing the surviving chimpanzees affected by the policy and thus, these individuals are still accounted

for in laboratory census figures (Bonifield and Cohen, 2015).

Changes in the figures were largely a consequence of transfers from a single laboratory in Louisiana, which had already planned to transfer approximately 100 chimpanzees to Chimp Haven, the national sanctuary system (A. Truitt, personal communication, 2014). The remaining changes in the population

TABLE 8.5

Number of Chimpanzees in Selected US Sanctuaries, 2013 and 2014

Sanctuary Name	2013	2014
Center for Great Apes	29	30
Chimp Haven	123	207
Chimpanzee Sanctuary Northwest	7	7
Chimps Inc.	8	7
Cleveland Amory Black Beauty Ranch	3	2
Primarily Primates	47	47
Primate Rescue Center	11	11
Save the Chimps	267	261
Wildlife Waystation	48	48
Total	**543**	**620**

Data source: ChimpCARE (n.d.); A. Truitt, personal communication, 2014

are the result of a small number of rescues and deaths. Since the federal government announced divestment of the chimpanzees it owns, this number is expected to decrease, accompanied by a corresponding increase in the number at sanctuaries (NIH, 2013). From 2013 to 2014, there were no changes in the number of orangutans in sanctuaries. For gibbons in US sanctuaries, there was one reported death and the addition of four adults from rescues (data not shown).

Discussion

This chapter has explored some of the most recent trends regarding apes in captivity, such as the increasing number of apes in sanctuaries in range countries across Asia and Africa, as well as some of the complex causes for this growth. Laws that regulate the trade in apes and market demand for the use of live, captive apes are part of the backdrop for understanding the number of apes in captivity outside of range states, as illustrated by the abovementioned figures of apes in captivity in the EU and the United States.

A number of other countries also house apes in captivity. For example, a handful of sanctuaries located in Brazil care for apes who have been retired from zoos and circuses (Projeto GAP, n.d.). Kumamoto Sanctuary, the sole ape sanctuary in Japan, houses 59 chimpanzees and six bonobos (Morimura, Idani and Matsuzawa, 2011; GAIN, n.d.). While the bonobos were transferred to Kumamoto from a zoo in the United States, the chimpanzees had been used in biomedical research until the law mandated their retirement (Morimura *et al.*, 2011; Kumamoto Sanctuary, 2013, 2014).

The exact number and global distribution of apes brought into captivity illegally is far harder to document. Regarding the trade in live apes and ape parts, a recent CITES report noted "Very limited information on this trade is available, and its impact on wild populations is currently unknown" (CITES, 2013, p. 8). The estimates that do exist suggest that the trade could exceed 3,000 apes per year (Stiles *et al.*, 2013).

There is a dearth of information on how many apes survive capture and transport, and on where survivors end up. Indeed, many experts agree that relatively few trafficked apes are ever confiscated and most traffickers commit crimes that go undetected (Ammann, 2011; Drori, 2012; Stiles *et al.*, 2013). In addition to buyers who seek private pets or performers, the demand for live apes by unscrupulous zoos in China and the Middle East accounts for hundreds of illegally trafficked apes (Stiles *et al.*, 2013). Surveys of enforcement officers and other research conducted by the Great Apes and Integrity (GAPIN) initiative also suggest that the detection and seizure of live apes is rare and that the lack of documentation and other evidence for illegal transactions represents a considerable challenge for law enforcement (CITES, 2013; WCO, 2013).

The laws governing the trade and captivity of apes vary and can change unpredictably. Whether international treaties or local rules agreed at town hall meetings, regulations on apes in captivity can impact the welfare of individual apes near and far in terms of their welfare and vulnerability to trafficking, exploitation and injury. In the same vein, legislation can affect the likelihood that apes will be captured and enter captivity, and subsequently, if they will be rescued, placed in a sanctuary and re-released.

This chapter considers a number of changes in the legal landscape concerning apes in captivity. Despite a plethora of laws, regulations and standards, sweeping changes regarding the treatment of apes in captivity —and, more importantly, regarding the well-being of the apes themselves—have yet to materialize. While there have been small steps in the right direction through collaborations among certain organizations and individuals, practices and attitudes do not appear to be catching up with science. What are the barriers to change and where are the opportunities?

While policy often plays an important role in change because it institutionalizes practices before the ideas or the behaviors are absorbed into the public consciousness, it is not the only option for advancing social change on behalf of apes. To identify areas in which targeted strategies might accelerate change, it is useful to consider human behavior and resistance to change. As science has revealed, people process information and make decisions in ways that can generate cognitive bias—which can lead to irrational decisions while also acting as a barrier to change.

Technology and science can be a tool for social change. The Institute of Medicine determined that chimpanzee experiments were largely unnecessary in view of advances in scientific knowledge and the availability of new and superior methods (Altevogt *et al.*, 2011). Meanwhile, movie studios and advertising agencies have shunned the use of apes as actors in favor of cutting-edge animatronics and CGI (Powell, 2014). Research that advances our understanding of apes and informs practice may further accelerate social change on behalf of apes, particularly through education and outreach.

Effective decision-making is dependent on access to complete and accurate information.

Photo: There is a dearth of information on how many apes survive capture and transport, and on where survivors end up. Relatively few are rescued. Mwanda kissing and grooming Lomela as a sign of welcome on her arrival at the Lola ya Bonobo sanctuary. © Vanessa Woods/ Lola ya Bonobo

Incomplete information and misinformation can lead reasonable people to misguided conclusions about apes and ape protection, which can result in harmful behaviors or suppress positive ones. Box 8.3 examines three organizations in Japan that illustrate how science, education and outreach can advance positive change on behalf of apes in captivity.

BOX 8.3

Effecting Positive Change for Apes in Captivity: Spotlight on Japanese Organizations

In Japan, there are more than 570 apes in zoos and sanctuaries (GAIN, n.d.). New policies and shifting social attitudes have effected a number of important changes for ape welfare, including zoo transparency and educational and scientific support for ape welfare and captive care. The work of three Japanese organizations that are working on behalf of apes is briefly discussed below.

The Great Ape Information Network (GAIN) is a cooperative project between universities and the Japanese government. In promoting the conservation and welfare of great apes, GAIN places emphasis on transparency and robust data (GAIN, n.d.). The scope, level of detail and accessibility of the GAIN database are exemplary. Not only is the database a valuable service for scientists and other stakeholders, but it is also a model for other countries and regulatory authorities.

Japan has had a small number of well-known ape performers in the past, but this practice has come under increased scrutiny in recent years. In 2006, Support for African/Asian Great Apes (SAGA), a primatological association, formally declared opposition to the use of apes in entertainment (SAGA, 2006). Following an incident in late 2012, during which a chimpanzee named Pan-kun bit a person, the association issued a position statement. SAGA has used its scientific expertise and authority to call out inaccurate media portrayals of apes and highlight the harmful effects of misguided beliefs about apes (SAGA, 2012).

The non-governmental organization Sanctuary Project has also initiated a program to raise awareness and promote change on behalf of captive apes, and particularly solitary chimpanzees. The organization's analysis points to a number of historical, practical and logistical factors that influence the prevalence of solitary apes. Among these, small size, aging or otherwise limited infrastructure and a poor legacy of husbandry practices are seen to play a role. The Sanctuary Project promotes enhanced enrichment and care practices at sites with solitary individuals alongside their efforts to advocate for long-term solutions (Sanctuary Project, n.d.).

GAIN, SAGA and the Sanctuary Project are examples of organizations that have been active in promoting the welfare of apes in captivity, supporting better practice and highlighting the need for improvement and change.

Conclusion

This chapter summarizes current information on apes in captivity in range states and surrounding regions as well as in some consumer countries of the global North. Zoos and sanctuaries account for most apes in captivity. In some jurisdictions, apes may be used in entertainment, kept as private pets or kept in laboratories.

This study reveals considerable variation in legal protections within and across countries. Such disparities can leave apes vulnerable to welfare risks and act as barriers to enforcement as well as the development of new legal protections for apes.

Agricultural expansion, extractive industries and other development activities in and near ape range states can impact ape sanctuaries. Land conversion, infrastructure development and the influx of people to live and work in previously remote areas can lead to increased levels of human–wildlife contact, conflict and zoonotic disease transfer, as well as greater hunting pressure; at the same time, these dynamics can reduce the availability of appropriate release sites, which are critical for ape sanctuaries and their residents. These factors have a direct impact on arrival and release rates, alongside other less obvious and indirect impacts. In seeking to mitigate the effects of development activities on apes and ape habitats, stakeholders and policy-makers have to consider the impacts on ape sanctuaries.

A number of factors can influence social attitudes and effect social change. With respect to efforts on behalf of apes, science, technology, education and outreach can be important instruments of change.

The illicit trade in apes is a global concern that is driven in part by the demand for captive apes in consumer countries. Policies and social attitudes about apes in captivity can affect all apes, both in their natural habitats and in captivity. Desensitization or misinformation about the urgency of ape

Photo: Agricultural expansion, extractive industries and other development activities in and near ape range states can impact ape sanctuaries. Land conversion, infrastructure development and the influx of people to live and work in previously remote areas have a direct impact on arrival and release rates. Rescued Grauer's gorilla, DRC. © Gorilla Rehabilitation and Conservation Education (GRACE) Center/ Deni Bechard

conservation and sanctuary care could hamper efforts aimed at decreasing demand in consumer countries or increasing support for conservation in range states. An ethical framework that acknowledges the value of apes regardless of their provenance or residence status could contribute both to stronger laws and to more public support for ape conservation and welfare programs.

Acknowledgments

Principal author: Debra Durham

Reviewers: Meredith Bastian and Kay Farmer

Author acknowledgments: The author is grateful for the information provided by the International Species Information System regarding the number of apes housed in its member institutions. Additional thanks are owed to A. Brulé, S. Speede and D. van Gennep for detailed interviews and facilitating access to data that were essential to the case studies; and also to the European Alliance of Rescue centres and Sanctuaries, In Defense of Animals–Africa, NAPSA and individual sanctuaries that provided information about rescues and their facilities.

Annex I

Apes and Industrial Agriculture Questionnaire Responses

THE PRESENCE OF INDUSTRIAL AGRICULTURE

Site no.	Ape species[1]	Country	Site name	Are apes using agricultural landscape?	Proximity of industrial agricultural activities to the ape population	How long has agro-industry been established or operating in your area?
1	Bonobo	DRC	Wamba, Luo Scientific Reserve	Partially	Adjacent	>20 years
2	Chimpanzee	Guinea-Bissau	Boé	Partially	More than 5 km	6–10 years
3		Uganda	Budongo Forest	Partially	Adjacent	16–20 years
4			Bulindi, Hoima district, 25 km from Budongo Forest	Entirely	Adjacent	11–15 years
5			Budongo Forest	Partially	Adjacent, within 1–5 km	16–20 years
6			Kalinzu Forest Central Reserve	Not at all	Adjacent	>20 years
7		Guinea	Seringbara, Nimba Mountains	Not at all	Within 1–5 km or more than 5 km	>20 years
8		Tanzania	Mahale	Partially	Adjacent	6–10 years
9	Chimpanzee and gorilla	Republic of Congo	Goualougo Triangle, Nouabalé-Ndoki National Park	Partially	Within 1–5 km	0–2 years or 3–5 years
10	Gibbon	Indonesia	Siberut Island, Mentawai Archipelago, West Sumatra	Not at all	Don't know	>20 years
11		Bangladesh	Lawachara National Park, Sylhet	Not at all	Within 1–5 km or more than 5 km	16–20 years
12	Gibbon, including siamang	Indonesia	Way Canguk	Not at all	Adjacent, within 1–5 km	11–15 years
13	Gibbon	Indonesia	Sokokembang Forest, Petungkriono, Pekalongan, Central Java	Partially	Adjacent, within 1–5 km	16–20 years
14		China	Mt. Wuliang, Mt. Ailao, Mt. Daxueshan, Bajiaohe, Yunnan	Not at all	Within 1–5 km	11–15 years

▶

Site no.	Ape species[1]	Country	Site name	Are apes using agricultural landscape?	Proximity of industrial agricultural activities to the ape population	How long has agro-industry been established or operating in your area?
15	Gibbon	Thailand	Khao Soi Dao Wildlife Sanctuary, Chantaburi Province and Mae Hong Son Province	Not at all	More than 5 km	>20 years
16		Thailand	Khao Yai National Park	Entirely	Adjacent	>20 years
17		India	Garo Hills, Meghalaya	Partially	Adjacent, within 1–5 km	11–15 years
18			Northeast India	Partially	Within 1–5 km or more than 5 km	>20 years
19		Indonesia	Mt. Dieng, Mt. Pegunugan Dieng, specifically Linggo Asri	Not at all	Adjacent, within 1–5 km	>20 years
20	Orangutan and gibbon	Indonesia	Cabang Panti Research Station, Gunung Palung National Park, West Kalimantan	Partially	Adjacent, within 1–5 km	16–20 years
21	Orangutan	Indonesia	Surya Hutani Jaya and Sumalindo Hutani Jaya plantations (partners with the SinarMas corporation), Muara Bengal, near Samarinda, East Kalimantan	Partially	Adjacent	>20 years
22	Orangutan and gibbon	Malaysia	Batang Ai, Lanjak Entimau, Tanjung Datu, Kubah (national park system of Sarawak)	Partially	Don't know	11–15 years or 16–20 years
23		Indonesia	Wehea Forest; PT[2] Surya Hutani Jaya and Sumalindo Hutani Jaya acacia plantations	Entirely	Adjacent, within 1–5 km or more than 5 km	0–2, 3–5, 6–10 or 11–15 years
24	Orangutan and gibbon, including siamang	Indonesia and Malaysia	Most protected areas in Malaysia (including Sarawak and Sabah), Central Kalimantan, East Java	Entirely	Adjacent	6–10, 11–15, 16–20 or >20 years
25		Indonesia	The Human Orangutan Conflict Response Unit roves through Aceh and North Sumatra provinces	Partially	Adjacent, within 1–5 km	0–2, 3–5, 6–10, 11–15, 16–20 or >20 years
26	Orangutan and gibbon	Malaysia	Lower Kinabatangan River floodplain	Partially	Adjacent	>20 years

Notes:

[1] The "Ape species" column specifies whether siamangs are among the gibbon species at a site.

[2] Limited liability company (Indonesian: *perseroan terbatas*).

APE USE OF CROPS*

Site no.	Ape species	Acacia	Banana	Cacao	Coffee	Eucalyptus	Industrial tree plantations (timber, etc.)
1	Bonobo				Not used by apes		
2	Chimpanzee	Feed on flowers	Feed on fruit				
3							
4		Not used by apes	Feed on fruit	Feed on fruit and use for nesting	Not used by apes	Use for nesting	Use for nesting
5							
6						Not used by apes	Not used by apes
7							
8							
9	Chimpanzee and gorilla						
10	Gibbon		Not used by apes	Not used by apes			
11		Not used by apes				Not used by apes	
12	Gibbon, including siamang			Not used by apes	Not used by apes		
13	Gibbon				Feed on fruit		Use for nesting
14							
15						Not used by apes	
16							Feed on kernel of nut
17			Feed on fruit		Not used by apes		Feed on fruit
18							
19					Don't know		Not used by apes
20	Orangutan and gibbon	Use for nesting	Don't know		Don't know		Use for nesting
21	Orangutan	Use for nesting	Feed on fruit			Use for nesting	Use for nesting
22	Orangutan and gibbon						Use for nesting
23		Use for nesting	Don't know	Don't know	Don't know	Use for nesting	Use for nesting
24	Orangutan and gibbon, including siamang	Not used by apes					
25			Feed on fruit	Not used by apes	Not used by apes	Don't know	Don't know
26	Orangutan and gibbon	Feed on bark and use for nesting	Don't know				Depending on species, feed on bark, use for nesting

Note: * Empty cells indicate an absence of crops within the apes' home range at the given site.

Oil palm	Pineapple	Rice	Rubber	Soy	Sugarcane	Tea	Tobacco
Not used by apes			Not used by apes				
Use for nesting		Not used by apes			Feed on leaves		
					Feed on pith		
	Not used by apes	Not used by apes			Feed on pith		Not used by apes
					Feed on stem		
						Not used by apes	
	Not used by apes	Don't know	Not used by apes				Don't know
						Not used by apes	
			Feed on flowers				
		Not used by apes				Not used by apes	
	Not used by apes	Not used by apes				Not used by apes	
	Don't know						
		Not used by apes	Not used by apes				
Feed on fruit	Don't know	Not used by apes	Don't know	Don't know			
Not used by apes			Don't know				
Not used by apes			Use for nesting				
Use for nesting	Don't know	Don't know	Don't know	Don't know	Don't know	Don't know	Don't know
Feed on fruit							
Feed on fruit		Not used by apes	Feed on bark		Don't know	Not used by apes	Not used by apes
Feed on petiole of leaves and fruit – directly on the bunches and on the ground							

ACRONYMS AND ABBREVIATIONS

~	approximately
AAF	African Agriculture Fund
AAP	AAP Rescue Center for Exotic Animals (Netherlands)
ACOP	Annual communication of progress (RSPO requirement from members)
A.P.E.S. Portal/Database	Ape Populations, Environments and Surveys Portal/Database
APL	Land for other uses (Indonesian: *Aerial Pengunaan Lainhas*)
ASEAN	Association of Southeast Asian Nations
asl	above sea level
BAT	British American Tobacco
BCI	Better Cotton Initiative
BEWG	Burma Environmental Working Group
BKSDA	Natural Resource Conservation Agency, Indonesia (Indonesian: *Balai Konservasi Sumber Daya Alam*)
BMP	Best Management Practices
Bonsucro	Better Sugar Cane Initiative
BOSF	Borneo Orangutan Survival Foundation
BPKEL	Leuser Ecosystem Management Authority (Indonesian: *Badan Pengelola Kawasan Ekosistem Leuser*)
CA	conservation agriculture
ca	circa (approximately)
CAMSUCO	Cameroon Sugar Company
CAP	Conservation Action Plan
CAR	Central African Republic
CBD	Convention on Biological Diversity
CBO	community-based organization
CIESIN	Center for International Earth Science Information Network, Columbia University
CIMTROP	Center for International Cooperation in Sustainable Management of Tropical Peatland
CIRAD	Agricultural Research for Development (French: *Centre de coopération Internationale en Recherche Agronomique pour le Développement*)
CITES	Convention on International Trade in Endangered Species of Wild Fauna and Flora
CKP	Wilmar's Central Kalimantan Project
CMS	Convention on Conservation of Migratory Species of Wild Animals
CO₂	carbon dioxide
COMIFAC	Central African Forest Commission (French: *Commission des Forêts d'Afrique Centrale*)
Congo	Republic of Congo
CPO	crude palm oil
CR	critically endangered (IUCN Red List classification)
CREF	Center for Research in Ecology and Forestry, DRC (French: *Centre de Recherche en Ecologie et Foresterie*)
CSPO	certified sustainable palm oil
DNA	deoxyribonucleic acid
DRC	Democratic Republic of Congo
EARS	European Association of Rescue centres and Sanctuaries
EAZA	European Association of Zoos and Aquariums
EIA	environmental impact assessment

EMA	Environmental Management Act (Indonesia)
EMP	environmental management plan
EN	endangered (IUCN Red List classification)
EPA	Environmental Protection Agency
EPO	Equatorial Palm Oil
ESIA	environmental and social impact assessment
ESMP	environmental and social management plan
ETM+	Landsat Enhanced Thematic Mapper Plus
EU	European Union
FAO	Food and Agriculture Organization of the United Nations
FCPF	Forest Carbon Partnership Facility
FDA	Forest Development Agency (Liberia)
FELCRA	Federal Land Rehabilitation and Consolidation Authority
FELDA	Federal Land Development Authority
FFI	Fauna & Flora International
FM	forest monitors
FPIC	free prior and informed consent
FPP	Forest Peoples Programme
FREL	Forest Reference Emission Level
FRL	Forest Reference Level
FSC	Forest Stewardship Council
GA	RSPO General Assembly
GAIN	Great Ape Information Network
GAPKI	Indonesian Palm Oil Association (Indonesian: *Gabungan Pengusaha Kelapa Sawit Indonesia*)
GAR	Golden Agri-Resources
GDP	gross domestic product
GFAS	Global Federation of Animal Sanctuaries
GFW	Global Forest Watch
GGE	Greater Gombe Ecosystem
GGE-CAP	Greater Gombe Ecosystem Conservation Action Plan
GHG	greenhouse gases
GIS	geographic information systems
GM	genetically modified
GMO	genetically modified organism
GPS	Global Positioning System
GRACE	Gorilla Rehabilitation and Conservation Education Center
GRASP	Great Apes Survival Partnership of the United Nations
GVL	Golden Veroleum
GW	Global Witness
ha	hectare
HCS	high carbon stock
HCV	high conservation value
HCVF	high conservation value forest
HOC	human–orangutan conflict
IAR	International Animal Rescue
ICCN	Congolese Institute for the Conservation of Nature
IDR	Indonesian Rupiah
IFAD	International Fund for Agricultural Development
IFC	International Finance Corporation
IIED	International Institute for Environment and Development
IM-FLEG	Independent Monitoring of Forest Law Enforcement and Governance
IMF	International Monetary Fund

IPPL	International Primate Protection League
ISIS	International Species Information System
ITOS	Information Technology Outreach Services, University of Georgia
ITP	industrial tree plantation
ITTA	International Tropical Timber Agreement
IUCN	International Union for Conservation of Nature
JGI	Jane Goodall Institute
JICA	Japanese International Cooperation Agency
JV	joint venture
km	kilometer
km²	square kilometer
KSWL	Kinyara Sugar Works Ltd
LCDL	low-carbon density land
LEITI	Liberia Extractive Industries Transparency Initiative
LPD	Liberia Palm Developments
LPF	low pole forest
m	meter
MAAIF	Ministry of Agriculture, Animal Industries and Fisheries (Uganda)
MFPED	Ministry of Finance, Planning and Economic Development (Uganda)
MPOA	Malaysian Palm Oil Association
MPOC	Malaysian Palm Oil Council
MSF	mixed peat swamp forest
Mt	mount(ain)
MWLE	Ministry of Water, Lands and Environment (Uganda)
N₂O	nitrous oxide
NAPSA	North American Primate Sanctuary Alliance
NES	Nucleus Estate Smallholder Project
NFRL	National Forestry Reform Law (Liberia)
NGO	non-governmental organization
NIH	National Institutes of Health
NRI	Sustainable Natural Rubber Initiative
NSA	National Strategic Area
NTFP	non-timber forest products
OPG	Olam Palm Gabon
ORG	Olam Rubber Gabon
OuTrop	Orangutan Tropical Peatland Project
P&C	RSPO Principles and Criteria
PIPIB	map indicating areas for which no new concession permits may be granted for the duration of the moratorium, Indonesia (Indonesian: *Peta Indikatif Penundaan Izin Baru*)
POIG	Palm Oil Innovation Group
PSG	Primate Specialist Group of the IUCN and SSC
PTSD	post-traumatic stress disorder
PTUN	Administrative Court (Indonesian: *Pengadilan Tata Usaha Negara*)
RAP	Regional Action Plan
REDD	Reducing Emissions from Deforestation and Forest Degradation
REDD+	Goes beyond REDD (deforestation and forest degradation), and includes the role of conservation, sustainable management of forests and enhancement of forest carbon stocks
RSB	Roundtable on Sustainable Biomaterials
RSPO	Roundtable on Sustainable Palm Oil
RTRS	Roundtable on Responsible Soy

SAFACAM	Cameroon Society of Forestry and Agriculture (French: *Société Africaine Forestière et Agricole du Cameroun*)
SAGA	Support for African/Asian Great Apes
SC	RSPO Standing Committee
SCA	Sabahmas Conservation Area
SCPI	sustainable crop production intensification
SD	Sime Darby
SGA	Section on Great Apes of the IUCN SSC Primate Specialist Group
SGSOC	Sithe Global Sustainable Oils Cameroon
SIA	social impact assessment
SIVcpz	simian immunodeficiency viruses
SMART	Spatial Monitoring and Reporting Tool
SOCP	Sumatran Orangutan Conservation Project
SOMDIAA	*Société d'Organisation de Management et de Développement des Industries Alimentaires et Agricoles* (an African agribusiness)
SOP	standard operating procedure
SOSUCAM	*Société Sucrière du Cameroun* (a sugar manufacturing company in Central Africa)
sp.	species (singular)
spp.	species (plural)
SPOTT	Sustainable Palm Oil Transparency Toolkit
SSA	Section on Small Apes of the IUCN SSC Primate Specialist Group
SSC	Species Survival Commission
SYRC	Sanaga-Yong Rescue Center
TACARE	Lake Tanganyika Catchment Reforestation and Education
TANAPA	Tanzania National Parks
TFT	The Forest Trust
TIF	tall interior forest
TM	Landsat Thematic Mapper
UBOS	Uganda Bureau of Statistics
UN	United Nations
UNECE	United Nations Economic Commission for Europe
UNEP	United Nations Environment Programme
UNEP-GEAS	UNEP Global Environmental Alert Service
UNFCC	United Nations Framework Convention on Climate Change
US	United States
USDA	United States Department of Agriculture
USFWS	United States Fish and Wildlife Service
VU	vulnerable (IUCN Red List classification)
WAZA	World Association of Zoos and Aquaria
WB	World Bank
WCBR	Wamba Committee for Bonobo Research
WCMC	United Nations Environment Programme World Conservation Monitoring Centre
WCS	Wildlife Conservation Society
WR	wildlife reserve
WRI	World Resources Institute
WWI	World War I
WWII	World War II
WWF	World Wildlife Fund/World Wide Fund for Nature
YKI	Gibbon Conservation Programme (Indonesian: *Yayasan Kelawait Indonesia*)
ZSL	Zoological Society of London

GLOSSARY

Accountability mechanisms: Means that incentivize organizations or individuals to take responsibility toward their constituents for their actions.

Advanced market commitment: A binding contract that provides a market once a product has been developed.

Afrotropics: The tropical belt in Africa, south of the Sahara Desert.

Age- or aging-in-place: Characterized by a focus on keeping individuals in their residence rather than moving them to specialized facilities for care.

Agribusiness: Agricultural activities conducted for commercial purposes and the companies involved in this industry.

Agroecology: The ecological study of agricultural landscapes.

Agroforestry: A method of farming that involves growing herbaceous and tree crops together to preserve or enhance the productivity of the land.

Agrofuel: Fuel that is produced from renewable resources, including plant biomass and vegetable oils, such as biogas or biodiesel. See also **biofuel**.

Analogous: Similar to; comparable to.

Anthropogenic: Resulting from humans or human activities.

Ape management plan: A document that outlines objectives for conserving a particular ape habitat and ways to achieve those objectives.

Aquifer recharge: The process by which surface water moves downward to groundwater.

Autonomous region: An administrative division of a country that has a degree of autonomy, meaning that it is free to make decisions on certain matters of public policy without approval from central authority.

Bimaturism: Development characterized by differing stages or timings within a species or within a sex; among orangutans, mature males are flanged or unflanged (see **flanged**).

Biodiversity: The variety of plant and animal life on Earth or in a particular habitat.

Biodiversity offset: Conservation activities that are designed to foster biodiversity in compensation for environmental damage caused by development projects.

Biofuel: Fuel produced from living organisms, most often plants or plant-derived materials; one example is bio-ethanol, an alcohol made by fermenting carbohydrates in crops such as corn or sugarcane. See also **agrofuels**.

Biofuel feedstock: Materials that are used to produce biofuel.

Biomass: The biological material of living (or recently living) organisms in a given area of an ecosystem at a given time; in the context of energy, a source of renewable energy derived from organisms, either alive or dead (see **biofuel**).

Brachiation: Arboreal locomotion that relies exclusively on the arms to propel the body forward.

Brownfield site: Land previously used for industrial or commercial purposes.

Business-as-usual model: A standard economic theory that discounts future earnings in favor of short-term profit-making.

Cambium: In woody plants, the layer that lies between the bark and wood of the stem.

Carbon fixation: The process by which inorganic carbon is converted into organic compounds, such as the conversion of carbon dioxide into glucose through photosynthesis.

Carbon neutrality: The state of net zero carbon emissions achieved by individuals or organizations that balance the amount of carbon they release with an equivalent amount sequestered, offset or bought in the form of carbon credits.

Carbon sequestration: The trapping of carbon by plants during the photosynthesis process.

Carbon sink: A natural or artificial store that absorbs more carbon than it releases, such as forests, soil and oceans.

Carbon storage: The process of capturing carbon dioxide from the atmosphere to mitigate global warming and other effects of high-carbon emission.

Catchment: An area that collects rainwater.

Civil society: The total array of non-governmental organizations that undertake collective activities in the name of particular communities or to further specific interests.

Class action: A lawsuit filed or defended by an individual who represents a group.

Climate change: Change in the Earth's weather on a regional or global scale, including fluctuations in wind patterns and rainfall, and especially with reference to rising temperatures in the earth's atmosphere, as caused by an increased production of greenhouse gases since the mid-20th century. See also **greenhouse gas**.

Cloud computing (or cloud technology): The use of a network of remote servers hosted on the Internet to store, manage and process data.

Cognitive bias: A lack of objectivity in information processing or reasoning that affects decision-making or other behavior, typically used to describe negative biases or those that lead to error.

Commodities: Raw materials or primary agricultural products that can be traded commercially.

Communal title to land: Statutory recognition of a community's rights to access, use and control of an area of land.

Compaction: The process of densely packing together, typically used to describe the compression of soil; the reduction in habitat available to wildlife, see **compression effect (or crowding effect)**.

Compliance mechanism: An official procedure through which government institutions (such as a regional agency, ministry or international organization) can check whether its officials or external actors adhere to binding rules and regulations. These procedures are normally specified in the same document that sets out the relevant rules (such as codes, implementing regulations and founding treaties).

Compression effect (or crowding effect): The process by which habitat disturbance and loss leads to greater population density within a particular area and reduced possibilities for species dispersal. See also **refugee crowding**.

Concession: A relatively large area of land that is allocated to agricultural investors for the industrialized production of crops, generally by a government.

Concessionaire: A group or company to whom a land concession has been granted to operate a business.

Conflict threshold: The point at which challenging situations turn into conflict.

Conservation corridor: A strip of natural habitat that connects two or more larger blocks of natural habitat, and that is left in place (or created) to enable roaming and dispersal of wildlife species and thereby to enhance or maintain the viability of specific wildlife populations.

Conspecific: A member of the same species.

Cover crop: A low-growing plant crop that is cultivated for the protection and enrichment of the soil.

Crop raiding: The movement of wild animals from their natural habitat into agricultural landscapes for the purpose of feeding on cultivated produce.

Crop residue: Plant materials that are left behind after harvesting, including leaves, stalks and roots.

Crude palm oil: Pre-purified oil that is extracted from the kernel and still contains trace metals, kernel shell pieces and products of oxidation. The purification process removes these components and makes the palm oil edible and salable.

Cultivar: A plant variety produced by selective breeding.

Customary occupancy: Use of an area of land by a group of people based on long-established, traditional patterns or norms.

Deciduous: Pertaining to trees that lose their leaves for part of the year.

Depauperate: Lacking in numbers or variety of species.

Developed countries: Industrialized countries that rank high on the Human Development Index.

Developing countries: Non-industrialized countries.

Dichromatic: Exhibiting two color variations independent of sex and age.

Dimorphic: Having two distinct forms.

Dipterocarp: A tall hardwood tree of the family *Dipterocarpaceae* that primarily grows in Asian rainforests and that is the source of valuable timber, aromatic oils and resins.

Diurnal: Daily or active during the day.

Downstream firm: A business that purchases products made by other companies, rather than the natural resources directly from the source.

Drone: An unmanned aerial vehicle.

Ecological gradient: Gradual change in abiotic factors, such as altitude, temperature, depth, ocean proximity and soil humidity, through space or time.

Ecological viability: The ability of an ecosystem or specific functions of the ecosystem to sustain themselves.

Endangered: Threatened with extinction.

Endemic: Native to or only found in a certain place; indigenous.

Energy balance: The relationship between the amount of energy consumed in food and the amount of energy used by the body for daily energy requirements.

Environmental impact assessment (EIA): An analytical tool used to assess the potential environmental impact of a project, development or policy.

Escarpment: The edge of a mountain range or cliff along a fault line.

Eutrophication: A state that is caused by an increase in natural or artificial nutrients in a body of water and that results in the unhindered growth of plants and algae and, consequently, the depletion of oxygen, which may lead to the death of fish and aquatic animals and a reduction in biodiversity.

Evergreen: Of trees and other plants, having green leaves throughout the year, as leaves of the past season are not shed until after new foliage has grown.

Executive: The branch of government responsible for putting parliamentary decisions and laws into effect.

Expropriation: The taking of land owned or used by individuals or communities by a government, in most instances to be used for "public interest" purposes.

Fallback foods: Food items that are always available but that are not preferred.

Fauna: Animals (members of the Animal Kingdom).

Faunal transect method: A survey technique designed to establish the density and distribution of wildlife by counting animals and animal signs along line transects.

Fission–fusion: Pertaining to communities whose size and composition are dynamic due to the coming together (fusion) and moving away (fission) of individuals.

Flagship species: A species selected to raise the profile of a particular habitat, issue, campaign or environmental cause so as to leverage greater support for biodiversity conservation at large.

Flanged: Pertaining to one of two morphs of adult male orangutan; characterized by large cheek pads, greater size, a long coat of dark hair on the back and a throat sac used for "long calls," as opposed to "unflanged."

Flood buffer: An area or strip of land that is forested or planted with shrubs and grass, and that is located between cropland or pasture and surface water courses to protect water quality, reduce erosion and minimize flooding.

Flora: Plants (members of the Plant Kingdom).

Folivore: An animal that eats primarily leaves. Related terms: folivorous, folivory.

Forest stand: A large number of trees growing in a specific area and recognizably uniform in species composition, size, age, arrangement or condition so as to be distinguishable from the forest or other growth in adjoining areas.

Frugivore: An animal that eats primarily fruit. Related terms: frugivorous, frugivory.

Functional connectivity: The degree to which the land that divides and separates natural habitats facilitates or impedes the habitats' ability to maintain ecological viability, allow movements of animals and perform ecosystem functions.

Fungible: Having multiple end uses, such as crops, which allows businesses to hedge against lower demand and prices in one sector by selling the same product to consumers in another sector.

G20: The Group of Twenty, an international forum for the governments and central bank governors of 20 major economies.

Genetic drift: Variation in the relative frequency of different genotypes (an individual's collection of genes) in a small population, due to the disappearance or loss of specific genes.

Genus (plural: genera): A principal taxonomic category that ranks above species and below family and that groups together closely related species; the first word of a species' scientific name.

Greenhouse gas (GHG): A gas in an atmosphere that absorbs and emits radiation within the thermal infrared range. The primary greenhouse gases in the Earth's atmosphere are water vapor, carbon dioxide, methane, nitrous oxide and ozone.

Gross concession area: In agricultural terms, the entire area awarded to a company, as opposed to the actual area on which crops are grown.

Gross domestic product (GDP): The total monetary value of all final goods produced and services provided within a country annually.

Habitat degradation: A reduction in the quality of a habitat such that it can no longer optimally support its fauna and flora. Natural degradation is generally localized in time and space, such as damage due to earthquakes, floods or landslides; in contrast, human-caused degradation can be irreversible and widespread, as is predominantly the case with degradation caused by industrial expansion.

Habitat fragmentation: A reduction in the size and continuity of an organism's preferred or required environment, resulting in patches of habitat. Natural fragmentation is generally localized and may be caused by storms or fire; fragmentation due to human activities can be extensive.

Habituation: The process by which wildlife becomes acustomed to the presence of humans.

Herbivore: An animal that eats only plants. Related terms: herbivorous, herbivory.

High carbon stock (HCS): Pertaining to natural habitats that have at least 35 tons of above-ground biomass.

High conservation value (HCV): Pertaining to natural habitats that are of critical importance due to their high biological, socioeconomic or landscape value.

Hybrid: The offspring of two different species or varieties of plant or animal; something that is formed by combining different elements.

Hydrological: Related to water.

Industrial agriculture (or industrial farming, intensive agriculture or farming, plantation agriculture, large-scale agriculture and commercial farming): A method of intensive crop production that is characterized by large monoculture farms and plantations that rely heavily on chemicals, pesticides, herbicides, fertilizers, intensive water use, and large-scale transport, storage and distribution infrastructure.

Infanticide: The act of killing an infant.

Infraction: A violation or infringement of a law or regulation.

Infrastructure: The basic physical and organizational structures and facilities needed for the operation of a society or enterprise.

Insolation: The amount of sunlight and solar radiation.

Intact forest landscape: An unbroken area of natural forest ecosystems that shows no signs of significant human activity and that is large enough to maintain all native biodiversity.

Interbirth interval: The biologically determined period of time between subsequent births.

Intergroup: Between groups.

Intraspecific: Within one species or among members of the same species.

Joint venture agreement: A business arrangement by which two or more parties decide to pool their resources for the purpose of accomplishing a specific task while retaining their distinct identities. Parties exercise control over the enterprise and consequently share profits, losses and costs.

Judicial proceeding: Any action involving or carried out in a court of law in order to determine or enforce legal rights.

Judicial review: An official procedure that is set out by the law and that permits competent national courts to check the legality of decisions made by state institutions. A decision under review may be deemed illegal if it was made or carried out in contravention of required procedures, the state constitution and other primary legislation.

Karst: A landscape formed through the dissolution of soluble rocks, such as limestone, dolomite and gypsum, and characterized by underground drainage systems with sinkholes, dolines and caves.

Keystone species: A species that plays a crucial role in the way an ecosystem functions, and whose presence and role has a disproportionately large effect on other organisms within the ecosystem.

Land acquisition: The concession, lease or purchase of land from a government or government entity by a third party, either public or private, for commercial use.

Land bank: The entirety of awarded concession land that a company can potentially develop.

Land tenure: Rules defining how rights to land are to be allocated within a specific society; they define how access is granted to rights to use, control and transfer land, as well as associated responsibilities and restraints.

Leaching: The process whereby water-soluble plant nutrients are lost from the soil due to rain and irrigation. Leaching can result in the contamination of groundwater if chemicals, such as those in fertilizers and pesticides, are dissolved and carried into the underground water supply.

Least developed country (LDC): A United Nations classification for countries that exhibit the lowest indicators of socioeconomic development.

Legal framework: System of laws and rules that governs and regulates a specific policy area.

Legal person: An entity, such as a corporation, non-governmental organization or administrative agency, that has legal rights and is subject to obligations.

Low bandwidth: Bandwidth defines the amount of data that can be sent or received over an electronic channel during a specific period of time. Low bandwidth services, such as dial-up Internet, are typically slow and may require a dedicated phone line for connection. They typically do not allow for uninterrupted video or audio streaming and file downloads and uploads are slow.

Low-carbon-density land: An area that has little biomass, such as fields of low-growing agricultural crops, grasslands and degraded forests in which only small trees, scrub or grass remains, as opposed to primary rainforest, which is high-carbon-density land.

Mantrap: A type of snare that is large enough to catch a human, such as a poacher, but may also be used to hunt other animals. The most common type is a large foothold trap whose springs are armed with metal teeth that close on the victim's leg.

Mast fruiting: The simultaneous production of fruit by large numbers of trees every 2–10 years, without any seasonal change in temperature or rainfall.

Medium spatial resolution: Satellite image quality in which each pixel represents an area of 20–100 m².

Mega-farms: Very large, highly mechanized industrial farms; in livestock farming, also known as "factory farms."

Metapopulation: A group of spatially separated populations of the same species that interact at some level.

Mitigation hierarchy: A tool that guides users toward minimizing the negative impact of development projects on biodiversity; often used as a precursor to **biodiversity offsets**.

Mobbing: Animal group behavior that involves surrounding and attacking a predator or other threat, in order to chase it off.

Monoculture: The cultivation of a single crop in a given area.

Monodominant: Dominated by a single species.

Monogamy: The practice of having a single mate over a period of time.

Monotonous forest: Forest ecosystems of similar type that extend over large areas.

Moratorium (plural: moratoria): A temporary prohibition of an activity.

Morph: A distinct form of an organism or species.

Mosaic landscape: A geographic area that encompasses a variety of land use types, such as urban, natural, industrial and agricultural.

Neopatrimonial: Characterized by a system of social hierarchy in which powerful patrons or parties use or distribute state resources to secure the loyalty of clients in the general population.

Neotropics: The tropical belt in the Americas.

Nest census: A research method for counting individuals indirectly by recording the number of nests in a given area and estimating population numbers based on these nest counts.

Normative arrangements: Laws or regulations that tell relevant actors what to do, and how to behave in certain situations.

Obligate crop feeder: An individual who depends entirely on foraging on crops for survival; in contrast, a semi-obligate crop feeder depends on crops along with other natural food types for survival.

Old-growth forest: Unlogged primary forest.

Ombrogenous, domed peat swamp: Peat that forms above groundwater level, highly acidic and dependent on rain-water for mineral nutrients. In the tropics these bog forests can form extensive domes more than 10 km in diameter.

Opportunity cost: Loss of income or benefit based on forgoing alternative options.

Outgrower scheme: The contracting of small-scale farms to sell some portion of their harvest to a buyer, often a large estate. See also **smallholder farm**.

Parasite: An organism that lives off or in another organism, to the detriment of the host organism.

Patrilineal: Related to or inheriting from the paternal side.

Pelage: Fur; coat.

Perforated forest: Forest in which there are relatively small, usually man-made, clearings.

Petiole: The stalk that joins a leaf to a stem.

Philopatric: The tendency of an organism to stay in, or return to, its home area.

Photosynthesis: The process that plants and some other organisms use to convert sunlight into food or other forms of chemical energy.

Physiochemical: Relating to physiological chemistry, or biochemistry, the chemical processes that occur in living organisms.

Pith: The spongy tissue in the stems and branches of many plants.

Pleistocene Era: The time period starting about 1.8 million years ago and lasting until just under 12,000 years ago.

Pleistocene refugium: A favorable area in which species survived periods of glaciation during the Pleistocene Era.

Poaching: Illegal hunting.

Polyandrous: Pertaining to a mating system that involves one female and two or more males.

Polygynandrous: Pertaining to an exclusive mating system that involves two or more males and two or more females. The numbers of males and females may not be equal.

Polygynous: Pertaining to a mating system that involves one male and two or more females.

Preputial: Relating to the foreskin or clitoral hood.

Primary forest: A natural forest of native tree species that lacks evidence of human activities and whose natural ecological processes are not significantly disturbed.

Public interest litigation: Legal action taken to advance the cause of a specific community or group, or issues of broad public concern.

Raindrop energy: The (kinetic) energy of falling raindrops.

Ramsar wetlands: Wetlands designated under the Convention on Wetlands, known as the Ramsar Convention, an intergovernmental treaty that provides the framework for national action and international cooperation for the conservation and wise use of wetlands and their resources.

Ratify: To sign or give formal consent to an agreement such as a treaty or contract, thereby formalizing its validity.

REDD+: Reducing Emissions from Deforestation and Forest Degradation (REDD) plus, a United Nations initiative that goes beyond reducing emissions and includes the role of conservation, sustainable management of forests and enhancement of forest carbon stocks.

Redress: Remedy or compensation for a wrong suffered.

Refugee crowding: The in-migration of individuals from areas of destroyed habitat or significant disturbance, resulting in crowded conditions in the remaining suitable habitat. See also **compression effect**.

Regeneration: The restoration or new growth of a forest or other vegetation that had been degraded or destroyed.

Regulatory framework: System of regulations that govern a specific policy area.

Rent-seeking behaviour: A company or organization's use of local resources to obtain an economic gain without reciprocating any benefits back to the community.

Riparian forest: A forest that grows along riverbanks.

Risk-mitigation tools: Actions and procedures designed to reduce exposure to the adverse effects of any given investment project.

Roundtable on Sustainable Palm Oil (RSPO): An association that brings together different market players to develop and implement global standards for sustainable palm oil.

Sanction: A penalty for violating a law or a rule.

Secondary forest: A forest that regenerates on the remains of native forests that have been cleared due to natural causes or human activity, such as agriculture.

Sedimentation: The process by which particles found in fluid settle and come to rest against a barrier.

Semi-deciduous: Relating to plants that lose their leaves for a very short period, when old leaves fall off and new growth is starting.

Sequester: To capture and store.

Silvicultural treatment: The practice of controlling the establishment, growth, composition, health and quality of forests to meet diverse needs and values (including practices such as enrichment planting, weeding, vine cutting, thinning and pruning).

Slash-and-burn agriculture: A farming technique that involves cutting and burning an area of forest or vegetation before planting. This technique is often associated with poor soil that is only cultivated for a few seasons before a new area of forest or vegetation is cut and burned to create new plots.

Smallholder farm: A small-scale plot, often less than 1 ha but sometimes up to 10 ha, cultivated both for subsistence purposes and to grow a limited number of cash crops.

Solitary apes: Apes who live alone or in isolation from other members of their species.

Spatial factor: A factor that relates to geography, topography or location.

Split-listing: A legal or regulatory status that recognizes some members of a species or population in a particular category, but not others, such as threatened versus endangered species with regard to extinction risk.

Stochastic: Occurring in a random pattern.

Sympatric: Pertaining to species or populations that occupy the same geographic ranges.

Taxon (plural: taxa): Any unit used in the science of biological classification or taxonomy.

Temporal factor: A factor that relates to time or season.

Topogenous peat swamps: Peat that forms in valley bottoms or other depressions as a result of poor drainage; they are usually slightly alkaline or neutral and receive mineral nutrients from runoff and seasonal flooding as well as rainwater.

Translocation: The human act of moving a living organism from one area to another.

Understory: Vegetation growing beneath the canopy of a forest.

Upstream production: Industrial growing of primary commodities, which are then processed by other firms.

Virology: The study of viruses.

Water table: The highest underground level below which the ground is completely saturated with water.

Wean: To accustom a young animal to nourishment other than the mother's milk.

Wildlife corridors: A strip of natural habitat that can be used by wildlife to move from one larger area of habitat to another.

Yield intensification: The process of increasing and intensifying the production of natural, agricultural or industrial products, particularly through improved practices that result in increased growth or production within an existing area, rather than through the expansion of cultivated land.

Zoonosis or zoonotic disease: An infectious disease that can be transmitted from non-human animals to humans.

REFERENCES

AAP (2011). *Former Circus Ape Regina Can Finally Live an Ape's Life.* Almere, the Netherlands: AAP Rescue Center for Exotic Animals. Available at: http://www.aap.nl/english/news/news/former-circus-ape-regina-can-finally-live-an-apes-life.html.

AAP (2013). *Milestone for Animal Welfare.* Almere, the Netherlands: AAP Rescue Center for Exotic Animals. Available at: http://www.aap.nl/english/news/news/milestone-for-animal-welfare.html.

AAP (2014). *Rescued: Chimpanzee Linda was Locked up Alone for Thirty Years.* Almere, the Netherlands: AAP Rescue Center for Exotic Animals. Available at: https://www.aap.nl/en/news/rescued-chimpanzee-linda-was-locked-alone-thirty-years.

AAP (2015). *Introduction: Chimpanzee Linda.* Almere, the Netherlands: AAP Rescue Center for Exotic Animals. Available at: https://www.youtube.com/watch?v=V4J66PPlUV8.

Abdullah, S.A. and Nakagoshi, N. (2008). Changes in agricultural landscape pattern and its spatial relationship with forestland in the State of Selangor, peninsular Malaysia. *Landscape and Urban Planning,* **87,** 147–55.

Abood, S.A., Lee, J.S.H., Burivalova, Z., Garcia-Ulloa, J. and Koh, L.P. (2015). Relative contributions of the logging, fiber, oil palm, and mining industries to forest loss in Indonesia. *Conservation Letters,* **8,** 58–67.

Abram, N.K., Meijaard, E., Wells, J.A., *et al.* (2015). Mapping perceptions of species' threats and population trends to inform conservation efforts: the Bornean orangutan case study. *Diversity and Distributions,* **21,** 487–99.

ACET (2013). *The Oil Palm Value Capture Opportunity in Africa.* Accra, Ghana: African Center for Economic Transformation (ACET). Available at: http://acetforafrica.org/wp-content/uploads/2013/09/130806LongPalm.pdf.

ActionAid (2012). *Biofuelling the Global Food Crisis: Why the EU Must Act at the G20.* Johannesburg, South Africa: ActionAid. Available at: https://www.actionaid.org.uk/sites/default/files/doc_lib/biofuelling_the_global_food_crisis.pdf.

Adams, W. (2004). *Against Extinction. The Story of Conservation.* London, UK: Earthscan.

ADB (2013). *Myanmar: Agriculture, Natural Resources, and Environment Initial Sector Assessment, Strategy, and Road Map.* Manila, Philippines: Asian Development Bank (ADB). Available at: http://www.gms-eoc.org/uploads/resources/349/attachment/ADB%202013%20Myanmar%20Agriculture%2C%20Environment%20Assement.pdf.

Adeney, J.M., Christensen, N. and Pimm, S.L. (2009). Reserves protect against deforestation fires in the Amazon. *PLoS One,* **4,** e5014.

AFDB (2008). *AfDB Signs €10 Million Private Sector Loan Agreement with SIAT-Gabon for Agricultural Expansion Project. February 20, 2008.* Abidjan, Ivory Coast: African Development Bank (AFDB). Available at: http://www.afdb.org/en/news-and-events/article/afdb-signs-eur-10-million-private-sector-loan-agreement-with-siat-gabon-for-agricultural-expansion-project-4050.

African Union (2003). *African Convention on the Conservation of Nature and Natural Resources. Signed in Maputo, Mozambique, July 11, 2003.* African Union. Available at: http://www.au.int/en/sites/default/files/african_convention_conservation_nature_natural_resources.pdf.

Agence France-Presse (2012). Olam gets $228 mn loan for Gabon palm oil operation. *Agence France-Presse,* July 19, 2012. Available at: https://sg.finance.yahoo.com/news/olam-gets-228-mn-loan-161950292.html.

Agrofin (n.d.). *Crude Palm Oil.* Manama, Kingdom of Bahrain: Agrofin. Available at: http://agrofin.net/vegetable-oil/crude-palm-oil/. Accessed November 10, 2014.

Aharikundira, M. and Tweheyo, M. (2011). Human–wildlife conflict and its implication for conservation around Bwindi Impenetrable National Park. *USDA Forest Service Proceedings,* 39–44.

Akers, A.A., Islam, M.A. and Nijman, V. (2013). Habitat characterization of western hoolock gibbons *Hoolock hoolock* by examining home range microhabitat use. *Primates,* **54,** 341–8.

Alden Wily, L. (2007). *'So Who Owns the Forest'. Investigation into Forest Ownership and Community Rights in Liberia.* Monrovia/Brussels/Moreton-in-Marsh: Sustainable Development Institute (SDI)/FERN. Available at: http://www.rightsandresources.org/wp-content/uploads/2014/01/doc_102.pdf.

Alden Wily, L. (2011). *Whose Land is It? The Status of Customary Land Tenure in Cameroon.* Centre for Environment and Development (CED), FERN and The Rainforest Foundation UK. Available at: http://www.fern.org/sites/fern.org/files/cameroon_eng_internet.pdf.

Alden Wily, L. (2012). *Land Rights in Gabon. Facing up to the Past and Present.* Brussels, Belgium/Moreton-in-Marsh, UK: FERN. Available at http://www.fern.org/sites/fern.org/files/fern_gabon_LR_EN.pdf.

Alexandratos, N. and Bruinsma, J. (2012). *World Food and Agriculture to 2030/2050: The 2012 Revision. ESA Working Paper No. 12–03, June.* Rome, Italy: Food and Agriculture Organization of the United Nations (FAO).

All Africa (2014). *Liberia: GVL Security Wanted Me Killed.* All Africa. Available at: http://allafrica.com/stories/201406240649.html?viewall=1.

Altevogt, B.M., Pankevich, D.E., Shelton-Davenport, M.K. and Kahn, J.P. (2011). *Committee on the Use of Chimpanzees in Biomedical and Behavioral Research: Assessing the Necessity.* Washington DC: National Academies Press. Available at: http://www.ncbi.nlm.nih.gov/books/NBK91443/. Accessed March 15, 2013.

Amianti, G.D. (2014). Indonesia struggles to clean up corrupt forestry sector. *Jakarta Globe,* January 1, 2014.

Ammann, K. (2011). *The Cairo Connection. Part II. Ape Trafficking, Nanyuki, Kenya.* Gerzensee, Switzerland: Pax Animalis. Available at: http://www.karlammann.com/pdf/cairo-connection-2.pdf.

Ancrenaz, M., Ambu, L., Sunjoto, I., *et al.* (2010). Recent surveys in the forests of Ulu Segama Malua, Sabah, Malaysia, show that orang-utans (*P. p. morio*) can be maintained in slightly logged forests. *PLoS One,* **5**, e11510.

Ancrenaz, M., Dabek, L. and O'Neil, S. (2007). The costs of exclusion: recognizing a role for local communities in biodiversity conservation. *PLoS Biol,* **5**, 2443–8.

Ancrenaz, M., Gimenez, O., Ambu, L., *et al.* (2005). Aerial surveys give new estimates for orangutans in Sabah, Malaysia. *PLoS Biol,* **3**, e3.

Ancrenaz, M., Marshall, A., Goossens, B., *et al.* (2008). *Pongo pygmaeus.* In *The IUCN Red List of Threatened Species, Version 2014.3.* Gland, Switzerland: International Union for Conservation of Nature (IUCN). Available at: http://www.iucnredlist.org/details/17975/0. Accessed February 26, 2015.

Ancrenaz, M., Oram, F., Ambu, L., *et al.* (2015). Of *Pongo,* palms and perceptions: a multidisciplinary assessment of Bornean orang-utans *Pongo pygmaeus* in an oil palm context. *Oryx,* **49**, 465–72.

Ancrenaz, M., Sollmann, R., Meijaard, E., *et al.* (2014). Coming down from the trees: is terrestrial activity in Bornean orangutans natural or disturbance driven? *Scientific Reports,* **4**, 4024.

Andayani, N., Brockelman, W., Geissmann, T., Nijman, V. and Supriatna, J. (2008). *Hylobates moloch.* In *The IUCN Red List of Threatened Species.* Gland, Switzerland: International Union for Conservation of Nature (IUCN). Available at: http://www.iucnredlist.org/details/10550/0.

Anderson, D.P., Nordheim, E.V. and Boesch, C. (2006). Environmental factors influencing the seasonality of estrus in chimpanzees. *Primates,* **47**, 43–50.

Animal Equality (2013). *Animal Suffering and Public Deception at Schwaben Park, Germany.* Los Angeles, CA: Animal Equality. Available at: http://www.zoocheck.com/wp-content/uploads/2015/06/SchwabenParkReport.pdf.

Animal Public eV, Born Free Foundation and Bund gegen Missbrauch der Tiere eV (2012). *The EU Zoo Inquiry 2011: An Evaluation of the Implementation and Enforcement of the EC Directive 1999/22, Relating to the Keeping of Wild Animals in Zoos – Germany.* Animal Public eV, Born Free Foundation and Bund gegen Missbrauch der Tiere eV. Available at: http://www.bornfree.org.uk/zooreports/Germany-En/germany-en.pdf.

Anseeuw, W., Alden Wily, L., Cotula, L. and Taylor, M. (2012a). *Land Rights and the Rush for Land: Findings of the Global Commercial Pressures on Land Research Project.* Rome, Italy: International Land Coalition (ILC).

Anseeuw, W., Boche, M., Breu, T., *et al.* (2012b). *Transnational Land Deals for Agriculture in the Global South. Analytical Report Based on the Land Matrix Database.* Bern/Montpellier/Hamburg: Centre for Development and Environment (CDE)/Centre de Coopération Internationale en Recherche Agronomique pour le Développement (CIRAD)/German Institute of Global and Area Studies (GIGA). Available at: http://www.landcoalition.org/sites/default/files/publication/1254/Analytical%20Report%20Web.pdf.

Anstey, S. (1991a). *Large Mammal Distribution in Liberia. Wildlife Survey Report.* World Wide Fund for Nature (WWF) and Forest Development Authority (FDA).

Anstey, S. (1991b). *Wildlife Utilisation in Liberia: The Findings of a National Survey 1989–1990. Wildlife Survey Report.* World Wide Fund for Nature (WWF) and Forest Development Authority (FDA).

Arandjelovic, M., Head, J., Boesch, C., Robbins, M.M. and Vigilant, L. (2014). Genetic inference of group dynamics and female kin structure in a western lowland gorilla population. *Primate Biology*, **1**, 29–38.

Arcus Foundation (2014). *State of the Apes: Extractive Industries and Ape Conservation.* Cambridge, UK: Cambridge University Press.

Aregheore, E.M. (2009). *Country Pasture/Forage Resource Profiles Cote D'Ivoire.* Rome, Italy: Food and Agriculture Organization of the United Nations (FAO).

ASEAN (1985). *Agreement on the Conservation of Nature and Natural Resources. Signed in Kuala Lumpur, Malaysia, July 9, 1985.* Jakarta, Indonesia: Association of Southeast Asian Nations (ASEAN). Available at: http://environment. asean.org/agreement-on-the-conservation-of-nature-and-natural-resources/.

Asquith, N.M. (1995). Javan gibbon conservation: why habitat protection is crucial. *Tropical Biodiversity*, **3**, 63–5.

Asquith, N.M., Martarinza and Sinaga, R. (1995). The Javan gibbon (*Hylobates moloch*): status and conservation recommendations. *Tropical Biodiversity*, **3**, 1–14.

Babweteera, F., Sheil, D., Reynolds, V., *et al.* (2011). Environmental and anthropogenic changes in and around Budongo Forest Reserve. In *The Ecological Impact of Long-Term Changes in Africa's Rift Valley*, ed. A.J. Plumptre. New York, NY: Nova Science Publishers, pp. 31–53.

Baldwin, P.J., McGrew, W.C. and Tutin, C.E.G. (1982). Wide-ranging chimpanzees at Mt Assirik. *International Journal of Primatology*, **3**, 367–83.

BankTrack (n.d.). *Golden Agri-Resources. List of Finance Institutions Involved.* Nijmegen, the Netherlands: BankTrack. Available at: http://www.banktrack.org/show/companyprofiles/golden_agri#tab_companyprofiles_finance. Accessed November 10, 2014.

Barral, S. (2012). *Le nouvel esprit du capitalisme agraire: les formes de l'autonomie ouvrière dans les plantations de palmier à huile en Indonésie.* PhD thesis. Paris, France: École des Hautes Etudes en Sciences Sociales (EHESS).

Bartlett, T.Q. (2007). The Hylobatidae: small apes of Asia. In *Primates in Perspective*, ed. C. Campbell, A. Fuentes, K.C. MacKinnon, M. Panger and S.K. Bearder. New York, NY: Oxford University Press, pp. 274–89.

Bartlett, T.Q. (2008). *The Gibbons of Khao Yai: Seasonal Variation in Behavior and Ecology.* London, UK: Routledge.

Bashaasha, B., Kraybill, D.S. and Southgate, D.D. (2001). Land use impacts of agricultural intensification and fuelwood taxation in Uganda. *Land Economics*, **77**, 241–9.

Beck, B., Walkup, K., Rodrigues, M., *et al.* (2007). *Best Practice Guidelines for the Re-Introduction of Great Apes.* Gland, Switzerland: World Conservation Union Species Survival Commission (SSC) Primate Specialist Group.

Bela, M. (2014). Production du caoutchouc: le Cameroun veut être une référence mondiale. *Come4News.* Available at: http://www.come4news.com/production-du-caoutchouc-le-cameroun-veut-etre-une-reference-mondiale-69681. Accessed September 3, 2014.

Benchimol, M. and Peres, C.A. (2013). Anthropogenic modulators of species-area relationships in Neotropical primates: a continental-scale analysis of fragmented forest landscapes. *Diversity and Distributions*, **19**, 1339–52.

Bene, J.K., Bitty, E.A., Bohoussou, K.H., *et al.* (2013). Current conservation status of large mammals in Sime Darby oil palm concession in Liberia. *Global Journal of Biology, Agriculture and Health Studies*, **2**, 93–102.

Bergl, R.A., Bradley, B.J., Nsubuga, A. and Vigilant, L. (2008). Effects of habitat fragmentation, population size and demographic history on genetic diversity: the Cross River gorilla in a comparative context. *American Journal of Primatology*, **70**, 848–59.

Bergl, R.A. and Vigilant, L. (2007). Genetic analysis reveals population structure and recent migration within the highly fragmented range of the Cross River gorilla (*Gorilla gorilla diehli*). *Molecular Ecology*, **16**, 501–16.

Bermejo, M. (1999). Status and conservation of primates in Odzala National Park, Republic of the Congo. *Oryx*, **33**, 323–31.

BirdLife International (n.d.). *Sites. Important Bird and Biodiversity Areas (IBAs): LR007 Cestos-Senkwen.* Cambridge, UK: BirdLife International. Available at: http://www.birdlife.org/datazone/sitefactsheet.php?id=6461. Accessed September 30, 2014.

Biy, V. (2013). *Cameroon: Chinese Group to Expand Rubber Production.* All Africa. Available at: http://allafrica.com/stories/201305280349.html. Accessed September 3, 2014.

Blake, S. (2002). *Ecology of forest elephant distribution and its implications for conservation.* PhD thesis. Edinburgh, UK: University of Edinburgh.

Blake, S., Strindberg, S., Boudjan, P., *et al.* (2007). Forest elephant crisis in the Congo Basin. *PLoS Biol*, **5**, e111.

Blakely, T., Hales, S. and Woodward, A. (2004). *Poverty: Assessing the Distribution of Health Risks by Socioeconomic Position at National and Local Levels. Environmental Burden of Disease Series No. 10.* Geneva, Switzerland: World Health Organization (WHO).

Blaser, J., Sarre, A., Poore, D. and Johnson, S. (2011). *Status of Tropical Forest Management 2011. ITTO Technical Series No. 38.* Yokohama, Japan: International Tropical Timber Organization (ITTO).

Bloomberg (n.d.). *Feronia Equity Holders.* Bloomberg. Available at: http://www.bloomberg.com/research/stocks/snapshot/snapshot.asp?ticker=FRNFF. Accessed September 26, 2014.

BMF (n.d.). *Bruno Manser's Biography.* Basel, Switzerland: Bruno Manser Fund (BMF). Available at: http://bmf.ch/en/about-us/bruno-mansers-biography/. Accessed March 18, 2015.

Boltanski, L. and Chiapello, E. (2011). *Le Nouvel Esprit du Capitalisme.* Paris, France: Gallimard.

Bonifield, J. and Cohen, E. (2015). Chimps still stuck in research labs despite promise of retirement. *CNN.com.* Available at: http://www.cnn.com/2015/02/06/health/research-chimps-stuck-in-labs/.

Born Free Foundation (2013). *Catalunya Proposes to Ban all Animals in Circuses.* Horsham, UK: Born Free Foundation. Available at: http://www.bornfree.org.uk/campaigns/zoo-check/circuses-performing-animals/circus-news/article/?no_cache=1&tx_ttnews%5Btt_news%5D=1445. Accessed April 8, 2015.

Born Free USA (2013). *Captive Primate Safety Act Fact Sheet.* Washington DC: Born Free USA. Available at: http://www.bornfreeusa.org/downloads/pdf/Fact-Sheet_Captive_Primates_Safety_Act.pdf.

BOS Foundation (2014). *Orphaned Orangutans Keep On Arriving.* Bogor, Indonesia: Borneo Orangutan Survival (BOS) Foundation. Available at: http://orangutan.or.id/orphaned-orangutans-keep-on-arriving/.

Boxer, B. (2013). *Captive Primate Safety Act.* US Congress. Available at: https://www.congress.gov/bill/113th-congress/senate-bill/1463.

Boyfield, K. (2013). *Commercial Agriculture: Cure or Curse? Malaysian and African Experience Contrasted. IEA Discussion Paper No. 48.* London, UK: Institute of Economic Affairs (IEA).

BPS (2012). *Statistik Kelapa Sawit Indonesia/Indonesian Oil Palm Statistics 2012.* Jakarta, Indonesia: Badan Pusat Statistik (BPS). Available at: http://www.bps.go.id/website/pdf_publikasi/watermark%20_Statistik%20Kelapa%20Sawit%20Indonesia%202012.pdf.

BPS (n.d.). *Population.* Jakarta, Indonesia: Badan Pusat Statistik (BPS). Available at: http://www.bps.go.id. Accessed June 25, 2014.

Brashares, J.S., Arcese, P. and Sam, M.K. (2001). Human demography and reserve size predict wildlife extinction in West Africa. *Proceedings of the Royal Society B: Biological Sciences*, **268**, 2473–8.

Brinkman, A. (2009). *Greenhouse Gas Emissions from Palm Oil Production.* Hoevelaken, the Netherlands: Brinkman Consultancy.

Brncic, T.M., Amarasekaran, B. and McKenna, A. (2010). *Final Report of the Sierra Leone National Chimpanzee Census Project.* Freetown, Sierra Leone: Tacugama Chimpanzee Sanctuary.

Brookfield, H., Potter, L. and Byron, Y. (1995). *In Place of the Forest. Environmental and Socio-economic Transformation in Borneo and the Eastern Malay Peninsula.* Tokyo, Japan: The United Nations University.

Brothwell, D. (1960). Upper Pleistocene human skull from Niah Caves, Sarawak. *Sarawak Museum Journal*, **9**, 323–50.

Brown, E., Dudley, N., Lindhe, A., *et al.* (2013). *Common Guidance for the Identification of High Conservation Values.* Oxford, UK: High Conservation Values (HCV) Resource Network.

Bruford, M.W., Ancrenaz, M., Chikhi, L., *et al.* (2010). Projecting genetic diversity and population viability for the fragmented orang-utan population in the Kinabatangan floodplain, Sabah, Malaysia. *Endangered Species Research*, **12**, 249.

Brundtland, G.H., Ehrlich, P., Goldemberg, J., *et al.* (2012). *Environment and development challenges: the imperative to act.* Presented at: The 12th Special Session of the Governing Council/Global Ministerial Environment Forum of the United Nations Environment Programme, February 20–22, 2012. Nairobi, Kenya: Millenium Alliance for Humanity and the Biosphere (MAHB). Available at: http://mahb.stanford.edu/wp-content/uploads/2012/02/Blue-Planet-Laureates-Environmental-and-Development-Challenges-The-Imperative-to-Act.pdf.

Budidarsono, S., Rahmanulloh, A. and Sofiyuddin, M. (2012). *Economics Assessment of Palm Oil Production. Technical Brief No. 26: Palm Oil Series.* Bogor, Indonesia: World Agroforestry Centre, ICRAF, SEA Regional Office.

Bunge (2014). *Bunge Global Palm Oil Sourcing Policy.* White Plains, NY: Bunge. Available at: http://www.bunge.com/citizenship/bunge-palm-oil-sourcing-policy.pdf.

Burgués Arrea, I., Brunner, A., Gleason, J. and Mitchell, L. (2014). *Moving Towards Greener Infrastructure: Innovative Legal Solutions to Common Challenges.* Sebastopol, CA: Environmental Law Alliance Worldwide and Conservation Strategy Fund. Available at: http://conservation-strategy.org/es/publication/moving-towards-greener-infrastructure-innovative-legal-solutions-common-challenges#.UodGK3hk5U.

Burma Environmental Working Group (2011). *Burma's Environment: People, Problems, Policies.* Chiang Mai, Thailand: Wanida Press.

Butler, R.A. (2006). *Rwanda Deforestation.* Menlo Park, CA: Mongabay.com. Available at: http://rainforests.mongabay.com/deforestation/archive/Rwanda.htm. Accessed September, 2014.

Butler, R.A. (2014). *After GAR Expands Policy, Over 50% of World's Palm Oil Bound by Zero Deforestation Commitments. March 3, 2014.* Menlo Park, CA: Mongabay.com. Available at: http://news.mongabay.com/2014/0303-gar-palm-oil.html.

Bwiza, D. (2013). Country report: Democratic Republic of Congo. *IUCNEL EJournal*, **5**, 141–8.

Caliman, J.P. (2011). Palmier à huile: le management environnemental des plantations. Dossier Biodiversité et cultures végétales (approches), économie-développement. *OCL-Oléagineux, Corps Gras Lipides*, **18**, 123–31.

Cambodia (1993a). *Constitution 1993.* Kingdom of Cambodia.

Cambodia (1993b). *Regulations on Creation and Designation of Protected Areas.* Kingdom of Cambodia.

Cambodia (1994). *Declaration (Prakas) on the Protection of Natural Areas 1994.* No. 1033. Kingdom of Cambodia.

Cambodia (1996). *Law on Environmental Protection and Natural Resource Management 1996.* Kingdom of Cambodia.

Cambodia (1999). *Sub-decree on Environmental Impact Assessment 1999.* Kingdom of Cambodia.

Cambodia (2001). *Land Law 2001.* Kingdom of Cambodia.

Cambodia (2002). *Law on Forestry 2002.* Kingdom of Cambodia.

Cambodia (2003). *Sub-decree on Community Forestry Management 2003.* No. 79. Kingdom of Cambodia.

Cambodia (2009). *Prakas on General Guidelines for Initial and Final Environmental Impact Assessment Reports 2009.* Kingdom of Cambodia.

Cambodia (2014). *The Fifth National Report to the Convention on Biological Diversity.* Kingdom of Cambodia.

Cameroon (1974). *Ordonnance Fixant le Régime Foncier.* No. 74–1. Republic of Cameroon.

Cameroon (1978). *Loi Relative à la Protection des Parcs Nationaux 1978.* No. 78–23. Republic of Cameroon.

Cameroon (1992). *Constitution 1992.* Republic of Cameroon.

Cameroon (1994). *Loi Portant Régime des Forêts, de la Faune et de la Pêche 1994.* No. 94/01. Republic of Cameroon.

Cameroon (1995a). *Décret Fixant les Modalités d'Application du Régime de la Faune 1995.* No. 95-466. Republic of Cameroon.

Cameroon (1995b). *Décret Fixant les Modalités d'Application du Régime des Forêts 1995.* No. 95-531/PM. Republic of Cameroon.

Cameroon (1996). *Loi Portant Loi-Cadre Relative à la Gestion de l'Environnement 1996.* No. 96-12. Republic of Cameroon.

Cameroon (2005). *Décret Fixant les Modalités de Réalisation des Études d'Impact Environnmental 2005.* No. 2005/0577. Republic of Cameroon.

Cameroon (2011). *Loi d'Orientation pour l'Aménagement et le Développement Durable au Cameroun 2011.* No. 2011-008. Republic of Cameroon.

Cameroon (2013). *Décret Fixant les Modalités de Réalisation des Études d'Impact Environnmental et Social 2013.* No. 2013/0171. Republic of Cameroon.

Campbell, C., Andayani, N., Cheyne, S., *et al.*, ed. (2008a). *Indonesian Gibbon Conservation and Management Workshop Final Report.* Apple Valley, MN: International Union for Conservation of Nature Species Survival Commission (IUCN SSC) Conservation Breeding Specialist Group.

Campbell, G., Kuehl, H., Kouame, P.N.G. and Boesch, C. (2008b). Alarming decline of West African chimpanzees in Côte d'Ivoire. *Current Biology*, **18**, 903–4.

Campbell-Smith, G., Campbell-Smith, M., Singleton, I. and Linkie, M. (2011a). Apes in space: saving an imperilled orangutan population in Sumatra. *PLoS One*, **6**, e17210.

Campbell-Smith, G., Campbell-Smith, M., Singleton, I. and Linkie, M. (2011b). Raiders of the lost bark: orangutan foraging strategies in a degraded landscape. *PLoS One*, **6**, e20962.

Campbell-Smith, G., Sembiring, R. and Linkie, M. (2012). Evaluating the effectiveness of human–orangutan conflict mitigation strategies in Sumatra. *Journal of Applied Ecology*, **49**, 367–75.

Campbell-Smith, G., Simanjorang, H.V.P., Leader-Williams, N. and Linkie, M. (2010). Local attitudes and perceptions toward crop-raiding by orangutans (*Pongo abelii*) and other nonhuman primates in Northern Sumatra, Indonesia. *American Journal of Primatology*, **72**, 866–76.

Cannon, C.H., Curran, L.M., Marshall, A.J. and Leighton, M. (2007). Long-term reproductive behaviour of woody plants across seven Bornean forest types in the Gunung Palung National Park (Indonesia): suprannual synchrony, temporal productivity and fruiting diversity. *Ecology Letters*, **10**, 956–69.

CAO (2009). CAO audit of IFC's investments. In *Wilmar Trading (IFC No. 20348), Delta-Wilmar CIS (IFC No. 24644), Wilmar WCap (IFC No. 25532), and Delta-Wilmar CIS Expansion (IFC No. 26271)*. Washington DC: Office of the Compliance Advisor/Ombudsman (CAO).

Cargill (2014). *Cargill Policy on Sustainable Palm Oil.* Minneapolis, MN: Cargill. Available at: https://www.cargill. com/wcm/groups/public/@ccom/documents/document/palm_oil_policy_statement.pdf.

Carlson, K., Curran, L., Ratnassari, D., *et al.* (2012). Committed carbon emissions, deforestation, and community land conversion from oil palm plantation expansion in West Kalimantan, Indonesia. *Proceedings of the National Academy of Sciences USA*, **109**, 7559–64.

Carne, C., Semple, S., Morrogh-Bernard, H., Zuberbühler, K. and Lehmann, J. (2014). The risk of disease to great apes: simulating disease spread in orang-utan (*Pongo pygmaeus wurmbii*) and chimpanzee (*Pan troglodytes schweinfurthii*) association networks. *PLoS One*, **9**, e95039.

Carrasco, L.R., Larrosa, C., Milner-Gulland, E.J. and Edwards, D.P. (2014). A double-edged sword for tropical forests. *Science*, **346**, 38–40.

Carrere, R. (2010). *Oil Palm in Africa: Past, Present and Future Scenarios.* Montevideo, Uruguay: World Rainforest Movement (WRM).

Carvalho, J.S., Marques, T.A. and Vicente, L. (2013). Population status of *Pan troglodytes verus* in Lagoas de Cufada Natural Park, Guinea-Bissau. *PLoS One*, **8**, e71527.

Cattau, M.E., Husson, S. and Cheyne, S.M. (2014). Population status of the Bornean orang-utan *Pongo pygmaeus* in a vanishing forest in Indonesia: the former Mega Rice Project. *Oryx*, **49**, 473–80.

CBD (2010). *Global Biodiversity Outlook 3.* Montreal, Canada: Convention on Biodiversity (CBD).

CBL (2014). *Central Bank of Liberia Annual Report 2013.* Monrovia, Liberia: Central Bank of Liberia (CBL). Available at: http://www.cbl.org.lr/doc/annualreports/cblannualreport2013.pdf.

CED and RELUFA (2013). *Above All Laws: How an American Company Operates Illegally in Cameroon.* Yaoundé, Cameroon: Centre pour l'Environnement et le Developpement (CED) and RELUFA. Available at: http://www. relufa.org/documents/AboveAllLaws-HowanAmericanCompanyOperatesIllegallyinCameroon-Final.pdf.

Centro de Rescate de Primates Rainfer (n.d.). *Los Primates.* Centro de Rescate de Primates Rainfer. Available at: http://rainfer.com/. Accessed January, 2015.

CEPF (2000). *Ecosystem Profile: Guinean Forests of West Africa Hotspot, Upper Guinean Forest Briefing Book.* Washington DC: Critical Ecosystem Partnership Fund (CEPF). Available at: http://www.cepf.net/Documents/ final.guineanforestwestafrica.upperguineanforest.briefingbook.pdf.

CFS (2013). *High Level Panel of Experts on Food Security and Nutrition. A Zero-Draft Consultation Paper on Biofuels and Food Security.* Rome, Italy: Committee on World Food Security (CFS). Available at: http://www.fao.org/ fsnforum/sites/default/files/files/86_Biofuels_v0/HLPE%20V0%20draft%20Biofuels%20and%20food%20 security%20-%2009%20Jan%202013.pdf.

Chalk, F. (1967). The anatomy of an investment: Firestone's 1927 loan to Liberia. *Journal of African Studies*, **1**, 12–32.

Chapin Metz, H. (1991). *Nigeria: A Country Study.* Washington DC: GPO for the Library of Congress.

Chapman, C.A., Balcomb, S.R., Gillespie, T.R., Skorupa, J.P. and Struhsaker, T.T. (2000). Long-term effects of logging on African primate communities: a 28-year comparison from Kibale National Park, Uganda. *Conservation Biology*, **14**, 207–17.

Chapman, C.A. and Lambert, J.E. (2000). Habitat alteration and the conservation of African primates: case study of Kibale National Park, Uganda. *American Journal of Primatology*, **50**, 169–85.

Chee, W.C. and Peng, C.C. (2006). *Country Pasture/Forage Resource Profiles Malaysia*. Rome, Italy: Food and Agriculture Organization of the United Nations (FAO).

Cheyne, S.M. (2008a). Effects of meteorology, astronomical variables, location and human disturbance on the singing apes: *Hylobates albibarbis*. *American Journal of Primatology*, **70**, 386–92.

Cheyne, S.M. (2008b). Feeding ecology, food choice and diet characteristics of gibbons in a disturbed peat-swamp forest, Indonesia. In *22nd Congress of the International Primatological Society (IPS), Edinburgh, UK*, ed. P.C. Lee, P. Honess, H. Buchanan-Smith, A. MaClarnon and W.I. Sellers. Bristol, UK: Top Copy, p. 342.

Cheyne, S.M. (2010). Behavioural ecology of gibbons (*Hylobates alibarbis*) in a degraded peat-swamp forest. In *Indonesian Primates. Developments in Primatology: Progress and Prospects*, ed. S. Gursky-Doyen and J. Supriatna. New York, Heidelberg and London: Springer Science, pp. 121–56.

Cheyne, S.M., Thompson, C.J.H. and Chivers, D.J. (2013). Travel adaptations of gibbons *Hylobates albibarbis* (Primates: Hylobatidae) in a degraded secondary forest, Indonesia. *Journal of Threatened Taxa*, **5**, 3963–8.

Cheyns, E. (2012). (Dé)politisation des standards dans les dispositifs de normalisation multiparties prenantes. Les cas du soja et de l'huile de palme. In *Normaliser au Nom du Développement Durable*, ed. P. Alphandéry, M. Djama, A. Fortier and È. Fouilleux. Versailles, France: Quae, pp. 101–18.

ChimpCARE (n.d.). *Where Are Our Amazing Chimpanzees in the United States?* ChimpCARE. Available at: http://www.chimpcare.org/map. Accessed September 3, 2014.

Choudhury, A. (1991). Ecology of the hoolock gibbon (*Hylobates hoolock*), a lesser ape in the tropical forests of north-eastern India. *Journal of Tropical Ecology*, **7**, 147–53.

Choudhury, A. (2009). The distribution, status and conservation of hoolock gibbon, *Hoolock hoolock*, in Karbi Anglong District, Assam, northeast India. *Primate Conservation*, **24**, 117–26.

Choudhury, A. (2013). Description of a new subspecies of hoolock gibbon, *Hoolock hoolock*, from north east India. *Newsletter and Journal of the Rhino Foundation for Nature in North East India*, **9**, 49–59.

Christie, T., Steininger, M., Juhn, D. and Peal, A. (2007). Fragmentation and clearance of Liberia's forests during 1986–2000. *Oryx*, **41**, 539–43.

Chung, A.Y.C., Ajik, M., Nilus, R. and Ong, R. (2007). *Forest pest occurrences: some recent evidences in Sabah*. Presented at: Proceedings FRIM Conference on Forestry and Forest Product Research, Kuala Lumpur.

CIESIN and ITOS (2013). *Global Roads Open Access Data Set, Version 1 (gROADSv1)*. Palisades, NY: NASA Socio-economic Data and Applications Center. Available at: http://dx.doi.org/10.7927/H4VD6WCT. Accessed May, 2015.

CIFOR (2015). *Socioecological Responsibility and Chinese Overseas Investments. The Case of Rubber Plantation Expansion in Cameroon. CIFOR Working Paper 176*. Bogor, Indonesia: Center for International Forestry Research (CIFOR). Available at: http://www.cifor.org/library/5474/socioecological-responsibility-and-chinese-overseas-investments-the-case-of-rubber-plantation-expansion-in-cameroon.

CIRMF (2014). *Transfert des Gorilles du vers le Sanctuaire du Projet Gorilles Fernan Vaz (PGFV)*. Centre International de Recherches Médicales de Franceville (CIRMF). Available at: http://www.cirmf.org/index.php?option=com_content&view=article&id=135%3Atransfert-des-gorilles-du-centre-international-de-recherches-medicales-de-franceville-cirmf-vers-le-sanctuaire-du-projet-gorilles-fernan-vaz-pgfv&catid=17%3Aactualites&Itemid=19&lang=en.

CITES (1973). *Convention on International Trade in Endangered Species of Wild Fauna and Flora (CITES). Signed in Washington DC, March 3, 1973*. Geneva, Switzerland: Convention on International Trade in Endangered Species of Wild Fauna and Flora (CITES). Available at: http://www.cites.org/eng/disc/text.php.

CITES (2013). *Technical Missions to Gorilla Range States to Assess Current Enforcement Activities and Initiatives: Annex 2 (Technical Report No. CoP16 Doc. 49 Annex 2)*. Geneva, Switzerland: Convention on International Trade in Endangered Species of Wild Fauna and Flora (CITES) Secretariat. Available at: http://www.cites.org/eng/cop/16/doc/E-CoP16-49-A2.pdf.

Clark, H. (2014). *Towards Joint Action by the International Community*. New York, NY: United Nations Development Programme (UNDP). Available at: http://www.undp.org/content/undp/en/home/presscenter/speeches/2014/09/26/helen-clark-speech-at-poaching-and-illicit-wildlife-trafficking-towards-joint-action-by-the-international-community.

Clay, J. (2004). *World Agriculture and the Environment: A Commodity-by-Commodity Guide to Impacts and Practices.* World Wide Fund for Nature (WWF)/Island Press.

CLUA (2014). *Disrupting the Global Commodity Business: How Strange Bedfellows Are Transforming a Trillion-Dollar Industry to Protect Forests, Benefit Local Communities, and Slow Global Warming.* San Francisco, CA: Climate and Land Use Alliance (CLUA). Available at: http://www.climateandlandusealliance.org/uploads/PDFs/Disrupting_Global_Commodity.pdf.

CMP (2013). *Open Standards for the Practice of Conservation.* Conservation Measures Partnership (CMP).

CMS (1979). *The Conservation of Migratory Species of Wild Animals. Signed in Bonn, Germany, June 23, 1979.* Bonn, Germany: Convention on Conservation of Migratory Species (CMS). Available at: http://www.cms.int/en/node/3916.

Coase, R.H. (1988). *The Firm, the Market and the Law.* Chicago, IL: Chicago University Press.

Colchester, M., Anderson, P., Jiwan, N., Andiko and Toh, S. (2009). *HCV and RSPO: Results of an Investigation. Report of an Independent Investigation into the Effectiveness of the Application of High Conservation Value Zoning in Palm Oil Development in Indonesia.* London, UK: Forest Peoples Programme (FFP), HuMa, Sawit Watch, Wild Asia.

Colchester, M., Chao, S., Dallinger, J., *et al.* (2011). *Oil Palm Expansion in South East Asia: Trends and Implications for Local Communities and Indigenous Peoples.* Moreton-in-Marsh, UK: Forest Peoples Programme (FPP) and Perkumpulan Sawit Watch. Available at: http://www.forestpeoples.org/oil-palm-expansion-in-south-east-asia-trends-implications-local-communities-indigenous-peoples. Accessed January, 2013.

Colin, C., Sherman, J., Lucas, D. and Byers, O. (2014). *Great Ape Reintroduction Workshop Report.* Chester, UK: Pan African Sanctuary Alliance (PASA) and International Union for Conservation of Nature Species Survival Commission (IUCN SSC) Conservation Breeding Specialist Group.

Collins, D.A. and McGrew, W.C. (1988). Habitats of three groups of chimpanzees (*Pan troglodytes*) in Tanzania compared. *Journal of Human Evolution*, **17**, 553–74.

COMIFAC (2005). Treaty on the Conservation and Sustainable Management of Forest Ecosystems in Central Africa and to Establish the Central African Forests Commission (COMIFAC). Signed in Brazzaville, Republic of Congo, February 5, 2005. *Law Environment and Development Journal*, **2**, 145–54.

Corley, R.H.V. and Tinker, P.B. (2003). *The Oil Palm*, 4th edn. *World Agriculture Series.* Oxford, UK: Wiley Blackwell.

Cotula, L. (2011). *Land Deals in Africa: What is in the Contracts?* London, UK: International Institute for Environment and Development (IIED).

Cotula, L. (2013). *The Great African Land Grab? Agricultural Investments and the Global Food System.* London, UK: Zed Books.

Cotula, L. and Mayers, J. (2009). *Tenure in REDD: Starting Point or Afterthought?* London, UK: International Institute for Environment and Development (IIED). Available at: http://pubs.iied.org/13554IIED.html.

Cotula, L., Vermeulen, S., Leonard, R. and Keeley, J. (2009). *Land Grab or Development Opportunity? Agricultural Investment and International Land Deals in Africa.* Rome, Italy: International Institute for Environment and Development (IIED)/Food and Agriculture Organization of the United Nations (FAO)/International Fund for Agricultural Development (IFAD).

Cuaron, A.D. (2000). Global perspective on habitat disturbance and tropical rainforest mammals. *Conservation Biology*, **14**, 1574–9.

Currey, D., Doherty, F., Lawson, S., Newman, J. and Ruwindrijarto, A. (2001). *Timber Trafficking. Illegal Logging in Indonesia, SE Asia and International Consumption of Illegally Sourced Timber.* Kenilworth, UK: Emmerson Press.

Danielsen, F., Beukema, H. and Burgess, N.D. (2009). Biofuel plantations on forested lands: double jeopardy for biodiversity and climate. *Conservation Biology*, **23**, 348–58.

Das, J., Biswas, J., Bhattacherjee, P.C. and Rao, S.S. (2009). Canopy bridges: an effective conservation tactic for supporting gibbon populations in forest fragments. In *The Gibbons: New Perspectives on Small Ape Socioecology and Population Biology*, ed. S. Lappan and D. Whittaker. New York, NY: Springer, pp. 467–75.

Das, J., Feeroz, M.M., Islam, M.A., *et al.* (2003). Distribution of hoolock gibbon (*Bunopithecus hoolock hoolock*) in India and Bangladesh. *Zoos' Print Journal*, **18**, 969–76.

Daszak, P., Zambrana-Torrelio, C., Bogich, T.L., *et al.* (2013). Interdisciplinary approaches to understanding disease emergence: the past, present, and future drivers of Nipah virus emergence. *Proceedings of the National Academy of Sciences USA*, **110**, 3681–8.

Davies, G. (1986). The orangutan in Sabah. *Oryx*, **20**, 40–5.

Davis, J.T., Mengersen, K., Abram, N.K., *et al.* (2013). It's not just conflict that motivates killing of orangutans. *PLoS One*, **8**, e75373.

Dayang Norwana, A.A.B., Kunjappan, R., Chin, M., *et al.* (2011). *The Local Impacts of Oil Palm Expansion in Malaysia: An Assessment Based on a Case Study in Sabah State*. Bogor, Indonesia: Center for International Forestry Research (CIFOR).

DD International (2012). *Research and Evidence Collection on Issues Related to Articles 17 and 18 of the Framework Convention on Tobacco Control. Report to British American Tobacco*. Haryana, India: DD International. Available at: http://ddinternational.org.uk/_uploads/document/51.pdf.

de Bruyn, M., Stelbrink, B., Morley, R.J., *et al.* (2014). Borneo and Indochina are major evolutionary hotspots for Southeast Asian biodiversity. *Systematic Biology*, **63**, 879–901.

De Lopez, T.T. (2002). Natural resource exploitation in Cambodia: an examination of use, appropriation, and exclusion. *Journal of Environment Development*, **11**, 355–79.

de Man, R. (2002). *Minutes of the preparatory meeting London, 20 September 2002*. Leyden, the Netherlands: Environmental Policy Consulting.

DeFries, R.S., Rudel, T., Uriarte, M. and Hansen, M. (2010). Deforestation driven by urban population growth and agricultural trade in the twenty-first century. *Nature Geoscience*, **3**, 178–81.

Delgado, R.A. (2010). Communication, culture and conservation in orangutans. In *Indonesian Primates. Developments in Primatology: Progress and Prospects*, ed. S. Gursky Doyen and J. Supriatna. New York, Heidelberg and London: Springer Science, pp. 23–40.

Delgado, R.A. and van Schaik, C.P. (2000). The behavioral ecology and conservation of the orangutan (*Pongo pygmaeus*): a tale of two islands. *Evolutionary Anthropology*, **9**, 201–18.

Dewi, H., Prasetyo, L.B. and Rinaldi, D. (2007). Pemetaan kesesuaian habitat owa jawa (*Hylobates moloch*) di TN Halimun-Salak. *Media Konservasi*, **12**, 1–9.

Di Marco, M., Buchanan, G.M., Szantoi, Z., *et al.* (2014). Drivers of extinction risk in African mammals: the interplay of distribution state, human pressure, conservation response and species biology. *Philosophical Transactions of the Royal Society of London B: Biological Sciences*, **369**, 20130198.

Dickman, A.J. (2010). Complexities of conflict: the importance of considering social factors for effectively resolving human–wildlife conflict. *Animal Conservation*, **13**, 458–66.

Dickman, A.J. (2012). From cheetahs to chimpanzees: a comparative review of the drivers of human–carnivore conflict and human–primate conflict. *Folia Primatologica*, **83**, 377–87.

Dinerstein, E., Baccini, A., Anderson, M., *et al.* (2014). Guiding agricultural expansion to spare tropical forests. *Conservation Letters*, **8**, 262–71. DOI: 10.1111/conl.12149.

Dixon, J., Tanyeri-Abur, A. and Wattenbach, H. (2004). Framework for analysing impacts of globalization on small-holders. In *Smallholders, Globalization and Policy Analysis. AGSF Occasional Paper 5*, ed. J. Dixon, K. Taniguchi, H. Wattenbach and A. TanyeriArbur. Rome, Italy: Food and Agriculture Organization of the United Nations (FAO), pp. 7–18.

Djanubudiman, G., Pambudi, J.A.A., Raharjo, B., Hidayat, M. and Wibisono, F. (2004). *Laporan Awal: Populasi, Distribusi dan Konservasi Owa Jawa (*Hylobates moloch *Audebert, 1798)*. Depok, Indonesia: YABSI and PSBK.

Doak, D.F., Bakker, V.J., Goldstein, B.E. and Hale, B. (2014). What is the future of conservation? *Trends in Ecology and Evolution*, **29**, 77–81.

Doran-Sheehy, D., Mongo, P., Lodwick, J. and Conklin-Brittain, N.L. (2009). Male and female western gorilla diet: preferred foods, use of fallback resources, and implications for ape versus Old World monkey foraging strategies. *American Journal of Physical Anthropology*, **140**, 727–38.

Dowd, D., Vergnes, V., Normand, E., Tweh, C. and Boesch, C. (2014). *Report on the Chimpanzee and Large Mammal Survey in the Kpayan Gross Concession Area of Investigation of Golden Veroleum, Liberia*. Cologny, Switzerland: Wild Chimpanzee Foundation. Available at: http://goldenveroleumliberia.com/upload/20140403_gvl_report__wcf_survey.pdf.

Doyle, S. (2006). *Crisis and Decline in Bunyoro: Population and Environment in Western Uganda 1860–1955.* Oxford, UK: The British Institute in Eastern Africa in association with James Currey.

DRC (1969). *Ordonnance-Loi Relative à la Conservation de la Nature 1969.* No. 69–041. Democratic Republic of the Congo.

DRC (1975). *Loi Relative à la Création des Secteurs Sauvegardés 1975.* No. 75–024. Democratic Republic of the Congo.

DRC (1982). *Loi Portant Réglementation de la Chasse 1982.* No. 82–002. Democratic Republic of the Congo.

DRC (2000). *Arrêté Portant Réglementation du Commerce International des Espèces de la Faune et de la Flore Menacés d'Extinction 2000.* No. 056/CAB/MIN/AFFECNPF/ 01/00. Democratic Republic of the Congo.

DRC (2002). *Loi Portant Code Forestier 2002.* No. 11–2002. Democratic Republic of the Congo.

DRC (2006a). *Arrêté Ministériel Portant Agrément de la Liste des Espèces Animales Protégées en République Démocratique du Congo 2006.* No. 020/CAB/MIN/ECNEF/ 2006. Democratic Republic of the Congo.

DRC (2006b). *Arrêté Ministériel Portant Dispositions Relatives à l'Obligation de l'Évaluation Environnementale et Sociale des Projets en RDC 2006.* No. 043/CAB/MIN/. Democratic Republic of the Congo.

DRC (2006c). *Constitution 2006.* Democratic Republic of the Congo.

DRC (2008a). *Décret Fixant la Procédure d'Attribution des Concessions Forestières 2008.* No. 08/09. Democratic Republic of the Congo.

DRC (2008b). *Décret Fixant la Procédure de Classement et de Déclassement des Forêts 2008.* No. 08/08. Democratic Republic of the Congo.

DRC (2011a). *Décret Fixant les Règles Spécifiques d'Attribution des Concessions Forestières de Conservation 2011.* No. 011/27. Democratic Republic of the Congo.

DRC (2011b). *Décret Portant Obligation de Publier tout Contrat Ayant pour Objet les Ressources Naturelles 2011.* No. 011/26. Democratic Republic of the Congo.

DRC (2011c). *Loi Portant Principes Fondamentaux Relatifs à l'Agriculture 2011.* No. 11–022. Democratic Republic of the Congo.

DRC (2011d). *Loi Portant Principes Fondamentaux Relatifs à Protection de l'Environnement 2011.* No. 11–009. Democratic Republic of the Congo.

Drori, O. (2012). *Trade in great apes and wildlife law enforcement: challenges and solutions.* Presented at: 2nd GRASP Council Meeting, November 6–8, 2012, Paris, France.

Dublin-Green, A. (2013). Opportunities inherent in palm oil industry. *BusinessDay*, May 8, 2013. Available at: http://businessdayonline.com/2013/05/opportunities-inherent-in-palm-oil-industry/#.VCQ16CldWyM.

Dudley, N. (2008). *Guidelines for Applying Protected Area Management Categories.* Gland, Switzerland: International Union for Conservation of Nature (IUCN). Available at: http://data.iucn.org/dbtw-wpd/edocs/PAPS-016.pdf.

Dulac, J. (2013). *Global Land Transport Infrastructure Requirements: Estimating Road and Railway Infrastructure Capacity and Costs to 2050.* Paris, France: International Energy Agency.

Dunn, A., Berg, R., Byler, D., *et al.* (2014). *Revised Regional Action Plan for the Conservation of the Cross River Gorilla (Gorilla gorilla diehli): 2014–2019.* New York, NY: International Union for Conservation of Nature Species Survival Commission (IUCN SSC) Primate Specialist Group and Wildlife Conservation Society.

Dupain, J., Fowler, A., Kasalevo, P., *et al.* (2013). The process of creation of a new protected area in the Democratic Republic of Congo: the case of the Iyondji Community Bonobo Reserve. *Pan Africa News*, **20**, 10–3.

Dupain, J. and Van Elsacker, L. (2001). The status of bonobo (*Pan paniscus*) in the Democratic Republic of Congo. In *All Apes Great and Small. Volume 1. African Apes*, ed. B.M.F. Galdikas, N.E. Briggs, L.K. Sheeran, G.L. Shapiro and J. Goodall. Berlin, Germany: Springer, pp. 57–74.

Durham, D.L. and Phillipson, A. (2014). Status of captive apes across Africa and Asia: the impact of extractive industry. In *State of the Apes: Extractive Industries and Ape Conservation*, ed. Arcus Foundation. Cambridge, UK: Cambridge University Press, pp. 278–306.

Ecobank (2014). *Middle Africa Briefing Note - Palm Oil - September 24.* Lomé, Togo: Ecobank. Available at: http://www.ecobank.com/upload/2014092411382365877P3PKDZWn4g.pdf.

Economist (2014). Grow but cherish your environment. *Economist*, August 16, 2014. Available at: http://www.economist.com/news/middle-east-and-africa/21612241-companies-wanting-make-palm-oil-face-angry-environmentalists-grow-cherish.

Economy Watch (2010). *Guinea-Bissau Economy*. Economy Watch. Available at: http://www.economywatch.com/world_economy/guinea-bissau/. Accessed September, 2014.

Elder, A.E. (2009). Hylobatid diets revisted: the importance of body mass, fruit availability, and interspecific competition. In *The Gibbons: New Perspectives on Small Ape Socioecology and Population Biology*, ed. S. Lappan and D.J. Whittaker. New York, NY: Springer, pp. 133–59.

Elmers, R.L. (2013). *Humane Care for Primates Act*. US Congress. Available at: https://www.congress.gov/bill/113th-congress/house-bill/3556.

Embrapa (2010). *Dendê*. Brasília, Brazil Ministério da Agricultura, Pecuária e Abastecimiento.

Emery Thompson, M., Jones, J.H., Pusey, A.E., *et al.* (2007a). Aging and fertility patterns in wild chimpanzees provide insights into the evolution of menopause. *Current Biology*, **17**, 2150–6.

Emery Thompson, M., Kahlenberg, S.M., Gilby, I.C. and Wrangham, R.W. (2007b). Core area quality is associated with variance in reproductive success among female chimpanzees at Kibale National Park. *Animal Behaviour*, **73**, 501–12.

Emery Thompson, M. and Wrangham, R.W. (2008). Diet and reproductive function in wild female chimpanzees (*Pan troglodytes schweinfurthii*) at Kibale National Park, Uganda. *American Journal of Physical Anthropology*, **135**, 171–81.

Emery Thompson, M. and Wrangham, R.W. (2013). *Pan troglodytes* robust chimpanzee. In *Mammals of Africa. Volume II. Primates*, ed. T.M. Butynski, J. Kingdon and J. Kalina. London, UK: Bloomsbury Publishing, pp. 55–64.

Emery Thompson, M., Zhou, A. and Knott, C.D. (2012). Low testosterone correlates with delayed development in male orangutans. *PLoS One*, **7**, e47282.

ENDCAP (n.d.). *Animals in Circuses*. Horsham, UK: ENDCAP. Available at: http://endcap.eu/animal-circuses/. Accessed May, 2015.

English, A. (2008). *Determinants for Liberian Farmgate Cocoa Prices*. Knoxville, TN: University of Tennessee.

Enthoven, J.J.K. (1903). *Bijdragen tot de Geografie van Borneo's Wester-afdeeling*. Leiden, the Netherlands: E.J. Brill.

Entwisle, B., Walsh, S.J., Rindfuss, R.R. and VanWey, L.K. (2005). Population and upland crop production in Nang Rong, Thailand. *Population and Environment*, **26**, 449–70.

Environment DG (n.d.). *The EU Approach to Combat Wildlife Trafficking*. Brussels, Belgium: Environment Directorate General (DG) of the European Commission. Available at: http://ec.europa.eu/environment/cites/trafficking_en.htm. Accessed September, 2014.

Equatorial Palm Oil PLC (2010). *Placing and Admission to AIM, London, February 23, 2010*. London, UK: Equatorial Palm Oil PLC. Available at: http://www.epoil.co.uk/uploads/epo-admission-document.pdf.

Etiendem, D.N., Tagg, N., Hens, L. and Pereboom, Z. (2013). Impact of human activities on Cross River gorilla (*Gorilla gorilla diehli*) habitats in the Mawambi Hills, southwest Cameroon. *Endangered Species Research*, **20**, 167–79.

ETP (2010). *Economic Transformation Plan*. Pemandu, Kuala Lumpur: Economic Transformation Programme (ETP).

EU (1999). *Council Directive 1999/22/EC of 29 March 1999 Relating to the Keeping of Wild Animals in Zoos*. Brussels, Belgium: European Union (EU). Available at: eur-lex.europa.eu/LexUriServ/LexUriServ.do?uri=OJ:L:1999:094:0024:0026:EN:PDF.

EU (2000). *Charter of Fundamental Rights of the European Union*. European Union (EU). Available at: http://eur-lex.europa.eu/legal-content/EN/TXT/HTML/?uri=CELEX:12010P&from=EN.

EU (2003). Directive 2003/30/EC of the European Parliament and of the Council of 8 May 2003 on the promotion of the use of biofuels or other renewable fuels for transport. *Official Journal of the European Union*. Available at: http://www.seai.ie/Renewables/Renewable_Energy_Policy/5_Biofuels_Transport.pdf.

EU (2005). *Commission Regulation (EC) No. 1739/2005 of 21 October 2005 Laying Down Animal Health Requirements for the Movement of Circus Animals between Member States*. Brussels, Belgium: European Union (EU). Available at: eur-lex.europa.eu/legal-content/EN/TXT/?uri=celex:32005R1739.

EU (2009). Directive 2009/28/EC of the European Parliament and of the Council of 23 April 2009 on the promotion of the use of energy from renewable sources and amending and subsequently repealing Directives 2001/77/EC and 2003/30/EC. *Official Journal of the European Union*. Available at: http://www.eur-lex.europa.eu/legal-content/EN/ALL/?uri=CELEX:32009L0028.

Eurogroup for Animals (2010). *Areas of Concern 2010: Analysis of Animal Welfare Issues in the European Union.* Brussels, Belgium: Eurogroup for Animals. Available at: http://eurogroupforanimals.org/files/publications/downloads/EurogroupForAnimals-AreasOfConcern2010.pdf.

European Commission (2012). *Commission Implementing Decision of 23 November 2012 on Recognition of the Roundtable on Sustainable Palm Oil RED Scheme for Demonstrating Compliance with the Sustainability Criteria under Directives 98/70/EC and 2009/28/EC of the European Parliament and of the Council, L 326/53, 23 November.* European Commission. Available at: eur-lex.europa.eu/legal-content/EN/TXT/?uri=CELEX:32012D0722.

European Commission (2014). *Everything But Arms (EBA): Who Benefits?* Brussels, Belgium: European Commission. Available at: http://trade.ec.europa.eu/doclib/docs/2014/october/tradoc_152839.pdf.

Evans, R. and Griffiths, G. (2013). *Palm Oil, Land Rights and Ecosystem Services in Gbarpolu County, Liberia. Research Note 3.* Reading, UK: Walker Institute for Climate System Research, University of Reading. Available at: http://www.walker-institute.ac.uk/publications/research_notes/WalkerInResNote3.pdf.

Fairet, E. (2012). *Vulnerability to crop-raiding: an interdisciplinary investigation in Loango National Park, Gabon.* PhD thesis. Durham, UK: Durham University.

Fan Peng-Fei, Fei Hanlan, Xiang Zoufu, *et al.* (2010). Social structure and group dynamics of the cao vit gibbon (*Nomascus nasutus*) in Bangliang, Jinxi, China. *Folia Primatologica*, **81**, 245–53.

Fan Peng-Fei and Jiang Xue-Long (2008). Effects of food and topography on ranging behavior of black crested gibbon (*Nomascus concolor jingdongensis*) in Wuliang Mountain, Yunnan, China. *American Journal of Primatology*, **70**, 871–8.

Fan Peng-Fei and Jiang Xue-Long (2010). Maintenance of multifemale social organization in a group of *Nomascus concolor* at Wuliang Mountain, Yunnan, China. *International Journal of Primatology*, **31**, 1–13.

Fan Peng-Fei, Jiang Xue-Long and Tian Chang-Cheng (2009). The critically endangered black crested gibbon *Nomascus concolor* on Wuliang Mountain, Yunnan, China: the role of forest types in the species conservation. *Oryx*, **43**, 1–6.

FAO (2001). *Non-Forest Tree Plantations. Forest Plantation Thematic Papers, Working Paper 6. FAO Forest Resources Development Service.* Rome, Italy: Food and Agriculture Organization of the United Nations (FAO). Available at: ftp://ftp.fao.org/docrep/fao/006/ac126e/ac126e00.pdf.

FAO (2002). *Small-Scale Palm Oil Processing in Africa. FAO Agricultural Services Bulletin 148.* Rome, Italy: Food and Agriculture Organization of the United Nations (FAO).

FAO (2009a). *FAOSTAT Online Statistical Service.* Rome, Italy: Food and Agriculture Organization of the United Nations (FAO). Available at: http://faostat.fao.org/. Accessed August, 2011.

FAO (2009b). *The Special Challenge for Sub-Saharan Africa. Brief for the High Level Expert Forum: How to Feed the World in 2050.* Rome, Italy: Food and Agriculture Organization of the United Nations (FAO). Available at: http://www.fao.org/fileadmin/templates/wsfs/docs/Issues_papers/HLEF2050_Africa.pdf.

FAO (2010). *Global Forest Resources Assessment: Main Report. FAO Forestry Paper No. 163.* Rome, Italy: Food and Agriculture Organization of the United Nations (FAO). Available at: http://www.fao.org/docrep/013/i1757e/i1757e00.htm.

FAO (2011). *State of the World's Forests 2011.* Rome, Italy: Food and Agriculture Organization of the United Nations (FAO).

FAO (2012a). *Foreign Agricultural Investment Country Profile: Democratic Republic of the Congo (DRC).* Rome, Italy: Food and Agriculture Organization of the United Nations (FAO). Available at: http://www.fao.org/fileadmin/user_upload/tcsp/docs/CONGO_Country_Profile_FINAL1.pdf.

FAO (2012b). Labour. In *Statistical Yearbook 2013. World Food and Agriculture*, ed. FAO. Rome, Italy: Food and Agriculture Organization of the United Nations (FAO), pp. 18–21. Available at: http://issuu.com/faosyb/docs/fao_statistical_yearbook_2012_issuu.

FAO (2013). *Rebuilding West Africa's Food Potential: Policies and Market Incentives for Smallholder-Inclusive Food Value Chains.* Rome, Italy: Food and Agriculture Organization of the United Nations (FAO). Available at: http://www.fao.org/docrep/018/i3222e/i3222e.pdf.

FAO (2014a). *FAOSTAT Database on Agriculture.* Rome, Italy: Food and Agriculture Organization of the United Nations (FAO). Available at: http://faostat.fao.org/. Accessed September, 2014.

FAO (2014b). *Liberia: Agriculture Sector.* Rome, Italy: Food and Agriculture Organization of the United Nations (FAO). Available at: http://www.fao.org/countryprofiles/index/en/?iso3=LBR&subject=4. Accessed August 22, 2014.

FAO (2015). *Cocoa Production Statistics by Country.* Rome, Italy: Food and Agriculture Organization of the United Nations (FAO). Available at: http://faostat3.fao.org/browse. Accessed May 19, 2015.

FAOSTAT (n.d.). *Datasets.* Rome, Italy: Food and Agriculture Organization of the United Nations (FAO) Statistics Division. Available at: http://faostat3.fao.org. Accessed November 10, 2014.

Farmer, K.H. (2002). Pan-African Sanctuary Alliance: status and range of activities for great ape conservation. *American Journal of Primatology*, **58**, 117–32.

Farole, T. and Winkler, D., ed. (2014). *Making Foreign Direct Investment Work for Sub-Saharan Africa: Local Spillovers and Competitiveness in Global Value Chains.* Washington DC: World Bank Publications.

Faust, L.J., Cress, D., Farmer, K.H., Ross, S.R. and Beck, B.B. (2011). Predicting capacity demand on sanctuaries for African chimpanzees (*Pan troglodytes*). *International Journal of Primatology*, **32**, 849–64.

Feintrenie, L. (2013). *Oil palm business models.* Presented at: 4th Conférence Internationale Biocarburants et Bio-énergies, 2ie CIRAD, November 21–23, 2013, Ouagadougou, Burkina Faso.

Feintrenie, L. (2014). Agro-industrial plantations in Central Africa, risks and opportunities. *Biodiversity and Conservation*, **23**, 1577–89.

Feintrenie, L., Chong, W.K. and Levang, P. (2010). Why do farmers prefer oil palm? Lessons learnt from Bungo District, Indonesia. *Small-Scale Forestry*, **9**, 379–96.

Felton, A.M., Engstrom, L.M., Felton, A. and Knott, C.D. (2003). Orangutan population density, forest structure and fruit availability in hand-logged and unlogged peat swamp forests in West Kalimantan, Indonesia. *Biological Conservation*, **114**, 91–101.

Ferdowsian, H.R., Durham, D.L., Johnson, C.M., *et al.* (2012). Signs of generalized anxiety and compulsive disorders in chimpanzees. *Journal of Veterinary Behavior: Clinical Applications and Research*, **7**, 353–61.

Ferdowsian, H.R., Durham, D.L., Kimwele, C., *et al.* (2011). Signs of mood and anxiety disorders in chimpanzees. *PLoS One*, **6**, e19855.

Fern (2013). UNCERD calls on Cameroon to respect international law. *EU Forest Watch*, **181**. Available at: http://www.fern.org/pt-br/node/5563.

Feronia (2014). *Management's Discussion and Analysis for the Three Months ended March 31, 2014.* Feronia Inc. Available at: http://www.feronia.com/md_and_a/categories/2014. Accessed November 3, 2014.

Ferrero (2014). *Ferrero Oil Palm Charter.* Ferrero. Available at: http://www.ferrero.com/group-news/Ferrero-palm-oil-progress-report---November-2014.

FFI and Forest Trends (2012). *Initial assessment: mitigating the environmental impacts of oil palm concessions on forests in Liberia.* Fauna & Flora International (FFI) and Forest Trends. Unpublished study.

Finkelstein, J.B. (2014). *The Chain: 96% of Global Palm Oil Trade Converted by Zero Deforestation, Chain Reaction Research, December 8, 2014.* Available at: http://skollworldforum.org/editor-pick/96-of-global-palm-oil-trade-covered-by-zero-deforestation/.

Fischer, J. and Lindenmayer, D.B. (2006). Beyond fragmentation: the continuum model for fauna research and conservation in human-modified landscapes. *Oikos*, **112**, 473–80.

Fitzherbert, E.B., Struebig, M., Morel, A., *et al.* (2008). How will oil palm expansion affect biodiversity? *Trends in Ecology and Evolution*, **23**, 538–45.

Fitzpatrick, M. (2013). *HR 2856 Captive Primate Safety Act.* US Congress. Available at: https://www.congress.gov/bill/113th-congress/house-bill/2856.

FNRC (2014). *Firestone and Liberia: About Firestone Natural Rubber Company.* Firestone Natural Rubber Company (FNRC). Available at: http://www.firestonenaturalrubber.com/about_fnrc.htm. Accessed August 22, 2014.

FOE Europe (2013). *Factsheet: Sime Darby and Land Grabs in Liberia, June, 2013.* Brussels, Belgium: Friends of the Earth (FOE) Europe. Available at: http://www.foeeurope.org/sites/default/files/news/foee_simedarby_factsheet_010213.pdf.

FOE Europe (2014). *Continuing to Exploit and Deforest: Wilmar's Ongoing Abuses, May, 2014.* Brussels, Belgium: Friends of the Earth (FOE) Europe. Available at: http://www.foeeurope.org/sites/default/files/publications/foee-wilmar-factsheet-220514.pdf.

FOE International (2013). *Land Grabbing for Palm Oil in Uganda, May, 2013.* Amsterdam, the Netherlands: Friends of the Earth (FOE) International. Available at: http://foeeurope.org/sites/default/files/press_releases/land_grabbing_for_palm_oil_in_uganda_0.pdf.

Forest Trust (2013). *Independent Assessment of Free Prior and Informed Consent Process: Golden Veroleum Liberia Inc., February, 2013*. Santa Fe, NM: Forest Trust. Available at: http://www.forestpeoples.org/sites/fpp/files/news/2012/10/TFT_GVL_Liberia_FPIC_Report_Final_Eng_low%20res.pdf.

Forman, R.T.T. (2006). Good and bad places for roads: effects of varying road and natural patterns on habitat loss, degradation, and fragmentation. In *Proceedings of the 2005 International Conference on Ecology and Transportation (CET)*, ed. C.L. Irwin, P. Garrett and K.P. McDermott. Raleigh, NC: North Carolina State University, pp. 164–74.

Formenty, P., Karesh, W., Froment, J.M. and Wallis, J. (2003). Infectious diseases in West Africa: a common threat to chimpanzees and humans. In *West African Chimpanzees Status Survey and Conservation Action Plan*, ed. R. Kormos, C. Boesch, M.I. Bakarr and T.M. Butynski. Gland, Switzerland and Cambridge, UK: International Union for Conservation of Nature Species Survival Commission (IUCN SSC) Primate Specialist Group, pp. 169–74.

Foster, W.A., Snaddon, J.L., Turner, E.C., *et al.* (2011). Establishing the evidence base for maintaining biodiversity and ecosystem function in the oil palm landscapes of South East Asia. *Philosophical Transactions of the Royal Society of London B: Biological Sciences*, **366**, 3277–91.

Fox, J. and Vogler, J.B. (2005). Land-use and land-cover change in montane mainland Southeast Asia. *Environmental Management*, **36**, 394–403.

Fox, J., Vogler, J.B., Sen, O.L., Giambelluca, T.W. and Ziegler, A.D. (2012). Simulating land-cover change in Montane mainland southeast Asia. *Environmental Management*, **49**, 968–79.

FPP (2012a). *Civil Society Raises Serious Concerns about Cameroon's Draft Revised Forest Code, December 10, 2012*. Moreton-in-Marsh, UK: Forest Peoples Programme (FPP). Available at: http://www.forestpeoples.org/topics/legal-human-rights/news/2012/12/civil-society-raises-serious-concerns-about-cameroon-s-draft.

FPP (2012b). *Human Rights-Based Analysis of the Agricultural Concession Agreements between Sime Darby and Golden Veroleum and the Government of Liberia*. Moreton-in-Marsh, UK: Forest Peoples Programme (FPP).

FPP (2014a). *Joint NGO Letter to UN Special Rapporteurs Calling for an Immediate Investigation into the Harassment of Local Organizations in Cameroon Protesting Against Herakles Farms, February 3, 2014*. Moreton-in-Marsh, UK: Forest Peoples Programme (FFP). Available at: http://www.forestpeoples.org/topics/palm-oil-rspo/publication/2014/joint-ngo-letter-un-special-rapporteurs-calling-immediate-inve.

FPP (2014b). *Liberia: UK's Equatorial Palm Oil Threatening to Seize Public Land Defying International Law, Government Orders and Human Rights*. Moreton-in-Marsh, UK: Forest Peoples Programme (FPP). Available at: http://www.globalresearch.ca/liberia-uks-equatorial-palm-oil-threatening-to-seize-public-land-defying-international-law-government-orders-and-human-rights/5388508.

FPP (2015). *Hollow Promises. An FPIC Assessment of Golden Veroleum and Golden Agri Resources Palm Oil Project in Southeastern Liberia*. Moreton-in-Marsh, UK: Forest Peoples Programme (FPP). Available at: http://www.forestpeoples.org/sites/fpp/files/news/2015/04/Golden%20Veroleum%20FINAL_1.pdf.

Francis, S. (2014). *Emaciated, Moaning and Scarred: Orangutan Rescued After Spending Two Years Tied Up*. Express.co.uk. Available at: http://www.express.co.uk/news/uk/507366/Orphaned-orangutan-rescued-after-spending-two-years-tied-up.

Freeman, H.D. and Ross, S.R. (2014). The impact of atypical early histories on pet or performer chimpanzees. *PeerJ*, **2**, e579.

Friends of Animals (2014). *Say NO to Captive Primate Safety Act*. Darien, CT: Friends of Animals. Available at: http://friendsofanimals.org/news/2014/august/say-no-captive-primate-safety-act.

Fruth, B., Benishay, J.M., Bila-Isia, I., *et al.* (2008). *Pan paniscus*. In *The IUCN Red List of Threatened Species, Version 2014.3*. Gland, Switzerland: International Union for Conservation of Nature (IUCN). Available at: http://www.iucnredlist.org/details/15932/0. Accessed February 24, 2015.

Fuglie, K. and Rada, N. (2013). *Resources, Policies, and Agricultural Productivity in Sub-Saharan Africa. Economic Research Report 145*. Washington DC: United States Department of Agriculture (USDA)/Economic Research Report (ERS).

Funwi-Gabga, N., Kuehl, H., Maisels, F., *et al.* (2014). The status of apes across Africa and Asia. In *State of the Apes: Extractive Industries and Ape Conservation*, ed. Arcus Foundation. Cambridge, UK: Cambridge University Press, pp. 252–77.

Fuo, O.N. and Semie, S.M. (2011). Cameroon's environmental framework law and the balancing of interests in socio-economic development. In *The Balancing of Interests in Environmental Law in Africa*, ed. M. Faure and W. du Plessis. Cape Town, South Africa: Pretoria University Law Press/ABC Press, pp. 75–94.

Furuichi, T. (2011). Female contributions to the peaceful nature of bonobo society. *Evolutionary Anthropology*, **20**, 131–42.

Furuichi, T., Idani, G., Ihobe, H., *et al.* (2012). Long-term studies on wild bonobos at Wamba, Luo Scientific Reserve, D. R. Congo: towards the understanding of female life history in a male-philopatric species. In *Long-Term Field Studies of Primates*, ed. P.M. Kappeler and D.P. Watts. Berlin/Heidelberg, Germany: Springer-Verlag, pp. 413–33.

Future Challenges (2011). *Land Grabs and Deforestation in South Sudan*. Berlin, Germany: Future Challenges. Available at: https://futurechallenges.org/local/land-grabs-and-deforestation-in-south-sudan/. Accessed October, 2014.

Gabon (1961). *Loi Réglementant l'Expropriation pour Cause d'Utilité Publique et Instituant des Servitudes pour l'Exécution des Travaux Publics (as amended in 1965 and 1976) 1961*. Republic of Gabon.

Gabon (1967). *Décret Réglementant l'Octroi des Concessions et Locations Domaniales 1967*. No. 77/PR/MF.DE. Republic of Gabon.

Gabon (1987a). *Décret Réglementant les Droits d'Usage Coutumiers 1987*. No. 192/PR/MEFCR. Republic of Gabon.

Gabon (1987b). *Décret Relatif aux Permis et Licences de Chasse 1987*. No. 188/PR/MEFCR. Republic of Gabon.

Gabon (1991). *Constitution 1991, last amended in 2000*. Republic of Gabon.

Gabon (1993). *Loi Relative à la Protection de l'Environnement 1993*. No. 16/93. Republic of Gabon.

Gabon (1994a). *Décret Complétant le Décret No. 189/PR/MEFCR du 4 Mars 1987, Relatif à la Protection de la Faune 1994*. No. 678/PR/MEFE. Republic of Gabon.

Gabon (1994b). *Décret Relatif à l'Agrément Spécial de Commerce des Produits de la Chasse 1994*. No. 677/PR/MEFE. Republic of Gabon.

Gabon (2001). *Loi Portant Code Forestier en République Gabonaise 2001*. No. 016–01. Republic of Gabon.

Gabon (2004). *Arrêté Portant Réglementation des Activités Forestières, Minières, Agricoles, Aquacoles, Cynégétiques et Touristiques à l'Intérieur d'une Zone Tampon 2004*. No. 000118/PR/MEFEPEPN. Republic of Gabon.

Gabon (2005). *Décret Réglementant les Etudes d'Impact sur l'Environnement 2005*. No. 000539/ PR/MEFEPEPN. Republic of Gabon.

Gabon (2007). *Loi Relative aux Parcs Nationaux 2007*. No. 003/2007. Republic of Gabon.

Gabon (2008). *Loi Portant Code Agricole en République Gabonaise 2008*. No. 022–2008. Republic of Gabon.

GAIN (n.d.). *Great Ape Information Network*. Great Ape Information Network (GAIN). Available at: http://www.shigen.nig.ac.jp/gain/index.jsp. Accessed July 2, 2014.

Ganas, J., Robbins, M.M., Nkurungi, J.B., Kaplin, B.A. and McNeilage, A. (2004). Dietary variability of mountain gorillas in Bwindi Impenetrable National Park, Uganda. *International Journal of Primatology*, **25**, 1043–72.

Gaveau, D.L.A., Curran, L.M., Paoli, G.D., *et al.* (2012). Examining protected area effectiveness in Sumatra: importance of regulations governing unprotected lands. *Conservation Letters*, **5**, 142–8.

Gaveau, D.L.A., Kshatriya, M., Sheil, D., *et al.* (2013). Reconciling forest conservation and logging in Indonesian Borneo. *PLoS One*, **8**, e69887.

Gaveau, D.L.A., Sloan, S., Molidena, E., *et al.* (2014). Four decades of forest persistence, clearance and logging on Borneo. *PLoS One*, **9**, e101654.

Geissmann, T. (1991). Reassessment of the age of sexual maturity in gibbons (*Hylobates* spp.). *American Journal of Primatology*, **23**, 11–22.

Geissmann, T., Grindley, M.E., Ngwe, L., *et al.* (2013). *The Conservation Status of Hoolock Gibbons in Myanmar*. Zurich, Switzerland: Gibbon Conservation Alliance.

Geissmann, T. and Nijman, V. (2006). Calling in wild silvery gibbons (*Hylobates moloch*) in Java (Indonesia): behavior, phylogeny, and conservation. *American Journal of Primatology*, **68**, 1–19.

Geist, H.J. (1999). Global assessment of deforestation related to tobacco farming. *Tobacco Control*, **8**, 18–28.

Georgiev, A.V., Lokasola, V., Emery Thompson, M., Lokasola, A. and Wrangham, R.W. (2013). Co-existing in the Congo: the impact of bonobo crop-raiding on subsistence farmers in Kokolopori. *American Journal of Primatology*, **75**, 41.

Gerasimchuk, I. (2013). *Biofuel Policies and Feedstock in the EU.* London, UK: Chatham House. Available at: http://www.chathamhouse.org/sites/files/chathamhouse/home/chatham/public_html/sites/default/files/Nov13Gerasimchuk.pdf.

Gerber, J.-F. (2008). *Résistances Contre deux Géants Industriels en Forêt Tropicale: Populations Locales versus Plantations Commerciales d'Hévéas et de Palmiers à Huile dans le Sud-Cameroun.* Montevideo, Uruguay: Mouvement Mondial pour les Forêts Tropicales. Available at: http://wrm.org.uy/wp-content/uploads/2013/02/Cameroun_fr.pdf.

Gerber, J.-F. (2011). Conflicts over industrial tree plantations in the South: who, how and why? *Global Environmental Change*, **21**, 165–76.

Gerber, J.-F., Veuthey, S. and Martínez-Alier, J. (2009). Linking political ecology with ecological economics in tree plantation conflicts in Cameroon and Ecuador. *Ecological Economics*, **68**, 2885–9.

Gerlach, L.W.C. (1881). Reis naar het meergebied van den Kapoeas in Borneo's Westerafdeeling. *Bijdragen tot de Taal-Land en Volkenkunde van Nederlandsch-Indië*, **5**, 285–322.

Germer, J. and Sauerborn, J. (2006). Estimation of the impact of oil palm plantation establishment on greenhouse gas balance. *Environment, Development and Sustainability*, **10**, 697–716.

GFAS (2013). *Who Can Apply.* Washington DC: Global Federation of Animal Sanctuaries (GFAS). Available at: http://www.sanctuaryfederation.org/gfas/for-sanctuaries/definitions/.

Ghai, R.R., Chapman, C.A., Omeja, P.A., Davies, T.J. and Goldberg, T.L. (2014). Nodule worm infection in humans and wild primates in Uganda: cryptic species in a newly identified region of human transmission. *PLoS Neglected Tropical Diseases*, **8**, e2641.

Ghobrial, L., Lankester, F., Kiyang, J.A., *et al.* (2010). Tracing the origins of rescued chimpanzees reveals widespread chimpanzee hunting in Cameroon. *BMC Ecology*, **10**, 2.

Ghosh, P. (2013). Anti-depressants help lab chimps. *BBC News*, Available at: http://www.bbc.co.uk/news/science-environment-21299657.

Gibbs, H.K., Ruesch, A.S., Achard, F., *et al.* (2010). Tropical forests were the primary sources of new agricultural land in the 1980s and 1990s. *Proceedings of the National Academy of Sciences USA*, **107**, 16732–7.

Gillespie, T.R. and Chapman, C.A. (2006). Prediction of parasite infection dynamics in primate metapopulations based on attributes of forest fragmentation. *Conservation Biology*, **20**, 441–8.

Gingold, B. (2011). *The World Bank Group, Palm Oil and Poverty.* Washington DC: World Resources Institute. Available at: http://www.wri.org/blog/2011/03/world-bank-group-palm-oil-and-poverty. Accessed September 5, 2014.

Ginoga, K., Cacho, O., Erwidodo, Lugina, M. and Djaenudin, D., ed. (2002). *Economic Performance of Common Agroforestry Systems in Southern Sumatra, Indonesia: Implications for Carbon Sequestration Services. Working Paper CC03, ACIAR Project ASEM 1999/093.* Armidale, New South Wales: University of New England.

Glendinning, L. (2008). Spanish parliament approves 'human rights' for apes. *The Guardian*, Available at: http://www.theguardian.com/world/2008/jun/26/humanrights.animalwelfare.

Global Roadmap (n.d.). *Global Roadmap.* Global Roadmap. Available at: http://www.global-roadmap.org. Accessed May, 2015.

Global Witness (2012). *Dealing with Disclosure: Improving Transparency in Decision-Making Over Large-Scale Land Acquisitions, Allocations and Investments. April, 2012.* London, UK: Global Witness. Available at http://www.globalwitness.org/library/dealing-disclosure.

GMG (n.d.). *Our Plantations and Processing Plants.* Singapore: GMG Global Ltd (GMG). Available at: http://www.gmg.sg/our_plantation.html. Accessed November, 2014.

Goldberg, T.L., Gillespie, T.R., Rwego, I.B., *et al.* (2007). Patterns of gastrointestinal bacterial exchange between chimpanzees and humans involved in research and tourism in western Uganda. *Biological Conservation*, **135**, 511–7.

Golden Agri-Resources (2011). *Golden Agri-Resources Initiates Industry Engagement for Forest Conservation, February 9, 2011.* Singapore: Golden Agri-Resources. Available at: http://www.goldenagri.com.sg/110209%20Golden%20Agri-Resources%20Initiates%20Industry%20Engagement%20for%20Forest%20Conservation.pdf.

Gonedelé Bi, S., Koné, I., Bitty, A.E., *et al.* (2012). Distribution and conservation status of catarrhine primates in Côte d'Ivoire (West Africa). *Folia Primatologica*, **83**, 11–23.

Goodall, J. (1986). *The Chimpanzees of Gombe: Patterns of Behavior.* Cambridge, MA: Belknap Press.

Goossens, B., Chikhi, L., Ancrenaz, M., *et al.* (2006). Genetic signature of anthropogenic population collapse in orang-utans. *PLoS Biol*, **4**, e25.

Goossens, B., Chikhi, L., Jalil, M.F., *et al.* (2005a). Patterns of genetic diversity and migration in increasingly fragmented and declining orang-utan (*Pongo pygmaeus*) populations from Sabah, Malaysia. *Molecular Ecology*, **14**, 441–56.

Goossens, B., Kapar, M.D., Kahar, S. and Ancrenaz, M. (2011). First sighting of Bornean orang-utan twins in the wild. *Asian Primates Journal*, **2**, 10–2.

Goossens, B., Setchell, J.M., Tchidongo, E., *et al.* (2005b). Survival, interactions with conspecifics and reproduction in 37 chimpanzees released into the wild. *Biological Conservation*, **123**, 461–75.

Gore, M.L. and Kahler, J.S. (2012). Gendered risk perceptions associated with human–wildlife conflict: implications for participatory conservation. *PLoS One*, **7**, e32901.

Gourichon, H. (2013). *Analysis of Incentives and Disincentives for Palm Oil in Nigeria. Technical Notes Series.* Rome, Italy: Food and Agriculture Organization of the United Nations (FAO).

GRASP (2014a). *GRASP Warns Illegal Ape Trade Remains Active.* Nairobi, Kenya: Great Apes Survival Partnership (GRASP). Available at: http://www.un-grasp.org/index.php?option=com_content&view=article&id=146:grasp-warns-illegal-ape-trade-remains-active&catid=7:press-releases&Itemid=55.

GRASP (2014b). *UN Peacekeepers Airlift Chimpanzees from Supermarket to Sanctuary.* Nairobi, Kenya: Great Apes Survival Partnership (GRASP). Available at: http://www.un-grasp.org/u-n-peacekeepers-airlift-chimpanzees-from-supermarket-sanctuary.

GRASP (n.d.). *GRASP Website.* Nairobi, Kenya: Great Apes Survival Partnership (GRASP). Available at: http://www.un-grasp.org. Accessed June, 2015.

Green Advocates and FPP (2012). *Customary Land Tenure in Grand Cape Mount and Community Recommendations for Reform of Liberia's Land Policy and Law.* Moreton-in-Marsh, UK: Green Advocates and Forest Peoples Programme (FPP).

Greengrass, E. (2011). *Exploring the Dynamics of Bushmeat Hunting and Trade in Sapo National Park.* Cambridge, UK: Fauna & Flora International.

Greenomics Indonesia (2015). *The Only Place on Earth is Being Bulldozed by Supplier of Two IPOP Signatories, May 6, 2015.* Greenomics Indonesia. Available at: http://www.greenomics.org/docs/IPOP-Implementation-Report-01_Greenomics.pdf.

Greenpeace (2013). *Palm Oil Giant Wilmar Caught in Forest Scandal.* Amsterdam, the Netherlands: Greenpeace. Available at: http://www.greenpeace.org/international/en/press/releases/Palm-oil-giant-Wilmar-caught-in-forest-scandal---Greenpeace/.

Greenpeace (2014). *P&G's Dirty Secret.* Amsterdam, the Netherlands: Greenpeace International.

Greenpeace (2015). *High Carbon Stock Approach Steering Group Launches Toolkit for Deforestation-Free Plantations.* Amsterdam, the Netherlands: Greenpeace International. Available at: http://www.greenpeace.org/seasia/Press-Centre/Press-Releases/High-Carbon-Stock-Toolkit/.

Greenpeace and Oakland Institute (2013). *Herakles Exposed: The Truth Behind Herakles Farms False Promises in Cameroon.* Oakland, CA: Greenpeace and Oakland Institute. Available at: http://www.oaklandinstitute.org/sites/oaklandinstitute.org/files/OI_Report_Herakles_Exposed.pdf.

Greenpeace International (2012). *Palm Oil's New Frontier: How Industrial Expansion Threatens Africa's Rainforests, September, 2012.* Amsterdam, the Netherlands: Greenpeace International. Available at: http://www.greenpeace.org/international/Global/international/publications/forests/2012/Congo/PalmOilsNewFrontier.pdf.

Greenpeace International (2013). *Identifying High Carbon Stock Forests for Protection. Towards Defining Natural Forests and Degraded Lands (Formerly Forest) in the Tropics, March, 2013.* Amsterdam, the Netherlands: Greenpeace International. Available at: http://www.goldenagri.com.sg/pdfs/misc/HCS%20Briefer%20FINAL%20with%20graphic%20Eng%20REVISED.pdf.

Greenpeace International (2014a). *Golden Agri Resources: A Progress Report. The Road to Good Oil: GAR's Progress Towards Responsible Palm Oil.* Amsterdam, the Netherlands: Greenpeace International. Available at: http://www.greenpeace.org/international/en/publications/Campaign-reports/Forests-Reports/GAR-Progress-Report.

Greenpeace International (2014b). *Licence to Launder. How Herakles' Farms Illegal Timber Trade Threatens Cameroon's Forests and VPA, May, 2014.* Amsterdam, the Netherlands: Greenpeace International. Available at: http://www.greenpeace.org/africa/Global/africa/publications/LicenceToLaunderFinal.pdf.

Greenpeace USA (2013). *Herakles Farms in Cameroon: A Showcase in Bad Palm Oil Production, February, 2013.* Washington DC: Greenpeace USA. Available at: http://www.greenpeace.org/usa/global/usa/planet3/pdfs/forests/heraklescrimefile.pdf.

Gregory, R., Long, G., Colligan, M., Geiger, J.G. and Laser, M. (2012). When experts disagree (and better science won't help much): using structured deliberations to support endangered species recovery planning. *Journal of Environmental Management*, **105**, 30–43.

Gregory, S.D., Ancrenaz, M., Brook, B.W., *et al.* (2014). Forecasts of habitat suitability improve habitat corridor efficacy in rapidly changing environments. *Diversity and Distributions*, **20**, 1044–57.

GRID-Arendal (2005). *Deforestation in West Africa: Case Cote-d'Ivoire. Vital Climate Graphics Africa.* Arendal, Norway: GRID-Arendal. Available at: http://www.grida.no/publications/vg/africa.

Guschanski, K., Vigilant, L., McNeilage, A., *et al.* (2009). Counting elusive animals: comparing field and genetic census of the entire mountain gorilla population of Bwindi Impenetrable National Park, Uganda. *Biological Conservation*, **142**, 290–300.

Gut Aiderbichl (2014). *Former Lab-Chimps.* Salzburg , Austria: Gut Aiderbichl. Available at: http://www.gut-aiderbichl.com/page.headline.php?cid=2580&redir=.

Gutiérrez-Vélez, V.H., DeFries, R., Pinedo-V'asquez, M., *et al.* (2011). High-yield oil palm expansion spares land at the expense of forests in the Peruvian Amazon. *Environmental Research Letters*, **6**, 044029.

Gwinner, V. (2013). From words to impacts: the research behind Cameroon's sustainable palm oil policy. *Reuters*, June 19, 2013. Available at: http://www.trust.org/item/20130619031630-gpfze/?source%20=%20hppartner.

Hadinaryanto, S.E. (2014). *Special Report: Palm Oil, Politics and Land Use in Indonesian Borneo.* Menlo Park, CA: Mongabay.com. Available at: http://news.mongabay.com/2014/0424-Hadinaryanto-palmoil-kalimantan.html#RhoLq1SvUzCAqpWx.99.

Halliday, J. (2010). *Dutch Palm Oil to be RSPO only by 2015.* Montpellier, France: Food Navigator. Available at: http://www.foodnavigator.com/Market-Trends/Dutch-palm-oil-to-be-RSPO-only-by-2015.

Hansen, M.C., Potapov, P.V., Moore, R., *et al.* (2013). High-resolution global maps of 21st-century forest cover change. *Science*, **342**, 850–3.

Harcourt, A.H. and Greenberg, J. (2001). Do gorilla females join males to avoid infanticide? A quantitative model. *Animal Behaviour*, **62**, 905–15.

Harcourt, A.H. and Parks, S.A. (2003). Threatened primates experience high human densities: adding an index of threat to the IUCN Red List criteria. *Biological Conservation*, **109**, 137–49.

Harcourt, A.H. and Stewart, K.J. (2007). *Gorilla Society: Conflict, Compromise, and Cooperation Between the Sexes.* Chicago, IL: University of Chicago Press.

Hardus, M.E., Lameira, A.R., Menken, S.B.J. and Wich, S.A. (2012). Effects of logging on orangutan behavior. *Biological Conservation*, **146**, 177–87.

Hashimoto, C., Tashiro, Y., Kimura, D., *et al.* (1998). Habitat use and ranging of wild bonobos (*Pan paniscus*) at Wamba. *International Journal of Primatology*, **19**, 1045–60.

Hawkins, D. (2012). *Opinion: Appetite for Rubber Opens up New Frontier.* Kings Pyon, UK: Agrimoney.com. Available at: http://www.agrimoney.com/feature/opinion-appetite-for-rubber-opens-up-new-frontier--147.html.

Hawkins, D. and Chen, Y. (2011). A growth story for Africa. *World Agriculture Report*, September 5.

Haynes, A. (2012). Thailand theme park continues to host orangutan kickboxing matches. *Earth Island Journal.* Available at: http://www.earthisland.org/journal/index.php/elist/eListRead/thailand_theme_park_continues_to_host_orangutan_kickboxing_matches.

Hays, M. and Hurowitz, G. (2013). *Investor survey: draft initial analysis and key findings.* Unpublished report prepared for the Union of Concerned Scientists.

Hayward, M.W. and Kerley, G.I.H. (2009). Fencing for conservation: restriction of evolutionary potential or a riposte to threatening processes? *Biological Conservation*, **142**, 1–13.

HCSS (n.d.). *High Carbon Stock Study (HCSS). About the HCS Study.* CarbonStockStudy.com. Available at: http://www.carbonstockstudy.com/HCS-Study/About-HCS-Study. Accessed May 15, 2015.

HCV Resource Network (2013). *Common Guidance for the High Conservation Values.* Oxford, UK: High Conservation Value (HCV) Resource Network. Available at: https://www.hcvnetwork.org/resources/cg-identification-sep-2014-english.

HCV Resource Network (n.d.). *About the Network.* Oxford, UK: High Conservation Value (HCV) Resource Network. Available at: https://www.hcvnetwork.org/resource-network. Accessed May 15, 2015.

Head, J., Boesch, C., Makaga, L. and Robbins, M.M. (2011). Sympatric chimpanzees and gorillas in Loango National Park, Gabon: dietary composition, seasonal changes and inter-site comparisons. *International Journal of Primatology*, **32**, 755–75.

Head, J.S., Boesch, C., Robbins, M.M., *et al.* (2013). Effective sociodemographic population assessment of elusive species in ecology and conservation management. *Ecology and Evolution*, **3**, 2903–16.

Head, J.S., Robbins, M.M., Mundry, R., Makaga, L. and Boesch, C. (2012). Remote video-camera traps measure habitat use and competitive exclusion among sympatric chimpanzee, gorilla and elephant in Loango National Park, Gabon. *Journal of Tropical Ecology*, **28**, 571–83.

Hickey, J.R., Carroll, J.P. and Nibbelink, N.P. (2012). Applying landscape metrics to characterize potential habitat of bonobos (*Pan paniscus*) in the Maringa-Lopori-Wamba landscape, Democratic Republic of Congo. *International Journal of Primatology*, **33**, 381–400.

Hickey, J., Nackoney, J., Nibbelink, N., *et al.* (2013). Human proximity and habitat fragmentation are key drivers of the rangewide bonobo distribution. *Biodiversity and Conservation*, **22**, 3085–104.

Hicks, C., Voladeth, S., Shi, W., *et al.* (2009). *Rubber Investments and Market Linkages in Lao PDR: Approaches for Sustainability.* Bangkok, Thailand: Sustainable Mekong Research Network. Available at: https://cmsdata.iucn.org/downloads/lao_rubber_investments___final_en___20_mar_09.pdf.

Hicks, T.C., Roessingh, P. and Menken, S.B.J. (2013). Impact of humans on long-distance communication behaviour of eastern chimpanzees (*Pan troglodytes schweinfurthii*) in the northern Democratic Republic of the Congo. *Folia Primatologica*, **84**, 135–56.

Hill, C.M. and Wallace, G.E. (2012). Crop protection and conflict mitigation: reducing the costs of living alongside non-human primates. *Biodiversity and Conservation*, **21**, 2569–87.

Hill, C.M. and Webber, A.D. (2010). Perceptions of nonhuman primates in human-wildlife conflict scenarios. *American Journal of Primatology*, **72**, 919–24.

Hilty, J.A., Brooks, C., Heaton, E. and Merenlender, A.M. (2006). Forecasting the effect of land-use change on native and non-native mammalian predator distributions. *Biodiversity and Conservation*, **15**, 2853–71.

Hockings, K.J. (2007). *Human–chimpanzee coexistence at Bossou, the Republic of Guinea: a chimpanzee perspective.* PhD thesis. Stirling, UK: University of Stirling.

Hockings, K.J., Anderson, J.R. and Matsuzawa, T. (2006). Road crossing in chimpanzees: a risky business. *Current Biology*, **16**, 668–70.

Hockings, K.J., Anderson, J.R. and Matsuzawa, T. (2009). Use of wild and cultivated foods by chimpanzees at Bossou, Republic of Guinea: feeding dynamics in a human-influenced environment. *American Journal of Primatology*, **71**, 636–46.

Hockings, K.J., Anderson, J.R. and Matsuzawa, T. (2012). Socioecological adaptations by chimpanzees, *Pan troglodytes verus*, inhabiting an anthropogenically impacted habitat. *Animal Behaviour*, **83**, 801–10.

Hockings, K.J. and Humle, T. (2009). *Best Practice Guidelines for the Prevention and Mitigation of Conflict Between Humans and Great Apes.* Gland, Switzerland: International Union for Conservation of Nature Species Survival Commission (IUCN SSC) Primate Specialist Group. Available at: http://www.primate-sg.org/best_practice_conflict/.

Hockings, K.J. and Matsuzawa, T. (2014). *Cocoa-Spread by Wild Chimpanzees: Do Chimpanzees Cultivate their own Gardens?* Hanoi, Vietnam: IPS XXV Congress.

Hockings, K.J. and McLennan, M.R. (2012). From forest to farm: systematic review of cultivar feeding by chimpanzees – management implications for wildlife in anthropogenic landscapes. *PLoS One*, **7**, e33391.

Hockings, K.J. and McLennan, M. (2013). Cultivar feeding by chimpanzees: from community variation to conflict mitigation. *Folia Primatologica*, **84**, 287–8.

Hockings, K.J., McLennan, M.R. and Hill, C.M. (2014). Fear beyond predators. *Science*, **344**, 981.

Hockings, K.J. and Sousa, C. (2012). Differential utilization of cashew – a low-conflict crop – by sympatric humans and chimpanzees. *Oryx*, **46**, 375–81.

Hoffman, T.S. and O'Riain, M.J. (2012). Landscape requirements of a primate population in a human-dominated environment. *Frontiers in Zoology*, **9**, 1.

Hohmann, G., Gerloff, U., Tautz, D. and Fruth, B. (1999). Social bonds and genetic ties: kinship, association and affiliation in a community of bonobos (*Pan paniscus*). *Behaviour*, **136**, 1219–35.

Hooijer, A., Silvius, M., Wösten, H. and Page, S. (2006). *PEAT-CO2, Assessment of CO2 Emissions from Drained Peatlands in SE Asia.Report Q3943 (2006).* Delft, the Netherlands: Delft Hydraulics.

Hourticq, J. and Megevand, C. (2013). *Deforestation Trends in the Congo Basin: Reconciling Economic Growth and Forest Protection. Working Paper 1: Agriculture.* Washington DC: World Bank Publications.

Hoyle, D. and Levang, P. (2012). *Oil Palm Development in Cameroon.* World Wide Fund for Nature (WWF) in partnership with IRD and Center for International Forestry Research (CIFOR).

Humle, T. (2003). *Culture and variation in wild chimpanzee behaviour: a study of three communities in West Africa.* PhD thesis. Stirling, UK: University of Stirling.

Humle, T. (2011a). The 2003 epidemic of a flu-like respiratory disease at Bossou. In *Chimpanzees of Bossou and Nimba*, ed. T. Matsuzawa, T. Humle and Y. Sugiyama. Tokyo, Japan: Springer-Verlag, pp. 325–33.

Humle, T. (2011b). Location and ecology. In *Chimpanzees of Bossou and Nimba*, ed. T. Matsuzawa, T. Humle and Y. Sugiyama. Tokyo, Japan: Springer-Verlag, pp. 371–80.

Humle, T., Colin, C., Laurans, M. and Raballand, E. (2011). Group release of sanctuary chimpanzees (*Pan troglodytes*) in the Haut Niger National Park, Guinea, West Africa: ranging patterns and lessons so far. *International Journal of Primatology*, **32**, 456–73.

Humle, T. and Matsuzawa, T. (2004). Oil palm use by adjacent communities of chimpanzees at Bossou and Nimba Mountains, West Africa. *International Journal of Primatology*, **25**, 551–81.

Husson, S.J., Wich, S.A., Marshall, A.J., *et al.* (2009). Orangutan distribution, density, abundance and impacts of disturbance. In *Orangutans: Geographic Variation in Behavioral Ecology and Conservation*, ed. S.A. Wich, S. Utami Atmoko, T.M. Setia and C.P. van Schaik. Oxford, UK: Oxford University Press, pp. 77–96.

IAWG (2011). *Options for Promoting Responsible Investment in Agriculture: Report to the High-Level Development Working Group.* Inter-Agency Working Group on the Food Security Pillar of the G20 Multi-Year Action Plan on Development (IAWG). Geneva, Switzerland: United Nations Conference on Trade and Development (UNCTAD). Available at: http://unctad.org/sections/dite_dir/docs/diae_dir_2011–06_G20_en.pdf.

ICCT (2014). *EU Energy Council Draft Directive on Indirect Land Use Change.* Washington DC: International Council on Clean Transportation (ICCT). Available at: http://www.theicct.org/sites/default/files/publications/ICCT update_EU_ILUC_july2014.pdf.

ICEM (2003). *Regional Report on Protected Areas and Development. Review of Protected Areas and Development in the Four Countries of the Lower Mekong River Region.* Indooroopilly, Australia: International Centre for Environmental Management (ICEM). Available at: https://portals.iucn.org/library/efiles/documents/2003–106–5.pdf.

Idani, G. (1990). Relations between unit-groups of bonobos at Wamba, Zaire: encounters and temporary fusions. *African Study Monographs*, **11**, 153–86.

IEA (2009). *The Impact of the Financial and Economic Crisis on Global Energy Investment.* Paris, France: International Energy Agency (IEA). Available at: https://www.iea.org/publications/freepublications/publication/the-impact-of-the-financial-and-economic-crisis-on-global-energy-investment.html.

IFAD (2011). *The Republic of Liberia Smallholder Tree Crop Revitalisation Support Project (STCRSP) Project Design Report: Main Report and Annexes.* The International Fund for Agricultural Development (IFAD) West Africa Division, Project Management Department.

IFC (2008). *Review of the Oil Palm Sector in Liberia.* Washington DC: International Financial Corporation (IFC), World Bank.

IIASA (2002). *IIASA.* Laxenburg, Austria: International Institute for Applied Systems Analysis (IIASA). Available at: http://www.iiasa.ac.at/.

IITA (2008). *Tree Crops to Ensure Income Generation and Sustainable Livelihoods in Liberia.* Ibadan, Nigeria: International Institute of Tropical Agriculture (IITA).

Ikbal, W., Prasetyo, L.B. and Risdiyanto, I. (2006). *Stand-alone GIS application for habitat suitability: case study Javan gibbon, Gunung Salak, West Java.* Presented at: Seminar on the Application of GIS & RS for Conservation, Bogor, Indonesia.

IMF (2008). *Central African Republic: Statistical Appendix International Monetary Fund.* Washington DC: International Monetary Fund (IMF).

IMF (2011). *Sierra Leone: Poverty Reduction Strategy Paper – Progress Report, 2008–2010. Country Report No. 11/95.* Washington DC: International Monetary Fund (IMF).

IMF (2014). *Liberia: Third Review Under the Extended Credit Facility Arrangement and Request for Waiver of Non-observance of Performance Criterion and Modification of Performance Criteria – Staff Report.* Washington DC: International Monetary Fund (IMF). Available at: http://www.imf.org/external/pubs/cat/longres.aspx?sk=41740.0. Accessed September 14, 2014.

IM-FLEG (2013). *Rapport No. 016/REM/CAGDF/FM. Independent Monitoring of Forest Law Enforcement and Governance (IM-FLEG).* Brazzaville, DRC: REM/CAGDF/Forests Monitor (FM). Available at: http://www.rem.org.uk/documents/OI_II_Rapport_016.pdf.

IM-FLEG (2014). *Rapport No. 01/CAGDF. Independent Monitoring of Forest Law Enforcement and Governance (IM-FLEG).* Brazzaville, DRC: REM/CAGDF/Forests Monitor (FM). Available at: http://www.rem.org.uk/documents/CAGDF_rapport1_Sangha.pdf.

Indonesia (1945). *Constitution 1945.* Republic of Indonesia.

Indonesia (1960). *National Agrarian Law 1960.* No. 5. Republic of Indonesia.

Indonesia (1990). *National Law 1990 on the Conservation of Living Resources and their Ecosystems.* No. 5. Republic of Indonesia.

Indonesia (1999). *National Law Forestry.* No. 41/1999. Republic of Indonesia.

Indonesia (2006a). *Decree of Minister of Forestry on Guidelines on the Borrowing of Forest Areas for Exploitation Purposes.* No. P.14/Menhut-II/2006. Republic of Indonesia.

Indonesia (2006b). *National Law on Aceh Governance.* No. 11/2006. Republic of Indonesia.

Indonesia (2007). *National Law on Spatial Planning.* No. 26/2007. Republic of Indonesia.

Indonesia (2008). *Government Regulation on the National Spatial Plan.* No. 26/2008. Republic of Indonesia.

Indonesia (2009). *National Law on Environmental Protection and Management.* No. 32/2009. Republic of Indonesia.

Indonesia (2010). *Regulation on Procedure for Changing Function of the Forest Zone 2010.* No. P.34/Menhut-II/2010. Republic of Indonesia.

Indrawan, M., Supriyadi, D., Supriatna, J. and Andayani, N. (1996). Javan gibbon surviving at a mined forest in Gunung Pongkor, Mount Halimun National Park, West Java: considerable tolerance to disturbances? *Asian Primates Journal,* **6,** 11–3.

INPE (2013). *Estimativa do Prodes 2013. Presentation.* San Jose dos Campos, Brazil: Instituto Nacional de Pesquisas Espaciais (INPE). Available at: http://www.obt.inpe.br/prodes/Prodes_Taxa2013.pdf.

International Development Association (2012). *Liberia: Smallholder Tree Crop Revitalisation Support Project – Project Appraisal.* Washington DC: World Bank. Available at: http://www-wds.worldbank.org/external/default/WDSContentServer/WDSP/IB/2012/05/18/000333037_20120518003436/Rendered/PDF/685240PAD0IDA00se00Only090Box369244B.pdf.

IRS (n.d.). *Yearly Average Currency Exchange Rates: Translating Foreign Currency into US Dollars.* Internal Revenue Service (IRS). Available at: http://www.irs.gov/Individuals/International-Taxpayers/Yearly-Average-Currency-Exchange-Rates. Accessed June, 2015.

ISIS (n.d.). *International Species Information System.* International Species Information System (ISIS). Available at: http://www2.isis.org/AboutISIS/Pages/About-ISIS.aspx. Accessed October, 2014.

Iskandar, E. (2007). *Habitat dan Populasi Owa Jawa (*Hylobates moloch *Audebert, 1797) di Taman Nasional Gunung Halimun-Salak Jawa Barat.* PhD thesis. Bogor, Indonesia: Institut Pertanian Bogor.

Islam, K. and Sato, N. (2012). Deforestation, land conversion and illegal logging in Bangladesh: the case of the Sal (*Shorea robusta*) forests. *iForest: Biogeosciences and Forestry*, **5**, 171–8.

ITC (2012). *Palm Products: Global Markets and Developments.* Geneva, Switzerland: International Trade Centre (ITC). Available at: http://www.intracen.org/uploadedFiles/intracenorg/Content/About_ITC/Where_are_ we_working/Multi-country_programmes/Pact_II/Palm%20Oil%20Report%202012.pdf.

ITTO (2011). *Status of Tropical Forest Management 2011. ITTO Technical Series No. 38.* Yokohama, Japan: International Tropical Timber Organization (ITTO). Available at: http://www.itto.int/en/sfm/.

IUCN (2012). *The IUCN Red List Categories and Criteria. Version 3.1,* 2nd edn. Gland, Switzerland, and Cambridge, UK: International Union for Conservation of Nature (IUCN).

IUCN (2014a). *The IUCN Red List of Threatened Species. Version 2014.2.* Gland, Switzerland: International Union for Conservation of Nature (IUCN). Available at: http://www.iucnredlist.org. Accessed June 10, 2014.

IUCN (2014b). *The IUCN Red List of Threatened Species. Version 2014.3.* Gland, Switzerland: International Union for Conservation of Nature (IUCN). Available at: http://www.iucnredlist.org.

IUCN (2014c). *Regional Action Plan for the Conservation of Western Lowland Gorillas and Central Chimpanzees 2015–2025.* Gland, Switzerland: International Union for Conservation of Nature Species Survival Commission (IUCN SSC) Primate Specialist Group.

IUCN (n.d.). *The IUCN Red List of Threatened Species. Spatial Data.* Gland, Switzerland: International Union for Conservation of Nature (IUCN). Available at: http://www.iucnredlist.org/. Accessed March 15, 2015.

IUCN and ICCN (2012). *Bonobo (*Pan paniscus*): Conservation Strategy 2012–2022.* Gland, Switzerland: International Union for Conservation of Nature Species Survival Commission (IUCN SSC) Primate Specialist Group and Institut Congolais pour la Conservation de la Nature (ICCN).

IUCN and UNEP (2014). *The World Database on Protected Areas (WDPA).* Cambridge, UK: United Nations Environment Programme (UNEP) World Conservation Monitoring Centre (WCMC). Available at: http://www. protectedplanet.net. Accessed August, 2014.

IUCN SSC (n.d.). *APES Database.* Gland, Switzerland: International Union for Conservation of Nature Species Survival Commission (IUCN SSC). Available at: http://apesportal.eva.mpg.de/database/archiveTable. Accessed June, 2015.

Jacquemard, J.-C. (2011). *Le Palmier à Huile. Agricultures Tropicales en Poche.* Versailles, France: Editions Quae et Presses agronomiques de Gembloux.

Jacquemard, J.-C., Suryana, E., Cochard, B., *et al.* (2010). *Intensification of oil palm (*Elaeis guineensis*) plantation efficiency through planting material: new results and developments.* Presented at: IOPC Transforming Oil Palm Industry, June 1–3, 2010, Jogja Expo Center, Yogyakarta, Indonesia.

Jacquemart, K. (2014). *Time to Stop the Harassment of Cameroon's NGOs. January 30, 2014.* Amsterdam, the Netherlands: Greenpeace International. Available at: http://www.greenpeace.org/international/en/news/Blogs/makingwaves/ time-to-stop-the-harassment-of-cameroons-ngos/blog/48051/.

Jansson, J. (2009). *Patterns of Chinese Investment, Aid and Trade in Central Africa (Cameroon, the DRC and Gabon). Briefing Paper, Centre for Chinese Studies.* Gland, Switzerland: World Wide Fund for Nature (WWF).

Jat, R.A., Sahrawat, K.L. and Kassam, A.H. (2013). *Conservation Agriculture: Global Perspectives and Challenges.* Wallingford, UK: CABI.

Jayaram, K., Riese, J. and Sanghvi, S. (2010). Agriculture: abundant opportunities. *McKinsey Quarterly.* Available at: http://www.mckinsey.com/insights/economic_studies/africas_path_to_growth_sector_by_sector.

Jayne, T.S., Chapoto, A., Sitko, N., *et al.* (2014). Is the scramble for land in Africa foreclosing a smallholder agricultural expansion strategy? *Journal of International Affairs*, **67**, 35–53.

JGI (2009). *Conservation Action Plan for the Greater Gombe Ecosystem, Western Tanzania 2009–2039.* Lymington, UK: Jane Goodall Institute (JGI).

Johns, A.D. and Skorupa, J.P. (1987). Responses of rain-forest primates to habitat disturbance: a review. *International Journal of Primatology*, **8**, 157–91.

Johns, J. (2005). The other connectivity: reaching beyond the choir. *Conservation Biology*, **19**, 1681–2.

Johnson, A.E., Knott, C.D., Pamungkas, B., Pasaribu, M. and Marshall, A.J. (2005). A survey of the orang-utan (*Pongo pygmaeus wurmbii*) population in and around Gunung Palung National Park, West Kalimantan, Indonesia based on nest counts. *Biological Conservation*, **121**, 495–507.

Johnson, J.A. (2012). *Assessing the Impact of Climate Change in Borneo.* Gland, Switzerland: World Wide Fund for Nature (WWF).

JPNN (2010). 7,3, Juta Ha Lahan Ternantar Ditertibkan. *Jawa Pos National Network (JPNN)*, March 22, 2010.

Junker, J., Blake, S., Boesch, C., *et al.* (2012). Recent decline in suitable environmental conditions for African great apes. *Diversity and Distributions*, **18**, 1077–91.

Kahlenberg, S.M., Emery Thompson, M., Muller, M.N. and Wrangham, R.W. (2008). Immigration costs for female chimpanzees and male protection as an immigrant counterstrategy to intrasexual aggression. *Animal Behaviour*, **76**, 1497–509.

Kakati, K. (2004). *Impact of forest fragmentation on the hoolock gibbon in Assam, India.* PhD thesis. Cambridge, UK: University of Cambridge.

Kalpers, J., Gray, M., Asuma, S., *et al.* (2010). *Buffer Zone and Human Wildlife Conflict Management: IGCP Lessons Learned.* Kigali, Rwanda: International Gorilla Conservation Programme (IGCP).

Kalyebara, M.R., Ragama, P.E., Kikulwe, E., *et al.* (2007). Economic importance of the banana bacterial wilt in Uganda. *African Crop Science Journal*, **14**, 93–103.

Kaminski, B. (2010). Kick-boxing orangutans at a theme park in Bangkok, Thailand. *The Telegraph*, Available at: http://www.telegraph.co.uk/earth/earthpicturegalleries/7571125/Kick-boxing-orangutans-at-a-theme-park-in-Bangkok-Thailand.html.

Kano, T. (1972). Distribution and adaptation of the chimpanzee on the eastern shore of Lake Tanganyika. *Kyoto University African Studies*, **VII**, 37–129.

Kano, T. (1992). *The Last Ape: Pygmy Chimpanzee Behavior and Ecology.* Stanford, CA: Stanford University Press.

Kano, T., Bongoli, L., Idani, G. and Hashimoto, C. (1996). The challenge of Wamba. *Etica and Animali*, **8**, 68–74.

Kappeler, M. (1984). The gibbon in Java. In *The Lesser Apes: Evolutionary and Behavioural Biology*, ed. H. Preuschoft, D.J. Chivers, W.Y. Brockelman and N. Creel. Edinburgh, UK: Edinburgh University Press, pp. 19–31.

Karesh, W.B., Dobson, A., Lloyd-Smith, J.O., *et al.* (2012). Ecology of zoonoses: natural and unnatural histories. *The Lancet*, **380**, 1936–45.

Kartodihardjo, H. and Supriono, A. (2000). *The Impact of Sectoral Development on Natural Forest Conversion and Degradation: the Case of Timber and Tree Crop Plantations in Indonesia. CIFOR Occasional Paper 26.* Bogor, Indonesia: Center for International Forestry Research (CIFOR).

Kavanagh, M. and Caldecott, J.O. (2013). Strategic guidelines for the translocation of primates and other animals. *Raffles Bulletin of Zoology*, 203–9.

Kayobyo, G., Hakiza, G.J. and Kucel, P. (2001). Cocoa (*Theobroma cacao*). In *Agriculture in Uganda. Volume II*, ed. J.K. Mukiibi. Kampala, Uganda: National Agricultural Research Organization, pp. 462–86.

KDNG (2010). *Tyrants, Tycoons and Tigers: Yuzana Company Ravages Burma's Hugawng Valley.* Kachin State: The Kachin Development Networking Group (KDNG). Available at: http://www.burmalibrary.org/docs09/TyrantsTycoonsandTigers.pdf.

Keele, B.F., Jones, J.H., Terio, K.A., *et al.* (2009). Increased mortality and AIDS-like immunopathology in wild chimpanzees infected with SIVcpz. *Nature*, **460**, 515–9.

Kennedy, K.B. (2011). The environmental law framework of the Democratic Republic of the Congo and the balancing of interests. In *The Balancing of Interests in Environmental Law in Africa*, ed. M. Faure and W. du Plessis. Cape Town, South Africa: Pretoria University Law Press/ABC Press, pp. 95–112.

Kenrick, J. and Lomax, T. (2013). Summary case study on the situation of Golden Veroleum Liberia's oil palm concession. Conflict or consent? In *The Oil Palm Sector at a Crossroads*, ed. M. Colchester and S. Chao. Moreton-in-Marsh, UK: Forest Peoples Programme (FPP), pp. 332–6. Available at: http://www.forestpeoples.org/sites/fpp/files/publication/2013/12/conflict-or-consent-chapter-13-summary-case-study-situation-golden-veroleum-liberia-s-oil-palm-conce.pdf.

Kenyon, M., Roos, C., Binh, V.T. and Chivers, D.J. (2011). Extrapair paternity in golden-cheeked gibbons (*Nomascus gabriellae*) in the secondary lowland forest of Cat Tien National Park, Vietnam. *Folia Primatologica*, **82**, 154–64.

Khan, S.A. and Baye, M. (2008). *China–Africa economic relations: the case of Cameroon.* Report submitted to the African Economic Research Consortium.

Kibria, M.G., Rahman, S.A., Imtiaj, A. and Sunderland, T. (2011). Extent and consequences of tropical forest degradation: successive policy options for Bangladesh. *Journal of Agricultural Science and Technology*, **1**, 29–37.

Kienzle, J., Ashburner, J.E. and Sims, B.G. (2013). *Mechanization for Rural Development: A Review of Patterns and Progress from Around the World. Integrated Crop Management 20–2013*. Rome, Italy: Food and Agriculture Organization of the United Nations (FAO).

Kim, H., Kim, H., Madhavan, M. and Suarez, A. (2013). *Measuring Environmental Externalities to Agriculture in Africa*. FAO and the George Washington University. Available at: https://elliott.gwu.edu/sites/elliott.gwu.edu/files/downloads/acad/ids/ghana-palm-oil-case-study.pdf.

Kim, S., Lappan, S. and Choe, J.C. (2011). Diet and ranging behavior of the endangered Javan gibbon (*Hylobates moloch*) in a submontane tropical rainforest. *American Journal of Primatology*, **73**, 270–80.

Kim, S., Lappan, S. and Choe, J.C. (2012). Responses of Javan gibbon (*Hylobates moloch*) groups in submontane forest to monthly variation in food availability: evidence for variation on a fine spatial scale. *American Journal of Primatology*, **74**, 1154–67.

Kindlmann, P. and Burel, F. (2008). Connectivity measures: a review. *Landscape Ecology*, **23**, 879–90.

KLK (2015). *KLK Clarifies the Findings in Chain Reaction Research's Report on KLK's Sustainability Risks, March 13, 2015*. Kalantan, Malaysia: Kuala Lumpur Kepong Berhad (KLK). Available at: http://www.klk.com.my/wp-content/uploads/2015/03/2015–03–13-Response-to-CRR-FINAL.pdf.

Knapen, H. (2001). *Forests of Fortune? The Environmental History of Southeast Borneo, 1600–1880*. Leiden, the Netherlands: KITLV Press.

Knight, A. (2008). The beginning of the end for chimpanzee experiments? *Philosophy, Ethics, and Humanities in Medicine*, **3**, 16.

Knop, E., Ward, P.I. and Wich, S.A. (2004). A comparison of orang-utan density in a logged and unlogged forest in Sumatra. *Biological Conservation*, **120**, 183–8.

Knott, C.D. (1998). Changes in orangutan caloric intake, energy balance, and ketones in response to fluctuating fruit availability. *International Journal of Primatology*, **19**, 1061–79.

Knott, C.D. (1999). *Reproductive, physiological and behavioural responses of orangutans in Borneo to fluctuations in food availability*. PhD thesis. Cambridge, MA: Harvard University.

Knott, C.D. (2005). Energetic responses to food availability in the great apes: implications for hominin evolution. In *Seasonality in Primates Studies of Living and Extinct Human and Non-Human Primates*, ed. D.K. Brockman and C.P. van Schaik. New York, NY: Cambridge University Press, pp. 351–78.

Knott, C.D., Emery Thompson, M. and Wich, S.A. (2009). The ecology of female reproduction in wild orangutans. In *Orangutans: Geographic Variation Behavioral Ecology and Conservation*, ed. S. Wich, S. Utami Atmoko, T. Setia and C.P. van Schaik. Oxford, UK: Oxford University Press, pp. 171–88.

Koh, L.P. and Ghazoul, J. (2010). Spatially explicit scenario analysis for reconciling agricultural expansion, forest protection, and carbon conservation in Indonesia. *Proceedings of the National Academy of Sciences USA*, **107**, 11140–4.

Koh, L.P., Miettinen, J., Soo Chin Liew and Ghazoul, J. (2011). Remotely sensed evidence of tropical peatland conversion to oil palm. *Proceedings of the National Academy of Sciences USA*, **108**, 5127–32.

Koh, L.P. and Wilcove, D.S. (2008a). Is oil palm agriculture really destroying tropical biodiversity? *Conservation Letters*, **1**, 60–4.

Koh, L.P. and Wilcove, D.S. (2008b). Oil palm: disinformation enables deforestation. *Trends in Ecology and Evolution*, **24**, 67–8.

Köndgen, S., Kühl, H., N'Goran, P.K., *et al.* (2008). Pandemic human viruses cause decline of endangered great apes. *Current Biology*, **18**, 260–4.

Konings, P. (1993). *Labour Resistance in Cameroon: Managerial Strategies and Labour Resistance in the Agro-Industrial Plantation of the Cameroon Development Corporation*. Leiden, the Netherlands: James Currey.

Kool, K.M. (1992). The status of endangered primates in Gunung Halimun reserve, Indonesia. *Oryx*, **26**, 29–33.

Kormos, R., Boesch, C., Bakarr, M.I. and Butynski, T.M. (2003). *West African Chimpanzees: Status, Survey and Conservation Action Plan*. Gland, Switzerland: International Union for Conservation of Nature (IUCN) World Conservation Union.

Kranendonk, G., van Bolhuis, H., Lange, A., *et al.* (2012). *Reduction of regurgitation and reingestion in retired laboratory chimpanzees* (Pan troglodytes). Presented at: XXIV Congress of the International Primatological Society, August 13, 2012, Mexico City, Mexico.

Krief, S., Cibot, M., Bortolamiol, S., *et al.* (2014). Wild chimpanzees on the edge: nocturnal activities in croplands. *PLoS One*, **9**, e109925.

Krieger, D.J. (2001). *Economic Value of Forest Ecosystem Services: A Review. An Analysis Prepared for The Wilderness Society.* Washington DC: The Wilderness Society.

Kuehl, H.S., Nzeingui, C., Yeno, S.L.D., *et al.* (2009). Discriminating between village and commercial hunting of apes. *Biological Conservation*, **142**, 1500–6.

Kumamoto Sanctuary (2013). *Four Bonobos have Arrived at Kumamoto Sanctuary.* Kyoto, Japan: Kumamoto Sanctuary, Wildlife Research Center, Kyoto University. Available at: http://www.wrc.kyoto-u.ac.jp/kumasan/en/report/bonobos/.

Kumamoto Sanctuary (2014). *Two Bonobos have Arrived at Kumamoto Sanctuary on May 21st, 2014.* Kyoto, Japan: Kumamoto Sanctuary, Wildlife Research Center, Kyoto University. Available at: http://www.wrc.kyoto-u.ac.jp/kumasan/en/report/bonobos/2014–05–21.html.

Kupsch, D., Serge, B.K. and Waltert, M. (2014). *Biodiversity, Carbon Stock and Market Value Assessment for the SGSOC Project Area, Southwest Region, Cameroon.* World Wide Fund for Nature (WWF) Germany and Greenpeace International.

Kusuma, A. (2011). Tersangka Bunuh 20 Orangutan dan Monyet Sejak 2008 [Suspect killed 20 orangutans and monkeys since 2008]. *Tribun Kaltim*, November 21, 2011.

Labes, E.M., Hegglin, D., Grimm, F., *et al.* (2010). Intestinal parasites of endangered orangutans (*Pongo pygmaeus*) in Central and East Kalimantan, Borneo, Indonesia. *Parasitology*, **137**, 123–35.

LAGA (2014). *The Last Great Ape Organization: November 2014 Report.* Cameroon: The Last Great Ape Organization (LAGA). Available at: http://www.laga-enforcement.org/Portals/0/Documents/Activity reports 2014/Activity Report -November 14.pdf.

Lambert, J.E. (1998). Primate frugivory in Kibale National Park, Uganda, and its implications for human use of forest resources. *African Journal of Ecology*, **36**, 234–40.

Land Matrix (n.d.). *Database of International Land Deals.* Land Matrix. Available at: http://www.landmatrix.org/. Accessed June, 2014.

Laporte, N.T., Stabach, J.A., Grosch, R., Lin, T.S. and Goetz, S.J. (2007). Expansion of industrial logging in central Africa. *Science*, **316**, 1451.

Lappan, S. (2008). Male care of infants in a siamang (*Symphalangus syndactylus*) population including socially monogamous and polyandrous groups. *Behavioral Ecology and Sociobiology*, **62**, 1307–17.

Lappan, S. (2009). Flowers are an important food for small apes in southern Sumatra. *American Journal of Primatology*, **71**, 624–35.

Laurance, W.F. (2007). Forest destruction: the road to ruin. *New Scientist*, 9 June, 25.

Laurance, W.F., Alonso, A., Lee, M. and Campbell, P. (2006). Challenges for forest conservation in Gabon, central Africa. *Futures*, **38**, 454–70.

Laurance, W.F. and Balmford, A. (2013). A global map for road building. *Nature*, **495**, 308–9.

Laurance, W.F., Clements, G.R., Sloan, S., *et al.* (2014a). A global strategy for road building. *Nature*, **513**, 229–32.

Laurance, W.F., Cochrane, M.A., Bergen, S., *et al.* (2001). The future of the Brazilian Amazon. *Science*, **291**, 438–9.

Laurance, W.F., Goosem, M. and Laurance, S.G.W. (2009). Impacts of roads and linear clearings on tropical forests. *Trends in Ecology and Evolution*, **24**, 659–69.

Laurance, W.F., Sayer, J. and Cassman, K.G. (2014b). Agricultural expansion and its impact on tropical nature. *Trends in Ecology and Evolution*, **29**, 107–16.

Laurance, W.F., Useche, D.C., Rendeiro, J., *et al.* (2012). Averting biodiversity collapse in tropical forest protected areas. *Nature*, **489**, 290–4.

Lawson, S. (2014). *Consumer Goods and Deforestation, An Analysis of the Extent and Nature of Illegality in Forest Conversion for Agriculture and Timber Plantations. Forest Trends Report Series.* Washington DC: Forest Trends. Available at: http://www.forest-trends.org/documents/files/doc_4718.pdf.

Leciak, E., Hladik, A. and Hladik, C.M. (2005). The oil palm (*Elaeis guineensis*) and the cores of high biodiversity in gallery forests of Guinea in relation to human and chimpanzees commensalism. *Revue D Ecologie-La Terre Et La Vie*, **60**, 179–84.

Leendertz, F.H., Lankester, F., Guislain, P., *et al.* (2006a). Anthrax in western and central African great apes. *American Journal of Primatology*, **68**, 928–33.

Leendertz, F.H., Pauli, G., Maetz-Rensing, K., *et al.* (2006b). Pathogens as drivers of population declines: the importance of systematic monitoring in great apes and other threatened mammals. *Biological Conservation*, **131**, 325–37.

Leighton, D.S.R. (1987). Gibbons: territoriality and monogamy. In *Primate Societies*, ed. B.B. Smuts, D.L. Cheyney, R.M. Seyfarth, R.W. Wrangham and T.T. Struhsaker. Chicago, IL: University of Chicago Press, pp. 135–45.

LEITI (n.d.). *Agriculture: 15 Books*. Liberia Extractive Industries Transparency Initiative (LEITI). Available at: https://www.scribd.com/collections/4297678/Agriculture. Accessed June, 2015.

Levin, J., Ng, G., Fortes, D., *et al.* (2012). *Profitability and Sustainability in Palm Oil Production. Analysis of Incremental Financial Costs and Benefits of RSPO Compliance*. Washington DC: World Wide Fund for Nature (WWF) US.

Liberia (1904). *Public Land Laws 1904 (as amended in 1972)*. Republic of Liberia.

Liberia (1956). *Aborigines Law 1956*. Republic of Liberia.

Liberia (1984). *Constitution 1984*. Republic of Liberia.

Liberia (1988). *Wildlife and National Parks Act 1988*. Republic of Liberia.

Liberia (2000). *National Forestry Law 2000*. Republic of Liberia.

Liberia (2002a). *Environment Protection Agency Act of Liberia 2002*. Republic of Liberia.

Liberia (2002b). *Environment Protection Law 2002*. Republic of Liberia.

Liberia (2003). *Act for the Establishment of a Protected Forest Area Network and Amending Chapter 1 and 9 of the New National Forestry Law, Part II of Title 23 of the Liberian Code of Laws Revised 2003*. Republic of Liberia.

Liberia (2006). *National Forestry Reform Law 2006*. Republic of Liberia.

Liberia (2008). *An Act Ratifying the Concession Agreement between the Republic of Liberia and LIBINC Oil Palm Inc.* Republic of Liberia.

Liberia (2009a). *Act Establishing the Liberia Extractive Industries Transparency Initiative 2009*. Republic of Liberia.

Liberia (2009b). *An Act Ratifying the Concession Agreement between the Republic of Liberia and Sime Darby Plantation (Liberia) Inc*. Republic of Liberia.

Liberia (2009c). *Community Rights Law 2009*. Republic of Liberia.

Liberia (2010a). *An Act Ratifying the Concession Agreement between the Republic of Liberia and Golden Veroleum (Liberia) Inc*. Republic of Liberia.

Liberia (2010b). *Amended and Restated Public Procurement and Concessions Act 2010*. Republic of Liberia.

Liberia (2010c). *Liberia Poverty Reduction Strategy*. Republic of Liberia.

Liberia (2011). *An Act Ratifying the Concession Agreement between the Republic of Liberia and Maryland Oil Palm Plantation*. Republic of Liberia.

Linder, J.M. (2013). African primate diversity threatened by 'new wave' of industrial oil palm expansion. *African Primates*, **8**, 25–38.

Lindsey, P., Balme, G., Becker, M., *et al.* (2012). *Illegal Hunting and the Bushmeat Trade in Savanna Africa: Drivers, Impacts and Solutions to Address the Problem*. New York, NY: Report by Panthera, Zoological Society of London (ZSL) and Wildlife Conservation Society. Available at: http://www.panthera.org/sites/default/files/bushmeat%20report%20v2%20lo.pdf.

LISGIS (2004). *Rubber Farms [map]*. Monrovia, Liberia: Liberia Institute of Statistics and Geo-Information Services (LISGIS).

Liu, Z.H., Zhang, R.Z., Jiang, H.S. and Southwick, C. (1989). Population structure of *Hylobates concolor* in Bawanglin Nature Reserve, Hainan, China. *American Journal of Primatology*, **19**, 247–54.

Loken, B., Spehar, S. and Rayadin, Y. (2013). Terrestriality in the Bornean orangutan (*Pongo pygmaeus morio*) and implications for their ecology and conservation. *American Journal of Primatology*, **75**, 1129–38.

Lonsdorf, E.V., Travis, D., Pusey, A.E. and Goodall, J. (2006). Using retrospective health data from the Gombe chimpanzee study to inform future monitoring efforts. *American Journal of Primatology*, **68**, 897–908.

Lorenti, G.A. (2014). *Assessing fragmentation characteristics at Bulindi, western Uganda: implications for primate conservation in a fragmented landscape*. MSc thesis. Oxford, UK: Oxford Brookes University.

Lynn, M. (1997). *Commerce and Economic Change in West Africa*. Cambridge, UK: Cambridge University Press.

MAAIF and MFPED (2000). *Plan for Modernisation of Agriculture: Eradicating Poverty in Uganda*. Kampala, Uganda: Ministry of Agriculture, Animal Industry and Fisheries (MAAIF) and Ministry of Finance, Planning and Economic Development (MFPED).

Mackey, B., DellaSala, D.A., Kormos, C., *et al.* (2015). Policy options for the world's primary forests in multilateral environmental agreements. *Conservation Letters*, **8**, 139–47.

MacKinnon, J. (1971). The orang-utan in Sabah today. *Oryx*, **11**, 141–91.

MacKinnon, J.R. (1972). *The behaviour and ecology of the orang-utan (*Pongo pygmaeus*) with relation to the other apes*. PhD thesis. Oxford, UK: University of Oxford.

MacKinnon, J. (1974). The behaviour and ecology of wild orang-utans. *Animal Behaviour*, **22**, 3–74.

Maddox, T., Priatna, D., Gemita, E. and Salampessy, A. (2007). *The Conservation of Tigers and other Wildlife in Oil Palm Plantations*. London, UK: The Zoological Society of London (ZSL).

Majid Cooke, F. (2006). *State, Communities and Forests in Contemporary Borneo. Asia-Pacific Environment Monograph 1*. Canberra, Australia: ANU E Press.

Majid Cooke, F., Toh, S. and Vaz, J. (2012). *Community-Investor Business Models: Lessons from the Oil Palm Sector in East Malaysia*. London/Rome/Kota Kinabalu: International Institute for Environment and Development (IIED)/International Fund for Agricultural Development (IFAD)/Food and Agriculture Organization of the United Nations (FAO)/University Malaysia Sabah.

Makana, J.R., Evans, T., Wieland, M., Leal, M. and Betts, P. (2014). *Certified Cocoa Production in Mambasa Territory, Eastern Democratic Republic of Congo. Project Report*. Kinshasa, DRC: Wildlife Conservation Society (WCS).

Malaysia (1930). *Sabah Land Ordinance 1930*. No. 68. Malaysia.

Malaysia (1957). *Constitution 1957 (as Amended 2006)*. Malaysia.

Malaysia (1963). *Sabah Fauna Conservation Ordinance 1963*. No. 11. Malaysia.

Malaysia (1965a). *Land Code 1965*. Malaysia.

Malaysia (1965b). *Sabah Fauna Conservation Rules 1965*. Malaysia.

Malaysia (1968a). *Forest Enactment 1968*. Malaysia.

Malaysia (1968b). *Sabah Forest Enactment 1968*. No. 2. Malaysia.

Malaysia (1973). *Sabah Fauna Conservation (Amendment) Enactment 1973*. No. 3. Malaysia.

Malaysia (1974). *Environmental Quality Act 1974*. No. 127. Malaysia.

Malaysia (1980). *National Parks Act 1980*. No. 226. Malaysia.

Malaysia (1984). *Sabah Parks Enactment 1984*. No. 6. Malaysia.

Malaysia (1987). *Environmental Quality (Prescribed Activities) (Environmental Impact Assessment) Order 1987*. Malaysia.

Malaysia (2000). *Environmental Quality (Prescribed Activities) (Environmental Impact Assessment) (Amendment) Order 2000*. Malaysia.

Malaysia (2002). *Sabah Environment Protection Enactment 2002*. Malaysia.

Malaysia (2008). *International Trade and Endangered Species Act 2008*. No. 686. Malaysia.

Malaysia (2010). *Wildlife Conservation Act 2010*. No. 716. Malaysia.

Malcolm, J.R. and Ray, J.C. (2000). Influence of timber extraction routes on central African small-mammal communities, forest structure, and tree diversity. *Conservation Biology*, **14**, 1623–38.

Manciana, E., Trucco, M. and Pineiro, M. (2009). *Large-Scale Acquisitions of Land for Rights for Agriculture and Natural Resource-based Use: Argentina*. Washington DC: World Bank Publications.

Marchal, V. and Hill, C. (2009). Primate crop-raiding: a study of local perceptions in four villages in North Sumatra, Indonesia. *Primate Conservation*, **24**, 107–16.

Marchini, S. and Macdonald, D.W. (2012). Predicting ranchers' intention to kill jaguars: case studies in Amazonia and Pantanal. *Biological Conservation*, **147**, 213–21.

Markham, A.C., Santymire, R.M., Lonsdorf, E.V., *et al.* (2014). Rank effects on social stress in lactating chimpanzees. *Animal Behaviour*, **87**, 195–202.

Marshall, A.J. (2009). Are montane forests demographic sinks for Bornean white-bearded gibbons *Hylobates albibarbis*? *Biotropica*, **41**, 257–67.

Marshall, A.J., Ancrenaz, M., Brearley, F.Q., *et al.* (2009a). The effects of forest phenology and floristics on populations of Bornean and Sumatran orangutans: are Sumatran forests more productive than Bornean forests? In *Orangutans: Geographic Variation in Behavioral Ecology and Conservation*, ed. S.A. Wich, S. Utami Atmoko, T. Mitra Setia and C.P. van Schaik. Oxford, UK: Oxford University Press, pp. 97–117.

Marshall, A.J., Lacy, R., Ancrenaz, M., *et al.* (2009b). Orangutan population biology, life history, and conservation. In *Orangutans: Geographic Variation in Behavioral Ecology and Conservation*, ed. S.A. Wich, S. Utami Atmoko, T. Mitra Setia and C.P. van Schaik. New York, NY: Oxford University Press, pp. 311–26.

Marshall, A.J. and Leighton, M. (2006). How does food availability limit the population density of white-bearded gibbons? In *Feeding Ecology of the Apes*, ed. G. Hohmann, M. Robbins and C. Boesch. Cambridge, UK: Cambridge University Press, pp. 313–35.

Marshall, A.J. and Meijaard, E. (2009). Orangutan nest surveys: the devil is in the details. *Oryx*, **43**, 416–8.

Marshall, A.J., Nardiyono, Engstrom, L.M., *et al.* (2006). The blowgun is mightier than the chainsaw in determining population density of Bornean orangutans (*Pongo pygmaeus morio*) in the forests of East Kalimantan. *Biological Conservation*, **129**, 566–78.

Masi, S., Cipolletta, C. and Robbins, M. (2009). Western lowland gorillas (*Gorilla gorilla gorilla*) change their activity patterns in response to frugivory. *American Journal of Primatology*, **71**, 91–100.

Matsuzawa, T., Humle, T. and Sugiyama, Y., ed. (2011). *Chimpanzees of Bossou and Nimba*. Tokyo, Japan: Springer-Verlag.

Mbodiam, B.R. (2014). *Cameroun: Justin Sugar Mills Dénonce une Cabale Contre son Projet Sucrier de Batouri*. Geneva, Switzerland: Agence Ecofin. Available at: http://www.agenceecofin.com/sucre/1208–22062-cameroun-justin-sugar-mills-denonce-une-cabale-contre-son-projet-sucrier-de-batouri. Accessed September 3, 2014.

McCarthy, J. (2012). Certifying in contested spaces: private regulation in Indonesian forestry and palm oil. *Third World Quarterly*, **33**, 1871–88.

McConkey, K.R. (2000). Primary seed shadow generated by gibbons in the rain forests of Barito Ulu, central Borneo. *American Journal of Primatology*, **52**, 13–29.

McConkey, K.R. (2005). The influence of gibbon primary seed shadows on post-dispersal seed fate in a lowland dipterocarp forest in central Borneo. *Journal of Tropical Ecology*, **21**, 255–62.

McConkey, K.R. and Chivers, D.J. (2007). Influence of gibbon ranging patterns on seed dispersal distance and deposition site in a Bornean forest. *Journal of Tropical Ecology*, **23**, 269–75.

McLennan, M.R. (2008). Beleaguered chimpanzees in the agricultural district of Hoima, western Uganda. *Primate Conservation*, **23**, 45–54.

McLennan, M.R. (2010). Case study of an unusual human–chimpanzee conflict at Bulindi, Uganda. *Pan Africa News*, **17**, 1–4.

McLennan, M.R. (2013). Diet and feeding ecology of chimpanzees (*Pan troglodytes*) in Bulindi, Uganda: foraging strategies at the forest–farm interface. *International Journal of Primatology*, **34**, 585–614.

McLennan, M.R. and Hill, C.M. (2010). Chimpanzee responses to researchers in a disturbed forest–farm mosaic at Bulindi, western Uganda. *American Journal of Primatology*, **72**, 907–18.

McLennan, M.R. and Hill, C.M. (2012). Troublesome neighbours: changing attitudes towards chimpanzees (*Pan troglodytes*) in a human-dominated landscape in Uganda. *Journal for Nature Conservation*, **20**, 219–27.

McLennan, M.R. and Hill, C.M. (2013). Ethical issues in the study and conservation of an African great ape in an unprotected, human-dominated landscape in western Uganda. In *Ethics in the Field: Contemporary Challenges*, ed. J. MacClancy and A. Fuentes. New York, NY: Berghahn Books, pp. 42–66.

McLennan, M.R. and Hockings, K.J. (2014). Wild chimpanzees show group differences in selection of agricultural crops. *Scientific Reports*, **4**, 5956.

McLennan, M.R. and Huffman, M.A. (2012). High frequency of leaf swallowing and its relationship to intestinal parasite expulsion in 'village' chimpanzees at Bulindi, Uganda. *American Journal of Primatology*, **74**, 642–50.

McLennan, M.R., Hyeroba, D., Asiimwe, C., Reynolds, V. and Wallis, J. (2012). Chimpanzees in mantraps: lethal crop protection and conservation in Uganda. *Oryx*, **46**, 598–603.

McLennan, M.R. and Plumptre, A.J. (2012). Protected apes, unprotected forest: composition, structure and diversity of riverine forest fragments and their conservation value in Uganda. *Tropical Conservation Science*, **5**, 79–103.

McShea, W.J., Steward, C., Peterson, L., *et al.* (2009). The importance of secondary forest blocks for terrestrial mammals within an Acacia/secondary forest matrix in Sarawak, Malaysia. *Biological Conservation*, **142**, 3108–19.

Médard, J.-F. (1977). L'état sous-développé au Cameroun. *Année Africaine*, 33–84.

Megevand, C. (2013). *Deforestation Trends in the Congo Basin: Reconciling Economic Growth and Forest Protection.* Washington DC: World Bank Publications.

Meijaard, E., Abram, N.K., Wells, J.A., *et al.* (2013). People's perceptions about the importance of forests on Borneo. *PLoS One*, **8**, e73008.

Meijaard, E., Albar, G., Nardiyono, *et al.* (2010). Unexpected ecological resilience in Bornean orangutans and implications for pulp and paper plantation management. *PLoS One*, **5**, e12813.

Meijaard, E., Buchori, D., Hadiprakoso, Y., *et al.* (2011). Quantifying killing of orangutans and human-orangutan conflict in Kalimantan, Indonesia *PLoS One*, **6**, e27491.

Meijaard, E., Sheil, D., Nasi, R., *et al.* (2005). *Life after Logging. Reconciling Wildlife Conservation and Production Forestry in Indonesian Borneo.* Jakarta, Indonesia: Center for International Forestry Research (CIFOR) and United Nations Educational, Scientific and Cultural Organization (UNESCO).

Meijaard, E. and Wich, S. (2007). Putting orang-utan population trends into perspective. *Current Biology*, **17**, R540.

Meijaard, E., Wich, S., Ancrenaz, M. and Marshall, A.J. (2012). Not by science alone: why orangutan conservationists must think outside the box. *Annals of the New York Academy of Sciences*, **1249**, 29–44.

Mendenhall, C.D., Karp, D.S., Meyer, C.F.J., Hadly, E.A. and Daily, G.C. (2014). Predicting biodiversity change and averting collapse in agricultural landscapes. *Nature*, **509**, 213.

Miettinen, J., Hooijer, A., Tollenaar, D., Page, S. and Malins, C. (2012). *Historical Analysis and Projection of Oil Palm Plantation Expansion on Peatland in Southeast Asia.* Washington DC: International Council on Clean Transportation (ICCT). Available at: http://www.theicct.org/sites/default/files/publications/ICCT_palm-expansion_Feb2012.pdf.

Miettinen, J., Shi, C. and Liew, S.C. (2011). Deforestation rates in insular Southeast Asia between 2000 and 2010. *Global Change Biology*, **17**, 2261–70.

Miller, J.A., Pusey, A.E., Gilby, I.C., *et al.* (2014). Competing for space: female chimpanzees are more aggressive inside than outside their core areas. *Animal Behaviour*, **87**, 147–52.

MINADER (2014). *Atelier de Redaction de la Strategie de Developpement Durable De La Filiere Huile de Palm Au Cameroun.* Yaoundé, Cameroon: Ministry of Agriculture and Rural Development of Cameroon (MINADER).

MINEPAT (2009). *Cameroon Vision 2035.* Yaoundé, Cameroon: Ministry of Economy, Planning, and Regional Development of Cameroon (MINEPAT).

Mitani, J.C. (2009). Male chimpanzees form enduring and equitable social bonds. *Animal Behaviour*, **77**, 633–40.

Mittermeier, R.A., Rylands, A.B. and Wilson, D.E. (2013). *Handbook of the Mammals of the World. Volume 3. Primates.* Barcelona, Spain: Lynx Edicions.

MOA Liberia (2007). *Comprehensive Assessment of the Agriculture Sector.* Rome, Italy: Food and Agriculture Organization of the United Nations (FAO). Available at: http://www.fao.org/docrep/010/ai562e/ai562e00.htm. Accessed September 14, 2014.

MOA Liberia (2008). *Food and Agriculture Policy and Strategy: From Subsistence to Sufficiency.* Liberia: Ministry of Agriculture (MOA). Available at: http://www.gafspfund.org/sites/gafspfund.org/files/Documents/Liberia_5_ of_ 7_FAPS_Food_Agriculture_Strategy_0.pdf.

MOF Indonesia (2009). *Orangutan Indonesia Conservation Strategies and Action Plan 2007–2017.* Jakarta, Indonesia: Ministry of Forestry (MOF) Indonesia. Available at: http://www.kemlu.go.id/Documents/Orangutan_National_ Action_Plan_2007–2017%28bilingual%29.pdf.

MONA Foundation (2013). *We Would Like to Introduce You to Linda.* Riudellots de la Selva, Spain: Mona Foundation. Available at: http://www.fundacionmona.org/news/en/2013/11/06/0004/we-would-like-to-introduce-you-to-linda.

MONA UK (2014). *Linda Cannot Come to MONA.* Riudellots de la Selva, Spain: MONA Foundation. Available at: http://www.mona-uk.org/linda-cannot-come-to-mona-2/.

Mongabay (2012). *Complaint Filed with Palm Oil Body over Orangutan Rescue Case.* Available at: http://news.mongabay.com/2012/1129-orangutans-sisirau-rspo-complaint.html.

Mongabay (2013). *Controversial Palm Oil Project Approved in Cameroon Rainforest.* Menlo Park, CA: Mongabay.com. Available at: http://news.mongabay.com/2013/1126-herakles-approved-in-cameroon.html. Accessed November 26, 2013.

Mongabay (2015). *Palm Oil Certification Body Purges Membership.* Menlo Park, CA: Mongaba.com. Available at: http://news.mongabay.com/2015/0305-rspo-purge.html.

Mongabay (n.d.). *Palm Oil Price Chart.* Menlo Park, CA: Mongabay.com. Available at: http://www.mongabay.com/commodities/prices/palm_oil.php. Accessed November 10, 2014.

Monkey World (2012). *Monkey World Rescue Centre: Meet Our Primates.* Monkey World Ape Rescue Centre. Available at: http://www.monkeyworld.org/meet-our-primates. Accessed March 27, 2013.

Monte Adone (n.d.). *Animali Esotici: Scimpanzé.* Sasso Marconi, Italy: Monte Adone. Available at: http://www.centrotutelafauna.org/animali_esotici_scimpanzé.xhtml. Accessed February, 2015.

Moore, J.J. (1996). Savanna chimpanzees, referential models and the last common ancestor. In *Great Ape Societies*, ed. W.C. McGrew, L. Marchant and T. Nishida. Cambridge, UK: Cambridge University Press, pp. 275–92.

Morgan, B.J., Adeleke, A., Bassey, T., *et al.* (2011). *Regional Action Plan for the Conservation of the Nigeria-Cameroon Chimpanzee (*Pan troglodytes ellioti*).* San Diego, CA: International Union for Conservation of Nature Species Survival Commission (IUCN SSC) Primate Specialist Group and Zoological Society of San Diego.

Morgan, D. and Sanz, C. (2006). Chimpanzee feeding ecology and comparisons with sympatric gorillas in the Goualougo Triangle, Republic of Congo. In *Primate Feeding Ecology in Apes and Other Primates: Ecological, Physiological, and Behavioural Aspects*, ed. G. Hohmann, M. Robbins and C. Boesch. Cambridge, UK: Cambridge University Press, pp. 97–122.

Morgan, D. and Sanz, C. (2007). *Best Practice Guidelines for Reducing the Impact of Commercial Logging on Great Apes in Western Equatorial Africa.* Gland, Switzerland: International Union for Conservation of Nature Species Survival Commission (IUCN SSC) Primate Specialist Group Available at: http://www.primate-sg.org/best_practice_logging/.

Morgan, D., Sanz, C., Onononga, J.R. and Strindberg, S. (2006). Ape abundance and habitat use in the Goualougo Triangle, Republic of Congo. *International Journal of Primatology*, **27**, 147–79.

Morgera, E. (2010). *Wildlife Law and the Empowerment of the Poor. FAO Legislative Study No. 103.* Rome, Italy: Food and Agriculture Organization of the United Nations (FAO).

Morgera, E. and Cirelli, M.T. (2009). *Wildlife Law and the Empowerment of the Poor in Sub-Saharan Africa. FAO Legislative Legal Papers No. 77.* Rome, Italy: Food and Agriculture Organization of the United Nations (FAO).

Morgera, E. and Tsioumani, E. (2010). *Wildlife Legislation and the Empowerment of the Poor in Asia and Oceania. FAO Legislative Legal Papers No. 83.* Rome, Italy: Food and Agriculture Organization of the United Nations (FAO).

Morimura, N., Idani, G. and Matsuzawa, T. (2011). The first chimpanzee sanctuary in Japan: an attempt to care for the 'surplus' of biomedical research. *American Journal of Primatology*, **73**, 226–32.

Morrison, J., Loucks, C., Long, B. and Wikramanayake, E. (2009). Landscape-scale spatial planning at WWF: a variety of approaches. *Oryx*, **43**, 499–507.

Morrogh-Bernard, H.C., Husson, S.J., Harsanto, F.A. and Chivers, D.J. (2014). Fine-scale habitat use by orang-utans in a disturbed peat swamp forest, Central Kalimantan, and implications for conservation management. *Folia Primatologica*, **85**, 135–53.

Morrogh-Bernard, H., Husson, S.J., Knott, C.D., *et al.* (2009). Orangutan activity budgets and diet. A comparison between species, populations and habitats. In *Orangutans. Geographic Variation in Behavioral Ecology and Conservation*, ed. S.A. Wich, S.U. Atmoko, T.M. Setia and C.P. van Schaik. Oxford, UK: Oxford University Press, pp. 119–33.

Morrogh-Bernard, H., Husson, S., Page, S.E. and Rieley, J.O. (2003). Population status of the Bornean orang-utan (*Pongo pygmaeus*) in the Sebangau peat swamp forest, Central Kalimantan, Indonesia. *Biological Conservation*, **110**, 141–52.

Moutondo, E.G. (2008). Les lois-cadres environnementales dans les pays francophones d'Afrique. In *Aspects Contemporains du Droit de l'Environnement en Afrique de l'Ouest et Centrale*, ed. L. Granier. Gland, Switzerland: International Union for Conservation of Nature (IUCN), pp. 57–70.

Muehlenbein, M.P. and Ancrenaz, M. (2009). Minimizing pathogen transmission at primate ecotourism destinations: the need for input from travel medicine. *Journal of Travel Medicine*, **16**, 229–32.

Muehlenbein, M.P. and Bribiescas, R.G. (2005). Testosterone-mediated immune functions and male life histories. *American Journal of Human Biology*, **17**, 527–58.

Mul, I.F., Paembonan, W., Singleton, I., Wich, S.A. and van Bolhuis, H.G. (2007). Intestinal parasites of free-ranging, semicaptive, and captive *Pongo abelii* in Sumatra, Indonesia. *International Journal of Primatology*, **28**, 407–20.

Murray, B., Lubowski, R. and Sohngen, B. (2009). *Including International Forest Carbon Incentives in Climate Policy: Understanding the Economics.* Durham, NC: Duke University and the Nicholas Institute for Environmental Policy Solutions.

Muzaffar, S.B., Islam, M.A., Kabir, D.S., *et al.* (2011). The endangered forests of Bangladesh: why the process of implementation of the Convention on Biological Diversity is not working. *Biodiversity and Conservation*, **20**, 1587–601.

Mwavu, E.N. and Witkowski, E.T.F. (2008). Land use and cover changes (1988–2002) around Budongo forest reserve, NW Uganda: implications for forest and woodland sustainability. *Land Degradation and Development*, **19**, 606–22.

MWLE (2002). *The National Forest Plan.* Kampala, Uganda: Ministry of Water, Lands and Environment (MWLE).

Myanmar (1894). *The Land Acquisition Act 1894.* Republic of the Union of Myanmar.

Myanmar (1992). *Forest Law 1992.* Republic of the Union of Myanmar.

Myanmar (1994). *Protection of Wild Life and Wild Plants and Conservation of Natural Areas Law 1994.* Republic of the Union of Myanmar.

Myanmar (2008). *Constitution 2008.* Republic of the Union of Myanmar.

Myanmar (2011). *Farmland Bill 2011.* Republic of the Union of Myanmar.

Myanmar (2012a). *Draft Environmental Impact Assessment Rules, Ministry of Environmental Conservation and Forestry 2012.* Republic of the Union of Myanmar.

Myanmar (2012b). *Environmental Conservation Law 2012.* Republic of the Union of Myanmar.

Myanmar (2012c). *Vacant, Fallow and Virgin Lands Management Law 2012.* Republic of the Union of Myanmar.

Myanmar (2014). *National Land Use Policy (Draft) 2014.* Republic of the Union of Myanmar. Available at: http://www.fdmoecaf.gov.mm/law

Myers Thompson, J. (1997). *The history, taxonomy and ecology of the bonobo* (Pan paniscus, *Schwarz, 1929) with a first description of a wild population living in a forest/savanna mosaic habitat.* PhD thesis. Oxford, UK: University of Oxford.

Myers Thompson, J.A. (2001). The status of bonobos in their southernmost geographic range. In *All Apes Great and Small*, ed. B.F. Galdikas, N. Briggs, L. Sheeran, G. Shapiro and J. Goodall. Berlin, Germany: Springer, pp. 75–81.

Nackoney, J., Molinario, G., Potapov, P., *et al.* (2014). Impacts of civil conflict on primary forest habitat in northern Democratic Republic of the Congo, 1990–2010. *Biological Conservation*, **170**, 321–8.

Nakamura, M., Corp, N., Fujimoto, M., *et al.* (2013). Ranging behavior of Mahale chimpanzees: a 16 year study. *Primates*, **54**, 171–82.

Nakott, J. (2012). Grundrechte für Menschenaffen. *National Geographic Deutschland*, 38–71. Available at: http://www.nationalgeographic.de/reportagen/grundrechte-fuer-menschenaffen. Accessed March 12, 2013.

Nantha, H.S. and Tisdell, C. (2009). The orangutan–oil palm conflict: economic constraints and opportunities for conservation. *Biodiversity and Conservation*, **18**, 487–502.

NAPSA (n.d.). *Membership Levels.* San Francisco, CA: North American Primate Sanctuary Alliance (NAPSA). Available at: http://www.primatesanctuaries.org/about-us/membership/membership-levels. Accessed October, 2014.

Naughton-Treves, L. (1997). Farming the forest edge: vulnerable places and people around Kibale National Park, Uganda. *Geographical Review*, **87**, 27–46.

Naughton-Treves, L. (1998). Predicting patterns of crop damage by wildlife around Kibale National Park, Uganda. *Conservation Biology*, **12**, 156–68.

Nduwamungu, J. (2011). *Forest Plantations and Woodlots in Burundi.* Nairobi, Kenya: African Forest Forum.

Nellemann, C., Miles, L., Kaltenborn, B.P., Viture, M. and Ahlenius, H. (2007). *The Last Stand of the Orangutan – State of Emergency: Illegal Logging, Fire and Palm Oil in Indonesia's National Parks.* Arendal, Norway: United Nations Environment Programme (UNEP), GRID-Arendal. Available at: http://www.grida.no.

Nepal, S.K. and Weber, K.E. (1995). Prospects for coexistence: wildlife and local people. *Ambio,* **24,** 238–45.

New Agriculturalist (2008). *Country Profile: Senegal.* New Agriculturalist. Available at: http://www.new-ag.info/en/country/profile.php?a=530. Accessed September, 2014.

Nguiffo, S. (2001). *Propos sur la Gestion Néo-Patrimoniale du Secteur Forestier au Cameroun.* Cambridge, UK: Forests Monitor. Available at: http://www.forestsmonitor.org/en/reports/549968/549979. Accessed September 3, 2014.

Nguiffo, S. and Schwartz, B. (2012a). *Herakles' 13th Labour? A Study of SGSOC's Land Concession in South-West Cameroon.* Yaoundé, Cameroon: Centre pour l'Environment et le Développement and RELUFA. Available at: http://www.forestpeoples.org/sites/fpp/files/publication/2012/02/herakles-13th-labour-english.pdf.

Nguiffo, S. and Schwartz, B. (2012b). *Illegalities in Forest Clearance for Large-Scale Commercial Agriculture: the Case of Cameroon.* Washington DC: Forest Trends.

Nguiffo, S., Schwartz, B. and Hoyle, D. (2012). *Emerging Trends in Land Use Conflicts in Cameroon. Overlapping Natural Resource Permits Threaten Protected Areas and Foreign Direct Investment.* World Wide Fund for Nature (WWF)/CED/RELUFA. Available at: http://wwf.panda.org/?205591/Land-use-conflicts-Cameroon.

Nguiffo, S. and Talla, M. (2010). Cameroon's wildlife regulation: local custom versus legal conception. In *Forests, People and Wildlife,* ed. A. Perlis. Rome, Italy: Food and Agriculture Organization of the United Nations, pp. 14–18.

NIH (2013). *Announcement of Agency Decision: Recommendations on the Use of Chimpanzees in NIH-Supported Research.* Washington DC: National Institutes of Health (NIH). Available at: http://dpcpsi.nih.gov/sites/default/files/NIH_response_to_Council_of_Councils_recommendations_62513.pdf.

Nijman, V. (1995). Remarks on the occurrence of gibbons in Central Java. *Primate Conservation,* **16,** 66–7.

Nijman, V. (2004). Conservation of the Javan gibbon *Hylobates moloch:* population estimates, local extinctions, and conservation priorities. *Raffles Bulletin of Zoology,* **52,** 271–80.

Nijman, V. (2005). *In Full Swing. An Assessment of the Trade in Gibbons and Orangutans on Java and Bali, Indonesia.* Petaling Jaya: TRAFFIC Southeast Asia.

Nijman, V. (2013). One hundred years of solitude: effects of long-term forest fragmentation on the primate community of Java, Indonesia. In *Primates in Fragments: Complexity and Resilience,* ed. L.K. Marsh and C.A. Chapman. New York, NY: Springer, pp. 33–45.

Nijman, V. and Shepherd, C.R. (2011). The role of Thailand in the international trade in CITES-listed live reptiles and amphibians. *PLoS One,* **6,** e17825.

Njoh, A.J. (2002). Development implications of colonial land and human settlement schemes in Cameroon. *Habitat International,* **26,** 399–415.

Njoh, A.J. and Akiwumi, F. (2012). Colonial legacies, land policies and the millennium development goals: lessons from Cameroon and Sierra Leone. *Habitat International,* **36,** 210–8.

Nkongho, N., Feintrenie, L. and Levang, P. (2014). *The Non-Industrial Palm Oil Sector in Cameroon. Working Paper 139.* Bogor, Indonesia: Center for International Forestry Research (CIFOR).

Noerjito, M. and Maryanti, I. (2001). *Jenis-jenis Hayati yang Dilindungi Perundang-undang Indonesia.* Cibinong, Indonesia: Indonesian Science Institute (LIPI).

Normand, E. and Boesch, C. (2009). Sophisticated Euclidean maps in forest chimpanzees. *Animal Behaviour,* **77,** 1195–201.

Norris, K., Asase, A., Collen, B., *et al.* (2010). Biodiversity in a forest-agriculture mosaic: the changing face of West African rainforests. *Biological Conservation,* **143,** 2341–50.

Norway (2014). *Press Release: Liberia and Norway Launch Climate and Forest Partnership.* Government of Norway. Available at: https://www.regjeringen.no/en/aktuelt/Liberia-and-Norway-launch-climate-and-forest-partnership/id2001145.

Norway and Liberia (2014). *Letter of Intent: Cooperation on Reducing Greenhouse Gas Emissions from Deforestation and Forest Degradation (REDD+) and Developing Liberia's Agriculture Sector.* Governments of Liberia and Norway. Available at: https://www.regjeringen.no/contentassets/b8b93fa03bda4ac893d065d26d64075b/letterofintentliberia.pdf.

Notohadiprawiro, T. (1998). *Conflict between problem-solving and optimising approach to land resources development policies: the case of Central Kalimantan wetlands.* Presented at: The Spirit of Peatlands: Proceedings of the International Peat Symposium, September 7–9, 1998, Finland. International Peat Society.

Nur Rofiq, H. (2013). *Economic analysis of oil palm plantation and oil palm productivity in effect on per capita income in Indonesia.* MA thesis. The Hague, the Netherlands: Erasmus International Institute of Social Studies.

Oakland Institute (2012). *Film: The Herakles Debacle, September 5, 2012.* Oakland, CA: Oakland Institute. Available at: http://www.oaklandinstitute.org/film-herakles-debacle.

Oates, J.F., Bergl, R.A., Sunderland-Groves, J. and Dunn, A. (2008a*). Gorilla gorilla* ssp. *diehli.* In *The IUCN Red List of Threatened Species, Version 2015.1.* Gland, Switzerland: International Union for Conservation of Nature (IUCN). Available at: http://www.iucnredlist.org. Accessed June 2, 2015.

Oates, J., Sunderland-Groves, J., Bergl, R., *et al.* (2007). *Regional Action Plan for the Conservation of the Cross River Gorilla (*Gorilla gorilla diehli*).* Arlington, VA: International Union for Conservation of Nature Species Survival Commission (IUCN SSC) Primate Specialist Group and Conservation International.

Oates, J.F., Tutin, C.E.G., Humle, T., *et al.* (2008b). *Pan troglodytes.* In *The IUCN Red List of Threatened Species.* Gland, Switzerland: International Union for Conservation of Nature (IUCN). Available at: http://www.iucnredlist.org. Accessed September 30, 2014.

Obama, B. (2013). *Executive Order 13648: Combating Wildlife Trafficking.* Washington DC: United States Government Printing Office. Available at: http://www.gpo.gov/fdsys/pkg/FR-2013–07–05/pdf/2013–16387.pdf.

Oberndorf, R.B. (2006). *Legal Analysis of Forest and Land Laws in Cambodia.* South Lake Tahoe, CA: Community Forest International (CFI). Available at: http://library.opendevelopmentcambodia.net:8080/newgenlibctxt/CatalogueRecords/LEGALA.pdf.

Oberndorf, R.B. (2012). *Legal Review of Recently Enacted Farmland Law and Vacant, Fallow and Virgin Lands Management Law. Improving Legal and Policy Frameworks Relating to Land Management in Myanmar.* Yangon, Myanmar: Food Security Working Group. Available at: http://www.forest-trends.org/documents/files/doc_3274.pdf.

O'Brien, T.G., Kinnaird, M.F., Nurcahyo, A., Prasetyaningrum, M. and Iqbal, M. (2003). Fire, demography and the persistence of Siamang (*Symphalangus syndactylus*: Hylobatidae) in a Sumatran rainforest. *Animal Conservation*, **6**, 115–21.

Ofon, A. (2014). *Crude Palm Oil: Africa's Burgeoning Market.* London, UK: Standard Chartered Bank. Available at: https://research.standardchartered.com/configuration/ROW%20Documents/Crude_palm_oil__Africa%E2%80%99s_burgeoning_market_25_06_14_01_52.pdf.

Ogawa, H., Moore, J. and Kamenya, S. (2006). Chimpanzees in the Ntakata and Kakungu Areas, Tanzania. *Primate Conservation*, **21**, 97–101.

Ohashi, G. (2015). Pestle-pounding and nut-cracking by wild chimpanzees at Kpala, Liberia. *Primates*, **56**, 113–7.

Olam (2010). *Investment in Greenfield Oil Palm Plantation in Gabon. Analyst and Media Briefing in Singapore, November 13, 2010.* Shanghai, China: Olam. Available at: http://www.olamonline.com/attachments/newsroom/gabon_palm_ap_vnov_12_-_final_%28short_version%29.pdf.

Olam (2014). *Rapport trimestriel en images Principales réalisations, Décembre 2014.* Shanghai, China: Olam. Available at: http://m.gabonews.com/IMG/pdf/rapport_trimestriel_olam_-_decembre_2014.pdf.

Olam (n.d.). *Palm FAQ.* Shanghai, China: Olam. Available at: http://olamgroup.com/products-services/food-staples-packaged-foods/palm/faq-and-reports. Accessed May 17, 2015.

Open Development Cambodia (2014). *Socio-Economic Data for Cambodia.* Open Development Cambodia (ODC). Available at: http://www.opendevelopmentcambodia.net/maps/downloads/. Accessed August, 2014.

Open Development Cambodia (2015a). *Economic Land Concession Briefing.* Open Development Cambodia (ODC). Available at: http://www.opendevelopmentcambodia.net/briefing/economic-land-concessions-elcs/. Accessed May 7, 2015.

Open Development Cambodia (2015b). *Forest Cover Briefing.* Open Development Cambodia (ODC). Available at: http://www.opendevelopmentcambodia.net/briefing/forest-cover/#Technical%20Notes. Accessed May 7, 2015.

Oppong-anane, K. (2006). *Country Pasture/Forage Resource Profiles Ghana.* Rome, Italy: Food and Agriculture Organization of the United Nations (FAO). Available at: http://www.fao.org/ag/agp/AGPC/doc/Counprof/PDF.

OuTrop (2013). *Nursery and Reforestation Strategy 2013–15.* Palangka Raya, Indonesia: The Orangutan Tropical Peatland Project (OuTrop).

Oyono, P.R. (2013). *The Narratives of Capitalist Land Accumulation and Recognition in Coastal Cameroon. Working Paper 29.* The Land Deal Politics Initiative.

Page, S., Hoscilo, A., Wosten, H., *et al.* (2009). Restoration ecology of lowland tropical peatlands in Southeast Asia: current knowledge and future research directions. *Ecosystems*, **12**, 888–905.

Page, S.E., Rieley, J.O., Shotyk, W. and Weiss, D. (1999). Interdependence of peat and vegetation in a tropical peat swamp forest. *Philosophical Transactions of the Royal Society of London B: Biological Sciences*, **354**, 1885–97.

Pakiam, R. (2014). Palm oil seen by UBS extending slump on outlook for supplies. *Bloomberg*, August 21, 2014. Available at: http://www.bloomberg.com/news/2014–08–20/palm-oil-seen-by-ubs-extending-declines-on-outlook-for-supplies.html.

Palacios, G., Lowenstine, L.J., Cranfield, M.R., *et al.* (2011). Human metapneumovirus infection in wild mountain gorillas, Rwanda. *Emerging Infectious Diseases*, **17**, 711–3.

PALMCI (2012). *PALMCI: Oil Palm Expert.* Abidjan, Ivory Coast: PALMCI. Available at: http://www.palmci.ci/DOC/entreprise/presentation/livret_palmci_2012.pdf.

Palombit, R.A. (1992). *Pair bonds and monogamy in wild siamang (*Hylobates syndactylus*) and white-handed gibbons (*Hylobates lar*) in northern Sumatra.* PhD thesis. Davis, CA: Animal Behavior, University of California.

Palombit, R.A. (1994). Dynamic pair bonds in hylobatids: implications regarding monogamous social systems. *Behaviour*, **128**, 65–101.

Palombit, R.A. (1997). Inter- and intra-specific variation in the diets of sympatric siamang (*Hylobates syndactylus*) and white-handed gibbons (*Hylobates lar*). *Folia Primatologica*, **68**, 321–37.

Paquette, N. (2014). *An overview of laws governing primates.* Presented at: North American Primate Sanctuary Alliance (NAPSA) Annual Meeting, October 1–3, 2014, San Antonio, TX.

Parid, M., Miyamoto, M., Aini, Z.N., Lim, H.F. and Michinaka, T. (2013). *Eradicating extreme poverty through land development strategy.* Presented at: Proceedings of REDD+ Research Project in Peninsular Malaysia, February 4, 2013, Kuala Lumpur.

Parnell, R.J. (2002). *The social structure and behaviour of western lowland gorillas (*Gorilla gorilla gorilla*) at Mbeli Bai, Republic of Congo.* PhD thesis. Stirling, UK: University of Stirling.

Parsons, M.B., Travis, D., Lonsdorf, E.V., *et al.* (2015). Epidemiology and molecular characterization of *Cryptosporidium* spp. in humans, wild primates, and domesticated animals in the Greater Gombe ecosystem, Tanzania. *PLoS Neglected Tropical Diseases*, **9**, e0003529.

Paustian, K., Antle, J.M., Sheehan, J. and Paul, E.A. (2006). *Agriculture's Role in Greenhouse Gas Mitigation.* Arlington, VA: Pew Center on Global Climate Change.

Pearce, F. (2007). Bog barons: Indonesia's carbon catastrophe. *New Scientist*, 1 December, 50–3.

Pedler, R., ed. (2010). *Best Management Practices for Orangutan Conservation: Natural Forest Concessions.* Jakarta, Indonesia: Orangutan Conservation Services Program (OCSP)/US Agency for International Development (USAID).

Pendleton, L.H. and Howe, E.L. (2002). Market integration, development, and smallholder forest clearance. *Land Economics*, **78**, 1–19.

Persey, S., Nussbaum, R., Hatchwell, M., Christie, S. and Crowley, H. (2011). *Towards Sustainable Palm Oil: A Framework for Action.* London, UK: Zoological Society of London (ZSL), Proforest, World Conservation Society.

Phatisa (n.d.). *African Agriculture Fund Portfolio Partners.* Nairobi, Kenya: Phatisa. Available at: http://www.phatisa.com/AAF/PortfolioPartners. Accessed November 10, 2014.

PHPA (1995). *Siberut National Park Integrated Conservation and Development Management Plan (1995–2020). Volume I. Current Conditions and Evaluation.* Jakarta, Indonesia: Chemonics International in association with PT Indeco Duta Utama and PT Nadya Karsa Amerta, for Ditjen Perlindungan Hutan dan Pelestarian Alam (PHPA), Departemen Kehutanan.

Pintea, L. (2007). *Applying remote sensing and GIS for chimpanzee habitat change detection, behaviour and conservation.* PhD thesis. Minneapolis, MN: University of Minnesota.

Pintea, L.P., Bauer, M.E., Bolstad, P.V. and Pusey, A. (2002). *Matching multiscale remote sensing data to interdisciplinary conservation needs: the case of chimpanzees in western Tanzania.* Presented at: Pecora 15/Land Satellite Information IV/ISPRS Commission I/FIEOS 2002.

Pintea, L., Pusey, A.E., Wilson, M.L., *et al.* (2011). Long-term ecological changes affecting the chimpanzees of Gombe National Park, Tanzania. In *The Ecological Impact of Long-Term Changes in Africa's Rift Valley*, ed. A.J. Plumptre. New York, NY: Nova Science Publishers, pp. 227–47.

Place, F. and Otsuka, K. (2000). Population pressure, land tenure, and tree resource management in Uganda. *Land Economics*, **76**, 233–51.

Platt, J.R. (2014). *Asia's Demand for Apes is Spurring a Deadly Illegal Trade.* TakePart. Available at: http://www.takepart.com/article/2014/06/19/asias-demand-apes-spurring-deadly-illegal-trade.

Plumptre, A.J., Rose, R., Nangendo, G., *et al.* (2010). *Eastern Chimpanzee (*Pan troglodytes schweinfurthii*): Status Survey and Conservation Action Plan 2010–2020.* Gland, Switzerland: International Union for Conservation of Nature (IUCN).

POIG (2013). *Palm Oil Innovation Group Charter, V1.0, November 13, 2013.* Palm Oil Innovation Group (POIG). Available at: http://www.greenpeace.org/international/Global/international/photos/forests/2013/Indonesia%20Forests/POIG%20Charter%2013%20November%202013.pdf.

Poulsen, J.R., Clark, C.J., Mavah, G. and Elkan, P.W. (2009). Bushmeat supply and consumption in a tropical logging concession in northern Congo. *Conservation Biology*, **23**, 1597–608.

Powell, C. (2014). *Deep Digital Science Behind 'Dawn of the Planet of the Apes'.* Available at: http://blogs.discovermagazine.com/outthere/2014/07/12/mind-blowing-digital-science-behind-new-planet-apes.

Prasetyo, L.B., Setiawan, Y. and Miuru, K. (2005). *Land-Use and Land Cover Changes during Regional Decentralization Policy Implementation: Study Case at Halimun National Park, Indonesia.* Bogor and Cibinong, Indonesia: IPB and JIKA.

Proforest (2014). *Summary Report for HCV Assessment for Olam Oil Palm Plantation Development in Gabon.* Oxford, UK: Proforest. Available at: http://olamgroup.com/wp-content/uploads/2014/01/Summary-Report-for-Olam-Palm-HCV-assessments.pdf.

Projeto GAP (n.d.). *Affiliated Sanctuaries.* São Paulo, Brazil: Projeto GAP Brazil. Available at: http://www.projetogap.org.br/en/affiliated-sanctuaries/. Accessed July, 2015.

ProtectedPlanet (n.d.-a). *Cross River National Park.* World Database on Protected Areas (WDPA). Available at: http://protectedplanet.net/sites/Cross_River_National_Park. Accessed May 27, 2014.

ProtectedPlanet (n.d.-b). *Ekinta River Forest Reserve.* World Database on Protected Areas (WDPA). Available at: http://protectedplanet.net/sites/Ekinta_River_Forest_Reserve. Accessed May 27, 2014.

Pruetz, J.D. and Bertolani, P. (2009). Chimpanzee (*Pan troglodytes verus*) behavioral responses to stresses associated with living in a savanna-mosaic environment: implications for hominin adaptations to open habitats. *Paleoanthropology*, **2009**, 252–62.

Pruetz, J.D., Marchant, L.F., Arno, J. and McGrew, W.C. (2002). Survey of savanna chimpanzees (*Pan troglodytes verus*) in southeastern Sénégal. *American Journal of Primatology*, **58**, 35–43.

Pryer, W.B. (1883). Notes on north-eastern Borneo and the Sulu Islands. *Proceedings Royal Geography Society*, **5**, 90–6.

Publish What You Pay (2013). *Publish What You Pay Denounces the Verdict Against Marc Ona, April 2, 2013.* London, UK: Publish What You Pay (PWYP). Available at: http://www.publishwhatyoupay.org/resources/publish-what-you-pay-denounces-verdict-against-marc-ona.

Pusey, A.E., Pintea, L., Wilson, M.L., Kamenya, S. and Goodall, J. (2007). The contribution of long-term research at Gombe National Park to chimpanzee conservation. *Conservation Biology*, **21**, 623–34.

Pusey, A., Williams, J. and Goodall, J. (1997). The influence of dominance rank on the reproductive success of female chimpanzees. *Science*, **277**, 828–31.

Quinten, M., Stirling, F., Schwarze, S., Dinata, Y. and Hodges, K. (2014). Knowledge, attitudes and practices of local people on Siberut Island (west-Sumatra, Indonesia) towards primate hunting and conservation. *Journal of Threatened Taxa*, **6**, 6389–98.

Rainforest Foundation (2013). *Seeds of Destruction. Expansion of Industrial Oil Palm in the Congo Basin: Potential Impacts on Forests and People.* London, UK: Rainforest Foundation UK.

Rao, M. and van Schaik, C.P. (1997). The behavioral ecology of Sumatran orangutans in logged and unlogged forest. *Tropical Biodiversity*, **4**, 173–85.

Rawson, B.M., Insua-Cao, P., Nguyen Manh Ha, *et al.* (2011). *The Conservation Status of Gibbons in Vietnam*. Hanoi: Fauna & Flora International and Conservation International.

Redford, K.H. (1992). The empty forest. *BioScience*, **42**, 414–22.

Reed, P.E., Mulangu, S., Cameron, K.N., *et al.* (2014). A new approach for monitoring ebolavirus in wild great apes. *PLoS Neglected Tropical Diseases*, **8**, e3143.

Reichard, U. (1995). Extra-pair copulations in a monogamous gibbon (*Hylobates lar*). *Ethology*, **100**, 99–112.

Reichard, U.H. (2009). The social organisation and mating system of Khao-Yai white-handed gibbons: 1992–2006. In *The Gibbons: New Perspectives on Small Ape Socioecology and Population Biology*, ed. S.W. Lappan and D.J. Whittaker. New York, NY: Springer, pp. 347–84.

Reichard, U. and Barelli, C. (2008). Life history and reproductive strategies of Khao Yai *Hylobates lar*: implications for social evolution in apes. *International Journal of Primatology*, **29**, 823–44.

Reichard, U. and Sommer, V. (1997). Group encounters in wild gibbons (*H. lar*): agonism, affiliation and the concept of infanticide. *Behaviour*, **134**, 1135–74.

Reinartz, G.E., Ingmanson, E.J. and Vervaecke, H. (2013). *Pan paniscus* gracile chimpanzee. In *Mammals of Africa. Volume II. Primates*, ed. T.M. Butynski, J. Kingdon and J. Kalina. London, UK: Bloomsbury Publishing, pp. 64–9.

Reynolds, V. (2005). *The Chimpanzees of the Budongo Forest*. Oxford, UK: Oxford University Press.

Reynolds, V., Wallis, J. and Kyamanywa, R. (2003). Fragments, sugar, and chimpanzees in Masindi District, western Uganda. In *Primates in Fragments: Ecology and Conservation*, ed. L.K. Marsh. New York, NY: Kluwer Academic/Plenum Publishers, pp. 309–20.

RFUK (2013). *Seeds of Destruction. Expansion of Industrial Oil Palm in the Congo Basin: Potential Impacts on Forests and People*. London, UK: Rainforest Foundation UK (RFUK). Available at: http://www.rainforestfoundationuk.org/palmoilreport?dm_i=D41,1AUCZ,44HZQH,4EOSV,1.

Richards, M.P. (2013). *Social and Environmental Impacts of Agricultural Large-Scale Land Acquisitions in Africa: With a Focus on West and Central Africa*. Washington DC: Rights and Resources Initiative.

Rights and Resources Initiative (2012). *Turning Point: What Future for Forest Peoples and Resources in the Emerging World Order?* Washington DC: Rights and Resources Initiative.

Rights and Resources Initiative (2014). *Lots of Words, Little Action: Will the Private Sector Tip the Scales for Community Land Rights?* Washington DC: Rights and Resources Initiative. Available at http://www.rightsandresources.org/publication/lots-of-words-little-action/.

Rijksen, H.D. and Meijaard, E. (1999). *Our Vanishing Relative. The Status of Wild Orang-utans at the Close of the Twentieth Century*. Dordrecht, the Netherlands: Kluwer Academic Publishers.

Rinaldi, D. (2003). The study of Javan gibbon (*Hylobates moloch* Audebert) in Gunung Halimun National Park (distribution, population and behavior). In *Research and Conservation of Biodiversity in Indonesia. Volume XI. Research on Endangered Species in Gunung Halimun National Park*, ed. N. Sakaguchi. Bogor, Indonesia: JIKA Biodiversity Conservation Project, pp. 30–48.

Rival, A. and Levang, P. (2014). *Palms of Controversies: Oil Palm and Development Challenges*. Bogor, Indonesia, and Paris, France: Center for International Forestry Research (CIFOR) and Editions Quae.

Robbins, A.M., Gray, M., Basabose, A., *et al.* (2013). Impact of male infanticide on the social structure of mountain gorillas. *PLoS One*, **8**, e78256.

Robbins, A.M., Stoinski, T., Fawcett, K. and Robbins, M.M. (2011). Lifetime reproductive success of female mountain gorillas. *American Journal of Physical Anthropology*, **146**, 582–93.

Robbins, M.M. (2010). Gorillas: diversity in ecology and behavior. In *Primates in Perspective*, 2nd edn, ed. C.J. Campbell, A. Fuentes, K.C. MacKinnon, S. Bearder and R.M. Stumpf. New York, NY: Oxford University Press, pp. 326–39.

Robbins, M.M. and Robbins, A.M. (2004). Simulation of the population dynamics and social structure of the Virunga mountain gorillas. *American Journal of Primatology*, **63**, 201–23.

Robbins, M. and Williamson, L. (2008). *Gorilla beringei*. In *The IUCN Red List of Threatened Species, Version 2014.3*. Gland, Switzerland: International Union for Conservation of Nature (IUCN). Available at: http://www.iucn redlist.org/details/39994/0. Accessed February 26, 2015.

Robson, S.L. and Wood, B. (2008). Hominin life history: reconstruction and evolution. *Journal of Anatomy*, **212**, 394–425.

Rogers, M.E., Abernethy, K., Bermejo, M., *et al.* (2004). Western gorilla diet: a synthesis from six sites. *American Journal of Primatology*, **64**, 173–92.

Ross, S.R. and Lukas, K.E. (2006). Use of space in a non-naturalistic environment by chimpanzees (*Pan troglodytes*) and lowland gorillas (*Gorilla gorilla gorilla*). *Applied Animal Behaviour Science*, **96**, 143–52.

Ross, S.R., Lukas, K.E., Lonsdorf, E.V., *et al.* (2008). Inappropriate use and portrayal of chimpanzees. *Science*, **319**, 1487.

Roy, J., Gray, M., Stoinski, T., Robbins, M.M. and Vigilant, L. (2014a). Fine-scale genetic structure analyses suggest further male than female dispersal in mountain gorillas. *BMC Ecology*, **14**, 21.

Roy, J., Vigilant, L., Gray, M., *et al.* (2014b). Challenges in the use of genetic mark–recapture to estimate the population size of Bwindi mountain gorillas (*Gorilla beringei beringei*). *Biological Conservation*, **180**, 249–61.

RSG and ISSG (2012). *IUCN Guidelines for Reintroductions and other Conservation Translocations*. Gland, Switzerland: International Union for Conservation of Nature Species Survival Commission (IUCN SSC). Available at: http://www.issg.org/pdf/publications/Translocation-Guidelines-2012.pdf.

RSPO (2004a). *Press Statement: New Global Initiative to Promote Sustainable Palm Oil*. Kuala Lumpur, Malaysia: Roundtable on Sustainable Palm Oil (RSPO).

RSPO (2004b). *Statutes: Roundtable on Sustainable Palm Oil*. Zurich, Switzerland: Roundtable on Sustainable Palm Oil (RSPO).

RSPO (2010a). *High Conservation Values in Non-Primary Forests, 7th RSPO General Assembly, November, 2010*. Kuala Lumpur, Malaysia: Roundtable on Sustainable Palm Oil (RSPO).

RSPO (2010b). *Non-Primary Forests Can Include High Conservation Values (HCV). Position Statement January 12, 2010*. Kuala Lumpur, Malaysia: Roundtable on Sustainable Palm Oil (RSPO). Available at: http://www.rspo.org/sites/default/files/RSPO_Statement_HCV%20Jan%202010%20FINAL.pdf.

RSPO (2012). *Term of Reference INA HCV Task Force Endorsed by the RSPO's Executive Board in July, 2012*. Kuala Lumpur, Malaysia: Roundtable on Sustainable Palm Oil (RSPO). Available at: http://www.rspo.org/file/Term%20of%20Reference_INA%20HCV%20TF%202012_Endorsed%20by%20EB%20in%20July%202012.pdf.

RSPO (2013a). *Case Tracker: Biase Plantation Limited (Ibiae Estate)/Wilmar International*. Kuala Lumpur, Malaysia: Roundtable on Sustainable Palm Oil (RSPO). Available at: http://www.rspo.org/members/complaints/status-of-complaints/view/26. Accessed July, 2015.

RSPO (2013b). *Principles and Criteria for the Production of Sustainable Palm Oil. Endorsed by Extraordinary RSPO GA, April 25, 2013*. Kuala Lumpur, Malaysia: Roundtable on Sustainable Palm Oil (RSPO). Available at: http://www.rspo.org/file/RSPO%20P&C2013_with%20Major%20Indicators_Endorsed%20by%20BOG_FINAL_A5_25thApril2014.pdf.

RSPO (2014a). *ACOP Digest 2012/13. A Snapshot of RSPO Members' Annual Communications of Progress*. Kuala Lumpur, Malaysia: Roundtable on Sustainable Palm Oil (RSPO).

RSPO (2014b). *Resolution 6f. 11th GA of the RSPO, Declaration of Mills*. Kuala Lumpur, Malaysia: Roundtable on Sustainable Palm Oil (RSPO). Available at: http://www.rspo.org/file/resolutions/GA11-Resolution6f.pdf.

RSPO (2014c). *RSPO Remediation and Compensation Procedures Related to Land Clearance without Prior HCV Assessment, May, 2014*. Kuala Lumpur, Malaysia: Roundtable on Sustainable Palm Oil (RSPO).

RSPO (2015a). *RSPO Impacts. Last Update June 17, 2015*. Kuala Lumpur, Malaysia: Roundtable on Sustainable Palm Oil (RSPO). Available at: http://www.rspo.org/about/impacts.

RSPO (2015b). *RSPO+ Voluntary Addendum to Strengthen the Standard on Peat, Deforestation and Social Requirements, May 5, 2015*. Kuala Lumpur, Malaysia: Roundtable on Sustainable Palm Oil (RSPO). Available at: http://www.rspo.org/news-and-events/news/rspo-voluntary-addendum-to-strengthen-the-standard-on-peat-deforestation-and-social-requirements.

RSPO (n.d.-a). *Board of Governors*. Kuala Lumpur, Malaysia: Roundtable on Sustainable Palm Oil (RSPO). Available at: http://www.rspo.org/about/who-we-are/board-of-governors. Accessed February 17, 2015.

RSPO (n.d.-b). *Case Tracker, PT Sisirau.* Kuala Lumpur, Malaysia: Roundtable on Sustainable Palm Oil (RSPO). Available at: http://www.rspo.org/members/complaints/status-of-complaints/view/22. Accessed July 7, 2015.

RSPO (n.d.-c). *New Planting Procedures.* Kuala Lumpur, Malaysia: Roundtable on Sustainable Palm Oil (RSPO). Available at: http://www.rspo.org/certification/new-planting-procedures. Accessed May 15, 2015.

RSPO (n.d.-d). *RSPO Ordinary Members.* Kuala Lumpur, Malaysia: Roundtable on Sustainable Palm Oil (RSPO). Available at: http://www.rspo.org/members?keywords=&member_type=Ordinary+Members&member_category=&member_country=All. Accessed February 17, 2015.

RSPO (n.d.-e). *RSPO Vision.* Kuala Lumpur, Malaysia: Roundtable on Sustainable Palm Oil (RSPO). Available at: http://www.rspo.org/en/vision_and_mission. Accessed July 15, 2014.

RSPO (n.d.-f). *Terminated and Suspended Members.* Kuala Lumpur, Malaysia: Roundtable on Sustainable Palm Oil (RSPO). Available at: http://www.rspo.org/members/terminated-and-suspended-members. Accessed March 4, 2015.

Rudel, T.K. (2013). The national determinants of deforestation in sub-Saharan Africa. *Philosophical Transactions of the Royal Society of London B: Biological Sciences*, **368**, 20120405.

Rudicell, R., Jones, J., Wroblewski, E., *et al.* (2010). Impact of simian immunodeficiency virus infection on chimpanzee population dynamics. *PLoS Pathogens*, **6**, e1001116.

Runting, R.K., Meijaard, E., Abram, N.K., *et al.* (2015). Alternative futures for Borneo show the value of integrating economic and conservation targets across borders. *Nature Communications*, **6**, 6819.

Rusmana, Y. and Listiyorini, E. (2014). Palm production in Indonesia rising for first time in six months. *Bloomberg*, March 21, 2014.

Russon, A.E., Wich, S.A., Ancrenaz, M., *et al.* (2009). Geographic variation in orangutan diets. In *Orangutans: Geographic Variation in Behavioral Ecology and Conservation*, ed. S.A. Wich, S. Utami Atmoko, T. Mitra Setia and C.P. van Schaik. Oxford, UK: Oxford University Press, pp. 135–56.

Rutherford, M.A. (2006). Current knowledge of coffee wilt disease, a major constraint to coffee production in Africa. *Phytopathology*, **96**, 663–6.

Ruysschaert, D. (2013). *Le Rôle des Organisations de Conservation dans la Construction et la Mise en Oeuvre de l'Agenda International de Conservation d'Espèces Emblématiques: le Cas de l'Orang-outan de Sumatra.* Toulouse, France: Toulouse-le-Mirail University. Available at: http://tel.archives-ouvertes.fr/tel-00951940.

Ruysschaert, D., Darsoyo, A., Zen, R., Gea, G. and Singleton, I. (2011). *Developing Palm-Oil Production on Degraded Land.* Medan, Indonesia: Foundation PanEco, YEL, World Agroforestry Centre.

Ruysschaert, D. and Salles, D. (2014). Towards global voluntary standards: questioning the effectiveness in attaining conservation goals. The case of the Roundtable on Sustainable Palm Oil (RSPO). *Ecological Economics*, **107**, 438–46.

Rwanda (2004). *Strategic Plan for Agricultural Transformation in Rwanda, October.* Rwanda: Ministry of Agriculture and Animal Resources.

Rwego, I.B., Isabirye-Basuta, G., Gillespie, T.R. and Goldberg, T.L. (2008). Gastrointestinal bacterial transmission among humans, mountain gorillas, and livestock in Bwindi Impenetrable National Park, Uganda. *Conservation Biology*, **22**, 1600–7.

SAGA (2006). *Demanding Statement About Forcing Chimpanzees to Perform in TV Entertainment Programs.* Aichi, Japan: Support for African/Asian Great Apes (SAGA), Primate Research Institute, Kyoto University. Available at: http://www.saga-jp.org/en/Demanding_Statement_about_Forcing_Chimpanzees_to_Perform_in_TV_Entertainment_Programs.html.

SAGA (2012). *Board Meeting of the 15th Symposium.* Aichi, Japan: Support for African/Asian Great Apes (SAGA), Primate Research Institute, Kyoto University. Available at: http://www.saga-jp.org/indexe.html.

Sakamaki, T., Kasalevo, P., Bokamba, M.B. and Bongoli, L. (2012). Iyondji Community Bonobo Reserve: a recently established reserve in the Democratic Republic of Congo. *African Study Monographs*, **19**, 16–9.

Sakamaki, T., Mulavwa, M. and Furuichi, T. (2009). Flu-like epidemics in wild bonobos (*Pan paniscus*) at Wamba, the Luo Scientific Reserve, Democratic Republic of Congo. *Pan Africa News*, **16**, 1.

Salafsky, N. (1993). Mammalian use of a buffer zone agroforestry system bordering Gunung-Palung National-Park, West Kalimantan, Indonesia. *Conservation Biology*, **7**, 928–33.

SAMFU (2008). *The Heavy Load: A Demand for Fundamental Changes at the Bridgestone/Firestone Rubber Plantation in Liberia.* Paynesville, Liberia: Save My Future Foundation (SAMFU). Available at: http://www.laborrights.org/sites/default/files/publications-and-resources/The%20Heavy%20Load.pdf.

Sánchez, K. (2015). *Oil palm industry and orangutan rescues.* Indonesia: International Animal Rescue (IAR). Unpublished paper provided to the Arcus Foundation.

Sanctuary Project (n.d.). *Chimpanzee Sanctuary Project.* Oita, Japan: Sanctuary Project. Available at: http://chimpsanctuary.org/indexE.htm. Accessed January 8, 2013.

Sarawak (1958). *Land Code 1958.* Malaysia.

Saudale, V. (2015). Ministry: Indonesia has only four decent zoos. *Jakarta Globe*, February 8, 2015. Available at: http://thejakartaglobe.beritasatu.com/news/ministry-indonesia-four-decent-zoos/

Savini, T., Boesch, C. and Reichard, U. (2008). Home-range characteristics and the influence of seasonality on female reproduction in white-handed gibbons (*Hylobates lar*) at Khao Yai National Park, Thailand. *American Journal of Physical Anthropology*, **135**, 1–12.

Sayer, J., Sunderland, T., Ghazoul, J., *et al.* (2013). Ten principles for a landscape approach to reconciling agriculture, conservation, and other competing land uses. *Proceedings of the National Academy of Sciences USA*, **110**, 8349–56.

Schoneveld, G.C. (2011). *The Anatomy of Large-Scale Farmland Acquisitions in Sub-Saharan Africa. CIFOR Working Paper 85.* Bogor, Indonesia: Center for International Forestry Research (CIFOR).

Schoneveld, G.C. (2014a). The geographic and sectoral patterns of large-scale farmland investments in sub-Saharan Africa. *Food Policy*, **48**, 34–50.

Schoneveld, G.C. (2014b). The politics of the forest frontier: negotiating between conservation, development, and indigenous rights in Cross River State, Nigeria. *Land Use Policy*, **38**, 147–62.

Schroeder, J. (2014). *Global Demand for Transportation Biofuels To Grow.* Cantonment, FL: ZimmComm New Media. Available at: http://www.Domesticfuel.com. Accessed February 10, 2014.

Schroepfer, K.K., Rosati, A.G., Chartrand, T. and Hare, B. (2011). Use of 'entertainment' chimpanzees in commercials distorts public perception regarding their conservation status. *PLoS One*, **6**, e26048.

Schwaben Park (2011). *Schwaben Park. YouTube video uploaded April 6, 2011.* Kaisersbach, Germany: Schwaben Park. Available at: https://www.youtube.com/watch?v=u09fgpJR5Es. Accessed July, 2015.

Schwaben Park (n.d.). *Schimpansenshow.* Kaisersbach, Germany: Schwaben Park. Available at: http://schwabenpark.com/index.php?id=43. Accessed July, 2015.

SDI (2010). *Liberia: The Promise Betrayed.* Monrovia, Liberia: Sustainable Development Institute (SDI).

SDI (2012a). *Golden Veroleum: What does the Contract Say?* Monrovia, Liberia: Sustainable Development Institute (SDI).

SDI (2012b). *Uncertain Futures: The Impacts of Sime Darby on Communities in Liberia.* Monrovia, Liberia: Sustainable Development Institute (SDI).

Seiler, N. and Robbins, M.M. (2015). Factors influencing ranging on community land and crop-raiding by mountain gorillas. *Animal Conservation*, in press. DOI: 10.1111/acv.12232.

SEnSOR (2012). *An integrated multi-disciplinary research programme for sustainability.* Presented at: RT10 Conference, October, Singapore. Socially and Environmentally Sustainable Oil Palm Research (SEnSOR).

Sha, J.C.M., Gumert, M.D., Lee, B., *et al.* (2009). Status of the long-tailed macaque *Macaca fascicularis* in Singapore and implications for management. *Biodiversity and Conservation*, **18**, 2909–26.

Sheil, D., Casson, A., Meijaard, E., *et al.* (2009). *The Impacts and Opportunities of Oil Palm in Southeast Asia. What Do We Know and What Do We Need to Know? CIFOR Occasional Paper 51.* Bogor, Indonesia: Center for International Forestry Research (CIFOR). Available at: http://www.cifor.org/publications/pdf_files/OccPapers/OP-51.pdf.

Shepherd, P.A., Rieley, J.O. and Page, S.E. (1997). The relationship between forest structure and peat characteristics in the upper catchment of the Sungai Sabangau, Central Kalimantan. In *Biodiversity and Sustainability of Tropical Peatlands*, ed. J.O. Rieley and S.E. Page. Cardigan, UK: Samara Publishing, pp. 191–210.

Shimada, M.K., Hayakawa, S., Humle, T., *et al.* (2004). Mitochondrial DNA genealogy of chimpanzees in the Nimba Mountains and Bossou, West Africa. *American Journal of Primatology*, **64**, 261–75.

Sicotte, P. (1993). Inter-group encounters and female transfer in mountain gorillas: influence of group composition on male behavior. *American Journal of Primatology*, **30**, 21–36.

Sime Darby (2013). *Plantation, June 2013.* Kuala Lumpur, Malaysia: Sime Darby. Available at: http://www.simedarby.com/upload/SD_FactSheet_Plantation.pdf.

Sims, B.G. (2011). *South Africa: Regional conservation agriculture symposium, Tanzania and Kenya: technical support to the regional CA-SARD Project, February 6–March 2.* Unpublished FAO mission report.

Singleton, I., Knott, C.D., Morrogh-Bernard, H.C., Wich, S.A. and van Schaik, C.P. (2009). Ranging behavior of orangutan females and social organization. In *Orangutans: Geographic Variation in Behavioral Ecology and Conservation,* ed. S.A. Wich, S. Utami Atmoko, T. Mitra Setia and C.P. van Schaik. Oxford, UK: Oxford University Press, pp. 205–13.

Singleton, I. and van Schaik, C.P. (2001). Orangutan home range size and its determinants in a Sumatran swamp forest. *International Journal of Primatology,* **22,** 877–911.

Singleton, I., Wich, S.A. and Griffiths, M. (2008). *Pongo abelii.* In *The IUCN Red List of Threatened Species, Version 2014.3.* Gland, Switzerland: International Union for Conservation of Nature (IUCN). Available at: http://www.iucnredlist.org/details/39780/0 Accessed February 26, 2015.

Singleton, I., Wich, S., Husson, S., *et al.* (2004). *Orangutan Population and Habitat Viability Assessment: Final Report.* Apple Valley, MN: International Union for Conservation of Nature Species Survival Commission (IUCN SSC) Conservation Breeding Specialist Group.

Small, R. (2013). *The Impact of Oil Palm Plantations on Conservation in Liberia.* Cambridge, UK: Fauna & Flora International. Available at: http://povertyandconservation.info/sites/default/files/10%20Rob%20Small%20%28FFI%29%20-%20The%20impact%20of%20oil%20palm%20plantations%20on%20conservation%20in%20Liberia.pdf.

Smalley, R. (2013). *Plantations, Contract Farming and Commercial Farming Areas in Africa: A Comparative Review. Land and Agricultural Commercialization in Africa (LACA) Working Paper 55.* Brighton, UK: Future Agricultures.

Smithsonian Institution (n.d.). *What Does it Mean to be Human?* Washington DC: Smithsonian Institution. Available at: http://humanorigins.si.edu/evidence/genetics. Accessed May, 2015.

Smuts, B., Cheney, D., Seyfarth, R., Wrangham, R. and Struhsaker, T. (1987). *Primate Societies,* 2nd edn. Chicago, IL: University of Chicago Press.

Sodhi, N.S., Koh, L.P., Clements, R., *et al.* (2010). Conserving Southeast Asian forest biodiversity in human-modified landscapes. *Biological Conservation,* **143,** 2375–84.

Solheim, E. and Natalegawa, R.M.M.M. (2010). *Letter of Intent: the Government of the Kingdom of Norway and the Government of the Republic of Indonesia on Cooperation on Reducing Greenhouse Gas Emissions from Deforestation and Forest Degradation.* Oslo, Norway: The Governments of Norway and the Republic of Indonesia.

SOMDIAA (n.d.). *SOMDIAA.* Paris, France: Société d'Organisation de Management et de Développement des Industries Alimentaires et Agricoles (SOMDIAA). Available at: http://www.somdiaa.com/en/. Accessed May, 2015.

Soumah, A.G., Humle, T. and Matsuzawa, T. (2014). *Oil palm use among the people and wild chimpanzees of Bossou, Guinea, West Africa.* Presented at: International Primatological Society, 25th Congress Paper August 11-16, 2014, Hanoi, Vietnam.

Sousa, J., Barata, A.V., Sousa, C., Casanova, C.C.N. and Vicente, L. (2011). Chimpanzee oil-palm use in Southern Cantanhez National Park, Guinea-Bissau. *American Journal of Primatology,* **73,** 485–97.

SPOM (n.d.). *Sustainable Palm Oil Manifesto (SPOM).* CarbonStockStudy.com. Available at: http://www.carbonstockstudy.com/Documents/Sustainable-Palm-Oil-Manifesto.aspx. Accessed May 13, 2015.

Steinmetz, R., Chutipong, W. and Seuaturien, N. (2006). Collaborating to conserve large mammals in Southeast Asia. *Conservation Biology,* **20,** 1391–401.

Stern, N.H. (2007). *The Economics of Climate Change: The Stern Review.* Cambridge, UK: Cambridge University Press.

Stevens, C., Winterbottom, R., Springer, J. and Reytar, K. (2014). *Securing Rights, Combating Climate Change: How Strengthening Community Forest Rights Mitigates Climate Change.* Washington DC: World Resources Institute. Available at: http://www.wri.org/securing-rights.

Stewart, C. (2014). *Industrial agriculture and apes: the experience of Olam International in Gabon.* Gabon: Olam International. Unpublished paper provided to the Arcus Foundation.

Stewart, K.J. (1988). Suckling and lactational anoestrus in wild gorillas (*Gorilla gorilla*). *Journal of Reproduction and Fertility,* **83,** 627–34.

Stiles, D., Redmond, I., Cress, D., Nellemann, C. and Formo, R.K. (2013). *Stolen Apes: The Illicit Trade in Chimpanzees, Gorillas, Bonobos and Orangutans. A Rapid Response Assessment.* United Nations Environment Programme. Available at: http://www.un-grasp.org/news/121-download.

Stokes, E.J., Strindberg, S., Bakabana, P.C., *et al.* (2010). Monitoring great ape and elephant abundance at large spatial scales: measuring effectiveness of a conservation landscape. *PLoS One,* **5**, e10294.

Strassburg, B., Micol, L., Ramos, F., *et al.* (2012). *Increasing Agricultural Output While Avoiding Deforestation: A Case Study for Mato Grosso, Brazil.* Rio de Janerio, Brazil: International Institute for Sustainability (IIS) and Instituto Centro de Vida (ICV). Available at: http://www.pcfisu.org/wp-content/uploads/2012/07/Mato_grosso_Final_Report.pdf.

Struebig, M., Kingston, T., Petit, E., *et al.* (2011). Parallel declines in species and genetic diversity in tropical forest fragments. *Ecology Letters,* **14**, 582–90.

Strum, S.C. (2010). The development of primate raiding: implications for management and conservation. *International Journal of Primatology,* **31**, 133–56.

Sugarjito, J. and Sinaga, M.H. (1999). Conservation status and population distribution of primates in Gunung Halimun National Park, West Java, Indonesia. In *Proceedings of the International Workshop on Javan Gibbon (*Hylobates moloch*): Rescue and Rehabilitation,* ed. J. Supriatna and B.O. Manullang. Jakarta, Indonesia: Conservation International Indonesia Program and Center for Biodiversity and Conservation Studies, pp. 6–12.

Sugiyama, Y. and Fujita, S. (2011). The demography and reproductive parameters of Bossou chimpanzees. In *Chimpanzees of Bossou and Nimba,* ed. T. Matsuzawa, T. Humle and Y. Sugiyama. Tokyo, Japan: Springer-Verlag, pp. 23–34.

Supriatna, J., Tilson, R., Gurmaya, K.J., *et al.* (1994). *Javan Gibbon and Javan Langur: Population and Habitat Viability Analysis Report.* Apple Valley, MN: International Union for Conservation of Nature Species Survival Commission (IUCN SSC) Conservation Breeding Specialist Group.

Susanto, A. (2014). Last orangutans evacuated from Solo Zoo. *Jakarta Globe,* July 2, 2014. Available at: http://thejakartaglobe.beritasatu.com/news/last-orangutans-evacuated-solo-zoo.

Sutomo (2006). *Potensi Keberadaan Mangsa Macan Tutul (*Panthera pardus melas *Cuvier, 1809) di Koridor antara Gunung Halimun dan Gunung Salak.* BSc thesis. Bogor, Indonesia: Institut Pertanian Bogor.

SWD (2012). *Sabah Wildlife Department Orangutan Action Plan 2012–2016.* Sabah, Malaysia: Sabah Wildlife Department (SWD).

Syarif, L. (2010). Current development of Indonesian environmental law. *IUCN Academy of Environmental Law E Journal,* Available at: http://www.iucnael.org/en/documents/485-indonesia-laode-syarif/file.

Takemoto, H. (2002). *Feeding ecology of chimpanzees in Bossou, Guinea: coping with the seasonal fluctuation of food supply and micrometeorology in the tropical forest.* PhD thesis. Kyoto, Japan: Kyoto University.

Takemoto, H. (2011). Microclimate and moving pattern. In *Chimpanzees of Bossou and Nimba,* ed. T. Matsuzawa, T. Humle and Y. Sugiyama. Tokyo, Japan: Springer-Verlag, pp. 335–8.

Tata, H., van Noordwijk, M., Ruysschaert, D., *et al.* (2014). Will funding to reduce emissions from deforestation and (forest) degradation (REDD+) stop conversion of peat swamps to oil palm in orangutan habitat in Tripa in Aceh, Indonesia? *Mitigation and Adaptation Strategies for Global Change,* **19**, 693–713.

Tchawa, P. (2012). *La Cession des Terres a Grande Échelle au Cameroun Etat de Lieux et Analyse Prospective du Cadre Règlementaire.* Yaoundé, Cameroon: Friedrich-Ebert-Stiftung.

TechnoServe (2011). *Technical Brief. Outgrower Scheme: Enhancing Profitability.* Washington DC: TechnoServe. Available at: http://www.technoserve.org/files/downloads/outgrower-brief-september.pdf.

Teleki, G. (1989). Population status of wild chimpanzees (*Pan troglodytes*) and threats to survival. In *Understanding Chimpanzees,* ed. P.G. Heltne and L.A. Marquardt. Cambridge, MA: Harvard University Press, pp. 312–53.

Terada, S., Nackoney, J., Sakamaki, T., *et al.* (2015). Habitat use of bonobos (*Pan paniscus*) at Wamba: selection of vegetation types for ranging, feeding, and night-sleeping. *American Journal of Primatology,* **77**, 701–13.

Texas Satutes (2001). *Health and Safety Code. Title 10. Health and Safety of Animals. Chapter 822. Regulation of Animals Subchapter E. Dangerous Wild Animals.* Texas Constitution and Statutes. Available at: http://www.statutes.legis.state.tx.us/Docs/HS/htm/HS.822.htm.

Teysmann, J.E. (1875). Verslag eener botanische reis naar de westkust van Borneo. *Natuurkundig Tijdschrift van Nederlandsch-Indië*, **35**, 271–568.

TFT (2014). *Palm Oil Industry Transformation: TFT's Perspective One Year Later.* Crassier, Switzerland: Tropical Forest Trust (TFT).

TFT (2015). *Wilmar Leads Path to Transformation. Palm Oil Giant Opens its Supply Chain to Customers and Stakeholders, Revealing Unprecedented Detail.* Crassier, Switzerland: Tropical Forest Trust (TFT). Available at: http://www.wilmar-international.com/wp-content/uploads/2015/01/TFT-Press-Release-Wilmar-Dashboard-22-January-2015.pdf.

The Inquirer Newspaper (2012). Liberia: SRC closes rubber factory. *The Inquirer Newspaper*, Accessed May 19, 2015. Available at: http://allafrica.com/stories/201209200977.html.

Thongmanivong, S. and Fujita, Y. (2006). Recent land use and livelihood transitions in northern Laos. *Mountain Research and Development*, **26**, 237–44.

Tieguhong, J.C. and Betti, J.L. (2008). Forest and protected area management. *ITTO Tropical Forest Update*, **18**, 6–9.

Tokuyama, N., Emikey, B., Bafike, B., *et al.* (2012). Bonobos apparently search for a lost member injured by a snare. *Primates*, **53**, 215–9.

Tranquilli, S., Abedi-Lartey, M., Abernethy, K., *et al.* (2014). Protected areas in tropical Africa: assessing threats and conservation activities. *PLoS One*, **9**, e114154.

Transparency International (2014). *Corruption Perceptions Index 2014.* Berlin, Germany: Transparency International. Available at: https://www.transparency.org/cpi2014/results. Accessed June, 2015.

Travis, D.A., Lonsdorf, E.V., Mlengeya, T. and Raphael, J. (2008). A science-based approach to managing disease risks for ape conservation. *American Journal of Primatology*, **70**, 745–50.

Treves, A. and Bruskotter, J. (2014). Tolerance for predatory wildlife. *Science*, **344**, 476–7.

Truitt, A. (2014). *An overview of laws governing primates.* Presented at: North American Primate Sanctuary Alliance (NAPSA) Annual Meeting, October 1–3, 2014, San Antonio, TX.

Trumper, K., Bertzky, M., Dickson, B., *et al.* (2009). *The Natural Fix? The Role of Ecosystems in Climate Mitigation. A UNEP Rapid Response Assessment.* Cambridge, UK: United Nations Environment Programme (UNEP) World Conservation Monitoring Centre (WCMC).

Tsoumou, C. (2011). Congo Republic wants $2.6 billion to replant forest. *Reuters*, August 5, 2011. Available at: http://www.reuters.com/article/2011/08/05/us-congo-republic-forest-idUSTRE77434320110805.

Tutin, C.E.G. (1996). Ranging and social structure of lowland gorillas in the Lopé Reserve, Gabon. In *Great Ape Societies*, ed. W.C. McGrew, L.F. Marchant and T. Nishida. Cambridge, UK: Cambridge University Press, pp. 58–70.

Tutin, C.E.G., Ancrenaz, M., Paredes, J., *et al.* (2001). Conservation biology framework for the release of wild-born orphaned chimpanzees into the Conkouati Reserve, Congo. *Conservation Biology*, **15**, 1247–57.

Tutin, C.E.G., Stokes, E., Boesch, C., *et al.* (2005). *Regional Action Plan for the Conservation of Chimpanzees and Gorillas in Western Equatorial Africa.* Washington DC: International Union for Conservation of Nature Species Survival Commission (IUCN SSC) Primate Specialist Group Conservation International.

Tweh, C.G., Lormie, M.M., Kouakou, C.Y., *et al.* (2014). Conservation status of chimpanzees *Pan troglodytes verus* and other large mammals in Liberia: a nationwide survey. *Oryx*. DOI: 10.1017/S0030605313001191.

Tweheyo, M., Lye, K.A. and Weladji, R.B. (2004). Chimpanzee diet and habitat selection in the Budongo Forest Reserve, Uganda. *Forest Ecology and Management*, **188**, 267–78.

UBOS (2006). *2002 Uganda Population and Housing Census: Analytical Report: Population Size and Distribution.* Kampala, Uganda: Uganda Bureau of Statistics. Available at: http://www.ubos.org/onlinefiles/uploads/ubos/pdf%20documents/2002%20CensusPopnSizeGrowthAnalyticalReport.pdf.

UBOS (2007). *Hoima District 2002 Population and Housing Census Analytical Report.* Kampala, Uganda: Uganda Bureau of Statistics (UBOS).

UBOS (2014). *National Population and Housing Census 2014: Provisional Results.* Kampala, Uganda: Uganda Bureau of Statistics. Available at: http://www.ubos.org/onlinefiles/uploads/ubos/NPHC/NPHC%202014%20PROVISIONAL%20RESULTS%20REPORT.pdf.

UN-REDD (n.d.-a). About REDD+. Available at: http://www.un-redd.org/AboutREDD/tabid/102614/ Default.aspx. Accessed May, 2015.

UN-REDD (n.d.-b). About the UN-REDD Programme. Available at: http://www.un-redd.org/AboutUN-REDD Programme/tabid/102613/Default.aspx. Accessed May, 2015.

UN (1992). *Convention on Biological Diversity. Signed in Rio de Janeiro, Brazil, June 5.* Blue Ridge Summit, PA: United Nations (UN). Available at: https://www.cbd.int/convention/text/default.shtml.

UN (2006). *International Tropical Timber Agreement. Signed in Geneva, Switzerland, January 27. TD/TIMBER.3/121.* Blue Ridge Summit, PA: United Nations (UN). Available at: http://www.itto.int/itta/.

UNECA (2013). *Making the Most of Africa's Commodities: Industrializing for Growth, Jobs and Economic Transformation. Economic Report on Africa 2013.* Addis Ababa, Ethiopia: United Nations Economic Commission for Africa (UNECA). Available at: http://www.uneca.org/sites/default/files/publications/unera_report_eng_final_web.pdf.

UNECA (2014). *Dynamic Industrial Policy in Africa. Economic Report on Africa 2014.* Addis Ababa, Ethiopia: United Nations Economic Commission for Africa (UNECA). Available at: http://repository.uneca.org/unecawebsite/sites/default/files/page_attachments/final_era2014_march25_en.pdf.

UNECE (2008). *Spatial Planning: Key Instrument for Development and Effective Governance with Special Reference to Countries in Transition.* Geneva, Switzerland: United Nations Economic Commission for Europe (UNECE).

UNEP (2011). Oil Palm Plantations: Threats And Opportunities For Tropical Ecosystems. Available at: http://na.unep.net/geas/archive/pdfs/Dec_11_Palm_Plantations.pdf.

UNEP (2014). *UNEP and Roundtable on Sustainable Palm Oil Sign New Agreement. November 14, 2014.* Nairobi, Kenya: United Nations Environment Programme (UNEP). Available at: http://www.unep.org/newscentre/Default.aspx?DocumentID=2812&ArticleID=11071.

UNESCO (n.d.). *Dja Faunal Reserve.* Paris, France: United Nations Educational, Scientific and Cultural Organization (UNESCO). Available at: http://whc.unesco.org/en/list/407. Accessed September 30, 2014.

US Senate Committee on Environment and Public Works (2014). *Senate Report 113–308, Captive Primate Safety Act.* US Congress. Available at: https://www.congress.gov/congressional-report/113th-congress/senate-report/308/1.

USAID (2008). *Nigeria Biodiversity and Tropical Forestry Assessment. Maximizing Agricultural Revenue in Key Enterprises for Targeted Sites (Markets).* Washington DC: US Agency for International Development (USAID).

USAID (2010a). *Country Profile on Property Rights and Natural Resource Governance: Democratic Republic of Congo.* Washington DC: US Agency for International Development (USAID). Available at: http://usaidlandtenure.net/democratic-republic-of-congo.

USAID (2010b). *Country Profile on Property Rights and Natural Resource Governance: Liberia.* Washington DC: US Agency for International Development (USAID). Available at: http://usaidlandtenure.net/liberia.

USAID (2011). *Country Profile on Property Rights and Natural Resource Governance: Cameroon.* Washington DC: US Agency for International Development (USAID). Available at: http://usaidlandtenure.net/cameroon.

USDA (2010). *Indonesia: Rising Global Demand Fuels Palm Oil Expansion.* Washington DC: United States Department of Agriculture (USDA).

USDA (2014a). *Land Values: 2014 Summary.* Washington DC: United States Department of Agriculture (USDA). Available at: http://www.nass.usda.gov/Publications/Todays_Reports/reports/land0814.pdf.

USDA (2014b). *United States Department of Agriculture PSD Database. Agricultural Production, Supply, and Distribution.* Washington DC: United States Department of Agriculture (USDA). Accessed June 25, 2014.

USDA (2015). *Oil Seeds: World Markets and Trade, June.* Washington DC: United States Department of Agriculture (USDA). Available at: https://apps.fas.usda.gov/psdonline/circulars/oilseeds.pdf.

USDA APHIS (2013). Petition to amend animal welfare act regulations to prohibit public contact with big cats, bears, and nonhuman primates, 9 CFR Part 2 and 9 CFR Part 3, Docket No. APHIS-2012–0107, 2013–18874. *Federal Register, Proposed Rule*, **78**, 47215–7.

USDA FAS (n.d.). *Global Agricultural Trade System.* Washington DC: United States Department of Agriculture (USDA) Foreign Agricultural Service (FAS). Available at: http://apps.fas.usda.gov/gats/default.aspx. Accessed September 2, 2014.

USDOI (2015). Endangered and threatened wildlife and plants; listing all chimpanzees as endangered species, 50 CFR Part 17, Docket No. FWS-R9-ES-2010-0086; 4500030115. *Federal Register*, **80**, 34500–25.

USFWS (2013). Listing all chimpanzees as endangered. *Federal Register*, **78**, 35201–17.

USFWS (2015a). *Endangered Species: Chimpanzee (*Pan troglodytes*).* Falls Church, VA: US Fish and Wildlife Service (USFWS). Available at: http://www.fws.gov/endangered/what-we-do/chimpanzee.html. Accessed July, 2015.

USFWS (2015b). *Final Rule to List All Chimpanzees as Captive and Wild as Endangered Questions and Answers.* Falls Church, VA: US Fish and Wildlife Service (USFWS). Available at: http://www.fws.gov/home/feature/2015/pdfs/ChimpanzeeFinalRuleFAQs.pdf.

USITC (2015). *Harmonized Tariff Schedule of the United States.* Washington DC: United States International Trade Commission (USITC). Available at: http://hts.usitc.gov. Accessed May 13, 2015.

van Kempen, J. and Mayifuila, N. (2013). *The Democratic Republic of the Congo New Agricultural Law No. 11/022 of December 24, 2011 is Currently Being amended and Supplemented.* EMW&A. Available at http://www.cabemery.org/2013/04/02/the-democratic-republic-of-the-congo-new-agricultural-law-n-11022-of-december-24–2011-is-currently-being-amended-and-supplemented/#.VDsDE_1waUk.

van Noordwijk, M.A., Sauren, S.E.B., Ahbam, N.A., *et al.* (2009). Development of independence: Sumatran and Bornean orangutans compared. In *Orangutans: Geographic Variation in Behavioral Ecology and Conservation*, ed. S.A. Wich, S. Utami Atmoko, T. Mitra Setia and C.P. van Schaik. Oxford, UK: Oxford University Press, pp. 189–203.

van Noordwijk, M.A., Willems, E.P., Utami Atmoko, S.S., Kuzawa, C.W. and van Schaik, C.P. (2013). Multi-year lactation and its consequences in Bornean orang-utan (*Pongo pygmaeus wurmbii*). *Behavioral Ecology and Sociobiology*, **67**, 805–14.

van Schaik, C. (2001). *Securing future for wild orangutans.* Presented at: The Apes: Challenges for the 21st Century, 10–13 May, 2000, Brookfield Zoo, Brookfield, IL.

van Schaik, C.P., Azwar and Priatna, D. (1995). Population estimates and habitat preferences of orang-utans based on line transects of nests. In *The Neglected Ape*, ed. R.D. Nadler, B.F.M. Galdikas, L.K. Sheeran and N. Rosen. New York, NY: Plenum Press, pp. 129–47.

van Vliet, N., Mertz, O., Heinimann, A., *et al.* (2012). Trends, drivers and impacts of changes in swidden cultivation in tropical forest-agriculture frontiers: a global assessment. *Global Environmental Change-Human and Policy Dimensions*, **22**, 418–29.

Varki, A. and Altheide, T.K. (2005). Comparing the human and chimpanzee genomes: searching for needles in a haystack. *Genome Research*, **15**, 1746–58.

Varkkey, H. (2013). Patronage politics, plantation fires and transboundary haze. *Environmental Hazards*, **12**, 200–17.

Vasudev, D. and Fletcher, R.J. (2015). Incorporating movement behavior into conservation prioritization in fragmented landscapes: an example of western hoolock gibbons in Garo Hills, India. *Biological Conservation*, **181**, 124–32.

Vietnam Briefing (2014). Vietnam's agricultural sector sees strong growth thanks to FDI. *Vietnam Briefing*, Accessed October, 2014. Available at: http://www.vietnam-briefing.com/news/vietnams-agricultural-sector-sees-strong-growth-thanks-fdi.html/.

Vis, J.K., Teoh, HC., Chandran, M.R., *et al.* (2012). Sustainable development of oil palm industry. In *Palm Oil: Production, Processing, Characterization, and Uses. AOCS Monograph Series on Oilseeds, Vol. 5*, ed. O.M. Lai, C.P. Tan and C.C. Akoh. Urbana, IL: AOCS Press, pp. 737–84.

von Maltitz, G. and Stafford, W. (2011). *Assessing Opportunities and Constraints for Biofuel Development in Sub-Saharan Africa.* Bogor, Indonesia: Center for International Forestry Research (CIFOR).

Wah Seong (2013). *Annual Report. Growing Today for a Better Tomorrow.* Kuala Lumpur, Malaysia: Wah Seong. Available at: http://announcements.bursamalaysia.com/EDMS/subweb.nsf/7f04516f8098680348256c6f0017a6bf/edf117d86cf56ff048257ce60015b8c7/$FILE/WASEONG-AnnualReport2013.pdf.

Wales Ape and Monkey Sanctuary (n.d.-a). *Chimpanzees.* Swansea Valley, UK: Wales Ape and Monkey Sanctuary. Available at: http://www.ape-monkey-rescue.org.uk/chimps.html. Accessed September, 2014.

Wales Ape and Monkey Sanctuary (n.d.-b). *Gibbons.* Swansea Valley, UK: Wales Ape and Monkey Sanctuary. Available at: http://www.ape-monkey-rescue.org.uk/gibbons.html. Accessed September, 2014.

Walsh, P.D., Abernethy, K.A., Bermejo, M., *et al.* (2003). Catastrophic ape decline in western equatorial Africa. *Nature*, **422**, 611–4.

Walsh, P.D., Tutin, C.E.G., Oates, J.F., *et al.* (2008). *Gorilla gorilla.* In *The IUCN Red List of Threatened Species, Version 2014.3.* Gland, Switzerland: International Union for Conservation of Nature (IUCN). Available at: http://www.iucnredlist.org/details/9404/0. Accessed February 26, 2015.

Waltert, M. (2013). *Large Mammal and Fish Fauna Assessments in the Planned Oil Palm Concession Area of Herakles Farms in SW Cameroon. Report to Save Wildlife Conservation Fund, Greenpeace, and WWF.* Göttingen, Germany: Georg-August-Universität, Department of Conservation Biology. Available at: http://www.greenpeace.org/international/Global/international/briefings/forests/2013/Waltert-Report-Herakles-June-2013.pdf.

Watts, D.P. (1984). Composition and variability of mountain gorilla diets in the central Virungas. *American Journal of Primatology*, 7, 325–56.

Watts, D.P. (1989). Infanticide in mountain gorillas: new cases and a reconsideration of the evidence. *Ethology*, 81, 1–18.

Watts, D.P., Muller, M., Amsler, S.J., Mbabazi, G. and Mitani, J.C. (2006). Lethal intergroup aggression by chimpanzees in Kibale National Park, Uganda. *American Journal of Primatology*, 68, 161–80.

WCO (2013). *Illicit Trade Report 2012 (No. D/2013/0448/7).* Brussels, Belgium: World Customs Organization (WCO). Available at: http://www.cites.org/fb/2013/wco_illicit_trade_report_2012.pdf.

WCS (2014). *New Park Protects 15,000 Gorillas.* Bronx, NY: Wildlife Conservation Society (WCS). Available at: http://www.wcs.org/press/press-releases/ntokou-pikounda-national-park.aspx. Accessed June 10, 2014.

Webber, A.D. and Hill, C.M. (2014). Using Participatory Risk Mapping (PRM) to identify and understand people's perceptions of crop loss to animals in Uganda. *PLoS One*, 9, e102912.

Webber, A.D., Hill, C.M. and Reynolds, V. (2007). Assessing the failure of a community-based human–wildlife conflict mitigation project in Budongo Forest Reserve, Uganda. *Oryx*, 41, 177–84.

WFFT (2015). *Canoe, The Bangkok Chimp, Getting Help From Authorities.* Petchaburi, Thailand: Wildlife Friends Foundation Thailand (WFFT). Available at: http://www.wfft.org/primates/canoe-the-bangkok-chimp-getting-help-form-authorities/.

White, L. and Tutin, C.E.G. (2001). Why chimpanzees and gorillas respond differently to logging: a cautionary tale from Gabon. In *African Rain Forest Ecology and Conservation: An Interdisciplinary Perspective*, ed. W. Weber, L.J.T. White, A. Vedder and L. Naughton-Treves. New Haven, CT: Yale University Press, pp. 449–62.

Wich, S.A. and Boyko, R.H. (2011). Which factors determine orangutan nests' detection probability along transects? *Tropical Conservation Science*, 4, 53–63.

Wich, S.A., de Vries, H., Ancrenaz, M., *et al.* (2009a). Orangutan life history variation. In *Orangutans: Geographic Variation in Behavioral Ecology and Conservation*, ed. S.A. Wich, S. Utami Atmoko, T. Mitra Setia and C.P. van Schaik. Oxford, UK: Oxford University Press, pp. 65–75.

Wich, S.A., Fredriksson, G.M., Usher, G., *et al.* (2012a). Hunting of Sumatran orang-utans and its importance in determining distribution and density. *Biological Conservation*, 146, 163–9.

Wich, S., Garcia-Ulloa, J., Kühl, H.S., *et al.* (2014). Will oil palm's homecoming spell doom for Africa's great apes? *Current Biology*, 24, 1–5.

Wich, S.A., Gaveau, D., Abram, N., *et al.* (2012b). Understanding the impacts of land-use policies on a threatened species: is there a future for the Bornean orang-utan? *PLoS One*, 7, e49142.

Wich, S.A., Geurts, M.L., Mitra Setia, T. and Utami Atmoko, S.S. (2006). Influence of fruit availability on Sumatran orangutan sociality and reproduction. In *Feeding Ecology in Apes and Other Primates: Ecological, Physical and Behavioral Aspects*, ed. G. Hohmann, M.M. Robbins and C. Boesch. New York, NY: Cambridge University Press, pp. 337–58.

Wich, S.A., Meijaard, E., Marshall, A.J., *et al.* (2008). Distribution and conservation status of the orang-utan (*Pongo* spp.) on Borneo and Sumatra: how many remain? *Oryx*, 42, 329–39.

Wich, S., Riswan, J., J., Refish, J. and Nelleman, C. (2011). *Orangutans and the Economics of Sustainable Forest Management in Sumatra.* Birkeland, Norway: UNEP/GRASP/PanEco/YEL/ICRAF/GRID-Arendal, Birkeland Trykkeri AS. Available at: http://www.grida.no/graphicslib/collection/orangutans-and-the-economics-of-sustainable-forest-management-in-sumatra. Accessed October 11, 2012.

Wich, S.A., Utami Atmoko, S.S., Mitra Setia, T., *et al.* (2004). Life history of wild Sumatran orangutans (*Pongo abelii*). *Journal of Human Evolution*, 47, 385–98.

Wich, S.A., Utami Atmoko, S., Mitra Setia, T. and van Schaik, C.P., ed. (2009b). *Orangutans: Geographic Variation in Behavioral Ecology and Conservation*. Oxford, UK: Oxford University Press.

Wicke, B., Sikkema, R., Dornburg, V. and Faaij, A. (2011). Exploring land use changes and the role of palm oil production in Indonesia and Malaysia. *Land Use Policy*, 28, 193–206.

Wilcove, D.S. and Koh, L.P. (2010). Addressing the threats to biodiversity from oil-palm agriculture. *Biodiversity and Conservation*, **19**, 999–1007.

Wilkie, D.S. and Carpenter, J.F. (1999). Bushmeat hunting in the Congo Basin: an assessment of impacts and options for mitigation. *Biodiversity and Conservation*, **8**, 927–55.

Wilkie, D., Shaw, E., Rotberg, F., Morelli, G. and Auzel, P. (2000). Roads, development and conservation in the Congo basin. *Conservation Biology*, **14**, 1614–22.

Williams, J.M., Lonsdorf, E.V., Wilson, M.L., *et al.* (2008). Causes of death in the Kasekela chimpanzees of Gombe National Park, Tanzania. *American Journal of Primatology*, **70**, 766–77.

Williams, J.M., Pusey, A.E., Carlis, J.V., Farm, B.P. and Goodall, J. (2002). Female competition and male territorial behavior influence female chimpanzees' ranging patterns. *Animal Behaviour*, **63**, 347–60.

Williamson, E.A. (2014). Mountain gorillas: a shifting demographic landscape. In *Primates and Cetaceans: Field Research and Conservation of Complex Mammalian Societies*, ed. J. Yamagiwa and L. Karczmarsk. Tokyo, Japan: Springer, pp. 273–88.

Williamson, E.A. and Butynski, T.M. (2013a). *Gorilla beringei* eastern gorilla. In *Mammals of Africa. Volume II. Primates*, ed. T.M. Butynski, J. Kingdon and J. Kalina. London, UK: Bloomsbury Publishing, pp. 45–53.

Williamson, E.A. and Butynski, T.M. (2013b). *Gorilla gorilla* western gorilla. In *Mammals of Africa. Volume II. Primates*, ed. T.M. Butynski, J. Kingdon and J. Kalina. London, UK: Bloomsbury Publishing, pp. 39–45.

Williamson, E.A., Maisels, F.G. and Groves, C.P. (2013). Hominidae. In *Handbook of the Mammals of the World. Volume 3. Primates*, ed. R.A. Mittermeier, A.B. Rylands and D.E. Wilson. Barcelona, Spain: Lynx Edicions, pp. 792–843.

Wilmar (2013a). *No Deforestation, No Peat, No Exploitation Policy*. Singapore: Wilmar International. Available at: http://www.wilmar-international.com/wp-content/uploads/2012/11/No-Deforestation-No-Peat-No-Exploitation-Policy.pdf.

Wilmar (2013b). *Wilmar Affirms Commitment to Open, Transparent and Responsible Practices*. Singapore: Wilmar International. Available at: http://www.wilmar-international.com/wp-content/uploads/2013/12/Wilmar-Affirms-Commitment-to-Open-Transparent-and-Responsible-Practices.pdf.

Wilson, D. and Reeder, D., ed. (2005). *Mammal Species of the World: A Taxonomic and Geographic Reference*, 3rd edn. Baltimore, MD: Johns Hopkins University Press.

Wilson, E.O. (1984). *Biophilia*. Cambridge, MA: Harvard University Press.

Wilson, H.B., Meijaard, E., Venter, O., Ancrenaz, M. and Possingham, H.P. (2014a). Conservation strategies for orangutans: reintroduction versus habitat preservation and the benefits of sustainably logged forest. *PLoS One*, **9**, e102174.

Wilson, K.A., Underwood, E.C., Morrison, S.A., *et al.* (2007a). Conserving biodiversity efficiently: what to do, where, and when. *PLoS Biol*, **5**, e223.

Wilson, M.L., Boesch, C., Fruth, B., *et al.* (2014b). Lethal aggression in *Pan* is better explained by adaptive strategies than human impacts. *Nature*, **513**, 414–7.

Wilson, M.L., Hauser, M.D. and Wrangham, R.W. (2007b). Chimpanzees (*Pan troglodytes*) modify grouping and vocal behaviour in response to location-specific risk. *Behaviour*, **144**, 1621–53.

Winrock International (2010). *Increased Productivity and Profitability of Liberia's Smallholder Oil Palm Sector*. Little Rock, AK: Winrock International.

Wolf, T.M., Sreevatsan, S., Travis, D., Mugisha, L. and Singer, R.S. (2014). The risk of tuberculosis transmission to free-ranging great apes. *American Journal of Primatology*, **76**, 2–13.

World Bank (1996). *Technical Annex to the Memorandum and Recommendation on a Proposed Credit in the Amount Equivalent to SDR 8.8 Million to the Republic of Cameroon for a Privatization and Private Sector Technical Assistance Project. Report No. P-6928-CM*. Washington DC: World Bank.

World Bank (2004). *Implementation Completion Report on a Credit in the Amount of US$180.0 Million to the Republic of Cameroon for a Third Structural Adjustment Credit. Report No. 29996*. Washington DC: World Bank.

World Bank (2011). *World Bank Group Adopts New Approach for Investment in Palm Oil Sector*. Washington DC: World Bank. Available at: http://www.worldbank.org/en/news/press-release/2011/04/03/world-bank-group-adopts-new-approach-investment-palm-oil-sector.

World Bank (2014). *State and Trends of Carbon Pricing 2014*. Washington DC: World Bank. DOI: 10.1596/978–1–4648–0268–3

World Bank (2015a). *Chapter 2: Sub-Saharan Africa. Global Economic Prospects 2015*. Washington DC: World Bank. Available at: http://www.worldbank.org/content/dam/Worldbank/GEP/GEP2015a/pdfs/GEP2015a_chapter2_regionaloutlook_SSA.pdf.

World Bank (2015b). *Liberia: Country Data*. Washington DC: World Bank. Available at: http://data.worldbank.org/country/liberia. Accessed May 19, 2015.

World Bank (n.d.-a). *Agricultural Land (% of Land Area)*. Washington DC: World Bank. Available at: data.worldbank.org/indicator/AG.LND.AGRI.ZS. Accessed May, 2015.

World Bank (n.d.-b). *Data: Indicators*. Washington DC: World Bank. Available at: http://data.worldbank.org/indicator Accessed May, 2015.

World Bank (n.d.-c). *Forest Area (% of Land Area)*. Washington DC: World Bank. Available at: data.worldbank.org/indicator/AG.LND.FRST.ZS. Accessed May, 2015.

World Bank (n.d.-d). *Gabon: Country at a Glance*. Washington DC: World Bank. Available at: http://www.worldbank.org/en/country/gabon. Accessed May 13, 2015.

World Bank (n.d.-e). *Terrestrial Protected Areas (% of Total Land Area)*. Washington DC: World Bank. Available at: data.worldbank.org/indicator/ER.LND.PTLD.ZS. Accessed May, 2015.

Wrangham, R.W. (1986). Ecology and social relationships in two species of chimpanzee. In *Ecological Aspects of Social Evolution: Birds and Mammals*, ed. D.I. Rubenstein and R.W. Wrangham. Princeton, NJ: Princeton University Press, pp. 352–78.

Wrangham, R.W. (1999). Evolution of coalitionary killing. *Yearbook of Physical Anthropology*, **42**, 1–30.

Wrangham, R.W. (2001). Moral decisions about wild chimpanzees. In *Great Apes and Humans: The Ethics of Coexistence*, ed. B.B. Beck, T.S. Stoinski, M. Hutchins, *et al.* Washington DC: Smithsonian Institution Press, pp. 230–44.

Wrangham, R., Crofoot, M., Lundy, R. and Gilby, I. (2007). Use of overlap zones among group-living primates: a test of the risk hypothesis. *Behaviour*, **144**, 1599–619.

WRI (2013). *RSPO Certified Mill Production Areas*. Washington DC: World Resources Institute (WRI). Available at: www.globalforestwatch.org. Accessed October, 2014.

WRI (2014a). *Agricultural Concession Data for Cameroon*. Washington DC: World Resources Institute (WRI). Available at: http://www.globalforestwatch.org. Accessed August 20, 2014.

WRI (2014b). *Logging*. Washington DC: World Resources Institute (WRI). Available at: http://www.globalforestwatch.org. Accessed August 20, 2014.

WRI (2014c). *Oil Palm*. Washington DC: World Resources Institute (WRI). Available at: http://www.globalforestwatch.org. Accessed August 20, 2014.

WRI (2014d). *Press Release: Unilever and WRI Announce Partnership to Increase Transparency of Key Commodity Supply Chains to Help End Tropical Deforestation*. Washington DC: World Resource Institute (WRI). Available at: http://www.wri.org/news/2014/09/release-unilever-and-wri-announce-partnership-increase-transparency-key-commodity.

WRI (2014e). *Wood Fiber*. Washington DC: World Resources Institute (WRI). Available at: http://www.globalforestwatch.org. Accessed August 20, 2014.

WRI (n.d.-a). *Forest Atlas of Cameroon*. Washington DC: World Resources Institute (WRI). Available at: http://www.wri.org/applications/maps/forestatlas/cmr/index.htm#v=atlas&l=fr&init=y. Accessed June, 2015.

WRI (n.d.-b). *Global Forest Watch*. Washington DC: World Resources Institute (WRI). Available at: http://www.globalforestwatch.org/. Accessed February 17, 2015.

Wright, S.P. and Tumbey, A.T. (2012). *Assessment of High Conservation Values Report. Golden Veroleum (Liberia) Inc.* Kuala Lumpur, Malaysia: Roundtable on Sustainable Palm Oil (RSPO). Available at: http://www.rspo.org/file/2012–12–07%20FINAL%20GVL%20BD%20KP%20ASSESSMENT%20of%20HCV%20REPORT%20%28GreenCons%29.pdf.

WWF (2013a). *Palm Oil Buyer's Scorecard: Measuring the Progress of Palm Oil Buyers*. Gland, Switzerland: World Wide Fund for Nature (WWF). Available at: http://wwf.panda.org/what_we_do/footprint/agriculture/palm_oil/solutions/responsible_purchasing/palm_oil_buyers_scorecard_2013/.

WWF (2013b). *WWF Assessment of RSPO Member Palm Oil Producers 2013*. Gland, Switzerland: World Wide Fund for Nature (WWF) International. Available at: http://wwf.panda.org/what_we_do/footprint/agriculture/palm_oil/solutions/responsible_purchasing/wwf_assessment_of_rspo_member_palm_oil_producers_2013/. Accessed July 16, 2014.

WWF (n.d.). *Palm Oil and Forest Conversion*. Gland, Switzerland: World Wide Fund for Nature (WWF) International. Available at: http://wwf.panda.org/what_we_do/footprint/agriculture/palm_oil/environmental_impacts/forest_conversion. Accessed March 14, 2015.

WWF-CIRAD (2014). *Compte-Rendu de Mission de la Délégation, March 11, 2014*. DRC: World Wildlife Fund and Centre de Coopération Internationale en Recherche Agronomique pour le Développement (WWF-CIRAD).

Xue, Y.L., Prado-Martinez, J., Sudmant, P.H., *et al.* (2015). Mountain gorilla genomes reveal the impact of long-term population decline and inbreeding. *Science*, **348**, 242–5.

Yamagiwa, J. and Basabose, A.K. (2009). Fallback foods and dietary partitioning among *Pan* and *Gorilla*. *American Journal of Physical Anthropology*, **140**, 739–50.

Yamagiwa, J., Kahekwa, J. and Basabose, A.K. (2003). Intra-specific variation in social organization of gorillas: implications for their social evolution. *Primates*, **44**, 359–69.

Yumarni, Alikodra, H.S., Budiprasetyo, L. and Soekmadi, R. (2011). Population analysis of Javan gibbon (*Hylobates moloch* Audebert 1797) in Gunung Halimun Salak National Park's corridor. *Media Konservasi*, **16**, 133–40.

Yuwono, E.H., Susanto, P., Saleh, C., *et al.* (2007). *Guidelines for the Better Management Practices on Avoidance, Mitigation and Management of Human–Orangutan Conflict in and around Oil Palm Plantations*. Jakarta, Indonesia: World Wide Fund for Nature (WWF) Indonesia.

Ywih, C.H., Ahmed, O.H., Majid, N.K. and Jalloh, M.B. (2009). Effects of converting secondary forest on tropical peat soil to oil palm plantation on carbon storage. *American Journal of Agricultural and Biological Sciences*, **4**, 123–30.

Zhang, M., Fellowes, J.R., Jiang, X., *et al.* (2010). Degradation of tropical forest in Hainan, China, 1991–2008: conservation implications for hainan gibbon (*Nomascus hainanus*). *Biological Conservation*, **143**, 1397–404.

Zhou, J., Wei, F., Li, M., *et al.* (2005). Hainan black-crested gibbon is headed for extinction. *International Journal of Primatology*, **26**, 453–65.

Zhou, J., Wei, F., Li, M., *et al.* (2008). Reproductive characters and mating behaviour of wild *Nomascus hainanus*. *International Journal of Primatology*, **29**, 1037–46.

Zommers, Z.A., Johnson, P.J. and Macdonald, D.W. (2012). Biofuels bonanza? Sugarcane production and poverty in villages surrounding Budongo Forest, Uganda. *Journal of Eastern African Studies*, **6**, 177–95.

ZSL (n.d.-a). *Africa RSPO Facts and Figures*. London, UK: Zoological Society of London (ZSL). Available at: http://www.sustainablepalmoil.org/palm-oil-by-region/africa/. Accessed November 10, 2014.

ZSL (n.d.-b). *Sustainable Palm Oil Transparency Toolkit (SPOTT)*. West Java, Indonesia: Zoological Society of London (ZSL) Indonesia. Available at: http://www.sustainablepalmoil.org/spott/. Accessed February 15, 2015.

Index

A

AAP sanctuary, Netherlands 246
AarhusKarlshamn 152
Abbott's gray gibbons (*Hylobates abbotti*) xiii, xvii, xx–xxi
Abundance Annex 2, 194, www.stateoftheapes.com
acacia plantations 168, 175, 176, 183
Aceh, Indonesia 128–130, 132, 133, 141, 156
Africa
agro-industry impacts 47–48, 94–95
ape distribution xviii
human–wildlife conflict mitigation strategies 35–36
land deals 43, 74, 75
responsible practices 100–101
sanctuaries 231
target for agro-industry 14–15, 34, 165–66
see also Central Africa; East Africa; sub-Saharan Africa; West Africa; *specific countries*
African Agriculture Fund 86
African apes xviii, 72, 93, 165–66, 184, Abundance Annex *see also* bonobos (*Pan paniscus*); chimpanzees (*Pan troglodytes*); gorillas (*Gorilla* spp.)
African Convention on the Conservation of Nature and Natural Resources 108
African Development Bank (AfDB) 86
African Export–Import Bank 86
agile gibbons (*Hylobates agilis*) xvii, xx–xxi, 239
Agreement on the Conservation of Nature and Natural Resources 108
ape distribution xviii, xx–xxi
ape index x–xiv
APES Database (Ape Populations, Environments and Surveys) xviii, xxi, 198, Abundance Annex (www.stateoftheapes.com)
apes and industrial agriculture questionnaire responses 260–63
APES Portal (Ape Populations, Environments and Surveys) xviii, xxi, 2, Abundance Annex (www.stateoftheapes.com)
areal penggunaan lain (APL) 128–130, 156
armed forces 199
Asia
agri-industry impacts 48–49
ape distribution xx–xxi
business expansion in Africa 86
crops, industrial 48–49
investors in African agribusinesses 85
land deals 43–45
see also specific countries

B

Asia Pulp and Paper 159
Asian apes xx–xxi, 165–66, 184, Abundance Annex *see also* gibbons (Hylobatidae); orangutans (*Pongo* spp.)
Atama 77, 86, 92, 94, 95

bananas 30, 170, 176
Bangladesh 48, 188
Benin 73
Best Management Practices for Orangutan Conservation (USAID) 147
Best Practice Guidelines for the Prevention and Mitigation of Conflict between Humans and Great Apes 33
BGFI Bank of Gabon 86
biodiversity
loss 1
protection
conservation agriculture (CA) 23, 24, 34
EIAs and EMPs 17, 31, 116–17, 118–19, 120–21, 140
low-carbon-density land (LCDL) 15
mitigation hierarchy 28
public–private partnerships 32–33
REDD+ project 22
RSPO *see* Roundtable on Sustainable Palm Oil (RSPO)
biofuels 21, 51, 76, 82–83, 85, 88–90, 137
Biopalm Energy 86
BNP Paribas 87
Bolloré Group 50
bonobos (*Pan paniscus*)
in captivity 231, 243, 256
case study *see* Luo Scientific Reserve/Wamba case study
crop raiding 170–72, 175
disease 184
distances travelled xxi, xxii
distribution xviii
ecology xxi
habitat, agro-industry impacts on 93, 170–72, 174, 177, 181–82, 188
home ranges and territoriality xxiii
overview x
range overlap with agro-industry 96
range overlaps of groups 180
reproduction xxiii–xxiv
socioecology xv
states found in xvi
trafficking death toll 234
Bornean gray gibbons (*Hylobates muelleri*) xiii, xvii, xx–xxi
Bornean orangutans (*Pongo pygmaeus*)
agro-industry impacts 24, 66–67, 173, 180
in captivity 233
case study *see* Sabangau peat swamp forest case study

crop raiding 168, 176, 185
distances travelled xxi, xxii
distribution xvi, xx–xxi
HCV Initiative 4 146–47
human–wildlife conflict 25–27
killings 185
overview xii
range overlap with agro-industry 66, 67
rescues 25–27, 32, 232, 233
survival criteria 67
Tabin Wildlife Reserve 144
see also orangutans (*Pongo* spp.)
Bornean white-bearded gibbons (*Hylobates albibarbis*) xvii, xx–xxi, 65, 239
Borneo
agro-industry impact on ape habitats 24, 65–67, 168, 172–73, 180
ape range – agro-industry overlap 66, 67
case study, long-term *see* Sabangau peat swamp forest case study
deforestation 46, 62–65, 68 *see also* Sabangau peat swamp forest case study
honorary wildlife rangers 144
human–wildlife conflict 25–27, 67, 180
industrial plantations 65
killing of apes 185
Mega Rice Project 201
orangutan conservation 146–47
overview 61–62
palm oil 24, 25, 62, 64–65, 67, 146–47, 176
protection strategies 69
rescues/rescue centers 25–27, 32, 232, 238
SMART for HCV 145
Tabin Wildlife Reserve 144
see also Indonesia; Kalimantan
Borneo Orangutan Survival Foundation (BOSF) 26–27, 146–47, 232
Bossou chimpanzees 177, 182
Brazil 82, 256
British American Tobacco (BAT) 30
Brunei 42, 61, 63, 64 *see also* Borneo
Budongo Forest Reserve, Uganda 29–31
Bugoma Forest Reserve, Uganda 29–31
Bukit Barisan Selatan National Park, Indonesia 122–23
Bukit Tigapuluh Ecosystem, Sumatra 141
Bulindi, Uganda 6, 29–31, 38
Bunge 86, 99
Burkina Faso 73
Burundi 47, 211, 214

C

cacao 22, 30, 58
Cambodia
ape range – agro-industry overlap 45
ape distribution xx–xxi
concession allocation 133
deforestation 44

EIAs 120–21
forest ownership 132
land deals 43, 44–45
land tenure 112
Law on Forestry 127, 133
multilateral treaties 108
palm oil 44
protected areas 44–45, 124–25
Cameroon
agro-industry, history of 49–51
agro-industry impact on ape habitats 54, 68–69, 94
agro-industry, potential sites 92, 93, 96
ape abundance 49
ape distribution xviii
ape range – agro-industry overlap 53, 54, 75
area under concession 74
concerns about agro-industry 54–55, 68–69
concession allocation 115
current agro-industry situation 54
deforestation 49, 54
EIAs 120–21
environmental protection 118
forest and ape status 46, 49
forest ownership 132
governance 101
land deals 43, 81
land/resource tenure 110, 111, 112, 113
Law on Environmental Management 118
multilateral treaties 108
national parks 133
palm oil 51–52, 70–71, 75, 77, 78, 79, 81, 92, 160
protected areas 53, 54, 124–25
public interest litigation 127
rescues/rescue centers 235–37
rubber 52–54, 83
Rural Sector Development Plan 81
smallholder farming 78, 98, 160
sugarcane 52, 83
Cameroon Development Corporation 50, 52, 78, 86
Cameroon Sugar Company (CAMSUCO) 52
Campo Ma'an National Park, Cameroon 52–53
Canary Islands 246
Cantanhez National Park, Guinea-Bissau 35–36
Cao Vit gibbons (*Nomascus nasutus*) xiv, xvii, xx–xxi
captive apes
information 257–58
key issues 246–47
in labs 232, 242, 254–55, 256
legislation 229–231, 241–42, 243, 246, 248–254, 256–57
in non-range states 241, 256
in non-range states: EU 241–42
circuses and entertainment 243–45
Linda's story 246–47
sanctuaries 245–48
zoos 242
in non-range states: Japan 258
in non-range states: US 248
Captive Primate Safety Act 248–49

Humane Care for Primates Act 249
  numbers 254–56
  public contact prohibition petition 250–51
  sanctuaries 249, 251, 252–53, 254, 255, 256
  split-listing of chimpanzees 249–250
  sub-national legislation 251–54
overview 195, 258–59
performers 230, 231, 243–47, 250–51
pets
  in range states 26, 126, 222, 238, 240
  in the US 250, 251–52, 254
  welfare risks 230, 233, 246–47
professional associations 231
in range state sanctuaries 231–32
rescue challenges 232–34
social attitudes 257
trafficking 232, 234, 235, 240, 256
see also rescues/rescue centers
carbon dioxide (CO_2) 20–21, 81
  see also greenhouse gas (GHG) emissions
carbon sequestration 20, 154
Cargill 86, 99
case studies, long-term 197–200, 226
  bonobos *see* Luo Scientific Reserve/Wamba
  case study
  Bornean orangutans *see* Sabangau peat swamp
  forest case study
  chimpanzees *see* Gombe Stream National Park
  case study
  silvery gibbons *see* Mount Halimun Salak
  National Park case study
cashews 35–36, 46
cassava 56, 216
Central Africa
  agro-industry threats 93
  forest administration resources 119
  infrastructure development 172
  land acquisitions 74, 75
  palm oil 58, 77, 79
  rubber 83
  see also specific countries
Central African Republic (CAR) 47, 75, 93
central chimpanzees (*Pan troglodytes troglodytes*)
  x, xvi, xviii, 49, 148, 150
Centre for International Cooperation in Sustainable
  Management of Tropical Peatlands (CIMTROP)
  202, 204
cereals 75, 83–85
certified sustainable palm oil (CSPO) 136, 137, 140,
  152–53, 157–58, 162, 163
chimpanzees (*Pan troglodytes*)
  Bossou community 177, 182
  Bulindi village 29–31, 38
  in captivity 231, 232, 243, 245–47, 248, 249–250,
  254–56, 258
  case study *see* Gombe Stream National Park
  case study
  crop raiding 30–31, 35–36, 170–72, 175, 177, 184,
  185, 237, 262–63
  deforestation impacts 174

diet xix, xxi
disease 184–85, 240
distances travelled xxi, xxii
ecology xix, xxi
habitat, agro-industry impacts on 29–31, 46,
  170–72, 174, 177, 181–82, 188
home ranges and territoriality xxii–xxiii, xxiii
human–wildlife conflict 30–31
intraspecific aggression 36, 180, 181, 212
killings 31
Linda's story 246–47
memory xxii
nest building 177
overview x–xi
range overlap with agro-industry 53, 54, 93, 96
regenerated forests 178
reproduction xxiii–xxiv
rescues/rescue centers 195, 230, 235–37
socioecology xv
states found in xvi
trafficking death toll 234
see also specific subspecies
China 48, 158, 188
China Development Bank Corporation 86
circuses 243–45
CITES Appendices xv
Citi 87
climate change 4, 19–21, 190, 207
coffee 30, 56, 58
compression effects 179–183, 198, 202
concession allocation 114–17
concessions, defined 3
Congo Basin 7–8, 14, 42, 72, 77, 91, 92, 98
conservation agriculture (CA) 23, 24, 34
conservation and mitigation strategies 33–37
consumer agency 38, 157
Convention on Biological Diversity (CBD) 108, 135–36
Convention on Conservation of Migratory Species of
  Wild Animals 108
Convention on International Trade in Endangered
  Species of Wild Fauna and Flora (CITES)
  108, 122, 135, 246
Convention on the Conservation of Migratory
  Species 135
Convention on Wetlands of International Importance
  (Ramsar Convention) 136
corn 83–84
corporate social responsibility (CSR) 99, 100
corruption 17, 101–2, 128, 129, 199, 221
Credit Suisse 87
Cress, Doug 234
Crookes Brothers 83
crop-protection measures 31, 37, 39
crop raiding 174–75, 183, 237, 262–63
  bonobos 170–72, 175
  chimpanzees 30–31, 35–36, 170–72, 175, 177, 184,
  185, 237, 262–63
  gibbons 175, 262–63
  gorillas 170, 184

orangutans 9, 26, 168, 175, 176, 183–84, 185, 262–63
crops grown 14, 40–41, 46, 167
    Africa 30, 47–48, 56, 73, 75, 90
    Asia 48–49, 62, 63
Cross River gorillas (*Gorilla gorilla diehli*) xi, xvi, xviii, 49, 93, 179, 181
Cross River National Park 95
crowding effect 179–183, 200, 202, 205–6

D

deforestation 14
    Africa, rates in 29–30
    agricultural expansion 30, 41, 92, 173–74
    Borneo 62–65, 68
    see also Sabangau peat swamp forest case study
    Cambodia 44
    Cameroon 49, 54
    DRC 29, 211
    GHGs released 20–21, 22
    human–wildlife conflict 26, 29–31
    impacts on ape populations 65–66, 166, 198, 238
    see also habitat, agro-industry impacts on Java 224
    Liberia 29, 55, 61
    sub-Saharan Africa 92
    Sumatra 196–97
    see also forest protection
demand for agricultural commodities 87–90
Democratic Republic of Congo (DRC)
    agro-industry impact on ape habitats 47, 188
    agro-industry, potential sites for 92, 93, 96
    ape distribution xviii
    ape range – agro-industry overlap 75, 93, 96
    area under concession 74
    case study *see* Luo Scientific Reserve/Wamba case study
    concession allocation 116
    corn 84
    deforestation 29, 211
    EIAs 120–21, 127
    Forestry Code 127
    gorillas 169, 170, 257
    land ownership 132
    land/resource tenure 110, 112, 113
    Law on Basic Principles of Environmental Protection 133
    multilateral treaties 108
    palm oil 75, 78, 86
    protected areas 124–25
    REDD+ project 22
    rescues/rescue centers 195, 232, 257
    restart of old plantations 171
    rubber 83
Development Bank of Central African States 86
diet xix, xxiv–xxv
disease 36, 166, 184–85, 211, 214, 238, 240
distances travelled by great apes xxi–xxii, xxii
Dja Faunal Reserve, Cameroon 52–53

E

East Africa 82, 84, 85, 172 *see also specific countries*
eastern chimpanzees (*Pan troglodytes schweinfurthii*) x, xvi, xviii, 29–31, 38
eastern gorillas (*Gorilla beringei*) xi, 93 *see also* Grauer's gorillas (*Gorilla beringei graueri*); mountain gorillas (*Gorilla beringei beringei*)
eastern hoolocks (*Hoolock leuconedys*) xii–xiii, xvii, xx–xxi
Ebola virus 55, 61, 80, 184
Ecobank 86
education 31, 37, 146, 212, 226, 257–58
employment 18, 56, 58, 71, 73, 220
encroachment 41–43, 67–69 *see also* deforestation
environmental impact assessments (EIAs) 17, 31, 116–17, 118–19, 120–21, 140
environmental management plans (EMPs) 17, 118
environmental protection 117–19, 133
Equatorial Palm Oil, Liberia 59, 94
Ethiopia 83, 84, 85
eucalyptus 168, 175, 176–77
European Union (EU)
    agro-industry investors 85, 86
    Biofuels Directive 88, 89
    captive apes 241–42
        circuses and entertainment 243–45
        Linda's story 246–47
        sanctuaries 245–48
        zoos 242
    Everything-but-Arms arrangement 91
    palm oil imports 79, 157–58
    Renewable Energy Directive 89–90
expansion drivers 87–92

F

Fernan-Vas Gorilla Project, Gabon 232
Feronia 86, 171
fertilizers 20, 21
fires 21, 62, 65, 81–82, 104, 129, 130, 138, 206–7
Firestone 57
foreign direct investment 51, 81, 85–86
forest protection
    Brazilian model 82
    Norway–Liberia Deal 61
    "passive protection" 96–97
    zero-deforestation commitments 99, 100, 113, 144, 159
Forest Stewardship Council 145
forests
    carbon sequestration 20, 21, 22
    Congo Basin 72
    FAO classification 20
    fragmentation 24
    high carbon stock (HCS) 100, 144
    high conservation value (HCV) 100, 140, 144
    land use planning 186
    loss *see* deforestation

management 205–6
protection *see* forest protection
REDD+ project 22
regeneration 200, 213
reserves 29
tenure 109–13
see also Sabangau peat swamp forest case study
free, prior and informed consent (FPIC) 17, 59, 61, 94–95, 100, 148
FRI-EL Green Power 86

G

G20 Inter-Agency Working Group 4
Gabon
agro-industry impact on ape habitats 47, 94
agro-industry, potential sites for 92, 93
agro-industry practices 100
ape abundance 148
ape distribution xviii
ape range – agro-industry overlap 75, 93, 96
area under concession 74
deforestation rates 147–48
EIAs 120–21
forest cover 147
gorillas 96, 151
HCV forests 148–151
human population 148
land deals 43
land/resource tenure 112, 113
multilateral treaties 108
national parks 122, 133
Olam International 147–151
palm oil 81, 86, 92, 148–151
protected areas 124–25
rescues/rescue centers 232
rubber 83
Strategic Plan for an Emerging Gabon 81
genetically modified organisms (GMOs) 4
Ghana 14, 47, 73, 74, 75, 78, 84, 85
gibbons (Hylobatidae)
in captivity 231, 242, 243, 245, 254, 255
case study *see* Mount Halimun Salak National Park case study
crop raiding 175, 262–63
deforestation impacts 65, 173
diet xxiv–xxv
disease 184
distribution xx–xxi
habitat, agro-industry impacts on 136, 169, 173, 176, 180–81, 188
home ranges and territoriality xxiii, xxv
overview xii–xiv
reproduction xxv
rescues/rescue centers 238–39
socioecology xxiv–xxv
states found in xvii
survival criteria 67

trafficking death toll 234
see also specific species
Global Forest Watch (GFW) 42, 158
Global Roadmap Project 16
Golden Agri-Resources (GAR) 86, 99, 100, 159
Golden Oil Holdings 86
Golden Veroleum Liberia (GVL) 59, 94, 95, 100
Gombe Stream National Park case study 198–99, 207–15
causes of population changes
disease 211
habitat change/loss 211
intraspecific aggression 212
killings 212
changes in population size and ranging patterns 209, 210
context and background 207, 209
Greater Gombe Ecosystem Conservation Action Plan (GGE– CAP) 212–13
map 208
methodology 209–10
recommendations 214–15
reducing threats 212–13
disease 214
habitat loss 213–14
hunting/poaching 214
gorillas (*Gorilla* spp.)
in captivity 231, 232, 243, 255
crop raiding 170, 184
diet xix
disease 184–85
distances travelled xxi
ecology xix
habitat, agro-industry impacts on 165, 169–170, 173–74, 175, 176–77, 181, 188
home ranges and territoriality xxii, xxiii
hunting/poaching 186–87
overview xi–xii
range overlap with agro-industry 54
reproduction xxiii–xxiv
socioecology xv
states found in xvi
trafficking death toll 234
see also specific species
governance 22, 67, 100–101 *see also* legal frameworks; legislation
Grauer's gorillas (*Gorilla beringei graueri*) xi, xvi, xviii, xxii, 93, 169, 170, 257
Great Ape Information Network (GAIN) 258
great apes *see* bonobos (*Pan paniscus*); chimpanzees (*Pan troglodytes*); gorillas (*Gorilla* spp.); orangutans (*Pongo* spp.)
Great Apes Survival Partnership (GRASP) 232, 234
greenhouse gas(es) (GHG) 4, 19–21, 22, 24, 90, 142, 154
GreenPalm certification 152–53, 157, 158
Greenpeace 138, 144, 157, 159
Guinea *see* Republic of Guinea
Guinea-Bissau 35–36, 46, 47, 177, 188
Gunung Leuser National Park, Sumatra 154

H

habitat, agro-industry impacts on
  by ape species 167–68
    bonobos 93, 170–72, 174, 177, 181–82, 188
    chimpanzees 29–31, 46, 170–72, 174, 177, 181–82, 188
    gibbons 136, 169, 173, 176, 180–81, 188
    gorillas 165, 169–170, 173–74, 175, 176–77, 181, 188
    orangutans 24, 136, 166, 168, 172–73, 180, 188
  Borneo 24, 65–67, 168, 172–73, 180
  Cameroon 54, 68–69, 94
  by crop type 167
  DRC 47, 188
  Gabon 47, 94
  habitat loss 165–66
  Indonesia 48, 188
  Ivory Coast 47
  key findings 166–67
  Liberia 59–60, 94
  long-term impacts 179–183
  Malaysia 48, 188
  Myanmar 49
  Nigeria 47, 95, 171
  by phase of production 177
    habitat destruction and clearance 173–74
    infrastructure development 172–73
    mature plantations 176–77
    young plantations 174–76
  remediations 177–79, 190–92
  Republic of Congo 20–21, 47, 94, 188
  research needed 166
  sub-Saharan Africa 92–96
  Sumatra 24, 104–5, 154, 156, 168, 190–91
  survey 188–190
  threats to apes 240
  types of impacts 165, 211
  Uganda 48, 95, 188
  West Africa 93
  see also deforestation; human–wildlife conflict
Hainan gibbons (*Nomascus hainanus*) xiv, xvii, xx–xxi
Herakles Farms, Cameroon 52, 86, 92, 94, 95
HEVECAM, Cameroon 53
high carbon stock (HCS) forests 100, 102, 142, 144, 148, 159
high conservation value (HCV) forests
  assessments 140
  Gabon 148–151
  Golden Veroleum Liberia 100
  HCS approach 159
  HCV areas 145
  Olam International 100
  RSPO clearance prohibition 154
  RSPO Principle 7 140
  RSPO task force 156
  set-aside system 178
  Wilmar International initiatives 144–47
home ranges and territoriality xxii

hoolocks (*Hoolock* spp.) xii–xiii, xvii, xxiv–xxv
human conflict impacts 218–19
human settlements 172, 206, 215–16, 235
human–wildlife conflict 39
  Borneo 25–27, 67, 180
  disease risks 184–85, 211
  Indonesia 25–27
  killing of apes 185, 212
  land use planning 186
  mitigation strategies 33–37, 39
  pets 240
  socioeconomic factors 183, 187–88
  Uganda 29–31, 82
  see also crop raiding
hunting/poaching 54, 55–56, 60, 166, 172, 185, 186–87, 199, 202, 214, 217, 218–19
Hylobates genus xiii, xxiv–xxv *see also specific species*

I

Illovo Sugar 83
Independent Monitoring of Forest Law Enforcement and Governance (IM-FLEG) 94
India 48, 90, 188
Indonesia
  agro-industry impact on ape habitats 48, 188
  ape distribution xx–xxi
  case study *see* Mount Halimun Salak National Park case study
  concession allocation 115, 133
  corruption 128, 221
  EIAs 120–21, 133
  forest protection laws 33–34
  greenhouse gas (GHG) emissions 21
  human–wildlife conflict 25–27
  infrastructure development 172
  land deals 43
  land prices 91
  land tenure 19, 112
  multilateral treaties 108
  national parks 122–23, 133
  Orangutan Indonesia Conservation Strategies and Action Plan 2007–2017 32
  palm oil 12–13, 18–19, 24, 25, 81–82, 134–35, 136, 137
  poverty 18–19
  productive use requirements 113
  proportion of land for expansion 64
  protected areas 124–25
  rescues/rescue centers 25–27, 32, 174–75, 238–39
  RSPO HCV task force 156
  species protection 125
  Tripa peat swamp forests, Aceh 128–130, 141
  Wilmar International 144
  zero-deforestation commitments 113
  see also Borneo; Sumatra
Indonesian Palm Oil Association 138
industrial agriculture, defined 3
industrial agriculture, overview 4–5

industrial tree plantations (ITPs) 65
infrastructure development 172–73
ING 87
Institute of Economic Affairs 4, 14
interbirth intervals xii, xxiv, xxv, 182, 186, 194, 199–200
International Animal Rescue (IAR) Indonesia 25–27, 174–75, 232, 240
International Finance Corporation 86
International Species Information System (ISIS) 242
International Tropical Timber Agreement 108
International Union for Conservation of Nature (IUCN) 32
investment sources 85–86
IUCN Red List Categories and Criteria xv
IUCN SSC APES Database 198
Ivory Coast
    agro-industry impact on ape habitats 47
    agro-industry, potential sites for 14
    ape distribution xviii
    ape range – agro-industry overlap 75, 92, 93
    palm oil 75, 77–78, 79, 80
    rubber 83
    sugarcane 83
    Wilmar International 144
Iyondji Community Bonobo Reserve, DRC 218

J

Jane Goodall Institute (JGI) 208, 212–13
Japan 225, 256, 258
jatropha 76, 85, 102
Java 221 see also Mount Halimun Salak National Park case study
Javan gibbons (Hylobates moloch) xvii, xx–xxi, 222 see also Mount Halimun Salak National Park case study
Justin Sugar Mills SA 52

K

Kalaweit rescue organization 145, 238–39
Kalimantan
    ape range – agro-industry overlap 66
    captive apes 233
    Central Kalimantan Project 146–47
    crop raiding 176
    human–wildlife conflict 25–27
    intact forest area 63
    killing of apes 67, 185
    land targeted for agro-industry 64
    orangutan conservation 146–47
    orangutan population 66–67
    palm oil 65
    rescues/rescue centers 25–27, 32, 232, 238–39
    SMART for HCV 145
    see also Borneo; Indonesia; Sabangau peat swamp forest case study

Kano, Takayoshi 215
Kenya 82, 84
key findings
    agro-industry expansion 42–43
    economic development and biodiversity conservation 15
    habitat, agro-industry impacts on 166–67
    Round Table on Sustainable Palm Oil (RSPO) 136–37
    sub-Saharan Africa 73
killing of apes, non-consumption 31, 67, 170–71, 180, 185, 186, 212, 237
Kinabatangan, Borneo 168, 172–73, 176, 180
Kinyara Sugar Works Ltd. (KSWL), Uganda 30, 31
Kloss' gibbons (Hylobates klossii) xvii, xx–xxi, 238, 239

L

land access 90–91
land deals 43–45, 72, 74, 81, 83, 109
Land Matrix 42, 43, 74, 76, 77, 83
land tenure 19, 51, 91, 109–13
land use planning 10, 33–36, 39, 69, 186, 212–13, 213–14, 226
Lao People's Democratic Republic (Lao PDR) xvii, xx, 44, 48
Lar gibbon (Hylobates lar) xvii, xx–xxi, 252–53
Latin America 14–15
law enforcement 82, 119, 124, 125, 126–131, 215, 220
legal challenges 127, 129–130
legal frameworks 105–9, 131–32
    concession allocation 114–17
    environmental protection provisions 117–19
    implementation and enforcement 119, 124, 125, 126–131
    land/resource tenure 109–13
    legal challenges 127, 129–130
    protected areas/species 119–125
    see also legislation
legislation
    ape captivity 229–231, 242, 243, 246, 248–254, 256–57
    different sets 115
    enforcement 118
    environmental protection 117–18
    forest protection 33–34, 55, 120
    international 107, 108, 135–36
    protected areas 119–122, 124–25, 128–29
    protected species 54, 122–25
    sustainable development 101–2
    transparency 116
    see also legal frameworks
Leuser Ecosystem, Aceh 128–130, 141, 156
Liberia
    agro-industry, history of 56
    agro-industry impact on ape habitats 59–60, 94
    agro-industry, potential sites for 92, 93
    agro-industry practices 100

ape abundance 55–56
ape distribution xviii
ape range – agro-industry overlap 75, 93
cacoa and coffee 58
concerns about agro-industry 60–61, 68
concession allocation 116
deforestation 29, 55, 61
Ebola virus 61
EIAs 120–21
Extractive Industries Transparency Initiative
    Act 116
forest ownership 132
forest protection laws 55
governance 101
land deals 43, 74
land tenure 112
multilateral treaties 108
National Forestry Reform Law 55
national parks 133
Norway–Liberia Deal 59, 61, 68, 83, 101
overview 55
palm oil 58–59, 77, 86
protected areas 124–25
rubber 56–58, 83
Liberia Palm Developments (LPD) 94, 95
Liberia Rubber Corporation 56–57
local communities
    agro-industry conflicts 82, 94–95, 100
    conservation education/efforts 212–15, 220
    free prior and informed consent (FPIC) 59
    free, prior and informed consent (FPIC)
    procedure 148
    involvement 226
    land rights 110–11
    land tenure 51, 91
    perception of wildlife 183
    see also human–wildlife conflict
logging 54, 62, 92, 166, 200, 202, 235 see also Sabangau
    peat swamp forest case study
long-term research 200, 226 see also case studies,
    long-term
low-carbon-density land (LCDL) 15
Luo Scientific Reserve/Wamba case study 199, 215–220
    civil war impacts 218–19
    context and background 215–16
    deforestation 216
    methodology 216–18
    population changes 217
    recommendations 220
    snares 219, 220
    survivorship 219–220
Lwiro sanctuary, DRC 232

M

Malawi 84
Malaysia
    agro-industry impact on ape habitats 48, 188
        agro-industry promotion 114
        ape distribution xx–xxi
        deforestation 65, 68, 69
        EIAs 17, 120–21, 133
        land/resource tenure 112, 113
        legal challenges, blocks to 127
        multilateral treaties 108
        palm oil 18, 24, 64, 65, 81–82, 134–35, 136, 137
        plantation establishment 17
        poverty 18
        protected areas 124–25
        rubber 20
        smallholder farming 63
        Wilmar International 144
        see also Borneo
Malaysian Palm Oil Association 138
Mali 73, 83
Max Planck Institute 198
Mbargue Forest, Cameroon 235–37
media coverage 129
Mega Rice Project, Borneo 201
Migros, Switzerland 138
Mishmi Hills hoolocks (Hoolock hoolock mishmiensis)
    xii–xiii
mitigation hierarchy 28
Moloch gibbon (Hylobates moloch) xvii, xx–xxi, 222
    see also Mount Halimun Salak National Park
    case study
MONA Foundation 246
monocultures x–1, 2–3 see also palm oil
Mount Halimun Salak National Park case study
    199, 221–226
    context and background 221
        population surveys and monitoring
            222–23
        silvery gibbons in western Java 222
    habitat estimates 223–24
    long-term monitoring challenges 224–25
    map 222
    recommendations and opportunities 225–26
mountain gorillas (Gorilla beringei beringei) xi, xvi,
    xviii, 93, 169–170
Mozambique 82, 83, 84, 85
Mueller's gray gibbon (Hylobates muelleri) xiii, xvii,
    65, 239
multilateral treaties 107, 108, 135–36
Myanmar
    agro-industry impact on ape habitats 49
    ape distribution xx–xxi
    EIAs 120–21
    Environmental Conservation Law 133
    environmental protection 118
    land ownership 132
    land/resource tenure 112, 113
    legal challenges, blocks to 127, 130
    multilateral treaties 108
    National Land Use Policy 132
    productive use requirements 133
    protected areas 124–25

N

national parks 49, 54, 94, 95, 121–22, 122–23, 133, 154, 170, 184 *see also* Gombe Stream National Park case study; Sabangau peat swamp forest case study
Nauvu 77–78
nest building xxi, 168, 171, 176, 177, 262–63
Nestlé 99
Nigeria
 agro-industry impact on ape habitats 47, 95, 171
 agro-industry practices 100
 ape distribution xviii
 ape range – agro-industry overlap 75
 corn 84
 land deals 75
 palm oil 75, 77
 rice 85
 rubber 83
 sugarcane 82
Nigeria–Cameroon chimpanzees (*Pan troglodytes ellioti*) x, xvi, xviii, 49, 52, 54, 171
nitrous oxide (N$_2$O) 20–21
Nomascus genus xiii–xiv, xvii, xxiv–xxv
 see also specific species
non-governmental organizations (NGOs) 82, 127, 138, 141, 157
Northeast Bornean orangutan (*Pongo pygmaeus morio*) xvi
northern white-cheeked gibbons (*Nomascus leucogenys*) xvii, xx–xxi
northern yellow-cheeked gibbon (*Nomascus annamensis*) xvii, xx–xxi, 45
northwest Bornean orangutan (*Pongo pygmaeus pygmaeus*) xvi
Norway–Liberia Deal 7, 59, 61, 68, 83, 101

O

Olam International 81, 86, 92, 94, 95, 100, 143, 147–151, 159
Orangutan Indonesia Conservation Strategies and Action Plan 2007–2017 32
Orangutan Tropical Peatland Project (OuTrop) 202
orangutans (*Pongo* spp.)
 Best Management Practices for Orangutan Conservation 147
 in captivity 126, 231, 232, 233, 240, 243, 245, 255
 case study, long-term *see* Sabangau peat swamp forest case study
 conservation projects 146–47
 crop protection measures 37
 crop raiding 9, 26, 168, 175, 176, 183–84, 185, 262–63
 deforestation impacts *see* Sabangau peat swamp forest case study
 diet xix
 disease 184
 distribution xx–xxi
 ecology xix, xxi
 habitat, agro-industry impacts on 24, 136, 166, 168, 172–73, 180, 188
 home ranges and territoriality xxii, xxiii
 human–wildlife conflict 25–27
 killings 185, 186
 nest building 168, 176
 overview xii
 population densities 153
 protective legislation 33–34
 reintroduction of rescued animals 32
 reproduction xxiii–xxiv
 rescues/rescue centers 25–27, 32–33, 34–35, 174–75, 232–33, 234
 socioecology xv, xix
 states found in xvi
 trafficking death toll 234
 translocation 32–33, 36, 154
 use of plantations 175, 176
 see also Bornean orangutans (*Pongo pygmaeus*); Sumatran orangutans (*Pongo abelii*)
Oxfam Novib 138

P

palm oil
 ape conservation practices 34
 Best Management Practices for Orangutan Conservation 147
 biodiesel 21
 Borneo 24, 25, 62, 64–65, 67, 146–47, 176
 Cambodia 44
 Cameroon 51–52, 70–71, 75, 77, 78, 79, 81, 92, 160
 carbon sequestration 20
 Central Africa 58, 77, 79
 crop rotation impacts 24
 CSPO 136, 137, 140, 152–53, 157–58, 162, 163
 demand for 90, 137
 DRC 75, 78, 86
 employment 18
 EU imports 79, 157–58
 expansion 5, 14, 42
 Gabon 81, 86, 92, 148–151
 global price declines 80
 greenhouse gas (GHG) emissions 20–21
 human–wildlife conflict 25–27
 impacts on ape habitats 24, 93, 94, 166
 Indonesia 12–13, 18–19, 24, 25, 81–82, 134–35, 136, 137
 investment sources 85–86
 Ivory Coast 75, 77–78, 79, 80
 Kalimantan 65
 key findings 15
 Liberia 58–59, 61, 77, 86
 Malaysia 18, 24, 64, 65, 81–82, 134–35, 136, 137
 mature plantations 176
 model of suitability for plantations 14
 national strategies 101
 Nigeria 75, 77
 Olam International 147–151

orangutan protection strategies 32–33
overlap with ape habitats 93
overlap with ape ranges 92–96, 136
and poverty 18–19
production amount 14, 18, 136
Republic of Congo 77, 81, 92
RSPO *see* Roundtable on Sustainable Palm Oil (RSPO)
smallholder farming 18, 19, 77, 160–61
sub-Saharan Africa 76–81, 90
Sumatra 24, 137, 160–61
surface cultivated 14
sustainable development 96–102
sustainable lending 87
trade 78–79, 80
uses 18
West Africa 58, 77, 79, 90
Wilmar International 144–47
yield intensification 24
Palm Oil Innovations Group (POIG) 100–101, 159
PALMCI group 77–78
Pamol 52, 78
peatlands 20, 21, 24, 154, 207 *see also* Sabangau peat swamp forest case study
pets *see* captive apes, pets
pileated gibbons (*Hylobates pileatus*) xvii, xx–xxi, 45
plantation establishment 17
plantations, mature 176–77
plantations, young 174–76
population crash 205–6
population recovery 206
poverty 18–19, 160
protected areas
benefits and limitations 198–99
Cambodia 44–45, 124–25
Cameroon 53, 54, 124–25
categories 46
DRC 124–25
Gabon 124–25
Global Roadmap Project 16
Indonesia 124–25
legislation 119–122
Liberia 55, 60, 124–25
Malaysia 124–25
management 226
Myanmar 124–25
see also Gombe Stream National Park case study; national parks; Sabangau peat swamp forest case study
protected species 122–25
public–private partnerships 32–33

R

Rabobank 87
Rainforest Alliance 136
REDD+ project 22
reforestation 178–79
regeneration of agricultural land 178–79

remediations 177–79
reproduction xxiii–xxiv, xxv
Republic of Congo
agro-industry impact on ape habitats 20–21, 47, 94, 188
agro-industry, potential sites for 92
ape distribution xviii
ape range – agro-industry overlap 75
area under concession 74
Atama plantation 77
land acquisitions 74
land deals 43
palm oil 77, 81, 92
sugarcane 83
Republic of Guinea 43, 47, 75, 92, 93, 177, 182
rescues/rescue centers
Africa 235–37, 257
Asia 25–27, 32–33, 34–35, 174–75, 225, 238–39
Asia and Africa 231–32
challenges 232–34
drivers and impacts 239–240
Europe 243, 245, 246–47
USA 248, 249, 251, 252–53, 254, 255
rice 18, 30, 52, 84–85
roads 16, 171, 172
Roundtable on Sustainable Palm Oil (RSPO)
architecture 140
Board of Governors 141, 142
General Assembly (GA) 140–42
Secretariat 142–43
Standing Committees (SCs) 141–42
certification categories 153
challenges 162
compensation 155
complementary initiatives 158–59
conservation impact, enhancing 157, 162–63
increasing demand for CSPO 157–58
traceability and transparency 158
costs to growers 152–53
creation 137–38
CSPO 136, 137, 140, 152–53, 157–58, 162, 163
industry applications 143
Olam International 147–151
Wilmar International 144–47
key findings 136–37
legitimacy 143
membership categories 138
operational challenges 152–53
Principles and Criteria 138–140
problems 59, 87
process-related obstacles 153–55
agreement, reaching 153–54
freeloading and non-compliance 156–57
interpretation 154
membership limitations 155–56
regulations, conflicting 156
stakeholder coverage, inadequate 156
sustainability promotion, steps towards 162–63
rubber 18, 44–45, 52–54, 56–58, 63, 83, 148, 171
Rwanda 47, 170

S

Sabah 63, 64, 65, 144
Sabahmas Conservation Area (SCA), Borneo 144
Sabangau peat swamp forest case study 198, 200–207
    catchment map 202
    context and background 200–202
    discussion
        impact of logging disturbance 203–5
        landscape 206–7
        population decline 206
        population recovery, post-logging 206
        timeline of population crash 204, 205–6
    methodology and results 202–3
    population densities 204
    population distribution shifts 203
Sanaga-Yong Rescue Center (SYRC),
    Cameroon 235–37
sanctuaries *see* rescues/rescue centers
Sanctuary Project 258
Sapo National Park, Liberia 94
Sarawak 63, 64, 65
Schwaben Park, Germany 243
Senegal 48, 75, 84
set-aside system 177–78
set-up costs 91–92
siamangs (*Symphlangus syndactylus*) xiv, xvii, xx–xxi,
    xxiv–xxv, 122–23, 145, 239
Siat Group 86
Sierra Leone 43, 48, 73, 74, 75, 77, 83, 85, 93
silvery gibbons (*Hylobates moloch*) xvii, xx–xxi, 222
    see also Mount Halimun Salak National Park
    case study
Sime Darby, Liberia 59, 83, 86, 94, 95
Sithe Global Sustainable Oils Cameroon (SGSOC) 52
smallholder farming
    African agricultural model 81, 92
    conservation initiatives 22, 23, 162–63
    defining 3, 72
    economic schemes 63, 86
    engagement 98
    palm oil 18, 19, 77, 160–61
    proliferation 73–74
    rubber 57–58
    sustainable economic development 4
social impact assessments (SIAs) 118, 140
Société Africaine Forestière et Agricole du Cameroun
    (SAFACAM) 50, 52, 78
Société Camerounaise de Palmeraies (SOCAPALM)
    52, 78
Société des Palmeraies de la Ferme Suisse 52
Société d'Organisation de Management et de
    Développement des Industries Alimentaires et
    Agricoles (SOMDIAA) 52
Société Financière des Caoutchoucs (SOCFIN) 78
Société Immobilière et Financière de la Côte Africaine
    (SIFCA) 77, 86
Société Sucrière du Cameroun (SOSUCAM) 52
socioecology xv
    gibbon socioecology xxiv–xxv
    great ape ecology xix, xxi–xxiii

great ape socioecology xv, xix
    reproduction xxiii–xxiv
socioeconomic values 183
sorghum 85
South Africa 82, 83, 84
South Sudan 48
southern white-cheeked gibbons
    (*Nomascus siki*) xvii
southern yellow-cheeked gibbons
    (*Nomascus gabriellae*) xvii, xx–xxi, 45
southwest Bornean orangutan
    (*Pongo pygmaeus wurmbii*) xvi
Spain 246
Spatial Monitoring and Reporting Tool (SMART) 145
species protection 32, 126
Standard Chartered 87
State of the Apes website 194
sub-Saharan Africa
    agricultural models, choice of 81–82
    agriculture's economic impact 73
    agro-industry 102
        crops 74–75
        expansion 71–73, 91–92
        impact on ape habitats 92–96
        investment sources 85–87
        land deals 74, 75–76
        overlap with ape ranges 74, 93
    ape distribution xviii
    cereals 83–85
    deforestation 92
    jatropha 76
    land prices 91
    land use changes 73–74
    palm oil
        demand for 90
        future expansion 79–81
        plantation area 76–77
        production 77–78
        trade 78–79, 80
    rubber 83
    smallholder farming 71–72, 73–74, 81
    sugarcane 82–83
    sustainable development 96–102
    see also specific countries
Sud-Cameroun Hevea, Cameroon 52, 94, 95
sugarcane 29–31, 46, 52, 82–83
Sumatra
    agricultural incomes 18
    agro-industry impact on ape habitats 24, 104–5,
    154, 156, 168, 190–91
    deforestation 196–97
    deterrent techniques 37
    legal protection 128–130
    palm oil 24, 137, 160–61
    rescues/rescue centers 26, 32, 34–35, 145, 238–39
    Tripa peat swamp forests, Aceh 128–130, 141, 156
    see also Indonesia
Sumatran orangutans (*Pongo abelii*) xii, xvi, xx–xxi,
    xxii, 26, 128, 136 *see also* orangutans (*Pongo* spp.)
Support for African/Asian Great Apes (SAGA) 258
survey methods 200

sustainable crop production intensification (SCPI) 23
sustainable development 96–102
sustainable lending 87
Sustainable Palm Oil Transparency Toolkit (SPOTT) 158
Swaziland 82, 83

T

Tabin Wildlife Reserve, Borneo 144
Tanzania 23, 48, 83, 84, 85, 188 *see also* Gombe Stream
    National Park case study
Thailand 44, 49, 188, 230–31
tobacco 6–7, 29–31
tools for surveys/monitoring 226
trafficking of live apes 234, 235, 238, 240, 256
translocation 32–33, 36
transparency 116, 119, 158
Treaty on the Conservation and Sustainable
    Management of Forest Ecosystems in Central
    Africa and to Establish the Central African
    Forest Commission 108
Tripa peat swamp forests, Aceh 128–130, 141, 156
tropical ecosystems 13
tuberculosis 240

U

Uganda
    agro-industry impact on ape habitats 48, 95, 188
    agro-industry practices 100
    ape distribution xviii
    cacao 30
    crop raiding 184
    crops 29, 30, 46
    deforestation 29–30
    forest reserves 29
    human–wildlife conflict 29–31, 38
    mountain gorillas 170
    Plan for Modernisation of Agriculture 29
    sugarcane 30–31, 82
    tobacco 6, 30–31
    Wilmar International 144
Unilever 86
United Nations Environment Programme World
    Conservation Monitoring Centre
    (UNEP-WCMC) 42
United States (USA)
    captive apes 248
        national legislation 248–251
        numbers 254–56
        sanctuaries 249, 251, 252–53, 254, 255, 256
        split-listing of chimpanzees 249–250
        sub-national legislation 251–54
    investors in African agribusinesses 85
    land prices 91
    Opportunities Act 91
University of Palangkaraya 202
Upper Guinea Forest 55

V

Vietnam 49

W

Walhi Aceh 129
Wamba, DRC *see* Luo Scientific Reserve/Wamba
    case study
West Africa
    agro-industry impact on ape habitats 93
    agro-industry, potential sites for 42, 92
    ape range – agro-industry overlap 75
    Ebola virus 80
    forest administration resources 119
    land acquisitions 74
    palm oil 58, 77, 79, 90
    rice 85
    rubber 83
    see also specific countries
western black-crested gibbons
    (*Nomascus concolor*) xiv, xvii, xx–xxi
western chimpanzees (*Pan troglodytes versus*) x, xvi,
    xviii, 46, 55–56, 59–60, 61, 94
western gorillas (*Gorilla gorilla*) xi, 93, 96, 169, 170
    see also Cross River gorillas (*Gorilla gorilla
    diehli*); western lowland gorillas (*Gorilla gorilla
    gorilla*)
western hoolocks (*Hoolock hoolock*) xii–xiii, xvii,
    xx–xxi
western lowland gorillas (*Gorilla gorilla gorilla*)
    Atama palm oil project 94
    in Cameroon 49
    crop raiding 170
    distances travelled xxi, xxii, 170
    distribution xviii
    habitat 169
    Olam International project 148, 150–51
    overview xi
    range states xvi
wheat 85
Wilmar International 86, 95, 99, 100, 144–47, 159
Wilson, E.O. 1
World Bank 18, 22, 86
World Heritage Convention 136
World Resources Institute (WRI) 158
World Wide Fund for Nature (WWF) 138, 159

Y

yield intensification 24, 160

Z

Zambia 83, 84
zero-deforestation commitments 99, 100, 113, 144, 159
Zimbabwe 82
zoos 242